The CERT® Oracle®
Secure Coding Standard
for Java™

The CERT® Oracle® Secure Coding Standard for Java™

Fred Long
Dhruv Mohindra
Robert C. Seacord
Dean F. Sutherland
David Svoboda

✦ Addison-Wesley

Upper Saddle River, NJ • Boston • Indianapolis • San Francisco
New York • Toronto • Montreal • London • Munich • Paris • Madrid
Capetown • Sydney • Tokyo • Singapore • Mexico City

≣ Software Engineering Institute | **Carnegie Mellon**

The SEI Series in Software Engineering

Many of the designations used by manufacturers and sellers to distinguish their products are claimed as trademarks. Where those designations appear in this book, and the publisher was aware of a trademark claim, the designations have been printed with initial capital letters or in all capitals.

CMM, CMMI, Capability Maturity Model, Capability Maturity Modeling, Carnegie Mellon, CERT, and CERT Coordination Center are registered in the U.S. Patent and Trademark Office by Carnegie Mellon University.

ATAM; Architecture Tradeoff Analysis Method; CMM Integration; COTS Usage-Risk Evaluation; CURE; EPIC; Evolutionary Process for Integrating COTS Based Systems; Framework for Software Product Line Practice; IDEAL; Interim Profile; OAR; OCTAVE; Operationally Critical Threat, Asset, and Vulnerability Evaluation; Options Analysis for Reengineering; Personal Software Process; PLTP; Product Line Technical Probe; PSP; SCAMPI; SCAMPI Lead Appraiser; SCAMPI Lead Assessor; SCE; SEI; SEPG; Team Software Process; and TSP are service marks of Carnegie Mellon University.

Special permission to reproduce portions of The CERT Oracle Secure Coding Standard for Java, © 2007–2011 by Carnegie Mellon University, in this book is granted by the Software Engineering Institute.

Many of the designations used by manufacturers and sellers to distinguish their products are claimed as trademarks. Where those designations appear in this book, and the publisher was aware of a trademark claim, the designations have been printed with initial capital letters or in all capitals.

The authors and publisher have taken care in the preparation of this book, but make no expressed or implied warranty of any kind and assume no responsibility for errors or omissions. No liability is assumed for incidental or consequential damages in connection with or arising out of the use of the information or programs contained herein.

The publisher offers excellent discounts on this book when ordered in quantity for bulk purchases or special sales, which may include electronic versions and/or custom covers and content particular to your business, training goals, marketing focus, and branding interests. For more information, please contact:

U.S. Corporate and Government Sales
(800) 382-3419
corpsales@pearsontechgroup.com

For sales outside the United States please contact:

International Sales
international@pearson.com

Visit us on the Web: informit.com/aw

Library of Congress Cataloging-in-Publication Data

The CERT Oracle secure coding standard for Java / Fred Long ... [et al.].
  p.   cm.—(The SEI series in software engineering)
Includes bibliographical references and index.
ISBN-13: 978-0-321-80395-5 (pbk. : alk. paper)
ISBN-10: 0-321-80395-7 (pbk. : alk. paper)
1. Java (Computer program language) 2. Computer security. 3. Oracle (Computer file) 4. Computer programming—Standards. I. Long, F. W. (Frederick W.), 1947- II. Carnegie-Mellon University. CERT Coordination Center.
QA76.73.J38C44 2012
005.8—dc23

                                  2011027284

ISBN-13:   978-0-321-80395-5
ISBN-10:   0-321-80395-7
Text printed in the United States on recycled paper at Edwards Brothers in Ann Arbor, Michigan.
First printing, September 2011

Contents

Foreword

James Gosling

Security in computer systems has been a serious issue for decades. This past decade's explosion in the dependence on networks and the computers connected to them has raised the issue to stratospheric levels. When Java was first designed, dealing with security was a key component. And in the years since then, all of the various standard libraries, frameworks, and containers that have been built have had to deal with security too. In the Java world, security is not viewed as an add-on feature. It is a pervasive way of thinking. Those who forget to think in a secure mindset end up in trouble.

But just because the facilities are there doesn't mean that security is assured automatically. A set of standard practices has evolved over the years. *The CERT® Oracle® Secure Coding Standard for Java™* is a compendium of these practices. These are not theoretical research papers or product marketing blurbs. This is all serious, mission-critical, battle-tested, enterprise-scale stuff.

Preface

An essential element of secure coding in the Java programming language is a well-documented and enforceable coding standard. The CERT Oracle Secure Coding Standard for Java provides rules for secure coding in the Java programming language. The goal of these rules is to eliminate insecure coding practices that can lead to exploitable vulnerabilities. The application of the secure coding standard leads to higher quality systems that are safe, secure, reliable, dependable, robust, resilient, available, and maintainable and can be used as a metric to evaluate source code for these properties (using manual or automated processes).

This coding standard affects a wide range of software systems developed in the Java programming language.

■ Scope

The CERT Oracle Secure Coding Standard for Java focuses on the Java Standard Edition 6 Platform (Java SE 6) environment and includes rules for secure coding using the Java programming language and libraries. *The Java Language Specification,* 3rd edition [JLS 2005] prescribes the behavior of the Java programming language and served as the primary reference for the development of this standard. This coding standard also addresses new features of the Java SE 7 Platform. Primarily, these features provide alternative compliant solutions to secure coding problems that exist in both the Java SE 6 and Java SE 7 platforms.

Languages such as C and C++ allow undefined, unspecified, or implementation-defined behaviors, which can lead to vulnerabilities when a programmer makes incorrect assumptions about the underlying behavior of an API or language construct. The Java Language Specification goes further to standardize language requirements because Java is designed to be a "write once, run anywhere" language. Even then, certain behaviors are left to the discretion of the implementor of the Java Virtual Machine (JVM) or the Java compiler. This standard identifies such language peculiarities and demonstrates secure coding practices to avoid them.

Focusing only on language issues does not translate to writing secure software. Design flaws in Java application programming interfaces (APIs) sometimes lead to their deprecation. At other times, the APIs or the relevant documentation may be interpreted incorrectly by the programming community. This standard identifies such problematic APIs and highlights their correct use. Examples of commonly used faulty design patterns (anti-patterns) and idioms are also included.

The Java language, its core and extension APIs, and the JVM provide security features such as the security manager, access controller, cryptography, automatic memory management, strong type checking, and bytecode verification. These features provide sufficient security for most applications, but their proper use is of paramount importance. This standard highlights the pitfalls and caveats associated with the security architecture and stresses its correct implementation. Adherence to this standard safeguards the confidentiality, integrity, and availability (CIA) of trusted programs and helps eliminate exploitable security flaws that can result in denial-of-service attacks, time-of-check-to-time-of-use attacks, information leaks, erroneous computations, and privilege escalation.

Software that complies with this standard provides its users the ability to define fine-grained security policies and safely execute trusted mobile code on untrusted systems or untrusted mobile code on trusted systems.

Included Libraries

This secure coding standard addresses security issues primarily applicable to the `lang` and `util` libraries, as well as to the Collections, Concurrency Utilities, Logging, Management, Reflection, Regular Expressions, Zip, I/O, JMX, JNI, Math, Serialization, and XML JAXP libraries. This standard avoids the inclusion of open bugs that have already been fixed or those that lack security ramifications. A functional bug is included only when it is likely that it occurs with high frequency, causes considerable security concerns, or affects most Java technologies that rely on the core platform. This standard is not limited to security issues specific to the Core API but also includes important security concerns pertaining to the standard extension APIs (`javax` package).

Issues Not Addressed

The following issues are not addressed by this standard:

- **Design and Architecture.** This standard assumes that the design and architecture of the product is secure—that is, that the product is free of design-level vulnerabilities that would otherwise compromise its security.

- **Content.** This coding standard does not address concerns specific to only one Java-based platform but applies broadly to all platforms. For example, rules that are applicable to Java Micro Edition (ME) or Java Enterprise Edition (EE) alone and not to Java SE are typically not included. Within Java SE, APIs that deal with the user interface (User Interface Toolkits) or with the web interface for providing features such as sound, graphical rendering, user account access control, session management, authentication, and authorization are beyond the scope of this standard. However, this does not preclude the standard from discussing networked Java systems given the risks associated with improper input validation and injection flaws and suggesting appropriate mitigation strategies.

- **Coding Style.** Coding style issues are subjective; it has proven impossible to develop a consensus on appropriate style rules. Consequently, *The CERT® Oracle® Secure Coding Standard for Java™* recommends only that the user define style rules and apply those rules consistently; requirements that mandate use of any particular coding style are deliberately omitted. The easiest way to consistently apply a coding style is with the use of a code formatting tool. Many integrated development environments (IDEs) provide such capabilities.

- **Tools.** As a federally funded research and development center (FFRDC), the Software Engineering Institute (SEI) is not in a position to recommend particular vendors or tools to enforce the restrictions adopted. Users of this document are free to choose tools; vendors are encouraged to provide tools to enforce these rules.

- **Controversial Rules.** In general, the CERT secure coding standards try to avoid the inclusion of controversial rules that lack a broad consensus.

■ Audience

The CERT® Oracle® Secure Coding Standard for Java™ is primarily intended for developers of Java language programs. While this standard focuses on the Java Platform SE 6, it should also be informative (although incomplete) for Java developers working with Java ME or Java EE and other Java language versions.

While primarily designed for secure systems, this standard is also useful for achieving other quality attributes such as safety, reliability, dependability, robustness, resiliency, availability, and maintainability.

This standard may also be used by

- Developers of analyzer tools who wish to diagnose insecure or nonconforming Java language programs

- Software development managers, software acquirers, or other software development and acquisition specialists to establish a proscriptive set of secure coding standards

- Educators as a primary or secondary text for software security courses that teach secure coding in Java

The rules in this standard may be extended with organization-specific rules. However, a program must comply with existing rules to be considered conforming to the standard.

Training may be developed to educate software professionals regarding the appropriate application of secure coding standards. After passing an examination, these trained programmers may also be certified as secure coding professionals.

■ Contents and Organization

The standard is organized into an introductory chapter and 17 chapters containing rules in specific topic areas. Each of the rule chapters contains a list of rules in that section, and a risk assessment summary for the rules. There is also a common glossary and bibliography. This preface is meant to be read first, followed by the introductory chapter. The rule chapters may be read in any order or used as reference material as appropriate. The rules are loosely organized in each chapter but, in general, may also be read in any order.

Rules have a consistent structure. Each rule has a unique identifier, which is included in the title. The title of the rules and the introductory paragraphs define the conformance requirements. This is typically followed by one or more sets of noncompliant code examples and corresponding compliant solutions. Each rule also includes a risk assessment and bibliographical references specific to that rule. When applicable, rules also list related vulnerabilities and related guidelines from the following sources:

- *The CERT® C Secure Coding Standard* [Seacord 2008]

- *The CERT® C++ Secure Coding Standard* [CERT 2011]

- ISO/IEC TR 24772. Information Technology—Programming Languages—Guidance to Avoiding Vulnerabilities in Programming Languages through Language Selection and Use [ISO/IEC TR 24772:2010]

- MITRE CWE [MITRE 2011]

- Secure Coding Rules for the Java Programming Language, version 3.0 [SCG 2009]
- *The Elements of Java™ Style* [Rogue 2000]

Identifiers

Each rule has a unique identifier, consisting of three parts:

- A three-letter mnemonic, representing the section of the standard, is used to group similar rules and make them easier to find.
- A two-digit numeric value in the range of 00 to 99, which ensures each rule has a unique identifier.
- The letter J, which indicates that this is a Java language rule and is included to prevent ambiguity with similar rules in CERT secure coding standards for other languages.

Identifiers may be used by static analysis tools to reference a particular rule in a diagnostic message or otherwise used as shorthand for the rule title.

■ System Qualities

Security is one of many system attributes that must be considered in the selection and application of a coding standard. Other attributes of interest include safety, portability, reliability, availability, maintainability, readability, and performance.

Many of these attributes are interrelated in interesting ways. For example, readability is an attribute of maintainability; both are important for limiting the introduction of defects during maintenance that can result in security flaws or reliability issues. In addition, readability facilitates code inspection by safety officers. Reliability and availability require proper resource management, which also contributes to the safety and security of the system. System attributes such as performance and security are often in conflict, requiring tradeoffs to be made.

The purpose of the secure coding standard is to promote software security. However, because of the relationship between security and other system attributes, the coding standards may include requirements and recommendations that deal primarily with other system attributes that also have a significant impact on security.

■ Priority and Levels

Each rule has an assigned priority. Priorities are assigned using a metric based on Failure Mode, Effects, and Criticality Analysis (FMECA) [IEC 60812]. Three values are assigned for each rule on a scale of 1 to 3 for

- Severity—How serious are the consequences of the rule being ignored:

  1 = low (denial-of-service attack, abnormal termination)

  2 = medium (data integrity violation, unintentional information disclosure)

  3 = high (run arbitrary code, privilege escalation)

- Likelihood—How likely is it that a flaw introduced by violating the rule could lead to an exploitable vulnerability:

  1 = unlikely

  2 = probable

  3 = likely

- Remediation cost—How expensive is it to remediate existing code to comply with the rule:

  1 = high (manual detection and correction)

  2 = medium (automatic detection and manual correction)

  3 = low (automatic detection and correction)

The three values are multiplied together for each rule. This product provides a measure that can be used in prioritizing the application of the rules. These products range from 1 to 27. Rules with a priority in the range of 1 to 4 are level 3 rules, 6 to 9 are level 2, and 12 to 27 are level 1. As a result, it is possible to claim level 1, level 2, or complete compliance (level 3) with a standard by implementing all rules in a level, as shown in Figure P–1.

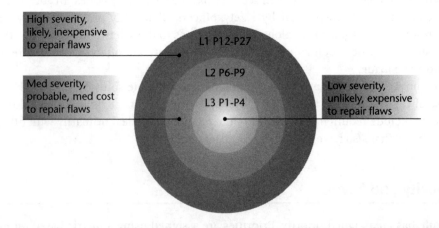

Figure P–1. Levels and priority ranges

The metric is designed primarily for remediation projects and does not apply to new development efforts that are implemented to the standard.

■ Conformance Testing

Software systems can be validated as conforming to *The CERT® Oracle® Secure Coding Standard for Java*™.

Normative vs. Nonnormative Text

Portions of this coding standard are intended to be normative; other portions are intended as good advice. The normative statements in these rules are the requirements for conformance with the standard. Normative statements use imperative language such as "must," "shall," and "require." Normative portions of each rule must be analyzable, although automated analysis is infeasible for some rules and not required.

The nonnormative portions of a rule describe good practices or useful advice. Nonnormative statements do not establish conformance requirements. Nonnormative statements use verbs such as "should" or phrases such as "is recommended" or "is good practice." Nonnormative portions of rules may be inappropriate for automated checking because such checking would likely report excessive false positives when applied to existing code. Automated checkers for these nonnormative portions might be useful when analyzing new code (that is, code that has been developed to this coding standard).

All of the rules in this standard have a normative component. Nonnormative recommendations are provided only when

- there is well-known good practice to follow
- the rule describes an approach that, if universally followed, would avoid violations where the normative part of the rule applies and would also be harmless when applied to code where the normative part of the rule is inapplicable

Entirely nonnormative guidelines are excluded from this coding standard. However, the authors of this book are planning a follow-on effort to publish these guidelines.

■ Automated Analysis

To ensure that the source code conforms to this secure coding standard, it is necessary to check for rule violations. The most effective means of checking is to use one or more analysis tools (analyzers). When a rule cannot be checked by a tool, manual review is required.

Many of the rules in this standard provide some indication as to whether or not existing analyzers can diagnose violations of the rule or even how amenable the rule is to automated analysis. This information is necessarily transitory because existing analyzers evolve and new analyzers are developed.

When choosing a source code analysis tool, it is clearly desirable that the tool be able to enforce as many of the rules in this document as possible. Not all rules are enforceable by automated analysis tools; some will require manual inspection.

■ Completeness and Soundness

To the greatest extent possible, an analyzer should be both complete and sound with respect to enforceable rules. An analyzer is considered sound (with respect to a specific rule) if it does not give a false-negative result, meaning it is able to find all violations of a rule within the entire program. An analyzer is considered complete if it does not issue false-positive results, or false alarms. The possibilities for a given rule are outlined in Table P–1.

Table P–1. Soundness and completeness

		False Positives	
		Y	N
False Negatives	N	Sound with false positives	Complete and sound
	Y	Unsound with false positives	Unsound

Tools with a high false-positive rate cause developers to waste their time, and they can lose interest in the results and consequently fail to realize value from the true bugs that are lost in the noise. Tools with a high number of false-negatives miss many defects that should be found and can foster a false sense of security. In practice, tools need to strike a balance between the two.

There are many tradeoffs in minimizing false-positives and false-negatives. It is obviously better to minimize both, and there are many techniques and algorithms that do both to some degree.

Analyzers are trusted processes, meaning that reliance is placed on the output of the tools. Consequently, developers must ensure that this trust is warranted. Ideally, this should be achieved by the tool supplier running appropriate validation tests. While it is possible to use a validation suite to test an analyzer, no formal validation scheme exists at this time.

■ CERT Source Code Analysis Laboratory

CERT has created the Source Code Analysis Laboratory (SCALe), which offers conformance testing of software systems to CERT secure coding standards, including The CERT Oracle Secure Coding Standard for Java.

SCALe evaluates client source code using multiple analyzers, including static analysis tools, dynamic analysis tools, and fuzz testing. CERT reports any violations of the secure coding rules to the developer. The developer may repair and resubmit the software for reevaluation.

After the developer has addressed these findings and the SCALe team determines that the product version tested conforms to the standard, CERT issues the developer a certificate and lists the system in a registry of conforming systems.

Successful conformance testing of a software system indicates that the SCALe analysis was unable to detect violations of rules defined by a CERT secure coding standard. Successful conformance testing does not provide any guarantees that these rules are not violated or that the software is entirely and permanently secure. SCALe does not test for unknown code-related vulnerabilities, high-level design and architectural flaws, the code's operational environment, or the code's portability. Conforming software systems can still be insecure, for example, if the software implements an insecure design or architecture.

Some rules in this standard include enumerated exceptions with discussion of the conditions under which each exception applies. When developers invoke an enumerated exception as a reason for deviating from a rule, they must document the relevant exception in the code at or near the point of deviation. A minimally acceptable form of documentation is a stylized comment containing the identifier of the exception being claimed, as in this example:

```
// MET12-EX0 applies here
```

The authors are currently developing a set of Java annotations that will permit programmers to indicate such exceptions in a form that is both human-readable and accessible to static analysis tools. For conformance testing purposes, determination of whether an exception applies in any particular case is made by the SCALe analyst.

Third-Party Libraries

Static analysis tools, such as FindBugs that analyze Java bytecode, can frequently discover violations of this secure coding standard in third-party libraries in addition to custom code. Violations of secure coding rules in third-party libraries are treated in the same manner as if they appeared in custom code.

Unfortunately, developers are not always in a position to modify third-party library code or perhaps even to convince the vendor to modify the code. This means that the system cannot pass conformance testing unless the problem is eliminated (possibly by replacing the library with another library or custom-developed code) or by documenting a deviation. The deviation procedure for third-party library code is the same as for custom code—that is, the developer must show that the violation does not cause a vulnerability. However, the costs may be different. For custom code, it may be more economical to repair the problem, whereas for third-party libraries, it might be easier to document a deviation.

Conformance Testing Process

For each secure coding standard, the source code is found to be provably nonconforming, conforming, or provably conforming against each rule in the standard.

- *Provably nonconforming.* The code is provably nonconforming if one or more violations of a rule are discovered for which no deviation has been allowed.
- *Conforming.* The code is conforming if no violations of a rule are identified.
- *Provably conforming.* The code is provably conforming if the code has been verified to adhere to the rule in all possible cases.

Deviation Procedure

Strict adherence to all rules is unlikely; consequently, deviations associated with specific rule violations are necessary. Deviations can be used in cases where a true positive finding is uncontested as a rule violation but the code is nonetheless determined to be secure. This may be the result of a design or architecture feature of the software or because the particular violation occurs for a valid reason that was unanticipated by the secure coding standard. In this respect, the deviation procedure allows for the possibility that secure coding rules are overly strict. Deviations cannot be used for reasons of performance, usability, or to achieve other nonsecurity attributes in the system. A software system that successfully passes conformance testing must not present known vulnerabilities resulting from coding errors.

Deviation requests are evaluated by the lead assessor; if the developer can provide sufficient evidence that deviation does not introduce a vulnerability, the deviation request is accepted. Deviations should be used infrequently because it is almost always easier to fix a coding error than it is to prove that the coding error does not result in a vulnerability.

Once the evaluation process has been completed, a report detailing the conformance or nonconformance of the code to the corresponding rules in the secure coding standard is provided to the developer.

CERT SCALe Seal

Developers of software that has been determined by CERT to conform to a secure coding standard may use the seal shown in Figure P–2 to describe the conforming software on the developer's website. The seal must be specifically tied to the software passing conformance testing and not applied to untested products, the company, or the organization.

Figure P-2. CERT SCALe Seal

Except for patches that meet the following criteria, any modification of software after it is designated as conforming voids the conformance designation. Until such software is retested and determined to be conforming, the new software cannot be associated with the CERT SCALe Seal.

Patches that meet all three of the following criteria do not void the conformance designation:

- The patch is necessary to fix a vulnerability in the code or is necessary for the maintenance of the software.
- The patch does not introduce new features or functionality.
- The patch does not introduce a violation of any of the rules in the secure coding standard to which the software has been determined to conform.

Use of the CERT SCALe Seal is contingent upon the organization entering into a service agreement with Carnegie Mellon University and upon the software being designated by CERT as conforming. For more information, email securecoding@cert.org.

Acknowledgments

Thanks to everyone who has contributed to making this effort a success.

Contributors

Siddarth Adukia, Lokesh Agarwal, Ron Bandes, Scott Bennett, Kalpana Chatnani, Steve Christey, Jose Sandoval Chaverri, Tim Halloran, Thomas Hawtin, Fei He, Ryan Hofler, Sam Kaplan, Georgios Katsis, Lothar Kimmeringer, Bastian Marquis, Michael Kross, Masaki Kubo, Christopher Leonavicius, Bocong Liu, Efstathios Mertikas, Aniket Mokashi, David Neville, Todd Nowacki, Vishal Patel, Jonathan Paulson, Justin Pincar, Michael Rosenman, Brendan Saulsbury, Eric Schwelm, Tamir Sen, Philip Shirey, Jagadish Shrinivasavadhani, Robin Steiger, Yozo Toda, Kazuya Togashi, John Truelove, Theti Tsiampali, Tim Wilson, and Weam Abu Zaki.

Reviewers

Daniel Bögner, James Baldo Jr., Hans Boehm, Joseph Bowbeer, Mark Davis, Sven Dietrich, Will Dormann, Chad R. Dougherty, Holger Ebel, Paul Evans, Hari Gopal, Klaus Havelund, David Holmes, Bart Jacobs, Sami Koivu, Niklas Matthies, Bill Michell, Philip Miller, Nick Morrott, Attila Mravik, Tim Peierls, Kirk Sayre, Thomas Scanlon, Steve Scholnick, Alex Snaps, David Warren, Ramon Waspitz, and Kenneth A. Williams.

Editors

Pamela Curtis, Shannon Haas, Carol Lallier, Tracey Tamules, Melanie Thompson, Paul Ruggerio, and Pennie Walters.

Addison-Wesley

Kim Boedigheimer, John Fuller, Stephane Nakib, Peter Gordon, Chuti Prasertsith, and Elizabeth Ryan.

Special Thanks

Archie Andrews, David Biber, Kim Boedigheimer, Peter Gordon, Frances Ho, Joe Jarzombek, Jason McNatt, Stephane Nakib, Rich Pethia, and Elizabeth Ryan.

About the Authors

Fred Long is a senior lecturer and director of learning and teaching in the Department of Computer Science, Aberystwyth University in the United Kingdom.

He lectures on formal methods; Java, C++, and C programming paradigms and programming-related security issues. He is chairman of the British Computer Society's Mid-Wales Sub-Branch.

Fred has been a Visiting Scientist at the Software Engineering Institute since 1992. Recently, his research has involved the investigation of vulnerabilities in Java.

Dhruv Mohindra is a senior software engineer at Persistent Systems Limited, India, where he develops monitoring software for widely used enterprise servers. He has worked for CERT at the Software Engineering Institute and continues to collaborate to improve the state of security awareness in the programming community.

Dhruv has also worked for Carnegie Mellon University, where he obtained his master of science degree in information security policy and management. He holds an undergraduate degree in computer engineering from Pune University, India, where he researched with Calsoft, Inc., during his academic pursuit.

A writing enthusiast, Dhruv occasionally contributes articles to technology magazines and online resources. He brings forth his experience and learning from developing and securing service oriented applications, server monitoring software, mobile device applications, web-based data miners, and designing user-friendly security interfaces.

Robert C. Seacord is a computer security specialist and writer. He is the author of books on computer security, legacy system modernization, and component-based software engineering.

Robert manages the Secure Coding Initiative at CERT, located in Carnegie Mellon's Software Engineering Institute in Pittsburgh, Pennsylvania. CERT, among other security-related activities, regularly analyzes software vulnerability reports and assesses the risk to the Internet and other critical infrastructure. Robert is an adjunct professor in the Carnegie Mellon University School of Computer Science and in the Information Networking Institute.

Robert started programming professionally for IBM in 1982, working in communications and operating system software, processor development, and software engineering. Robert also has worked at the X Consortium, where he developed and maintained code for the Common Desktop Environment and the X Window System.

Robert has a bachelor's degree in computer science from Rensselaer Polytechnic Institute.

Dean F. Sutherland is a senior software security engineer at CERT. Dean received his Ph.D. in software engineering from Carnegie Mellon in 2008. Before his return to academia, he spent 14 years working as a professional software engineer at Tartan, Inc. He spent the last six of those years as a senior member of the technical staff and a technical lead for compiler back-end technology. He was the primary active member of the corporate R&D group, was a key instigator of the design and deployment of a new software development process for Tartan, led R&D projects, and provided both technical and project leadership for the 12-person compiler back-end group.

David Svoboda is a software security engineer at CERT. David has been the primary developer on a diverse set of software development projects at Carnegie Mellon since 1991, ranging from hierarchical chip modeling and social organization simulation to automated machine translation (AMT). His KANTOO AMT software, developed in 1996, is still in production use at Caterpillar. He has over 13 years of Java development experience, starting with Java 2, and his Java projects include Tomcat servlets and Eclipse plug-ins. David is also actively involved in several ISO standards groups: the JTC1/SC22/WG14 group for the C programming language and the JTC1/SC22/WG21 group for C++.

Chapter 1

Introduction

Software vulnerability reports and reports of software exploitations continue to grow at an alarming rate. A significant number of these reports result in technical security alerts. To address this growing threat to corporations, educational institutions, governments, and individuals, systems must be developed that are free of software vulnerabilities.

Coding errors cause the majority of software vulnerabilities. For example, 64 percent of the nearly 2,500 vulnerabilities in the National Vulnerability Database in 2004 were caused by programming errors [Heffley 2004].

Java is a relatively secure language. There is no explicit pointer manipulation; array and string bounds are automatically checked; attempts at referencing a null pointer are trapped; and the arithmetic operations are well defined and platform independent, as are the type conversions. The built-in bytecode verifier ensures that these checks are always in place. Moreover, Java provides comprehensive, fine-grained security mechanisms that can control access to individual files, sockets, and other sensitive resources. To take advantage of the security mechanisms, the Java Virtual Machine (JVM) must have a security manager in place. This is an ordinary Java object of class `java.lang.SecurityManager` (or a subclass) that can be put in place programmatically but is more commonly specified via a command-line argument.

Java program safety, however, can be compromised. The remainder of this chapter describes use cases under which Java programs might be exploited and examples of rules that mitigate against these attacks. Not all of the rules apply to all Java language programs; frequently, their applicability depends on how the software is deployed and assumptions concerning trust.

■ Misplaced Trust

Software programs often contain multiple components that act as subsystems, where each component operates in one or more trusted domains. For example, one component may have access to the file system but lack access to the network, while another component has access to the network but lacks access to the file system. *Distrustful decomposition* and *privilege separation* [Dougherty 2009] are examples of secure design patterns that reduce the amount of code that runs with special privileges by designing the system using mutually untrusting components.

While software components can obey policies that allow them to transmit data across trust boundaries, they cannot specify the level of trust given to any component. The deployer of the application must define the trust boundaries with the help of a systemwide security policy. A security auditor can use that definition to determine whether the software adequately supports the security objectives of the application.

A Java program can contain both internally developed and third-party code. Java was designed to allow the execution of untrusted code; consequently, third-party code can operate in its own trusted domain. The public API of such third-party code can be considered to be a trust boundary. Data that crosses a trust boundary should be validated unless the code that produces this data provides guarantees of validity. A subscriber or client may omit validation when the data flowing into its trust boundary is appropriate for use as is. In all other cases, inbound data must be validated.

■ Injection Attacks

Data received by a component from a source outside the component's trust boundary can be malicious and can result in an injection attack, as shown in the scenario in Figure 1–1.

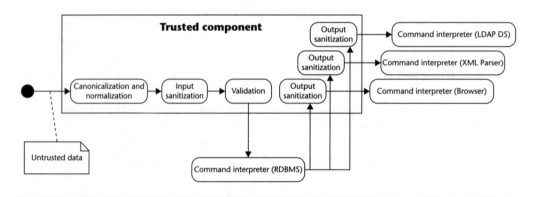

Figure 1–1. Injection attacks

Programs must take steps to ensure that data received across a trust boundary is appropriate and not malicious. These steps can include the following:

Validation: Validation is the process of ensuring that input data falls within the expected domain of valid program input. This requires that inputs conform to type and numeric range requirements as well as to input invariants for the class or subsystem.

Sanitization: In many cases, data is passed directly to a component in a different trusted domain. Data sanitization is the process of ensuring that data conforms to the requirements of the subsystem to which it is passed. Sanitization also involves ensuring that data conforms to security-related requirements regarding leaking or exposure of sensitive data when output across a trust boundary. Sanitization may include the elimination of unwanted characters from the input by means of removing, replacing, encoding, or escaping the characters. Sanitization may occur following input (input sanitization) or before the data is passed across a trust boundary (output sanitization). Data sanitization and input validation may coexist and complement each other. See rule IDS01-J for more details on data sanitization.

Canonicalization and Normalization: Canonicalization is the process of lossless reduction of the input to its equivalent simplest known form. Normalization is the process of lossy conversion of input data to the simplest known (and anticipated) form. Canonicalization and normalization must occur *before* validation to prevent attackers from exploiting the validation routine to strip away invalid characters and, as a result, constructing an invalid (and potentially malicious) character sequence. See rule IDS02-J for more information. Normalization should be performed only on fully assembled user input. Never normalize partial input or combine normalized input with nonnormalized input.

Complex subsystems that accept string data that specify commands or instructions are a special concern. String data passed to these components may contain special characters that can trigger commands or actions, resulting in a software vulnerability.

These are examples of components that can interpret commands or instructions:

- Operating system command interpreter (see rule IDS07-J)
- A data repository with a SQL-compliant interface
- XML parser
- XPath evaluators
- Lightweight Directory Access Protocol (LDAP) directory service
- Script engines
- Regular expression (regex) compilers

When data must be sent to a component in a different trusted domain, the sender must ensure that the data is suitable for the receiver's trust boundary by properly encoding and escaping any data flowing across the trust boundary. For example, if a system is infiltrated by malicious code or data, many attacks are rendered ineffective if the system's output is appropriately escaped and encoded.

■ Leaking Sensitive Data

A system's security policy determines which information is *sensitive*. Sensitive data may include user information such as social security or credit card numbers, passwords, or private keys. When components with differing degrees of trust share data, the data is said to flow across a trust boundary. Because Java allows components under different trusted domains to communicate with each other in the same program, data can be transmitted across a trust boundary. Systems must ensure that data is not transmitted to a component in a different trusted domain if authorized users in that domain are not permitted access to the data. This may be as simple as not transmitting the data, or it may involve filtering sensitive data from data that can flow across a trust boundary, as shown in Figure 1–2.

Java software components provide many opportunities to output sensitive information. Rules that address the mitigation of sensitive information disclosure include the following:

Rule	Page
ERR01-J. Do not allow exceptions to expose sensitive information	263
FIO13-J. Do not log sensitive information outside a trust boundary	516
IDS03-J. Do not log unsanitized user input	41
MSC03-J. Never hard code sensitive information	635
SER03-J. Do not serialize unencrypted, sensitive data	541
SER04-J. Do not allow serialization and deserialization to bypass the security manager	546
SER06-J. Make defensive copies of private mutable components during deserialization	551

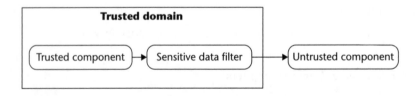

Figure 1–2. Filtering data

Interfaces, classes, and class members (such as fields and methods) are access-controlled in Java. The access is indicated by an access modifier (public, protected, or private) or by the absence of an access modifier (the default access, also called package-private access).

Java's type safety means that fields that are declared private or protected or that have default (package) protection should not be globally accessible. However, there are a number of vulnerabilities *built in* to Java that enable this protection to be overcome such as the misuse of Java reflection. These should come as no surprise to the Java expert because they are well-documented, but they may trap the unwary. For example, a field that is declared public may be directly accessed by any part of a Java program and may be modified from anywhere in a Java program (unless the field is also declared final). Clearly, sensitive information must not be stored in a public field because it could be compromised by anyone who could access the JVM running the program.

Table 1–1 presents a simplified view of the access control rules. An x indicates that the particular access is permitted from within that domain. For example, an x in the "Class" column means that the member is accessible to code present within the same class in which it is declared. Similarly, the "Package" column indicates that the member is accessible from any class (or subclass) defined in the same package, provided that the referring class (or subclass) and the class containing the member were loaded by the same class loader. The same class loader condition applies only to package-private member access.

Classes and class members should be given the minimum possible access so that malicious code has the least opportunity to compromise security. As far as possible, classes should avoid using interfaces to expose methods that contain (or invoke) sensitive code; interfaces allow only publicly accessible methods, and such methods are part of the public application programming interface (API) of the class. (Note that this is the opposite of Bloch's recommendation to prefer interfaces for APIs [Bloch 2008, Item 16].) One exception

Table 1–1. Access control rules

Access Specifier	Class	Package	Subclass	World
Private	x			
None	x	x	x*	
Protected	x	x	x**	
Public	x	x	x	x

*Subclasses within the same package can also access members that have no access specifiers (default or package-private visibility). An additional requirement for access is that the subclasses must be loaded by the class loader that loaded the class containing the package-private members. Subclasses in a different package cannot access such package-private members.

**To reference a protected member, the accessing code must be contained in either the class that defines the protected member or in a subclass of that defining class. Subclass access is permitted without regard to the package location of the subclass.

to this is implementing an *unmodifiable* interface that exposes a public immutable view of a mutable object. (See rule OBJ04-J.) Additionally, note that even when a nonfinal class's visibility is package-private, it remains susceptible to misuse if it contains public methods. Methods that perform all necessary security checks, as well as sanitize all inputs, can also be exposed through interfaces.

Protected accessibility is invalid for top-level classes, although nested classes may be declared protected. Fields of nonfinal public classes must not be declared protected to prevent untrusted code in another package from subclassing the class and accessing the member. Furthermore, protected members are part of the API of the class and require continued support. Rule OBJ01-J requires declaring fields private.

When a class, interface, method, or field is part of a published API, such as a web service end point, it may be declared public. Other classes and members should be declared either package-private or private. For example, classes that are not critical to security are encouraged to provide public static factories to implement instance control with a private constructor.

■ Leaking Capabilities

A capability is a communicable, unforgeable token of authority. The term *capability* was introduced by Dennis and Van Horn [Dennis 1966]. It refers to a value that references an object along with an associated set of access rights. A user program on a capability-based operating system must use a capability to access an object.

Each Java object has an unforgeable identity. Because the Java == operator tests for reference equality, it can be used to test this identity. This unforgeable identity allows use of a reference to an object as a token, serving as an unforgeable proof of authorization to perform some action [Mettler 2010a].

Authority is embodied by object references, which serve as capabilities. Authority refers to any effects that running code can have other than to perform side-effect-free computations. Authority includes effects not only on external resources such as files or network sockets but also on mutable data structures that are shared with other parts of the program [Mettler 2010b].

References to objects whose methods can perform sensitive operations can serve as capabilities that enable the holder to perform those operations (or to request that the object perform those operations on behalf of the holder). Consequently, such references must themselves be treated as sensitive data and must not be leaked to untrusted code.

An often surprising source of leaked capabilities and leaked data is inner classes, which have access to all the fields of their enclosing class. Java bytecodes lack built-in support for inner classes; consequently, inner classes are compiled into ordinary classes with stylized names, such as `OuterClass$InnerClass`. Because inner classes must be able to access the private fields of their enclosing class, the access control for those fields is changed to package access in the bytecode. Consequently, handcrafted bytecode can access these nominally private fields (see "Security Aspects in Java Bytecode Engineering" [Schönefeld 2002] for an example).

Rules regarding capabilities include the following:

Rule	Page
ERR09-J. Do not allow untrusted code to terminate the JVM	296
MET04-J. Do not increase the accessibility of overridden or hidden methods	218
OBJ08-J. Do not expose sensitive private members of an outer class from within a nested class	192
SEC00-J. Do not allow privileged blocks to leak sensitive information across a trust boundary	570
SEC04-J. Protect sensitive operations with security manager checks	582
SER08-J. Minimize privileges before deserializing from a privileged context	558

■ Denial of Service

Denial-of-service attacks attempt to make a computer resource unavailable or insufficiently available to its intended users. Such attacks are generally of greater concern for persistent, server-type systems than for desktop applications; nevertheless, denial-of-service issues can arise for all classes of application.

Denial of Service through Resource Exhaustion

Denial of service can occur when resource usage is disproportionately large in comparison to the input data that causes the resource usage. Checking inputs for excessive resource consumption may be unjustified for client software that expects the user to handle resource-related problems. Even such client software, however, should check for inputs that could cause persistent denial of service, such as filling up the file system.

Secure Coding Guidelines for the Java Programming Language [SCG 2009] lists some examples of possible attacks:

- Requesting a large image size for vector graphics, such as SVG and font files
- "Zip bombs," where small files, such as ZIPs, GIFs, or gzip-encoded HTML content consume excessive resources when uncompressed because of extreme compression
- "Billion laughs attack," whereby XML entity expansion causes an XML document to grow dramatically during parsing. This can be mitigated by setting the XMLConstants. FEATURE_SECURE_PROCESSING feature to enforce reasonable limits

- Using excessive disk space
- Inserting many keys with the same hash code into a hash table, consequently triggering worst-case performance ($O(n^2)$)) rather than average-case performance ($O(n)$))
- Initiating many connections where the server allocates significant resources for each (the traditional SYN flood attack, for example)

Rules regarding denial-of-service attacks and their prevention resulting from resource exhaustion include the following:

Rule	Page
FIO03-J. Remove temporary files before termination	483
FIO04-J. Close resources when they are no longer needed	487
FIO07-J. Do not let external processes block on input and output streams	500
FIO14-J. Perform proper cleanup at program termination	519
IDS04-J. Limit the size of files passed to `ZipInputStream`	43
MET12-J. Do not use finalizers	248
MSC04-J. Do not leak memory	638
MSC05-J. Do not exhaust heap space	647
SER10-J. Avoid memory and resource leaks during serialization	563
TPS00-J. Use thread pools to enable graceful degradation of service during traffic bursts	418
TPS01-J. Do not execute interdependent tasks in a bounded thread pool	421
VNA03-J. Do not assume that a group of calls to independently atomic methods is atomic	317

Concurrency-Related Denial of Service

Some denial-of-service attacks operate by attempting to induce concurrency-related problems, such as thread deadlock, thread starvation, and race conditions.

Rules regarding prevention of denial-of-service attacks resulting from concurrency issues include the following:

Rule	Page
LCK00-J. Use private final lock objects to synchronize classes that may interact with untrusted code	332
LCK01-J. Do not synchronize on objects that may be reused	339

Other Denial-of-Service Attacks

Additional rules regarding prevention of denial-of-service attacks include the following:

Precursors to Denial of Service

A number of additional rules address vulnerabilities that can enable denial-of-service attacks but are insufficient to cause denial of service on their own:

■ Serialization

Serialization enables object state in a Java program to be captured and written out to a byte stream [Sun 2004b]. This allows for the object state to be preserved so that it can be reinstated in the future (by deserialization). Serialization also enables Java method calls to be transmitted over a network using remote method invocation (RMI), wherein objects are *marshalled* (serialized), exchanged between distributed virtual machines, and *unmarshalled* (deserialized). Serialization is also extensively used in JavaBeans.

An object can be serialized as follows:

```
ObjectOutputStream oos = new ObjectOutputStream(
    new FileOutputStream("SerialOutput"));
oos.writeObject(someObject);
oos.flush();
```

The object can then be deserialized as follows:

```
ObjectInputStream ois = new ObjectInputStream(
    new FileInputStream("SerialOutput"));
someObject = (SomeClass) ois.readObject();
```

Serialization captures all the nontransient fields of an object, including the nonpublic fields that are normally inaccessible, provided that the object's class implements the Serializable interface. If the byte stream to which the serialized values are written is readable, the values of the normally inaccessible fields may be deduced. Moreover, it may be possible to modify or forge the preserved values so that when the class is deserialized, the values become corrupted.

Introducing a security manager fails to prevent normally inaccessible fields from being serialized and deserialized (although permission must be granted to write to and read from the file or network if the byte stream is being stored or transmitted). Network traffic (including RMI) can be protected, however, by using SSL/TLS (Secure Sockets Layer/Transport Layer Security).

Classes that require special handling during object serialization or deserialization can implement the following methods with precisely the following signatures [API 2006]:

```
private void writeObject(java.io.ObjectOutputStream out)
  throws IOException;
private void readObject(java.io.ObjectInputStream in)
  throws IOException, ClassNotFoundException;
```

When a Serializable class lacks an overriding implementation of writeObject(), the object is serialized using a default method, which serializes all its public, protected, package-private, and private fields, except for transient fields. Similarly, when a `Serializable` class lacks an overriding implementation of `readObject()`, the object is deserialized by deserializing all its public, protected, and private fields, with the exception of transient fields. This issue is described further in rule SER01-J.

■ Concurrency, Visibility, and Memory

Memory that can be shared between threads is called *shared memory* or *heap memory*. The term *variable* as used in this section refers to both fields and array elements [JLS 2005]. Variables that are shared between threads are referred to as shared variables. All instance fields, static fields, and array elements are shared variables and are stored in heap memory. Local variables, formal method parameters, and exception handler parameters are never shared between threads and are unaffected by the memory model.

In modern shared-memory multiprocessor architectures, each processor has one or more levels of cache that are periodically reconciled with main memory, as shown in Figure 1–3.

The visibility of writes to shared variables can be problematic because the value of a shared variable may be cached, and writing its value to main memory may be delayed. Consequently, another thread may read a stale value of the variable.

A further concern is not only that concurrent executions of code are typically interleaved, but also that the compiler or runtime system may reorder statements to optimize performance. This results in execution orders that are difficult to discern by examination

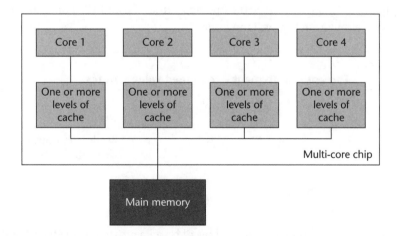

Figure 1–3. Shared-memory multiprocessor architectures

of the source code. Failure to account for possible reorderings is a common source of data races.

Consider the following example in which a and b are (shared) global variables or instance fields, but r1 and r2 are local variables that are inaccessible to other threads.

Initially, let a = 0 and b = 0.

Thread 1	Thread 2
a = 10;	b = 20;
r1 = b;	r2 = a;

In Thread 1, the two assignments a = 10; and r1 = b; are unrelated, so the compiler or runtime system is free to reorder them. The two assignments in Thread 2 may also be freely reordered. Although it may seem counterintuitive, the Java memory model allows a read to see the value of a write that occurs later in the apparent execution order.

This is a possible execution order showing actual assignments:

Execution Order (Time)	Thread#	Assignment	Assigned Value	Notes
1.	t_1	a = 10;	10	
2.	t_2	b = 20;	20	
3.	t_1	r1 = b;	0	Reads initial value of b, that is, 0
4.	t_2	r2 = a;	0	Reads initial value of a, that is, 0

In this ordering, r1 and r2 read the original values of the variables b and a respectively, even though they are expected to see the updated values, 20 and 10. This is another possible execution order showing actual assignments:

Execution Order (Time)	Thread#	Statement	Assigned Value	Notes
1.	t_1	r1 = b;	20	Reads later value (in step 4) of write, that is, 20
2.	t_2	r2 = a;	10	Reads later value (in step 3) of write, that is, 10
3.	t_1	a = 10;	10	
4.	t_2	b = 20;	20	

In this ordering, r1 and r2 read the values of b and a written from steps 4 and 3 respectively, even before the statements corresponding to these steps have executed.

Restricting the set of possible reorderings makes it easier to reason about the correctness of the code.

Even when statements execute in the order of their appearance in a thread, caching can prevent the latest values from being reflected in the main memory.

The *Java Language Specification (JLS)* defines the Java Memory Model (JMM), which provides certain guarantees to the Java programmer. The JMM is specified in terms of actions, including variable reads and writes, monitor locks and unlocks, and thread starts and joins. The JMM defines a partial ordering called *happens-before* on all actions within the program. To guarantee that a thread executing action B can see the results of action A, for example, there must be a happens-before relationship defined such that A happens-before B.

According to the JLS, §17.4.5, "Happens-before Order" [JLS 2005]:

1. An unlock on a monitor happens-before every subsequent lock on that monitor.
2. A write to a volatile field happens-before every subsequent read of that field.
3. A call to `Thread.start()` on a thread happens-before any actions in the started thread.
4. All actions in a thread happen-before any other thread successfully returns from a `Thread.join()` on that thread.
5. The default initialization of any object happens-before any other actions (other than default writes) of a program.
6. A thread calling interrupt on another thread happens-before the interrupted thread detects the interrupt.
7. The end of a constructor for an object happens-before the start of the finalizer for that object.

When two operations lack a happens-before relationship, the JVM is free to reorder them. A data race occurs when a variable is written to by at least one thread and read by at least one other thread and the reads and writes lack a happens-before relationship. A correctly synchronized program is one that lacks data races. The JMM guarantees *sequential consistency* for correctly synchronized programs. Sequential consistency means that the result of any execution is the same as if the reads and writes on shared data by all threads were executed in some sequential order, and the operations of each individual thread appear in this sequence in the order specified by its program [Tanenbaum 2003]. In other words:

1. Take the read and write operations performed by each thread and put them in the order the thread executes them (thread order).
2. Interleave the operations in some way allowed by the happens-before relationships to form an execution order.

3. Read operations must return most recently written data in the total program order for the execution to be sequentially consistent.

4. This implies that all threads see the same total ordering of reads and writes of shared variables.

The actual execution order of instructions and memory accesses can vary as long as the actions of the thread appear to that thread *as if* program order were followed and provided all values read are allowed for by the memory model. This allows programmers to understand the semantics of the programs they write and allows compiler writers and virtual machine implementors to perform various optimizations [JPL 2006].

There are several concurrency primitives that can help a programmer reason about the semantics of multithreaded programs.

The `volatile` Keyword

Declaring shared variables as volatile ensures visibility and limits reordering of accesses. Volatile accesses do not guarantee the atomicity of composite operations such as incrementing a variable. Consequently, use of volatile is insufficient when the atomicity of composite operations must be guaranteed (see rule CON02-J for more information).

Declaring variables as volatile establishes a happens-before relationship such that a write to a volatile variable is always seen by threads performing subsequent reads of the same variable. Statements that occur before the write to the volatile field also happen-before any reads of the volatile field.

Consider two threads that are executing some statements, as shown in Figure 1–4.

Thread 1 and Thread 2 have a happens-before relationship such that Thread 2 cannot start before Thread 1 finishes.

Thread 1

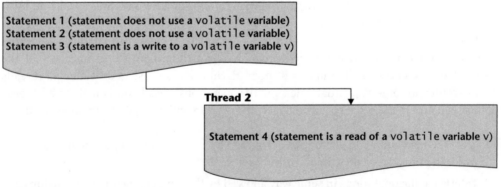

Statement 1 (statement does not use a `volatile` variable)
Statement 2 (statement does not use a `volatile` variable)
Statement 3 (statement is a write to a `volatile` variable v)

Thread 2

Statement 4 (statement is a read of a `volatile` variable v)

Figure 1–4. Volatile read and write operations

In this example, Statement 3 writes to a volatile variable, and Statement 4 (in Thread 2) reads the same volatile variable. The read sees the most recent write (to the same variable v) from Statement 3.

Volatile read and write operations cannot be reordered either with respect to each other or with respect to nonvolatile variable accesses. When Thread 2 reads the volatile variable, it sees the results of all the writes occurring before the write to the volatile variable in Thread 1. Because of the relatively strong guarantees of volatile, the performance overhead of volatile is almost the same as that of synchronization.

The previous example lacks a guarantee that Statements 1 and 2 will be executed in the order in which they appear in the program. They may be freely reordered by the compiler because of the absence of a happens-before relationship between these two statements.

The possible reorderings between volatile and nonvolatile variables are summarized in Table 1–2. Load and store operations are synonymous with read and write operations, respectively [Lea 2008].

Note that the visibility and ordering guarantees provided by the `volatile` keyword apply specifically to the variable; that is, they apply only to primitive fields and object references. For the purposes of these guarantees, the actual member is the object reference itself; the objects referred to by volatile object references (referents) are beyond the scope of the guarantees. Consequently, declaring an object reference volatile is insufficient to guarantee that changes to the members of the referent are visible. That is, a thread may fail to observe a recent write from another thread to a member field of such a referent. Furthermore, when the referent is mutable and lacks thread-safety, other threads might see a partially constructed object or an object in a (temporarily) inconsistent state [Goetz 2007]. However, when the referent is immutable, declaring the reference volatile suffices to guarantee visibility of the members of the referent.

Table 1–2. Possible reorderings between volatile and nonvolatile variables

Can Reorder	2nd Operation			
1st Operation	Normal Load	Normal Store	Volatile Load	Volatile Store
Normal load	Yes	Yes	Yes	No
Normal store	Yes	Yes	Yes	No
Volatile load	No	No	No	No
Volatile store	Yes	Yes	No	No

Synchronization

A correctly synchronized program is one whose sequentially consistent executions lack data races. The example shown here uses a nonvolatile variable x and a volatile variable y. It is incorrectly synchronized.

Thread 1	Thread 2
x = 1	r1 = y
y = 2	r2 = x

There are two sequentially consistent execution orders of this example:

Step (Time)	Thread#	Statement	Comment
1.	t_1	x = 1	Write to nonvolatile variable
2.	t_1	y = 2	Write to volatile variable
3.	t_2	r1 = y	Read of volatile variable
4.	t_2	r2 = x	Read of nonvolatile variable

and

Step (Time)	Thread#	Statement	Comment
1.	t_2	r1 = y	Read of volatile variable
2.	t_2	r2 = x	Read of nonvolatile variable
3.	t_1	x = 1	Write to nonvolatile variable
4.	t_1	y = 2	Write to volatile variable

In the first case, there is a happens-before relationship between actions such that Steps 1 and 2 always occur before Steps 3 and 4. However, the second sequentially consistent execution case lacks a happens-before relationship between any of the steps. Consequently, this example contains data races.

Correct visibility guarantees that multiple threads accessing shared data can view each other's results but fails to establish the order in which each thread reads or writes the data. Correct synchronization provides correct visibility and also guarantees that threads access data in a proper order. For example, the following code ensures that there is only one sequentially consistent execution order that performs all the actions of Thread 1 before Thread 2.

```
class Assign {
  public synchronized void doSomething() {
    // If in Thread 1, perform Thread 1 actions
    x = 1;
    y = 2;
    // If in Thread 2, perform Thread 2 actions
    r1 = y;
    r2 = x;
  }
}
```

When using synchronization, it is unnecessary to declare the variable y volatile. Synchronization involves acquiring a lock, performing operations, and then releasing the lock. In the previous example, the doSomething() method acquires the intrinsic lock of the class object Assign. This example can also be written to use block synchronization:

```
class Assign {
  public void doSomething() {
    synchronized (this) {
      // If in Thread 1, perform Thread 1 actions
      x = 1;
      y = 2;
      // If in Thread 2, perform Thread 2 actions
      r1 = y;
      r2 = x;
    }
  }
}
```

The intrinsic lock used in both examples is the same. An object's intrinsic lock is also known as its monitor. Releasing an object's intrinsic lock always has a happens-before relationship with the next acquisition of the object's intrinsic lock.

The java.util.concurrent Classes

Atomic Classes   Volatile variables are useful for guaranteeing visibility. However, they are insufficient for ensuring atomicity. Synchronization addresses this requirement but incurs overheads of context switching and frequently causes lock contention. The atomic classes of package java.util.concurrent.atomic provide a mechanism for reducing contention in most practical environments while at the same time ensuring atomicity. According to Goetz and colleagues, "With low to moderate contention, atomics offer better scalability; with high contention, locks offer better contention avoidance" [Goetz 2006a].

The atomic classes expose commonly needed functionality to the programmer while providing efficient execution by taking advantage of the *compare-and-swap* instruction(s) provided by modern processors. For example, the `AtomicInteger.incrementAndGet()` method supports atomic increment of a variable. Other high-level methods such as `java.util.concurrent.atomic.Atomic*.compareAndSet()` (where the asterisk can be, for example, an `Integer`, `Long`, or `Boolean`) also provide a clean abstract interface for programmers while making efficient use of processor facilities.

The `java.util.concurrent` utilities are preferred over traditional synchronization primitives such as the `synchronized` keyword and volatile variables because the utilities abstract away the underlying details, provide a cleaner and less error-prone API, are easier to scale, and can be enforced using policies.

The Executor Framework   The `java.util.concurrent` package provides a mechanism for concurrent execution of tasks through use of the executor framework. A task is a logical unit of work encapsulated by a class that implements `Runnable` or `Callable`. The executor framework decouples task submission from low-level scheduling and thread management details. It also provides a thread pool mechanism that allows a system to degrade gracefully when presented with more requests than the system can handle simultaneously.

The core interface of the framework is the `Executor` interface. It is extended by the `ExecutorService` interface, which provides facilities for thread pool termination and for obtaining return values of tasks. The `ExecutorService` interface is further extended by the `ScheduledExecutorService` interface, which provides a mechanism for running tasks either periodically or after some delay. The `Executors` class provides several factory and utility methods that provide commonly used configurations of `Executor`, `ExecutorService`, and other related interfaces. For example, the `Executors.newFixedThreadPool()` method returns a fixed-size thread pool with an upper limit on the number of concurrently executing tasks and maintains an unbounded queue for holding tasks while the thread pool is full. The base (actual) implementation of the thread pool is provided by the `ThreadPoolExecutor` class. This class can be instantiated to customize the task execution policy.

Explicit Locking   The `ReentrantLock` class from the `java.util.concurrent` package provides additional features that are missing from intrinsic locks. For example, the `ReentrantLock.tryLock()` method returns immediately when another thread is already holding the lock. The JMM semantics for acquiring and releasing a `ReentrantLock` are identical to those for acquiring and releasing an intrinsic lock.

■ Principle of Least Privilege

According to the principle of least privilege, every program and every user of the system should operate using the least set of privileges necessary to complete their particular task [Saltzer 1974, Saltzer 1975]. The *Build Security In* website [DHS 2006] provides additional definitions of this principle. Executing with minimal privileges reduces the severity of exploitation in case a vulnerability is discovered in the code.

Specific rules that enforce the principle of least privilege include the following:

Rule	Page
ENV03-J. Do not grant dangerous combinations of permissions	613
SEC00-J. Do not allow privileged blocks to leak sensitive information across a trust boundary	570
SEC01-J. Do not allow tainted variables in privileged blocks	574

The security policy that defines the set of permissions should be as restrictive as possible. When a Java program is run with a security manager in place, the default security policy file grants permissions sparingly; however, Java's flexible security model allows the user to grant additional permissions to applications by defining a custom security policy.

Java uses code signing as a requirement for granting elevated privileges to code. Many security policies permit signed code to operate with elevated privileges. Only code that requires elevated privileges should be signed; other code should not be signed. (See rule ENV00-J.)

Code that needs to be signed may coexist with unsigned classes in the same JAR file. It is recommended that all privileged code be packaged together. (See rule ENV01-J for more information.) Furthermore, it is possible to grant privileges to code on the basis of the code base and/or its signer using a security policy.

Privileged operations should be limited to the smallest possible code blocks that require such privileges. The Java `AccessController` mechanism allows only certain parts of code to acquire elevated privileges. When a class needs to assert its privileges, it executes the privileged code in a `doPrivileged()` block. The `AccessController` mechanism works in conjunction with the security policy in effect. Because users may be unaware of the details of the security model and incapable of correctly configuring security policies tailored to their requirements, privileged code present within the `doPrivileged()` blocks must be kept to a minimum to avoid security vulnerabilities.

■ Security Managers

`SecurityManager` is a Java class that defines a security policy for Java code. When a program runs with no security manager installed, it has no restrictions; it may use any classes or methods provided by the Java API. When a security manager is present, it specifies which potentially unsafe or sensitive actions are permitted. Any actions not allowed by the security policy cause a `SecurityException` to be thrown; code can query its security manager to discover which actions are allowed. The security manager can also control the functions that the trusted Java API can perform. When untrusted code is disallowed from accessing system classes, it should be granted only limited permissions that prevent it from accessing trusted classes in the specified packages. The `accessClassInPackage` permission provides the required functionality.

Several predefined security managers are available for certain types of applications. The applet security manager is used to manage all Java applets. It denies applets all but the most essential privileges. It is designed to protect inadvertent system modification, information leakage, and user impersonation.

The use of security managers is not limited to client-side protection. Web servers, such as Tomcat and WebSphere, use this facility to isolate Trojan servlets and malicious Java Server Page (JSP) code, as well as to protect sensitive system resources from inadvertent access.

For Java applications that run from the command line, a custom security manager can be set using a special flag. It is also possible to install a security manager programmatically. This helps create a default sandbox that permits or denies sensitive actions based on the security policy in effect.

Prior to the Java 2 SE Platform, the `SecurityManager` class was `abstract`. Because it is no longer `abstract`, there is no explicit requirement to override its methods. To create and use a security manager programmatically, the code must have the runtime permissions `createSecurityManager` to instantiate a `SecurityManager` and `setSecurityManager` to install it. These permissions are checked only when a security manager is already installed. This is useful for situations in which a global-default security manager is in place, such as on a virtual host, and individual hosts need to be denied the requisite permissions for overriding the default security manager with a custom one.

The security manager is closely tied to the `AccessController` class. The former is used as a hub for access control, whereas the latter is the actual implementer of the access control algorithm. The security manager supports

- Providing backward compatibility: Legacy code often contains custom implementations of the security manager class because it was originally `abstract`.
- Defining custom policies: Subclassing the security manager permits definition of custom security policies (multilevel, coarse, or fine-grained, for example).

Regarding the implementation and use of custom security managers, as opposed to default ones, the *Java Security Architecture Specification* [SecuritySpec 2008] states:

> We encourage the use of `AccessController` in application code, while customization of a security manager (via subclassing) should be the last resort and should be done with extreme care. Moreover, a customized security manager, such as one that always checks the time of the day before invoking standard security checks, could and should utilize the algorithm provided by `AccessController` whenever appropriate.

Many of the Java SE APIs perform security manager checks by default before performing sensitive operations. For example, the constructor of class `java.io.FileInputStream` throws a `SecurityException` when the caller lacks permission to read a file. Because `SecurityException` is a subclass of `RuntimeException`, the declarations of some API methods are not required to declare that they throw `RuntimeException`, and some indeed fail to do so. For example, the `java.io.FileReader` class lacks a `throws SecurityException` clause. Avoid depending on the presence or absence of security manager checks unless they are specified in the API method's documentation.

■ Class Loaders

The `java.lang.ClassLoader` class and its descendent classes are the means by which new code is dynamically loaded into the JVM. Every class provides a link to the `ClassLoader` that loaded it; furthermore, every class loader class also has its own parent class loader that loaded it, down to a single root class loader. `ClassLoader` is abstract, so it cannot be instantiated. All class loaders inherit from `SecureClassLoader`, which itself inherits from `ClassLoader`. `SecureClassLoader` performs security checks on its methods, as do its descendents. `SecureClassLoader` defines a `getPermissions()` method, which indicates the privileges available to classes loaded by the class loader. This serves to provide protection mechanisms limiting what additional classes may be loaded by untrusted code.

Fortunately, classes loaded by different class loaders are always different. For the purposes of the security of untrusted code, package-private (that is, default) access can be considered the same as private access.

■ Summary

Although it is a relatively secure language, the Java programming language and libraries are still prone to a large variety of programming errors that can leave systems vulnerable to attack. It is an error of the first magnitude to assume that the features provided by Java to mitigate common programming mistakes suffice to render Java programs inherently secure, and that further measures are unnecessary. Maintaining a security mindset is essential to developing and deploying systems that are free from exploitable software vulnerabilities because any implementation bug can have serious security ramifications.

To minimize the likelihood of security vulnerabilities caused by programmer error, Java developers should adhere to the secure coding rules specified by this coding standard and follow other applicable secure coding guidelines.

Chapter 2

Input Validation and Data Sanitization (IDS)

■ Rules

■ Risk Assessment Summary

Rule	Severity	Likelihood	Remediation Cost	Priority	Level
IDS00-J	high	probable	medium	P12	L1
IDS01-J	high	probable	medium	P12	L1
IDS02-J	medium	unlikely	medium	P4	L3
IDS03-J	medium	probable	medium	P8	L2
IDS04-J	low	probable	high	P2	L3
IDS05-J	medium	unlikely	medium	P4	L3
IDS06-J	medium	unlikely	medium	P4	L3
IDS07-J	high	probable	medium	P12	L1
IDS08-J	medium	unlikely	medium	P4	L3
IDS09-J	medium	probable	medium	P8	L2
IDS10-J	low	unlikely	medium	P2	L3
IDS11-J	high	probable	medium	P12	L1
IDS12-J	low	probable	medium	P4	L3
IDS13-J	low	unlikely	medium	P2	L3

■ IDS00-J. Sanitize untrusted data passed across a trust boundary

Many programs accept untrusted data originating from unvalidated users, network connections, and other untrusted sources and then pass the (modified or unmodified) data across a trust boundary to a different trusted domain. Frequently the data is in the form of a string with some internal syntactic structure, which the subsystem must parse. Such data must be sanitized both because the subsystem may be unprepared to handle the malformed input and because unsanitized input may include an injection attack.

In particular, programs must sanitize all string data that is passed to command interpreters or parsers so that the resulting string is innocuous in the context in which it is parsed or interpreted.

Many command interpreters and parsers provide their own sanitization and validation methods. When available, their use is preferred over custom sanitization techniques because custom developed sanitization can often neglect special cases or hidden complexities in the parser. Another problem with custom sanitization code is that it may not be adequately maintained when new capabilities are added to the command interpreter or parser software.

SQL Injection

A SQL injection vulnerability arises when the original SQL query can be altered to form an altogether different query. Execution of this altered query may result in information leaks or data modification. The primary means of preventing SQL injection are sanitizing and validating untrusted input and parameterizing queries.

Suppose a database contains user names and passwords used to authenticate users of the system. The user names have a string size limit of 8. The passwords have a size limit of 20.

A SQL command to authenticate a user might take the form:

```
SELECT * FROM db_user WHERE username='<USERNAME>' AND
                            password='<PASSWORD>'
```

If it returns any records, the user name and password are valid.

However, if an attacker can substitute arbitrary strings for <USERNAME> and <PASSWORD>, they can perform a SQL injection by using the following string for <USERNAME>:

```
validuser' OR '1'='1
```

When injected into the command, the command becomes:

```
SELECT * FROM db_user WHERE username='validuser' OR '1'='1' AND
password=<PASSWORD>
```

If validuser is a valid user name, this SELECT statement selects the validuser record in the table. The password is never checked because username='validuser' is true; consequently the items after the OR are not tested. As long as the components after the OR generate a syntactically correct SQL expression, the attacker is granted the access of validuser.

Likewise, an attacker could supply a string for <PASSWORD> such as:

```
' OR '1'='1
```

This would yield the following command:

```
SELECT * FROM db_user WHERE username='' AND password='' OR '1'='1'
```

This time, the '1'='1' tautology disables both user name and password validation, and the attacker is falsely logged in without a correct login ID or password.

Noncompliant Code Example

This noncompliant code example shows JDBC code to authenticate a user to a system. The password is passed as a char array, the database connection is created, and then the passwords are hashed.

Unfortunately, this code example permits a SQL injection attack because the SQL statement `sqlString` accepts unsanitized input arguments. The attack scenario outlined previously would work as described.

```
class Login {
  public Connection getConnection() throws SQLException {
    DriverManager.registerDriver(new
          com.microsoft.sqlserver.jdbc.SQLServerDriver());
    String dbConnection =
      PropertyManager.getProperty("db.connection");
    // can hold some value like
    // "jdbc:microsoft:sqlserver://<HOST>:1433,<UID>,<PWD>"
    return DriverManager.getConnection(dbConnection);
  }

  String hashPassword(char[] password) {
    // create hash of password
  }

  public void doPrivilegedAction(String username, char[] password)
                            throws SQLException {
    Connection connection = getConnection();
    if (connection == null) {
      // handle error
    }
    try {
      String pwd = hashPassword(password);

      String sqlString = "SELECT * FROM db_user WHERE username = '"
                        + username +
                        "' AND password = '" + pwd + "'";
      Statement stmt = connection.createStatement();
      ResultSet rs = stmt.executeQuery(sqlString);

      if (!rs.next()) {
        throw new SecurityException(
          "User name or password incorrect"
        );
      }

      // Authenticated; proceed
    } finally {
      try {
        connection.close();
      } catch (SQLException x) {
        // forward to handler
      }
    }
  }
}
```

Compliant Solution (`PreparedStatement`)

Fortunately, the JDBC library provides an API for building SQL commands that sanitize untrusted data. The `java.sql.PreparedStatement` class properly escapes input strings, preventing SQL injection when used properly. This is an example of component-based sanitization.

This compliant solution modifies the `doPrivilegedAction()` method to use a `PreparedStatement` instead of `java.sql.Statement`. This code also validates the length of the `username` argument, preventing an attacker from submitting an arbitrarily long user name.

```java
public void doPrivilegedAction(
  String username, char[] password
) throws SQLException {
  Connection connection = getConnection();
  if (connection == null) {
    // Handle error
  }
  try {
    String pwd = hashPassword(password);

    // Ensure that the length of user name is legitimate
    if ((username.length() > 8) {
      // Handle error
    }

    String sqlString =
      "select * from db_user where username=? and password=?";
    PreparedStatement stmt = connection.prepareStatement(sqlString);
    stmt.setString(1, username);
    stmt.setString(2, pwd);
    ResultSet rs = stmt.executeQuery();
    if (!rs.next()) {
      throw new SecurityException("User name or password incorrect");
    }

    // Authenticated, proceed
  } finally {
    try {
      connection.close();
    } catch (SQLException x) {
      // forward to handler
    }
  }
}
```

Use the `set*()` methods of the `PreparedStatement` class to enforce strong type checking. This mitigates the SQL injection vulnerability because the input is properly escaped by automatic entrapment within double quotes. Note that prepared statements must be used even with queries that insert data into the database.

XML Injection

Because of its platform independence, flexibility, and relative simplicity, the extensible markup language (XML) has found use in applications ranging from remote procedure calls to systematic storage, exchange, and retrieval of data. However, because of its versatility, XML is vulnerable to a wide spectrum of attacks. One such attack is called *XML injection*.

A user who has the ability to provide structured XML as input can override the contents of an XML document by injecting XML tags in data fields. These tags are interpreted and classified by an XML parser as executable content and, as a result, may cause certain data members to be overridden.

Consider the following XML code snippet from an online store application, designed primarily to query a back-end database. The user has the ability to specify the quantity of an item available for purchase.

```
<item>
  <description>Widget</description>
  <price>500.0</price>
  <quantity>1</quantity>
</item>
```

A malicious user might input the following string instead of a simple number in the `quantity` field.

```
1</quantity><price>1.0</price><quantity>1
```

Consequently, the XML resolves to the following block:

```
<item>
  <description>Widget</description>
  <price>500.0</price>
  <quantity>1</quantity><price>1.0</price><quantity>1</quantity>
</item>
```

A Simple API for XML (SAX) parser (`org.xml.sax` and `javax.xml.parsers.` `SAXParser`) interprets the XML such that the second price field overrides the first, leaving the price of the item as $1. Even when it is not possible to perform such an attack, the attacker may be able to inject special characters, such as comment blocks and `CDATA` delimiters, which corrupt the meaning of the XML.

Noncompliant Code Example

In this noncompliant code example, a client method uses simple string concatenation to build an XML query to send to a server. XML injection is possible because the method performs no input validation.

```
private void createXMLStream(BufferedOutputStream outStream,
                            String quantity) throws IOException {
  String xmlString;
  xmlString = "<item>\n<description>Widget</description>\n" +
              "<price>500.0</price>\n" +
              "<quantity>" + quantity + "</quantity></item>";
  outStream.write(xmlString.getBytes());
  outStream.flush();
}
```

Compliant Solution (Whitelisting)

Depending on the specific data and command interpreter or parser to which data is being
sent, appropriate methods must be used to sanitize untrusted user input. This compliant
solution uses whitelisting to sanitize the input. In this compliant solution, the method
requires that the quantity field must be a number between 0 and 9.

```
private void createXMLStream(BufferedOutputStream outStream,
                            String quantity) throws IOException {
  // Write XML string if quantity contains numbers only.
  // Blacklisting of invalid characters can be performed
  // in conjunction.

  if (!Pattern.matches("[0-9]+", quantity)) {
    // Format violation
  }

  String xmlString = "<item>\n<description>Widget</description>\n" +
                     "<price>500</price>\n" +
                     "<quantity>" + quantity + "</quantity></item>";
  outStream.write(xmlString.getBytes());
  outStream.flush();
}
```

Compliant Solution (XML Schema)

A more general mechanism for checking XML for attempted injection is to validate it using
a Document Type Definition (DTD) or schema. The schema must be rigidly defined to prevent injections from being mistaken for valid XML. Here is a suitable schema for validating
our XML snippet:

```
<xs:schema xmlns:xs="http://www.w3.org/2001/XMLSchema">
<xs:element name="item">
```

```
   <xs:complexType>
    <xs:sequence>
      <xs:element name="description" type="xs:string"/>
      <xs:element name="price" type="xs:decimal"/>
      <xs:element name="quantity" type="xs:integer"/>
    </xs:sequence>
   </xs:complexType>
</xs:element>
</xs:schema>
```

The schema is available as the file `schema.xsd`. This compliant solution employs this schema to prevent XML injection from succeeding. It also relies on the `CustomResolver` class to prevent XXE attacks. This class, as well as XXE attacks, are described in the subsequent code examples.

```java
private void createXMLStream(BufferedOutputStream outStream,
                            String quantity) throws IOException {
  String xmlString;
  xmlString = "<item>\n<description>Widget</description>\n" +
              "<price>500.0</price>\n" +
              "<quantity>" + quantity + "</quantity></item>";
  InputSource xmlStream = new InputSource(
    new StringReader(xmlString)
  );

  // Build a validating SAX parser using our schema
  SchemaFactory sf
    = SchemaFactory.newInstance(XMLConstants.W3C_XML_SCHEMA_NS_URI);
  DefaultHandler defHandler = new DefaultHandler() {
      public void warning(SAXParseException s)
        throws SAXParseException {throw s;}
      public void error(SAXParseException s)
        throws SAXParseException {throw s;}
      public void fatalError(SAXParseException s)
        throws SAXParseException {throw s;}
    };
  StreamSource ss = new StreamSource(new File("schema.xsd"));
  try {
    Schema schema = sf.newSchema(ss);
    SAXParserFactory spf = SAXParserFactory.newInstance();
    spf.setSchema(schema);
    SAXParser saxParser = spf.newSAXParser();
    // To set the custom entity resolver,
    // an XML reader needs to be created
    XMLReader reader = saxParser.getXMLReader();
    reader.setEntityResolver(new CustomResolver());
    saxParser.parse(xmlStream, defHandler);
```

```
  } catch (ParserConfigurationException x) {
    throw new IOException("Unable to validate XML", x);
  } catch (SAXException x) {
    throw new IOException("Invalid quantity", x);
  }

  // Our XML is valid, proceed
  outStream.write(xmlString.getBytes());
  outStream.flush();
}
```

Using a schema or DTD to validate XML is convenient when receiving XML that may have been loaded with unsanitized input. If such an XML string has not yet been built, sanitizing input before constructing XML yields better performance.

XML External Entity Attacks (XXE)

An XML document can be dynamically constructed from smaller logical blocks called entities. Entities can be internal, external, or parameter-based. External entities allow the inclusion of XML data from external files.

According to XML W3C Recommendation [W3C 2008], Section 4.4.3, "Included If Validating":

> When an XML processor recognizes a reference to a parsed entity, to validate the document, the processor MUST include its replacement text. If the entity is external, and the processor is not attempting to validate the XML document, the processor MAY, but need not, include the entity's replacement text.

An attacker may attempt to cause denial of service or program crashes by manipulating the URI of the entity to refer to special files existing on the local file system, for example, by specifying /dev/random or /dev/tty as input URIs. This may crash or block the program indefinitely. This is called an XML external entity (XXE) attack. Because inclusion of replacement text from an external entity is optional, not all XML processors are vulnerable to external entity attacks.

Noncompliant Code Example

This noncompliant code example attempts to parse the file evil.xml, reports any errors, and exits. However, a SAX or a DOM (Document Object Model) parser will attempt to access the URL specified by the SYSTEM attribute, which means it will attempt to read the contents of the local /dev/tty file. On POSIX systems, reading this file causes the program to block until input data is supplied to the machine's console. Consequently, an attacker can use this malicious XML file to cause the program to hang.

```java
class XXE {
  private static void receiveXMLStream(InputStream inStream,
                                       DefaultHandler defaultHandler)
      throws ParserConfigurationException, SAXException, IOException {
    SAXParserFactory factory = SAXParserFactory.newInstance();
    SAXParser saxParser = factory.newSAXParser();
    saxParser.parse(inStream, defaultHandler);
  }

  public static void main(String[] args)
      throws ParserConfigurationException, SAXException, IOException {
    receiveXMLStream(new FileInputStream("evil.xml"),
                     new DefaultHandler());
  }
}
```

This program is subject to a remote XXE attack if the `evil.xml` file contains the following:

```xml
<?xml version="1.0"?>
<!DOCTYPE foo SYSTEM "file:/dev/tty">
<foo>bar</foo>
```

This noncompliant code example may also violate rule ERR06-J if the information contained in the exceptions is sensitive.

Compliant Solution (`EntityResolver`)

This compliant solution defines a `CustomResolver` class that implements the interface `org.xml.sax.EntityResolver`. This enables a SAX application to customize handling of external entities. The `setEntityResolver()` method registers the instance with the corresponding SAX driver. The customized handler uses a simple whitelist for external entities. The `resolveEntity()` method returns an empty `InputSource` when an input fails to resolve to any of the specified, safe entity source paths. Consequently, when parsing malicious input, the empty `InputSource` returned by the custom resolver causes a `java.net.MalformedURLException` to be thrown. Note that you must create an `XMLReader` object on which to set the custom entity resolver.

This is an example of component-based sanitization.

```java
class CustomResolver implements EntityResolver {
  public InputSource resolveEntity(String publicId, String systemId)
    throws SAXException, IOException {

    // check for known good entities
    String entityPath = "/home/username/java/xxe/file";
    if (systemId.equals(entityPath)) {
      System.out.println("Resolving entity: " + publicId +
                         " " + systemId);
      return new InputSource(entityPath);
    } else {
      return new InputSource(); // Disallow unknown entities
                                // by returning a blank path
    }
  }
}

class XXE {
  private static void receiveXMLStream(InputStream inStream,
                                       DefaultHandler defaultHandler)
    throws ParserConfigurationException, SAXException, IOException {
    SAXParserFactory factory = SAXParserFactory.newInstance();
    SAXParser saxParser = factory.newSAXParser();

    // To set the Entity Resolver, an XML reader needs to be created
    XMLReader reader = saxParser.getXMLReader();
    reader.setEntityResolver(new CustomResolver());
    reader.setErrorHandler(defaultHandler);

    InputSource is = new InputSource(inStream);
    reader.parse(is);
  }

  public static void main(String[] args)
      throws ParserConfigurationException, SAXException, IOException {
    receiveXMLStream(new FileInputStream("evil.xml"),
                     new DefaultHandler());
  }
}
```

Risk Assessment

Failure to sanitize user input before processing or storing it can result in injection attacks.

Rule	Severity	Likelihood	Remediation Cost	Priority	Level
IDS00-J	high	probable	medium	P12	L1

Related Vulnerabilities   CVE-2008-2370 describes a vulnerability in Apache Tomcat 4.1.0 through 4.1.37, 5.5.0 through 5.5.26, and 6.0.0 through 6.0.16. When a `RequestDispatcher` is used, Tomcat performs path normalization before removing the query string from the URI, which allows remote attackers to conduct directory traversal attacks and read arbitrary files via a .. (dot dot) in a request parameter.

Related Guidelines

CERT C Secure Coding Standard	STR02-C. Sanitize data passed to complex subsystems
CERT C++ Secure Coding Standard	STR02-CPP. Sanitize data passed to complex subsystems
ISO/IEC TR 24772:2010	Injection [RST]
MITRE CWE	CWE-116. Improper encoding or escaping of output

Bibliography

[OWASP 2005]	
[OWASP 2007]	
[OWASP 2008]	Testing for XML Injection (OWASP-DV-008)
[W3C 2008]	4.4.3, Included If Validating

■ IDS01-J. Normalize strings before validating them

Many applications that accept untrusted input strings employ input filtering and validation mechanisms based on the strings' character data.

For example, an application's strategy for avoiding cross-site scripting (XSS) vulnerabilities may include forbidding `<script>` tags in inputs. Such blacklisting mechanisms are a useful part of a security strategy, even though they are insufficient for complete input validation and sanitization. When implemented, this form of validation must be performed only after normalizing the input.

Character information in Java SE 6 is based on the Unicode Standard, version 4.0 [Unicode 2003]. Character information in Java SE 7 is based on the Unicode Standard, version 6.0.0 [Unicode 2011].

According to the Unicode Standard [Davis 2008a], annex #15, Unicode Normalization Forms:

> When implementations keep strings in a normalized form, they can be assured that equivalent strings have a unique binary representation.
>
> Normalization Forms KC and KD must not be blindly applied to arbitrary text. Because they erase many formatting distinctions, they will prevent round-trip conversion to and from many legacy character sets, and unless supplanted by

formatting markup, they may remove distinctions that are important to the semantics of the text. It is best to think of these Normalization Forms as being like uppercase or lowercase mappings: useful in certain contexts for identifying core meanings, but also performing modifications to the text that may not always be appropriate. They can be applied more freely to domains with restricted character sets.

Frequently, the most suitable normalization form for performing input validation on arbitrarily encoded strings is KC (NFKC) because normalizing to KC transforms the input into an equivalent canonical form that can be safely compared with the required input form.

Noncompliant Code Example

This noncompliant code example attempts to validate the `String` before performing normalization. Consequently, the validation logic fails to detect inputs that should be rejected because the check for angle brackets fails to detect alternative Unicode representations.

```
// String s may be user controllable
// \uFE64 is normalized to < and \uFE65 is normalized to > using NFKC
String s = "\uFE64" + "script" + "\uFE65";

// Validate
Pattern pattern = Pattern.compile("[<>]"); // Check for angle brackets
Matcher matcher = pattern.matcher(s);
if (matcher.find()) {
  // Found black listed tag
  throw new IllegalStateException();
} else {
  // ...
}

// Normalize
s = Normalizer.normalize(s, Form.NFKC);
```

The `normalize()` method transforms Unicode text into an equivalent composed or decomposed form, allowing for easier searching of text. The normalize method supports the standard normalization forms described in Unicode Standard Annex #15—Unicode Normalization Forms.

Compliant Solution

This compliant solution normalizes the string before validating it. Alternative representations of the string are normalized to the canonical angle brackets. Consequently, input validation correctly detects the malicious input and throws an `IllegalStateException`.

```
String s = "\uFE64" + "script" + "\uFE65";

// Normalize
s = Normalizer.normalize(s, Form.NFKC);

// Validate
Pattern pattern = Pattern.compile("[<>]");
Matcher matcher = pattern.matcher(s);
if (matcher.find()) {
  // Found black listed tag
  throw new IllegalStateException();
} else {
  // ...
}
```

Risk Assessment

Validating input before normalization affords attackers the opportunity to bypass filters and other security mechanisms. This can result in the execution of arbitrary code.

Rule	Severity	Likelihood	Remediation Cost	Priority	Level
IDS01-J	high	probable	medium	P12	L1

Related Guidelines

ISO/IEC TR 24772:2010	Cross-site scripting [XYT]
MITRE CWE	CWE-289. Authentication bypass by alternate name
	CWE-180. Incorrect behavior order: Validate before canonicalize

Bibliography

[API 2006]
[Davis 2008a]
[Weber 2009]

▪ IDS02-J. Canonicalize path names before validating them

According to the Java API [API 2006] for class `java.io.File`:

> A path name, whether abstract or in string form, may be either absolute or relative. An absolute path name is complete in that no other information is required to locate the file that it denotes. A relative path name, in contrast, must be interpreted in terms of information taken from some other path name.

Absolute or relative path names may contain file links such as symbolic (soft) links, hard links, shortcuts, shadows, aliases, and junctions. These file links must be fully resolved before any file validation operations are performed. For example, the final target of a symbolic link called `trace` might be the path name `/home/system/trace`. Path names may also contain special file names that make validation difficult:

1. "." refers to the directory itself.
2. Inside a directory, the special file name ".." refers to the directory's parent directory.

In addition to these specific issues, there are a wide variety of operating system–specific and file system–specific naming conventions that make validation difficult.

The process of canonicalizing file names makes it easier to validate a path name. More than one path name can refer to a single directory or file. Further, the textual representation of a path name may yield little or no information regarding the directory or file to which it refers. Consequently, all path names must be fully resolved or *canonicalized* before validation.

Validation may be necessary, for example, when attempting to restrict user access to files within a particular directory or otherwise make security decisions based on the name of a file name or path name. Frequently, these restrictions can be circumvented by an attacker by exploiting a *directory traversal* or *path equivalence* vulnerability. A directory traversal vulnerability allows an I/O operation to escape a specified operating directory. A path equivalence vulnerability occurs when an attacker provides a different but equivalent name for a resource to bypass security checks.

Canonicalization contains an inherent race window between the time the program obtains the canonical path name and the time it opens the file. While the canonical path name is being validated, the file system may have been modified and the canonical path name may no longer reference the original valid file. Fortunately, this race condition can be easily mitigated. The canonical path name can be used to determine whether the referenced file name is in a secure directory (see rule FIO00-J for more information). If the referenced file is in a secure directory, then, by definition, an attacker cannot tamper with it and cannot exploit the race condition.

This rule is a specific instance of rule IDS01-J.

Noncompliant Code Example

This noncompliant code example accepts a file path as a command-line argument and uses the `File.getAbsolutePath()` method to obtain the absolute file path. It also uses the `isInSecureDir()` method defined in rule FIO00-J to ensure that the file is in a secure directory. However, it neither resolves file links nor eliminates equivalence errors.

```
public static void main(String[] args) {
  File f = new File(System.getProperty("user.home") +
    System.getProperty("file.separator") + args[0]);
```

```
    String absPath = f.getAbsolutePath();

    if (!isInSecureDir(Paths.get(absPath))) {
      throw new IllegalArgumentException();
    }
    if (!validate(absPath)) { // Validation
      throw new IllegalArgumentException();
    }
  }
}
```

The application intends to restrict the user from operating on files outside of their home directory. The `validate()` method attempts to ensure that the path name resides within this directory, but can be easily circumvented. For example, a user can create a link in their home directory that refers to a directory or file outside of their home directory. The path name of the link might appear to the `validate()` method to reside in their home directory and consequently pass validation, but the operation will actually be performed on the final target of the link, which resides outside the intended directory.

Note that `File.getAbsolutePath()` does resolve symbolic links, aliases, and short cuts on Windows and Macintosh platforms. Nevertheless, the *Java Language Specification* (JLS) lacks any guarantee that this behavior is present on *all* platforms or that it will continue in future implementations.

Compliant Solution (`getCanonicalPath()`)

This compliant solution uses the `getCanonicalPath()` method, introduced in Java 2, because it resolves all aliases, shortcuts, and symbolic links consistently across all platforms. Special file names such as dot dot (. .) are also removed so that the input is reduced to a canonicalized form before validation is carried out. An attacker cannot use `../` sequences to break out of the specified directory when the `validate()` method is present.

```
public static void main(String[] args) throws IOException {
  File f = new File(System.getProperty("user.home") +
  System.getProperty("file.separator")+ args[0]);
  String canonicalPath = f.getCanonicalPath();

  if (!isInSecureDir(Paths.get(canonicalPath))) {
    throw new IllegalArgumentException();
  }
  if (!validate(canonicalPath)) { // Validation
   throw new IllegalArgumentException();
  }
}
```

The getCanonicalPath() method throws a security exception when used within applets because it reveals too much information about the host machine. The getCanonicalFile() method behaves like getCanonicalPath() but returns a new File object instead of a String.

Compliant Solution (Security Manager)

A comprehensive way of handling this issue is to grant the application the permissions to operate only on files present within the intended directory—the user's home directory in this example. This compliant solution specifies the absolute path of the program in its security policy file and grants java.io.FilePermission with target ${user.home}/* and actions read and write.

```
grant codeBase "file:/home/programpath/" {
  permission java.io.FilePermission "${user.home}/*", "read, write";
};
```

This solution requires that the user's home directory is a secure directory as described in rule FIO00-J.

Noncompliant Code Example

This noncompliant code example allows the user to specify the absolute path of a file name on which to operate. The user can specify files outside the intended directory (/img in this example) by entering an argument that contains ../ sequences and consequently violate the intended security policies of the program.

```
FileOutputStream fis =
  new FileOutputStream(new File("/img/" + args[0]));
// ...
```

Noncompliant Code Example

This noncompliant code example attempts to mitigate the issue by using the File.getCanonicalPath() method, which fully resolves the argument and constructs a canonicalized path. For example, the path /img/../etc/passwd resolves to /etc/passwd. Canonicalization without validation is insufficient because an attacker can specify files outside the intended directory.

```
File f = new File("/img/" + args[0]);
String canonicalPath = f.getCanonicalPath();
FileOutputStream fis = new FileOutputStream(f);
// ...
```

Compliant Solution

This compliant solution obtains the file name from the untrusted user input, canonicalizes it, and then validates it against a list of benign path names. It operates on the specified file only when validation succeeds; that is, only if the file is one of the two valid files file1.txt or file2.txt in /img/java.

```
File f = new File("/img/" + args[0]);
String canonicalPath = f.getCanonicalPath();

if (!canonicalPath.equals("/img/java/file1.txt") &&
    !canonicalPath.equals("/img/java/file2.txt")) {
  // Invalid file; handle error
}

FileInputStream fis = new FileInputStream(f);
```

The /img/java directory must be secure to eliminate any race condition.

Compliant Solution (Security Manager)

This compliant solution grants the application the permissions to read only the intended files or directories. For example, read permission is granted by specifying the absolute path of the program in the security policy file and granting java.io.FilePermission with the canonicalized absolute path of the file or directory as the target name and with the action set to read.

```
// All files in /img/java can be read
grant codeBase "file:/home/programpath/" {
  permission java.io.FilePermission "/img/java", "read";
};
```

Risk Assessment

Using path names from untrusted sources without first canonicalizing them and then validating them can result in directory traversal and path equivalence vulnerabilities.

Rule	Severity	Likelihood	Remediation Cost	Priority	Level
IDS02-J	medium	unlikely	medium	P4	L3

Related Vulnerabilities CVE-2005-0789 describes a directory traversal vulnerability in LimeWire 3.9.6 through 4.6.0 that allows remote attackers to read arbitrary files via a .. (dot dot) in a magnet request.

CVE-2008-5518 describes multiple directory traversal vulnerabilities in the web administration console in Apache Geronimo Application Server 2.1 through 2.1.3 on Windows that allow remote attackers to upload files to arbitrary directories.

Related Guidelines

The CERT C Secure Coding Standard	FIO02-C. Canonicalize path names originating from untrusted sources
The CERT C++ Secure Coding Standard	FIO02-CPP. Canonicalize path names originating from untrusted sources
ISO/IEC TR 24772:2010	Path Traversal [EWR]
MITRE CWE	CWE-171. Cleansing, canonicalization, and comparison errors
	CWE-647. Use of non-canonical URL paths for authorization decisions

Bibliography

[API 2006]	Method `getCanonicalPath()`
[Harold 1999]	

■ IDS03-J. Do not log unsanitized user input

A log injection vulnerability arises when a log entry contains unsanitized user input. A malicious user can insert fake log data and consequently deceive system administrators as to the system's behavior [OWASP 2008]. For example, a user might split a legitimate log entry into two log entries by entering a carriage return and line feed (CRLF) sequence, either of which might be misleading. Log injection attacks can be prevented by sanitizing and validating any untrusted input sent to a log.

Logging unsanitized user input can also result in leaking sensitive data across a trust boundary, or storing sensitive data in a manner that violates local law or regulation. For example, if a user can inject an unencrypted credit card number into a log file, the system could violate PCI DSS regulations [PCI 2010]. See rule IDS00-J for more details on input sanitization.

Noncompliant Code Example

This noncompliant code example logs the user's login name when an invalid request is received. No input sanitization is performed.

```
if (loginSuccessful) {
  logger.severe("User login succeeded for: " + username);
} else {
  logger.severe("User login failed for: " + username);
}
```

Without sanitization, a log injection attack is possible. A standard log message when username is david might look like this:

```
May 15, 2011 2:19:10 PM java.util.logging.LogManager$RootLogger log
SEVERE: User login failed for: david
```

If the username that is used in a log message was not david, but rather a multiline string like this:

```
david
May 15, 2011 2:25:52 PM java.util.logging.LogManager$RootLogger log
SEVERE: User login succeeded for: administrator
```

the log would contain the following misleading data:

```
May 15, 2011 2:19:10 PM java.util.logging.LogManager$RootLogger log
SEVERE: User login failed for: david
May 15, 2011 2:25:52 PM java.util.logging.LogManager$RootLogger log
SEVERE: User login succeeded for: administrator
```

Compliant Solution

This compliant solution sanitizes the username input before logging it, preventing injection attacks. Refer to rule IDS00-J for more details on input sanitization.

```
if (!Pattern.matches("[A-Za-z0-9_]+", username)) {
  // Unsanitized username
  logger.severe("User login failed for unauthorized user");
} else if (loginSuccessful) {
  logger.severe("User login succeeded for: " + username);
} else {
  logger.severe("User login failed for: " + username);
}
```

Risk Assessment

Allowing unvalidated user input to be logged can result in forging of log entries, leaking secure information, or storing sensitive data in a manner that violates a local law or regulation.

Rule	Severity	Likelihood	Remediation Cost	Priority	Level
IDS03-J	medium	probable	medium	P8	L2

Related Guidelines

ISO/IEC TR 24772:2010	Injection [RST]
MITRE CWE	CWE-144. Improper neutralization of line delimiters
	CWE-150. Improper neutralization of escape, meta, or control sequences

Bibliography

[API 2006]

[OWASP 2008]

[PCI DSS Standard]

■ IDS04-J. Limit the size of files passed to `ZipInputStream`

Check inputs to `java.util.ZipInputStream` for cases that cause consumption of excessive system resources. Denial of service can occur when resource usage is disproportionately large in comparison to the input data that causes the resource usage. The nature of the zip algorithm permits the existence of *zip bombs* where a small file, such as ZIPs, GIFs, or gzip-encoded HTTP content consumes excessive resources when uncompressed because of extreme compression.

The zip algorithm is capable of producing very large compression ratios [Mahmoud 2002]. Figure 2–1 shows a file that was compressed from 148MB to 590KB, a ratio of more than 200 to 1. The file consists of arbitrarily repeated data: alternating lines of *a* characters and *b* characters. Even higher compression ratios can be easily obtained using input data that is targeted to the compression algorithm, or using more input data (that is untargeted), or other compression methods.

Any entry in a zip file whose uncompressed file size is beyond a certain limit must not be uncompressed. The actual limit is dependent on the capabilities of the platform.

This rule is a specific instance of the more general rule MSC07-J.

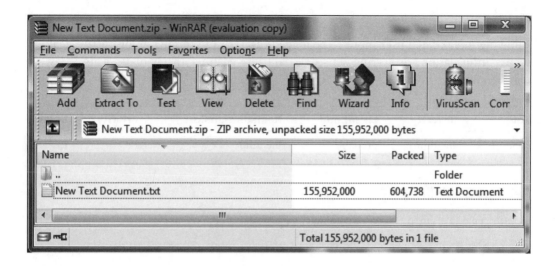

Figure 2–1. Very large compression ratios in a Zip file.

Noncompliant Code Example

This noncompliant code fails to check the resource consumption of the file that is being unzipped. It permits the operation to run to completion or until local resources are exhausted.

```
static final int BUFFER = 512;
// ...

// external data source: filename
BufferedOutputStream dest = null;
FileInputStream fis = new FileInputStream(filename);
ZipInputStream zis = new ZipInputStream(new BufferedInputStream(fis));
ZipEntry entry;
while ((entry = zis.getNextEntry()) != null) {
  System.out.println("Extracting: " + entry);
  int count;
  byte data[] = new byte[BUFFER];
  // write the files to the disk
  FileOutputStream fos = new FileOutputStream(entry.getName());
  dest = new BufferedOutputStream(fos, BUFFER);
  while ((count = zis.read(data, 0, BUFFER)) != -1) {
    dest.write(data, 0, count);
  }
  dest.flush();
  dest.close();
}
zis.close();
```

Compliant Solution

In this compliant solution, the code inside the while loop uses the `ZipEntry.getSize()` method to find the uncompressed file size of each entry in a zip archive before extracting the entry. It throws an exception if the entry to be extracted is too large—100MB in this case.

```
static final int TOOBIG = 0x6400000; // 100MB

// ...

// write the files to the disk, but only if file is not insanely big
if (entry.getSize() > TOOBIG) {
  throw new IllegalStateException("File to be unzipped is huge.");
}
if (entry.getSize() == -1) {
  throw new IllegalStateException(
          "File to be unzipped might be huge.");
}
FileOutputStream fos = new FileOutputStream(entry.getName());
dest = new BufferedOutputStream(fos, BUFFER);
while ((count = zis.read(data, 0, BUFFER)) != -1) {
  dest.write(data, 0, count);
}
```

Risk Assessment

Rule	Severity	Likelihood	Remediation Cost	Priority	Level
IDS04-J	low	probable	high	P2	L3

Related Guidelines

MITRE CWE	CWE-409. Improper handling of highly compressed data (data amplification)
Secure Coding Guidelines for the Java Programming Language, Version 3.0	Guideline 2-5. Check that inputs do not cause excessive resource consumption

Bibliography

[Mahmoud 2002]   Compressing and Decompressing Data Using Java APIs

■ IDS05-J. Use a subset of ASCII for file and path names

File and path names containing particular characters can be troublesome and can cause unexpected behavior resulting in vulnerabilities. The following characters and patterns can be problematic when used in the construction of a file or path name:

- Leading dashes: Leading dashes can cause problems when programs are called with the file name as a parameter because the first character or characters of the file name might be interpreted as an option switch.
- Control characters, such as newlines, carriage returns, and escape: Control characters in a file name can cause unexpected results from shell scripts and in logging.
- Spaces: Spaces can cause problems with scripts and when double quotes aren't used to surround the file name.
- Invalid character encodings: Character encodings can make it difficult to perform proper validation of file and path names. (See rule IDS11-J.)
- Name-space separation characters: Including name-space separation characters in a file or path name can cause unexpected and potentially insecure behavior.
- Command interpreters, scripts, and parsers: Some characters have special meaning when processed by a command interpreter, shell, or parser and should consequently be avoided.

As a result of the influence of MS-DOS, file names of the form xxxxxxxx.xxx, where x denotes an alphanumeric character, are generally supported by modern systems. On some platforms, file names are case sensitive; while on other platforms, they are case insensitive. VU#439395 is an example of a vulnerability in C resulting from a failure to deal appropriately with case sensitivity issues [VU#439395].

This rule is a specific instance of rule IDS00-J.

Noncompliant Code Example

In the following noncompliant code example, unsafe characters are used as part of a file name.

```
File f = new File("A\uD8AB");
OutputStream out = new FileOutputStream(f);
```

A platform is free to define its own mapping of unsafe characters. For example, when tested on an Ubuntu Linux distribution, this noncompliant code example resulted in the following file name:

A?

Compliant Solution

Use a descriptive file name containing only the subset of ASCII previously described.

```
File f = new File("name.ext");
OutputStream out = new FileOutputStream(f);
```

Noncompliant Code Example

This noncompliant code example creates a file with input from the user without sanitizing the input.

```
public static void main(String[] args) throws Exception {
  if (args.length < 1) {
    // handle error
  }
  File f = new File(args[0]);
  OutputStream out = new FileOutputStream(f);
  // ...
}
```

No checks are performed on the file name to prevent troublesome characters. If an attacker knew this code was in a program used to create or rename files that would later be used in a script or automated process of some sort, the attacker could choose particular characters in the output file name to confuse the later process for malicious purposes.

Compliant Solution

In this compliant solution, the program uses a whitelist to reject unsafe file names.

```
public static void main(String[] args) throws Exception {
  if (args.length < 1) {
    // handle error
  }
  String filename = args[0];

  Pattern pattern = Pattern.compile("[^A-Za-z0-9%&+,.:=_]");
  Matcher matcher = pattern.matcher(filename);
  if (matcher.find()) {
    // filename contains bad chars, handle error
  }
```

```
    File f = new File(filename);
    OutputStream out = new FileOutputStream(f);
    // ...
}
```

All file names originating from untrusted sources must be sanitized to ensure they contain only safe characters.

Risk Assessment

Failing to use only a safe subset of ASCII can result in misinterpreted data.

Rule	Severity	Likelihood	Remediation Cost	Priority	Level
IDS05-J	medium	unlikely	medium	P4	L3

Related Guidelines

CERT C Secure Coding Standard	MSC09-C. Character encoding—Use subset of ASCII for safety
CERT C++ Secure Coding Standard	MSC09-CPP. Character encoding—Use subset of ASCII for safety
ISO/IEC TR 24772:2010	Choice of filenames and other external identifiers [AJN]
MITRE CWE	CWE-116. Improper encoding or escaping of output

Bibliography

ISO/IEC 646-1991	ISO 7-bit coded character set for information interchange
[Kuhn 2006]	UTF-8 and Unicode FAQ for UNIX/Linux
[Wheeler 2003]	5.4, File Names
[VU#439395]	

▪ IDS06-J. Exclude user input from format strings

Interpretation of Java format strings is stricter than in languages such as C [Seacord 2005]. The standard library implementations throw appropriate exceptions when any conversion argument fails to match the corresponding format specifier. This approach reduces opportunities for malicious exploits. Nevertheless, malicious user input can exploit format strings and can cause information leaks or denial of service. As a result, strings from an untrusted source should not be incorporated into format strings.

Noncompliant Code Example

This noncompliant code example demonstrates an information leak issue. It accepts a credit card expiration date as an input argument and uses it within the format string.

```
class Format {
  static Calendar c =
    new GregorianCalendar(1995, GregorianCalendar.MAY, 23);
  public static void main(String[] args) {
    // args[0] is the credit card expiration date
    // args[0] can contain either %1$tm, %1$te or %1$tY as malicious
    // arguments
    // First argument prints 05 (May), second prints 23 (day)
    // and third prints 1995 (year)
    // Perform comparison with c, if it doesn't match print the
    // following line
    System.out.printf(args[0] +
    " did not match! HINT: It was issued on %1$terd of some month", c);
  }
}
```

In the absence of proper input validation, an attacker can determine the date against which the input is being verified by supplying an input that includes one of the format string arguments %1$tm, %1$te, or %1$tY.

Compliant Solution

This compliant solution ensures that user-generated input is excluded from format strings.

```
class Format {
  static Calendar c =
    new GregorianCalendar(1995, GregorianCalendar.MAY, 23);
  public static void main(String[] args) {
    // args[0] is the credit card expiration date
    // Perform comparison with c,
    // if it doesn't match print the following line
    System.out.printf ("%s did not match! "
        + " HINT: It was issued on %1$terd of some month", args[0], c);
  }
}
```

Risk Assessment

Allowing user input to taint a format string may cause information leaks or denial of service.

Rule	Severity	Likelihood	Remediation Cost	Priority	Level
IDS06-J	medium	unlikely	medium	P4	L3

Automated Detection Static analysis tools that perform taint analysis can diagnose some violations of this rule.

Related Guidelines

CERT C Secure Coding Standard	FIO30-C. Exclude user input from format strings
CERT C++ Secure Coding Standard	FIO30-CPP. Exclude user input from format strings
ISO/IEC TR 24772:2010	Injection [RST]
MITRE CWE	CWE-134. Uncontrolled format string

Bibliography

[API 2006]	Class Formatter
[Seacord 2005]	Chapter 6, Formatted Output

■ IDS07-J. Do not pass untrusted, unsanitized data to the `Runtime.exec()` method

External programs are commonly invoked to perform a function required by the overall system. This is a form of reuse and might even be considered a crude form of component-based software engineering. Command and argument injection vulnerabilities occur when an application fails to sanitize untrusted input and uses it in the execution of external programs.

Every Java application has a single instance of class `Runtime` that allows the application to interface with the environment in which the application is running. The current runtime can be obtained from the `Runtime.getRuntime()` method. The semantics of `Runtime.exec()` are poorly defined, so it's best not to rely on its behavior any more than necessary, but typically it invokes the command directly without a shell. If you want a shell, you can use `/bin/sh -c` on POSIX or `cmd.exe` on Windows. The variants of `exec()` that take the command line as a single string split it using a `StringTokenizer`. On Windows, these tokens are concatenated back into a single argument string before being executed.

Consequently, command injection attacks cannot succeed unless a command interpreter is explicitly invoked. However, argument injection attacks can occur when arguments have spaces, double quotes, and so forth, or start with a - or / to indicate a switch.

This rule is a specific instance of rule IDS00-J. Any string data that originates from outside the program's trust boundary must be sanitized before being executed as a command on the current platform.

Noncompliant Code Example (Windows)

This noncompliant code example provides a directory listing using the dir command. This is implemented using Runtime.exec() to invoke the Windows dir command.

```java
class DirList {
  public static void main(String[] args) throws Exception {
    String dir = System.getProperty("dir");
    Runtime rt = Runtime.getRuntime();
    Process proc = rt.exec("cmd.exe /C dir " + dir);
    int result = proc.waitFor();
    if (result != 0) {
      System.out.println("process error: " + result);
    }
    InputStream in = (result == 0) ? proc.getInputStream() :
                                     proc.getErrorStream();
    int c;
    while ((c = in.read()) != -1) {
      System.out.print((char) c);
    }
  }
}
```

Because Runtime.exec() receives unsanitized data originating from the environment, this code is susceptible to a command injection attack.

An attacker can exploit this program using the following command:

```
java -Ddir='dummy & echo bad' Java
```

The command executed is actually two commands:

```
cmd.exe /C dir dummy & echo bad
```

which first attempts to list a nonexistent dummy folder and then prints bad to the console.

Noncompliant Code Example (POSIX)

This noncompliant code example provides the same functionality but uses the POSIX ls command. The only difference from the Windows version is the argument passed to Runtime.exec().

```
class DirList {
  public static void main(String[] args) throws Exception {
    String dir = System.getProperty("dir");
    Runtime rt = Runtime.getRuntime();
    Process proc = rt.exec(new String[] {"sh", "-c", "ls " + dir});
    int result = proc.waitFor();
    if (result != 0) {
      System.out.println("process error: " + result);
    }
    InputStream in = (result == 0) ? proc.getInputStream() :
                                     proc.getErrorStream();
    int c;
    while ((c = in.read()) != -1) {
      System.out.print((char) c);
    }
  }
}
```

The attacker can supply the same command shown in the previous noncompliant code example with similar effects. The command executed is actually:

```
sh -c 'ls dummy & echo bad'
```

Compliant Solution (Sanitization)

This compliant solution sanitizes the untrusted user input by permitting only a small group of whitelisted characters in the argument that will be passed to `Runtime.exec()`; all other characters are excluded.

```
// ...
if (!Pattern.matches("[0-9A-Za-z@.]+", dir)) {
  // Handle error
}
// ...
```

Although this is a compliant solution, this sanitization approach rejects valid directories. Also, because the command interpreter invoked is system dependent, it is difficult to establish that this solution prevents command injections on every platform on which a Java program might run.

Compliant Solution (Restricted User Choice)

This compliant solution prevents command injection by passing only trusted strings to `Runtime.exec()`. While the user has control over which string is used, the user cannot provide string data directly to `Runtime.exec()`.

```
// ...
String dir = null;
// only allow integer choices
int number = Integer.parseInt(System.getproperty("dir"));
switch (number) {
  case 1:
    dir = "data1"
    break; // Option 1
  case 2:
    dir = "data2"
    break; // Option 2
  default: // invalid
    break;
}
if (dir == null) {
  // handle error
}
```

This compliant solution hard codes the directories that may be listed.

This solution can quickly become unmanageable if you have many available directories. A more scalable solution is to read all the permitted directories from a properties file into a `java.util.Properties` object.

Compliant Solution (Avoid `Runtime.exec()`)

When the task performed by executing a system command can be accomplished by some other means, it is almost always advisable to do so. This compliant solution uses the `File.list()` method to provide a directory listing, eliminating the possibility of command or argument injection attacks.

```
import java.io.File;

class DirList {
  public static void main(String[] args) throws Exception {
    File dir = new File(System.getProperty("dir"));
    if (!dir.isDirectory()) {
      System.out.println("Not a directory");
    } else {
      for (String file : dir.list()) {
        System.out.println(file);
      }
    }
  }
}
```

Risk Assessment

Passing untrusted, unsanitized data to the `Runtime.exec()` method can result in command and argument injection attacks.

Rule	Severity	Likelihood	Remediation Cost	Priority	Level
IDS07-J	high	probable	medium	P12	L1

Related Vulnerabilities

[CVE-2010-0886]	Sun Java Web Start plugin command line argument injection
[CVE-2010-1826]	Command injection in `updateSharingD`'s handling of Mach RPC messages
[T-472]	Mac OS X Java command injection flaw in `updateSharingD` lets local users gain elevated privileges

Related Guidelines

The CERT C Secure Coding Standard	ENV03-C. Sanitize the environment when invoking external programs
	ENV04-C. Do not call `system()` if you do not need a command processor
The CERT C++ Secure Coding Standard	ENV03-CPP. Sanitize the environment when invoking external programs
	ENV04-CPP. Do not call `system()` if you do not need a command processor
ISO/IEC TR 24772:2010	Injection [RST]
MITRE CWE	CWE-78. Improper neutralization of special elements used in an OS command ("OS command injection")

Bibliography

[Chess 2007]	Chapter 5, Handling Input, "Command Injection"
[OWASP 2005]	
[Permissions 2008]	

■ IDS08-J. Sanitize untrusted data passed to a regex

Regular expressions are widely used to match strings of text. For example, the POSIX `grep` utility supports regular expressions for finding patterns in the specified text.

For introductory information on regular expressions, see the Java Tutorials [Tutorials 08]. The `java.util.regex` package provides the `Pattern` class that encapsulates a compiled representation of a regular expression and the `Matcher` class, which is an engine that uses a `Pattern` to perform matching operations on a `CharSequence`.

Java's powerful regular expression (regex) facilities must be protected from misuse. An attacker may supply a malicious input that modifies the original regular expression in such a way that the regex fails to comply with the program's specification. This attack vector, called a *regex injection*, might affect control flow, cause information leaks, or result in denial-of-service (DoS) vulnerabilities.

Certain constructs and properties of Java regular expressions are susceptible to exploitation:

- Matching flags: Untrusted inputs may override matching options that may or may not have been passed to the `Pattern.compile()` method.

- Greediness: An untrusted input may attempt to inject a regex that changes the original regex to match as much of the string as possible, exposing sensitive information.

- Grouping: The programmer can enclose parts of a regular expression in parentheses to perform some common action on the group. An attacker may be able to change the groupings by supplying untrusted input.

Untrusted input should be sanitized before use to prevent regex injection. When the user must specify a regex as input, care must be taken to ensure that the original regex cannot be modified without restriction. Whitelisting characters (such as letters and digits) before delivering the user-supplied string to the regex parser is a good input sanitization strategy. A programmer must provide only a very limited subset of regular expression functionality to the user to minimize any chance of misuse.

Regex Injection Example

Suppose a system log file contains messages output by various system processes. Some processes produce public messages and some processes produce sensitive messages marked "private." Here is an example log file:

```
10:47:03 private[423] Successful logout name: usr1 ssn: 111223333
10:47:04 public[48964] Failed to resolve network service
10:47:04 public[1] (public.message[49367]) Exited with exit code: 255
10:47:43 private[423] Successful login name: usr2 ssn: 444556666
10:48:08 public[48964] Backup failed with error: 19
```

A user wishes to search the log file for interesting messages but must be prevented from seeing the private messages. A program might accomplish this by permitting the user to provide search text that becomes part of the following regex:

```
(.*? +public\[\d+\] +.*<SEARCHTEXT>.*)
```

However, if an attacker can substitute any string for <SEARCHTEXT>, he can perform a regex injection with the following text:

```
.*)|(.*
```

When injected into the regex, the regex becomes:

```
(.*? +public\[\d+\] +.*.*)|(.*.*)
```

This regex will match any line in the log file, including the private ones.

Noncompliant Code Example

This noncompliant code example periodically loads the log file into memory and allows clients to obtain keyword search suggestions by passing the keyword as an argument to `suggestSearches()`.

```java
public class Keywords {
  private static ScheduledExecutorService scheduler
    = Executors.newSingleThreadScheduledExecutor();
  private static CharBuffer log;
  private static final Object lock = new Object();

  // Map log file into memory, and periodically reload
  static
    try {
      FileChannel channel = new FileInputStream(
        "path").getChannel();

      // Get the file's size and map it into memory
      int size = (int) channel.size();
      final MappedByteBuffer mappedBuffer = channel.map(
        FileChannel.MapMode.READ_ONLY, 0, size);

      Charset charset = Charset.forName("ISO-8859-15");
      final CharsetDecoder decoder = charset.newDecoder();

      log = decoder.decode(mappedBuffer); // Read file into char buffer
```

```
      Runnable periodicLogRead = new Runnable() {
        @Override public void run() {
          synchronized(lock) {
            try {
              log = decoder.decode(mappedBuffer);
            } catch (CharacterCodingException e) {
              // Forward to handler
            }
          }
        }
      };
      scheduler.scheduleAtFixedRate(periodicLogRead,
                                    0, 5, TimeUnit.SECONDS);
    } catch (Throwable t) {
      // Forward to handler
    }
  }

  public static Set<String> suggestSearches(String search) {
    synchronized(lock) {
      Set<String> searches = new HashSet<String>();

      // Construct regex dynamically from user string
      String regex = "(.*? +public\\[\\d+\\] +.*" + search + ".*)";

      Pattern keywordPattern = Pattern.compile(regex);
      Matcher logMatcher = keywordPattern.matcher(log);
      while (logMatcher.find()) {
        String found = logMatcher.group(1);
        searches.add(found);
      }
      return searches;
    }
  }

}
```

This code permits a trusted user to search for public log messages such as "error." However, it also allows a malicious attacker to perform the regex injection previously described.

Compliant Solution (Whitelisting)

This compliant solution filters out nonalphanumeric characters (except space and single quote) from the search string, which prevents regex injection previously described.

```java
public class Keywords {
  // ...
  public static Set<String> suggestSearches(String search) {
    synchronized(lock) {
      Set<String> searches = new HashSet<String>();

      StringBuilder sb = new StringBuilder(search.length());
      for (int i = 0; i < search.length(); ++i) {
        char ch = search.charAt(i);
        if (Character.isLetterOrDigit(ch) ||
            ch == ' ' ||
            ch == '\'') {
          sb.append(ch);
        }
      }
      search = sb.toString();

      // Construct regex dynamically from user string
      String regex = "(.*? +public\\[\\d+\\] +.*" + search + ".*)";
      // ...
    }
  }
}
```

This solution also limits the set of valid search terms. For instance, a user may no longer search for "name =" because the = character would be sanitized out of the regex.

Compliant Solution

Another method of mitigating this vulnerability is to filter out the sensitive information prior to matching. Such a solution would require the filtering to be done every time the log file is periodically refreshed, incurring extra complexity and a performance penalty. Sensitive information may still be exposed if the log format changes but the class is not also refactored to accommodate these changes.

Risk Assessment

Failing to sanitize untrusted data included as part of a regular expression can result in the disclosure of sensitive information.

Rule	Severity	Likelihood	Remediation Cost	Priority	Level
IDS08-J	medium	unlikely	medium	P4	L3

Related Guidelines

MITRE CWE   CWE-625. Permissive regular expression

Bibliography

[Tutorials 08]   Regular Expressions
[CVE 05]   CVE-2005-1949

■ IDS09-J. Do not use locale-dependent methods on locale-dependent data without specifying the appropriate locale

Using locale-dependent methods on locale-dependent data can produce unexpected results when the locale is unspecified. Programming language identifiers, protocol keys, and HTML tags are often specified in a particular locale, usually `Locale.ENGLISH`. It may even be possible to bypass input filters by changing the default locale, which can alter the behavior of locale-dependent methods. For example, when a string is converted to uppercase, it may be declared valid; however, changing the string back to lowercase during subsequent execution may result in a blacklisted string.

Any program which invokes locale-dependent methods on untrusted data must explicitly specify the locale to use with these methods.

Noncompliant Code Example

This noncompliant code example uses the locale-dependent `String.toUpperCase()` method to convert an HTML tag to uppercase. While the English locale would convert "title" to "TITLE," the Turkish locale will convert "title" to "T?TLE," where "?" is the Latin capital letter "I" with a dot above the character [API 2006].

```
"title".toUpperCase();
```

Compliant Solution (Explicit Locale)

This compliant solution explicitly sets the locale to English to avoid unexpected results.

```
"title".toUpperCase(Locale.ENGLISH);
```

This rule also applies to the `String.equalsIgnoreCase()` method.

Compliant Solution (Default Locale)

This compliant solution sets the default locale to English before proceeding with string operations.

```
Locale.setDefault(Locale.ENGLISH);
"title".toUpperCase();
```

Risk Assessment

Failure to specify the appropriate locale when using locale-dependent methods on locale-dependent data may result in unexpected behavior.

Rule	Severity	Likelihood	Remediation Cost	Priority	Level
IDS09-J	medium	probable	medium	P8	L2

Bibliography

[API 2006]   Class `String`

■ IDS10-J. Do not split characters between two data structures

Legacy software frequently assumes that every character in a string occupies 8 bits (a Java `byte`). The Java language assumes that every character in a string occupies 16 bits (a Java `char`). Unfortunately, neither the Java `byte` nor Java `char` data types can represent all possible Unicode characters. Many strings are stored or communicated using encodings such as UTF-8 that support characters with varying sizes.

While Java strings are stored as an array of characters and can be represented as an array of bytes, a single character in the string might be represented by two or more consecutive elements of type `byte` or of type `char`. Splitting a `char` or `byte` array risks splitting a multibyte character.

Ignoring the possibility of supplementary characters, multibyte characters, or combining characters (characters that modify other characters) may allow an attacker to bypass input validation checks. Consequently, characters must not be split between two data structures.

Multibyte Characters

Multibyte encodings are used for character sets that require more than one byte to uniquely identify each constituent character. For example, the Japanese encoding Shift-JIS (shown below) supports multibyte encoding where the maximum character length is two bytes (one leading and one trailing byte).

Byte Type	Range
single-byte	0x00 through 0x7F and 0xA0 through 0xDF
lead-byte	0x81 through 0x9F and 0xE0 through 0xFC
trailing-byte	0x40–0x7E and 0x80–0xFC

The trailing byte ranges overlap the range of both the single-byte and lead-byte characters. When a multibyte character is separated across a buffer boundary, it can be interpreted differently than if it were not separated across the buffer boundary; this difference arises because of the ambiguity of its composing bytes [Phillips 2005].

Supplementary Characters

According to the Java API [API 2006] class `Character` documentation (Unicode Character Representations):

> The `char` data type (and consequently the value that a `Character` object encapsulates) are based on the original Unicode specification, which defined characters as fixed-width 16-bit entities. The Unicode standard has since been changed to allow for characters whose representation requires more than 16 bits. The range of legal code points is now \u0000 to \u10FFFF, known as Unicode scalar value.
>
> The Java 2 platform uses the UTF-16 representation in `char` arrays and in the `String` and `StringBuffer` classes. In this representation, supplementary characters are represented as a pair of `char` values, the first from the high-surrogates range, (\uD800-\uDBFF), the second from the low-surrogates range (\uDC00-\uDFFF).
>
> An `int` value represents all Unicode code points, including supplementary code points. The lower (least significant) 21 bits of `int` are used to represent Unicode code points, and the upper (most significant) 11 bits must be zero. Unless otherwise specified, the behavior with respect to supplementary characters and surrogate char values is as follows:

- The methods that only accept a `char` value cannot support supplementary characters. They treat `char` values from the surrogate ranges as undefined characters. For example, `Character.isLetter('\uD840')` returns `false`, even though this specific value if followed by any low-surrogate value in a string would represent a letter.

■ The methods that accept an `int` value support all Unicode characters, including supplementary characters. For example, `Character.isLetter(0x2F81A)` returns `true` because the code point value represents a letter (a CJK ideograph).

Noncompliant Code Example (Read)

This noncompliant code example tries to read up to 1024 bytes from a socket and build a `String` from this data. It does this by reading the bytes in a while loop, as recommended by rule FIO10-J. If it ever detects that the socket has more than 1024 bytes available, it throws an exception. This prevents untrusted input from potentially exhausting the program's memory.

```java
public final int MAX_SIZE = 1024;

public String readBytes(Socket socket) throws IOException {
  InputStream in = socket.getInputStream();
  byte[] data = new byte[MAX_SIZE+1];
  int offset = 0;
  int bytesRead = 0;
  String str = new String();
  while ((bytesRead = in.read(data, offset, data.length - offset))
          != -1) {
    offset += bytesRead;
    str += new String(data, offset, data.length - offset, "UTF-8");
    if (offset >= data.length) {
      throw new IOException("Too much input");
    }
  }
  in.close();
  return str;
}
```

This code fails to account for the interaction between characters represented with a multibyte encoding and the boundaries between the loop iterations. If the last byte read from the data stream in one `read()` operation is the leading byte of a multibyte character, the trailing bytes are not encountered until the next iteration of the `while` loop. However, multibyte encoding is resolved during construction of the new `String` within the loop. Consequently, the multibyte encoding can be interpreted incorrectly.

Compliant Solution (Read)

This compliant solution defers creation of the string until all the data is available.

```
public final int MAX_SIZE = 1024;

public String readBytes(Socket socket) throws IOException {
  InputStream in = socket.getInputStream();
  byte[] data = new byte[MAX_SIZE+1];
  int offset = 0;
  int bytesRead = 0;
  while ((bytesRead = in.read(data, offset, data.length - offset))
         != -1) {
    offset += bytesRead;
    if (offset >= data.length) {
      throw new IOException("Too much input");
    }
  }
  String str = new String(data, "UTF-8");
  in.close();
  return str;
}
```

This code avoids splitting multibyte-encoded characters across buffers by deferring construction of the result string until the data has been read in full.

Compliant Solution (Reader)

This compliant solution uses a Reader rather than an InputStream. The Reader class converts bytes into characters on the fly, so it avoids the hazard of splitting multibyte characters. This routine aborts if the socket provides more than 1024 characters rather than 1024 bytes.

```
public final int MAX_SIZE = 1024;

public String readBytes(Socket socket) throws IOException {
  InputStream in = socket.getInputStream();
  Reader r = new InputStreamReader(in, "UTF-8");
  char[] data = new char[MAX_SIZE+1];
  int offset = 0;
  int charsRead = 0;
  String str = new String(data);
```

```
  while ((charsRead = r.read(data, offset, data.length - offset))
         != -1) {
    offset += charsRead;
    str += new String(data, offset, data.length - offset);
    if (offset >= data.length) {
      throw new IOException("Too much input");
    }
  }
  in.close();
  return str;
}
```

Noncompliant Code Example (Substring)

This noncompliant code example attempts to trim leading letters from the string. It fails to accomplish this task because Character.isLetter() lacks support for supplementary and combining characters [Hornig 2007].

```
// Fails for supplementary or combining characters
public static String trim_bad1(String string) {
  char ch;
  int i;
  for (i = 0; i < string.length(); i += 1) {
    ch = string.charAt(i);
    if (!Character.isLetter(ch)) {
      break;
    }
  }
  return string.substring(i);
}
```

Noncompliant Code Example (Substring)

This noncompliant code example attempts to correct the problem by using the String.codePointAt() method, which accepts an int argument. This works for supplementary characters but fails for combining characters [Hornig 2007].

```
// Fails for combining characters
public static String trim_bad2(String string) {
  int ch;
  int i;
  for (i = 0; i < string.length(); i += Character.charCount(ch)) {
    ch = string.codePointAt(i);
    if (!Character.isLetter(ch)) {
      break;
    }
  }
  return string.substring(i);
}
```

Compliant Solution (Substring)

This compliant solution works both for supplementary and for combining characters [Hornig 2007]. According to the Java API [API 2006] class `java.text.BreakIterator` documentation:

> The `BreakIterator` class implements methods for finding the location of boundaries in text. Instances of `BreakIterator` maintain a current position and scan over text returning the index of characters where boundaries occur.

The boundaries returned may be those of supplementary characters, combining character sequences, or ligature clusters. For example, an accented character might be stored as a base character and a diacritical mark.

```
public static String trim_good(String string) {
  BreakIterator iter = BreakIterator.getCharacterInstance();
  iter.setText(string);
  int i;
  for (i = iter.first(); i != BreakIterator.DONE; i = iter.next()) {
    int ch = string.codePointAt(i);
    if (!Character.isLetter(ch)) {
      break;
    }
  }
  // Reached first or last text boundary
  if (i == BreakIterator.DONE) {
    // The input was either blank or had only (leading) letters
    return "";
  } else {
    return string.substring(i);
  }
}
```

To perform locale-sensitive `String` comparisons for searching and sorting, use the `java.text.Collator` class.

Risk Assessment

Failure to correctly account for supplementary and combining characters can lead to unexpected behavior.

Rule	Severity	Likelihood	Remediation Cost	Priority	Level
IDS10-J	low	unlikely	medium	P2	L3

Bibliography

[API 2006]	Classes `Character` and `BreakIterator`
[Hornig 2007]	Problem Areas: Characters

▪ IDS11-J. Eliminate noncharacter code points before validation

In some versions prior to Unicode 5.2, conformance clause C7 allows the deletion of noncharacter code points. For example, conformance clause C7 from Unicode 5.1 states [Unicode 2007]:

> C7. When a process purports not to modify the interpretation of a valid coded character sequence, it shall make no change to that coded character sequence other than the possible replacement of character sequences by their canonical-equivalent sequences or the deletion of noncharacter code points.

According to the Unicode Technical Report #36, Unicode Security Considerations [Davis 2008b], Section 3.5, "Deletion of Noncharacters":

> Whenever a character is invisibly deleted (instead of replaced), such as in this older version of C7, it may cause a security problem. The issue is the following: A gateway might be checking for a sensitive sequence of characters, say "delete." If what is passed in is "deXlete," where X is a noncharacter, the gateway lets it through: The sequence "deXlete" may be in and of itself harmless. However, suppose that later on, past the gateway, an internal process invisibly deletes the X. In that case, the sensitive sequence of characters is formed, and can lead to a security breach.

Any string modifications, including the removal or replacement of noncharacter code points, must be performed before any validation of the string is performed.

Noncompliant Code Example

This noncompliant code example accepts only valid ASCII characters and deletes any non-ASCII characters. It also checks for the existence of a <script> tag.

Input validation is being performed before the deletion of non-ASCII characters. Consequently, an attacker can disguise a <script> tag and bypass the validation checks.

```
// "\uFEFF" is a non-character code point
String s = "<scr" + "\uFEFF" + "ipt>";
s = Normalizer.normalize(s, Form.NFKC);
// Input validation
Pattern pattern = Pattern.compile("<script>");
Matcher matcher = pattern.matcher(s);
if (matcher.find()) {
  System.out.println("Found black listed tag");
} else {
  // ...
}

// Deletes all non-valid characters
s = s.replaceAll("^\\p{ASCII}]", "");
// s now contains "<script>"
```

Compliant Solution

This compliant solution replaces the unknown or unrepresentable character with Unicode sequence \uFFFD, which is reserved to denote this condition. It also does this replacement before doing any other sanitization, in particular, checking for <script>. This ensures that malicious input cannot bypass filters.

```
String s = "<scr" + "\uFEFF" + "ipt>";

s = Normalizer.normalize(s, Form.NFKC);
// Replaces all non-valid characters with unicode U+FFFD
s = s.replaceAll("^\\p{ASCII}]", "\uFFFD");

Pattern pattern = Pattern.compile("<script>");
Matcher matcher = pattern.matcher(s);
if (matcher.find()) {
  System.out.println("Found blacklisted tag");
} else {
  // ...
}
```

According to the Unicode Technical Report #36, Unicode Security Considerations [Davis 2008b], "U+FFFD is usually unproblematic, because it is designed expressly for this kind of purpose. That is, because it doesn't have syntactic meaning in programming languages or structured data, it will typically just cause a failure in parsing. Where the output character set is not Unicode, though, this character may not be available."

Risk Assessment

Deleting noncharacter code points can allow malicious input to bypass validation checks.

Rule	Severity	Likelihood	Remediation Cost	Priority	Level
IDS11-J	high	probable	medium	P12	L1

Related Guidelines

MITRE CWE	CWE-182. Collapse of data into unsafe value

Bibliography

[API 2006]	
[Davis 2008b]	3.5, Deletion of Noncharacters
[Weber 2009]	Handling the Unexpected: Character-Deletion
[Unicode 2007]	
[Unicode 2011]	

■ IDS12-J. Perform lossless conversion of String data between differing character encodings

Performing conversions of String objects between different character encodings may result in loss of data.

According to the Java API [API 2006], String.getBytes(Charset) method documentation:

> This method always replaces malformed-input and unmappable-character sequences with this charset's default replacement byte array.

When a String must be converted to bytes, for example, for writing to a file, and the string might contain unmappable character sequences, proper character encoding must be performed.

Noncompliant Code Example

This noncompliant code example [Hornig 2007] corrupts the data when `string` contains characters that are not representable in the specified `charset`.

```
// Corrupts data on errors
public static byte[] toCodePage_bad(String charset, String string)
  throws UnsupportedEncodingException {
  return string.getBytes(charset);
}

// Fails to detect corrupt data
public static String fromCodePage_bad(String charset, byte[] bytes)
  throws UnsupportedEncodingException {
  return new String(bytes, charset);
}
```

Compliant Solution

The `java.nio.charset.CharsetEncoder` class can transform a sequence of 16-bit Unicode characters into a sequence of bytes in a specific `Charset`, while the `java.nio.charset.Character-Decoder` class can reverse the procedure [API 2006]. Also see rule FIO11-J for more information.

This compliant solution [Hornig 2007] uses the `CharsetEncoder` and `CharsetDecoder` classes to handle encoding conversions.

```
public static byte[] toCodePage_good(String charset, String string)
  throws IOException {

  Charset cs = Charset.forName(charset);
  CharsetEncoder coder = cs.newEncoder();
  ByteBuffer bytebuf = coder.encode(CharBuffer.wrap(string));
  byte[] bytes = new byte[bytebuf.limit()];
  bytebuf.get(bytes);
  return bytes;
}

public static String fromCodePage_good(String charset,byte[] bytes)
  throws CharacterCodingException {

  Charset cs = Charset.forName(charset);
  CharsetDecoder coder = cs.newDecoder();
  CharBuffer charbuf = coder.decode(ByteBuffer.wrap(bytes));
  return charbuf.toString();
}
```

Noncompliant Code Example

This noncompliant code example [Hornig 2007] attempts to append a string to a text file in the specified encoding. This is erroneous because the String may contain unrepresentable characters.

```
// Corrupts data on errors
public static void toFile_bad(String charset, String filename,
                             String string) throws IOException {

  FileOutputStream stream = new FileOutputStream(filename, true);
  OutputStreamWriter writer = new OutputStreamWriter(stream, charset);
  writer.write(string, 0, string.length());
  writer.close();
}
```

Compliant Solution

This compliant solution [Hornig 2007] uses the CharsetEncoder class to perform the required function.

```
public static void toFile_good(String filename, String string,
                               String charset) throws IOException {

  Charset cs = Charset.forName(charset);
  CharsetEncoder coder = cs.newEncoder();
  FileOutputStream stream = new FileOutputStream(filename, true);
  OutputStreamWriter writer = new OutputStreamWriter(stream, coder);
  writer.write(string, 0, string.length());
  writer.close();
}
```

Use the FileInputStream and InputStreamReader objects to read back the data from the file. The InputStreamReader accepts an optional CharsetDecoder argument, which must be the same as that previously used for writing to the file.

Risk Assessment

Use of nonstandard methods for performing character-set-related conversions can lead to loss of data.

Rule	Severity	Likelihood	Remediation Cost	Priority	Level
IDS12-J	low	probable	medium	P4	L3

Related Guidelines

MITRE CWE	CWE-838. Inappropriate encoding for output context
	CWE-116. Improper encoding or escaping of output

Bibliography

[API 2006]	Class `String`
[Hornig 2007]	Global Problem Areas: Character Encodings

■ IDS13-J. Use compatible encodings on both sides of file or network I/O

Every Java platform has a default character encoding. The available encodings are listed in the *Supported Encodings* document [Encodings 2006]. A conversion between characters and sequences of bytes requires a character encoding to specify the details of the conversion. Such conversions use the system default encoding in the absence of an explicitly specified encoding. When characters are converted into an array of bytes to be sent as output, transmitted across some communication channel, input, and converted back into characters, compatible encodings must be used on both sides of the conversation. Disagreement over character encodings can cause data corruption.

According to the Java API [API 2006] for the `String` class:

> The length of the new `String` is a function of the charset, and for that reason may not be equal to the length of the byte array. The behavior of this constructor when the given bytes are not valid in the given charset is unspecified.

> Binary data that is expected to be a valid string may be read and converted to a string by exception FIO11-EX0.

Noncompliant Code Example

This noncompliant code example reads a byte array and converts it into a `String` using the platform's default character encoding. When the default encoding differs from the encoding that was used to produce the byte array, the resulting `String` is likely to be incorrect. Undefined behavior can occur when some of the input lacks a valid character representation in the default encoding.

```
FileInputStream fis = null;
try {
  fis = new FileInputStream("SomeFile");
  DataInputStream dis = new DataInputStream(fis);
```

```
    byte[] data = new byte[1024];
    dis.readFully(data);
    String result = new String(data);
} catch (IOException x) {
    // handle error
} finally {
    if (fis != null) {
        try {
            fis.close();
        } catch (IOException x) {
            // Forward to handler
        }
    }
}
```

Compliant Solution

This compliant solution explicitly specifies the intended character encoding in the second argument to the String constructor.

```
FileInputStream fis = null;
try {
    fis = new FileInputStream("SomeFile");
    DataInputStream dis = new DataInputStream(fis);
    byte[] data = new byte[1024];
    dis.readFully(data);
    String encoding = "SomeEncoding"; // for example, "UTF-16LE"
    String result = new String(data, encoding);
} catch (IOException x) {
    // handle error
} finally {
    if (fis != null) {
        try {
            fis.close();
        } catch (IOException x) {
            // Forward to handler
        }
    }
}
```

Exceptions

IDS13-EX0: An explicit character encoding may be omitted on the receiving side when the data is produced by a Java application that uses the same platform and default character encoding and is communicated over a secure communication channel (see MSC00-J for more information).

Risk Assessment

Failure to specify the character encoding while performing file or network I/O can result in corrupted data.

Rule	Severity	Likelihood	Remediation Cost	Priority	Level
IDS13-J	low	unlikely	medium	P2	L3

Automated Detection Sound automated detection of this vulnerability is not feasible.

Bibliography

[Encodings 2006]

Chapter 3

Declarations and Initialization (DCL)

■ Rules

Rule	Page
DCL00-J. Prevent class initialization cycles	75
DCL01-J. Do not reuse public identifiers from the Java Standard Library	79
DCL02-J. Declare all enhanced for statement loop variables final	81

■ Risk Assessment Summary

Rule	Severity	Likelihood	Remediation Cost	Priority	Level
DCL00-J	low	unlikely	medium	P2	L3
DCL01-J	low	unlikely	medium	P2	L3
DCL02-J	low	unlikely	low	P3	L3

■ DCL00-J. Prevent class initialization cycles

According to the *Java Language Specification* (JLS), §12.4, "Initialization of Classes and Interfaces" [JLS 2005]:

> Initialization of a class consists of executing its static initializers and the initializers for static fields (class variables) declared in the class.

In other words, the presence of a `static` field triggers the initialization of a class. However, a static field could also depend on the initialization of another class, possibly creating an initialization cycle. The JLS also states in §8.3.2.1, "Initializers for Class Variables" [JLS 2005]:

> At run time, `static` variables that are `final` and that are initialized with compile-time constant values are initialized first.

This statement can be misleading because it is inapplicable to instances that use values of `static final` fields that are initialized at a later stage. Declaring a field to be `static final` is insufficient to guarantee that it is fully initialized before being read.

Programs in general should—and security-sensitive programs must—eliminate all class initialization cycles.

Noncompliant Code Example (Intraclass Cycle)

This noncompliant code example contains an intraclass initialization cycle.

```java
public class Cycle {
  private final int balance;
  private static final Cycle c = new Cycle();
  // Random deposit
  private static final int deposit = (int) (Math.random() * 100);

  public Cycle() {
    balance = deposit - 10; // Subtract processing fee
  }

  public static void main(String[] args) {
    System.out.println("The account balance is: " + c.balance);
  }
}
```

The `Cycle` class declares a `private static final` class variable, which is initialized to a new instance of the `Cycle` class. Static initializers are guaranteed to be invoked once before the first use of a static class member or the first invocation of a constructor.

The programmer's intent is to calculate the account balance by subtracting the processing fee from the deposited amount. However, the initialization of the `c` class variable happens before the `deposit` field is initialized because it appears lexically before the initialization of the `deposit` field. Consequently, the value of `deposit` seen by the constructor, when invoked during the static initialization of c, is the initial value of deposit (0) rather than the random value. As a result, the balance is always computed to be -10.

The JLS permits implementations to ignore the possibility of such recursive initialization cycles [Bloch 2005a].

Compliant Solution (Intraclass Cycle)

This compliant solution changes the initialization order of the class Cycle so that the fields are initialized without creating any dependency cycles. Specifically, the initialization of c is placed lexically *after* the initialization of deposit so that it occurs temporally after deposit is fully initialized.

```java
public class Cycle {
  private final int balance;
  // Random deposit
  private static final int deposit = (int) (Math.random() * 100);
  // Inserted after initialization of required fields
  private static final Cycle c = new Cycle();
  public Cycle() {
    balance = deposit - 10; // Subtract processing fee
  }

  public static void main(String[] args) {
    System.out.println("The account balance is: " + c.balance);
  }
}
```

Such initialization cycles become insidious when many fields are involved. Consequently, it is important to ensure that the control flow lacks such cycles.

Although this compliant solution prevents the initialization cycle, it depends on declaration order and is consequently fragile; later maintainers of the software may be unaware that the declaration order must be maintained to preserve correctness. Consequently, such dependencies must be clearly documented in the code.

Noncompliant Code Example (Interclass Cycle)

This noncompliant code example declares two classes with static variables whose values depend on each other. The cycle is obvious when the classes are seen together (as here) but is easy to miss when viewing the classes separately.

```
class A {
  public static final int a = B.b + 1;
  // ...
}

class B {
  public static final int b = A.a + 1;
  // ...
}
```

The initialization order of the classes can vary and, consequently, cause computation of different values for A.a and B.b. When class A is initialized first, A.a will have the value 2, and B.b will have the value 1. These values will be reversed when class B is initialized first.

Compliant Solution (Interclass Cycle)

This compliant solution breaks the interclass cycle by eliminating one of the dependencies.

```
class A {
  public static final int a = 2;
  // ...
}
// class B unchanged: b = A.a + 1
```

With the cycle broken, the initial values will always be A.a = 2 and B.b = 3, regardless of initialization order.

Risk Assessment

Initialization cycles may lead to unexpected results.

Rule	Severity	Likelihood	Remediation Cost	Priority	Level
DCL00-J	low	unlikely	medium	P2	L3

Related Guidelines

The CERT C++ Secure Coding Standard	DCL14-CPP. Avoid assumptions about the initialization order between translation units
ISO/IEC TR 24772:2010	Initialization of variables [LAV]

Bibliography

[JLS 2005]	§8.3.2.1, Initializers for Class Variables
	§12.4, Initialization of Classes and Interfaces
[Bloch 2005a]	Puzzle 49. Larger than life
[MITRE 2009]	CWE-665. Improper initialization

■ DCL01-J. Do not reuse public identifiers from the Java Standard Library

Do not reuse the names of publicly visible identifiers, public utility classes, interfaces, or packages in the Java Standard Library.

When a developer uses an identifier that has the same name as a public class, such as `Vector`, a subsequent maintainer might be unaware that this identifier does not actually refer to `java.util.Vector` and might unintentionally use the custom `Vector` rather than the original `java.util.Vector` class. The custom type `Vector` can shadow a class name from `java.util.Vector`, as specified by the JLS, §6.3.2, "Obscured Declarations" [JLS 2005]. This can result in unexpected program behavior.

Well-defined import statements can resolve these issues. However, when reused name definitions are imported from other packages, use of the *type-import-on-demand declaration* (see the JLS, §7.5.2, "Type-Import-on-Demand Declaration" [JLS 2005]) can complicate a programmer's attempt to determine which specific definition was intended to be used. Additionally, a common practice that can lead to errors is to produce the import statements *after* writing the code, often via automatic inclusion of import statements by an IDE. This creates further ambiguity with respect to the names. When a custom type is found earlier than the intended type in the Java include path, no further searches are conducted. Consequently, the wrong type is silently adopted.

Noncompliant Code Example (Class Name)

This noncompliant code example implements a class that reuses the name of the class `java.util.Vector`. It attempts to introduce a different condition for the `isEmpty()` method for interfacing with native legacy code by overriding the corresponding method in `java.util.Vector`. Unexpected behavior can arise if a maintainer confuses the `isEmpty()` method with the `java.util.Vector.isEmpty()` method.

```java
class Vector {
  private int val = 1;

  public boolean isEmpty() {
    if (val == 1) {    // compares with 1 instead of 0
      return true;
    } else {
      return false;
    }
  }
  // other functionality is same as java.util.Vector
}

// import java.util.Vector; omitted
public class VectorUser {
  public static void main(String[] args) {
    Vector v = new Vector();
    if (v.isEmpty()) {
      System.out.println("Vector is empty");
    }
  }
}
```

Compliant Solution (Class Name)

This compliant solution uses a different name for the class, preventing any potential shadowing of the class from the Java Standard Library.

```java
class MyVector {
  // other code
}
```

When the developer and organization control the original shadowed class, it may be preferable to change the design strategy of the original in accordance with Bloch's *Effective Java* [Bloch 2008], Item 16, *Prefer interfaces to abstract classes*. Changing the original class into an interface would permit class `MyVector` to declare that it implements the hypothetical

Vector interface. This would permit client code that intended to use MyVector to remain compatible with code that uses the original implementation of Vector.

Risk Assessment

Public identifier reuse decreases the readability and maintainability of code.

Rule	Severity	Likelihood	Remediation Cost	Priority	Level
DCL01-J	low	unlikely	medium	P2	L3

Automated Detection   An automated tool can easily detect reuse of the set of names representing public classes or interfaces from the Java Standard Library.

Related Guidelines

The CERT C Secure Coding Standard	PRE04-C. Do not reuse a standard header file name
The CERT C++ Secure Coding Standard	PRE04-CPP. Do not reuse a standard header file name

Bibliography

[JLS 2005]	§6.3.2, Obscured Declarations
	§6.3.1, Shadowing Declarations
	§7.5.2, Type-Import-on-Demand Declaration
	§14.4.3, Shadowing of Names by Local Variables
[FindBugs 2008]	
[Bloch 2005a]	Puzzle 67. All strung out
[Bloch 2008]	Item 16. Prefer interfaces to abstract classes

■ DCL02-J. Declare all enhanced for statement loop variables final

The enhanced for statement introduced in Java 5 (also known as the for-each idiom) is primarily used for iterating over collections of objects. Unlike the basic for statement, assignments to the loop variable fail to affect the loop's iteration order over the underlying set of objects. Consequently, assignments to the loop variable can have an effect other than what is intended by the developer. This provides yet another reason to avoid assigning to the loop variable in a for loop.

As detailed in the JLS, §14.14.2, "The Enhanced for Statement" [JLS 2005]:

An enhanced for statement of the form

```
for (ObjType obj : someIterableItem) {
  // ...
}
```

is equivalent to a basic for loop of the form

```
for (Iterator myIterator = someIterableItem.iterator();
     myIterator.hasNext();) {
  ObjType obj = myIterator.next();
  // ...
}
```

Consequently, an assignment to the loop variable is equivalent to modifying a variable local to the loop body whose initial value is the object referenced by the loop iterator. This modification is not necessarily erroneous, but can obscure the loop functionality or indicate a misunderstanding of the underlying implementation of the enhanced for statement.

Declare all enhanced for statement loop variables final. The final declaration causes Java compilers to flag and reject any assignments made to the loop variable.

Noncompliant Code Example

This noncompliant code example attempts to process a collection of objects using an enhanced for loop. It further intends to skip processing one item in the collection.

```
Collection<ProcessObj> processThese = // ...

for (ProcessObj processMe: processThese) {
  if (someCondition) { // found the item to skip
    someCondition = false;
    processMe = processMe.getNext(); // attempt to skip to next item
  }
  processMe.doTheProcessing(); // process the object
}
```

The attempt to skip to the next item appears to succeed because the assignment is successful and the value of processMe is updated. Unlike a basic for loop, however, the assignment leaves the overall iteration order of the loop unchanged. Consequently, the object following the skipped object is processed twice.

Note that if `processMe` were declared final, a compiler error would result at the attempted assignment.

Compliant Solution

This compliant solution correctly processes each object in the collection no more than once.

```
Collection<ProcessObj> processThese = // ...

for (final ProcessObj processMe: processThese) {
  if (someCondition) { // found the item to skip
    someCondition = false;
    continue; // skip by continuing to next iteration
  }
  processMe.doTheProcessing(); // process the object
}
```

Risk Assessment

Assignments to the loop variable of an enhanced `for` loop (for-each idiom) fail to affect the overall iteration order, lead to programmer confusion, and can leave data in a fragile or inconsistent state.

Rule	Severity	Likelihood	Remediation Cost	Priority	Level
DCL02-J	low	unlikely	low	P3	L3

Automated Detection   This rule is easily enforced with static analysis.

Bibliography

[JLS 2005]   §14.14.2, The Enhanced `for` Statement

Chapter 4

Expressions (EXP)

■ Rules

■ Risk Assessment Summary

Rule	Severity	Likelihood	Remediation Cost	Priority	Level
EXP00-J	medium	probable	medium	P8	L2
EXP01-J	low	likely	high	P3	L3
EXP02-J	low	likely	low	P9	L2
EXP03-J	low	likely	medium	P6	L2
EXP04-J	low	probable	low	P6	L2
EXP05-J	low	unlikely	medium	P2	L3
EXP06-J	low	unlikely	low	P3	L2

▪ EXP00-J. Do not ignore values returned by methods

Methods can return values to communicate failure or success or to update local objects or fields. Security risks can arise when method return values are ignored or when the invoking method fails to take suitable action. Consequently, programs must not ignore method return values.

When getter methods are named after an action, a programmer could fail to realize that a return value is expected. For example, the only purpose of the `ProcessBuilder.redirectErrorStream()` method is to report via return value whether the process builder successfully merged standard error and standard output. The method that actually performs redirection of the error stream is the overloaded single-argument method `ProcessBuilder.redirectErrorStream(boolean)`.

Noncompliant Code Example (File Deletion)

This noncompliant code example attempts to delete a file but fails to check whether the operation has succeeded.

```
public void deleteFile() {
  File someFile = new File("someFileName.txt");
  // do something with someFile
  someFile.delete();
}
```

Compliant Solution

This compliant solution checks the `boolean` value returned by the `delete()` method and handles any resulting errors.

```
public void deleteFile() {
  File someFile = new File("someFileName.txt");
  // do something with someFile
  if (!someFile.delete()) {
    // handle failure to delete the file
  }
}
```

Noncompliant Code Example (String Replacement)

This noncompliant code example ignores the return value of the `String.replace()` method, failing to update the original string. The `String.replace()` method cannot modify the state of the `String` (because `String` objects are immutable); rather, it returns a reference to a new `String` object containing the modified string.

```
public class Replace {
  public static void main(String[] args) {
    String original = "insecure";
    original.replace('i', '9');
    System.out.println(original);
  }
}
```

It is especially important to process the return values of immutable object methods. While many methods of mutable objects operate by changing some internal state of the object, methods of immutable objects cannot change the object and often return a mutated new object, leaving the original object unchanged.

Compliant Solution

This compliant solution correctly updates the String reference original with the return value from the String.replace() method.

```
public class Replace {
  public static void main(String[] args) {
    String original = "insecure";
    original = original.replace('i', '9');
    System.out.println(original);
  }
}
```

Risk Assessment

Ignoring method return values can lead to unexpected program behavior.

Rule	Severity	Likelihood	Remediation Cost	Priority	Level
EXP00-J	medium	probable	medium	P8	L2

Related Guidelines

CERT C Secure Coding Standard	EXP12-C. Do not ignore values returned by functions
CERT C++ Secure Coding Standard	EXP12-CPP. Do not ignore values returned by functions or methods
ISO/IEC TR 24772:2010	Passing Parameters and Return Values [CSJ]
MITRE CWE	CWE-252. Unchecked return value

Bibliography

[API 2006]   Method `delete()`

                Method `replace()`

[Green 2008]   `String.replace`

[Pugh 2009]   Misusing `putIfAbsent`

■ EXP01-J. Never dereference null pointers

Null pointer dereferencing occurs when a `null` variable is treated as if it were a valid object reference and used without checking its state. This condition results in a `NullPointer-Exception`, and can also result in denial of service. Consequently, null pointers must never be dereferenced.

Noncompliant Code Example

This noncompliant example shows a bug in Tomcat version 4.1.24, initially discovered by Reasoning [Reasoning 2003]. The `cardinality` method was designed to return the number of occurrences of object `obj` in collection `col`. One valid use of the `cardinality` method is to determine how many objects in the collection are `null`. However, because membership in the collection is checked using the expression `obj.equals(elt)`, a null pointer dereference is guaranteed whenever `obj` is `null` and `elt` is not `null`.

```
public static int cardinality(Object obj, final Collection col) {
  int count = 0;
  Iterator it = col.iterator();
  while (it.hasNext()) {
    Object elt = it.next();
    // null pointer dereference
    if ((null == obj && null == elt) || obj.equals(elt)) {
      count++;
    }
  }
  return count;
}
```

Compliant Solution

This compliant solution eliminates the `null` pointer dereference.

```
public static int cardinality(Object obj, final Collection col) {
  int count = 0;
  Iterator it = col.iterator();
  while (it.hasNext()) {
    Object elt = it.next();
    if ((null == obj && null == elt) ||
        (null != obj && obj.equals(elt))) {
      count++;
    }
  }
  return count;
}
```

Explicit null checks as shown here are an acceptable approach to eliminating null pointer dereferences.

Risk Assessment

Dereferencing a `null` pointer can lead to a denial of service. In multithreaded programs, null pointer dereferences can violate cache coherency policies and can cause resource leaks.

Rule	Severity	Likelihood	Remediation Cost	Priority	Level
EXP01-J	low	likely	high	P3	L3

Automated Detection   Null pointer dereferences can happen in path-dependent ways. Limitations of automatic detection tools can require manual inspection of code [Hovemeyer 2007] to detect instances of null pointer dereferences. Annotations for method parameters that must be non-null can reduce the need for manual inspection by assisting automated null pointer dereference detection; use of these annotations is strongly encouraged.

Related Vulnerabilities   Java Web Start applications and applets particular to JDK version 1.6, prior to update 4, were affected by a bug that had some noteworthy security consequences. In some isolated cases, the application or applet's attempt to establish an HTTPS connection with a server generated a `NullPointerException` [SDN 2008]. The resulting failure to establish a secure HTTPS connection with the server caused a denial of service. Clients were temporarily forced to use an insecure HTTP channel for data exchange.

Related Guidelines

CERT C Secure Coding Standard	EXP34-C. Do not dereference null pointers
CERT C++ Secure Coding Standard	EXP34-CPP. Ensure a null pointer is not dereferenced
ISO/IEC TR 24772:2010	Null Pointer Dereference [XYH]
MITRE CWE	CWE-476. NULL pointer dereference

Bibliography

[API 2006]	Method doPrivileged()
[Hovemeyer 2007]	
[Reasoning 2003]	Defect ID 00-0001
	Null Pointer Dereference
[SDN 2008]	Bug ID 6514454

■ EXP02-J. Use the two-argument `Arrays.equals()` method to compare the contents of arrays

Arrays do not override the `Object.equals()` method; the implementation of the `equals()` method compares array *references* rather than their *contents*. Programs must use the two-argument `Arrays.equals()` method to compare the contents of two arrays. Programs must use the reference equality operators, `==` and `!=`, when intentionally testing reference equality. Programs also must not use the array `equals()` method because it can lead to unexpected results.

Noncompliant Code Example

This noncompliant code example incorrectly uses the `Object.equals()` method to compare two arrays.

```java
public void arrayEqualsExample() {
  int[] arr1 = new int[20]; // initialized to 0
  int[] arr2 = new int[20]; // initialized to 0
  arr1.equals(arr2); // false
}
```

Compliant Solution

This compliant solution compares the two arrays using the two-argument `Arrays.equals()` method.

```
public void arrayEqualsExample() {
  int[] arr1 = new int[20]; // initialized to 0
  int[] arr2 = new int[20]; // initialized to 0
  Arrays.equals(arr1, arr2); // true
}
```

Risk Assessment

Using the `equals()` method or relational operators with the intention of comparing array contents produces incorrect results, which can lead to vulnerabilities.

Rule	Severity	Likelihood	Remediation Cost	Priority	Level
EXP02-J	low	likely	low	P9	L2

Automated Detection   Static detection of calls to `Arrays.equals(...)` is straightforward.

Related Guidelines

MITRE CWE   CWE-595. Comparison of object references instead of object contents

Bibliography

[API 2006]   Class `Arrays`

■ EXP03-J. Do not use the equality operators when comparing values of boxed primitives

The *values* of boxed primitives cannot be directly compared using the `==` and `!=` operators because these operators compare object references rather than object values. Programmers can find this behavior surprising because autoboxing memoizes, or caches, the values of some primitive variables. Consequently, reference comparisons and value comparisons produce identical results for the subset of values that are memoized.

Autoboxing automatically wraps a value of a primitive type with the corresponding wrapper object. The *Java Language Specification* (JLS) §5.1.7, "Boxing Conversion" [JLS 2005], explains which primitive values are memoized during autoboxing:

> If the value p being boxed is `true`, `false`, a `byte`, a `char` in the range `\u0000` to `\u007f`, or an `int` or `short` number between –128 and 127, then let `r1` and `r2` be the results of any two boxing conversions of p. It is always the case that `r1 == r2`.

Primitive Type	Boxed Type	Fully Memoized
`boolean, byte`	`Boolean, Byte`	yes
`char, short, int`	`Char, Short, Int`	no

Use of the `==` and `!=` operators for comparing the values of fully memoized boxed primitive types is permitted.

Use of the `==` and `!=` operators for comparing the *values* of boxed primitive types that are not fully memoized is permitted only when the range of values represented is guaranteed to be within the ranges specified by the JLS to be fully memoized.

Use of the `==` and `!=` operators for comparing the *values* of boxed primitive types is not allowed in all other cases.

Note that JVM implementations are allowed, but not required, to memoize additional values:

> Less memory-limited implementations could, for example, cache all characters and shorts, as well as integers and longs in the range of –32K to +32K.

Code that depends on implementation-defined behavior is nonportable.

Noncompliant Code Example

This noncompliant code example defines a `Comparator` with a `compare()` method [Bloch 2009]. The `compare()` method accepts two boxed primitives as arguments. The `==` operator is used to compare the two boxed primitives. In this context, however, it compares the *references* to the wrapper objects rather than comparing the *values* held in those objects.

```
static Comparator<Integer> cmp = new Comparator<Integer>() {
  public int compare(Integer i, Integer j) {
    return i < j ? -1 : (i == j ? 0 : 1);
  }
};
```

Note that primitive integers are also accepted by this declaration because they are auto-boxed at the call site.

Compliant Solution

This compliant solution uses the comparison operators, <, >, <=, or >=, because these cause automatic unboxing of the primitive values. The == and != operators should not be used to compare boxed primitives.

```
public int compare(Integer i, Integer j) {
  return i < j ? -1 : (i > j ? 1 : 0);
}
```

Noncompliant Code Example

This noncompliant code example uses the == operator in an attempt to compare the values of pairs of Integer objects. However, the == operator compares object references rather than object values.

```
public class Wrapper {
  public static void main(String[] args) {
    Integer i1 = 100;
    Integer i2 = 100;
    Integer i3 = 1000;
    Integer i4 = 1000;
    System.out.println(i1 == i2);
    System.out.println(i1 != i2);
    System.out.println(i3 == i4);
    System.out.println(i3 != i4);
  }
}
```

The Integer class is only guaranteed to cache integer values from -128 to 127, which can result in equivalent values outside this range comparing as unequal when tested using the equality operators. For example, a Java Virtual Machine (JVM) that did not cache any other values when running this program would output

```
true
false
false
true
```

Compliant Solution

This compliant solution uses the `equals()` method instead of the `==` operator to compare the values of the objects. The program now prints `true`, `false`, `true`, `false` on all platforms, as expected.

```java
public class Wrapper {
  public static void main(String[] args) {
    Integer i1 = 100;
    Integer i2 = 100;
    Integer i3 = 1000;
    Integer i4 = 1000;
    System.out.println(i1.equals(i2));
    System.out.println(!i1.equals(i2));
    System.out.println(i3.equals(i4));
    System.out.println(!i3.equals(i4));
  }
}
```

Noncompliant Code Example

Java Collections contain only objects; they cannot contain primitive types. Further, the type parameters of all Java generics must be object types rather than primitive types. That is, attempting to declare an `ArrayList<int>` (which would, presumably, contain values of type `int`) fails at compile time because type `int` is not an object type. The appropriate declaration would be `ArrayList<Integer>`, which makes use of the wrapper classes and autoboxing.

This noncompliant code example attempts to count the number of indices in arrays `list1` and `list2` that have equivalent values. Recall that class `Integer` is required to memoize only those integer values in the range –128 to 127; it might return a nonunique object for any value outside that range. Consequently, when comparing autoboxed integer values outside that range, the `==` operator might return `false` and the example could deceptively output 0.

```java
public class Wrapper {
  public static void main(String[] args) {
    // Create an array list of integers, where each element
    // is greater than 127
    ArrayList<Integer> list1 = new ArrayList<Integer>();
    for (int i = 0; i < 10; i++) {
      list1.add(i + 1000);
    }

    // Create another array list of integers, where each element
    // has the same value as the first list
```

```
    ArrayList<Integer> list2 = new ArrayList<Integer>();
    for (int i = 0; i < 10; i++) {
      list2.add(i + 1000);
    }

    // Count matching values.
    int counter = 0;
    for (int i = 0; i < 10; i++) {
      if (list1.get(i) == list2.get(i)) {  // uses '=='
        counter++;
      }
    }

    // Print the counter: 0 in this example
    System.out.println(counter);
  }
}
```

However, if the particular JVM running this code memoized integer values from -32,768 to 32,767, all of the int values in the example would have been autoboxed to singleton Integer objects, and the example code would have operated as expected. Using reference equality instead of object equality requires that all values encountered fall within the interval of values memoized by the JVM. The JLS lacks a specification of this interval; rather, it specifies a minimum range that must be memoized. Consequently, successful prediction of this program's behavior would require implementation-specific details of the JVM.

Compliant Solution

This compliant solution uses the equals() method to perform value comparisons of wrapped objects. It produces the correct output 10.

```
public class Wrapper {
  public static void main(String[] args) {
    // Create an array list of integers
    ArrayList<Integer> list1 = new ArrayList<Integer>();

    for (int i = 0; i < 10; i++) {
      list1.add(i + 1000);
    }

    // Create another array list of integers, where each element
    // has the same value as the first one
    ArrayList<Integer> list2 = new ArrayList<Integer>();
```

```
      for (int i = 0; i < 10; i++) {
        list2.add(i + 1000);
      }

      // Count matching values
      int counter = 0;
      for (int i = 0; i < 10; i++) {
        if (list1.get(i).equals(list2.get(i))) {  // uses 'equals()'
          counter++;
        }
      }

      // Print the counter: 10 in this example
      System.out.println(counter);
    }
  }
```

Noncompliant Code Example (new `Boolean`)

In this noncompliant code example, constructors for class `Boolean` return distinct, newly instantiated objects. Using the reference equality operators in place of value comparisons will yield unexpected results.

```
public void exampleEqualOperator() {
  Boolean b1 = new Boolean("true");
  Boolean b2 = new Boolean("true");

  if (b1 == b2) {          // never equal
    System.out.println("Never printed");
  }
}
```

Compliant Solution (new `Boolean`)

In this compliant solution, the values of autoboxed `Boolean` variables may be compared using the reference equality operators because the Java language guarantees that the `Boolean` type is fully memoized. Consequently, these objects are guaranteed to be singletons.

```
public void exampleEqualOperator() {
  Boolean b1 = true; // Or Boolean.True
  Boolean b2 = true; // Or Boolean.True
```

```
if (b1 == b2) {        // always equal
  System.out.println("Will always be printed");
  }
}
```

Exceptions

EXP03-EX0: In the unusual case where a program is guaranteed to execute only on a single implementation, it is permissible to depend on implementation-specific ranges of memoized values.

Risk Assessment

Using the equivalence operators to compare values of boxed primitives can lead to erroneous comparisons.

Rule	Severity	Likelihood	Remediation Cost	Priority	Level
EXP03-J	low	likely	medium	P6	L2

Automated Detection Detection of all uses of the reference equality operators on boxed primitive objects is straightforward. Determining the correctness of such uses is infeasible in the general case.

Related Guidelines

MITRE CWE	CWE-595. Comparison of object references instead of object contents
	CWE-597. Use of wrong operator in string comparison

Bibliography

[Bloch 2009]	4, Searching for the One
[JLS 2005]	§5.1.7, Boxing Conversion
[Pugh 2009]	Using == to Compare Objects Rather than `.equals`

■ EXP04-J. Ensure that autoboxed values have the intended type

A boxing conversion converts the value of a primitive type to the corresponding value of the reference type. One example is the automatic conversion from `int` to `Integer` [JLS 2005]. This is convenient in cases where an object parameter is required, such as with collection classes like Map and List. Another use case is for interoperation with methods that require their parameters to be object references rather than primitive types. Automatic conversion to the resulting wrapper types also reduces clutter in code.

Expressions autobox into the intended type when the reference type causing the boxing conversion is one of the specific numeric wrapper types (for example, Boolean, Byte, Character, Short, Integer, Long, Float, or Double). However, autoboxing can produce unexpected results when the reference type causing the boxing conversion is nonspecific (for example, Number or Object) and the value being converted is the result of an expression that mixes primitive numeric types. In this latter case, the specific wrapper type that results from the boxing conversion is chosen on the basis of the numeric promotion rules governing the expression evaluation. Consequently, programs that use primitive arithmetic expressions as actual arguments passed to method parameters that have nonspecific reference types must cast the expression to the intended primitive numeric type before the boxing conversion takes place (unless the intended type is the resulting type of the expression).

Noncompliant Code Example

This noncompliant code example prints 100 as the size of the HashSet rather than the expected result (1). The combination of values of types short and int in the operation i-1 causes the result to be autoboxed into an object of type Integer rather than one of type Short. The HashSet contains only values of type Short; the code attempts to remove objects of type Integer. Consequently, the remove() operation accomplishes nothing.

```
public class ShortSet {
  public static void main(String[] args) {
    HashSet<Short> s = new HashSet<Short>();
    for (short i = 0; i < 100; i++) {
      s.add(i);
      s.remove(i - 1);  // tries to remove an Integer
    }
    System.out.println(s.size());
  }
}
```

The language's type checking guarantees that only values of type Short can be inserted into the HashSet. Nevertheless, programmers are free to attempt to remove an object of *any* type because Collections<E>.remove() accepts an argument of type Object rather than of type E. Such behavior can result in unintended object retention or memory leaks [Techtalk 2007].

Compliant Solution

Objects removed from a collection must share the type of the elements of the collection. Numeric promotion and autoboxing can produce unexpected object types. This compliant solution uses an explicit cast to short that matches the intended boxed type.

```
public class ShortSet {
  public static void main(String[] args) {
    HashSet<Short> s = new HashSet<Short>();
    for (short i = 0; i < 100; i++) {
      s.add(i);
      s.remove((short)(i - 1));  // removes a Short
    }
    System.out.println(s.size());
  }
}
```

Risk Assessment

Allowing autoboxing to produce objects of an unintended type can cause silent failures with some APIs, such as the Collections library. These failures can result in unintended object retention, memory leaks, or incorrect program operation.

Rule	Severity	Likelihood	Remediation Cost	Priority	Level
EXP04-J	low	probable	low	P6	L2

Automated Detection Detection of invocations of Collection.remove() whose operand fails to match the type of the elements of the underlying collection is straightforward. It is possible, although unlikely, that some of these invocations could be intended. The remainder are heuristically likely to be in error. Automated detection for other APIs could be possible.

Bibliography

[Core Java 2004]   Chapter 5

[JLS 2005]   §5.1.7, Boxing Conversions

[Techtalk 2007]   The Joy of Sets

■ EXP05-J. Do not write more than once to the same variable within an expression

According to the JLS, §15.7, "Evaluation Order" [JLS 2005]:

> The Java programming language guarantees that the operands of operators appear to be evaluated in a specific evaluation order, namely, from left to right.

Section 15.7.3, "Evaluation Respects Parentheses and Precedence" adds:

> Java programming language implementations must respect the order of evaluation as indicated explicitly by parentheses and implicitly by operator precedence.

When an expression contains side effects, these two requirements can yield unexpected results. Evaluation of the *operands* proceeds left-to-right, without regard to operator precedence rules and indicative parentheses; evaluation of the *operators*, however, obeys precedence rules and parentheses.

Expressions must not write to memory that they subsequently read and also must not write to any memory twice. Note that memory reads and writes can occur either directly in the expression from assignments or indirectly through side effects in methods called in the expression.

Noncompliant Code Example (Order of Evaluation)

This noncompliant code example shows how side effects in expressions can lead to unanticipated outcomes. The programmer intends to write access control logic based on different threshold levels. Each user has a rating that must be above the threshold to be granted access. As shown, a simple method can calculate the rating. The get() method is expected to return a nonzero factor for users who are authorized and a zero value for those who are unauthorized.

In this case, the programmer expects the rightmost subexpression to evaluate first because the * operator has a higher precedence than the + operator. The parentheses reinforce this belief. These ideas lead to the incorrect conclusion that the right-hand side evaluates to zero whenever the get() method returns zero. The programmer expects number to be assigned 0 because of the rightmost number = get() subexpression. Consequently, the test in the left-hand subexpression is expected to reject the unprivileged user because the rating value (number) is below the threshold of 10.

However, the program grants access to the unauthorized user because evaluation of the side-effect-infested subexpressions follows the left-to-right ordering rule.

```
class BadPrecedence {
  public static void main(String[] args) {
    int number = 17;
    int[] threshold = new int[20];
    threshold[0] = 10;
    number = (number > threshold[0]? 0 : -2)
             + ((31 * ++number) * (number = get()));
    // ...
    if (number == 0) {
      System.out.println("Access granted");
    } else {
      System.out.println("Denied access"); // number = -2
    }
  }

  public static int get() {
    int number = 0;
    // Assign number to non zero value if authorized else 0
    return number;
  }
}
```

Noncompliant Code Example (Order of Evaluation)

This noncompliant code example reorders the previous expression so that the left-to-right evaluation order of the operands corresponds with the programmer's intent.

Although this code performs as expected, it still represents poor practice by writing to number three times in a single expression.

```
int number = 17;
number = ((31 * ++number) * (number = get()))
         + (number > threshold[0]? 0 : -2);
```

Compliant Solution (Order of Evaluation)

This compliant solution uses equivalent code with no side effects and performs not more than one write per expression. The resulting expression can be reordered without concern for the evaluation order of the component expressions, making the code easier to understand and maintain.

```
int number = 17;

final int authnum = get();
number = ((31 * (number + 1)) * authnum)
         + (authnum > threshold[0]? 0 : -2);
```

Exceptions

EXP05-EX0: The increment and decrement operators (++) and (--) read a numeric variable, and then assign a new value to the variable. These are well-understood and are an exception to this rule.

EXP05-EX1: The logical operators || and && have well-understood short-circuit semantics, so expressions involving these operators do not violate this rule. Consider the following code:

```
public void exampleMethod(InputStream in) {
  int i;
  // Skip one char, process next
  while ((i = in.read()) != -1 && (i = in.read()) != -1) {
    // …
  }

}
```

Although the conditional expression appears to violate this rule, this code is compliant because the subexpressions on either side of the && operator do not violate it. Each subexpression has exactly one assignment and one side effect (the reading of a character from in).

Risk Assessment

Failure to understand the evaluation order of expressions containing side effects can result in unexpected output.

Rule	Severity	Likelihood	Remediation Cost	Priority	Level
EXP05-J	low	unlikely	medium	P2	L3

Automated Detection   Detection of all expressions involving both side effects and multiple operator precedence levels is straightforward. Determining the correctness of such uses is infeasible in the general case; heuristic warnings could be useful.

Related Guidelines

CERT C Secure Coding Standard	EXP30-C. Do not depend on order of evaluation between sequence points
CERT C++ Secure Coding Standard	EXP30-CPP. Do not depend on order of evaluation between sequence points
ISO/IEC TR 24772:2010	Side Effects and Order of Evaluation [SAM]

Bibliography

[JLS 2005]	§15.7, Evaluation Order
	§15.7.3, Evaluation Respects Parentheses and Precedence

■ EXP06-J. Do not use side-effecting expressions in assertions

The `assert` statement is a convenient mechanism for incorporating diagnostic tests in code. Expressions used with the standard `assert` statement must avoid side effects. Typically, the behavior of the `assert` statement depends on the status of a runtime property. When enabled, the `assert` statement is designed to evaluate its expression argument and throw an `AssertionError` if the result of the expression is `false`. When disabled, `assert` is defined to be a no-op; any side effects resulting from evaluation of the expression in the assertion are lost when assertions are disabled. Consequently, programs must not use side-effecting expressions in assertions.

Noncompliant Code Example

This noncompliant code is attempting to delete all the null names from the list in an assertion. However, the `boolean` expression is not evaluated when assertions are disabled.

```
private ArrayList<String> names;

void process(int index) {
  assert names.remove(null); // side-effect
  // ...
}
```

Compliant Solution

Avoid the possibility of side effects in assertions. This can be achieved by decoupling the `boolean` expression from the assertion.

```
private ArrayList<String> names;

void process(int index) {
  boolean nullsRemoved = names.remove(null);
  assert nullsRemoved; // no side-effect
  // …
}
```

Risk Assessment

Side effects in assertions result in program behavior that depends on whether assertions are enabled or disabled.

Rule	Severity	Likelihood	Remediation Cost	Priority	Level
EXP06-J	low	unlikely	low	P3	L3

Automated Detection Automated detection of assertion operands that contain locally visible side effects is straightforward. Some analyses could require programmer assistance to determine which method invocations lack side effects.

Related Guidelines

CERT C Secure Coding Standard   EXP31-C. Avoid side effects in assertions

CERT C++ Secure Coding Standard   EXP31-CPP. Avoid side effects in assertions

Bibliography

[Tutorials 2008]   Programming with Assertions

Chapter 5

Numeric Types and Operations (NUM)

■ Rules

■ Risk Assessment Summary

Rule	Severity	Likelihood	Remediation Cost	Priority	Level
NUM00-J	medium	unlikely	medium	P4	L3
NUM01-J	medium	unlikely	medium	P4	L3
NUM02-J	low	likely	medium	P6	L2
NUM03-J	low	unlikely	medium	P2	L3
NUM04-J	low	probable	high	P2	L3
NUM05-J	low	probable	high	P2	L3
NUM06-J	low	unlikely	high	P1	L3
NUM07-J	low	probable	medium	P4	L3
NUM08-J	low	probable	medium	P4	L3
NUM09-J	low	probable	low	P6	L2
NUM10-J	low	probable	low	P6	L2
NUM11-J	low	likely	medium	P6	L2
NUM12-J	low	unlikely	medium	P2	L3
NUM13-J	low	unlikely	medium	P2	L3

■ NUM00-J. Detect or prevent integer overflow

Programs must not allow mathematical operations to exceed the integer ranges provided by their primitive integer data types. According to the *Java Language Specification* (JLS), §4.2.2, "Integer Operations" [JLS 2005]:

> The built-in integer operators do not indicate overflow or underflow in any way. Integer operators can throw a `NullPointerException` if unboxing conversion of a `null` reference is required. Other than that, the only integer operators that can throw an exception are the integer divide operator/and the integer remainder operator %, which throw an `ArithmeticException` if the right-hand operand is zero, and the increment and decrement operators ++ and --, which can throw an `OutOfMemoryError` if boxing conversion is required and there is insufficient memory to perform the conversion.

The integral types in Java, representation, and inclusive ranges are shown in the following table taken from the JLS, §4.2.1, "Integral Types and Values" [JLS 2005]:

Type	Representation	Inclusive Range
byte	8-bit signed two's-complement	-128 to 127
short	16-bit signed two's-complement	-32,768 to 32,767
int	32-bit signed two's-complement	-2,147,483,648 to 2,147,483,647
long	64-bit signed two's-complement	-9,223,372,036,854,775,808 to 9,223,372,036,854,775,807
char	16-bit unsigned integers representing UTF-16 code units	\u0000 to \uffff (0 to 65,535)

The following table shows the integer overflow behavior of the integral operators.

Operator	Overflow	Operator	Overflow	Operator	Overflow	Operator	Overflow
+	yes	-=	yes	<<	no	<	no
-	yes	*=	yes	>>	no	>	no
*	yes	/=	yes	&	no	>=	no
/	yes	%=	no	\	no	<=	no
%	no	<<=	no	^	no	==	no
++	yes	>>=	no	~	no	!=	no
--	yes	&=	no	!	no		
=	no	|=	no	unary +	no		
+=	yes	^=	no	unary -	yes		

Because the ranges of Java types are not symmetric (the negation of each minimum value is one more than each maximum value), even operations like unary negation can overflow if applied to a minimum value. Because the java.lang.math.abs() method returns the absolute value of any number, it can also overflow if given the minimum int or long as an argument.

When a mathematical operation cannot be represented using the supplied integer types, Java's built-in integer operators silently wrap the result without indicating overflow. This can result in incorrect computations and unanticipated outcomes. Failure to account for integer overflow has resulted in failures of real systems, for example, when implementing the compareTo() method. The meaning of the return value of the compareTo() method is defined only in terms of its sign and whether it is zero; the magnitude of the return value is irrelevant. Consequently, an apparent but incorrect optimization would be to subtract the operands and return the result. For operands of opposite signs, this can result in integer overflow, consequently violating the compareTo() contract [Bloch 2008, Item 12].

Comparison of Compliant Techniques

Following are the three main techniques for detecting unintended integer overflow:

- *Precondition testing.* Check the inputs to *each* arithmetic operator to ensure that overflow cannot occur. Throw an ArithmeticException when the operation would overflow if it were performed; otherwise, perform the operation.

- *Upcasting.* Cast the inputs to the next larger primitive integer type and perform the arithmetic in the larger size. Check each intermediate result for overflow of the original smaller type, and throw an ArithmeticException if the range check fails. Note that the range check must be performed after *each* arithmetic operation; larger expressions without per-operation bounds checking can overflow the larger type. Downcast the final result to the original smaller type before assigning to a variable of the original smaller type. This approach cannot be used for type long because long is already the largest primitive integer type.

- *BigInteger.* Convert the inputs into objects of type BigInteger and perform all arithmetic using BigInteger methods. Type BigInteger is the standard arbitrary-precision integer type provided by the Java standard libraries. The arithmetic operations implemented as methods of this type cannot overflow; instead, they produce the numerically correct result. Consequently, compliant code performs only a single range check just before converting the final result to the original smaller type and throws an ArithmeticException if the final result is outside the range of the original smaller type.

The precondition testing technique requires different precondition tests for each arithmetic operation. This can be somewhat more difficult to implement and to audit than either of the other two approaches.

The upcast technique is the preferred approach when applicable. The checks it requires are simpler than those of the previous technique; it is substantially more efficient than using BigInteger. Unfortunately, it cannot be applied to operations involving type long, as there is no bigger type to upcast to.

The BigInteger technique is conceptually the simplest of the three techniques because arithmetic operations on BigInteger cannot overflow. However, it requires the use of method calls for each operation in place of primitive arithmetic operators, which can obscure the intended meaning of the code. Operations on objects of type `BigInteger` can also be significantly less efficient than operations on the original primitive integer type.

Precondition Testing

The following code example shows the necessary precondition checks required for each arithmetic operation on arguments of type `int`. The checks for the other integral types are analogous. These methods throw an exception when an integer overflow would otherwise occur; any other conforming error handling is also acceptable.

```java
static final int safeAdd(int left, int right)
            throws ArithmeticException {
  if (right > 0 ? left > Integer.MAX_VALUE - right
            : left < Integer.MIN_VALUE - right) {
    throw new ArithmeticException("Integer overflow");
  }
  return left + right;
}

static final int safeSubtract(int left, int right)
            throws ArithmeticException {
  if (right > 0 ? left < Integer.MIN_VALUE + right
            : left > Integer.MAX_VALUE + right) {
    throw new ArithmeticException("Integer overflow");
  }
  return left - right;
}

static final int safeMultiply(int left, int right)
            throws ArithmeticException {
  if (right > 0 ? left > Integer.MAX_VALUE/right
            || left < Integer.MIN_VALUE/right
            : (right < -1 ? left > Integer.MIN_VALUE/right
                        || left < Integer.MAX_VALUE/right
                    : right == -1
                      && left == Integer.MIN_VALUE) ) {
    throw new ArithmeticException("Integer overflow");
  }
  return left * right;
}

static final int safeDivide(int left, int right)
            throws ArithmeticException {
```

```
  if ((left == Integer.MIN_VALUE) && (right == -1)) {
    throw new ArithmeticException("Integer overflow");
  }
  return left / right;
}
static final int safeNegate(int a) throws ArithmeticException {
  if (a == Integer.MIN_VALUE) {
    throw new ArithmeticException("Integer overflow");
  }
  return -a;
}
static final int safeAbs(int a) throws ArithmeticException {
  if (a == Integer.MIN_VALUE) {
    throw new ArithmeticException("Integer overflow");
  }
  return Math.abs (a)
}
```

These method calls are likely to be inlined by most just-in-time systems (JITs).

These checks can be simplified when the original type is char. Because the range of type char includes only positive values, all comparisons with negative values may be omitted.

Noncompliant Code Example

Either operation in this noncompliant code example could result in an overflow. When overflow occurs, the result will be incorrect.

```
public static int multAccum(int oldAcc, int newVal, int scale) {
  // May result in overflow
  return oldAcc + (newVal * scale);
}
```

Compliant Solution (Precondition Testing)

This compliant solution uses the safeAdd() and safeMultiply() methods defined in the Precondition Testing section to perform secure integral operations or throw Arithmetic-Exception on overflow.

```
public static int multAccum(int oldAcc, int newVal, int scale)
                throws ArithmeticException {
  return safeAdd(oldAcc, safeMultiply(newVal, scale));
}
```

Compliant Solution (Upcasting)

This compliant solution shows the implementation of a method for checking whether value of type long falls within the representable range of an int using the upcasting technique. The implementations of range checks for the smaller primitive integer types are similar.

```java
public static long intRangeCheck(long value)
                throws ArithmeticException {
  if ((value < Integer.MIN_VALUE) || (value > Integer.MAX_VALUE)) {
    throw new ArithmeticException("Integer overflow");
  }
  return value;
}

public static int multAccum(int oldAcc, int newVal, int scale)
                throws ArithmeticException {
  final long res = intRangeCheck(
    ((long) oldAcc) + intRangeCheck((long) newVal * (long) scale)
  );
  return (int) res; // safe down-cast
}
```

Note that this approach cannot be applied to values of type long because long is the largest primitive integral type. Use the BigInteger technique instead when the original variables are of type long.

Compliant Solution (BigInteger)

This compliant solution uses the BigInteger technique to detect overflow.

```java
private static final BigInteger bigMaxInt =
  BigInteger.valueOf(Integer.MAX_VALUE);
private static final BigInteger bigMinInt =
  BigInteger.valueOf(Integer.MIN_VALUE);

public static BigInteger intRangeCheck(BigInteger val)
                throws ArithmeticException {
  if (val.compareTo(bigMaxInt) == 1 ||
      val.compareTo(bigMinInt) == -1) {
    throw new ArithmeticException("Integer overflow");
  }
  return val;
}

public static int multAccum(int oldAcc, int newVal, int scale)
                throws ArithmeticException {
  BigInteger product =
```

```
    BigInteger.valueOf(newVal).multiply(BigInteger.valueOf(scale));
    BigInteger res =
      intRangeCheck(BigInteger.valueOf(oldAcc).add(product));
    return res.intValue(); // safe conversion
  }
```

Noncompliant Code Example (`AtomicInteger`)

Operations on objects of type `AtomicInteger` suffer from the same overflow issues as other integer types. The solutions are generally similar to the solutions already presented; however, concurrency issues add additional complications. First, potential issues with time-of-check, time-of-use (TOCTOU) race conditions must be avoided; see rule VNA02-J for more information. Second, use of an `AtomicInteger` creates happens-before relationships between the various threads that access it. Consequently, changes to the number of accesses or order of accesses can alter the execution of the overall program. In such cases, you must either choose to accept the altered execution or carefully craft your implementation to preserve the exact number of accesses and order of accesses to the `AtomicInteger`.

This noncompliant code example uses an `AtomicInteger`, which is part of the concurrency utilities. The concurrency utilities lack integer overflow checks.

```
class InventoryManager {
  private final AtomicInteger itemsInInventory =
    new AtomicInteger(100);

  //...
  public final void nextItem() {
    itemsInInventory.getAndIncrement();
  }
}
```

Consequently, `itemsInInventory` can wrap around to `Integer.MIN_VALUE` when the `nextItem()` method is invoked when `itemsInInventory == Integer.MAX_VALUE`.

Compliant Solution (`AtomicInteger`)

This compliant solution uses the `get()` and `compareAndSet()` methods provided by `AtomicInteger` to guarantee successful manipulation of the shared value of `itemsInInventory`. This solution has the following characteristics:

■ The number and order of accesses to `itemsInInventory` remain unchanged from the noncompliant code example.

- All operations on the value of `itemsInInventory` are performed on a temporary local copy of its value.
- The overflow check in this example is performed in inline code rather than encapsulated in a method call. This is an acceptable alternative implementation. The choice of method call versus inline code should be made according to your organization's standards and needs.

```
class InventoryManager {
  private final AtomicInteger itemsInInventory =
    new AtomicInteger(100);

  public final void nextItem() {
    while (true) {
      int old = itemsInInventory.get();
      if (old == Integer.MAX_VALUE) {
        throw new ArithmeticException("Integer overflow");
      }
      int next = old + 1; // Increment
      if (itemsInInventory.compareAndSet(old, next)) {
        break;
      }
    } // end while
  } // end nextItem()
}
```

The two arguments to the `compareAndSet()` method are the expected value of the variable when the method is invoked and the intended new value. The variable's value is updated only when the current value and the expected value are equal [API 2006]. Refer to rule VNA02-J for more details.

Exceptions

NUM00-EX0: Depending on circumstances, integer overflow could be benign. For example, many algorithms for computing hash codes use modular arithmetic, intentionally allowing overflow to occur. Such benign uses must be carefully documented.

NUM00-EX1: Prevention of integer overflow is unnecessary for numeric types that undergo bitwise operations and not arithmetic operations. See rule NUM01-J for more information.

Risk Assessment

Failure to perform appropriate range checking can lead to integer overflows, which can cause unexpected program control flow or unanticipated program behavior.

Rule	Severity	Likelihood	Remediation Cost	Priority	Level
NUM00-J	medium	unlikely	medium	P4	L3

Automated Detection Automated detection of integer operations that can potentially overflow is straightforward. Automatic determination of which potential overflows are true errors and which are intended by the programmer is infeasible. Heuristic warnings might be helpful.

Related Guidelines

The CERT C Secure Coding Standard	INT32-C. Ensure that operations on signed integers do not result in overflow
The CERT C++ Secure Coding Standard	INT32-CPP. Ensure that operations on signed integers do not result in overflow
ISO/IEC TR 24772:2010	Wrap-around Error [XYY]
MITRE CWE	CWE-682. Incorrect calculation
	CWE-190. Integer overflow or wraparound
	CWE-191. Integer underflow (wrap or wraparound)

Bibliography

[API 2006]	Class `AtomicInteger`
[Bloch 2005]	Puzzle 27. Shifty i's
[JLS 2005]	§4.2.2, Integer Operations
	§15.22, Bitwise and Logical Operators
[Seacord 2005]	Chapter 5, Integers
[Tutorials 2008]	Primitive Data Types

■ NUM01-J. Do not perform bitwise and arithmetic operations on the same data

Integer variables are frequently intended to represent either a numeric value or a bit collection. Numeric values must be exclusively operated on using arithmetic operations, while bit collections should be exclusively operated on using logical operations. However, static analyzers are frequently unable to determine the intended use of a particular integer variable.

Performing bitwise and arithmetic operations on the same data indicates confusion regarding the purpose of the data stored in the variable. Unfortunately, bitwise operations are frequently performed on arithmetic values as a form of premature optimization. Bitwise operators include the unary operator ~ and the binary operators <<, >>, >>>, &, ^, and |. Although such operations are valid and will compile, they can reduce code readability.

Noncompliant Code Example (Left Shift)

Left- and right-shift operators are often employed to multiply or divide a number by a power of two. This compromises code readability and portability for the sake of often-illusory speed gains. The Java Virtual Machine (JVM) usually makes such optimizations automatically, and, unlike a programmer, the JVM can optimize for the implementation details of the current platform. This noncompliant code example includes both bitwise and arithmetic manipulations of the integer x that conceptually contains a numeric value. The result is a prematurely optimized statement that assigns the value 5x + 1 to x, which is what the programmer intended to express.

```
int x = 50;
x += (x << 2) + 1;
```

Noncompliant Code Example (Left Shift)

This noncompliant code example segregates arithmetic and bitwise operators by variables. The x variable participates only in bitwise operations, and y participates only in arithmetic operations.

```
int x = 50;
int y = x << 2;
x += y + 1;
```

This example is noncompliant because the actual data has both bitwise and arithmetic operations performed on it, even though the operations are performed on different variables.

Compliant Solution (Left Shift)

In this compliant solution, the assignment statement is modified to reflect the arithmetic nature of x, resulting in a clearer indication of the programmer's intentions.

```
int x = 50;
x = 5 * x + 1;
```

A reviewer could now recognize that the operation should also be checked for overflow. This might not have been apparent in the original, noncompliant code example. See rule NUM00-J for more information.

Noncompliant Code Example (Logical Right Shift)

In this noncompliant code example, the programmer wishes to divide x by 4. In a misguided attempt to optimize performance, the programmer uses a right-shift operation rather than a division operation.

```
int x = -50;
x >>>= 2;
```

The >>>= operator is a logical right shift; it fills the leftmost bits with zeroes, regardless of the number's original sign. After execution of this code sequence, x contains a large positive number (specifically, 0x3FFFFFF3). Using logical right shift for division produces an incorrect result when the dividend (x in this example) contains a negative value.

Noncompliant Code Example (Arithmetic Right Shift)

In this noncompliant code example, the programmer attempts to correct the previous example by using an arithmetic right shift (the >>= operator):

```
int x = -50;
x >>= 2;
```

After this code sequence is run, x contains the value −13 rather than the expected −12. Arithmetic right shift truncates the resulting value towards negative infinity, whereas integer division truncates toward zero.

Compliant Solution (Right Shift)

In this compliant solution, the right shift is replaced by division.

```
int x = -50;
x /= 4;
```

Noncompliant Code Example

In this noncompliant code example, a programmer is attempting to fetch four values from a byte array and pack them into the integer variable `result`. The integer value in this example represents a bit collection, not a numeric value.

```
// b[] is a byte array, initialized to 0xFF
byte[] b = new byte[] {-1, -1, -1, -1};
int result = 0;
for (int i = 0; i < 4; i++) {
  result = ((result << 8) + b[i]);
}
```

In the bitwise operation, the value of the byte array element `b[i]` is promoted to an `int` by sign-extension. When a byte array element contains a negative value (for example, 0xFF), the sign-extension propagates 1-bits into the upper 24 bits of the `int`. This behavior might be unexpected if the programmer is assuming that `byte` is an unsigned type. In this example, adding the promoted byte values to `result` fails to result in a packed integer representation of the bytes [FindBugs 2008].

Noncompliant Code Example

This noncompliant code example masks off the upper 24 bits of the promoted byte array element before performing the addition. The number of bits required to mask the sizes of `byte` and `int` are specified by the JLS. Although this code calculates the correct result, it violates this rule by combining bitwise and arithmetic operations on the same data.

```
byte[] b = new byte[] {-1, -1, -1, -1};
int result = 0;
for (int i = 0; i < 4; i++) {
  result = ((result << 8) + (b[i] & 0xFF));
}
```

Compliant Solution

This compliant solution masks off the upper 24 bits of the promoted byte array element. The result is then combined with `result` using a logical OR operation.

```
byte[] b = new byte[] {-1, -1, -1, -1};
int result = 0;
for (int i = 0; i < 4; i++) {
  result = ((result << 8) | (b[i] & 0xFF));
}
```

Exceptions

NUM01-EX0: Bitwise operations may be used to construct constant expressions.

```
int limit = 1 << 17 - 1; // 2^17 - 1 = 131071
```

Nevertheless, as a matter of style, it is preferable to replace such constant expressions with the equivalent hexadecimal constants.

```
int limit = 0x1FFFF; // 2^17 - 1 = 131071
```

NUM01-EX1: Data that is normally treated arithmetically may be treated with bitwise opera-tions for the purpose of serialization or deserialization. This is often required for reading or writing the data from a file or network socket. Bitwise operations are also permitted when reading or writing the data from a tightly packed data structure of bytes.

```
int value = /* interesting value */
Byte[] bytes = new Byte[4];
for (int i = 0; i < bytes.length; i++) {
  bytes[i] = value >> (i*8) & 0xFF;
}
/* bytes[] now has same bit representation as value */
```

Risk Assessment

Performing bitwise manipulation and arithmetic operations on the same variable obscures the programmer's intentions and reduces readability. This, in turn, makes it more difficult for a security auditor or maintainer to determine which checks must be performed to elimi-nate security flaws and ensure data integrity. For instance, overflow checks are critical for numeric types that undergo arithmetic operations but less critical for numeric types that undergo bitwise operations.

Rule	Severity	Likelihood	Remediation Cost	Priority	Level
NUM01-J	medium	unlikely	medium	P4	L3

Related Guidelines

CERT C Secure Coding Standard   INT14-C. Avoid performing bitwise and arithmetic operations on the same data

CERT C++ Secure Coding Standard   INT14-CPP. Avoid performing bitwise and arithmetic operations on the same data

Bibliography

[Steele 1977]

■ NUM02-J. Ensure that division and modulo operations do not result in divide-by-zero errors

Division and modulo operations are susceptible to divide-by-zero errors. Consequently, the divisor in a division or modulo operation must be checked for zero prior to the operation.

Noncompliant Code Example (Division)

The result of the / operator is the quotient from the division of the first arithmetic operand by the second arithmetic operand. Division operations are susceptible to divide-by-zero errors. Overflow can also occur during two's-complement signed integer division when the dividend is equal to the minimum (negative) value for the signed integer type and the divisor is equal to –1. See rule NUM00-J for more information. This noncompliant code example can result in a divide-by-zero error during the division of the signed operands num1 and num2.

```
long num1, num2, result;

/* Initialize num1 and num2 */

result = num1 / num2;
```

Compliant Solution (Division)

This compliant solution tests the divisor to guarantee there is no possibility of divide-by-zero errors.

```
long num1, num2, result;

/* Initialize num1 and num2 */

if (num2 == 0) {
  // handle error
} else {
  result = num1 / num2;
}
```

Noncompliant Code Example (Modulo)

The % operator provides the remainder when two operands of integer type are divided. This noncompliant code example can result in a divide-by-zero error during the remainder operation on the signed operands num1 and num2.

```
long num1, num2, result;

/* Initialize num1 and num2 */

result = num1 % num2;
```

Compliant Solution (Modulo)

This compliant solution tests the divisor to guarantee there is no possibility of a divide-by-zero error.

```
long num1, num2, result;

/* Initialize num1 and num2 */

if (num2 == 0) {
  // handle error
} else {
  result = num1 % num2;
}
```

Risk Assessment

A division or modulo by zero can result in abnormal program termination and denial of service (DoS).

Rule	Severity	Likelihood	Remediation Cost	Priority	Level
NUM02-J	low	likely	medium	P6	L2

Automated Detection   Automated detection exists for C and C++ but not for Java yet.

Related Guidelines

CERT C Secure Coding Standard	INT33-C. Ensure that division and modulo operations do not result in divide-by-zero errors
CERT C++ Secure Coding Standard	INT33-CPP. Ensure that division and modulo operations do not result in divide-by-zero errors
MITRE CWE	CWE-369. Divide by zero

Bibliography

[ISO/IEC 9899:1999]	Section 6.5.5, Multiplicative Operators
[Seacord 05]	Chapter 5, Integers
[Warren 02]	Chapter 2, Basics

■ NUM03-J. Use integer types that can fully represent the possible range of unsigned data

The only unsigned primitive integer type in Java is the 16-bit char data type; all of the other primitive integer types are signed. To interoperate with native languages, such as C or C++, that use unsigned types extensively, any unsigned values must be read and stored into a Java integer type that can fully represent the possible range of the unsigned data. For example, the Java long type can be used to represent all possible unsigned 32-bit integer values obtained from native code.

Noncompliant Code Example

This noncompliant code example uses a generic method for reading integer data without considering the signedness of the source. It assumes that the data read is always signed and treats the most significant bit as the sign bit. When the data read is unsigned, the actual sign and magnitude of the values may be misinterpreted.

```
public static int getInteger(DataInputStream is) throws IOException {
  return is.readInt();
}
```

Compliant Solution

This compliant solution requires that the values read are 32-bit unsigned integers. It reads an unsigned integer value using the `readInt()` method. The `readInt()` method assumes signed values and returns a signed `int`; the return value is converted to a `long` with sign extension. The code uses an `&` operation to mask off the upper 32 bits of the `long` producing a value in the range of a 32-bit unsigned integer, as intended. The mask size should be chosen to match the size of the unsigned integer values being read.

```
public static long getInteger(DataInputStream is) throws IOException {
  return is.readInt() & 0xFFFFFFFFL; // mask with 32 one-bits
}
```

As a general principle, you should always be aware of the signedness of the data you are reading.

Risk Assessment

Treating unsigned data as though it were signed produces incorrect values and can lead to lost or misinterpreted data.

Rule	Severity	Likelihood	Remediation Cost	Priority	Level
NUM03-J	low	unlikely	medium	P2	L3

Automated Detection   Automated detection is infeasible in the general case.

Bibliography

[API 2006]	Class `DataInputStream`, method `readInt`
[Harold 1997]	Chapter 2, Primitive Data Types, Cross Platform Issues, Unsigned Integers
[Hitchens 2002]	2.4.5, Accessing Unsigned Data

▪ NUM04-J. Do not use floating-point numbers if precise computation is required

The Java language provides two primitive floating-point types, `float` and `double`, which are associated with the single-precision 32-bit and double-precision 64-bit format values and operations specified by IEEE 754 [IEEE 754]. Each of the floating-point types has a fixed, limited number of mantissa bits. Consequently, it is impossible to precisely represent any irrational number (for example, π). Further, because these types use a binary mantissa, they cannot precisely represent many finite decimal numbers, such as 0.1, because these numbers have repeating binary representations.

When precise computation is necessary, such as when performing currency calculations, floating-point types must not be used. Instead, use an alternative representation that can completely represent the necessary values.

When precise computation is unnecessary, floating-point representations may be used. In these cases, you must carefully and methodically estimate the maximum cumulative error of the computations to ensure that the resulting error is within acceptable tolerances. Consider using numerical analysis to properly understand the problem. See Goldberg's work for an introduction to this topic [Goldberg 1991].

Noncompliant Code Example

This noncompliant code example performs some basic currency calculations.

```
double dollar = 1.00;
double dime = 0.10;
int number = 7;
System.out.println("A dollar less " + number + " dimes is $" +
                   (dollar - number * dime) );
```

Because the value 0.10 lacks an exact representation in either Java floating-point type (or *any* floating-point format that uses a binary mantissa), on most platforms, this program prints:

```
A dollar less 7 dimes is $0.29999999999999993
```

Compliant Solution

This compliant solution uses an integer type (such as long) and works with cents rather than dollars.

```
long dollar = 100;
long dime = 10;
int number = 7;
System.out.println("A dollar less " + number + " dimes is " +
                   (dollar - number * dime) + " cents" );
```

This code correctly outputs:

```
A dollar less 7 dimes is 30 cents
```

Compliant Solution

This compliant solution uses the `BigDecimal` type, which provides exact representation of decimal values. Note that on most platforms, computations performed using `BigDecimal` are less efficient than those performed using primitive types. The importance of this reduced efficiency is application specific.

```
import java.math.BigDecimal;

BigDecimal dollar = new BigDecimal("1.0");
BigDecimal dime = new BigDecimal("0.1");
int number = 7;
System.out.println("A dollar less " + number + " dimes is $" +
        (dollar.subtract(new BigDecimal(number).multiply(dime) )) );
```

This code outputs:

```
A dollar less 7 dimes is $0.3
```

Risk Assessment

Using floating-point representations when precise computation is required can result in a loss of precision and incorrect values.

Rule	Severity	Likelihood	Remediation Cost	Priority	Level
NUM04-J	low	probable	high	P2	L3

Automated Detection   Automated detection of floating-point arithmetic is straightforward. However, determining which code suffers from insufficient precision is not feasible in the general case. Heuristic checks, such as flagging floating-point literals that cannot be represented precisely, could be useful.

Related Guidelines

The CERT C Secure Coding Standard	FLP02-C. Avoid using floating point numbers when precise computation is needed
The CERT C++ Secure Coding Standard	FLP02-CPP. Avoid using floating point numbers when precise computation is needed
ISO/IEC TR 24772:2010	Floating Point Arithmetic [PLF]

Bibliography

[Bloch 2008]	Item 48. Avoid **float** and **double** if exact answers are required
[Bloch 2005]	Puzzle 2. Time for a change
[Goldberg 1991]	
[IEEE 754]	
[JLS 2005]	§4.2.3, Floating-Point Types, Formats, and Values

■ NUM05-J. Do not use denormalized numbers

Java uses the IEEE 754 standard for floating-point representation. In this representation, floats are encoded using 1 sign bit, 8 exponent bits, and 23 mantissa bits. Doubles are encoded and used exactly the same way, except they use 1 sign bit, 11 exponent bits, and 52 mantissa bits. These bits encode the values of s, the sign; M, the significand; and E, the exponent. Floating-point numbers are then calculated as $(-1)^s * M * 2^E$.

Ordinarily, all of the mantissa bits are used to express significant figures, in addition to a leading 1, which is implied and consequently omitted. As a result, floats have 24 significant bits of precision, and doubles have 53 significant bits of precision. Such numbers are called normalized numbers.

When the value to be represented is too small to encode normally, it is encoded in *denormalized* form, indicated by an exponent value of **Float.MIN_EXPONENT - 1** or **Double. MIN_EXPONENT - 1**. Denormalized floating-point numbers have an assumed 0 in the one's place and have one or more leading zeros in the represented portion of their mantissa. These leading zero bits no longer function as significant bits of precision; consequently, the total precision of denormalized floating-point numbers is less than that of normalized floating-point numbers. Note that even using normalized numbers where precision is required can pose a risk. See rule NUM04-J for more information.

Using denormalized numbers can severely impair the precision of floating-point calculations; as a result, denormalized numbers must not be used.

Detecting Denormalized Numbers

The following code tests whether a **float** value is denormalized in FP-strict mode or for platforms that lack extended range support. Testing for denormalized numbers in the presence of extended range support is platform dependent; see rule NUM06-J for additional information.

```
strictfp public static boolean isDenormalized(float val) {
  if (val == 0) {
    return false;
  }
  if ((val > -Float.MIN_NORMAL) && (val < Float.MIN_NORMAL)) {
    return true;
  }
  return false;
}
```

Testing whether values of type `double` are denormalized is analogous.

Print Representation of Denormalized Numbers

Denormalized numbers can also be troublesome because their printed representation is unusual. Floats and normalized doubles, when formatted with the %a specifier, begin with a leading nonzero digit. Denormalized doubles can begin with a leading zero to the left of the decimal point in the mantissa.

Here is a small program, along with its output, that demonstrates the print representation of denormalized numbers.

```
strictfp class FloatingPointFormats {
  public static void main(String[] args) {
    float x = 0x1p-125f;
    double y = 0x1p-1020;
    System.out.format("normalized float with %%e    : %e\n", x);
    System.out.format("normalized float with %%a    : %a\n", x);
    x = 0x1p-140f;
    System.out.format("denormalized float with %%e  : %e\n", x);
    System.out.format("denormalized float with %%a  : %a\n", x);
    System.out.format("normalized double with %%e   : %e\n", y);
    System.out.format("normalized double with %%a   : %a\n", y);
    y = 0x1p-1050;
    System.out.format("denormalized double with %%e: %e\n", y);
    System.out.format("denormalized double with %%a: %a\n", y);
  }
}
```

```
normalized float with %e    : 2.350989e-38
normalized float with %a    : 0x1.0p-125
denormalized float with %e  : 7.174648e-43
denormalized float with %a  : 0x1.0p-140
normalized double with %e   : 8.900295e-308
normalized double with %a   : 0x1.0p-1020
denormalized double with %e: 8.289046e-317
denormalized double with %a: 0x0.0000001p-1022
```

Noncompliant Code Example

This noncompliant code example attempts to reduce a floating-point number to a denormalized value and then restore the value.

```
float x = 1/3.0f;
System.out.println("Original    : " + x);
x = x * 7e-45f;
System.out.println("Denormalized: " + x);
x = x / 7e-45f;
System.out.println("Restored    : " + x);
```

Because this operation is imprecise, this code produces the following output when run in FP-strict mode:

```
Original    : 0.33333334
Denormalized: 2.8E-45
Restored    : 0.4
```

Compliant Solution

Do not use code that could use denormalized numbers. When calculations using float produce denormalized numbers, use of double can provide sufficient precision.

```
double x = 1/3.0;
System.out.println("Original    : " + x);
x = x * 7e-45;
System.out.println("Denormalized: " + x);
x = x / 7e-45;
System.out.println("Restored    : " + x);
```

This code produces the following output in FP-strict mode:

```
Original    : 0.3333333333333333
Denormalized: 2.333333333333333E-45
Restored    : 0.3333333333333333
```

Exceptions

NUM05-EX0: Denormalized numbers are acceptable when suitable numerical analysis demonstrates that the computed values meet all accuracy and behavioral requirements appropriate to the application.

Risk Assessment

Floating-point numbers are an approximation; denormalized floating-point numbers are a less precise approximation. Use of denormalized numbers can cause unexpected loss of precision, possibly leading to incorrect or unexpected results. Although the severity for violations of this rule is low, applications that require accurate results should make every attempt to comply.

Rule	Severity	Likelihood	Remediation Cost	Priority	Level
NUM05-J	low	probable	high	P2	L3

Related Vulnerabilities CVE-2010-4476 [CVE 2008] reports a vulnerability in the `Double.parseDouble()` method in Java 1.6 update 23 and earlier, Java 1.5 update 27 and earlier, and 1.4.2_29 and earlier. This vulnerability causes a denial of service when this method is passed a crafted string argument. The value 2.2250738585072012e-308 is close to the minimum normalized, positive, double-precision floating-point number, and when encoded as a string, it triggers an infinite loop of estimations during conversion to a normalized or denormalized `double`.

Related Guidelines

The CERT C Secure Coding Standard	FLP05-C. Don't use denormalized numbers

Bibliography

[Bryant 2003]	Computer Systems: A Programmer's Perspective, Section 2.4, Floating Point
[CVE 2008]	CVE-2010-4476
[IEEE 754]	

■ NUM06-J. Use the `strictfp` modifier for floating-point calculation consistency across platforms

The Java language allows platforms to use available floating-point hardware that can provide *extended floating-point support* with exponents that contain more bits than the standard Java primitive type `double` (in the absence of the `strictfp` modifier). Consequently, these platforms can represent a superset of the values that can be represented by the standard floating-point types. Floating-point computations on such platforms can produce different results than would be obtained if the floating-point computations were restricted to the standard representations of float and double. According to the JLS, §15.4, "FP-strict Expressions" [JLS 2005]:

> The net effect [of non-fp-strict evaluation], roughly speaking, is that a calculation might produce "the correct answer" in situations where exclusive use of the float value set or double value set might result in overflow or underflow.

Programs that require consistent results from floating-point operations across different JVMs and platforms must use the strictfp modifier. This modifier requires the JVM and the platform to behave as though all floating-point computations were performed using values limited to those that can be represented by a standard Java float or double, guaranteeing that the result of the computations will match exactly across all JVMs and platforms.

Using the strictfp modifier leaves execution unchanged on platforms that lack platform-specific floating-point behavior. It can have substantial impact, however, on both the efficiency and the resulting values of floating-point computations when executing on platforms that provide extended floating-point support. On these platforms, using the strictfp modifier increases the likelihood that intermediate operations will overflow or underflow because it restricts the range of intermediate values that can be represented; it can also reduce computational efficiency. These issues are unavoidable when portability is the main concern.

The strictfp modifier can be used with a class, method, or interface:

Usage	Applies to
Class	All code in the class (instance, variable, static initializers) and code in nested classes
Method	All code within the method
Interface	All code in any class that implements the interface

An expression is *FP-strict* when any of the containing classes, methods, or interfaces is declared to be strictfp. Constant expressions containing floating-point operations are also evaluated strictly. All compile-time constant expressions are by default FP-strict.

Strict behavior is not inherited by a subclass that extends an FP-strict superclass. An overriding method can independently choose to be FP-strict when the overridden method is not, or vice versa.

Noncompliant Code Example

This noncompliant code example does not mandate FP-strict computation. Double.MAX_VALUE is multiplied by 1.1 and reduced back by dividing by 1.1, according to the evaluation order. If Double.MAX_VALUE is the maximum value permissible by the platform, the calculation will yield the result infinity.

However, if the platform provides extended floating-point support, this program might print a numeric result roughly equivalent to `Double.MAX_VALUE`.

The JVM may choose to treat this case as FP-strict; if it does so, overflow occurs. Because the expression is not FP-strict, an implementation may use an extended exponent range to represent intermediate results.

```java
class Example {
  public static void main(String[] args) {
    double d = Double.MAX_VALUE;
    System.out.println("This value \"" + ((d * 1.1) / 1.1) +
                    "\" cannot be represented as double.");
  }
}
```

Compliant Solution

For maximum portability, use the `strictfp` modifier within an expression (class, method, or interface) to guarantee that intermediate results do not vary because of implementation-defined behavior. The calculation in this compliant solution is guaranteed to produce `infinity` because of the intermediate overflow condition, regardless of what floating-point support is provided by the platform.

```java
strictfp class Example {
  public static void main(String[] args) {
    double d = Double.MAX_VALUE;
    System.out.println("This value \"" + ((d * 1.1) / 1.1) +
                    "\" cannot be represented as double.");
  }
}
```

Noncompliant Code Example

Native floating-point hardware provides greater range than `double`. On these platforms, the JIT is permitted to use floating-point registers to hold values of type `float` or type `double` (in the absence of the `strictfp` modifier), even though the registers support values with greater exponent range than that of the primitive types. Consequently, conversion from `float` to `double` can cause an *effective* loss of magnitude.

```
class Example {
  double d = 0.0;

  public void example() {
    float f = Float.MAX_VALUE;
    float g = Float.MAX_VALUE;
    this.d = f * g;
    System.out.println("d (" + this.d + ") might not be equal to " +
                       (f * g));
  }

  public static void main(String[] args) {
    Example ex = new Example();
    ex.example();
  }
}
```

Magnitude loss would also occur if the value were stored to memory—for example, to a field of type float.

Compliant Solution

This compliant solution uses the `strictfp` keyword to require exact conformance with standard Java floating point. Consequently, the intermediate value of both computations of f * g is identical to the value stored in `this.d`, even on platforms that support extended range exponents.

```
strictfp class Example {
  double d = 0.0;
  public void example() {
    float f = Float.MAX_VALUE;
    float g = Float.MAX_VALUE;
    this.d = f * g;
    System.out.println("d (" + this.d + ") might not be equal to " +
                       (f * g));
  }

  public static void main(String[] args) {
    Example ex = new Example();
    ex.example();
  }
}
```

Exceptions

NUM06-EX0: This rule applies only to calculations that require consistent floating-point results on all platforms. Applications that lack this requirement need not comply.

NUM06-EX1: The `strictfp` modifier may be omitted when suitable numerical analysis demonstrates that the computed values meet all accuracy and behavioral requirements appropriate to the application.

Risk Assessment

Failure to use the `strictfp` modifier can result in implementation-defined behavior with respect to the behavior of floating-point operations.

Rule	Severity	Likelihood	Remediation Cost	Priority	Level
NUM06-J	low	unlikely	high	P1	L3

Automated Detection   Sound automated detection of violations of this rule is not feasible in the general case.

Related Guidelines

The CERT C Secure Coding Standard	FLP00-C. Understand the limitations of floating point numbers
CERT C++ Secure Coding Standard	FLP00-CPP. Understand the limitations of floating point numbers

Bibliography

[Darwin 2004]	Ensuring the Accuracy of Floating-Point Numbers
[JLS 2005]	§15.4, FP-strict Expressions
[JPL 2006]	9.1.3, Strict and Non-Strict Floating-Point Arithmetic
[McCluskey 2001]	Making Deep Copies of Objects, Using `strictfp`, and Optimizing String Performance

▪ NUM07-J. Do not attempt comparisons with NaN

According to the JLS, §4.2.3, "Floating-Point Types, Formats, and Values" [JLS 2005]:

> NaN (not-a-number) is unordered, so the numerical comparison operators <, <=, >, and >= return `false` if either or both operands are NaN. The equality operator == returns `false` if either operand is NaN, and the inequality operator != returns `true` if either operand is NaN.

Because this unordered property is often unexpected, direct comparisons with NaN must not be performed. Problems can arise when programmers write code that compares floating-point values without considering the semantics of NaN. For example, input validation checks that fail to consider the possibility of a NaN value as input can produce unexpected results. See rule NUM08-J for additional information.

Noncompliant Code Example

This noncompliant code example attempts a direct comparison with NaN. In accordance with the semantics of NaN, all comparisons with NaN yield false (with the exception of the != operator, which returns true). Consequently, this comparison always returns false, and the "result is NaN" message is never printed.

```java
public class NaNComparison {
  public static void main(String[] args) {
    double x = 0.0;
    double result = Math.cos(1/x); // returns NaN if input is infinity
    if (result == Double.NaN) { // comparison is always false!
      System.out.println("result is NaN");
    }
  }
}
```

Compliant Solution

This compliant solution uses the method Double.isNaN() to check whether the expression corresponds to a NaN value.

```java
public class NaNComparison {
  public static void main(String[] args) {
    double x = 0.0;
    double result = Math.cos(1/x); // returns NaN when input is infinity
    if (Double.isNaN(result)) {
      System.out.println("result is NaN");
    }
  }
}
```

Risk Assessment

Comparisons with NaN values can lead to unexpected results.

Rule	Severity	Likelihood	Remediation Cost	Priority	Level
NUM07-J	low	probable	medium	P4	L3

Automated Detection   Automated detection of floating-point comparison operators is straightforward. Sound determination of whether the possibility of an unordered result has been correctly handled is not feasible in the general case. Heuristic checks could be useful.

Bibliography

[FindBugs 2008]	FE: Doomed test for equality to NaN
[JLS 2005]	§4.2.3, Floating-Point Types, Formats, and Values

■ NUM08-J. Check floating-point inputs for exceptional values

Floating-point numbers can take on three exceptional values: infinity, -infinity, and NaN (not-a-number). These values are produced as a result of exceptional or otherwise unresolvable floating-point operations, such as division by zero. These exceptional values can also be obtained directly from user input through methods such as Double.valueOf(String s). Failure to detect and handle such exceptional values can result in inconsistent behavior.

The method Double.valueOf(String s) can return NaN or an infinite double, as specified by its contract. Programs must ensure that all floating-point inputs (especially those obtained from the user) are free of unexpected exceptional values. The methods Double.isNaN(double d) and Double.isInfinite(double d) can be used for this purpose.

NaN values are particularly problematic because they are unordered. That is, the expression NaN == NaN always returns false. See rule NUM07-J for more information.

Noncompliant Code Example

This noncompliant code example accepts user data without validating it.

```
double currentBalance; // User's cash balance

void doDeposit(String userInput) {
  double val;
  try {
   val = Double.valueOf(userInput);
  } catch (NumberFormatException e) {
    // Handle input format error
  }
```

```
  if (val >= Double.MAX_VALUE - currentBalance) {
    // Handle range error
  }

  currentBalance += val;
}
```

This code will produce unexpected results when an exceptional value is entered for `val` and subsequently used in calculations or as control values. The user could, for example, input the strings `infinity` or `NaN` on the command line, which would be parsed by `Double.valueOf(String s)` into the floating-point representations of either `infinity` or `NaN`. All subsequent calculations using these values would be invalid, possibly causing runtime exceptions or enabling DoS attacks.

In this noncompliant code example, entering `NaN` for `val` would cause `currentBalance` to be set to `NaN`, corrupting its value. If this value were used in other expressions, every resulting value would also become `NaN`, possibly corrupting important data.

Compliant Solution

This compliant solution validates the floating-point input before using it. The value is tested to ensure that it is neither `infinity`, `-infinity`, nor `NaN`.

```
double currentBalance; // User's cash balance

void doDeposit(String s){
  double val;
  try {
    val = Double.valueOf(userInput);
  } catch (NumberFormatException e) {
    // Handle input format error
  }

  if (Double.isInfinite(val)){
    // Handle infinity error
  }

  if (Double.isNaN(val)) {
    // Handle NaN error
  }

  if (val >= Double.MAX_VALUE - currentBalance) {
    // Handle range error
  }
  currentBalance += val;
}
```

Exceptions

NUM08-EX0: Occasionally, `NaN`, `infinity`, or `-infinity` may be acceptable as expected inputs to a program. In such cases, explicit checks might not be necessary. However, such programs must be prepared to handle these exceptional values gracefully and should prevent propagation of the exceptional values to other code that fails to handle exceptional values. The choice to permit input of exceptional values during ordinary operation should be explicitly documented.

Risk Assessment

Incorrect or missing validation of floating-point input can result in miscalculations and unexpected results, possibly leading to inconsistent program behavior and denial of service.

Rule	Severity	Likelihood	Remediation Cost	Priority	Level
NUM08-J	low	probable	medium	P4	L3

Automated Detection Automated detection is infeasible in the general case. It could be possible to develop a *taint*-like analysis that detects many interesting cases.

Related Guidelines

The CERT C Secure Coding Standard	FLP04-C. Check floating point inputs for exceptional values
The CERT C++ Secure Coding Standard	FLP04-CPP. Check floating point inputs for exceptional values

Bibliography

[IEEE 754]

[IEEE 1003.1, 2004]

▪ NUM09-J. Do not use floating-point variables as loop counters

Floating-point variables must not be used as loop counters. Limited-precision IEEE 754 floating-point types cannot represent

- all simple fractions exactly.
- all decimals precisely, even when the decimals can be represented in a small number of digits.
- all digits of large values, meaning that incrementing a large floating-point value might not change that value within the available precision.

Noncompliant Code Example

This noncompliant code example uses a floating-point variable as a loop counter. The decimal number 0.1 cannot be precisely represented as a float or even as a double.

```
for (float x = 0.1f; x <= 1.0f; x += 0.1f) {
  System.out.println(x);
}
```

Because 0.1f is rounded to the nearest value that can be represented in the value set of the float type, the actual quantity added to x on each iteration is somewhat larger than 0.1. Consequently, the loop executes only nine times and typically fails to produce the expected output.

Compliant Solution

This compliant solution uses an integer loop counter from which the desired floating-point value is derived.

```
for (int count = 1; count <= 10; count += 1) {
  float x = count/10.0f;
  System.out.println(x);
}
```

Noncompliant Code Example

This noncompliant code example uses a floating-point loop counter that is incremented by an amount that is typically too small to change its value given the precision.

```
for (float x = 100000001.0f; x <= 100000010.0f; x += 1.0f) {
  /* ... */
}
```

The code loops forever on execution.

Compliant Solution

This compliant solution uses an integer loop counter from which the floating-point value is derived. Additionally, it uses a double to ensure that the available precision suffices to represent the desired values. The solution also runs in FP-strict mode to guarantee portability of its results. See NUM06-J for more information.

```
for (int count = 1; count <= 10; count += 1) {
  double x = 100000000.0 + count;
  /* ... */
}
```

Risk Assessment

Using floating-point loop counters can lead to unexpected behavior.

Rule	Severity	Likelihood	Remediation Cost	Priority	Level
NUM09-J	low	probable	low	P6	L2

Automated Detection   Automated detection of floating-point loop counters is straightforward.

Related Guidelines

The CERT C Secure Coding Standard	FLP30-C. Do not use floating point variables as loop counters
The CERT C++ Secure Coding Standard	FLP30-CPP. Do not use floating point variables as loop counters
ISO/IEC TR 24772:2010	Floating-Point Arithmetic [PLF]

Bibliography

[Bloch 2005]	Puzzle 34. Down for the count
[JLS 2005]	§4.2.3, Floating-Point Types, Formats, and Values

▪ NUM10-J. Do not construct `BigDecimal` objects from floating-point literals

Literal decimal floating-point numbers cannot always be precisely represented as an IEEE 754 floating-point value. Consequently, the `BigDecimal(double val)` constructor must not be passed a floating-point literal as an argument when doing so results in an unacceptable loss of precision.

Noncompliant Code Example

This noncompliant code example passes a `double` value to the `BigDecimal` constructor. Because the decimal literal `0.1` cannot be precisely represented by a `double`, precision of the `BigDecimal` is affected.

```
// prints 0.1000000000000000055511151231257827021181583404541015625
// when run in FP-strict mode System.out.println(new BigDecimal(0.1));
```

Compliant Solution

This compliant solution passes the decimal literal as a `String` so that the `BigDecimal(String val)` constructor is invoked and the precision is preserved.

```
// prints 0.1
// when run in FP-strict mode System.out.println(new BigDecimal("0.1"));
```

Risk Assessment

Using the `BigDecimal(double val)` constructor with decimal floating-point literals can lead to loss of precision.

Rule	Severity	Likelihood	Remediation Cost	Priority	Level
NUM10-J	low	probable	low	P6	L2

Automated Detection   Automated detection is straightforward.

Bibliography

[JLS 2005]

■ NUM11-J. Do not compare or inspect the string representation of floating-point values

String representations of floating-point numbers must not be compared or inspected.

Noncompliant Code Example (String Comparison)

This noncompliant code example compares the string representations of two floating-point values.

```
int i = 1;
String s = Double.valueOf(i / 1000.0).toString();
if (s.equals("0.001")) {
  // ...
}
```

The comparison unexpectedly fails because s contains the string "0.0010".

Noncompliant Code Example (Regex)

This noncompliant code example attempts to mitigate the extra trailing zero by using a regular expression on the string before comparing it.

```
int i = 1;
String s = Double.valueOf(i / 1000.0).toString();
s = s.replaceFirst("[.0]*$", "");
if (s.equals("0.001")) {
  // ...
}
```

While the comparison does succeed on the code above, it fails on the similar code below, which uses 1/10000.0 instead of 1/1000.0. The string produced is not 0.00010 but rather 1.0E-4.

```
int i = 1;
String s = Double.valueOf(i / 10000.0).toString();
s = s.replaceFirst("[.0]*$", "");
if (s.equals("0.0001")) {
  // ...
}
```

Compliant Solution (String Comparison)

This compliant solution uses the BigDecimal class to avoid precision loss. It then performs a numeric comparison, which passes as expected.

```
int i = 1;
BigDecimal d = new BigDecimal(Double.valueOf(i / 1000.0).toString());
if (d.compareTo(new BigDecimal("0.001")) == 0) {
  // ...
}
```

Risk Assessment

Comparing or inspecting the string representation of floating-point values may have unexpected results.

Rule	Severity	Likelihood	Remediation Cost	Priority	Level
NUM11-J	low	likely	medium	P6	L2

Related Vulnerabilities   Hibernate Validator bug report HV-192[1] describes a violation of this rule.

Bibliography

[API 2006]

[JLS 2005]

■ NUM12-J. Ensure conversions of numeric types to narrower types do not result in lost or misinterpreted data

Conversions of numeric types to narrower types can result in lost or misinterpreted data if the value of the wider type is outside the range of values of the narrower type. As a result, all narrowing conversions must be guaranteed safe by range-checking the value before conversion.

There are 22 possible *narrowing primitive conversions* in Java. According to the JLS, §5.1.3, "Narrowing Primitive Conversions" [JLS 2005]:

- short to byte or char
- char to byte or short
- int to byte, short, or char
- long to byte, short, char, or int
- float to byte, short, char, int, or long
- double to byte, short, char, int, long, or float

Narrowing primitive conversions are allowed in cases where the value of the wider type is within the range of the narrower type.

Integer Narrowing

Integer type ranges are defined by the JLS, §4.2.1, "Integral Types and Values" [JLS 2005], and are also described in rule NUM00-J.

The following table presents the rules for narrowing primitive conversions of integer types. In the table, for an integer type T, n represents the number of bits used to represent the resulting type T (precision).

---

1. http://opensource.atlassian.com/projects/hibernate/browse/HV-192

From	To	Description	Possible Resulting Errors
signed integer	integral type T	Keeps only n lower-order bits	Lost or misinterpreted data
char	integral type T	Keeps only n lower-order bits	Magnitude error; negative number even though char is 16-bit unsigned

When integers are cast to narrower data types, the magnitude of the numeric value and the corresponding sign can be affected. Consequently, data can be lost or misinterpreted.

Floating-Point to Integer Conversion

Floating-point conversion to an integral type T is a two-step procedure:

1. When converting a floating-point value to an int or long and the value is a NaN, a zero value is produced. Otherwise, if the value is not infinity, it is rounded towards zero to an integer value V:

- If T is long and V can be represented as a long, the long value V is produced.
- If V can be represented as an int, then the int value V is produced.

Otherwise,

- The value is negative infinity or a value too negative to be represented, and Integer.MIN_VALUE or Long.MIN_VALUE is produced.
- The value is positive infinity or a value too positive to be represented, Integer.MAX_VALUE or Long.MAX_VALUE is produced.

2. If T is byte, char, or short, the result of the conversion is the result of a narrowing conversion to type T of the result of the first step

See the JLS, §5.1.3, "Narrowing Primitive Conversions," [JLS 2005] for more information.

Other Conversions

Narrower primitive types can be cast to wider types without affecting the magnitude of numeric values. See the JLS, §5.1.2, "Widening Primitive Conversion" [JLS 2005], for more information. Conversion from int or long to float or from long to double can lead to loss of precision (loss of least significant bits). No runtime exception occurs despite this loss.

Note that conversions from float to double or from double to float can also lose information about the overall magnitude of the converted value. See rule NUM06-J for additional information.

Noncompliant Code Example (Integer Narrowing)

In this noncompliant code example, a value of type int is converted to a value of type byte without range checking.

```java
class CastAway {
  public static void main(String[] args) {
    int i = 128;
    workWith(i);
  }

  public static void workWith(int i) {
    byte b = (byte) i;  // b has value -128
    // work with b
  }
}
```

The resulting value may be unexpected because the initial value (128) is outside of the range of the resulting type.

Compliant Solution (Integer Narrowing)

This compliant solution validates that the value stored in the wider integer type is within the range of the narrower type before converting to the narrower type.

```java
class CastAway {
  public static void workWith(int i) {
    // check if i is within byte range
    if ((i < Byte.MIN_VALUE) || (i > Byte.MAX_VALUE)) {
      throw new ArithmeticException("Value is out of range");
    }

    byte b = (byte) i;
    // work with b
  }
}
```

Noncompliant Code Example (Floating-Point Conversion to Integer)

The narrowing primitive conversions in this noncompliant code example suffer from loss in the magnitude of the numeric value as well as a loss of precision.

```
float i  = Float.MIN_VALUE;
float j  = Float.MAX_VALUE;
short b = (short) i;
short c = (short) j;
```

The minimum and maximum float values are converted to minimum and maximum int values (0x80000000 and 0x7FFFFFFF respectively). The resulting short values are the lower 16 bits of these values (0x0000 and 0xFFFF). The resulting final values (0 and −1) might be unexpected.

Compliant Solution (Floating-Point to Integer Conversion)

This compliant solution range-checks both the i and j variables before converting to the resulting integer type. Because both values are out of the valid range for a short, this code will always throw an ArithmeticException.

```
float i = Float.MIN_VALUE;
float j = Float.MAX_VALUE;
if ((i < Short.MIN_VALUE) || (i > Short.MAX_VALUE) ||
    (j < Short.MIN_VALUE) || (j > Short.MAX_VALUE)) {
  throw new ArithmeticException ("Value is out of range");
}

short b = (short) i;
short c = (short) j;
// other operations
```

Noncompliant Code Example (double to float Conversion)

The narrowing primitive conversions in this noncompliant code example suffer from a loss in the magnitude of the numeric value as well as a loss of precision. Because Double.MAX_VALUE is larger than Float.MAX_VALUE, c receives the value infinity, and because Double.MIN_VALUE is smaller than Float.MIN_VALUE, b receives the value 0.

```
double i = Double.MIN_VALUE;
double j = Double.MAX_VALUE;
float b = (float) i;
float c = (float) j;
```

Compliant Solution (double to float Conversion)

This compliant solution performs range checks on both i and j before proceeding with the conversions. Because both values are out of the valid range for a float, this code will always throw an ArithmeticException.

```
double i = Double.MIN_VALUE;
double j = Double.MAX_VALUE;
if ((i < Float.MIN_VALUE) || (i > Float.MAX_VALUE) ||
    (j < Float.MIN_VALUE) || (j > Float.MAX_VALUE)) {
  throw new ArithmeticException ("Value is out of range");
}

float b = (float) i;
float c = (float) j;
// other operations
```

Exceptions

NUM12-EX0: Java's narrowing conversions are both well defined and portable. The effects of narrowing on integral types can be easily reproduced in code; however, the effects of narrowing on floating-point types and between floating-point types and integral types cannot be easily represented. Knowledgeable programmers may intentionally apply narrowing conversions involving floating-point types in contexts where their output is both expected and reasonable. Consequently, narrowing conversions are permitted when the code contains comments that document both the use of narrowing conversions and the anticipated truncation. A suitable comment might read:

```
// Deliberate narrowing cast of i; possible truncation OK
```

This exception does not permit narrowing conversions without range-checking among integral types. The following code example demonstrates how to perform explicit narrowing from a long to an int where range-checking is not required.

```
long value = /* initialize */;
int i = (int) (value % 0x100000000); // 2^32
```

The range-checking is unnecessary because the truncation that is normally implicit in a narrowing conversion is made explicit. The compiler will optimize the operation away, and for that reason, no performance penalty is incurred.

Similar operations may be used for converting to other integral types.

Risk Assessment

Casting a numeric value to a narrower type can result in information loss related to the sign and magnitude of the numeric value. As a result, data can be misrepresented or interpreted incorrectly.

Rule	Severity	Likelihood	Remediation Cost	Priority	Level
NUM12-J	low	unlikely	medium	P2	L3

Automated Detection   Automated detection of narrowing conversions on integral types is straightforward. Determining whether such conversions correctly reflect the intent of the programmer is infeasible in the general case. Heuristic warnings could be useful.

Related Guidelines

The CERT C Secure Coding Standard	INT31-C. Ensure that integer conversions do not result in lost or misinterpreted data
	FLP34-C. Ensure that floating point conversions are within range of the new type
The CERT C++ Secure Coding Standard	INT31-CPP. Ensure that integer conversions do not result in lost or misinterpreted data
	FLP34-CPP. Ensure that floating point conversions are within range of the new type
ISO/IEC TR 24772:2010	Numeric Conversion Errors [FLC]
MITRE CWE	CWE-681. Incorrect conversion between numeric types
	CWE-197. Numeric truncation error

Bibliography

[Harold 1999]	
[JLS 2005]	§5.1.3, Narrowing Primitive Conversions

■ NUM13-J. Avoid loss of precision when converting primitive integers to floating-point

The following 19 specific conversions on primitive types are called the widening primitive conversions:

- byte to short, int, long, float, or double
- short to int, long, float, or double

- char to int, long, float, or double
- int to long, float, or double
- long to float or double
- float to double

Conversion from int or long to float or from long to double can lead to loss of precision (loss of least significant bits). In these cases, the resulting floating-point value is a rounded version of the integer value, using IEEE 754 round-to-nearest mode. Despite this loss of precision, the JLS requires that the conversion and rounding occur silently, that is, without any runtime exception. See the JLS, §5.1.2, "Widening Primitive Conversion" [JLS 2005] for more information. Conversions from integral types smaller than int to a floating-point type and conversions from int to double can never result in a loss of precision. Consequently, programs must ensure that conversions from an int or long to a floating-point type or from long to double do not result in a loss of required precision.

Note that conversions from float to double can also lose information about the overall magnitude of the converted value. See rule NUM06-J for additional information.

Noncompliant Code Example

In this noncompliant code example, two identical large integer literals are passed as arguments to the subFloatFromInt() method. The second argument is coerced to float, cast back to int, and subtracted from a value of type int. The result is returned as a value of type int.

This method could have unexpected results because of the loss of precision. In FP-strict mode, values of type float have 23 mantissa bits, a sign bit, and an 8-bit exponent. See NUM06-J for more information about FP-strict mode. The exponent allows type float to represent a larger range than that of type int. However, the 23-bit mantissa means that float supports exact representation only of integers whose representation fits within 23 bits; float supports only approximate representation of integers outside that range.

```
strictfp class WideSample {
  public static int subFloatFromInt(int op1, float op2) {
    return op1 - (int)op2;
  }

  public static void main(String[] args) {
    int result = subFloatFromInt(1234567890, 1234567890);
    // This prints -46, and not 0 as may be expected
    System.out.println(result);
  }

}
```

Note that conversions from `long` to either `float` or `double` can lead to similar loss of precision.

Compliant Solution (`ArithmeticException`)

This compliant solution range checks the argument of the integer argument (`op1`) to ensure it can be represented as a value of type `float` without a loss of precision.

```
strictfp class WideSample {
  public static int subFloatFromInt(int op1, float op2)
                  throws ArithmeticException {

    // The significand can store at most 23 bits
    if ((op1 > 0x007FFFFF) || (op1 < -0x800000)) {
      throw new ArithmeticException("Insufficient precision");
    }
    return op1 - (int)op2;
  }

  public static void main(String[] args) {
    int result = subFloatFromInt(1234567890, 1234567890);
    System.out.println(result);
  }
}
```

In this example, the `subFloatFromInt()` method throws `ArithmeticException`. This general approach, with appropriate range checks, can be used for conversions from `long` to either `float` or `double`.

Compliant Solution (Wider Type)

This compliant solution accepts an argument of type `double` instead of an argument of type `float`. In FP-strict mode, values of type `double` have 52 mantissa bits, a sign bit, and an 11-bit exponent. Integer values of type `int` and narrower can be converted to `double` without a loss of precision.

```
strictfp class WideSample {
  public static int subDoubleFromInt(int op1, double op2) {
    return op1 - (int)op2;
  }
  public static void main(String[] args) {
```

```
    int result = subDoubleFromInt(1234567890, 1234567890);
    // Works as expected
    System.out.println(result);
  }

}
```

Note that this compliant solution cannot be used when the primitive integers are of type `long` because Java lacks a primitive floating-point type whose mantissa can represent the full range of a `long`.

Exceptions

NUM13-EX0: Conversion from integral types to floating-point types without a range check is permitted when suitable numerical analysis demonstrates that the loss of the least significant bits of precision is acceptable.

Risk Assessment

Converting integer values to floating-point types whose mantissa has fewer bits than the original integer value can result in a rounding error.

Rule	Severity	Likelihood	Remediation Cost	Priority	Level
NUM13-J	low	unlikely	medium	P2	L3

Automated Detection   Automatic detection of casts that can lose precision is straightforward. Sound determination of whether those casts correctly reflect the intent of the programmer is infeasible in the general case. Heuristic warnings could be useful.

Related Guidelines

The CERT C Secure Coding Standard	FLP36-C. Beware of precision loss when converting integral types to floating point
The CERT C++ Secure Coding Standard	FLP36-CPP. Beware of precision loss when converting integral types to floating point

Bibliography

[JLS 2005]	§5.1.2, Widening Primitive Conversion

Object Orientation (OBJ)

■ Rules

■ Risk Assessment Summary

Rule	Severity	Likelihood	Remediation Cost	Priority	Level
OBJ00-J	medium	likely	medium	P12	L1
OBJ01-J	medium	likely	medium	P12	L1
OBJ02-J	medium	probable	high	P4	L3
OBJ03-J	low	probable	medium	P4	L3
OBJ04-J	low	likely	medium	P6	L2
OBJ05-J	high	probable	medium	P12	L1
OBJ06-J	medium	probable	high	P4	L3
OBJ07-J	medium	probable	medium	P8	L2
OBJ08-J	medium	probable	medium	P8	L2
OBJ09-J	high	unlikely	low	P9	L2
OBJ10-J	medium	probable	medium	P8	L2
OBJ11-J	high	probable	medium	P12	L1

■ OBJ00-J. Limit extensibility of classes and methods with invariants to trusted subclasses only

Many methods offer *invariants*, which can be any or all of the guarantees made about what the method can do, requirements about the required state of the object when the method is invoked, or guarantees about the state of the object when the method completes. For instance, the % operator, which computes the remainder of a number, provides the invariant that

$$0 < = abs(a \% b) < abs(b), \text{ for all integers } a, b \text{ where } b\ ! = 0$$

Many classes also offer invariants, which are guarantees made about the state of their objects' fields upon the completion of any of their methods. For instance, classes whose member fields may not be modified once they have assumed a value are called *immutable classes*. An important consequence of immutability is that the invariants of instances of these classes are preserved throughout their lifetimes.

A fundamental principle of object-oriented design is that a subclass that extends a superclass must preserve the invariants provided by the superclass. Unfortunately, design principles fail to constrain attackers, who can (and do) construct malicious classes that extend benign classes and provide methods that deliberately violate the invariants of the benign classes.

For instance, an immutable class that lacks the final qualifier can be extended by a malicious subclass that can modify the state of the supposedly immutable object. Furthermore, a malicious subclass object can impersonate the immutable object while actually remaining mutable. Such malicious subclasses can violate program invariants on which clients depend, consequently introducing security vulnerabilities.

To prevent misuse, classes with invariants on which other code depends should be declared final. Furthermore, immutable classes must be declared final.

Some superclasses must *permit* extension by trusted subclasses while simultaneously *preventing* extension by untrusted code. Declaring such superclasses to be final is infeasible because it would prevent the required extension by trusted code. Such problems require careful design for inheritance.

Consider two classes belonging to different protection domains: One is malicious and extends the other, which is trusted. Consider an object of the malicious subclass with a fully qualified invocation of a method defined by the trusted superclass, not overridden by the malicious class. In this case, the trusted superclass's permissions are examined to execute the method, and as a result, the malicious object gets the method invoked inside the protection domain of the trusted superclass [Gong 2003].

One commonly suggested solution is to place code at each point where the superclass can be instantiated to ensure that the instance being created has the same type as the superclass. When the type is found to be that of a subclass rather than the superclass's type, the checking code performs a security manager check to ensure that malicious classes cannot misuse the superclass. This approach is insecure because it allows a malicious class to add a finalizer and obtain a partially initialized instance of the superclass. This attack is detailed in rule OBJ11-J.

For nonfinal classes, the method that performs the security manager check must be invoked as an argument to a private constructor to ensure that the security check is performed *before* any superclass's constructor can exit. For an example of this technique, see rule OBJ11-J.

A method that receives an untrusted, nonfinal input argument must beware that other methods or threads might concurrently modify the input object. Some methods attempt to prevent modification by making a local copy of the input object. This is insufficient because a shallow copy of an object can still allow it to refer to mutable subobjects that can be modified by other methods or threads. Some methods go further and perform a deep copy of the input object. Although this mitigates the problem of modifiable subobjects, the method could still receive as an argument a mutable object that extends the input object class and provides inadequate copy functionality.

Noncompliant Code Example (`BigInteger`)

This noncompliant code example uses the `java.math.BigInteger` class. This class is nonfinal and consequently extendable. This can be a problem when operating on an instance of `BigInteger` that was obtained from an untrusted client. For example, a malicious client could construct a spurious mutable `BigInteger` instance by overriding `BigInteger`'s member functions [Bloch 2008].

The following code example demonstrates such an attack.

```
BigInteger msg = new BigInteger("123");
msg = msg.modPow(exp, m);  // Always returns 1

// Malicious subclassing of java.math.BigInteger
class BigInteger extends java.math.BigInteger {
  private int value;

  public BigInteger(String str) {
    super(str);
    value = Integer.parseInt(str);
  }

  public void setValue(int value) {
    this.value = value;
  }

  @Override public java.math.BigInteger modPow(
  java.math.BigInteger exponent, java.math.BigInteger m) {
    this.value = ((int) (Math.pow(this.doubleValue(),
                exponent.doubleValue()))) % m.intValue();
    return this;
  }
}
```

This malicious `BigInteger` class is clearly mutable because of the `setValue()` method. Furthermore, the `modPow()` method is subject to precision loss. (See rules NUM00-J, NUM08-J, NUM12-J, and NUM13-J for more information.) Any code that receives an object of this class and assumes that the object is immutable will behave unexpectedly. This is particularly important because the `BigInteger.modPow()` method has several useful cryptographic applications.

Noncompliant Code Example (Security Manager)

This noncompliant code example installs a security manager check in the constructor of the `BigInteger` class. The security manager denies access when it detects that a subclass without the requisite permissions is attempting to instantiate the superclass [SCG 2009]. It also compares class types, in compliance with rule OBJ09-J.

```java
public class BigInteger {
  public BigInteger(String str) {
    // java.lang.Object.getClass(), which is final
    Class c = getClass();
    // Confirm class type
    if (c != java.math.BigInteger.class) {
      // Check the permission needed to subclass BigInteger
      // throws a security exception if not allowed
      securityManagerCheck();
    }
    // ...
  }
}
```

Unfortunately, throwing an exception from the constructor of a non-final class is insecure because it allows a finalizer attack. (See rule OBJ11-J.)

Compliant Solution (Final)

This compliant solution prevents creation of malicious subclasses by declaring the immutable `BigInteger` class to be final. Although this solution would be appropriate for locally maintained code, it cannot be used in the case of `java.math.BigInteger` because it would require changing the Java SE API, which has already been published and must remain compatible with previous versions.

```java
final class BigInteger {
  // ...
}
```

Compliant Solution (Class Sanitization)

The instances of nonfinal classes obtained from untrusted sources must be used with care because their methods might be overridden by malicious methods. This potential vulnerability can be mitigated by making defensive copies of the acquired instances prior to use. This compliant solution demonstrates this technique for a `BigInteger` argument [Bloch 2008].

```
public static BigInteger safeInstance(BigInteger val) {
  // create a defensive copy if it is not java.math.BigInteger
  if (val.getClass() != java.math.BigInteger.class) {
    return new BigInteger(val.toByteArray());
  }
  return val;
}
```

Rules OBJ04-J and OBJ06-J discuss defensive copying in great depth.

Compliant Solution (Java SE 6, Public and Private Constructors)

This compliant solution invokes a security manager check as a side effect of computing the Boolean value passed to a private constructor (as seen in rule OBJ11-J). The rules for order of evaluation require that the security manager check must execute before invocation of the private constructor. Consequently, the security manager check also executes before invocation of any superclass's constructor. Note that the security manager check is made without regard to whether the object under construction has the type of the parent class or the type of a subclass (whether trusted or not).

This solution prevents the finalizer attack; it applies to Java SE 6 and later versions, where throwing an exception before the `java.lang.Object` constructor exits prevents execution of finalizers [SCG 2009].

```
public class BigInteger {
  public BigInteger(String str) {
    // throws a security exception if not allowed
    this(str, check(this.getClass()));
  }

  private BigInteger(String str, boolean securityManagerCheck) {
    // regular construction goes here
  }

  private static boolean check(Class c) {
    // Confirm class type
    if (c != java.math.BigInteger.class) {
      // Check the permission needed to subclass BigInteger
      // throws a security exception if not allowed
      securityManagerCheck();
    }
    return true;
  }
}
```

Noncompliant Code Example (Data-Driven Execution)

Code in privileged blocks should be as simple as possible, both to improve reliability and to simplify security audits. Invocation of overridable methods permits modification of the code that is executed in the privileged context without modification of previously audited classes. Furthermore, calling overridable methods disperses the code over multiple classes, making it harder to determine which code must be audited. Malicious subclasses cannot directly exploit this issue because privileges are dropped as soon as unprivileged code is executed. Nevertheless, maintainers of the subclasses might unintentionally violate the requirements of the base class. For example, even when the base class's overridable method is thread-safe, a subclass might provide an implementation that lacks this property, leading to security vulnerabilities.

This noncompliant code example invokes an overridable `getMethodName()` method in the privileged block using the reflection mechanism.

```java
public class MethodInvoker {
  public void invokeMethod() {
    AccessController.doPrivileged(new PrivilegedAction<Object>() {
      public Object run() {
        try {
          Class<?> thisClass = MethodInvoker.class;
          String methodName = getMethodName();
          Method method = thisClass.getMethod(methodName, null);
          method.invoke(new MethodInvoker(), null);
        } catch (Throwable t) {
          // Forward to handler
        }
        return null;
      }
    }
    );
  }

  String getMethodName() {
    return "someMethod";
  }

  public void someMethod() {
    // ...
  }
  // Other methods
}
```

A subclass can override `getMethodName()` to return a string other than `"someMethod"`. If an object of such a subclass runs `invokeMethod()`, control flow will divert to a method other than `someMethod()`.

Compliant Solution (Final)

This compliant solution declares the getMethodName() method final so that it cannot be overridden.

```
final String getMethodName() {
  // ...
}
```

Alternative approaches that prevent overriding of the getMethodName() method include declaring it as private or declaring the enclosing class as final.

Compliant Solution (Disallow Polymorphism)

This compliant solution specifically invokes the correct getMethodName(), preventing diversion of control flow.

```
public void invokeMethod() {
  AccessController.doPrivileged(new PrivilegedAction<Object>() {
    public Object run() {
      try {
        Class<?> thisClass = MethodInvoker.class;
        String methodName = MethodInvoker.this.getMethodName();
        Method method = thisClass.getMethod(methodName, null);
        method.invoke(new MethodInvoker(), null);
      } catch (Throwable t) {
        // Forward to handler
      }
      return null;
    }
  }
  );
}
```

Risk Assessment

Permitting a nonfinal class or method to be inherited without checking the class instance allows a malicious subclass to misuse the privileges of the class.

Rule	Severity	Likelihood	Remediation Cost	Priority	Level
OBJ00-J	medium	likely	medium	P12	L1

Related Guidelines

Secure Coding Guidelines for the Java Programming Language, Version 3.0	Guideline 1-2. Limit the extensibility of classes and methods

Bibliography

[API 2006]	Class `BigInteger`
[Bloch 2008]	Item 1. Consider static factory methods instead of constructors
[Gong 2003]	Chapter 6, Enforcing Security Policy
[Lai 2008]	Java Insecurity, Accounting for Subtleties That Can Compromise Code
[McGraw 1999]	Chapter Seven, Rule 3, Make everything final, unless there's a good reason not to
[Ware 2008]	

■ OBJ01-J. Declare data members as private and provide accessible wrapper methods

It is difficult to control how data members declared public or protected are accessed. Attackers can manipulate such members in unexpected ways. As a result, data members must be declared private. Use wrapper accessor methods to expose class members that are to be accessed outside of the package in which their class is declared. Using wrapper methods enables appropriate monitoring and control of the modification of data members (for example, by defensive copying, validating input, and logging). The wrapper methods can preserve class invariants.

Noncompliant Code Example (Public Primitive Field)

In this noncompliant code example, the data member `total` keeps track of the total number of elements as they are added and removed from a container using the methods `add()` and `remove()` respectively.

```java
public class Widget {
  public int total; // Number of elements
  void add() {
    if (total < Integer.MAX_VALUE) {
      total++;
      // ...
    } else {
```

```
      throw new ArithmeticException("Overflow");
    }
  }

  void remove() {
    if (total > 0) {
      total--;
      // ...
    } else {
      throw new ArithmeticException("Overflow");
    }
  }
}
```

As a public data member, total can be altered by external code independently of the add() and remove() methods. It is bad practice to expose fields from a public class [Bloch 2008].

Compliant Solution (Private)

This compliant solution declares total as private and provides a public accessor so that the required member can be accessed beyond the current package. The add() and remove() methods modify its value without violating any class invariants.

Note that care must be taken when providing references to private mutable objects from accessor methods; see rule OBJ05-J for more information.

```
public class Widget {
  private int total; // Declared private

  public int getTotal () {
    return total;
  }

  // definitions for add() and remove() remain the same
}
```

It is good practice to use methods such as add(), remove(), and getTotal() to manipulate the private internal state. These methods can perform additional functions, such as input validation and security manager checks, prior to manipulating the state.

Noncompliant Code Example (Public Mutable Field)

This noncompliant code example shows a static mutable hash map with public accessibility.

```
public static final HashMap<Integer, String> hm =
    new HashMap<Integer, String>();
```

Compliant Solution (Provide Wrappers and Reduce Accessibility of Mutable Members)

Mutable data members that are static must be declared private.

```
private static final HashMap<Integer, String> hm =
    new HashMap<Integer, String>();

public static String getElement(int key) {
  return hm.get(key);
}
```

Depending on the required functionality, wrapper methods may retrieve either a reference to the HashMap, a *copy* of the HashMap, or a value contained by the HashMap. This compliant solution adds a wrapper method to return the value of an element given its index in the HashMap.

Exceptions

OBJ01-EX0: According to Sun's Code Conventions document [Conventions 2009]:

> One example of appropriate public instance variables is the case where the class is essentially a data structure, with no behavior. In other words, if you would have used a struct instead of a class (if Java supported struct), then it's appropriate to make the class's instance variables public.

OBJ01-EX1: "If a class is package-private or is a private nested class, there is nothing inherently wrong with exposing its data fields—assuming they do an adequate job of describing the abstraction provided by the class. This approach generates less visual clutter than the accessor-method approach, both in the class definition and in the client code that uses it" [Bloch 2008]. This exception applies to both mutable and immutable fields.

OBJ01-EX2: Static final fields that contain mathematical constants may be declared public.

Risk Assessment

Failing to declare data members private can defeat encapsulation.

Rule	Severity	Likelihood	Remediation Cost	Priority	Level
OBJ01-J	medium	likely	medium	P12	L1

Automated Detection Detection of public and protected data members is trivial; heuristic detection of the presence or absence of accessor methods is straightforward. However, simply reporting all detected cases without suppressing those cases covered by the exceptions to this rule would produce excessive false positives. Sound detection and application of the exceptions to this rule is infeasible; however, heuristic techniques may be useful.

Related Guidelines

CERT C++ Secure Coding Standard	OOP00-CPP. Declare data members private
MITRE CWE	CWE-766. Critical variable declared public
Secure Coding Guidelines for the Java Programming Language, Version 3.0	Guideline 3-2. Define wrapper methods around modifiable internal state

Bibliography

[Bloch 2008]	Item 13. Minimize the accessibility of classes and members; Item 14. In public classes, use accessor methods, not public fields
[JLS 2005]	§6.6, Access Control
[Long 2005]	§2.2, Public Fields

■ OBJ02-J. Preserve dependencies in subclasses when changing superclasses

Developers often separate program logic across multiple classes or files to modularize code and to increase reusability. When developers modify a superclass (during maintenance, for example), the developer must ensure that changes in superclasses preserve all the program invariants on which the subclasses depend. Failure to maintain all relevant invariants can cause security vulnerabilities.

Noncompliant Code Example

This noncompliant code example relies on a class `Account` that stores banking-related information without any inherent security. Security is delegated to the subclass `BankAccount`. The client application is required to use `BankAccount` because it contains the security mechanism.

```
private class Account {
  // Maintains all banking related data such as account balance
  private double balance = 100;

  boolean withdraw(double amount) {
    if ((balance - amount) >= 0) {
      balance -= amount;
      System.out.println("Withdrawal successful. The balance is : "
                         + balance);
      return true;
    }
    return false;
  }
}

public class BankAccount extends Account {
  // Subclass handles authentication
  @Override boolean withdraw(double amount) {
    if (!securityCheck()) {
      throw new IllegalAccessException();
    }
    return super.withdraw(amount);
  }
  private final boolean securityCheck() {
    // check that account management may proceed
  }
}

public class Client {
  public static void main(String[] args) {
    Account account = new BankAccount();
    // Enforce security manager check
    boolean result = account.withdraw(200.0);
    System.out.println("Withdrawal successful? " + result);
  }
}
```

At a later date, the maintainer of the class Account added a new method called overdraft(). However, the BankAccount class maintainer was unaware of the change. Consequently, the client application became vulnerable to malicious invocations. For example, the overdraft() method could be invoked directly on a BankAccount object, avoiding the security checks that should have been present. The following noncompliant code example shows this vulnerability.

```
private class Account {
  // Maintains all banking related data such as account balance
  boolean overdraft() {
    balance += 300;    // Add 300 in case there is an overdraft
    System.out.println("Added back-up amount. The balance is :"
                      + balance);
    return true;
  }

  // other Account methods
}
public class BankAccount extends Account {
  // Subclass handles authentication
  // NOTE: unchanged from previous version
  // NOTE: lacks override of overdraft method
}
public class Client {
  public static void main(String[] args) {
    Account account = new BankAccount();
    // Enforce security manager check
    boolean result = account.withdraw(200.0);
    if (!result) {
      result = account.overdraft();
    }
    System.out.println("Withdrawal successful? " + result);
  }
}
```

While this code works as expected, it adds a dangerous attack vector. Because there is no security check on the `overdraft()` method, a malicious client can invoke it without authentication:

```
public class MaliciousClient {
  public static void main(String[] args) {
    Account account = new BankAccount();
    // No security check performed
    boolean result = account.overdraft();
    System.out.println("Withdrawal successful? " + result);
  }
}
```

Compliant Solution

In this compliant solution, the `BankAccount` class provides an overriding version of the `overdraft()` method that immediately fails, preventing misuse of the overdraft feature. All other aspects of the compliant solution remain unchanged.

```
class BankAccount extends Account {
  // ...
  @Override void overdraft() { // override
    throw new IllegalAccessException();
  }
}
```

Alternatively, when the intended design permits the new method in the parent class to be invoked directly from a subclass without overriding, install a security manager check directly in the new method.

Noncompliant Code Example (`Calendar`)

This noncompliant code example overrides the methods `after()` and `compareTo()` of the class `java.util.Calendar`. The `Calendar.after()` method returns a `boolean` value that indicates whether or not the `Calendar` represents a time *after* that represented by the specified `Object` parameter. The programmer wishes to extend this functionality so that the `after()` method returns `true` even when the two objects represent the same date. The programmer also overrides the method `compareTo()` to provide a "comparisons by day" option to clients (for example, comparing today's date with the first day of the week, which differs from country to country, to check whether it is a weekday).

```
class CalendarSubclass extends Calendar {
  @Override public boolean after(Object when) {
    // correctly calls Calendar.compareTo()
    if (when instanceof Calendar &&
        super.compareTo((Calendar) when) == 0) {
      return true;
    }
    return super.after(when);
  }
  @Override public int compareTo(Calendar anotherCalendar) {
    return compareDays(this.getFirstDayOfWeek(),
                       anotherCalendar.getFirstDayOfWeek());
  }
  private int compareDays(int currentFirstDayOfWeek,
                          int anotherFirstDayOfWeek) {
    return (currentFirstDayOfWeek > anotherFirstDayOfWeek) ? 1
         : (currentFirstDayOfWeek == anotherFirstDayOfWeek) ? 0 : -1;
  }
  public static void main(String[] args) {
    CalendarSubclass cs1 = new CalendarSubclass();
```

```
   cs1.setTime(new Date());
   // Date of last Sunday (before now)
   cs1.set(Calendar.DAY_OF_WEEK, Calendar.SUNDAY);
   // Wed Dec 31 19:00:00 EST 1969
   CalendarSubclass cs2 = new CalendarSubclass();
   // expected to print true
   System.out.println(cs1.after(cs2));
  }

  // Implementation of other Calendar abstract methods
}
```

The java.util.Calendar class provides a compareTo() method and an after() method. The after() method is documented in the *Java API Reference* [API 2006] as follows:

The after() method returns whether this Calendar represents a time after the time represented by the specified Object. This method is equivalent to compareTo(when) > 0 if and only if when is a Calendar instance. Otherwise, the method returns false.

The documentation fails to state whether after() invokes compareTo() or whether compareTo() invokes after(). In the Oracle JDK 1.6 implementation, the source code for after() is as follows:

```
public boolean after(Object when) {
  return when instanceof Calendar
        && compareTo((Calendar) when) > 0;
}
```

In this case, the two objects are initially compared using the overriding Calendar-Subclass.after() method. This invokes the superclass's Calendar.after() method to perform the remainder of the comparison. But the Calendar.after() method internally calls the compareTo() method, which delegates to CalendarSubclass.compareTo(). Consequently, CalendarSubclass.after() actually calls CalendarSub-class.compareTo() and returns false.

The developer of the subclass was unaware of the implementation details of Calendar.after() and incorrectly assumed that the superclass's after() method would invoke only the superclass's methods without invoking overriding methods from the subclass. Rule MET05-J describes similar programming errors.

Such errors generally occur because the developer made assumptions about the implementation-specific details of the superclass. Even when these assumptions are initially correct, implementation details of the superclass may change without warning.

Compliant Solution (`Calendar`)

This compliant solution uses a design pattern called composition and forwarding (some-times also called delegation) [Lieberman 1986], [Gamma 1995, p. 20]. The compliant solution introduces a new *forwarder* class that contains a private member field of the `Calendar` type; this is *composition* rather than inheritance. In this example, the field refers to `CalendarImplementation`, a concrete instantiable implementation of the `abstract` `Calendar` class. The compliant solution also introduces a wrapper class called `Composite-Calendar` that provides the same overridden methods found in the `CalendarSubclass` from the preceding noncompliant code example.

```
class CalendarImplementation extends Calendar {
  // ...
}

// Class ForwardingCalendar
public class ForwardingCalendar {
  private final CalendarImplementation c;

  public ForwardingCalendar(CalendarImplementation c) {
    this.c = c;
  }

  CalendarImplementation getCalendarImplementation() {
    return c;
  }

  public boolean after(Object when) {
    return c.after(when);
  }

  public int compareTo(Calendar anotherCalendar) {
    // CalendarImplementation.compareTo() will be called
    return c.compareTo(anotherCalendar);
  }
}

class CompositeCalendar extends ForwardingCalendar {
  public CompositeCalendar(CalendarImplementation ci) {
    super(ci);
  }

  @Override public boolean after(Object when) {
    // This will call the overridden version, i.e.
    // CompositeClass.compareTo();
    if (when instanceof Calendar &&
        super.compareTo((Calendar)when) == 0) {
      // Return true if it is the first day of week
      return true;
    }
```

```
      // Does not compare with first day of week any longer;
      // Uses default comparison with epoch
      return super.after(when);
    }

    @Override public int compareTo(Calendar anotherCalendar) {
      return compareDays(
              super.getCalendarImplementation().getFirstDayOfWeek(),
              anotherCalendar.getFirstDayOfWeek());
    }

    private int compareDays(int currentFirstDayOfWeek,
                            int anotherFirstDayOfWeek) {
      return (currentFirstDayOfWeek > anotherFirstDayOfWeek) ? 1
          : (currentFirstDayOfWeek == anotherFirstDayOfWeek) ? 0 : -1;
    }

  public static void main(String[] args) {
    CalendarImplementation ci1 = new CalendarImplementation();
    ci1.setTime(new Date());
    // Date of last Sunday (before now)
    ci1.set(Calendar.DAY_OF_WEEK, Calendar.SUNDAY);

    CalendarImplementation ci2 = new CalendarImplementation();
    CompositeCalendar c = new CompositeCalendar(ci1);
    // expected to print true
    System.out.println(c.after(ci2));
  }
}
```

Note that each method of the class `ForwardingCalendar` redirects to methods of the contained `CalendarImplementation` class, from which it receives return values; this is the *forwarding* mechanism. The `ForwardingCalendar` class is largely independent of the implementation of the class `CalendarImplementation`. Consequently, future changes to `CalendarImplementation` are unlikely to break `ForwardingCalendar` and are also unlikely to break `CompositeCalendar`. Invocations of the overriding `after()` method of `CompositeCalendar` perform the necessary comparison by using the `CalendarImplementation.compareTo()` method as required. Using `super.after(when)` forwards to `ForwardingCalendar`, which invokes the `CalendarImplementation.after()` method as required. As a result, `java.util.Calendar.after()` invokes the `CalendarImplementation.compareTo()` method as required, resulting in the program correctly printing `true`.

Risk Assessment

Modifying a superclass without considering the effect on subclasses can introduce vulnerabilities. Subclasses that are developed without awareness of the superclass implementation can be subject to erratic behavior, resulting in inconsistent data state and mismanaged control flow.

Rule	Severity	Likelihood	Remediation Cost	Priority	Level
OBJ02-J	medium	probable	high	P4	L3

Automated Detection   Sound automated detection is not currently feasible.

Related Vulnerabilities   The introduction of the entrySet() method in the java.util. Hashtable superclass in JDK 1.2 left the java.security.Provider subclass vulnerable to a security attack. The Provider class extends java.util.Properties, which in turn extends Hashtable. The Provider class maps a cryptographic algorithm name (for example, "RSA") to a class that provides its implementation.

The Provider class inherits the put() and remove() methods from Hashtable and adds security manager checks to each. These checks ensure that malicious code cannot add or remove the mappings. When entrySet() was introduced, it became possible for untrusted code to remove the mappings from the Hashtable because Provider failed to override this method to provide the necessary security manager check [SCG 2009]. This is commonly known as the *fragile class hierarchy* problem.

Related Guidelines

Secure Coding Guidelines for the Java Programming Language, Version 3.0	Guideline 1-3. Understand how a superclass can affect subclass behavior

Bibliography

[API 2006]	Class Calendar
[Bloch 2008]	Item 16. Favor composition over inheritance
[Gamma 1995]	Design Patterns, Elements of Reusable Object-Oriented Software
[Lieberman 1986]	Using prototypical objects to implement shared behavior in object-oriented systems

■ OBJ03-J. Do not mix generic with nongeneric raw types in new code

Generically typed code can be freely used with raw types when attempting to preserve compatibility between nongeneric legacy code and newer generic code. Using raw types with generic code causes most Java compilers to issue "unchecked" warnings but still compile the code. When generic and nongeneric types are used together correctly, these warnings can be ignored; at other times, these warnings can denote potentially unsafe operations. According to the *Java Language Specification*, §4.8, "Raw Types" [JLS 2005]:

> The use of raw types is allowed only as a concession to compatibility of legacy code. The use of raw types in code written after the introduction of genericity into the Java programming language is strongly discouraged. It is possible that future versions of the Java programming language will disallow the use of raw types.

When a parameterized type tries to access an object that is not of the parameterized type, heap pollution occurs. For instance, consider the following code snippet.

```
List l = new ArrayList();
List<String> ls = l; // Produces unchecked warning
```

It is insufficient to rely on unchecked warnings alone to detect violations of this rule. According to the *Java Language Specification*, §4.12.2.1, "Heap Pollution" [JLS 2005]:

> Note that this does not imply that heap pollution only occurs if an unchecked warning actually occurred. It is possible to run a program where some of the binaries were compiled by a compiler for an older version of the Java programming language, or by a compiler that allows the unchecked warnings to be suppressed. This practice is unhealthy at best.

Extending legacy classes and making the overriding methods generic fails because this is disallowed by the *Java Language Specification*.

Noncompliant Code Example

This noncompliant code example compiles but produces an unchecked warning because the raw type of the List.add() method is used (the list parameter in the addToList() method) rather than the parameterized type.

```java
class ListUtility {
  private static void addToList(List list, Object obj) {
    list.add(obj); // Unchecked warning
  }

  public static void main(String[] args) {
    List<String> list = new ArrayList<String> ();
    addToList(list, 1);
    System.out.println(list.get(0));
  }
}
```

When executed, this code throws an exception. This happens not because a List<String> receives an Integer but because the value returned by list.get(0) is an improper type (an Integer rather than a String). In other words, the code throws an exception some time after the execution of the operation that actually caused the error, complicating debugging.

Compliant Solution (Parameterized Collection)

This compliant solution enforces type safety by changing the addToList() method signature to enforce proper type checking.

```
class ListUtility {
  private static void addToList(List<String> list, String str) {
    list.add(str);    // No warning generated
  }

  public static void main(String[] args) {
    List<String> list = new ArrayList<String> ();
    addToList(list, "1");
    System.out.println(list.get(0));
  }
}
```

The compiler prevents insertion of an Object to the parameterized list, because addToList() cannot be called with an argument whose type produces a mismatch. The code has consequently been changed to add a String to the list instead of an Integer.

Compliant Solution (Legacy Code)

While the previous compliant solution eliminates use of raw collections, it may be infeasible to implement this solution when interoperating with legacy code.

Suppose that the addToList() method was legacy code that could not be changed. The following compliant solution creates a checked view of the list by using the Collections. checkedList() method. This method returns a wrapper collection that performs runtime type checking in its implementation of the add() method before delegating to the backend List<String>. The wrapper collection can be safely passed to the legacy addToList() method.

```
class ListUtility {
  private static void addToList(List list, Object obj) {
    list.add(obj); // Unchecked warning
  }
```

```
public static void main(String[] args) {
  List<String> list = new ArrayList<String> ();
  List<String> checkedList =
    Collections.checkedList(list, String.class);
  addToList(checkedList, 1);
  System.out.println(list.get(0));
  }
}
```

The compiler still issues the unchecked warning, which may still be ignored. However, the code now fails when it attempts to add the Integer to the list, consequently preventing the program from proceeding with invalid data.

Noncompliant Code Example

This noncompliant code example compiles and runs cleanly because it suppresses the unchecked warning produced by the raw List.add() method. The printOne() method intends to print the value 1 either as an int or as a double depending on the type of the variable type.

```
class ListAdder {
  @SuppressWarnings("unchecked")
  private static void addToList(List list, Object obj) {
    list.add(obj);      // Unchecked warning
  }

  private static <T> void printOne(T type) {
    if (!(type instanceof Integer || type instanceof Double)) {
      System.out.println("Cannot print in the supplied type");
    }
    List<T> list = new ArrayList<T>();
    addToList(list, 1);
    System.out.println(list.get(0));
  }

  public static void main(String[] args) {
    double d = 1;
    int i = 1;
    System.out.println(d);
    ListAdder.printOne(d);
    System.out.println(i);
    ListAdder.printOne(i);
  }
}
```

However, despite `list` being correctly parameterized, this method prints 1 and never 1.0 because the `int` value 1 is always added to `list` without being type checked. This code produces the following output:

```
1.0
1
1
1
```

Compliant Solution

This compliant solution generifies the `addToList()` method, eliminating any possible type violations.

```java
class ListAdder {
  private static <T> void addToList(List<T> list, T t) {
    list.add(t);      // No warning generated
  }

  private static <T> void printOne(T type) {
    if (type instanceof Integer) {
      List<Integer> list = new ArrayList<Integer>();
      addToList(list, 1);
      System.out.println(list.get(0));
    } else if (type instanceof Double) {
      List<Double> list = new ArrayList<Double>();

      // This will not compile if addToList(list, 1) is used
      addToList(list, 1.0);
      System.out.println(list.get(0));
    } else {
      System.out.println("Cannot print in the supplied type");
    }
  }

  public static void main(String[] args) {
    double d = 1;
    int i = 1;
    System.out.println(d);
    ListAdder.printOne(d);
    System.out.println(i);
    ListAdder.printOne(i);
  }
}
```

This code compiles cleanly and produces the correct output:

```
1.0
1.0
1
1
```

If the method addToList() is externally defined (such as in a library or as an upcall method) and cannot be changed, the same compliant method printOne() can be used, but no warnings result if addToList(1) is used instead of addToList(1.0). Great care must be taken to ensure type safety when generics are mixed with nongeneric code.

Exceptions

OBJ03-EX0: Raw types must be used in class literals. For example, because List<Integer>.class is invalid, it is permissible to use the raw type List.class [Bloch 2008].

OBJ03-EX1: The instanceof operator cannot be used with generic types. It is permissible to mix generic and raw code in such cases [Bloch 2008].

```
if (o instanceof Set) { // Raw type
  Set<?> m = (Set<?>) o; // Wildcard type
  // ...
}
```

Risk Assessment

Mixing generic and nongeneric code can produce unexpected results and exceptional conditions.

Rule	Severity	Likelihood	Remediation Cost	Priority	Level
OBJ03-J	low	probable	medium	P4	L3

Bibliography

[Bloch 2008]   Item 23. Don't use raw types in new code

[Bloch 2007]

[Bloch 2005a]   Puzzle 88. Raw deal

[Darwin 2004]   8.3, Avoid Casting by Using Generics

[JavaGenerics 2004]

[JLS 2005]   Chapter 5, Conversions and Promotions

§4.8, Raw Types

§5.1.9, Unchecked Conversion

[Langer 2008]   Topic 3, Coping with Legacy

[Naftalin 2006a]   Chapter 8, Effective Generics

[Naftalin 2006b]   Principle of Indecent Exposure

[Schildt 2007]   Create a Checked Collection

■ OBJ04-J. Provide mutable classes with copy functionality to safely allow passing instances to untrusted code

Mutable classes allow code external to the class to alter their instance or class fields. Provide means for creating copies of mutable classes so that *disposable* instances of such classes can be passed to untrusted code. This functionality is useful when methods in other classes must create copies of the particular class instance; see rules OBJ05-J and OBJ06-J for additional details.

Mutable classes must provide either a copy constructor or a public static factory method that returns a copy of an instance. Alternatively, final classes may advertise their copy functionality by overriding the `clone()` method of `java.lang.Object`. Use of the `clone()` method is secure *only* for final classes; nonfinal classes must *not* take this approach.

Trusted callers can be trusted to use the provided copy functionality to make defensive copies before passing object instances to untrusted code. Untrusted callers cannot be trusted to make such defensive copies. Consequently, providing copy functionality does not obviate the need for making defensive copies of inputs received from untrusted code or outputs returned to untrusted code.

Noncompliant Code Example

In this noncompliant code example, `MutableClass` uses a mutable field `date` of type `Date`. Class `Date` is also a mutable class. The example is noncompliant because the `MutableClass` objects lack copy functionality.

```
public final class MutableClass {
  private Date date;

  public MutableClass(Date d) {
    this.date = d;
  }
}
```

```
public void setDate(Date d) {
  this.date = d;
}

public Date getDate() {
  return date;
}
}
```

When a trusted caller passes an instance of `MutableClass` to untrusted code, and the untrusted code modifies that instance (perhaps by incrementing the month or changing the time zone), the object's state can be made inconsistent with respect to its previous state. Similar problems can arise in the presence of multiple threads, even in the absence of untrusted code.

Compliant Solution (Copy Constructor)

This compliant solution uses a copy constructor that initializes a `MutableClass` instance when an argument of the same type (or subtype) is passed to it.

```
public final class MutableClass { // Copy Constructor
  private final Date date;

  public MutableClass(MutableClass mc)  {
    this.date = new Date(mc.date.getTime());
  }

  public MutableClass(Date d) {
    this.date = new Date(d.getTime());  // Make defensive copy
  }

  public Date getDate() {
    return (Date) date.clone(); // Copy and return
  }
}
```

This approach is useful when the instance fields are declared final. Callers request a copy by invoking the copy constructor with an existing `MutableClass` instance as its argument.

Compliant Solution (Public Static Factory Method)

This compliant solution exports a public static factory method `getInstance()` that creates and returns a copy of a given `MutableClass` object instance.

```
class MutableClass {
  private final Date date;
  private MutableClass(Date d) {
    // Noninstantiable and nonsubclassable
    this.date = new Date(d.getTime());  // Make defensive copy
  }

  public Date getDate() {
    return (Date) date.clone(); // Copy and return
  }

  public static MutableClass getInstance(MutableClass mc)  {
    return new MutableClass(mc.getDate());
  }
}
```

This approach is useful when the instance fields are declared final.

Compliant Solution (`clone()`)

This compliant solution provides the needed copy functionality by declaring `MutableClass` to be final, implementing the `Cloneable` interface, and providing an `Object.clone()` method that performs a deep copy of the object.

```
public final class MutableClass implements Cloneable {
  private Date date;

  public MutableClass(Date d) {
    this.date = new Date(d.getTime());
  }

  public Date getDate() {
    return (Date) date.clone();
  }

  public void setDate(Date d) {
    this.date = (Date) d.clone();
  }

  public Object clone() throws CloneNotSupportedException {
    final MutableClass cloned = (MutableClass) super.clone();
    // manually copy mutable Date object
    cloned.date = (Date) date.clone();
    return cloned;
  }
}
```

Note that the `clone()` method must manually clone the `Date` object. This step is usually unnecessary when the object contains only primitive fields or fields that refer to immutable objects. However, when the fields contain data such as unique identifiers or object creation times, the `clone()` method must calculate and assign appropriate new values for such fields [Bloch 2008].

Mutable classes that define a `clone()` method must be declared final. This ensures that untrusted code cannot declare a subclass that overrides the `clone()` method to create a spurious instance. The `clone()` method should copy all internal mutable state as necessary—in this compliant example, the `Date` object.

When untrusted code can call accessor methods passing mutable arguments, create defensive copies of the arguments before they are stored in any instance fields. See rule OBJ06-J for additional information. When retrieving internal mutable state, make a defensive copy of that state before returning it to untrusted code. See rule OBJ05-J for additional information.

Defensive copies would be unnecessary if untrusted code always invoked an object's `clone()` method on mutable state received from mutable classes and operated only on the cloned copy. Unfortunately, untrusted code has little incentive to do so, and malicious code has every incentive to misbehave. This compliant solution provides a `clone()` method to trusted code and also guarantees that the state of the object cannot be compromised when the accessor methods are called directly from untrusted code.

Compliant Solution (`clone()` with final members)

When a mutable class's instance fields are declared final and lack accessible copy methods, provide a `clone()` method, as shown in this compliant solution.

```java
public final class MutableClass implements Cloneable {
  private final Date date; // final field

  public MutableClass(Date d) {
    this.date = new Date(d.getTime());  // copy-in
  }

  public Date getDate() {
    return (Date) date.clone(); // copy and return
  }

  public Object clone() {
    Date d = (Date) date.clone();
    MutableClass cloned = new MutableClass(d);
    return cloned;
  }
}
```

Callers can use the clone() method to obtain an instance of such a mutable class. The clone() method must create a new instance of the final member class and copy the original state to it. The new instance is necessary because there might not be an accessible copy method available in the member class. If the member class evolves in the future, it is critical to include the new state in the manual copy. Finally, the clone() method must create and return a new instance of the enclosing class (MutableClass) using the newly created member instance (d) [SCG 2009].

Mutable classes that define a clone() method must be declared final.

Compliant Solution (Unmodifiable Date Wrapper)

If cloning or copying a mutable object is infeasible or expensive, one alternative is to create an unmodifiable view class. This class overrides mutable methods to throw an exception, protecting the mutable class.

```
class UnmodifiableDateView extends Date {
  private Date date;

  public UnmodifiableDateView(Date date) {
    this.date = date;
  }

  public void setTime(long date) {
    throw new UnsupportedOperationException();
  }

  // Override all other mutator methods
  // to throw UnsupportedOperationException
}

public final class MutableClass {
  private Date date;

  public MutableClass(Date d) {
    this.date = d;
  }

  public void setDate(Date d) {
    this.date = (Date) d.clone();
  }

  public UnmodifiableDateView getDate() {
    return new UnmodifiableDateView(date);
  }
}
```

Exceptions

OBJ04-EX0: Sensitive classes should not be cloneable, per rule OBJ07-J.

Risk Assessment

Creating a mutable class without providing copy functionality can result in the data of its instance becoming corrupted when the instance is passed to untrusted code.

Rule	Severity	Likelihood	Remediation Cost	Priority	Level
OBJ04-J	low	likely	medium	P6	L2

Automated Detection Sound automated detection is infeasible in the general case. Heuristic approaches could be useful.

Related Guidelines

MITRE CWE	CWE-374. Passing mutable objects to an untrusted method
	CWE-375. Returning a mutable object to an untrusted caller
Secure Coding Guidelines for the Java Programming Language, Version 3.0	Guideline 2-3. Support copy functionality for a mutable class

Bibliography

[API 2006]	Method `clone()`
[Bloch 2008]	Item 39. Make defensive copies when needed; Item 11. Override clone judiciously
[Security 2006]	

■ OBJ05-J. Defensively copy private mutable class members before returning their references

Returning references to internal mutable members of a class can compromise an application's security both by breaking encapsulation and by providing the opportunity to corrupt the internal state of the class (whether accidentally or maliciously). As a result, programs must not return references to internal mutable classes.

Returning a reference to a defensive copy of mutable internal state ensures that the caller cannot modify the original internal state, although the copy remains mutable.

Noncompliant Code Example

This noncompliant code example shows a getDate() accessor method that returns the sole instance of the private Date object.

```
class MutableClass {
  private Date d;

  public MutableClass() {
    d = new Date();
  }

  public Date getDate() {
    return d;
  }
}
```

An untrusted caller can manipulate a private Date object because returning the reference exposes the internal mutable component beyond the trust boundaries of MutableClass.

Compliant Solution (clone())

This compliant solution returns a clone of the Date object from the getDate() accessor method. While Date can be extended by an attacker, this is safe because the Date object returned by getDate() is controlled by MutableClass and is known to be a nonmalicious subclass.

```
public Date getDate() {
  return (Date)d.clone();
}
```

Note that defensive copies performed during execution of a constructor must avoid use of the clone() method when the class could be subclassed by untrusted code. This restriction prevents execution of a maliciously crafted overriding of the clone() method. See rule OBJ07-J for more details.

Classes that have public setter methods, that is, methods whose purpose is to change class fields, must follow the related advice found in rule OBJ06-J. Note that setter methods can (and usually should) perform input validation and sanitization before setting internal fields.

Noncompliant Code Example (Mutable Member Array)

In this noncompliant code example, the getDate() accessor method returns an array of Date objects. The method fails to make a defensive copy of the array before returning it. Because the array contains references to Date objects that are mutable, a shallow copy of the array is insufficient because an attacker can modify the Date objects in the array.

```
class MutableClass {
  private Date[] date;

  public MutableClass() {
    date = new Date[20];
    for (int i = 0; i < date.length; i++) {
      date[i] = new Date();
    }
  }

  public Date[] getDate() {
    return date; // or return date.clone()
  }
}
```

Compliant Solution (Deep Copy)

This compliant solution creates a deep copy of the date array and returns the copy, thereby protecting both the date array and the individual Date objects.

```
class MutableClass {
  private Date[] date;

  public MutableClass() {
    date = new Date[20];
    for(int i = 0; i < date.length; i++) {
      date[i] = new Date();
    }
  }

  public Date[] getDate() {
    Date[] dates = new Date[date.length];
    for (int i = 0; i < date.length; i++) {
      dates[i] = (Date) date[i].clone();
    }
    return dates;
  }
}
```

Noncompliant Code Example (Mutable Member Containing Immutable Objects)

In this noncompliant code example, class `ReturnRef` contains a private `Hashtable` instance field. The hash table stores immutable but sensitive data (for example, social security numbers [SSNs]). The `getValues()` method gives the caller access to the hash table by returning a reference to it. An untrusted caller can use this method to gain access to the hash table; as a result, hash table entries can be maliciously added, removed, or replaced. Furthermore, multiple threads can perform these modifications, providing ample opportunities for race conditions.

```java
class ReturnRef {
  // Internal state, may contain sensitive data
  private Hashtable<Integer,String> ht =
    new Hashtable<Integer,String>();

  private ReturnRef() {
    ht.put(1, "123-45-6666");
  }

  public Hashtable<Integer,String> getValues() {
    return ht;
  }

  public static void main(String[] args) {
    ReturnRef rr = new ReturnRef();
    // Prints sensitive data 123-45-6666
    Hashtable<Integer, String> ht1 = rr.getValues();
    // Untrusted caller can remove entries
    ht1.remove(1);
    // Now prints null, original entry is removed
    Hashtable<Integer, String> ht2 = rr.getValues();
  }
}
```

In returning a reference to the `ht` hash table, this example also hinders efficient garbage collection.

Compliant Solution (Shallow Copy)

Make defensive copies of private internal mutable object state. For mutable fields that contain immutable data, a shallow copy is sufficient. Fields that refer to mutable data generally require a deep copy.

This compliant solution creates and returns a shallow copy of the hash table containing immutable SSNs. Consequently, the original hash table remains private, and any attempts to modify it are ineffective.

```java
class ReturnRef {
  // ...
  private Hashtable<Integer,String> getValues() {
    return (Hashtable<Integer, String>) ht.clone(); // shallow copy
  }

  public static void main(String[] args) {
    ReturnRef rr = new ReturnRef();
    // Prints non-sensitive data
    Hashtable<Integer,String> ht1 = rr.getValues();
    // Untrusted caller can only modify copy
    ht1.remove(1);
    // Prints non-sensitive data
    Hashtable<Integer,String> ht2 = rr.getValues();
  }
}
```

When a hash table contains references to mutable data such as `Date` objects, each of those objects must also be copied by using a copy constructor or method. For further details, refer to rules OBJ04-J and OBJ06-J.

Note that making deep copies of the keys of a hash table is unnecessary; shallow copying of the references suffices because a hash table's contract dictates that its keys must produce consistent results to the `equals()` and `hashCode()` methods. Mutable objects whose `equals()` or `hashCode()` method results may be modified are not suitable keys.

Exceptions

OBJ05-EX0: When a method is called with only an unmodifiable view of an object, that method may freely use the unmodifiable view without defensive copying. This decision should be made early in the design of the API. Note that new callers of such methods must also expose only unmodifiable views.

Risk Assessment

Returning references to internal object state (mutable or immutable) can render an application susceptible to information leaks and corruption of its objects' states, which consequently violates class invariants. Control flow can also be affected in some cases.

Rule	Severity	Likelihood	Remediation Cost	Priority	Level
OBJ05-J	high	probable	medium	P12	L1

Automated Detection Sound automated detection is infeasible; heuristic checks could be useful.

Related Vulnerabilities Pugh [Pugh 2009] cites a vulnerability discovered by the Findbugs static analysis tool in the early betas of JDK 1.7 where the sun.security.x509. InvalidityDateExtension class returned a Date instance through a public accessor without creating defensive copies.

Related Guidelines

CERT C++ Secure Coding Standard   OOP35-CPP. Do not return references to private data.

MITRE CWE   CWE-375. Returning a mutable object to an untrusted caller

Bibliography

[API 2006]   Method clone()

[Bloch 2008]   Item 39. Make defensive copies when needed

[Goetz 2006a]   3.2, Publication and Escape: Allowing Internal Mutable State to Escape

[Gong 2003]   9.4, Private Object State and Object Immutability

[Haggar 2000]   Practical Java Praxis 64. Use clone for immutable objects when passing or receiving object references to mutable objects

[Security 2006]

■ OBJ06-J. Defensively copy mutable inputs and mutable internal components

A mutable input has the characteristic that its value may vary; that is, multiple accesses may see differing values. This characteristic enables potential attacks that exploit race conditions. For example, a time-of-check, time-of-use (TOCTOU) vulnerability may result when a field contains a value that passes validation and security checks but changes before use.

Returning references to an object's internal mutable components provides an attacker with the opportunity to corrupt the state of the object. Consequently, accessor methods must return defensive copies of internal mutable objects (see rule OBJ05-J for more information).

Noncompliant Code Example

This noncompliant code example contains a TOCTOU vulnerability. Because cookie is a mutable input, an attacker can cause it to expire between the initial check (the hasExpired() call) and the actual use (the doLogic() call).

```
public final class MutableDemo {
  // java.net.HttpCookie is mutable
  public void useMutableInput(HttpCookie cookie) {
    if (cookie == null) {
      throw new NullPointerException();
    }

    // Check whether cookie has expired
    if (cookie.hasExpired()) {
      // Cookie is no longer valid,
      // handle condition by throwing an exception
    }

    // Cookie may have expired since time of check
    doLogic(cookie);
  }
}
```

Compliant Solution

This compliant solution avoids the TOCTOU vulnerability by copying the mutable input and performing all operations on the copy. Consequently, an attacker's changes to the mutable input cannot affect the copy. Acceptable techniques include using a copy constructor or implementing the java.lang.Cloneable interface and declaring a public clone method (for classes not declared final). In cases like HttpCookie where the mutable class is declared final—that is, it cannot provide an accessible copy method—perform a manual copy of the object state within the caller. See rule OBJ04-J for more information. Note that any input validation must be performed on the *copy* rather than on the original object.

```
public final class MutableDemo {
  // java.net.HttpCookie is mutable
  public void useMutableInput(HttpCookie cookie) {
    if (cookie == null) {
      throw new NullPointerException();
    }

    // Create copy
    cookie = (HttpCookie)cookie.clone();

    // Check whether cookie has expired
    if (cookie.hasExpired()) {
      // Cookie is no longer valid,
```

```
      // handle condition by throwing an exception
    }

    doLogic(cookie);
  }
}
```

Compliant Solution

Some copy constructors and clone() methods perform a shallow copy of the original instance. For example, invocation of clone() on an array results in creation of an array instance whose elements have the same values as the original instance. This shallow copy is sufficient for arrays of primitive types but fails to protect against TOCTOU vulnerabilities when the elements are references to mutable objects, such as an array of cookies. Such cases require a deep copy that also duplicates the referenced objects.

This compliant solution demonstrates correct use both of a shallow copy (for the array of int) and of a deep copy (for the array of cookies).

```
public void deepCopy(int[] ints, HttpCookie[] cookies) {
  if (ints == null || cookies == null) {
    throw new NullPointerException();
  }

  // Shallow copy
  int[] intsCopy = ints.clone();

  // Deep copy
  HttpCookie[] cookiesCopy = new HttpCookie[cookies.length];
  for (int i = 0; i < cookies.length; i++) {
    // Manually create copy of each element in array
    cookiesCopy[i] = (HttpCookie)cookies[i].clone();
  }

  doLogic(intsCopy, cookiesCopy);
}
```

Noncompliant Code Example

When the class of a mutable input is nonfinal or is an interface an attacker can write a subclass that maliciously overrides the parent class's clone() method. The attacker's clone() method can subsequently subvert defensive copying. This noncompliant code example demonstrates this weakness.

```
// java.util.Collection is an interface
public void copyInterfaceInput(Collection<String> collection) {
  doLogic(collection.clone());
}
```

Compliant Solution

This compliant solution protects against potential malicious overriding by creating a new instance of the nonfinal mutable input, using the expected class rather than the class of the potentially malicious argument. The newly created instance can be forwarded to any code capable of modifying it.

```
public void copyInterfaceInput(Collection<String> collection) {
  // Convert input to trusted implementation
  collection = new ArrayList(collection);
  doLogic(collection);
}
```

Some objects appear to be immutable because they have no mutator methods. For example, the java.lang.CharSequence interface describes an immutable sequence of characters. Note, however, that a variable of type CharSequence is a reference to an underlying object of some other class that implements the CharSequence interface; that other class may be mutable. When the underlying object changes, the CharSequence changes. Essentially, the CharSequence interface omits methods that would permit object mutation *through that interface* but lacks any guarantee of true immutability. Such objects must still be defensively copied before use. For the case of the CharSequence interface, one permissible approach is to obtain an immutable copy of the characters by using the toString() method. Mutable fields should not be stored in static variables. When there is no other alternative, create defensive copies of the fields to avoid exposing them to untrusted code.

Risk Assessment

Failing to create a copy of a mutable input may result in a TOCTOU vulnerability or expose internal mutable components to untrusted code.

Rule	Severity	Likelihood	Remediation Cost	Priority	Level
OBJ06-J	medium	probable	high	P4	L3

Related Guidelines

Secure Coding Guidelines for the Java Programming Language, Version 3.0

Guideline 2-2. Create copies of mutable outputs

Bibliography

[Bloch 2008]   Item 39. Make defensive copies when needed

[Pugh 2009]   Returning References to Internal Mutable State

■ OBJ07-J. Sensitive classes must not let themselves be copied

Classes containing private, confidential, or otherwise sensitive data are best not copied. If a class is not meant to be copied, then failing to define copy mechanisms, such as a copy constructor, is insufficient to prevent copying.

Java's object cloning mechanism allows an attacker to manufacture new instances of a class by copying the memory images of existing objects rather than by executing the class's constructor. Often this is an unacceptable way of creating new objects. An attacker can misuse the clone feature to manufacture multiple instances of a singleton class, create thread-safety issues by subclassing and cloning the subclass, bypass security checks within the constructor, and violate the invariants of critical data.

Classes that have security checks in their constructors must beware of finalization attacks, as explained in rule OBJ11-J.

Classes that are not sensitive but maintain other invariants must be sensitive to the possibility of malicious subclasses accessing or manipulating their data and possibly invalidating their invariants. See rule OBJ04-J for more information.

Noncompliant Code Example

This noncompliant code example defines class SensitiveClass, which contains a character array used to hold a file name, along with a Boolean *shared* variable, initialized to false. This data is not meant to be copied; consequently, SensitiveClass lacks a copy constructor.

```java
class SensitiveClass {
  private char[] filename;
  private Boolean shared = false;

  SensitiveClass(String filename) {
    this.filename = filename.toCharArray();
  }

  final void replace() {
    if (!shared) {
      for(int i = 0; i < filename.length; i++) {
        filename[i]= 'x'; }
    }
  }
}
```

```java
  final String get() {
    if (!shared) {
      shared = true;
      return String.valueOf(filename);
    } else {
      throw new IllegalStateException("Failed to get instance");
    }
  }

  final void printFilename() {
    System.out.println(String.valueOf(filename));
  }
}
```

When a client requests a `String` instance by invoking the `get()` method, the `shared` flag is set. To maintain the array's consistency with the returned `String` object, operations that can modify the array are subsequently prohibited. As a result, the `replace()` method designed to replace all elements of the array with an x cannot execute normally when the flag is set. Java's cloning feature provides a way to circumvent this constraint even though `SensitiveClass` does not implement the `Cloneable` interface.

This class can be exploited by a malicious class, shown in the following noncompliant code example, that subclasses the nonfinal `SensitiveClass` and provides a `public clone()` method.

```java
class MaliciousSubclass extends SensitiveClass implements Cloneable {
  protected MaliciousSubclass(String filename) {
    super(filename);
  }

  @Override public MaliciousSubclass clone() {
  // Well-behaved clone() method
    MaliciousSubclass s = null;
    try {
      s = (MaliciousSubclass)super.clone();
    } catch(Exception e) {
      System.out.println("not cloneable");
    }
    return s;
  }

  public static void main(String[] args) {
    MaliciousSubclass ms1 = new MaliciousSubclass("file.txt");
```

```
      MaliciousSubclass ms2 = ms1.clone(); // Creates a copy
      String s = ms1.get();   // Returns filename
      System.out.println(s); // Filename is "file.txt"
      ms2.replace();          // Replaces all characters with 'x'
      // Both ms1.get() and ms2.get() will subsequently
      // return filename = 'xxxxxxxx'
      ms1.printFilename();   // Filename becomes 'xxxxxxxx'
      ms2.printFilename();   // Filename becomes 'xxxxxxxx'
   }
}
```

The malicious class creates an instance ms1 and produces a second instance ms2 by cloning the first. It then obtains a new filename by invoking the get() method on the first instance. At this point, the shared flag is set to true. Because the second instance ms2 does not have its shared flag set to true, it is possible to alter the first instance ms1 using the replace() method. This obviates any security efforts and severely violates the class's invariants.

Compliant Solution (Final Class)

The easiest way to prevent malicious subclasses is to declare SensitiveClass to be final.

```
final class SensitiveClass {
  // ...
}
```

Compliant Solution (Final clone())

Sensitive classes should neither implement the Cloneable interface nor provide a copy constructor. Sensitive classes that extend from a superclass that implements Cloneable (and are cloneable as a result) must provide a clone() method that throws a CloneNotSupportedException. This exception must be caught and handled by the client code. A sensitive class that does not implement Cloneable must also follow this advice because it inherits the clone() method from Object. The class can prevent subclasses from being made cloneable by defining a final clone() method that always fails.

```
class SensitiveClass {
  // ...
  public final SensitiveClass clone()
                            throws CloneNotSupportedException {
    throw new CloneNotSupportedException();
  }
}
```

This class fails to prevent malicious subclasses but does protect the data in `Sensitive-Class`. Its methods are protected by being declared final. For more information on handling malicious subclasses, see rule OBJ04-J.

Risk Assessment

Failure to make sensitive classes noncopyable can permit violations of class invariants and provide malicious subclasses with the opportunity to exploit the code to create new instances of objects, even in the presence of the default security manager (in the absence of custom security checks).

Rule	Severity	Likelihood	Remediation Cost	Priority	Level
OBJ07-J	medium	probable	medium	P8	L2

Bibliography

[McGraw 1998]	Twelve rules for developing more secure Java code
[MITRE 2009]	CWE-498. Cloneable class containing sensitive information; CWE-491. Public `cloneable()` method without final (aka "object hijack")
[Wheeler 2003]	10.6, Java

■ OBJ08-J. Do not expose private members of an outer class from within a nested class

A nested class is any class whose declaration occurs within the body of another class or interface [JLS 2005]. The use of a nested class is error prone unless the semantics are well understood. A common notion is that only the nested class may access the contents of the outer class. Not only does the nested class have access to the private fields of the outer class, the same fields can be accessed by any other class within the package when the nested class is declared public or if it contains public methods or constructors. As a result, the nested class must not expose the private members of the outer class to external classes or packages.

According to the *Java Language Specification*, §8.3, "Field Declarations" [JLS 2005]:

> Note that a private field of a superclass might be accessible to a subclass (for example, if both classes are members of the same class). Nevertheless, a private field is never inherited by a subclass.

Noncompliant Code Example

This noncompliant code example exposes the private (x,y) coordinates through the `getPoint()` method of the inner class. Consequently, the `AnotherClass` class that belongs to the same package can also access the coordinates.

```
class Coordinates {
  private int x;
  private int y;

  public class Point {
    public void getPoint() {
      System.out.println("(" + x + "," + y + ")");
    }
  }
}

class AnotherClass {
  public static void main(String[] args) {
    Coordinates c = new Coordinates();
    Coordinates.Point p = c.new Point();
    p.getPoint();
  }
}
```

Compliant Solution

Use the private access specifier to hide the inner class and all contained methods and constructors.

```
class Coordinates {
  private int x;
  private int y;

  private class Point {
    private void getPoint() {
      System.out.println("(" + x + "," + y + ")");
    }
  }
}

class AnotherClass {
  public static void main(String[] args) {
    Coordinates c = new Coordinates();
    Coordinates.Point p = c.new Point();    // fails to compile
    p.getPoint();
  }
}
```

Compilation of AnotherClass now results in a compilation error because the class attempts to access a private nested class.

Risk Assessment

The Java language system weakens the accessibility of private members of an outer class when an inner class is present, which can result in an information leak.

Rule	Severity	Likelihood	Remediation Cost	Priority	Level
OBJ08-J	medium	probable	medium	P8	L2

Automated Detection Automated detection of nonprivate inner classes that define nonprivate members and constructors that leak private data from the outer class is straightforward.

Related Guidelines

MITRE CWE	CWE-492. Use of Inner Class Containing Sensitive Data

Bibliography

[JLS 2005]	§8.1.3, Inner Classes and Enclosing Instances
	§8.3, Field Declarations
[Long 2005]	§2.3, Inner Classes
[McGraw 1999]	Securing Java, Getting Down to Business with Mobile Code

■ OBJ09-J. Compare classes and not class names

In a JVM, "Two classes are the same class (and consequently the same type) if they are loaded by the same class loader, and they have the same fully qualified name" [JVMSpec 1999]. Two classes with the same name but different package names are distinct, as are two classes with the same fully qualified name loaded by different class loaders.

It could be necessary to check whether a given object has a specific class type or whether two objects have the same class type associated with them, for example, when implementing the `equals()` method. If the comparison is performed incorrectly, the code could assume that the two objects are of the same class when they are not. As a result, class names must not be compared.

Depending on the function that the insecure code performs, it could be vulnerable to a mix-and-match attack. An attacker could supply a malicious class with th e same fully qualified name as the target class. If access to a protected resource is granted based on the comparison of class names alone, the unprivileged class could gain unwarranted access to the resource.

Conversely, the assumption that two classes deriving from the same code base are the same is error prone. While this assumption is commonly observed to be true in desktop applications, it is typically not the case with J2EE servlet containers. The containers can use different class loader instances to deploy and recall applications at runtime without having to restart the JVM. In such situations, two objects whose classes come from the same code base could appear to the JVM to be two different classes. Also note that the equals() method might not return true when comparing objects originating from the same code base.

Noncompliant Code Example

This noncompliant code example compares the name of the class of object auth to the string "com.application.auth.DefaultAuthenticationHandler" and branches on the result of the comparison.

```
// Determine whether object auth has required/expected class object
if (auth.getClass().getName().equals(
    "com.application.auth.DefaultAuthenticationHandler")) {
  // ...
}
```

Comparing fully qualified class names is insufficient because distinct class loaders can load differing classes with identical fully qualified names into a single JVM.

Compliant Solution

This compliant solution compares the class object auth to the class object that the current class loader loads, instead of comparing just the class names.

```
// Determine whether object auth has required/expected class name
if (auth.getClass() == this.getClass().getClassLoader().loadClass(
    "com.application.auth.DefaultAuthenticationHandler")) {
  // ...
}
```

The call to loadClass() returns the class with the specified name in the current name space (consisting of the class name and the defining class loader), and the comparison is correctly performed on the two class objects.

Noncompliant Code Example

This noncompliant code example compares the names of the class objects of x and y using the equals() method. Again, it is possible that x and y are distinct classes with the same name if they come from different class loaders.

```
// Determine whether objects x and y have the same class name
if (x.getClass().getName().equals(y.getClass().getName())) {
  // Objects have the same class
}
```

Compliant Solution

This compliant solution correctly compares the two objects' classes.

```
// Determine whether objects x and y have the same class
if (x.getClass() == y.getClass()) {
  // Objects have the same class
}
```

Risk Assessment

Comparing classes solely using their names can allow a malicious class to bypass security checks and gain access to protected resources.

Rule	Severity	Likelihood	Remediation Cost	Priority	Level
OBJ09-J	high	unlikely	low	P9	L2

Related Guidelines

MITRE CWE	CWE-486. Comparison of classes by name

Bibliography

[Christudas 2005]	Internals of Java Class Loading
[JVMSpec 1999]	§2.8.1, Class Names
[McGraw 1998]	Twelve Rules for Developing More Secure Java Code
[Wheeler 2003]	Java Secure Programming for Linux and UNIX HOW TO

■ OBJ10-J. Do not use public static nonfinal variables

Client code can trivially access public static fields. Neither reads nor writes to such variables are checked by a security manager. Furthermore, new values cannot be validated programmatically before they are stored in these fields.

In the presence of multiple threads, nonfinal public static fields can be modified in inconsistent ways. See rule TSM01-J for an example.

Improper use of public static fields can also result in type-safety issues. For example, untrusted code can supply an unexpected subtype with malicious methods when the variable is defined to be of a more general type, such as `java.lang.Object` [Gong 2003]. As a result, classes must not contain nonfinal public static fields.

Noncompliant Code Example

This noncompliant code example is adopted from JDK v1.4.2 [FT 2008]. It declares a function table containing a public static field.

```
package org.apache.xpath.compiler;

public class FunctionTable {
  public static FuncLoader m_functions;
}
```

An attacker can replace the function table as follows:

```
FunctionTable.m_functions = new_table;
```

Replacing the function table gives the attacker access to `XPathContext`, which is used to set the reference node for evaluating `XPath` expressions. Manipulating `XPathContext` can cause XML fields to be modified in inconsistent ways, resulting in unexpected behavior. Also, because static variables are global across the Java Runtime Environment (JRE), they can be used as a covert communication channel between different application domains (for example, through code loaded by different class loaders).

This vulnerability was repaired in JDK v1.4.2_05.

Compliant Solution

This compliant solution declares the `FuncLoader` static field final and treats it as a constant.

```
public static final FuncLoader m_functions;
// Initialize m_functions in a constructor
```

Fields declared static and final are also safe for multithreaded use. (See rule TSM03-J.) However, remember that simply changing the modifier to final might not prevent attackers from indirectly retrieving an incorrect value from the static final variable before its initialization. (See rule DCL00-J for more information.) Furthermore, individual members of the referenced object can also be changed if the object itself is mutable.

It is also permissible to use a wrapper method to retrieve the value of m_functions, allowing m_functions to be declared private. See rule OBJ01-J for more information.

Noncompliant Code Example (`serialVersionUID`)

This noncompliant code example uses a public static nonfinal `serialVersionUID` field in a class designed for serialization.

```
class DataSerializer implements Serializable {
  public static long serialVersionUID = 1973473122623778747L;
  // ...
}
```

Compliant Solution

This compliant solution declares the `serialVersionUID` field final and private.

```
class DataSerializer implements Serializable {
  private static final long serialVersionUID = 1973473122623778747L;
}
```

The serialization mechanism uses the `serialVersionUID` field internally, so accessible wrapper methods are unnecessary.

Risk Assessment

Unauthorized modifications of public static variables can result in unexpected behavior and violation of class invariants. Furthermore, because static variables can be visible to code loaded by different class loaders when those class loaders are in the same delegation chain, such variables can be used as a covert communication channel between different application domains.

Rule	Severity	Likelihood	Remediation Cost	Priority	Level
OBJ10-J	medium	probable	medium	P8	L2

Related Guidelines

MITRE CWE   CWE-493. Critical public variable without final modifier

                                      CWE-500. Public static field not marked final

Secure Coding Guidelines for the Java   Guideline 3-1. Treat public static fields as constants
Programming Language, Version 3.0

Bibliography

[FT 2008]   Function Table, Class Function Table

[Gong 2003]   9.3, Static Fields

[Nisewanger 2007]   Antipattern 5, Misusing Public Static Variables

[Sterbenz 2006]   Antipattern 5, Misusing Public Static Variables

■ OBJ11-J. Be wary of letting constructors throw exceptions

An object is partially initialized if a constructor has begun building the object but has not finished. As long as the object is not fully initialized, it must be hidden from other classes.

Other classes might access a partially initialized object from concurrently running threads. This rule is a specific instance of rule TSM01-J but focuses only on single-threaded programs. Multithreaded programs must also comply with rule TSM03-J.

Some uses of variables require *failure atomicity*. This requirement typically arises when a variable constitutes an aggregation of different objects, for example, a composition-and-forwarding-based approach, as described in rule OBJ02-J. In the absence of failure atomicity, the object can be left in an inconsistent state as a result of partial initialization.

There are three common approaches to dealing with the problem of partially initialized objects:

- *Exception in constructor.* One approach is to throw an exception in the object's constructor. Unfortunately, an attacker can maliciously obtain the instance of such an object. For example, an attack that uses the finalizer construct allows the attacker to invoke arbitrary methods within the class even when the class methods are protected by a security manager.

- *Final field.* Declaring the variable that is initialized to the object as final prevents the object from being partially initialized. The compiler produces a warning when there is a possibility that the variable's object might not be fully initialized. This also guarantees initialization safety in multithreaded code. According to the *Java Language Specification,* §17.5, "Final Field Semantics" [JLS 2005], "An object is considered to be completely initialized when its constructor finishes. A thread that can only see a reference to an object after that object has been completely initialized is guaranteed to see the correctly initialized values for that object's final fields." In other words, when a constructor executing in one thread initializes a final field to a known safe value, other threads are unable to see any *preinitialized* values of the object.

■ *Initialized flag.* This approach allows uninitialized or partially initialized objects to exist in a known failed state; such objects are commonly known as *zombie objects*. This solution is error prone because any access to such a class must first check whether or not the object has been correctly initialized. The following table summarizes these three approaches.

Solution	Uninitialized values	Partially-initialized objects
Exception in constructor	prevents	does not prevent
Final field	prevents	prevents
Initialized flag	detects	detects

Noncompliant Code Example (Finalizer Attack)

This noncompliant code example, based on an example by Kabutz [Kabutz 2001], defines the constructor of the BankOperations class so that it performs SSN verification using the method performSSNVerification(). The implementation of the performSSNVerification() method assumes that an attacker does not know the correct SSN and trivially returns false.

```
public class BankOperations {
  public BankOperations() {
    if (!performSSNVerification()) {
      throw new SecurityException("Access Denied!");
    }
  }

  private boolean performSSNVerification() {
    return false;
    // Returns true if data entered is valid, else false.
    // Assume that the attacker always enters an invalid SSN.
  }
```

```
  public void greet() {
    System.out.println(
    "Welcome user! You may now use all the features.");
  }
}

public class Storage {
  private static BankOperations bop;

  public static void store(BankOperations bo) {
  // Only store if it is initialized
    if (bop == null) {
      if (bo == null) {
        System.out.println("Invalid object!");
        System.exit(1);
      }
      bop = bo;
    }
  }
}

public class UserApp {
  public static void main(String[] args) {
    BankOperations bo;
    try {
      bo = new BankOperations();
    } catch (SecurityException ex) { bo = null; }

    Storage.store(bo);
    System.out.println("Proceed with normal logic");
  }
}
```

The constructor throws a `SecurityException` when SSN verification fails. The User-App class appropriately catches this exception and displays an "Access Denied" message. However, these precautions fail to prevent a malicious program from invoking methods of the partially initialized class `BankOperations`.

The goal of the attack is to capture a reference to the partially initialized object of the `BankOperations` class. If a malicious subclass catches the `SecurityException` thrown by the `BankOperations` constructor, it is unable to further exploit the vulnerable code because the new object instance has gone out of scope. Instead, an attacker can exploit this code by extending the `BankOperations` class and overriding the `finalize()` method. This intentionally violates rule MET12-J.

When the constructor throws an exception, the garbage collector waits to grab the object reference. However, the object cannot be garbage-collected until *after* the finalizer completes its execution. The attacker's finalizer obtains and stores a reference by using the this keyword. Consequently, the attacker can maliciously invoke any instance method on the base class by using the stolen instance reference. This attack can even bypass a check by a security manager.

```
public class Interceptor extends BankOperations {
  private static Interceptor stealInstance = null;

  public static Interceptor get() {
    try {
      new Interceptor();
    } catch (Exception ex) {/* ignore exception */}
    try {
      synchronized (Interceptor.class) {
        while (stealInstance == null) {
          System.gc();
          Interceptor.class.wait(10);
        }
      }
    } catch (InterruptedException ex) { return null; }
    return stealInstance;
  }

  public void finalize() {
    synchronized (Interceptor.class) {
      stealInstance = this;
      Interceptor.class.notify();
    }
    System.out.println("Stole the instance in finalize of " + this);
  }
}

public class AttackerApp { // Invoke class and gain access
                           // to the restrictive features
  public static void main(String[] args) {
    Interceptor i = Interceptor.get(); // stolen instance

    // Can store the stolen object even though this should have printed
    // "Invalid Object!"
    Storage.store(i);

    // Now invoke any instance method of BankOperations class
    i.greet();
  }
  UserApp.main(args); // Invoke the original UserApp
  }
}
```

Compliance with rules ERR00-J and ERR03-J can help to ensure that fields are appropriately initialized in catch blocks. A developer who explicitly initializes the variable to null is more likely to document this behavior so that other programmers or clients include the appropriate null reference checks where required. Moreover, this guarantees initialization safety in a multithreaded scenario.

Compliant Solution (Final)

This compliant solution declares the partially initialized class final so that it cannot be extended.

```
public final class BankOperations {
  // ...
}
```

Compliant Solution (Final `finalize()`)

If the class itself cannot be declared final, it can still thwart the finalizer attack by declaring its own `finalize()` method and making it final.

```
public class BankOperations {
  public final void finalize() {
    // do nothing
  }
}
```

This solution is allowed under exception MET12-EX1, which permits a class to use an empty final finalizer to prevent a finalizer attack.

Compliant Solution (Java SE 6, Public and Private Constructors)

This compliant solution applies to Java SE 6 and later versions, where a finalizer is prevented from being executed when an exception is thrown before the `java.lang.Object` constructor exits [SCG 2009].

In the public constructor, the result of the method call `performSSNVerification()` is passed as an argument to a private constructor. Also, the `performSSNVerification()` method throws an exception rather than returning false if the security check fails.

```
public class BankOperations {
  public BankOperations() {
    this( performSSNVerification());
  }

  private BankOperations(boolean secure) {
    // secure is always true
    // constructor without any security checks
  }

  private static boolean performSSNVerification() {
    // Returns true if data entered is valid, else throws
    // a SecurityException
    // Assume that the attacker just enters invalid SSN;
    // so this method always throws the exception
    throw new SecurityException("Access Denied!");
  }

  // ...remainder of BankOperations class definition
}
```

The first statement in any constructor must be a call to either a superclass's constructor or another constructor in the same class. If a constructor call was not provided in the public constructor, the default constructor of the superclass executes. Unfortunately, this could allow a finalizer to be added and executed if the superclass constructor exited before the security check.

Compliant Solution (Initialized Flag)

Rather than throwing an exception, this compliant solution uses an *initialized flag* to indicate whether an object was successfully constructed. The flag is initialized to false and set to true when the constructor finishes successfully.

```
class BankOperations {
  private volatile boolean initialized = false;

  public BankOperations() {
    if (!performSSNVerification()) {
      throw new SecurityException("Access Denied!");
    }
```

```
    this.initialized = true; // object construction successful
  }

  private boolean performSSNVerification() {
    return false;
  }

  public void greet() {
    if (!this.initialized) {
      throw new SecurityException("Access Denied!");
    }

    System.out.println(
        "Welcome user! You may now use all the features.");
  }
}
```

The `initialized` flag prevents any attempt to access the object's methods if the object is not fully constructed. Because each method must check the `initialized` flag to detect a partially constructed object, this solution imposes a speed penalty on the program. It is also harder to maintain because it is easy for a maintainer to add a method that fails to check the `initialized` flag.

According to Charlie Lai [Lai 2008]:

> If an object is only partially initialized, its internal fields likely contain safe default values such as `null`. Even in an untrusted environment, such an object is unlikely to be useful to an attacker. If the developer deems the partially initialized object state secure, then the developer doesn't have to pollute the class with the flag. The flag is necessary only when such a state isn't secure or when accessible methods in the class perform sensitive operations without referencing any internal field.

Noncompliant Code Example (Static Variable)

This noncompliant code example uses a nonfinal static variable. The *Java Language Specification* does not mandate complete initialization and safe publication even though a static initializer has been used. Note that in the event of an exception during initialization, the variable can be incorrectly initialized.

```
class Trade {
  private static Stock s;
  static {
    try {
      s = new Stock();
    } catch (IOException e) {
```

```
        /* does not initialize s to a safe state */
      }
    }
    // ...
  }
```

Compliant Solution (Final Static Variable)

This compliant solution guarantees safe publication by declaring the Stock field final.

```
  private static final Stock s;
```

Unlike the previous compliant solution, however, this approach permits a possibly null value but guarantees that a non-null value refers to a completely initialized object.

Risk Assessment

Allowing access to a partially initialized object can provide an attacker with an opportunity to resurrect the object before or during its finalization; as a result, the attacker can bypass security checks.

Rule	Severity	Likelihood	Remediation Cost	Priority	Level
OBJ11-J	high	probable	medium	P12	L1

Automated Detection Automated detection for this rule is infeasible in the general case. Some instances of nonfinal classes whose constructors can throw exceptions could be straightforward to diagnose.

Related Vulnerabilities Vulnerability CVE-2008-5339 describes a collection of vulnerabilities in Java. In one of the vulnerabilities, an applet causes an object to be deserialized using ObjectInputStream.readObject(), but the input is controlled by an attacker. The object actually read is a serializable subclass of ClassLoader, and it has a readObject() method that stashes the object instance into a static variable; consequently, the object survives the serialization. As a result, the applet manages to construct a ClassLoader object by passing the restrictions against this in an applet, and the ClassLoader allows it to construct classes that are not subject to the security restrictions of an applet. This vulnerability is described in depth in rule SER08-J.

Related Guidelines

Secure Coding Guidelines for the Java
Programming Language, Version 3.0

Guideline 1-2. Limit the extensibility of classes
and methods

Guideline 4-3. Defend against partially initialized
instances of non-final classes

Bibliography

[API 2006]

[Darwin 2004]

[Flanagan 2005]

[JLS 2005]

[Kabutz 2001]

[Lai 2008]

`finalize()`

§9.5, The Finalize Method

§3.3, Destroying and Finalizing Objects

§12.6, Finalization of Class Instances

§8.3.1, Field Modifiers

§17.5, Final Field Semantics

Issue 032. Exceptional constructors—resurrecting
the dead

Java Insecurity: Accounting for Subtleties That Can
Compromise Code

Chapter 7

Methods (MET)

■ Risk Assessment Summary

Rule	Severity	Likelihood	Remediation Cost	Priority	Level
MET00-J	high	likely	high	P9	L2
MET01-J	medium	probable	medium	P8	L2
MET02-J	high	likely	medium	P18	L1
MET03-J	medium	probable	medium	P8	L2
MET04-J	medium	probable	medium	P8	L2
MET05-J	medium	probable	medium	P8	L2
MET06-J	medium	probable	low	P12	L1
MET07-J	low	unlikely	medium	P2	L3
MET08-J	low	unlikely	medium	P2	L3
MET09-J	low	unlikely	high	P1	L3
MET10-J	medium	unlikely	medium	P4	L3
MET11-J	low	probable	high	P2	L3
MET12-J	medium	probable	medium	P8	L2

■ MET00-J. Validate method arguments

Validate method arguments to ensure that they fall within the bounds of the method's intended design. This practice ensures that operations on the method's parameters yield valid results. Failure to validate method arguments can result in incorrect calculations, runtime exceptions, violation of class invariants, and inconsistent object state.

Redundant testing of arguments by both the caller and the callee is a style of *defensive programming* that is largely discredited within the programming community, in part for reasons of performance. Instead, normal practice requires validation on only one side of each interface.

Caller validation of arguments can result in faster code because the caller may be aware of invariants that prevent invalid values from being passed. Conversely, callee validation of arguments encapsulates the validation code in a single location, reducing the size of the code and raising the likelihood that the validation checks are performed consistently and correctly.

Methods that receive arguments across a trust boundary must perform callee validation of their arguments for safety and security reasons. This applies to all public methods of a library, for example. Other methods, including private methods, should validate arguments that are both untrusted and unvalidated when those arguments may propagate from a public method via its arguments.

When defensive copying is necessary, make the defensive copies *before* argument validation, and validate the copies rather than the original arguments. See rule SER06-J for additional information.

Noncompliant Code Example

In this noncompliant code example, `setState()` and `useState()` fail to validate their arguments. A malicious caller could pass an invalid state to the library, consequently corrupting the library and exposing a vulnerability.

```
private Object myState = null;

// Sets some internal state in the library
void setState(Object state) {
  myState = state;
}

// Performs some action using the file passed earlier
void useState() {
  // Perform some action here
}
```

Such vulnerabilities are particularly severe when the internal state contains or refers to sensitive or system-critical data.

Compliant Solution

This compliant solution both validates the method arguments and verifies the internal state before use. This promotes consistency in program execution and reduces the potential for vulnerabilities.

```
private Object myState = null;

// Sets some internal state in the library
void setState(Object state) {
  if (state == null) {
    // Handle null state
  }

  // Defensive copy here when state is mutable

  if (isInvalidState(state)) {
   // Handle invalid state
  }
```

```
  myState = state;
}

// Performs some action using the state passed earlier
void useState() {
  if (myState == null) {
    // Handle no state (e.g. null) condition
  }
  //...
}
```

Exceptions

MET00-EX0: Argument validation inside a method may be omitted when the stated contract of a method requires that the *caller* must validate arguments passed to the method. In this case, the validation must be performed by the caller for all invocations of the method.

MET00-EX1: Argument validation may be omitted for arguments whose type adequately constrains the state of the argument. This constraint should be clearly documented in the code.

This may include arguments whose values (as permitted by their type) are not necessarily valid but are still correctly handled by the method. In the following code, the arguments x and y are not validated even though their product might not be a valid int. The code is safe because it adequately handles all int values for x and y.

```
public int product(int x, int y) {
  long result = (long) x * y;
  if (result < Integer.MIN_VALUE || result > Integer.MAX_VALUE) {
    // handle error
  }
  return (int) result;
}
```

MET00-EX2: Complete validation of all arguments of all methods may introduce added cost and complexity that exceeds its value for all but the most critical code. In such cases, consider argument validation at API boundaries, especially those that may involve interaction with untrusted code.

Risk Assessment

Failure to validate method arguments can result in inconsistent computations, runtime exceptions, and control flow vulnerabilities.

Rule	Severity	Likelihood	Remediation Cost	Priority	Level
MET00-J	high	likely	high	P9	L2

Related Guidelines

ISO/IEC TR 24772:2010   Argument passing to library functions [TRJ]

Bibliography

[Bloch 2008]   Item 38. Check parameters for validity

■ MET01-J. Never use assertions to validate method arguments

Never use assertions to validate arguments of public methods. According to the *Java Language Specification*, §14.10, "The `assert` Statement" [JLS 2005]:

> ... assertions should not be used for argument-checking in public methods. Argument-checking is typically part of the contract of a method, and this contract must be upheld whether assertions are enabled or disabled.

Another problem with using assertions for argument checking is that erroneous arguments should result in an appropriate runtime exception (such as `IllegalArgumentException`, `IndexOutOfBoundsException`, or `NullPointerException`). An assertion failure will not throw an appropriate exception.

Noncompliant Code Example

The method `getAbsAdd()` computes and returns the sum of the absolute value of parameters x and y. It lacks argument validation, in violation of rule MET00-J. Consequently, it can produce incorrect results because of integer overflow or when either or both of its arguments are `Integer.MIN_VALUE`.

```
public static int getAbsAdd(int x, int y) {
  return Math.abs(x) + Math.abs(y);
}
getAbsAdd(Integer.MIN_VALUE, 1);
```

Noncompliant Code Example

This noncompliant code example uses assertions to validate arguments of a public method.

```
public static int getAbsAdd(int x, int y) {
  assert x != Integer.MIN_VALUE;
  assert y != Integer.MIN_VALUE;
  int absX = Math.abs(x);
  int absY = Math.abs(y);
  assert (absX <= Integer.MAX_VALUE - absY);
  return absX + absY;
}
```

The conditions checked by the assertions are reasonable. However, the validation code is not executed when assertions are disabled.

Compliant Solution

This compliant solution validates the method arguments by ensuring that values passed to Math.abs() exclude Integer.MIN_VALUE and also by checking for integer overflow.

```
public static int getAbsAdd(int x, int y) {
  if (x == Integer.MIN_VALUE || y == Integer.MIN_VALUE) {
    throw new IllegalArgumentException();
  }
  int absX = Math.abs(x);
  int absY = Math.abs(y);
  if (absX > Integer.MAX_VALUE - absY) {
    throw new IllegalArgumentException();
  }
  return absX + absY;
}
```

Alternatively, the addition could be performed using type long and the result of the addition stored in a local variable of type long. This alternate implementation would require a check to ensure that the resulting long can be represented in the range of the type int. Failure of this latter check would indicate that an int version of the addition would have overflowed.

Risk Assessment

Failure to validate method arguments can result in inconsistent computations, runtime exceptions, and control flow vulnerabilities.

Rule	Severity	Likelihood	Remediation Cost	Priority	Level
MET01-J	medium	probable	medium	P8	L2

Related Guidelines

MITRE CWE	CWE-617. Reachable assertion

Bibliography

[Daconta 2003]	Item 7. My assertions are not gratuitous
[ESA 2005]	Rule 68. Explicitly check method parameters for validity, and throw an adequate exception in case they are not valid. Do not use the `assert` statement for this purpose
[JLS 2005]	§14.10, The `assert` Statement

■ MET02-J. Do not use deprecated or obsolete classes or methods

Never use deprecated fields, methods, or classes in new code. The Java SE 6 documentation provides a complete list of deprecated APIs [API 2006]. Java also provides a `@deprecated` annotation to indicate the deprecation of specific fields, methods, and classes. For instance, many methods of `java.util.Date`, such as `Date.getYear()`, have been explicitly deprecated. Rule THI05-J describes issues that can result from using the deprecated `Thread.stop()` method.

Obsolete fields, methods, and classes should not be used. Java lacks any annotation that indicates obsolescence; nevertheless, several classes and methods are documented as obsolete. For instance, the `java.util.Dictionary` class is marked as obsolete; new code should use `java.util.Map<K,V>` instead [API 2006].

Finally, several classes and methods impose particular limitations on their use. For instance, all of the subclasses of the `abstract` class `java.text.Format` are thread-unsafe. These classes must be avoided in multithreaded code.

Obsolete Methods and Classes

The following methods and classes must not be used:

Class or Method	Replacement	Rule
`java.lang.Character.isJavaLetter()`	`java.lang.Character.isJavaIdentifierStart()`	
`java.lang.Character.isJavaLetterOrDigit()`	`java.lang.Character.isJavaIdentifierPart()`	

(continued)

Class or Method	Replacement	Rule
`java.lang.Character.isSpace()`	`java.lang.Character.isWhitespace()`	
`java.lang.Class.newInstance()`	`java.lang.reflect.Constructor.newInstance()`	ERR06-J
`java.util.Date` (many methods)	`java.util.Calendar`	
`java.util.Dictionary`	`java.util.Map<K,V>`	
`java.util.Properties.save()`	`java.util.Properties.store()`	
`java.lang.Thread.run()`	`java.lang.Thread.start()`	THI00-J
`java.lang.Thread.stop()`	`java.lang.Thread.interrupt()`	THI05-J
`java.lang.ThreadGroup` (many methods)	`java.util.concurrent.Executor`	THI01-J

The Java Virtual Machine (JVM) Profiler Interface (JVMPI) and JVM Debug Interface (JVMDI) are also deprecated and have been replaced by the JVM Tool Interface (JVMTI). See rule ENV05-J for more information.

Risk Assessment

Using deprecated or obsolete classes or methods in program code can lead to erroneous behavior.

Rule	Severity	Likelihood	Remediation Cost	Priority	Level
MET02-J	high	likely	medium	P18	L1

Automated Detection   Detecting uses of deprecated methods is straightforward. Obsolete methods and thread-unsafe methods have no automatic means of detection.

Related Guidelines

ISO/IEC TR 24772:2010	Deprecated language features [MEM]
MITRE CWE	CWE-589. Call to non-ubiquitous API

Bibliography

[API 2006]	Deprecated API, Dictionary
[SDN 2008]	Bug database, Bug ID 4264153

■ MET03-J. Methods that perform a security check must be declared private or final

Member methods of nonfinal classes that perform security checks can be compromised when a malicious subclass overrides the methods and omits the checks. Consequently, such methods must be declared private or final to prevent overriding.

Noncompliant Code Example

This noncompliant code example allows a subclass to override the readSensitiveFile() method and omit the required security check.

```java
public void readSensitiveFile() {
  try {
    SecurityManager sm = System.getSecurityManager();
    if (sm != null) {  // Check for permission to read file
      sm.checkRead("/temp/tempFile");
    }
    // Access the file
  } catch (SecurityException se) {
    // Log exception
  }
}
```

Compliant Solution

This compliant solution prevents overriding of the readSensitiveFile() method by declaring it final.

```java
public final void readSensitiveFile() {
  try {
    SecurityManager sm = System.getSecurityManager();
    if (sm != null) {  // Check for permission to read file
      sm.checkRead("/temp/tempFile");
    }
    // Access the file
  } catch (SecurityException se) {
    // Log exception
  }
}
```

Compliant Solution

This compliant solution prevents overriding of the `readSensitiveFile()` method by declaring it private.

```
private void readSensitiveFile() {
  try {
    SecurityManager sm = System.getSecurityManager();
    if (sm != null) {  // Check for permission to read file
      sm.checkRead("/temp/tempFile");
    }
    // Access the file
  } catch (SecurityException se) {
    // Log exception
  }
}
```

Exceptions

MET03-EX0: Classes that are declared final are exempt from this rule because their member methods cannot be overridden.

Risk Assessment

Failure to declare a class's method private or final affords the opportunity for a malicious subclass to bypass the security checks performed in the method.

Rule	Severity	Likelihood	Remediation Cost	Priority	Level
MET03-J	medium	probable	medium	P8	L2

Bibliography

[Ware 2008]

■ MET04-J. Do not increase the accessibility of overridden or hidden methods

Increasing the accessibility of overridden or hidden methods permits a malicious subclass to offer wider access to the restricted method than was originally intended. Consequently, programs must override methods only when necessary and must declare methods final whenever possible to prevent malicious subclassing. When methods cannot be declared final, programs must refrain from increasing the accessibility of overridden methods.

The access modifier of an overriding or hiding method must provide at least as much access as the overridden or hidden method (*Java Language Specification*, §8.4.8.3, "Requirements in Overriding and Hiding" [JLS 2005]). The following are the allowed accesses:

Overridden/hidden method modifier	Overriding/hiding method modifier
public	public
protected	protected or public
default	default or protected or public
private	Cannot be overridden

Noncompliant Code Example

This noncompliant code example demonstrates how a malicious subclass Sub can both override the doLogic() method of its superclass and increase the accessibility of the overriding method. Any user of Sub can invoke the doLogic() method because the base class Super defines it to be protected, consequently allowing class Sub to increase the accessibility of doLogic() by declaring its own version of the method to be public.

```
class Super {
  protected void doLogic() {
    System.out.println("Super invoked");
  }
}

public class Sub extends Super {
  public void doLogic() {
    System.out.println("Sub invoked");
    // Do sensitive operations
  }
}
```

Compliant Solution

This compliant solution declares the doLogic() method final to prevent malicious overriding.

```
class Super {
  protected final void doLogic() { // declare as final
    System.out.println("Super invoked");
    // Do sensitive operations
  }
}
```

Exceptions

MET04-EX0: For classes that implement the `java.lang.Cloneable` interface, the accessibility of the `Object.clone()` method should be increased from protected to public [SCG 2009].

Risk Assessment

Subclassing allows weakening of access restrictions, which can compromise the security of a Java application.

Rule	Severity	Likelihood	Remediation Cost	Priority	Level
MET04-J	medium	probable	medium	P8	L2

Automated Detection Detecting violations of this rule is straightforward.

Related Guidelines

MITRE CWE	CWE-487. Reliance on package-level scope
Secure Coding Guidelines for the Java Programming Language, Version 3.0	Guideline 1-1. Limit the accessibility of classes, interfaces, methods, and fields

Bibliography

[JLS 2005]	§8.4.8.3, Requirements in Overriding and Hiding

■ MET05-J. Ensure that constructors do not call overridable methods

According to the *Java Language Specification*, §12.5, "Creation of New Class Instances" [JLS 2005]:

> Unlike C++, the Java programming language does not specify altered rules for method dispatch during the creation of a new class instance. If methods are invoked that are overridden in subclasses in the object being initialized, then these overriding methods are used, even before the new object is completely initialized.

Invocation of an overridable method during object construction may result in the use of uninitialized data, leading to runtime exceptions or to unanticipated outcomes. Calling overridable methods from constructors can also leak the `this` reference before object construction is complete, potentially exposing uninitialized or inconsistent data to other threads. See rule TSM01-J for additional information. As a result, constructors must invoke only methods that are final or private.

Noncompliant Code Example

This noncompliant code example results in the use of uninitialized data by the doLogic() method.

```java
class SuperClass {
  public SuperClass () {
    doLogic();
  }

  public void doLogic() {
    System.out.println("This is superclass!");
  }
}

class SubClass extends SuperClass {
  private String color = null;
  public SubClass() {
    super();
    color = "Red";
  }

  public void doLogic() {
    System.out.println("This is subclass! The color is :" + color);
    // ...
  }
}

public class Overridable {
  public static void main(String[] args) {
    SuperClass bc = new SuperClass();
    // Prints "This is superclass!"
    SuperClass sc = new SubClass();
    // Prints "This is subclass! The color is :null"
  }
}
```

The doLogic() method is invoked from the superclass's constructor. When the superclass is constructed directly, the doLogic() method in the superclass is invoked and executes successfully. However, when the subclass initiates the superclass's construction, the subclass's doLogic() method is invoked instead. In this case, the value of color is still null because the subclass's constructor has not yet concluded.

Compliant Solution

This compliant solution declares the doLogic() method as final so that it cannot be overridden.

```
class SuperClass {
  public SuperClass() {
    doLogic();
  }
  public final void doLogic() {
    System.out.println("This is superclass!");
  }
}
```

Risk Assessment

Allowing a constructor to call overridable methods can provide an attacker with access to the this reference before an object is fully initialized, which could lead to a vulnerability.

Rule	Severity	Likelihood	Remediation Cost	Priority	Level
MET05-J	medium	probable	medium	P8	L2

Automated Detection   Automated detection of constructors that contain invocations of overridable methods is straightforward.

Related Guidelines

ISO/IEC TR 24772:2010	Inheritance [RIP]

Bibliography

[ESA 2005]	Rule 62. Do not call nonfinal methods from within a constructor
[JLS 2005]	Chapter 8, Classes, §12.5 Creation of New Class Instances
[Rogue 2000]	Rule 81. Do not call non-final methods from within a constructor
Secure Coding Guidelines for the Java Programming Language, Version 3.0	Guideline 4-4. Prevent constructors from calling methods that can be overridden

■ MET06-J. Do not invoke overridable methods in clone()

Calling overridable methods from the clone() method is insecure. First, a malicious subclass could override the method and affect the behavior of the clone() method. Second, a trusted subclass could observe (and potentially modify) the cloned object in a partially initialized state before its construction has concluded. In either case, the subclass could leave the clone, the object being cloned, or both, in an inconsistent state. Consequently, clone() methods may invoke only methods that are final or private.

This rule is closely related to rule MET05-J.

Noncompliant Code Example

This noncompliant code example shows two classes, CloneExample and Sub. The class CloneExample calls an overridable method doSomething(). The overridden method sets the value of the cookies; the overriding method sets the values of the domain names. The doSomething() method of the subclass Sub is erroneously executed twice at runtime because of polymorphism. The first invocation comes from CloneExample.clone(), and the other comes from Sub.clone(). Consequently, the values of the cookies are never initialized, while the domains are initialized twice.

Furthermore, the subclass not only sees the clone in an inconsistent state but also modifies the clone in a manner that creates inconsistent copies. This is because the deepCopy() method occurs after the call to the doSomething() method, and the overriding doSomething() implementation erroneously modifies the object.

```
class CloneExample implements Cloneable {
  HttpCookie[] cookies;

  CloneExample(HttpCookie[] c) {
    cookies = c;
  }

  public Object clone() throws CloneNotSupportedException {
    final CloneExample clone = (CloneExample) super.clone();
    clone.doSomething(); // Invokes overridable method
    clone.cookies = clone.deepCopy();
    return clone;
  }

  void doSomething() { // Overridable
    for (int i = 0; i < cookies.length; i++) {
      cookies[i].setValue("" + i);
    }
  }
}
```

```java
  HttpCookie[] deepCopy() {
    if (cookies == null) {
      throw new NullPointerException();
    }

    // deep copy
    HttpCookie[] cookiesCopy = new HttpCookie[cookies.length];

    for (int i = 0; i < cookies.length; i++) {
      // Manually create a copy of each element in array
      cookiesCopy[i] = (HttpCookie) cookies[i].clone();
    }
    return cookiesCopy;
  }
}

class Sub extends CloneExample {
  Sub(HttpCookie[] c) {
    super(c);
  }

  public Object clone() throws CloneNotSupportedException {
    final Sub clone = (Sub) super.clone();
    clone.doSomething();
    return clone;
  }

  void doSomething() { // Erroneously executed
    for (int i = 0;i < cookies.length; i++) {
      cookies[i].setDomain(i + ".foo.com");
    }
  }

  public static void main(String[] args)
      throws CloneNotSupportedException {
    HttpCookie[] hc = new HttpCookie[20];
    for (int i = 0 ; i < hc.length; i++){
      hc[i] = new HttpCookie("cookie" + i,"" + i);
    }
    CloneExample bc = new Sub(hc);
    bc.clone();
  }
}
```

When an overridable method is invoked on a shallow copy of the object, the original object is also modified.

Compliant Solution

This compliant solution declares both the doSomething() and the deepCopy() methods final, preventing overriding of these methods.

```
class CloneExample implements Cloneable {
  final void doSomething() {
    // ...
  }
  final HttpCookie[] deepCopy() {
    // ...
  }

  // ...
}
```

Alternative solutions that prevent invocation of overridden methods include declaring these methods private or final, or declaring the class containing these methods final.

Risk Assessment

Calling overridable methods on the clone under construction can expose class internals to malicious code or violate class invariants by exposing the clone to trusted code in a partially initialized state, affording the opportunity to corrupt the state of the clone, the object being cloned, or both.

Rule	Severity	Likelihood	Remediation Cost	Priority	Level
MET06-J	medium	probable	low	P12	L1

Automated Detection   Automated detection is straightforward.

Bibliography

[Bloch 2008]   Item 11. Override clone judiciously
[Gong 2003]

■ MET07-J. Never declare a class method that hides a method declared in a superclass or superinterface

When a class declares a static method m, the declaration of m hides any method m', where the signature of m is a subsignature of the signature of m', and the declaration of m' is both in the superclasses and superinterfaces of the declaring class and also would otherwise be accessible to code in the declaring class (*Java Language Specification*, §8.4.8.2, "Hiding (by Class Methods)" [JLS 2005]).

An instance method defined in a subclass overrides another instance method in the superclass when both have the same name, number and type of parameters, and return type.

Hiding and overriding differ in the determination of which method is invoked from a call site. For overriding, the method invoked is determined at runtime on the basis of the specific object instance in hand. For hiding, the method invoked is determined at compile time on the basis of the specific qualified name or method invocation expression used at the call site. Although the Java language provides unambiguous rules for determining which method is invoked, the results of these rules are often unexpected. Additionally, programmers sometimes expect method overriding in cases where the language provides method hiding. Consequently, programs must never declare a class method that hides a method declared in a superclass or superinterface.

Noncompliant Code Example

In this noncompliant example, the programmer hides the static method rather than overriding it. Consequently, the code invokes the `displayAccountStatus()` method of the superclass at two different call sites instead of invoking the superclass method at one call site and the subclass method at the other.

```java
class GrantAccess {
  public static void displayAccountStatus() {
    System.out.println("Account details for admin: XX");
  }
}

class GrantUserAccess extends GrantAccess {
  public static void displayAccountStatus() {
    System.out.println("Account details for user: XX");
  }
}

public class StatMethod {
  public static void choose(String username) {
```

```
      GrantAccess admin = new GrantAccess();
      GrantAccess user = new GrantUserAccess();
      if (username.equals("admin")) {
        admin.displayAccountStatus();
      } else {
        user.displayAccountStatus();
      }
    }

    public static void main(String[] args) {
      choose("user");
    }
  }
```

Compliant Solution

In this compliant solution, the programmer declares the `displayAccountStatus()` methods as instance methods by removing the `static` keyword. Consequently, the dynamic dispatch at the call sites produces the expected result. The `@Override` annotation indicates intentional overriding of the parent method.

```
class GrantAccess {
  public void displayAccountStatus() {
    System.out.print("Account details for admin: XX");
  }
}

class GrantUserAccess extends GrantAccess {
  @Override
  public void displayAccountStatus() {
    System.out.print("Account details for user: XX");
  }
}

public class StatMethod {
  public static void choose(String username) {
    GrantAccess admin = new GrantAccess();
    GrantAccess user = new GrantUserAccess();

    if (username.equals("admin")) {
      admin.displayAccountStatus();
    } else {
      user.displayAccountStatus();
```

```
    }
  }

  public static void main(String[] args) {
    choose("user");
  }
}
```

The methods inherited from the superclass can also be overloaded in a subclass. Overloaded methods are new methods unique to the subclass and neither hide nor override the superclass method [Tutorials 2008].

Technically, a private method cannot be hidden or overridden. There is no requirement that private methods with the same signature in the subclass and the superclass bear any relationship in terms of having the same return type or throws clause, the necessary conditions for hiding [JLS 2005]. Consequently, hiding cannot occur when private methods have different return types or throws clauses.

Exceptions

MET07-EX0: Occasionally, an API provides hidden methods. Invoking those methods is not a violation of this rule, provided that all invocations of hidden methods use qualified names or method invocation expressions that *explicitly* indicate which specific method is invoked. If the displayAccountStatus() were a hidden method, for example, the following implementation of the choose() method would be an acceptable alternative:

```
public static void choose(String username) {
  if (username.equals("admin")) {
    GrantAccess.displayAccountStatus();
  } else {
    GrantUserAccess.displayAccountStatus();
  }
}
```

Risk Assessment

Confusing overriding and hiding can produce unexpected results.

Rule	Severity	Likelihood	Remediation Cost	Priority	Level
MET07-J	low	unlikely	medium	P2	L3

Automated Detection Automated detection of violations of this rule is straightforward. Automated determination of cases where method hiding is unavoidable is infeasible. However, determining whether all invocations of hiding or hidden methods explicitly indicate which specific method is invoked is straightforward.

Bibliography

[Bloch 2005a]   Puzzle 48. All I get is static
[JLS 2005]   §8.4.8.2, Hiding (by Class Methods)
[Tutorials 2008]   Overriding and Hiding Methods

■ MET08-J. Ensure objects that are equated are equatable

Composition or inheritance may be used to create a new class that both encapsulates an existing class and adds one or more fields. When one class extends another in this way, the concept of equality for the subclass may or may not involve its new fields. That is, when comparing two subclass objects for equality, sometimes their respective fields must also be equal, and other times they need not be equal. Depending on the concept of equality for the subclass, the subclass might override `equals()`. Furthermore, this method must follow the general contract for `equals()` as specified by the *Java Language Specification* [JLS 2005].

An object is characterized both by its identity (location in memory) and by its state (actual data). The == operator compares only the identities of two objects (to check whether the references refer to the same object); the `equals()` method defined in `java.lang.Object` can be overridden to compare the state as well. When a class defines an `equals()` method, it implies that the method compares state. When the class lacks a customized `equals()` method (either locally declared or inherited from a parent class), it uses the default `Object.equals()` implementation inherited from `Object`. The default `Object.equals()` implementation compares only the references and may produce unexpected results.

The `equals()` method applies only to objects, not primitives.

Enumerated types have a fixed set of distinct values that may be compared using == rather than the `equals()` method. Note that enumerated types provide an `equals()` implementation that uses == internally; this default cannot be overridden. More generally, subclasses that both inherit an implementation of `equals()` from a superclass and lack a requirement for additional functionality need not override the `equals()` method.

The general usage contract for `equals()` as specified by the *Java Language Specification* establishes five requirements:

1. It is reflexive: For any reference value x, x.equals(x) must return `true`.

2. It is symmetric: For any reference values x and y, x.equals(y) must return `true` if and only if y.equals(x) returns `true`.

3. It is transitive: For any reference values x, y, and z, if x.equals(y) returns true and y.equals(z) returns true, then x.equals(z) must return true.

4. It is consistent: For any reference values x and y, multiple invocations of x.equals(y) consistently return true or consistently return false, provided no information used in equals() comparisons on the object is modified.

5. For any non-null reference value x, x.equals(null) must return false.

Never violate any of these requirements when overriding the equals() method.

Noncompliant Code Example (Symmetry)

This noncompliant code example defines a CaseInsensitiveString class that includes a String and overrides the equals() method. The CaseInsensitiveString class knows about ordinary strings, but the String class has no knowledge of case-insensitive strings. Consequently, the CaseInsensitiveString.equals() method should not attempt to inter-operate with objects of the String class.

```
public final class CaseInsensitiveString {
  private String s;

  public CaseInsensitiveString(String s) {
    if (s == null) {
      throw new NullPointerException();
    }
    this.s = s;
  }

  // This method violates symmetry
  public boolean equals(Object o) {
    if (o instanceof CaseInsensitiveString) {
      return s.equalsIgnoreCase(((CaseInsensitiveString)o).s);
    }

    if (o instanceof String) {
      return s.equalsIgnoreCase((String)o);
    }
    return false;
  }

  // Comply with MET09-J
  public int hashCode() {/* ... */}
```

```
  public static void main(String[] args) {
    CaseInsensitiveString cis = new CaseInsensitiveString("Java");
    String s = "java";
    System.out.println(cis.equals(s)); // Returns true
    System.out.println(s.equals(cis)); // Returns false
  }
}
```

By operating on String objects, the CaseInsensitiveString.equals() method violates the second contract requirement (symmetry). Because of the asymmetry, given a String object s and a CaseInsensitiveString object cis that differ only in case, cis.equals(s) returns true, while s.equals(cis) returns false.

Compliant Solution

In this compliant solution, the CaseInsensitiveString.equals() method is simplified to operate only on instances of the CaseInsensitiveString class, consequently preserving symmetry.

```
public final class CaseInsensitiveString {
  private String s;

  public CaseInsensitiveString(String s) {
    if (s == null) {
      throw new NullPointerException();
    }
    this.s = s;
  }

  public boolean equals(Object o) {
    return o instanceof CaseInsensitiveString &&
      ((CaseInsensitiveString)o).s.equalsIgnoreCase(s);
  }

  public int hashCode() {/* ... */}

  public static void main(String[] args) {
    CaseInsensitiveString cis = new CaseInsensitiveString("Java");
    String s = "java";
    System.out.println(cis.equals(s)); // Returns false now
    System.out.println(s.equals(cis)); // Returns false now
  }
}
```

Noncompliant Code Example (Transitivity)

This noncompliant code example defines an XCard class that extends the Card class.

```java
public class Card {
  private final int number;

  public Card(int number) {
    this.number = number;
  }

  public boolean equals(Object o) {
    if (!(o instanceof Card)) {
      return false;
    }

    Card c = (Card)o;
    return c.number == number;
  }

  public int hashCode() {/* ... */}
}

class XCard extends Card {
  private String type;
  public XCard(int number, String type) {
    super(number);
    this.type = type;
  }

  public boolean equals(Object o) {
    if (!(o instanceof Card)) {
      return false;
    }

    // Normal Card, do not compare type
    if (!(o instanceof XCard)) {
      return o.equals(this);
    }

    // It is an XCard, compare type as well
    XCard xc = (XCard)o;
    return super.equals(o) && xc.type == type;
  }

  public int hashCode() {/* ... */}

  public static void main(String[] args) {
    XCard p1 = new XCard(1, "type1");
    Card p2 = new Card(1);
    XCard p3 = new XCard(1, "type2");
    System.out.println(p1.equals(p2)); // Returns true
```

```
      System.out.println(p2.equals(p3)); // Returns true
      System.out.println(p1.equals(p3)); // Returns false
                                         // violating transitivity
    }
}
```

In the noncompliant code example, p1 and p2 compare equal and p2 and p3 compare equal, but p1 and p3 compare unequal, violating the transitivity requirement. The problem is that the Card class has no knowledge of the XCard class and consequently cannot determine that p2 and p3 have different values for the field type.

Compliant Solution

Unfortunately, in this case it is impossible to extend an instantiable class (as opposed to an abstract class) by adding a value or field in the subclass while preserving the equals() contract. Use composition rather than inheritance to achieve the desired effect [Bloch 2008]. This compliant solution adopts this approach by adding a private card field to the XCard class and providing a public viewCard() method.

```java
class XCard {
  private String type;
  private Card card; // Composition

  public XCard(int number, String type) {
    card = new Card(number);
    this.type = type;
  }

  public Card viewCard() {
    return card;
  }

  public boolean equals(Object o) {
    if (!(o instanceof XCard)) {
      return false;
    }

    XCard cp = (XCard)o;
    return cp.card.equals(card) && cp.type.equals(type);
  public int hashCode() {/* ... */}

  public static void main(String[] args) {
    XCard p1 = new XCard(1, "type1");
    Card p2 = new Card(1);
```

```
    XCard p3 = new XCard(1, "type2");
    XCard p4 = new XCard(1, "type1");
    System.out.println(p1.equals(p2)); // Prints false
    System.out.println(p2.equals(p3)); // Prints false
    System.out.println(p1.equals(p3)); // Prints false
    System.out.println(p1.equals(p4)); // Prints true
  }
}
```

Noncompliant Code Example (Consistency)

A uniform resource locator (URL) specifies both the location of a resource and also a method to access it. According to the Java API documentation for class URL [API 2006]:

> Two URL objects are equal if they have the same protocol, reference equivalent hosts, have the same port number on the host, and the same file and fragment of the file.
>
> Two hosts are considered equivalent if both host names can be resolved into the same IP addresses; else if either host name can't be resolved, the host names must be equal without regard to case; or both host names equal to null.

The defined behavior for the equals() method is known to be inconsistent with *virtual hosting* in HTTP.

Virtual hosting allows a web server to host multiple websites on the same computer, sometimes sharing the same IP address. Unfortunately, this technique was unanticipated when the URL class was designed. Consequently, when two completely different URLs resolve to the same IP address, the URL class considers them to be equal.

Another risk associated with the equals() method for URL objects is that the logic it uses when connected to the Internet differs from that used when disconnected. When connected to the Internet, the equals() method follows the steps described in the Java API; when disconnected, it performs a string compare on the two URLs. Consequently, the URL. equals() method violates the consistency requirement for equals().

Consider an application that allows an organization's employees to access an external mail service via http://mailwebsite.com. The application is designed to deny access to other websites by behaving as a makeshift firewall. However, a crafty or malicious user could nevertheless access an illegitimate website http://illegitimatewebsite.com if it were hosted on the same computer as the legitimate website and consequently shared the same IP address. Even worse, an attacker could register multiple websites (for phishing purposes) until one was registered on the same computer, consequently defeating the firewall.

```
public class Filter {
  public static void main(String[] args) throws MalformedURLException {
    final URL allowed = new URL("http://mailwebsite.com");
    if (!allowed.equals(new URL(args[0]))) {
      throw new SecurityException("Access Denied");
    }
    // Else proceed
  }
}
```

Compliant Solution (Strings)

This compliant solution compares two URLs' string representations, thereby avoiding the pitfalls of URL.equals().

```
public class Filter {
  public static void main(String[] args) throws MalformedURLException {
    final URL allowed = new URL("http://mailwebsite.com");
    if (!allowed.toString().equals(new URL(args[0]).toString())) {
      throw new SecurityException("Access Denied");
    }
    // Else proceed
  }
}
```

This solution still has problems. Two URLs with different string representation can still refer to the same resource. However, the solution fails safely in this case because the equals() contract is preserved, and the system will never allow a malicious URL to be accepted by mistake.

Compliant Solution (URI.equals())

A Uniform Resource Identifier (URI) contains a string of characters used to identify a resource; this is a more general concept than an URL. The java.net.URI class provides string-based equals() and hashCode() methods that satisfy the general contracts for Object.equals() and Object.hashCode(); they do not invoke hostname resolution and are unaffected by network connectivity. URI also provides methods for normalization and canonicalization that URL lacks. Finally, the URL.toURI() and URI.toURL() methods provide easy conversion between the two classes. Programs should use URIs instead of URLs whenever possible. According to the Java API [API 2006] URI class documentation:

> A URI may be either absolute or relative. A URI string is parsed according to the generic syntax without regard to the scheme, if any, that it specifies. No lookup of the host, if any, is performed, and no scheme-dependent stream handler is constructed.

This compliant solution uses a URI object instead of a URL. The filter appropriately blocks the website when presented with any string other than http://mailwebsite.com because the comparison fails.

```java
public class Filter {
  public static void main(String[] args)
                  throws MalformedURLException, URISyntaxException {
    final URI allowed = new URI("http://mailwebsite.com");
    if (!allowed.equals(new URI(args[0]))) {
      throw new SecurityException("Access Denied");
    }
    // Else proceed
  }
}
```

Additionally, the URI class performs normalization (removing extraneous path segments like "..") and relativization of paths [API 2006] and [Darwin 2004].

Noncompliant Code Example (`java.security.Key`)

The method `java.lang.Object.equals()` by default is unable to compare composite objects such as cryptographic keys. Most Key classes lack an `equals()` implementation that would override Object's default implementation. In such cases, the components of the composite object must be compared individually to ensure correctness.

This noncompliant code example compares two keys using the `equals()` method. The comparison may return `false` even when the key instances represent the same logical key.

```java
private static boolean keysEqual(Key key1, Key key2) {
  if (key1.equals(key2)) {
    return true;
  }
}
```

Compliant Solution (`java.security.Key`)

This compliant solution uses the `equals()` method as a first test and then compares the encoded version of the keys to facilitate provider-independent behavior. For example, this code can determine whether a `RSAPrivateKey` and `RSAPrivateCrtKey` represent equivalent private keys [Sun 2006].

```java
private static boolean keysEqual(Key key1, Key key2) {
  if (key1.equals(key2)) {
    return true;
  }

  if (Arrays.equals(key1.getEncoded(), key2.getEncoded())) {
    return true;
  }

  // More code for different types of keys here.
  // For example, the following code can check if
  // an RSAPrivateKey and an RSAPrivateCrtKey are equal:
  if ((key1 instanceof RSAPrivateKey) &&
      (key2 instanceof RSAPrivateKey)) {

   if ((((RSAKey)key1).getModulus().equals(
       ((RSAKey)key2).getModulus())) &&
      (((RSAPrivateKey) key1).getPrivateExponent().equals(
      ((RSAPrivateKey) key2).getPrivateExponent())))) {
     return true;
    }
  }
  return false;
}
```

Exceptions

METO8-EX0: Requirements of this rule may be violated provided that the incompatible types are never compared. There are classes in the Java platform libraries (and elsewhere) that extend an instantiable class by adding a value component. For example, `java.sql.Timestamp` extends `java.util.Date` and adds a nanoseconds field. The `equals()` implementation for `Timestamp` violates symmetry and can cause erratic behavior when `Timestamp` and `Date` objects are used in the same collection or are otherwise intermixed [Bloch 2008].

Risk Assessment

Violating the general contract when overriding the `equals()` method can lead to unexpected results.

Rule	Severity	Likelihood	Remediation Cost	Priority	Level
MET08-J	low	unlikely	medium	P2	L3

Related Guidelines

MITRE CWE	CWE-697. Insufficient comparison

Bibliography

[API 2006]	Method `equals()`
[Bloch 2008]	Item 8. Obey the general contract when overriding equals
[Darwin 2004]	9.2, Overriding the `equals` Method
[Harold 1997]	Chapter 3, Classes, Strings, and Arrays, The Object Class (Equality)
[Sun 2006]	Determining If Two Keys Are Equal (JCA Reference Guide)
[Techtalk 2007]	More Joy of Sets

■ MET09-J. Classes that define an `equals()` method must also define a `hashCode()` method

Classes that override the `Object.equals()` method must also override the `Object.hashCode()` method. The `java.lang.Object` class requires that any two objects that compare equal using the `equals()` method must produce the same integer result when the `hashCode()` method is invoked on the objects [API 2006].

The `equals()` method is used to determine logical equivalence between object instances. Consequently, the `hashCode()` method must return the same value for all equivalent objects. Failure to follow this contract is a common source of defects.

Noncompliant Code Example

This noncompliant code example associates credit card numbers with strings using a `HashMap` and subsequently attempts to retrieve the string value associated with a credit card number. The expected retrieved value is 4111111111111111; the actual retrieved value is `null`.

```
public final class CreditCard {
  private final int number;

  public CreditCard(int number) {
    this.number = (short) number;
  }
```

```
   public boolean equals(Object o) {
     if (o == this) {
       return true;
     }
     if (!(o instanceof CreditCard)) {
       return false;
     }
     CreditCard cc = (CreditCard)o;
     return cc.number == number;
   }

   public static void main(String[] args) {
     Map<CreditCard, String> m = new HashMap<CreditCard, String>();
     m.put(new CreditCard(100), "4111111111111111");
     System.out.println(m.get(new CreditCard(100)));
   }
}
```

The cause of this erroneous behavior is that the `CreditCard` class overrides the `equals()` method but fails to override the `hashCode()` method. Consequently, the default `hashCode()` method returns a different value for each object, even though the objects are logically equivalent; these differing values lead to examination of different hash buckets, which prevents the `get()` method from finding the intended value.

Note that by specifying the credit card number in `main()`, these code examples violate rule MSC03-J for the sake of brevity.

Compliant Solution

This compliant solution overrides the `hashCode()` method so that it generates the same value for any two instances that are considered to be equal by the `equals()` method. Bloch discusses the recipe to generate such a hash function in detail [Bloch 2008].

```
public final class CreditCard {
  private final int number;

  public CreditCard(int number) {
    this.number = (short) number;
  }

  public boolean equals(Object o) {
    if (o == this) {
      return true;
```

```
    }
    if (!(o instanceof CreditCard)) {
      return false;
    }
    CreditCard cc = (CreditCard)o;
    return cc.number == number;
  }

  public int hashCode() {
    int result = 17;
    result = 31 * result + number;
    return result;
  }

  public static void main(String[] args) {
    Map<CreditCard, String> m = new HashMap<CreditCard, String>();
    m.put(new CreditCard(100), "4111111111111111");
    System.out.println(m.get(new CreditCard(100)));
  }
}
```

Risk Assessment

Overriding the equals() method without overriding the hashCode() method can lead to unexpected results.

Rule	Severity	Likelihood	Remediation Cost	Priority	Level
MET09-J	low	unlikely	high	P1	L3

Automated Detection   Automated detection of classes that override only one of equals() and hashCode() is straightforward. Sound static determination that the implementations of equals() and hashCode() are mutually consistent is not feasible in the general case, although heuristic techniques may be useful.

Related Guidelines

MITRE CWE   CWE-581. Object model violation: Just one of equals and hashcode defined

Bibliography

[API 2006]   Class Object
[Bloch 2008]   Item 9. Always override hashCode when you override equals

■ MET10-J. Follow the general contract when implementing the compareTo() method

Choosing to implement the Comparable interface represents a commitment that the implementation of the compareTo() method adheres to the general usage contract for that method. Library classes such as TreeSet and TreeMap accept Comparable objects and use the associated compareTo() methods to sort the objects. However, a class that implements the compareTo() method in an unexpected way can cause undesirable results.

The general usage contract for compareTo() from Java SE 6 API [API 2006] (numbering added) states that

1. The implementor must ensure sgn(x.compareTo(y)) == -sgn(y.compareTo(x)) for all x and y. (This implies that x.compareTo(y) must throw an exception if y.compareTo(x) throws an exception.)

2. The implementor must also ensure that the relation is transitive: (x.compareTo(y) > 0 && y.compareTo(z) > 0) implies x.compareTo(z) > 0.

3. Finally, the implementor must ensure that x.compareTo(y) == 0 implies that sgn(x.compareTo(z)) == sgn(y.compareTo(z)) for all z.

4. It is strongly recommended, but not strictly required, that (x.compareTo(y) == 0) == x.equals(y). Generally speaking, any class that implements the Comparable interface and violates this condition should clearly indicate this fact. The recommended language is "Note: this class has a natural ordering that is inconsistent with equals."

In the foregoing description, the notation sgn(expression) designates the mathematical *signum* function, which is defined to return either –1, 0, or 1 depending on whether the value of the expression is negative, zero, or positive.

Implementations must never violate any of the first three conditions when implementing the compareTo() method. Implementations should conform to the fourth condition whenever possible.

Noncompliant Code Example (Rock-Paper-Scissors)

This program implements the classic game of rock-paper-scissors, using the compareTo() operator to determine the winner of a game.

```
class GameEntry implements Comparable {
  public enum Roshambo {ROCK, PAPER, SCISSORS}
  private Roshambo value;

  public GameEntry(Roshambo value) {
```

```
    this.value = value;
  }

  public int compareTo(Object that) {
    if (!(that instanceof Roshambo)) {
      throw new ClassCastException();
    }
    GameEntry t = (GameEntry) that;
    return (value == t.value) ? 0
      : (value == Roshambo.ROCK && t.value == Roshambo.PAPER) ? -1
      : (value == Roshambo.PAPER && t.value == Roshambo.SCISSORS) ? -1
      : (value == Roshambo.SCISSORS && t.value == Roshambo.ROCK) ? -1
      : 1;
  }
}
```

However, this game violates the required transitivity property because rock beats scissors, and scissors beats paper, but rock does not beat paper.

Compliant Solution (Rock-Paper-Scissors)

This compliant solution implements the same game without using the `Comparable` interface.

```
class GameEntry {
  public enum Roshambo {ROCK, PAPER, SCISSORS}
  private Roshambo value;

  public GameEntry(Roshambo value) {
    this.value = value;
  }

  public int beats(Object that) {
    if (!(that instanceof Roshambo)) {
      throw new ClassCastException();
    }
    GameEntry t = (GameEntry) that;
    return (value == t.value) ? 0
      : (value == Roshambo.ROCK && t.value == Roshambo.PAPER) ? -1
      : (value == Roshambo.PAPER && t.value == Roshambo.SCISSORS) ? -1
      : (value == Roshambo.SCISSORS && t.value == Roshambo.ROCK) ? -1
      : 1;
  }
}
```

Risk Assessment

Violating the general contract when implementing the compareTo() method can result in unexpected results, possibly leading to invalid comparisons and information disclosure.

Rule	Severity	Likelihood	Remediation Cost	Priority	Level
MET10-J	medium	unlikely	medium	P4	L3

Automated Detection   Automated detection of violations of this rule is infeasible in the general case.

Related Guidelines

CERT C++ Secure Coding Standard	ARR40-CPP. Use a valid ordering rule
MITRE CWE	CWE-573. Improper following of specification by caller

Bibliography

[API 2006]	Method compareTo()
[JLS 2005]	

■ MET11-J. Ensure that keys used in comparison operations are immutable

Objects that serve as keys in ordered sets and maps should be immutable. When some fields must be mutable, the equals(), hashCode(), and compareTo() methods must consider only immutable state when comparing objects. Violations of this rule can produce inconsistent orderings in collections. The documentation of java.util.Interface Set<E> and java.util.Interface Map<K,V> warns against this. For example, the documentation for the Interface Map states [API 2006]:

> Note: Great care must be exercised [when] mutable objects are used as map keys. The behavior of a map is not specified if the value of an object is changed in a manner that affects equals comparisons while the object is a key in the map. A special case of this prohibition is that it is not permissible for a map to contain itself as a key. While it is permissible for a map to contain itself as a value, extreme caution is advised: the equals and hashCode methods are no longer well defined on such a map.

Noncompliant Code Example

This noncompliant code example defines a mutable class Employee that consists of the fields name and salary, whose values can be changed using the setEmployeeName() and setSalary() methods. The equals() method is overridden to provide a comparison facility by employee name.

```java
// Mutable class Employee
class Employee {
  private String name;
  private double salary;

  Employee(String empName, double empSalary) {
    this.name = empName;
    this.salary = empSalary;
  }

  public void setEmployeeName(String empName) {
    this.name = empName;
  }

 public void Salary(double empSalary) {
    this.Salary = empSalary;
  }

  @Override
  public boolean equals(Object o) {
    if (!(o instanceof Employee)) {
      return false;
    }

    Employee emp = (Employee)o;
    return emp.name.equals(name);
  }
public int hashCode() {/* ... */}

// Client code
Map<Employee, Calendar> map =
  new ConcurrentHashMap<Employee, Calendar>();
// ...
```

Use of the Employee object as a key to the map is insecure because the properties of the object could change after an ordering has been established. For example, a client could modify the name field when the last name of an employee changes. As a result, clients would observe nondeterministic behavior.

Compliant Solution

This compliant solution adds a final field `employeeID` that is immutable after initialization. The `equals()` method compares `Employee` objects on the basis of this field.

```
// Mutable class Employee
class Employee {
  private String name;
  private double salary;
  private final long employeeID;  // Unique for each Employee

  Employee(String name, double salary, long empID) {
    this.name = name;
    this.salary = salary;
    this.employeeID = empID;
  }

  // ... other methods

  @Override
  public boolean equals(Object o) {
   if (!(o instanceof Employee)) {
     return false;
   }

   Employee emp = (Employee)o;
   return emp.employeeID == employeeID;
  }
}

// Client code remains same
Map<Employee, Calendar> map =
  new ConcurrentHashMap<Employee, Calendar>();
// ...
```

The `Employee` class can now be safely used as a key for the map in the client code.

Noncompliant Code Example

Many programmers are surprised by an instance of hash code mutability that arises because of serialization. The contract for the `hashCode()` method lacks any requirement that hash codes remain consistent across different executions of an application. Similarly, when an object is serialized and subsequently deserialized, its hash code after deserialization may be inconsistent with its original hash code.

This noncompliant code example uses the `MyKey` class as the key index for the `Hashtable`. The `MyKey` class overrides `Object.equals()`, but uses the default `Object.hashCode()`. According to the Java API [API 2006] class `Hashtable` documentation:

> To successfully store and retrieve objects from a hash table, the objects used as keys must implement the `hashCode` method and the `equals` method.

This noncompliant code example follows that advice but can nevertheless fail after serialization and deserialization. Consequently, it may be impossible to retrieve the value of the object after deserialization by using the original key.

```java
class MyKey implements Serializable {
  // Does not override hashCode()
}

class HashSer {
  public static void main(String[] args)
                    throws IOException, ClassNotFoundException {
    Hashtable<MyKey,String> ht = new Hashtable<MyKey, String>();
    MyKey key = new MyKey();
    ht.put(key, "Value");
    System.out.println("Entry: " + ht.get(key));
    // Retrieve using the key, works

    // Serialize the Hashtable object
    FileOutputStream fos = new FileOutputStream("hashdata.ser");
    ObjectOutputStream oos = new ObjectOutputStream(fos);
    oos.writeObject(ht);
    oos.close();

    // Deserialize the Hashtable object
    FileInputStream fis = new FileInputStream("hashdata.ser");
    ObjectInputStream ois = new ObjectInputStream(fis);
    Hashtable<MyKey, String> ht_in =
       (Hashtable<MyKey, String>)(ois.readObject());
    ois.close();

    if (ht_in.contains("Value"))
      // Check whether the object actually exists in the hash table
      System.out.println("Value was found in deserialized object.");

    if (ht_in.get(key) == null) // Gets printed
      System.out.println(
          "Object was not found when retrieved using the key.");
  }
}
```

Compliant Solution

This compliant solution changes the type of the key value to be an `Integer` object. Consequently, key values remain consistent across multiple runs of the program, across serialization and deserialization, and also across multiple JVMs.

```
class HashSer {
  public static void main(String[] args)
                    throws IOException, ClassNotFoundException {
    Hashtable<Integer, String> ht = new Hashtable<Integer, String>();
    ht.put(new Integer(1), "Value");
    System.out.println("Entry: " + ht.get(1)); // Retrieve using the key

    // Serialize the Hashtable object
    FileOutputStream fos = new FileOutputStream("hashdata.ser");
    ObjectOutputStream oos = new ObjectOutputStream(fos);
    oos.writeObject(ht);
    oos.close();

    // Deserialize the Hashtable object
    FileInputStream fis = new FileInputStream("hashdata.ser");
    ObjectInputStream ois = new ObjectInputStream(fis);
    Hashtable<Integer, String> ht_in =
        (Hashtable<Integer, String>)(ois.readObject());
    ois.close();

    if (ht_in.contains("Value"))
      // Check whether the object actually exists in the Hashtable
      System.out.println("Value was found in deserialized object.");

    if (ht_in.get(1) == null)  // Not printed
      System.out.println(
          "Object was not found when retrieved using the key.");
  }
}
```

This problem could also have been avoided by overriding the `hashCode()` method in the `MyKey` class, though it is best to avoid serializing hash tables that are known to use implementation-defined parameters.

Risk Assessment

Failure to ensure that the keys used in a comparison operation are immutable can lead to nondeterministic behavior.

Rule	Severity	Likelihood	Remediation Cost	Priority	Level
MET11-J	low	probable	high	P2	L3

Automated Detection   Some available static analysis tools can detect instances where the `compareTo()` method reads from a nonconstant field. If the nonconstant field were modified, the value of `compareTo()` might change, which could break program invariants.

Bibliography

[API 2006]   `java.util.Interface Set<E>` and `java.util.Interface Map<K,V>`

■ MET12-J. Do not use finalizers

The garbage collector invokes object finalizer methods after it determines that the object is unreachable but before it reclaims the object's storage. Execution of the finalizer provides an opportunity to release resources such as open streams, files, and network connections that might not otherwise be released automatically through the normal action of the garbage collector.

A sufficient number of problems are associated with finalizers to restrict their use to exceptional conditions:

- There is no fixed time at which finalizers must be executed because this depends on the JVM. The only guarantee is that any finalizer method that executes will do so sometime after the associated object has become unreachable (detected during the first cycle of garbage collection) and sometime before the garbage collector reclaims the associated object's storage (during the garbage collector's second cycle). Execution of an object's finalizer may be delayed for an *arbitrarily* long time after the object becomes unreachable. Consequently, invoking time-critical functionality such as closing file handles in an object's `finalize()` method is problematic.

- The JVM may terminate without invoking the finalizer on some or all unreachable objects. Consequently, attempts to update critical persistent state from finalizer methods can fail without warning. Similarly, Java lacks any guarantee that finalizers will execute on process termination. Methods such as `System.gc()`, `System.runFinalization()`, `System.runFinalizersOnExit()`, and `Runtime.runFinalizersOnExit()` either lack such guarantees or have been deprecated because of lack of safety and potential for deadlock.

- According to the *Java Language Specification*, §12.6.2, "Finalizer Invocations Are Not Ordered" [JLS 2005]:

  > The Java programming language imposes no ordering on finalize() method calls. Finalizers [of different objects] may be called in any order, or even concurrently.
  >
  > One consequence is that slow-running finalizers can delay execution of other finalizers in the queue. Further, the lack of guaranteed ordering can lead to substantial difficulty in maintaining desired program invariants.

- Uncaught exceptions thrown during finalization are ignored. When an exception thrown in a finalizer propagates beyond the finalize() method, the process itself immediately stops and consequently fails to accomplish its sole purpose. This termination of the finalization process may or may not prevent all subsequent finalization from executing. The *Java Language Specification* fails to define this behavior, leaving it to the individual implementations.

- Coding errors that result in memory leaks can cause objects to incorrectly remain reachable; consequently, their finalizers are never invoked.

- A programmer can unintentionally resurrect an object's reference in the finalize() method. When this occurs, the garbage collector must determine yet again whether the object is free to be deallocated. Further, because the finalize() method has executed once, the garbage collector cannot invoke it a second time.

- Garbage collection usually depends on memory availability and usage rather than on the scarcity of some other particular resource. Consequently, when memory is readily available, a scarce resource may be exhausted in spite of the presence of a finalizer that could release the scarce resource if it were executed. See rules FIO04-J and TPS00-J for more details on handling scarce resources correctly.

- It is a common myth that finalizers aid garbage collection. On the contrary, they increase garbage-collection time and introduce space overheads. Finalizers interfere with the operation of modern generational garbage collectors by extending the lifetimes of many objects. Incorrectly programmed finalizers could also attempt to finalize reachable objects, which is always counterproductive and can violate program invariants.

- Use of finalizers can introduce synchronization issues even when the remainder of the program is single-threaded. The finalize() methods are invoked by the garbage collector from one or more threads of its choice; these threads are typically distinct from the main() thread, although this property is not guaranteed. When a finalizer is necessary, any required cleanup data structures must be protected from concurrent access. See the JavaOne presentation by Hans J. Boehm [Boehm 2005] for additional information.

■ Use of locks or other synchronization-based mechanisms within a finalizer can cause deadlock or starvation. This possibility arises because neither the invocation order nor the specific executing thread or threads for finalizers can be guaranteed or controlled.

Because of these problems, finalizers must not be used in new classes.

Noncompliant Code Example (Superclass `finalizer()`)

Superclasses that use finalizers impose additional constraints on their extending classes. Consider an example from JDK 1.5 and earlier. The following noncompliant code example allocates a 16MB buffer used to back a Swing `JFrame` object. Although the `JFrame` APIs lack `finalize()` methods, `JFrame` extends `AWT.Frame`, which does have a `finalize()` method. When a `MyFrame` object becomes unreachable, the garbage collector cannot reclaim the storage for the byte buffer because code in the inherited `finalize()` method might refer to it. Consequently, the byte buffer must persist *at least* until the inherited `finalize()` method for class `MyFrame` completes its execution and cannot be reclaimed until the following garbage-collection cycle.

```
class MyFrame extends JFrame {
  private byte[] buffer = new byte[16 * 1024 * 1024];
  // persists for at least two GC cycles
}
```

Compliant Solution (Superclass `finalizer()`)

When a superclass defines a `finalize()` method, make sure to decouple the objects that can be immediately garbage-collected from those that must depend on the finalizer. This compliant solution ensures that the `buffer` can be reclaimed as soon as the object becomes unreachable.

```
class MyFrame {
  private JFrame frame;
  private byte[] buffer = new byte[16 * 1024 * 1024]; // now decoupled
}
```

Noncompliant Code Example (`System.runFinalizersOnExit()`)

This noncompliant code example uses the `System.runFinalizersOnExit()` method to simulate a garbage-collection run. Note that this method is deprecated because of thread-safety issues; see rule MET02-J.

According to the Java API [API 2006] class `System`, `runFinalizersOnExit()` method documentation:

> Enable or disable finalization on exit; doing so specifies that the finalizers of all objects that have finalizers that have not yet been automatically invoked are to be run before the Java runtime exits. By default, finalization on exit is disabled.

The class `SubClass` overrides the `protected finalize()` method and performs cleanup activities. Subsequently, it calls `super.finalize()` to make sure its superclass is also finalized. The unsuspecting `BaseClass` calls the `doLogic()` method, which happens to be overridden in the `SubClass`. This resurrects a reference to `SubClass` that not only prevents it from being garbage-collected but also prevents it from calling its finalizer to close new resources that may have been allocated by the called method. As detailed in rule MET05-J, if the subclass's finalizer has terminated key resources, invoking its methods from the superclass might result in the observation of object in an inconsistent state. In some cases, this can result in a `NullPointerException`.

```java
class BaseClass {
  protected void finalize() throws Throwable {
    System.out.println("Superclass finalize!");
    doLogic();
  }

  public void doLogic() throws Throwable {
    System.out.println("This is super-class!");
  }
}

class SubClass extends BaseClass {
  private Date d; // mutable instance field

  protected SubClass() {
    d = new Date();
  }

  protected void finalize() throws Throwable {
    System.out.println("Subclass finalize!");
    try {
```

```
      // cleanup resources
      d = null;
    } finally {
      super.finalize();  // Call BaseClass's finalizer
    }
  }

  public void doLogic() throws Throwable {
    // any resource allocations made here will persist

    // inconsistent object state
    System.out.println(
        "This is sub-class! The date object is: " + d);
    // 'd' is already null
  }
}

public class BadUse {
  public static void main(String[] args) {
    try {
      BaseClass bc = new SubClass();
      // Artificially simulate finalization (do not do this)
      System.runFinalizersOnExit(true);
    } catch (Throwable t) {
      // handle error
    }
  }
}
```

This code outputs:

```
Subclass finalize!
Superclass finalize!
This is sub-class! The date object is: null
```

Compliant Solution

Joshua Bloch [Bloch 2008] suggests implementing a stop() method explicitly such that it leaves the class in an unusable state beyond its lifetime. A private field within the class can signal whether the class is unusable. All the class methods must check this field prior to operating on the class. This is akin to the "initialized flag"–compliant solution discussed in rule OBJ11-J. As always, a good place to call the termination logic is in the finally block.

Exceptions

MET12-EX0: Finalizers may be used when working with native code because the garbage collector cannot reclaim memory used by code written in another language and because the lifetime of the object is often unknown. Again, the native process must not perform any critical jobs that require immediate resource deallocation.

Any subclass that overrides finalize() must explicitly invoke the method for its superclass as well. There is no automatic *chaining* of finalizers. The correct way to handle this is as follows.

```java
protected void finalize() throws Throwable {
  try {
    //...
  } finally {
    super.finalize();
  }
}
```

A more expensive solution is to declare an anonymous class so that the finalize() method is guaranteed to run for the superclass. This solution is applicable to public nonfinal classes. "The finalizer guardian object forces super.finalize to be called if a subclass overrides finalize() and does not explicitly call super.finalize" [JLS 2005].

```java
public class Foo {
  // The finalizeGuardian object finalizes the outer Foo object
  private final Object finalizerGuardian = new Object() {
    protected void finalize() throws Throwable {
      // Finalize outer Foo object
    }
  };
  //...
}
```

The ordering problem can be dangerous when dealing with native code. For example, if object A references object B (either directly or reflectively) and the latter gets finalized first, A's finalizer may end up dereferencing dangling native pointers. To impose an explicit ordering on finalizers, make sure that B remains reachable until A's finalizer has concluded. This can be achieved by adding a reference to B in some global state variable and removing it when A's finalizer executes. An alternative is to use the `java.lang.ref` references.

MET12-EX1: A class may use an empty final finalizer to prevent a finalizer attack, as specified in rule OBJ11-J.

Risk Assessment

Improper use of finalizers can result in resurrection of garbage-collection-ready objects and result in denial-of-service vulnerabilities.

Rule	Severity	Likelihood	Remediation Cost	Priority	Level
MET12-J	medium	probable	medium	P8	L2

Related Vulnerabilities   AXIS2-4163 describes a vulnerability in the `finalize()` method in the Axis web services framework. The finalizer incorrectly calls `super.finalize()` before doing its own cleanup. This leads to errors in `GlassFish` when the garbage collector runs.

Related Guidelines

MITRE CWE	CWE-586. Explicit call to `Finalize()`
	CWE-583. `finalize()` method declared public
	CWE-568. `finalize()` method without `super.finalize()`

Bibliography

[API 2006]	`finalize()`
[Bloch 2008]	Item 7. Avoid finalizers
[Boehm 2005]	
[Coomes 2007]	"Sneaky" Memory Retention
[Darwin 2004]	Section 9.5, The Finalize Method
[Flanagan 2005]	Section 3.3, Destroying and Finalizing Objects
[JLS 2005]	§12.6, Finalization of Class Instances

Chapter 8

Exceptional Behavior (ERR)

■ Rules

■ Risk Assessment Summary

Rule	Severity	Likelihood	Remediation Cost	Priority	Level
ERR00-J	low	probable	medium	P4	L3
ERR01-J	medium	probable	high	P4	L3

(continued)

Rule	Severity	Likelihood	Remediation Cost	Priority	Level
ERR02-J	medium	likely	high	P6	L2
ERR03-J	low	probable	high	P2	L3
ERR04-J	low	probable	medium	P4	L3
ERR05-J	low	unlikely	medium	P2	L3
ERR06-J	low	unlikely	high	P1	L3
ERR07-J	low	likely	medium	P6	L2
ERR08-J	medium	likely	medium	P12	L1
ERR09-J	low	unlikely	medium	P2	L3

■ ERR00-J. Do not suppress or ignore checked exceptions

Programmers often suppress checked exceptions by catching exceptions with an empty or trivial `catch` block. Each `catch` block must ensure that the program continues only with valid invariants. Consequently, the `catch` block must either recover from the exceptional condition, rethrow the exception to allow the next nearest enclosing `catch` clause of a `try` statement to recover, or throw an exception that is appropriate to the context of the `catch` block.

Exceptions disrupt the expected control flow of the application. For example, no part of any expression or statement that occurs in the `try` block after the point from which the exception is thrown is evaluated. Consequently, exceptions must be handled appropriately. Many reasons for suppressing exceptions are invalid. For example, when the client cannot be expected to recover from the underlying problem, it is good practice to allow the exception to propagate outwards rather than to catch and suppress the exception.

Noncompliant Code Example

This noncompliant code example simply prints the exception's stack trace.

```
try {
  //...
} catch (IOException ioe) {
  ioe.printStacktrace();
}
```

Printing the exception's stack trace can be useful for debugging purposes, but the resulting program execution is equivalent to suppressing the exception. Printing the stack trace can also leak information about the structure and state of the process to an attacker. (See rule ERR01-J for more information.) Note that even though this noncompliant code example reacts to the exception by printing out a stack trace, it then proceeds as though the exception were not thrown. That is, the behavior of the application is unaffected by the exception being thrown, except that any expressions or statements that occur in the `try` block after the point from which the exception is thrown are not evaluated.

Compliant Solution (Interactive)

This compliant solution handles a `FileNotFoundException` by requesting that the user specify another file name.

```
boolean volatile validFlag = false;
do {
  try {
    // If requested file does not exist, throws FileNotFoundException
    // If requested file exists, sets validFlag to true
    validFlag = true;
  } catch (FileNotFoundException e) {
    // Ask the user for a different file name
  }
} while (validFlag != true);
// Use the file
```

To comply with rule ERR01-J, the user should only be allowed to access files in a user-specific directory. This prevents any other `IOException` that escapes the loop from leaking sensitive file system information.

Compliant Solution (Exception Reporter)

Proper reporting of exceptional conditions is context-dependent. For example, GUI applications should report the exception in a graphical manner, such as in an error dialog box. Most library classes should be able to objectively determine how an exception should be reported to preserve modularity; they cannot rely on `System.err`, on any particular logger, or on the availability of the windowing environment. As a result, library classes that wish to report exceptions should specify the API they use to report exceptions. This compliant solution specifies both an interface for reporting exceptions, which exports the `report()` method, and a default exception reporter class that the library can use. The exception reporter can be overridden by subclasses.

```java
public interface Reporter {
  public void report(Throwable t);
}

public class ExceptionReporter {

  // Exception reporter that prints the exception
  // to the console (used as default)
  private static final Reporter PrintException = new Reporter() {
    public void report(Throwable t) {
      System.err.println(t.toString());
    }
  };

  // Stores the default reporter.
  // The default reporter can be changed by the user.
  private static Reporter Default = PrintException;

  // Helps change the default reporter back to
  // PrintException in the future
  public static Reporter getPrintException() {
    return PrintException;
  }

  public static Reporter getExceptionReporter() {
    return Default;
  }

  // May throw a SecurityException (which is unchecked)
  public static void setExceptionReporter(Reporter reporter) {
    // Custom permission
    ExceptionReporterPermission perm = new
    ExceptionReporterPermission("exc.reporter");
    SecurityManager sm = System.getSecurityManager();
    if (sm != null) {
    // Check whether the caller has appropriate permissions
    sm.checkPermission(perm);
    }
    // Change the default exception reporter
    Default = reporter;
  }
}
```

The `setExceptionReporter()` method prevents hostile code from maliciously installing a more verbose reporter that leaks sensitive information or that directs exception reports to an inappropriate location, such as the attacker's computer, by limiting attempts to change the exception reporter to callers that have the custom permission `Exception-ReporterPermission` with target `exc.reporter`.

The library may subsequently use the exception reporter in `catch` clauses:

```java
try {
  // ...
} catch (IOException warning) {
  ExceptionReporter.getExceptionReporter().report(warning);
  // Recover from the exception...
}
```

Any client code that possesses the required permissions can override the `Exception-Reporter` with a handler that logs the error or provides a dialog box, or both. For example, a GUI client using Swing may require exceptions to be reported using a dialog box:

```java
ExceptionReporter.setExceptionReporter(new ExceptionReporter() {
  public void report(Throwable exception) {
    JOptionPane.showMessageDialog(frame,
                                  exception.toString,
                                  exception.getClass().getName(),
                                  JOptionPane.ERROR_MESSAGE);
  });
}
```

Compliant Solution (Subclass Exception Reporter and Filter Sensitive Exceptions)

Sometimes exceptions must be hidden from the user for security reasons (see rule ERR01-J for more information). In such cases, one acceptable approach is to subclass the `ExceptionReporter` class and add a `filter()` method in addition to overriding the default `report()` method.

```java
class MyExceptionReporter extends ExceptionReporter {
    private static final Logger logger =
        Logger.getLogger("com.organization.Log");
```

```java
public static void report(Throwable t) {
  try {
    final Throwable filteredException =
        (t instanceof NonSensitiveException_1) ? t : filter(t);
  } finally {
    // Do any necessary user reporting
    // (show dialog box or send to console)
    if (filteredException instanceof NonSensitiveCommonException) {
      logger.log(Level.FINEST, "Loggable exception occurred", t);
    }
  }
}

public static Exception filter(Throwable t) {
  if (t instanceof SensitiveForLoggingException_1) {
    // Do not log sensitive information (blacklist)
    return SensitiveCommonException();
  }
  // ...
  // Return for reporting to the user
  return new NonSensitiveCommonException();
}
}
```

The `report()` method accepts a `Throwable` instance and consequently handles all errors, checked exceptions, and unchecked exceptions. The filtering mechanism is based on a *whitelisting* approach wherein only nonsensitive exceptions are propagated to the user. Exceptions that are forbidden to appear in a log file can be filtered in the same fashion (see rule FIO13-J for more information). This approach provides the benefits of exception chaining by reporting exceptions tailored to the abstraction while also logging the low-level cause for future failure analysis [Bloch 2008].

Noncompliant Code Example

If a thread is interrupted while sleeping or waiting, it causes a `java.lang.Interrupted-Exception` to be thrown. However, the `run()` method of interface `Runnable` cannot throw a checked exception and must handle `InterruptedException`. This noncompliant code example catches and suppresses `InterruptedException`.

```
class Foo implements Runnable {
  public void run() {
    try {
      Thread.sleep(1000);
    } catch (InterruptedException e) {
      // Ignore
    }
  }
}
```

This code prevents callers of the run() method from determining that an interrupted exception occurred. Consequently, the caller methods such as Thread.start() cannot act on the exception [Goetz 2006a]. Likewise, if this code were called in its own thread, it would prevent the calling thread from knowing that the thread was interrupted.

Compliant Solution

This compliant solution catches the InterruptedException and restores the interrupted status by calling the interrupt() method on the current thread.

```
class Foo implements Runnable {
  public void run() {
    try {
      Thread.sleep(1000);
    } catch (InterruptedException e) {
      Thread.currentThread().interrupt(); // Reset interrupted status
    }
  }
}
```

Consequently, calling methods (or code from a calling thread) can determine that an interrupt was issued [Goetz 2006a].

Exceptions

ERROO-EXO: Exceptions that occur during the freeing of a resource may be suppressed in those cases where failure to free the resource cannot affect future program behavior. Examples of freeing resources include closing files, network sockets, shutting down threads, and so forth. Such resources are often freed in catch or finally blocks and never reused during subsequent execution. Consequently, the exception cannot influence future program behavior through any avenue other than resource exhaustion. When resource exhaustion is adequately handled, it is sufficient to sanitize and log the exception for future improvement; additional error handling is unnecessary in this case.

ERR00-EX1: When recovery from an exceptional condition is impossible at a particular abstraction level, code at that level must not handle that exceptional condition. In such cases, an appropriate exception must be thrown so that higher level code can catch the exceptional condition and can attempt recovery. The most common implementation for this case is to omit a `catch` block and allow the exception to propagate normally:

```
// When recovery is possible at higher levels
private void doSomething() throws FileNotFoundException {
  // Requested file does not exist; throws FileNotFoundException
  // Higher level code can handle it by displaying a
  // dialog box and asking the user for the file name
}
```

Some APIs may limit the permissible exceptions thrown by particular methods. In such cases, it may be necessary to catch an exception and either wrap it in a permitted exception or translate it to one of the permitted exceptions.

```
public void myMethod() throws MyProgramException {
  // ...
  try {
    // Requested file does not exist
    // User is unable to supply the file name
  } catch (FileNotFoundException e) {
    throw new MyProgramException(e);
  }
  // ...
}
```

Alternatively, when higher level code is also unable to recover from a particular exception, the checked exception may be wrapped in an unchecked exception and rethrown.

ERR00-EX2: An `InterruptedException` may be caught and suppressed when extending class `Thread` [Goetz 2006a]. An interruption request may also be suppressed by code that implements a thread's interruption policy [Goetz 2006a, p. 143].

Risk Assessment

Ignoring or suppressing exceptions can result in inconsistent program state.

Rule	Severity	Likelihood	Remediation Cost	Priority	Level
ERR00-J	low	probable	medium	P4	L3

Automated Detection Detection of suppressed exceptions is straightforward. Sound determination of which specific cases represent violations of this rule and which represent permitted exceptions to the rule is infeasible. Heuristic approaches may be effective.

Related Vulnerabilities AMQ-1272[1] describes a vulnerability in the ActiveMQ service. When ActiveMQ receives an invalid username and password from a Stomp client, a security exception is generated but is subsequently ignored, leaving the client connected with full and unrestricted access to ActiveMQ.

Related Guidelines

MITRE CWE   CWE-390. Detection of error condition without action

Bibliography

[Bloch 2008]   Item 65. Don't ignore exceptions; Item 62. Document all exceptions thrown
                  by each method

[Goetz 2006a]   5.4, Blocking and Interruptible Methods

[JLS 2005]   Chapter 11, Exceptions

■ ERR01-J. Do not allow exceptions to expose sensitive information

Failure to filter sensitive information when propagating exceptions often results in information leaks that can assist an attacker's efforts to develop further exploits. An attacker may craft input arguments to expose internal structures and mechanisms of the application. Both the exception message text and the type of an exception can leak information. For example, the `FileNotFoundException` message reveals information about the file system layout, and the exception type reveals the absence of the requested file.

This rule applies to server-side applications as well as to clients. Attackers can glean sensitive information not only from vulnerable web servers but also from victims who use vulnerable web browsers. In 2004, Schönefeld discovered an exploit for the Opera v7.54

---

1. https://issues.apache.org/jira/browse/AMQ-1272

web browser in which an attacker could use the `sun.security.krb5.Credentials` class in an applet as an oracle to "retrieve the name of the currently logged in user and parse his home directory from the information which is provided by the thrown `java.security.AccessControlException`" [Schönefeld 2004].

All exceptions reveal information that can assist an attacker's efforts to carry out a denial of service (DoS) against the system. Consequently, programs must filter both exception messages and exception types that can propagate across trust boundaries. The following table lists several problematic exceptions:

Exception Name	Description of Information Leak or Threat
`java.io.FileNotFoundException`	Underlying file system structure, user name enumeration
`java.sql.SQLException`	Database structure, user name enumeration
`java.net.BindException`	Enumeration of open ports when untrusted client can choose server port
`java.util.ConcurrentModification-Exception`	May provide information about thread-unsafe code
`javax.naming.InsufficientResources-Exception`	Insufficient server resources (may aid DoS)
`java.util.MissingResourceException`	Resource enumeration
`java.util.jar.JarException`	Underlying file system structure
`java.security.acl.NotOwnerException`	Owner enumeration
`java.lang.OutOfMemoryError`	DoS
`java.lang.StackOverflowError`	DoS

Printing the stack trace can also result in unintentionally leaking information about the structure and state of the process to an attacker. When a Java program that is run within a console terminates because of an uncaught exception, the exception's message and stack trace are displayed on the console; the stack trace may itself leak sensitive information about the program's internal structure. Consequently, command-line programs must never abort because of an uncaught exception.

Noncompliant Code Example (Leaks from Exception Message and Type)

In this noncompliant code example, the program must read a file supplied by the user, but the contents and layout of the file system are sensitive. The program accepts a file name as an input argument but fails to prevent any resulting exceptions from being presented to the user.

```
class ExceptionExample {
  public static void main(String[] args) throws FileNotFoundException {
    // Linux stores a user's home directory path in
    // the environment variable $HOME, Windows in %APPDATA%
    FileInputStream fis =
        new FileInputStream(System.getenv("APPDATA") + args[0]);
  }
}
```

When a requested file is absent, the `FileInputStream` constructor throws a `FileNotFoundException`, allowing an attacker to reconstruct the underlying file system by repeatedly passing fictitious path names to the program.

Noncompliant Code Example (Wrapping and Rethrowing Sensitive Exception)

This noncompliant code example logs the exception and then wraps it in a more general exception before rethrowing it.

```
try {
  FileInputStream fis =
      new FileInputStream(System.getenv("APPDATA") + args[0]);
} catch (FileNotFoundException e) {
  // Log the exception
  throw new IOException("Unable to retrieve file", e);
}
```

Even when the logged exception is not accessible to the user, the original exception is still informative and can be used by an attacker to discover sensitive information about the file system layout.

Note that this example also violates rule FIO04-J, as it fails to close the input stream in a `finally` block. Subsequent code examples also omit this `finally` block for brevity.

Noncompliant Code Example (Sanitized Exception)

This noncompliant code example logs the exception and throws a custom exception that does not wrap the `FileNotFoundException`.

```
class SecurityIOException extends IOException {/* ... */};

try {
  FileInputStream fis =
      new FileInputStream(System.getenv("APPDATA") + args[0]);
} catch (FileNotFoundException e) {
  // Log the exception
  throw new SecurityIOException();
}
```

While this exception is less likely than the previous noncompliant code examples to leak useful information, it still reveals that the specified file cannot be read. More specifically, the program reacts differently to nonexistent file paths than it does to valid ones, and an attacker can still infer sensitive information about the file system from this program's behavior. Failure to restrict user input leaves the system vulnerable to a brute-force attack in which the attacker discovers valid file names by issuing queries that collectively cover the space of possible file names. File names that cause the program to return the sanitized exception indicate nonexistent files, while file names that do not return exceptions reveal existing files.

Compliant Solution (Security Policy)

This compliant solution implements the policy that only files that live in c:\homepath may be opened by the user and that the user is not allowed to discover anything about files outside this directory. The solution issues a terse error message when the file cannot be opened or the file does not live in the proper directory. Any information about files outside c:\homepath is concealed.

The compliant solution also uses the File.getCanonicalFile() method to canonicalize the file to simplify subsequent path name comparisons (see rule IDS02-J).

```
class ExceptionExample {
  public static void main(String[] args) {

    File file = null;
    try {
      file = new File(System.getenv("APPDATA") +
            args[0]).getCanonicalFile();
      if (!file.getPath().startsWith("c:\\homepath")) {
        System.out.println("Invalid file");
        return;
      }
```

```
      } catch (IOException x) {
        System.out.println("Invalid file");
        return;
      }

      try {
        FileInputStream fis = new FileInputStream(file);
      } catch (FileNotFoundException x) {
        System.out.println("Invalid file");
        return;
      }
    }
  }
```

Compliant Solution (Restricted Input)

This compliant solution operates under the policy that only c:\homepath\file1 and c:\homepath\file2 are permitted to be opened by the user.

It also catches Throwable, as permitted by exception ERR08-EX0. It uses the MyExceptionReporter class described in rule ERR00-J, which filters sensitive information from any resulting exceptions.

```
class ExceptionExample {
  public static void main(String[] args) {
    FileInputStream fis = null;
    try {
      switch(Integer.valueOf(args[0])) {
        case 1:
          fis = new FileInputStream("c:\\homepath\\file1");
          break;
        case 2:
          fis = new FileInputStream("c:\\homepath\\file2");
          break;
        //...
        default:
          System.out.println("Invalid option");
          break;
      }
    } catch (Throwable t) {
      MyExceptionReporter.report(t); // Sanitize
    }
  }
}
```

Compliant solutions must ensure that security exceptions such as `java.security.` `AccessControlException` and `java.lang.SecurityException` continue to be logged and sanitized appropriately. See rule ERR02-J for additional information. The `MyException-Reporter` class from rule ERR00-J demonstrates an acceptable approach for this logging and sanitization.

For scalability, the switch statement should be replaced with some sort of mapping from integers to valid file names or at least an enum type representing valid files.

Risk Assessment

Exceptions may inadvertently reveal sensitive information unless care is taken to limit the information disclosure.

Rule	Severity	Likelihood	Remediation Cost	Priority	Level
ERR01-J	medium	probable	high	P4	L3

Related Vulnerabilities CVE-2009-2897 describes several cross-site scripting (XSS) vulnerabilities in several versions of SpringSource Hyperic HQ. These vulnerabilities allow remote attackers to inject arbitrary web script or HTML via invalid values for numerical parameters. They are demonstrated by an uncaught `java.lang.NumberFormatException` exception resulting from entering several invalid numeric parameters to the web interface.

Related Guidelines

C++ Secure Coding Standard	ERR12-CPP. Do not allow exceptions to transmit sensitive information
MITRE CWE	CWE-209. Information exposure through an error message
	CWE-600. Uncaught exception in servlet
	CWE-497. Exposure of system data to an unauthorized control sphere

Bibliography

[Gong 2003]	9.1, Security Exceptions

■ ERR02-J. Prevent exceptions while logging data

Exceptions that are thrown while logging is in progress can prevent successful logging unless special care is taken. Failure to account for exceptions during the logging process can cause security vulnerabilities, such as allowing an attacker to conceal critical security exceptions by preventing them from being logged. Consequently, programs must ensure that data logging continues to operate correctly even when exceptions are thrown during the logging process.

Noncompliant Code Example

This noncompliant code example writes a critical security exception to the standard error stream.

```
try {
  // ...
} catch (SecurityException se) {
  System.err.println(e);
  // Recover from exception
}
```

Writing such exceptions to the standard error stream is inadequate for logging purposes. First, the standard error stream may be exhausted or closed, preventing recording of subsequent exceptions. Second, the trust level of the standard error stream may be insufficient for recording certain security-critical exceptions or errors without leaking sensitive information. If an I/O error were to occur while writing the security exception, the `catch` block would throw an `IOException` and the critical security exception would be lost. Finally, an attacker may disguise the exception so that it occurs with several other innocuous exceptions.

Similarly, using `Console.printf()`, `System.out.print*()`, or `Throwable.print-StackTrace()` to output a security exception also constitutes a violation of this rule.

Compliant Solution

This compliant solution uses `java.util.logging.Logger`, the default logging API provided by JDK 1.4 and later. Use of other compliant logging mechanisms, such as log4j, is also permitted.

```
try {
  // ...
} catch(SecurityException se) {
  logger.log(Level.SEVERE, se);
  // Recover from exception
}
```

Typically, only one logger is required for the entire program.

Risk Assessment

Exceptions thrown during data logging can cause loss of data and can conceal security problems.

Rule	Severity	Likelihood	Remediation Cost	Priority	Level
ERR02-J	medium	likely	high	P6	L2

Related Vulnerabilities HARMONY-5981[2] describes a vulnerability in the HARMONY implementation of Java. In this implementation, the `FileHandler` class can receive log messages, but if one thread closes the associated file, a second thread will throw an exception when it tries to log a message.

Bibliography

[API 2006]	Class Logger
[JLS 2005]	Chapter 11, Exceptions
[Ware 2008]	

■ ERR03-J. Restore prior object state on method failure

Objects in general should—and security-critical objects *must*—be maintained in a consistent state even when exceptional conditions arise. Common techniques for maintaining object consistency include

- Input validation (on method arguments, for example)
- Reordering logic so that code that can result in the exceptional condition executes before the object is modified
- Using rollbacks in the event of failure
- Performing required operations on a temporary copy of the object and committing changes to the original object only after their successful completion
- Avoiding the need to modify the object at all

Noncompliant Code Example

This noncompliant code example shows a `Dimensions` class that contains three internal attributes, the `length`, `width`, and `height` of a rectangular box. The `getVolumePackage()`

2. https://issues.apache.org/jira/browse/HARMONY-5981

method is designed to return the total volume required to hold the box after accounting for packaging material, which adds 2 units to the dimensions of each side. Nonpositive values of the dimensions of the box (exclusive of packaging material) are rejected during input validation. No dimension can be larger than 10. Also, the weight of the object is passed in as an argument and cannot be more than 20 units.

Consider the case where the weight is more than 20 units. This causes an Illegal-ArgumentException, which is intercepted by the custom error reporter. While the logic restores the object's original state in the absence of this exception, the rollback code fails to execute in the event of an exception. Consequently, subsequent invocations of getVolumePackage() produce incorrect results.

```
class Dimensions {
  private int length;
  private int width;
  private int height;
  static public final int PADDING = 2;
  static public final int MAX_DIMENSION = 10;

  public Dimensions(int length, int width, int height) {
    this.length = length;
    this.width = width;
    this.height = height;
  }

  protected int getVolumePackage(int weight) {
    length += PADDING;
    width  += PADDING;
    height += PADDING;
    try {
      if (length <= PADDING || width <= PADDING
          || height <= PADDING || length > MAX_DIMENSION + PADDING
          || width > MAX_DIMENSION + PADDING ||
        height > MAX_DIMENSION + PADDING || weight <= 0 ||
        weight > 20) {
        throw new IllegalArgumentException();
      }
      // 12 * 12 * 12 = 1728
      int volume = length * width * height;
      // Revert
      length -= PADDING; width -= PADDING; height -= PADDING;
      return volume;
    } catch (Throwable t) {
      MyExceptionReporter mer = new MyExceptionReporter();
      mer.report(t); // Sanitize
      return -1; // Non-positive error code
    }
  }
}
```

```
public static void main(String[] args) {
  Dimensions d = new Dimensions(10, 10, 10);
  // Prints -1 (error)
  System.out.println(d.getVolumePackage(21));
  // Prints 2744 instead of 1728
  System.out.println(d.getVolumePackage(19));
  }
}
```

The `catch` clause is permitted by exception ERR00-EX0 because it serves as a general filter passing exceptions to the `MyExceptionReporter` class, which is dedicated to safely reporting exceptions as recommended by rule ERR00-J. While this code only throws `IllegalArgumentException`, the catch clause is general enough to handle any exception in case the `try` block should be modified to throw other exceptions.

Compliant Solution (Rollback)

This compliant solution replaces the `catch` block in the `getVolumePackage()` method with code that restores prior object state in the event of an exception.

```
// ...
} catch (Throwable t) {
  MyExceptionReporter mer = new MyExceptionReporter();
  // Sanitize
  mer.report(t);
  // Revert
  length -= PADDING; width -= PADDING; height -= PADDING;
  return -1;
}
```

Compliant Solution (`finally` Clause)

This compliant solution uses a `finally` clause to perform rollback, guaranteeing that rollback occurs whether or not an error occurs.

```
protected int getVolumePackage(int weight) {
  length += PADDING;
  width  += PADDING;
  height += PADDING;
  try {
   if (length <= PADDING || width <= PADDING || height <= PADDING ||
     length > MAX_DIMENSION + PADDING ||
```

```
      width > MAX_DIMENSION + PADDING ||
      height > MAX_DIMENSION + PADDING ||
      weight <= 0 || weight > 20) {
      throw new IllegalArgumentException();
    }

    int volume = length * width * height; // 12 * 12 * 12 = 1728
    return volume;
  } catch (Throwable t) {
    MyExceptionReporter mer = new MyExceptionReporter();
    mer.report(t); // Sanitize
    return -1; // Non-positive error code
  } finally {
    // Revert
    length -= PADDING; width -= PADDING; height -= PADDING;
  }
}
```

Compliant Solution (Input Validation)

This compliant solution improves on the previous solution by performing input validation before modifying the state of the object. Note that the try block contains only those statements that could throw the exception; all others have been moved outside the try block.

```
protected int getVolumePackage(int weight) {
  try {
    if (length <= 0 || width <= 0 || height <= 0 ||
        length > MAX_DIMENSION || width > MAX_DIMENSION ||
        height > MAX_DIMENSION ||
        weight <= 0 || weight > 20) {
      throw new IllegalArgumentException(); // Validate first
    }
  } catch (Throwable t) {
    MyExceptionReporter mer = new MyExceptionReporter();
    mer.report(t); // Sanitize
    return -1;
  }

  length += PADDING;
  width  += PADDING;
  height += PADDING;

  int volume = length * width * height;
  length -= PADDING; width -= PADDING; height -= PADDING;
  return volume;
}
```

Compliant Solution (Unmodified Object)

This compliant solution avoids the need to modify the object. The object's state cannot be made inconsistent, and rollback is consequently unnecessary. This approach is preferred to solutions that modify the object but may be infeasible for complex code.

```
protected int getVolumePackage(int weight) {
  try {
    if (length <= 0 || width <= 0 || height <= 0 ||
        length > MAX_DIMENSION || width > MAX_DIMENSION ||
        height > MAX_DIMENSION || weight <= 0 || weight > 20) {
      throw new IllegalArgumentException(); // Validate first
    }
  } catch (Throwable t) {
    MyExceptionReporter mer = new MyExceptionReporter();
    mer.report(t); // Sanitize
    return -1;
  }

  int volume = (length + PADDING) * (width + PADDING) *
               (height + PADDING);
  return volume;
}
```

Risk Assessment

Failure to restore prior object state on method failure can leave the object in an inconsistent state and can violate required state invariants.

Rule	Severity	Likelihood	Remediation Cost	Priority	Level
ERR03-J	low	probable	high	P2	L3

Related Vulnerabilities CVE-2008-0002 describes a vulnerability in several versions of Apache Tomcat. If an exception occurs during parameter processing, the program can be left in the context of the wrong request, which might allow remote attackers to obtain sensitive information. An exception can be triggered by disconnecting from Tomcat during this processing.

Related Guidelines

MITRE CWE   CWE-460. Improper cleanup on thrown exception

Bibliography

[Bloch 2008]   Item 64. Strive for failure atomicity

■ ERR04-J. Do not exit abruptly from a `finally` block

Never use `return`, `break`, `continue`, or `throw` statements within a `finally` block. When program execution enters a `try` block that has a `finally` block, the `finally` block always executes, regardless of whether the `try` block (or any associated `catch` blocks) executes to completion. Statements that cause the `finally` block to terminate abruptly also cause the `try` block to terminate abruptly and consequently suppress any exception thrown from the `try` or `catch` blocks [JLS 2005].

Noncompliant Code Example

In this noncompliant code example, the `finally` block completes abruptly because of a `return` statement in the block.

```
class TryFinally {
  private static boolean doLogic() {
    try {
      throw new IllegalStateException();
    } finally {
      System.out.println("logic done");
      return true;
    }
  }
}
```

The `IllegalStateException` is suppressed by the abrupt termination of the `finally` block caused by the `return` statement.

Compliant Solution

This compliant solution removes the `return` statement from the `finally` block.

```
class TryFinally {
  private static boolean doLogic() {
    try {
      throw new IllegalStateException();
    } finally {
      System.out.println("logic done");
    }
    // Any return statements must go here;
    // applicable only when exception is thrown conditionally
  }
}
```

Exceptions

ERR04-EX0: Control flow statements whose destination is within the `finally` block are perfectly acceptable.

For example, the following code does not violate this rule, because the `break` statement exits the `while` loop but not the `finally` block.

```
class TryFinally {
  private static boolean doLogic() {
    try {
      throw new IllegalStateException();
    } finally {
      int c;
      try {
        while ((c = input.read()) != -1) {
          if (c > 128) {
            break;
          }
        }
      } catch (IOException x) {
        // forward to handler
      }
      System.out.println("logic done");
    }
    // Any return statements must go here;
    // applicable only when exception is thrown conditionally
  }
}
```

Risk Assessment

Exiting abruptly from a `finally` block masks any exceptions thrown inside the associated try and catch blocks.

Rule	Severity	Likelihood	Remediation Cost	Priority	Level
ERR04-J	low	probable	medium	P4	L3

Related Guidelines

MITRE CWE	CWE-459. Incomplete cleanup
	CWE-584. Return inside finally block

Bibliography

[Bloch 2005a]   Puzzle 36. Indecision

[Chess 2007]   8.2, Managing Exceptions, "The Vanishing Exception"

[JLS 2005]   §14.20.2, Execution of try-catch-finally

■ ERR05-J. Do not let checked exceptions escape from a `finally` block

Methods invoked from within a `finally` block can throw an exception. Failure to catch and handle such exceptions results in the abrupt termination of the entire `try` block. This causes any exception thrown in the `try` block to be lost, preventing any possible recovery method from handling that specific problem. Additionally, the transfer of control associated with the exception may prevent execution of any expressions or statements that occur after the point in the `finally` block from which the exception is thrown. Consequently, programs must appropriately handle checked exceptions that are thrown from within a `finally` block.

Allowing checked exceptions to escape a `finally` block also violates rule ERR04-J.

Noncompliant Code Example

This noncompliant code example contains a `finally` block that closes the `reader` object. The programmer incorrectly assumes that the statements in the `finally` block cannot throw exceptions and consequently fails to appropriately handle any exception that may arise.

```java
public class Operation {
  public static void doOperation(String some_file) {
    // ... code to check or set character encoding ...
    try {
      BufferedReader reader =
          new BufferedReader(new FileReader(some_file));
      try {
        // Do operations
      } finally {
        reader.close();
        // ... Other cleanup code ...
      }
    } catch (IOException x) {
      // Forward to handler
    }
  }
}
```

The close() method can throw an IOException, which, if thrown, would prevent execution of any subsequent cleanup statements. The compiler correctly fails to diagnose this problem because any IOException would be caught by the outer catch block. Also, an exception thrown from the close() operation can mask any exception that gets thrown during execution of the Do operations block, preventing proper recovery.

Compliant Solution (Handle Exceptions in finally Block)

This compliant solution encloses the close() method invocation in a try-catch block of its own within the finally block. Consequently, the potential IOException can be handled without allowing it to propagate further.

```java
public class Operation {
  public static void doOperation(String some_file) {
    // ... code to check or set character encoding ...
    try {
      BufferedReader reader =
        new BufferedReader(new FileReader(some_file));
      try {
        // Do operations
      } finally {
        try {
          reader.close();
        } catch (IOException ie) {
          // Forward to handler
        }
        // ... Other clean-up code ...
      }
    } catch (IOException x) {
      // Forward to handler
    }
  }
}
```

Compliant Solution (Java 1.7: try-with-resources)

Java 1.7 introduced a new feature, called *try-with-resources*, that can close certain resources automatically in the event of an error. This compliant solution uses try-with-resources to properly close the file.

```
public class Operation {
  public static void doOperation(String some_file) {
    // ... code to check or set character encoding ...
    try ( // try-with-resources
      BufferedReader reader =
        new BufferedReader(new FileReader(some_file))) {
      // Do operations
    } catch (IOException ex) {
      System.err.println("thrown exception: " + ex.toString());
      Throwable[] suppressed = ex.getSuppressed();
      for (int i = 0; i < suppressed.length; i++) {
        System.err.println("suppressed exception: "
          + suppressed[i].toString());
      }
      // Forward to handler
    }
  }

  public static void main(String[] args) {
    if (args.length < 1) {
      System.out.println("Please supply a path as an argument");
      return;
    }
    doOperation(args[0]);
  }
}
```

When an IOException occurs in the try block of the doOperation() method, it is caught by the catch block and printed as the *thrown exception*. This includes exceptions that occur while creating the BufferedReader. When an IOException occurs while closing the reader, that exception is also caught by the catch block and printed as the thrown exception. If both the try block and closing the reader throw an IOException, the catch clause catches both exceptions and prints the try block exception as the thrown exception. The close exception is suppressed and printed as the *suppressed exception*. In all cases the reader is safely closed.

Risk Assessment

Failure to handle an exception in a finally block may have unexpected results.

Rule	Severity	Likelihood	Remediation Cost	Priority	Level
ERR05-J	low	unlikely	medium	P2	L3

Related Guidelines

MITRE CWE	CWE-460. Improper cleanup on thrown exception
	CWE-584. Return inside `finally` block
	CWE-248. Uncaught exception
	CWE-705. Incorrect control flow scoping

Bibliography

[Bloch 2005a]	Puzzle 41. Field and stream
[Chess 2007]	8.3, Preventing Resource Leaks (Java)
[Harold 1999]	
[J2SE 2011]	The try-with-resources statement

■ ERR06-J. Do not throw undeclared checked exceptions

Java requires that each method address every checked exception that can be thrown during its execution either by handling the exception within a `try-catch` block or by declaring that the exception can propagate out of the method (via the `throws` clause). Unfortunately, there are a few techniques that permit undeclared checked exceptions to be thrown at runtime. Such techniques defeat the ability of caller methods to use the `throws` clause to determine the complete set of checked exceptions that could propagate from an invoked method. Consequently such techniques must not be used to throw undeclared checked exceptions.

Noncompliant Code Example (`Class.newInstance()`)

This noncompliant code example throws undeclared checked exceptions. The `unde-claredThrow()` method takes a `Throwable` argument, and invokes a function that will throw the argument without declaring it. While `undeclaredThrow()` catches any exceptions the function declares that it might throw, it nevertheless throws the argument it is given without regard to whether the argument is one of the declared exceptions.

This noncompliant code example also violates rule ERR07-J. However, because of exception ERR08-EX0, it does not violate rule ERR08-J. Any checked exception thrown by the default constructor of `java.lang.Class.newInstance()` is propagated to the caller, even though `Class.newInstance()` declares that it throws only `InstantiationException` and `IllegalAccessException`. This noncompliant code example demonstrates one way to use `Class.newInstance()` to throw arbitrary checked and unchecked exceptions.

```
public class NewInstance {
  private static Throwable throwable;

  private NewInstance() throws Throwable {
    throw throwable;
  }

  public static synchronized void undeclaredThrow(Throwable throwable) {
    // These exceptions should not be passed
    if (throwable instanceof IllegalAccessException ||
        throwable instanceof InstantiationException) {
      // Unchecked, no declaration required
      throw new IllegalArgumentException();
    }

    NewInstance.throwable = throwable;
    try {
      // next line throws the Throwable argument passed in above,
      // even though the throws clause of class.newInstance fails
      // to declare that this may happen
      NewInstance.class.newInstance();
    } catch (InstantiationException e) { /* unreachable */
    } catch (IllegalAccessException e) { /* unreachable */
    } finally { // Avoid memory leak
      NewInstance.throwable = null;
    }
  }
}

public class UndeclaredException {
  public static void main(String[] args) {
    // No declared checked exceptions
    NewInstance.undeclaredThrow(
        new Exception("Any checked exception"));
  }
}
```

Noncompliant Code Example (Class.newInstance() Workarounds)

When the programmer wishes to catch and handle the possible undeclared checked exceptions, the compiler refuses to believe that any can be thrown in the particular context.

This noncompliant code example attempts to catch undeclared checked exceptions thrown by `Class.newInstance()`. It catches `Exception` and dynamically checks whether the caught exception is an instance of the possible checked exception (carefully rethrowing all other exceptions).

```
public static void main(String[] args) {
  try {
    NewInstance.undeclaredThrow(
        new IOException("Any checked exception"));
  } catch (Throwable e) {
    if (e instanceof IOException) {
      System.out.println("IOException occurred");
    } else if (e instanceof RuntimeException) {
      throw (RuntimeException) e;
    } else {
      // forward to handler
    }
  }
}
```

Compliant Solution (`Constructor.newInstance()`)

This compliant solution uses `java.lang.reflect.Constructor.newInstance()` rather than `Class.newInstance()`. The `Constructor.newInstance()` method wraps any exceptions thrown from within the constructor into a checked exception called `InvocationTargetException`.

```
public static synchronized void undeclaredThrow(Throwable throwable) {
  // These exceptions should not be passed
  if (throwable instanceof IllegalAccessException ||
      throwable instanceof InstantiationException){
    // Unchecked, no declaration required
    throw new IllegalArgumentException();
  }

  NewInstance.throwable = throwable;
  try {
    Constructor constructor =
        NewInstance.class.getConstructor(new Class<?>[0]);
    constructor.newInstance();
```

```
      } catch (InstantiationException e) { /* unreachable */
      } catch (IllegalAccessException e) { /* unreachable */
      } catch (InvocationTargetException e) {
        System.out.println("Exception thrown: "
            + e.getCause().toString());
      } finally { // Avoid memory leak
        NewInstance.throwable = null;
      }
    }
}
```

Noncompliant Code Example (`sun.misc.Unsafe`)

This noncompliant code example is insecure both because it can throw undeclared checked exceptions and because it uses the `sun.misc.Unsafe` class. All `sun.*` classes are unsupported and undocumented because their use can cause portability and backward compatibility issues.

Classes loaded by the bootstrap class loader have the permissions needed to call the static factory method `Unsafe.getUnsafe()`. Arranging to have an arbitrary class loaded by the bootstrap class loader without modifying the `sun.boot.class.path` system property can be difficult. However, an alternative way to gain access is to change the accessibility of the field that holds an instance of `Unsafe` through the use of reflection. This works only when permitted by the current security manager (which would violate rule ENV03-J). Given access to `Unsafe`, a program can throw an undeclared checked exception by calling the `Unsafe.throwException()` method.

```
import java.io.IOException;
import java.lang.reflect.Field;
import sun.misc.Unsafe;

public class UnsafeCode {
  public static void main(String[] args)
      throws SecurityException, NoSuchFieldException,
             IllegalArgumentException, IllegalAccessException {
    Field f = Unsafe.class.getDeclaredField("theUnsafe");
    f.setAccessible(true);
    Unsafe u = (Unsafe) f.get(null);
    u.throwException(
      new IOException("No need to declare this checked exception"));
  }
}
```

Noncompliant Code Example (Generic Exception)

An unchecked cast of a generic type with parameterized exception declaration can also result in unexpected checked exceptions. All such casts are diagnosed by the compiler unless the warnings are suppressed.

```
interface Thr<EXC extends Exception> {
  void fn() throws EXC;
}

public class UndeclaredGen {
  static void undeclaredThrow() throws RuntimeException {
    @SuppressWarnings("unchecked")  // Suppresses warnings
    Thr<RuntimeException> thr = (Thr<RuntimeException>)(Thr)
      new Thr<IOException>() {
        public void fn() throws IOException {
          throw new IOException();
        }
      };
    thr.fn();
  }

  public static void main(String[] args) {
    undeclaredThrow();
  }
}
```

Noncompliant Code Example (`Thread.stop(Throwable)`)

According to the Java API [API 2006], class `Thread`:

> [`Thread.stop()`] may be used to generate exceptions that its target thread is unprepared to handle (including checked exceptions that the thread could not possibly throw, were it not for this method). For example, the following method is behaviorally identical to Java's throw operation but circumvents the compiler's attempts to guarantee that the calling method has declared all of the checked exceptions that it may throw:

```
static void sneakyThrow(Throwable t) {
  Thread.currentThread().stop(t);
}
```

Note that both versions of `Thread.stop()` are deprecated, so this code also violates rule MET02-J.

Noncompliant Code Example (Bytecode Manipulation)

It is also possible to disassemble a class, remove any declared checked exceptions, and reassemble the class so that checked exceptions are thrown at runtime when the class is used [Roubtsov 2003a]. Compiling against a class that declares the checked exception and supplying at runtime a class that lacks the declaration can also result in undeclared checked exceptions. Undeclared checked exceptions can also be produced through crafted use of the `sun.corba.Bridge` class. All these practices are violations of this rule.

Risk Assessment

Failure to document undeclared checked exceptions can result in checked exceptions that the caller is unprepared to handle, consequently violating the safety property.

Rule	Severity	Likelihood	Remediation Cost	Priority	Level
ERR06-J	low	unlikely	high	P1	L3

Related Guidelines

MITRE CWE	CWE-703. Improper check or handling of exceptional conditions
	CWE-248. Uncaught exception

Bibliography

[Bloch 2008]	Item 2. Consider a builder when faced with many constructor parameters
[Goetz 2004b]	
[JLS 2005]	Chapter 11, Exceptions
[Roubtsov 2003a]	
[Schwarz 2004]	
[Venners 2003]	Scalability of Checked Exceptions

■ ERR07-J. Do not throw `RuntimeException`, `Exception`, or `Throwable`

Methods must not throw `RuntimeException`, `Exception`, or `Throwable`. Handling these exceptions requires catching `RuntimeException`, which is disallowed by rule ERR08-J. Moreover, throwing a `RuntimeException` can lead to subtle errors; for example, a caller cannot examine the exception to determine why it was thrown and consequently cannot attempt recovery.

Methods can throw a specific exception subclassed from `Exception` or `RuntimeException`. Note that it is permissible to construct an exception class specifically for a single `throw` statement.

Noncompliant Code Example

The `isCapitalized()` method in this noncompliant code example accepts a string and returns `true` when the string consists of a capital letter followed by lowercase letters. The method also throws a `RuntimeException` when passed a null string argument.

```java
boolean isCapitalized(String s) {
  if (s == null) {
    throw new RuntimeException("Null String");
  }
  if (s.equals("")) {
    return true;
  }
  String first = s.substring(0, 1);
  String rest = s.substring(1);
  return (first.equals(first.toUpperCase()) &&
          rest.equals(rest.toLowerCase()));
}
```

A calling method must also violate rule ERR08-J to determine whether the `RuntimeException` was thrown.

Compliant Solution

This compliant solution throws `NullPointerException` to denote the specific exceptional condition.

```java
boolean isCapitalized(String s) {
  if (s == null) {
    throw new NullPointerException();
  }
  if (s.equals("")) {
    return true;
  }
  String first = s.substring(0, 1);
  String rest = s.substring(1);
  return (first.equals(first.toUpperCase())
          rest.equals(rest.toLowerCase()));
}
```

Note that the null check is redundant; if it were removed, the subsequent call to `s.equals("")` would throw a `NullPointerException` when `s` is null. However, the null check explicitly indicates the programmer's intent. More complex code may require explicit testing of invariants and appropriate throw statements.

Noncompliant Code Example

This noncompliant code example specifies the `Exception` class in the `throws` clause of the method declaration for the `doSomething()` method.

```java
private void doSomething() throws Exception {
  //...
}
```

Compliant Solution

This compliant solution declares a more specific exception class in the `throws` clause of the method declaration for the `doSomething()` method.

```java
private void doSomething() throws IOException {
  //...
}
```

Exceptions

ERR07-EX0: Classes that sanitize exceptions to comply with a security policy are permitted to translate specific exceptions into more general exceptions. This translation could potentially result in throwing `RuntimeException`, `Exception`, or `Throwable` in some cases, depending on the requirements of the security policy.

Risk Assessment

Throwing `RuntimeException`, `Exception`, or `Throwable` prevents classes from catching the intended exceptions without catching other unintended exceptions as well.

Rule	Severity	Likelihood	Remediation Cost	Priority	Level
ERR07-J	low	likely	medium	P6	L2

Related Guidelines

MITRE CWE	CWE-397. Declaration of throws for generic exception

Bibliography

[Goetz 2004b]

[Tutorials 2008]   Unchecked Exceptions—The Controversy

■ ERR08-J. Do not catch NullPointerException or any of its ancestors

Programs must not catch `java.lang.NullPointerException`. A `NullPointerException` exception thrown at runtime indicates the existence of an underlying null pointer dereference that must be fixed in the application code (see rule EXP01-J for more information). Handling the underlying null pointer dereference by catching the `NullPointerException` rather than fixing the underlying problem is inappropriate for several reasons. First, catching `NullPointerException` adds significantly more performance overhead than simply adding the necessary null checks [Bloch 2008]. Second, when multiple expressions in a `try` block are capable of throwing a `NullPointerException`, it is difficult or impossible to determine which expression is responsible for the exception because the `NullPointerException` catch block handles any `NullPointerException` thrown from any location in the `try` block. Third, programs rarely remain in an expected and usable state after a `NullPointerException` has been thrown. Attempts to continue execution after first catching and logging (or worse, suppressing) the exception rarely succeed.

Likewise, programs must not catch `RuntimeException`, `Exception`, or `Throwable`. Few, if any, methods are capable of handling all possible runtime exceptions. When a method catches `RuntimeException`, it may receive exceptions unanticipated by the designer, including `NullPointerException` and `ArrayIndexOutOfBoundsException`. Many catch clauses simply log or ignore the enclosed exceptional condition and attempt to resume normal execution; this practice often violates rule ERR00-J. Runtime exceptions often indicate bugs in the program that should be fixed by the developer and often cause control flow vulnerabilities.

Noncompliant Code Example (NullPointerException)

This noncompliant code example defines an `isName()` method that takes a `String` argument and returns `true` if the given string is a valid name. A valid name is defined as two capitalized words separated by one or more spaces. Rather than checking to see whether the given string is `null`, the method catches `NullPointerException` and returns `false`.

```
boolean isName(String s) {
  try {
    String names[] = s.split(" ");

    if (names.length != 2) {
      return false;
    }
    return (isCapitalized(names[0]) && isCapitalized(names[1]));
  } catch (NullPointerException e) {
    return false;
  }
}
```

Compliant Solution

This compliant solution explicitly checks the String argument for null rather than catching NullPointerException.

```
boolean isName(String s) {
  if (s == null) {
    return false;
  }
  String names[] = s.split(" ");
  if (names.length != 2) {
    return false;
  }
  return (isCapitalized(names[0]) && isCapitalized(names[1]));
}
```

Compliant Solution

This compliant solution omits an explicit check for a null reference and permits a NullPointerException to be thrown.

```
boolean isName(String s) /* throws NullPointerException */ {
  String names[] = s.split(" ");
  if (names.length != 2) {
    return false;
  }
  return (isCapitalized(names[0]) && isCapitalized(names[1]));
}
```

Omitting the null check means that the program fails more quickly than if the program had returned `false` and lets an invoking method discover the null value. A method that throws a `NullPointerException` without a null check must provide a precondition that the argument being passed to it is not `null`.

Noncompliant Code Example (Explicit Null Checks)

This noncompliant code example is derived from the logging service null object design pattern described by Henney [Henney 2003]. The logging service is composed of two classes: one that prints the triggering activity's details to a disk file using the `FileLog` class and another that prints to the console using the `ConsoleLog` class. An interface, `Log`, defines a `write()` method that is implemented by the respective log classes. Method selection occurs polymorphically at runtime. The logging infrastructure is subsequently used by a `Service` class.

```
public interface Log {
  void write(String messageToLog);
}

public class FileLog implements Log {
  private final FileWriter out;

  FileLog(String logFileName) throws IOException {
    out = new FileWriter(logFileName, true);
  }

  public void write(String messageToLog) {
    // write message to file
  }
}

public class ConsoleLog implements Log {
  public void write(String messageToLog) {
    System.out.println(messageToLog); // write message to console
  }
}

class Service {
  private Log log;

  Service() {
    this.log = null; // no logger
  }

  Service(Log log) {
    this.log = log; // set the specified logger
  }
```

```
  public void handle() {
    try {
      log.write("Request received and handled");
    } catch (NullPointerException npe) {
      // Ignore
    }
  }

  public static void main(String[] args) throws IOException {
    Service s = new Service(new FileLog("logfile.log"));
    s.handle();

    s = new Service(new ConsoleLog());
    s.handle();
  }
}
```

Each `Service` object must support the possibility that a `Log` object may be `null` because clients may choose not to perform logging. This noncompliant code example eliminates null checks by using a `try-catch` block that ignores `NullPointerException`.

This design choice suppresses genuine occurrences of `NullPointerException` in violation of rule ERR00-J. It also violates the design principle that exceptions should be used only for exceptional conditions because ignoring a null `Log` object is part of the ordinary operation of a server.

Compliant Solution (Null Object Pattern)

The null object design pattern provides an alternative to the use of explicit null checks in code. It reduces the need for explicit null checks through the use of an explicit, safe *null object* rather than a null reference.

This compliant solution modifies the no-argument constructor of class `Service` to use the *do nothing* behavior provided by an additional class, `Log.NULL`; it leaves the other classes unchanged.

```
  public interface Log {

    public static final Log NULL = new Log() {
      public void write(String messageToLog) {
        // do nothing
      }
    };
```

```
  void write(String messageToLog);
}

class Service {

  private final Log log = Log.NULL;

  // ...
}
```

Declaring the log reference final ensures that its value is assigned during initialization.

An acceptable alternative implementation uses accessor methods to control all interaction with the reference to the current log. The *accessor method to set a log* ensures use of the null object in place of a null reference. The *accessor method to get a log* ensures that any retrieved instance is either an actual logger or a null object (but never a null reference). Instances of the null object are immutable and are inherently thread-safe.

Some system designs require returning a value from a method rather than implementing do-nothing behavior. One acceptable approach is use of an exceptional value object that throws an exception before the method returns [Cunningham 1995]. This can be a useful alternative to returning null.

In distributed environments, the null object must be passed by copy to ensure that remote systems avoid the overhead of a remote call argument evaluation on every access to the null object. Null object code for distributed environments must also implement the Serializable interface.

Code that uses this pattern must be clearly documented to ensure that security-critical messages are never discarded because the pattern has been misapplied.

Noncompliant Code Example (Division)

This noncompliant code example assumes that the original version of the division() method was declared to throw only ArithmeticException. However, the caller catches the more general Exception type to report arithmetic problems rather than catching the specific ArithmeticException type. This practice is risky because future changes to the method signature could add to the more exceptions list of potential exceptions the caller must handle. In this example, a revision of the division() method can throw IOException in addition to ArithmeticException. However, the compiler will not diagnose the lack of a corresponding handler because the invoking method already catches IOException as a result of catching Exception. Consequently, the recovery process might be inappropriate for the specific exception type that is thrown. Furthermore, the developer has failed to anticipate that catching Exception also catches unchecked exceptions.

```
public class DivideException {
  public static void division(int totalSum, int totalNumber)
    throws ArithmeticException, IOException  {
    int average  = totalSum / totalNumber;
    // Additional operations that may throw IOException...
    System.out.println("Average: " + average);
  }
}

  public static void main(String[] args) {
    try {
      division(200, 5);
      division(200, 0); // Divide by zero
    } catch (Exception e) {
      System.out.println("Divide by zero exception : "
                            + e.getMessage());
    }
  }
```

Noncompliant Code Example

This noncompliant code example attempts to solve the problem by specifically catching `ArithmeticException`. However, it continues to catch `Exception` and consequently catches both unanticipated checked exceptions and unanticipated runtime exceptions.

```
try {
  division(200, 5);
  division(200, 0); // Divide by zero
} catch (ArithmeticException ae) {
  throw new DivideByZeroException();
} catch (Exception e) {
  System.out.println("Exception occurred :" + e.getMessage());
}
```

Note that `DivideByZeroException` is a custom exception type that extends `Exception`.

Compliant Solution

This compliant solution catches only the specific anticipated exceptions (`ArithmeticException` and `IOException`). All other exceptions are permitted to propagate up the call stack.

```
import java.io.IOException;

public class DivideException {
  public static void main(String[] args) {
    try {
      division(200, 5);
      division(200, 0); // Divide by zero
    } catch (ArithmeticException ae) {
      // DivideByZeroException extends Exception so is checked
      throw new DivideByZeroException();
    } catch (IOException ex) {
      ExceptionReporter.report(ex);
    }
  }

  public static void division(int totalSum, int totalNumber)
                            throws ArithmeticException, IOException  {
    int average  = totalSum / totalNumber;
    // Additional operations that may throw IOException...
    System.out.println("Average: "+ average);
  }
}
```

The ExceptionReporter class is documented in rule ERR00-J.

Compliant Solution (Java 1.7)

Java 1.7 allows a single catch block to catch multiple exceptions of different types, which prevents redundant code. This compliant solution catches the specific anticipated exceptions (ArithmeticException and IOException) and handles them with one catch clause. All other exceptions are permitted to propagate to the next catch clause of a try statement on the stack.

```
import java.io.IOException;

public class DivideException {
  public static void main(String[] args) {
    try {
      division(200, 5);
      division(200, 0); // Divide by zero
    } catch (ArithmeticException | IOException ex) {
      ExceptionReporter.report(ex);
    }
  }
}
```

```
   public static void division(int totalSum, int totalNumber)
                           throws ArithmeticException, IOException {
     int average  = totalSum / totalNumber;
     // Additional operations that may throw IOException...
     System.out.println("Average: "+ average);
   }
 }
```

Exceptions

ERR08-EX0: A catch block may catch all exceptions to process them before rethrowing them (filtering sensitive information from exceptions before the call stack leaves a trust boundary, for example). Refer to rule ERR01-J and weaknesses CWE 7 and CWE 388 for more information. In such cases, a catch block should catch Throwable rather than Exception or RuntimeException.

This code sample catches all exceptions and wraps them in a custom DoSomething-Exception before rethrowing them.

```
class DoSomethingException extends Exception {
  public DoSomethingException(Throwable cause) {
    super(cause);
  }

  // other methods

};

private void doSomething() throws DoSomethingException {
  try {
    // code that might throw an Exception
  } catch (Throwable t) {
    throw new DoSomethingException(t);
  }
}
```

Exception wrapping is a common technique to safely handle unknown exceptions. For another example, see rule ERR06-J.

ERR08-EX1: Task processing threads such as worker threads in a thread pool or the Swing event dispatch thread are permitted to catch RuntimeException when they call untrusted code through an abstraction such as the Runnable interface [Goetz 2006a, p. 161].

ERR08-EX2: Systems that require substantial fault tolerance or graceful degradation are permitted to catch and log general exceptions such as `Throwable` at appropriate levels of abstraction. For example:

- A real-time control system that catches and logs all exceptions at the outermost layer, followed by warm-starting the system so that real-time control can continue. Such approaches are clearly justified when program termination would have safety-critical or mission-critical consequences.

- A system that catches all exceptions that propagate out of each major subsystem, logs the exceptions for later debugging, and subsequently shuts down the failing subsystem (perhaps replacing it with a much simpler, limited-functionality version) while continuing other services.

Risk Assessment

Catching `NullPointerException` may mask an underlying null dereference, degrade application performance, and result in code that is hard to understand and maintain. Likewise, catching `RuntimeException`, `Exception`, or `Throwable` may unintentionally trap other exception types and prevent them from being handled properly.

Rule	Severity	Likelihood	Remediation Cost	Priority	Level
ERR08-J	medium	likely	medium	P12	L1

■ ERR09-J. Do not allow untrusted code to terminate the JVM

Invocation of `System.exit()` terminates the Java Virtual Machine (JVM), consequently terminating all running programs and threads. This can result in denial of service (DoS) attacks. For example, a call to `System.exit()` that is embedded in Java Server Pages (JSP) code can cause a web server to terminate, preventing further service for users. Programs must prevent both inadvertent and malicious calls to `System.exit()`. Additionally, programs should perform necessary cleanup actions when forcibly terminated (for example, by using the Windows Task Manager, POSIX `kill` command, or other mechanisms).

Noncompliant Code Example

This noncompliant code example uses `System.exit()` to forcefully shutdown the JVM and terminate the running process. The program lacks a security manager; consequently, it lacks the capability to check whether the caller is permitted to invoke `System.exit()`.

```
public class InterceptExit {
  public static void main(String[] args) {
    // ...
    System.exit(1);  // Abrupt exit
    System.out.println("This never executes");
  }
}
```

Compliant Solution

This compliant solution installs a custom security manager PasswordSecurityManager that overrides the checkExit() method defined in the SecurityManager class. This override is required to enable invocation of cleanup code before allowing the exit. The default checkExit() method in the SecurityManager class lacks this facility.

```
class PasswordSecurityManager extends SecurityManager {
  private boolean isExitAllowedFlag;

  public PasswordSecurityManager(){
    super();
    isExitAllowedFlag = false;
  }

  public boolean isExitAllowed(){
    return isExitAllowedFlag;
  }

  @Override
    public void checkExit(int status) {
    if (!isExitAllowed()) {
      throw new SecurityException();
    }
    super.checkExit(status);
  }

  public void setExitAllowed(boolean f) {
    isExitAllowedFlag = f;
  }
}
public class InterceptExit {
  public static void main(String[] args) {
    PasswordSecurityManager secManager =
        new PasswordSecurityManager();
    System.setSecurityManager(secManager);
    try {
      // ...
```

```
      System.exit(1);  // Abrupt exit call
    } catch (Throwable x) {
      if (x instanceof SecurityException) {
        System.out.println("Intercepted System.exit()");
        // Log exception
      } else {
        // Forward to exception handler
      }
    }

    // ...
    secManager.setExitAllowed(true);  // Permit exit
    // System.exit() will work subsequently
    // ...
  }
}
```

This implementation uses an internal flag to track whether the exit is permitted. The method setExitAllowed() sets this flag. The checkExit() method throws a SecurityException when the flag is unset (that is, false). Because this flag is not initially set, normal exception processing bypasses the initial call to System.exit(). The program catches the SecurityException and performs mandatory cleanup operations, including logging the exception. The System.exit() method is enabled only after cleanup is complete.

Exceptions

ERR09-EX0: It is permissible for a command-line utility to call System.exit(), for example, when the required number of arguments are not input [Bloch 2008, ESA 2005].

Risk Assessment

Allowing unauthorized calls to System.exit() may lead to denial of service.

Rule	Severity	Likelihood	Remediation Cost	Priority	Level
ERR09-J	low	unlikely	medium	P2	L3

Related Guidelines

MITRE CWE   CWE-382. J2EE bad practices: Use of System.exit()

Bibliography

[API 2006]	Method `checkExit()`, class `Runtime`, method `addShutdownHook`
[Austin 2000]	Writing a Security Manager
[Darwin 2004]	9.5, The Finalize Method
[ESA 2005]	Rule 78. Restrict the use of the `System.exit` method
[Goetz 2006a]	7.4, JVM Shutdown
[Kalinovsky 2004]	Chapter 16, Intercepting a Call to `System.exit`

Chapter 9

Visibility and Atomicity (VNA)

■ Rules

■ Risk Assessment Summary

Rule	Severity	Likelihood	Remediation Cost	Priority	Level
VNA00-J	medium	probable	medium	P8	L2
VNA01-J	low	probable	medium	P4	L3
VNA02-J	medium	probable	medium	P8	L2

Continued

Rule	Severity	Likelihood	Remediation Cost	Priority	Level
VNA03-J	low	probable	medium	P4	L3
VNA04-J	low	probable	medium	P4	L3
VNA05-J	low	unlikely	medium	P2	L3

■ VNA00-J. Ensure visibility when accessing shared primitive variables

Reading a shared primitive variable in one thread may not yield the value of the most recent write to the variable from another thread. Consequently, the thread may observe a stale value of the shared variable. To ensure the visibility of the most recent update, either the variable must be declared volatile or the reads and writes must be synchronized.

Declaring a shared variable volatile guarantees visibility in a thread-safe manner only when both of the following conditions are met:

- A write to a variable is independent from its current value.
- A write to a variable is independent from the result of any nonatomic compound operations involving reads and writes of other variables. (See rule VNA02-J for more information.)

The first condition can be relaxed when you can be sure that only one thread will ever update the value of the variable [Goetz 2006a]. However, code that relies on single-thread confinement is error prone and difficult to maintain. This design approach is permitted under this rule but is discouraged.

Synchronizing the code makes it easier to reason about its behavior and is frequently more secure than simply using the volatile keyword. However, synchronization has somewhat higher performance overhead and can result in thread contention and deadlocks when used excessively.

Declaring a variable volatile or correctly synchronizing the code both guarantee that 64-bit primitive long and double variables are accessed atomically. For more information on sharing those variables among multiple threads, see rule VNA05-J.

Noncompliant Code Example (Nonvolatile Flag)

This noncompliant code example uses a shutdown() method to set the nonvolatile done flag that is checked in the run() method.

```
final class ControlledStop implements Runnable {
  private boolean done = false;

  @Override public void run() {
    while (!done) {
      try {
        // ...
        Thread.currentThread().sleep(1000); // Do something
      } catch(InterruptedException ie) {
        Thread.currentThread().interrupt(); // Reset interrupted status
      }
    }
  }

  public void shutdown() {
    done = true;
  }
}
```

If one thread invokes the shutdown() method to set the flag, a second thread might not observe that change. Consequently, the second thread might observe that done is still false and incorrectly invoke the sleep() method. Compilers and just-in-time compilers (JITs) are allowed to optimize the code when they determine that the value of done is never modified by the same thread, resulting in an infinite loop.

Compliant Solution (Volatile)

In this compliant solution, the done flag is declared volatile to ensure that writes are visible to other threads.

```
final class ControlledStop implements Runnable {
  private volatile boolean done = false;

  @Override public void run() {
    while (!done) {
      try {
        // ...
        Thread.currentThread().sleep(1000); // Do something
      } catch(InterruptedException ie) {
```

```
              Thread.currentThread().interrupt(); // Reset interrupted status
        }
      }
    }

  public void shutdown() {
    done = true;
  }
}
```

Compliant Solution (`AtomicBoolean`)

In this compliant solution, the done flag is declared to be of type `java.util.concurrent.` `atomic.AtomicBoolean`. Atomic types also guarantee that writes are visible to other threads.

```java
final class ControlledStop implements Runnable {
  private final AtomicBoolean done = new AtomicBoolean(false);

  @Override public void run() {
    while (!done.get()) {
      try {
        // ...
        Thread.currentThread().sleep(1000); // Do something
      } catch(InterruptedException ie) {
        Thread.currentThread().interrupt(); // Reset interrupted status
      }
    }
  }

  public void shutdown() {
    done.set(true);
  }
}
```

Compliant Solution (`synchronized`)

This compliant solution uses the intrinsic lock of the `Class` object to ensure that updates are visible to other threads.

```
final class ControlledStop implements Runnable {
  private boolean done = false;

  @Override public void run() {
    while (!isDone()) {
      try {
        // ...
        Thread.currentThread().sleep(1000); // Do something
      } catch(InterruptedException ie) {
        Thread.currentThread().interrupt(); // Reset interrupted status
      }
    }
  }

  public synchronized boolean isDone() {
    return done;
  }

  public synchronized void shutdown() {
    done = true;
  }
}
```

While this is an acceptable compliant solution, intrinsic locks cause threads to block and may introduce contention. On the other hand, volatile-qualified shared variables do not block. Excessive synchronization can also make the program prone to deadlock.

Synchronization is a more secure alternative in situations where the volatile keyword or a java.util.concurrent.atomic.Atomic* field is inappropriate, such as when a variable's new value depends on its current value. See rule VNA02-J for more information.

Compliance with rule LCK00-J can reduce the likelihood of misuse by ensuring that untrusted callers cannot access the lock object.

Exceptions

VNA00-EX0: Class objects are created by the virtual machine; their initialization always precedes any subsequent use. Consequently, cross-thread visibility of Class objects is already assured by default.

Risk Assessment

Failing to ensure the visibility of a shared primitive variable may result in a thread observing a stale value of the variable.

Rule	Severity	Likelihood	Remediation Cost	Priority	Level
VNA00-J	medium	probable	medium	P8	L2

Automated Detection Some static analysis tools are capable of detecting violations of this rule.

Related Guidelines

MITRE CWE   CWE-667. Improper locking

        CWE-413. Improper resource locking

        CWE-567. Unsynchronized access to shared data in a multithreaded context

Bibliography

[Bloch 2008]   Item 66. Synchronize access to shared mutable data

[Goetz 2006a] 3.4.2, Example: Using Volatile to Publish Immutable Objects

[JLS 2005]   Chapter 17, Threads and Locks

        §17.4.5, Happens-Before Order

        §17.4.3, Programs and Program Order

        §17.4.8, Executions and Causality Requirements

[JPL 2006]   14.10.3, The Happens-Before Relationship

■ VNA01-J. Ensure visibility of shared references to immutable objects

A common misconception is that shared references to immutable objects are immediately visible across multiple threads as soon as they are updated. For example, a developer can mistakenly believe that a class containing fields that refer only to immutable objects is itself immutable and consequently thread-safe.

Section 14.10.2, "Final Fields and Security," of *Java Programming Language*, Fourth Edition [JPL 2006], states:

> The problem is that, while the shared object is immutable, the reference used to access the shared object is itself shared and often mutable. Consequently, a correctly synchronized program must synchronize access to that shared reference,

but often programs do not do this, because programmers do not recognize the need to do it.

References to both immutable and mutable objects must be made visible to all the threads. Immutable objects can be shared safely among multiple threads. However, references to mutable objects can be made visible before the objects are fully constructed. Rule TSM03-J describes object construction and visibility issues specific to mutable objects.

Noncompliant Code Example

This noncompliant code example consists of the immutable Helper class:

```java
// Immutable Helper
public final class Helper {
  private final int n;

  public Helper(int n) {
    this.n = n;
  }
  // ...
}
```

and a mutable Foo class:

```java
final class Foo {
  private Helper helper;

  public Helper getHelper() {
    return helper;
  }

  public void setHelper(int num) {
    helper = new Helper(num);
  }
}
```

The getHelper() method publishes the mutable helper field. Because the Helper class is immutable, it cannot be changed after it is initialized. Furthermore, because Helper is immutable, it is always constructed properly before its reference is made visible, in compliance with rule TSM03-J. Unfortunately, a separate thread could observe a stale reference in the helper field of the Foo class.

Compliant Solution (Synchronization)

This compliant solution synchronizes the methods of the Foo class to ensure that no thread sees a stale Helper reference.

```
final class Foo {
  private Helper helper;

  public synchronized Helper getHelper() {
    return helper;
  }

  public synchronized void setHelper(int num) {
    helper = new Helper(num);
  }
}
```

The immutable Helper class remains unchanged.

Compliant Solution (Volatile)

References to immutable member objects can be made visible by declaring them volatile.

```
final class Foo {
  private volatile Helper helper;

  public Helper getHelper() {
    return helper;
  }

  public void setHelper(int num) {
    helper = new Helper(num);
  }
}
```

The immutable Helper class remains unchanged.

Compliant Solution (`java.util.concurrent` Utilities)

This compliant solution wraps the mutable reference to the immutable Helper object within an AtomicReference wrapper that can be updated atomically.

```
final class Foo {
  private final AtomicReference<Helper> helperRef =
      new AtomicReference<Helper>();

  public Helper getHelper() {
    return helperRef.get();
  }

  public void setHelper(int num) {
    helperRef.set(new Helper(num));
  }
}
```

The immutable `Helper` class remains unchanged.

Risk Assessment

The incorrect assumption that classes that contain only references to immutable objects are themselves immutable can cause serious thread-safety issues.

Rule	Severity	Likelihood	Remediation Cost	Priority	Level
VNA01-J	low	probable	medium	P4	L3

Bibliography

[API 2006]

[JPL 2006]   14.10.2, Final Fields and Security

■ VNA02-J. Ensure that compound operations on shared variables are atomic

Compound operations are operations that consist of more than one discrete operation. Expressions that include postfix or prefix increment (++), postfix or prefix decrement (--), or compound assignment operators always result in compound operations. Compound assignment expressions use operators such as *=, /=, %=, +=, -=, <<=, >>=, >>>=, ^=, and |= [JLS 2005]. Compound operations on shared variables must be performed atomically to prevent data races and race conditions.

For information about the atomicity of a grouping of calls to independently atomic methods that belong to thread-safe classes, see rule VNA03-J.

The *Java Language Specification* also permits reads and writes of 64-bit values to be nonatomic. For more information, see rule VNA05-J.

Noncompliant Code Example (Logical Negation)

This noncompliant code example declares a shared `boolean` `flag` variable and provides a `toggle()` method that negates the current value of `flag`.

```java
final class Flag {
  private boolean flag = true;

  public void toggle() { // Unsafe
    flag = !flag;
  }

  public boolean getFlag() { // Unsafe
    return flag;
  }
}
```

Execution of this code may result in a data race because the value of `flag` is read, negated, and written back.

Consider, for example, two threads that call `toggle()`. The expected effect of toggling `flag` twice is that it is restored to its original value. However, the following scenario leaves `flag` in the incorrect state:

Time	flag=	Thread	Action
1	true	t_1	reads the current value of `flag`, true, into a temporary variable
2	true	t_2	reads the current value of `flag`, (still) true, into a temporary variable
3	true	t_1	toggles the temporary variable to false
4	true	t_2	toggles the temporary variable to false
5	false	t_1	writes the temporary variable's value to `flag`
6	false	t_2	writes the temporary variable's value to `flag`

As a result, the effect of the call by t_2 is not reflected in `flag`; the program behaves as if `toggle()` were called only once, not twice.

Noncompliant Code Example (Bitwise Negation)

The `toggle()` method may also use the compound assignment operator ^= to negate the current value of `flag`.

```
final class Flag {
  private boolean flag = true;

  public void toggle() { // Unsafe
    flag ^= true; // Same as flag = !flag;
  }

  public boolean getFlag() { // Unsafe
    return flag;
  }
}
```

This code is also not thread-safe. A data race exists because ^= is a nonatomic compound operation.

Noncompliant Code Example (Volatile)

Declaring `flag` volatile also fails to solve the problem:

```
final class Flag {
  private volatile boolean flag = true;

  public void toggle() { // Unsafe
    flag ^= true;
  }

  public boolean getFlag() { // Safe
    return flag;
  }
}
```

This code remains unsuitable for multithreaded use because declaring a variable volatile fails to guarantee the atomicity of compound operations on the variable.

Compliant Solution (Synchronization)

This compliant solution declares both the `toggle()` and `getFlag()` methods as synchronized.

```
final class Flag {
  private boolean flag = true;

  public synchronized void toggle() {
    flag ^= true; // Same as flag = !flag;
  }

  public synchronized boolean getFlag() {
    return flag;
  }
}
```

This solution guards reads and writes to the flag field with a lock on the instance, that is, this. Furthermore, synchronization ensures that changes are visible to all threads. Now, only two execution orders are possible, one of which is shown in the following scenario:

Time	flag=	Thread	Action
1	true	t_1	reads the current value of flag, true, into a temporary variable
2	true	t_1	toggles the temporary variable to false
3	false	t_1	writes the temporary variable's value to flag
4	false	t_2	reads the current value of flag, false, into a temporary variable
5	false	t_2	toggles the temporary variable to true
6	true	t_2	writes the temporary variable's value to flag

The second execution order involves the same operations, but t_2 starts and finishes before t_1.

Compliance with rule LCK00-J can reduce the likelihood of misuse by ensuring that untrusted callers cannot access the lock object.

Compliant Solution (Volatile-Read, Synchronized-Write)

In this compliant solution, the getFlag() method is not synchronized, and flag is declared as volatile. This solution is compliant because the read of flag in the getFlag() method is an atomic operation and the volatile qualification assures visibility. The toggle() method still requires synchronization because it performs a nonatomic operation.

```
final class Flag {
  private volatile boolean flag = true;

  public synchronized void toggle() {
    flag ^= true; // Same as flag = !flag;
  }

  public boolean getFlag() {
    return flag;
  }
}
```

This approach must not be used for getter methods that perform any additional operations other than returning the value of a volatile field without use of synchronization. Unless read performance is critical, this technique may lack significant advantages over synchronization [Goetz 2006a].

Compliant Solution (Read-Write Lock)

This compliant solution uses a read-write lock to ensure atomicity and visibility.

```
final class Flag {
  private boolean flag = true;
  private final ReadWriteLock lock = new ReentrantReadWriteLock();
  private final Lock readLock = lock.readLock();
  private final Lock writeLock = lock.writeLock();

  public void toggle() {
    writeLock.lock();
    try {
      flag ^= true; // Same as flag = !flag;
    } finally {
      writeLock.unlock();
    }
  }

  public boolean getFlag() {
    readLock.lock();
    try {
      return flag;
    } finally {
      readLock.unlock();
    }
  }
}
```

Read-write locks allow shared state to be accessed by multiple readers or a single writer, but never both. According to Goetz [Goetz 2006a]:

> In practice, read-write locks can improve performance for frequently accessed read-mostly data structures on multiprocessor systems; under other conditions they perform slightly worse than exclusive locks due to their greater complexity.

Profiling the application can determine the suitability of read-write locks.

Compliant Solution (`AtomicBoolean`)

This compliant solution declares `flag` to be of type `AtomicBoolean`.

```java
import java.util.concurrent.atomic.AtomicBoolean;

final class Flag {
  private AtomicBoolean flag = new AtomicBoolean(true);

  public void toggle() {
    boolean temp;
    do {
      temp = flag.get();
    } while (!flag.compareAndSet(temp, !temp));
  }

  public AtomicBoolean getFlag() {
    return flag;
  }
}
```

The `flag` variable is updated using the `compareAndSet()` method of the `AtomicBoolean` class. All updates are visible to other threads.

Noncompliant Code Example (Addition of Primitives)

In this noncompliant code example, multiple threads can invoke the `setValues()` method to set the a and b fields. Because this class fails to test for integer overflow, users of the `Adder` class must ensure that the arguments to the `setValues()` method can be added without overflow. (See rule NUM00-J for more information.)

```java
final class Adder {
  private int a;
  private int b;
```

```
  public int getSum() {
    return a + b;
  }

  public void setValues(int a, int b) {
    this.a = a;
    this.b = b;
  }
}
```

The getSum() method contains a race condition. For example, when a and b currently have the values 0 and Integer.MAX_VALUE, respectively, and one thread calls getSum() while another calls setValues(Integer.MAX_VALUE, 0), the getSum() method might return either 0 or Integer.MAX_VALUE, or it might overflow. Overflow will occur when the first thread reads a and b after the second thread has set the value of a to Integer.MAX_ VALUE but before it has set the value of b to 0.

Note that declaring the variables as volatile fails to resolve the issue because these compound operations involve reads and writes of multiple variables.

Noncompliant Code Example (Addition of Atomic Integers)

In this noncompliant code example, a and b are replaced with atomic integers.

```
final class Adder {
  private final AtomicInteger a = new AtomicInteger();
  private final AtomicInteger b = new AtomicInteger();

  public int getSum() {
    // Check for overflow
    return a.get() + b.get();
  }

  public void setValues(int a, int b) {
    this.a.set(a);
    this.b.set(b);
  }
}
```

The simple replacement of the two int fields with atomic integers fails to eliminate the race condition because the compound operation a.get() + b.get() is still nonatomic.

Compliant Solution (Addition)

This compliant solution synchronizes the `setValues()` and `getSum()` methods to ensure atomicity.

```
final class Adder {
  private int a;
  private int b;

  public synchronized int getSum() {
    // Check for overflow
    return a + b;
  }

  public synchronized void setValues(int a, int b) {
    this.a = a;
    this.b = b;
  }
}
```

The operations within the synchronized methods are now atomic with respect to other synchronized methods that lock on that object's *monitor* (that is, its intrinsic lock). It is now possible, for example, to add overflow checking to the synchronized `getSum()` method without introducing the possibility of a race condition.

Risk Assessment

When operations on shared variables are not atomic, unexpected results can be produced. For example, information can be disclosed inadvertently because one user can receive information about other users.

Rule	Severity	Likelihood	Remediation Cost	Priority	Level
VNA02-J	medium	probable	medium	P8	L2

Automated Detection Some available tools can diagnose violations of this rule by detecting instance fields with empty locksets.

Some available static analysis tools can detect the instances of nonatomic update of a concurrently shared value. The result of the update is determined by the interleaving of thread execution. These tools can detect the instances where thread-shared data is accessed without holding an appropriate lock, possibly causing a race condition.

Related Guidelines

MITRE CWE   CWE-667. Improper locking

CWE-413. Improper resource locking

CWE-366. Race condition within a thread

CWE-567. Unsynchronized access to shared data in a multithreaded context

Bibliography

[API 2006]   Class `AtomicInteger`

[Bloch 2008]   Item 66. Synchronize access to shared mutable data

[Goetz 2006a]   2.3, Locking

[JLS 2005]   Chapter 17, Threads and Locks

§17.4.5, Happens-Before Order

§17.4.3, Programs and Program Order

§17.4.8, Executions and Causality Requirements

[Lea 2000a]   Section 2.2.7, The Java Memory Model

Section 2.1.1.1, Objects and Locks

[Tutorials 2008]   Java Concurrency Tutorial

■ VNA03-J. Do not assume that a group of calls to independently atomic methods is atomic

A consistent locking policy guarantees that multiple threads cannot simultaneously access or modify shared data. When two or more operations must be performed as a single atomic operation, a consistent locking policy must be implemented using either intrinsic synchronization or `java.util.concurrent` utilities. In the absence of such a policy, the code is susceptible to race conditions.

Given an invariant involving multiple objects, a programmer might incorrectly assume that a group of individually atomic operations is collectively atomic without additional locking. Similarly, programmers might incorrectly assume that use of a thread-safe `Collection` is sufficient to preserve an invariant that involves the collection's elements without additional synchronization. A thread-safe class can only guarantee atomicity of its individual methods. A grouping of calls to such methods requires additional synchronization.

Consider, for example, a scenario where the standard thread-safe API lacks a single method to both find a particular person's record in a `Hashtable` and also update that person's payroll information. In such cases, the two method invocations must be performed atomically.

Enumerations and iterators also require either explicit synchronization on the collection object (client-side locking) or use of a private final lock object.

Compound operations on shared variables are also nonatomic. See rule VNA02-J for more information.

Rule VNA04-J describes a specialized case of this rule.

Noncompliant Code Example (`AtomicReference`)

This noncompliant code example wraps references to `BigInteger` objects within thread-safe `AtomicReference` objects.

```
final class Adder {
  private final AtomicReference<BigInteger> first;
  private final AtomicReference<BigInteger> second;

  public Adder(BigInteger f, BigInteger s) {
    first = new AtomicReference<BigInteger>(f);
    second = new AtomicReference<BigInteger>(s);
  }

  public void update(BigInteger f, BigInteger s) { // Unsafe
    first.set(f);
    second.set(s);
  }

  public BigInteger add() { // Unsafe
    return first.get().add(second.get());
  }
}
```

`AtomicReference` is an object reference that can be updated atomically. However, operations that combine more than one atomic reference are nonatomic. In this noncompliant code example, one thread may call `update()` while a second thread may call `add()`. This might cause the `add()` method to add the new value of `first` to the old value of `second`, yielding an erroneous result.

Compliant Solution (Method Synchronization)

This compliant solution declares the `update()` and `add()` methods synchronized to guarantee atomicity.

```
final class Adder {
  // ...
  private final AtomicReference<BigInteger> first;
  private final AtomicReference<BigInteger> second;

  public Adder(BigInteger f, BigInteger s) {
    first = new AtomicReference<BigInteger>(f);
    second = new AtomicReference<BigInteger>(s);
  }

  public synchronized void update(BigInteger f, BigInteger s){
    first.set(f);
    second.set(s);
  }

  public synchronized BigInteger add() {
    return first.get().add(second.get());
  }
}
```

Noncompliant Code Example (synchronizedList())

This noncompliant code example uses a java.util.ArrayList<E> collection, which is not thread-safe. However, the example uses Collections.synchronizedList() as a synchronization wrapper for the ArrayList. It subsequently uses an array, rather than an iterator, to iterate over the ArrayList to avoid a ConcurrentModificationException.

```
final class IPHolder {
  private final List<InetAddress> ips =
      Collections.synchronizedList(new ArrayList<InetAddress>());

  public void addAndPrintIPAddresses(InetAddress address) {
    ips.add(address);
    InetAddress[] addressCopy =
        (InetAddress[]) ips.toArray(new InetAddress[0]);
    // Iterate through array addressCopy ...
  }
}
```

Individually, the add() and toArray() collection methods are atomic. However, when called in succession (as shown, in the addAndPrintIPAddresses() method), there is no guarantee that the *combined* operation is atomic. The addAndPrintIPAddresses() method contains a race condition that allows one thread to add to the list and a second thread to race in and modify the list before the first thread completes. Consequently, the addressCopy array may contain more IP addresses than expected.

Compliant Solution (Synchronized Block)

The race condition can be eliminated by synchronizing on the underlying list's lock. This compliant solution encapsulates all references to the array list within synchronized blocks.

```
final class IPHolder {
  private final List<InetAddress> ips =
    Collections.synchronizedList(new ArrayList<InetAddress>());

  public void addAndPrintIPAddresses(InetAddress address) {
    synchronized (ips) {
      ips.add(address);
      InetAddress[] addressCopy =
          (InetAddress[]) ips.toArray(new InetAddress[0]);
      // Iterate through array addressCopy ...
    }
  }
}
```

This technique is also called client-side locking [Goetz 2006a] because the class holds a lock on an object that might be accessible to other classes. Client-side locking is not always an appropriate strategy; see rule LCK11-J for more information.

This code does not violate rule LCK04-J because, while it does synchronize on a collection view (the synchronizedList() result), the backing collection is inaccessible and consequently cannot be modified by any code.

Note that this compliant solution does not actually use the synchronization offered by Collections.synchronizedList(). If no other code in this solution used it, it could be eliminated.

Noncompliant Code Example (synchronizedMap())

This noncompliant code example defines the KeyedCounter class that is not thread-safe. Although the HashMap is wrapped in a synchronizedMap(), the overall increment operation is not atomic [Lee 2009].

```
final class KeyedCounter {
  private final Map<String, Integer> map =
    Collections.synchronizedMap(new HashMap<String, Integer>());

  public void increment(String key) {
    Integer old = map.get(key);
    int oldValue = (old == null) ? 0 : old.intValue();
    if (oldValue == Integer.MAX_VALUE) {
      throw new ArithmeticException("Out of range");
    }
    map.put(key, oldValue + 1);
  }

  public Integer getCount(String key) {
    return map.get(key);
  }
}
```

Compliant Solution (Synchronization)

This compliant solution ensures atomicity by using an internal private lock object to synchronize the statements of the increment() and getCount() methods.

```
final class KeyedCounter {
  private final Map<String, Integer> map =
    new HashMap<String, Integer>();
  private final Object lock = new Object();

  public void increment(String key) {
    synchronized (lock) {
      Integer old = map.get(key);
      int oldValue = (old == null) ? 0 : old.intValue();
      if (oldValue == Integer.MAX_VALUE) {
        throw new ArithmeticException("Out of range");
      }
      map.put(key, oldValue + 1);
    }
  }

  public Integer getCount(String key) {
    synchronized (lock) {
      return map.get(key);
    }
  }
}
```

This compliant solution avoids using `Collections.synchronizedMap()` because locking on the unsynchronized map provides sufficient thread-safety for this application. Rule LCK04-J provides more information about synchronizing on `synchronizedMap()` objects.

Compliant Solution (ConcurrentHashMap)

The previous compliant solution is safe for multithreaded use but does not scale because of excessive synchronization, which can lead to contention and deadlock.

The `ConcurrentHashMap` class used in this compliant solution provides several utility methods for performing atomic operations and is often a good choice for algorithms that must scale [Lee 2009].

```
final class KeyedCounter {
  private final ConcurrentMap<String, AtomicInteger> map =
    new ConcurrentHashMap<String, AtomicInteger>();

  public void increment(String key) {
    AtomicInteger value = new AtomicInteger();
    AtomicInteger old = map.putIfAbsent(key, value);

    if (old != null) {
      value = old;
    }

    if (value.get() == Integer.MAX_VALUE) {
      throw new ArithmeticException("Out of range");
    }

    value.incrementAndGet(); // Increment the value atomically
  }

  public Integer getCount(String key) {
    AtomicInteger value = map.get(key);
    return (value == null) ? null : value.get();
  }

  // Other accessors ...
}
```

According to § 5.2.1., "ConcurrentHashMap," of the work of Goetz and colleagues [Goetz 2006a]:

ConcurrentHashMap, along with the other concurrent collections, further improve on the synchronized collection classes by providing iterators that do not throw

`ConcurrentModificationException`, as a result eliminating the need to lock the collection during iteration. The iterators returned by `ConcurrentHashMap` are weakly consistent instead of fail-fast. A weakly consistent iterator can tolerate concurrent modification, traverses elements as they existed when the iterator was constructed, and may (but is not guaranteed to) reflect modifications to the collection after the construction of the iterator.

Note that methods such as `ConcurrentHashMap.size()` and `ConcurrentHashMap. isEmpty()` are allowed to return an approximate result for performance reasons. Code should avoid relying on these return values when exact results are required.

Risk Assessment

Failure to ensure the atomicity of two or more operations that must be performed as a single atomic operation can result in race conditions in multithreaded applications.

Rule	Severity	Likelihood	Remediation Cost	Priority	Level
VNA03-J	low	probable	medium	P4	L3

Related Guidelines

MITRE CWE	CWE-362. Concurrent execution using shared resource with improper synchronization ("race condition")
	CWE-366. Race condition within a thread
	CWE-662. Improper synchronization

Bibliography

[API 2006]	
[Goetz 2006a]	Section 4.4.1, Client-side Locking
	Section 5.2.1, ConcurrentHashMap
[JavaThreads 2004]	Section 8.2, Synchronization and Collection Classes
[Lee 2009]	Map & Compound Operation

■ VNA04-J. Ensure that calls to chained methods are atomic

Method chaining is a convenient mechanism that allows multiple method invocations on the same object to occur in a single statement. A method-chaining implementation consists of a series of methods that return the `this` reference. This implementation allows a caller to invoke methods in a chain by performing the next method invocation on the return value of the previous method in the chain.

While the methods used in method chaining can be atomic, the chain they comprise is inherently nonatomic. Consequently, callers of methods that are involved in method chaining must provide sufficient locking to guarantee that the entire chain of invocations is atomic, as shown in rule VNA03-J.

Noncompliant Code Example

Method chaining is a useful design pattern for building an object and setting its optional fields. A class that supports method chaining provides several setter methods that each return the this reference. However, if accessed concurrently, a thread may observe shared fields to contain inconsistent values. This noncompliant code example shows the JavaBeans pattern, which is not thread-safe.

```
final class USCurrency {
  // Change requested, denomination (optional fields)
  private int quarters = 0;
  private int dimes = 0;
  private int nickels = 0;
  private int pennies = 0;
  public USCurrency() {}

  // Setter methods
  public USCurrency setQuarters(int quantity) {
    quarters = quantity;
    return this;
  }
  public USCurrency setDimes(int quantity) {
    dimes = quantity;
    return this;
  }
  public USCurrency setNickels(int quantity) {
    nickels = quantity;
    return this;
  }
  public USCurrency setPennies(int quantity) {
    pennies = quantity;
    return this;
  }
}

// Client code:
class exampleClientCode {
```

```
    private final USCurrency currency = new USCurrency();
    // ...

    public exampleClientCode() {

      Thread t1 = new Thread(new Runnable() {
          @Override public void run() {
            currency.setQuarters(1).setDimes(1);
          }
      });
      t1.start();

      Thread t2 = new Thread(new Runnable() {
          @Override public void run() {
            currency.setQuarters(2).setDimes(2);
          }
      });
      t2.start();

      //...
    }
  }
```

The JavaBeans pattern uses a no-argument constructor and a series of parallel setter methods to build an object. This pattern is not thread-safe and can lead to inconsistent object state when the object is modified concurrently. In this noncompliant code example, the client constructs a USCurrency object and starts two threads that use method chaining to set the optional values of the USCurrency object. This example code might result in the USCurrency instance being left in an inconsistent state, for example, with two quarters and one dime or one quarter and two dimes.

Compliant Solution

This compliant solution uses the variant of the Builder pattern [Gamma 1995], suggested by Bloch [Bloch 2008], to ensure the thread-safety and atomicity of object creation.

```
final class USCurrency {
  private final int quarters;
  private final int dimes;
  private final int nickels;
  private final int pennies;
```

```
  public USCurrency(Builder builder) {
    this.quarters = builder.quarters;
    this.dimes = builder.dimes;
    this.nickels = builder.nickels;
    this.pennies = builder.pennies;
  }

  // Static class member
  public static class Builder {
    private int quarters = 0;
    private int dimes = 0;
    private int nickels = 0;
    private int pennies = 0;

    public static Builder newInstance() {
      return new Builder();
    }

    private Builder() {}

    // Setter methods
    public Builder setQuarters(int quantity) {
      this.quarters = quantity;
      return this;
    }
    public Builder setDimes(int quantity) {
      this.dimes = quantity;
      return this;
    }
    public Builder setNickels(int quantity) {
      this.nickels = quantity;
      return this;
    }
    public Builder setPennies(int quantity) {
      this.pennies = quantity;
      return this;
    }

    public USCurrency build() {
      return new USCurrency(this);
    }
  }
}

// Client code:
class exampleClientCode {
```

```
     private volatile USCurrency currency;
     // ...

     public exampleClientCode() {

       Thread t1 = new Thread(new Runnable() {
           @Override public void run() {
             currency = USCurrency.Builder.newInstance().
                          setQuarters(1).setDimes(1).build();
           }
       });
       t1.start();

       Thread t2 = new Thread(new Runnable() {
           @Override public void run() {
             currency = USCurrency.Builder.newInstance().
                          setQuarters(2).setDimes(2).build();
           }
       });
       t2.start();

       //...
     }
   }
```

The `Builder.newInstance()` factory method is called with any required arguments to obtain a `Builder` instance. The optional parameters are set using the setter methods of the builder. The object construction concludes with the invocation of the `build()` method. This pattern makes the `USCurrency` class immutable and consequently thread-safe.

Note that the `currency` field cannot be declared final because it is assigned a new immutable object. It is, however, declared volatile in compliance with rule VNA01-J.

When input must be validated, ensure that the values are defensively copied prior to validation. (See rule OBJ06-J for more information.) The `builder` class also complies with rule OBJ08-J because it maintains a copy of the variables defined in the scope of the containing class. The private members within the nested class take precedence and, as a result, maintain encapsulation.

Risk Assessment

Using method chaining in multithreaded environments without performing external locking can lead to nondeterministic behavior.

Rule	Severity	Likelihood	Remediation Cost	Priority	Level
VNA04-J	low	probable	medium	P4	L3

Bibliography

[API 2006]

[Bloch 2008]   Item 2. Consider a builder when faced with many constructor parameters

■ VNA05-J. Ensure atomicity when reading and writing 64-bit values

The *Java Language Specification* allows 64-bit `long` and `double` values to be treated as two 32-bit values. For example, a 64-bit write operation could be performed as two separate 32-bit operations.

According to the *Java Language Specification*, §17.7, "Non-Atomic Treatment of `double` and `long`" [JLS 2005]:

> This behavior is implementation specific; Java virtual machines are free to perform writes to `long` and `double` values atomically or in two parts. For the purposes of the Java programming language memory model, a single write to a non-volatile `long` or `double` value is treated as two separate writes: one to each 32-bit half. This can result in a situation where a thread sees the first 32 bits of a 64-bit value from one write, and the second 32 bits from another write.

This behavior can result in indeterminate values being read in code that is required to be thread-safe. Consequently, multithreaded programs must ensure atomicity when reading or writing 64-bit values.

Noncompliant Code Example

In this noncompliant code example, if one thread repeatedly calls the `assignValue()` method and another thread repeatedly calls the `printLong()` method, the `printLong()` method could occasionally print a value of `i` that is neither zero nor the value of the `j` argument.

```java
class LongContainer {
  private long i = 0;

  void assignValue(long j) {
    i = j;
  }
```

```
  void printLong() {
    System.out.println("i = " + i);
  }
}
```

A similar problem can occur when i is declared double.

Compliant Solution (Volatile)

This compliant solution declares i volatile. Writes and reads of long and double volatile values are always atomic.

```
class LongContainer {
  private volatile long i = 0;

  void assignValue(long j) {
    i = j;
  }

  void printLong() {
    System.out.println("i = " + i);
  }
}
```

It is important to ensure that the argument to the assignValue() method is obtained from a volatile variable or obtained as the result of an atomic read. Otherwise, a read of the variable argument can itself expose a vulnerability.

The semantics of volatile explicitly exclude any guarantee of the atomicity of compound operations that involve read-modify-write sequences such as incrementing a value. See rule VNA02-J for more information.

Exceptions

VNA05-EX0: If all reads and writes of 64-bit long and double values occur within a synchronized region, the atomicity of the read/write is guaranteed. This requires both that the value is exposed only through synchronized methods in the class and that the value is inaccessible from other code (whether directly or indirectly). For more information, see rule VNA02.

VNA05-EX1: This rule can be ignored for platforms that guarantee that 64-bit long and double values are read and written as atomic operations. Note, however, that such guarantees are not portable across different platforms.

Risk Assessment

Failure to ensure the atomicity of operations involving 64-bit values in multithreaded applications can result in reading and writing indeterminate values. However, many JVMs read and write 64-bit values atomically even though the specification does not require them to.

Rule	Severity	Likelihood	Remediation Cost	Priority	Level
VNA05-J	low	unlikely	medium	P2	L3

Automated Detection   Some static analysis tools are capable of detecting violations of this rule.

Related Guidelines

MITRE CWE	CWE-667. Improper Locking

Bibliography

[Goetz 2006a]	3.1.2, Non-atomic 64-Bit Operations
[Goetz 2004c]	
[JLS 2005]	§17.7, Non-atomic Treatment of double and long

Chapter 10

Locking (LCK)

◼ Rules

■ Risk Assessment Summary

Rule	Severity	Likelihood	Remediation Cost	Priority	Level
LCK00-J	low	probable	medium	P4	L3
LCK01-J	medium	probable	medium	P8	L2
LCK02-J	medium	probable	medium	P8	L2
LCK03-J	medium	probable	medium	P8	L2
LCK04-J	low	probable	medium	P4	L3
LCK05-J	low	probable	medium	P4	L3
LCK06-J	medium	probable	medium	P8	L2
LCK07-J	low	likely	high	P3	L3
LCK08-J	low	likely	low	P9	L2
LCK09-J	low	probable	high	P2	L3
LCK10-J	low	probable	medium	P4	L3
LCK11-J	low	probable	medium	P4	L3

■ LCK00-J. Use private final lock objects to synchronize classes that may interact with untrusted code

There are two ways to synchronize access to shared mutable variables: method synchronization and block synchronization. Methods declared as synchronized and blocks that synchronize on the this reference both use the object's *monitor* (that is, its intrinsic lock). An attacker can manipulate the system to trigger contention and deadlock by obtaining and indefinitely holding the intrinsic lock of an accessible class, consequently causing a denial of service (DoS).

One technique for preventing this vulnerability is the *private lock object* idiom [Bloch 2001]. This idiom uses the intrinsic lock associated with the instance of a private final java.lang.Object declared within the class instead of the intrinsic lock of the object itself. This idiom requires the use of synchronized blocks within the class's methods rather than the use of synchronized methods. Lock contention between the class's methods and those of a hostile class becomes impossible because the hostile class cannot access the private final lock object.

Static methods and state also share this vulnerability. When a static method is declared synchronized, it acquires the intrinsic lock of the class object before any statements in its body are executed, and it releases the intrinsic lock when the method completes. Untrusted code that has access to an object of the class, or of a subclass, can use the `getClass()` method to gain access to the class object and consequently manipulate the class object's intrinsic lock. Protect static data by locking on a private static final `Object`. Reducing the accessibility of the class to package-private provides further protection against untrusted callers.

The private lock object idiom is also suitable for classes that are designed for inheritance. When a superclass requests a lock on the object's monitor, a subclass can interfere with its operation. For example, a subclass may use the superclass object's intrinsic lock for performing unrelated operations, causing lock contention and deadlock. Separating the locking strategy of the superclass from that of the subclass ensures that they do not share a common lock and also permits fine-grained locking by supporting the use of multiple lock objects for unrelated operations. This increases the overall responsiveness of the application.

Objects that require synchronization must use the private lock object idiom rather than their own intrinsic lock in any case where untrusted code could:

- Subclass the class.
- Create an object of the class or of a subclass.
- Access or acquire an object instance of the class or of a subclass.

Subclasses whose superclasses use the private lock object idiom must themselves use the idiom. However, when a class uses intrinsic synchronization on the class object without documenting its locking policy, subclasses must not use intrinsic synchronization on their own class object. When the superclass documents its policy by stating that client-side locking is supported, the subclasses have the option to choose between intrinsic locking and using the private lock object idiom. Subclasses must document their locking policy regardless of which locking option is chosen. See rule TSM00-J for related information.

When any of these restrictions are violated, the object's intrinsic lock cannot be trusted. But when these restrictions are obeyed, the private lock object idiom fails to add any additional security. Consequently, objects that comply with *all* of the restrictions are permitted to synchronize using their own intrinsic lock. However, block synchronization using the private lock object idiom is superior to method synchronization for methods that contain nonatomic operations that could either use a more fine-grained locking scheme involving multiple private final lock objects or that lack a requirement for synchronization. Nonatomic operations can be decoupled from those that require synchronization and can be executed outside the synchronized block. Both for this reason and for simplification of maintenance, block synchronization using the private lock object idiom is generally preferred over intrinsic synchronization.

Noncompliant Code Example (Method Synchronization)

This noncompliant code example exposes instances of the SomeObject class to untrusted code.

```
public class SomeObject {

  // Locks on the object's monitor
  public synchronized void changeValue() {
    // ...
  }
}

// Untrusted code
SomeObject someObject = new SomeObject();
synchronized (someObject) {
  while (true) {
    // Indefinitely delay someObject
    Thread.sleep(Integer.MAX_VALUE);
  }
}
```

The untrusted code attempts to acquire a lock on the object's monitor and, upon succeeding, introduces an indefinite delay that prevents the synchronized changeValue() method from acquiring the same lock. Note that in the untrusted code, the attacker intentionally violates rule LCK09-J.

Noncompliant Code Example (Public Nonfinal Lock Object)

This noncompliant code example locks on a public nonfinal object in an attempt to use a lock other than SomeObject's intrinsic lock.

```
public class SomeObject {
  public Object lock = new Object();

  public void changeValue() {
    synchronized (lock) {
      // ...
    }
  }
}
```

This change fails to protect against malicious code. For example, untrusted or malicious code could disrupt proper synchronization by changing the value of the lock object.

Noncompliant Code Example (Publicly Accessible Nonfinal Lock Object)

This noncompliant code example synchronizes on a publicly accessible nonfinal field. The lock field is declared volatile so that changes are visible to other threads.

```
public class SomeObject {
  private volatile Object lock = new Object();

  public void changeValue() {
    synchronized (lock) {
      // ...
    }
  }

  public void setLock(Object lockValue) {
    lock = lockValue;
  }
}
```

Any thread can modify the field's value to refer to a different object in the presence of an accessor such as setLock(). That modification might cause two threads that intend to lock on the same object to lock on different objects, thereby permitting them to execute two critical sections in an unsafe manner. For example, if the lock were changed when one thread was in its critical section, a second thread would lock on the new object instead of the old one and would enter its critical section erroneously.

A class that lacks accessible methods to change the lock is secure against untrusted manipulation. However, it remains susceptible to inadvertent modification by the programmer.

Noncompliant Code Example (Public Final Lock Object)

This noncompliant code example uses a public final lock object.

```
public class SomeObject {
  public final Object lock = new Object();

  public void changeValue() {
    synchronized (lock) {
      // ...
```

```
      }
    }
  }

// Untrusted code
SomeObject someObject = new SomeObject();
someObject.lock.wait()
```

Untrusted code that has the ability to create an instance of the class or has access to an already created instance can invoke the `wait()` method on the publicly accessible `lock`, causing the lock in the `changeValue()` method to be released immediately. Furthermore, if the method were to invoke `lock.wait()` from its body and not test a condition predicate, it would be vulnerable to malicious notifications. (See rule THI03-J for more information.)

This noncompliant code example also violates rule OBJ01-J.

Compliant Solution (Private Final Lock Object)

Thread-safe public classes that may interact with untrusted code must use a private final lock object. Existing classes that use intrinsic synchronization must be refactored to use block synchronization on such an object. In this compliant solution, calling `changeValue()` obtains a lock on a private final `Object` instance that is inaccessible to callers that are outside the class's scope.

```
public class SomeObject {
  private final Object lock = new Object(); // private final lock object

  public void changeValue() {
    synchronized (lock) { // Locks on the private Object
      // ...
    }
  }
}
```

A private final lock object can be used only with block synchronization. Block synchronization is preferred over method synchronization because operations without a requirement for synchronization can be moved outside the synchronized region, reducing lock contention and blocking. Note that it is unnecessary to declare the `lock` field volatile because of the strong visibility semantics of final fields. When granularity issues require the use of multiple locks, declare and use multiple private final lock objects to satisfy the granularity requirements rather than using a mutable reference to a lock object along with a setter method.

Noncompliant Code Example (Static)

This noncompliant code example exposes the class object of SomeObject to untrusted code.

```
public class SomeObject {
  // changeValue locks on the class object's monitor
  public static synchronized void changeValue() {
    // ...
  }
}

// Untrusted code
synchronized (SomeObject.class) {
  while (true) {
    Thread.sleep(Integer.MAX_VALUE); // Indefinitely delay someObject
  }
}
```

The untrusted code attempts to acquire a lock on the class object's monitor and, upon succeeding, introduces an indefinite delay that prevents the synchronized changeValue() method from acquiring the same lock.

A compliant solution must also comply with rule LCK05-J. In the untrusted code, the attacker intentionally violates rule LCK09-J.

Compliant Solution (Static)

Thread-safe public classes that both use intrinsic synchronization over the class object and may interact with untrusted code must be refactored to use a static private final lock object and block synchronization.

```
public class SomeObject {
  private static final Object lock = new Object();
  public static void changeValue() {
    synchronized (lock) { // Locks on the private Object
      // ...
    }
  }
}
```

In this compliant solution, changeValue() obtains a lock on a private static Object that is inaccessible to the caller.

Exceptions

LCK00-EX0: A class may violate this rule when *all* of the following conditions are met:

- It sufficiently documents that callers must not pass objects of this class to untrusted code.
- The class cannot invoke methods, directly or indirectly, on objects of any untrusted classes that violate this rule.
- The synchronization policy of the class is documented properly.

Clients are permitted to use a class that violates this rule when *all* of the following conditions are met:

- Neither the client class nor any other class in the system passes objects of the violating class to untrusted code.
- The violating class cannot invoke methods, directly or indirectly, from untrusted classes that violate this rule.

LCK00-EX1: When a superclass of the class documents that it supports client-side locking and synchronizes on its class object, the class can support client-side locking in the same way and document this policy.

LCK00-EX2: Package-private classes are exempt from this rule because their accessibility protects against untrusted callers. However, use of this exemption should be documented explicitly to ensure that trusted code within the same package neither reuses the lock object nor changes the lock object inadvertently.

Risk Assessment

Exposing the lock object to untrusted code can result in DoS.

Rule	Severity	Likelihood	Remediation Cost	Priority	Level
LCK00-J	low	probable	medium	P4	L3

Related Guidelines

MITRE CWE	CWE-412. Unrestricted externally accessible lock
	CWE-413. Improper resource locking

Bibliography

[Bloch 2001]	Item 52. Document thread safety

▪ LCK01-J. Do not synchronize on objects that may be reused

Misuse of synchronization primitives is a common source of concurrency issues. Synchronizing on objects that may be reused can result in deadlock and nondeterministic behavior. Consequently, programs must never synchronize on objects that may be reused.

Noncompliant Code Example (Boolean Lock Object)

This noncompliant code example synchronizes on a `Boolean` lock object.

```
private final Boolean initialized = Boolean.FALSE;

public void doSomething() {
  synchronized (initialized) {
    // ...
  }
}
```

The `Boolean` type is unsuitable for locking purposes because it allows only two values: true and false. Boolean literals containing the same value share unique instances of the `Boolean` class in the Java Virtual Machine (JVM). In this example, `initialized` refers to the instance corresponding to the value `Boolean.FALSE`. If any other code were to inadvertently synchronize on a `Boolean` literal with this value, the lock instance would be reused and the system could become unresponsive or could deadlock.

Noncompliant Code Example (Boxed Primitive)

This noncompliant code example locks on a boxed `Integer` object.

```
int lock = 0;
private final Integer Lock = lock; // Boxed primitive Lock is shared

public void doSomething() {
  synchronized (Lock) {
    // ...
  }
}
```

Boxed types may use the same instance for a range of integer values; consequently, they suffer from the same reuse problem as `Boolean` constants. The wrapper objects are reused when the value can be represented as a byte; JVM implementations are also permitted to reuse wrapper objects for larger ranges of values. While use of the intrinsic lock associated with the boxed `Integer` wrapper object is insecure, instances of the `Integer` object constructed using the `new` operator (`new Integer(value)`) are unique and not reused. In general, locks on any data type that contains a boxed value are insecure.

Compliant Solution (Integer)

This compliant solution locks on a nonboxed `Integer`, using a variant of the private lock object idiom. The `doSomething()` method synchronizes using the intrinsic lock of the `Integer` instance, `Lock`.

```
int lock = 0;
private final Integer Lock = new Integer(lock);

public void doSomething() {
  synchronized (Lock) {
    // ...
  }
}
```

When explicitly constructed, an `Integer` object has a unique reference and its own intrinsic lock that is distinct not only from other `Integer` objects but also from boxed integers that have the same value. While this is an acceptable solution, it can cause maintenance problems because developers can incorrectly assume that boxed integers are also appropriate lock objects. A more appropriate solution is to synchronize on a private final lock object as described in the final compliant solution for this rule.

Noncompliant Code Example (Interned `String` Object)

This noncompliant code example locks on an interned `String` object.

```
private final String lock = new String("LOCK").intern();

public void doSomething() {
  synchronized (lock) {
    // ...
  }
}
```

According to the Java API class java.lang.String documentation [API 2006]:

When the intern() method is invoked, if the pool already contains a string equal to this String object as determined by the equals(Object) method, then the string from the pool is returned. Otherwise, this String object is added to the pool and a reference to this String object is returned.

Consequently, an interned String object behaves like a global variable in the JVM. As demonstrated in this noncompliant code example, even when every instance of an object maintains its own lock field, the fields all refer to a common String constant. Locking on String constants has the same reuse problem as locking on Boolean constants.

Additionally, hostile code from any other package can exploit this vulnerability if the class is accessible. See rule LCK00-J for more information.

Noncompliant Code Example (String Literal)

This noncompliant code example locks on a final String literal.

```
// This bug was found in jetty-6.1.3 BoundedThreadPool
private final String lock = "LOCK";

public void doSomething() {
  synchronized (lock) {
    // ...
  }
}
```

String literals are constant and are automatically interned. Consequently, this example suffers from the same pitfalls as the preceding noncompliant code example.

Compliant Solution (String Instance)

This compliant solution locks on a noninterned String instance.

```
private final String lock = new String("LOCK");

public void doSomething() {
  synchronized (lock) {
    // ...
  }
}
```

A `String` instance differs from a `String` literal. The instance has a unique reference and its own intrinsic lock that is distinct from other `String` object instances or literals. Nevertheless, a better approach is to synchronize on a private final lock object, as shown in the following compliant solution.

Compliant Solution (Private Final Lock `Object`)

This compliant solution synchronizes on a private final lock object. This is one of the few cases in which a `java.lang.Object` instance is useful.

```java
private final Object lock = new Object();

public void doSomething() {
  synchronized (lock) {
    // ...
  }
}
```

For more information on using an `Object` as a lock, see rule LCK00-J.

Risk Assessment

A significant number of concurrency vulnerabilities arise from locking on the wrong kind of object. It is important to consider the properties of the lock object rather than simply scavenging for objects on which to synchronize.

Rule	Severity	Likelihood	Remediation Cost	Priority	Level
LCK01-J	medium	probable	medium	P8	L2

Automated Detection   Some static analysis tools can detect violations of this rule.

Bibliography

[API 2006]   Class String, Collections

[Findbugs 2008]

[Miller 2009]   Locking

[Pugh 2008]   Synchronization

[Tutorials 2008]   Wrapper Implementations

■ LCK02-J. Do not synchronize on the class object returned by getClass()

Synchronizing on the return value of the `Object.getClass()` method can lead to unexpected behavior. Whenever the implementing class is subclassed, the subclass locks on the subclass's type. The `Class` object of the subclass is entirely distinct from the `Class` object of the parent class.

According to the *Java Language Specification*, §4.3.2, "The Class Object" [JLS 2005]:

> A class method that is declared `synchronized` synchronizes on the lock associated with the `Class` object of the class.

Programmers who interpret this to mean that a subclass using `getClass()` will synchronize on the `Class` object of the base class are incorrect. The subclass will actually lock on its own `Class` object; which may or may not be what the programmer intended. Consequently, programs must not synchronize on the class object returned by `getClass()`.

The programmer's actual intent should be clearly documented or annotated. Note that when a subclass fails to override an accessible noncompliant superclass's method, it inherits the method, which may lead to the false conclusion that the superclass's intrinsic lock is available in the subclass.

When synchronizing on a class literal, the corresponding lock object should be inaccessible to untrusted code. Callers from other packages cannot access class objects that are package-private; consequently, synchronizing on the intrinsic lock object of such classes is permitted. For more information, see rule LCK00-J.

Noncompliant Code Example (getClass() Lock Object)

In this noncompliant code example, the `parse()` method of the `Base` class parses a date and synchronizes on the class object returned by `getClass()`. The `Derived` class also inherits the `parse()` method. However, this inherited method synchronizes on `Derived`'s class object because the inherited parse method's invocation of `getClass()` is really an invocation of `this.getClass()`, and the `this` argument is a reference to the instance of the `Derived` class.

The `Derived` class also adds a `doSomethingAndParse()` method that locks on the class object of the `Base` class because the developer misconstrued that the `parse()` method in `Base` always obtains a lock on the `Base` class object, and `doSomethingAndParse()` must follow the same locking policy. Consequently, the `Derived` class has two different locking strategies and fails to be thread-safe.

```
class Base {
  static DateFormat format =
    DateFormat.getDateInstance(DateFormat.MEDIUM);

  public Date parse(String str) throws ParseException {
    synchronized (getClass()) {
      return format.parse(str);
    }
  }
}

class Derived extends Base {
  public Date doSomethingAndParse(String str) throws ParseException {
    synchronized (Base.class) {
      // ...
      return format.parse(str);
    }
  }
}
```

Compliant Solution (Class Name Qualification)

In this compliant solution, the class name providing the lock (Base) is fully qualified.

```
class Base {
  static DateFormat format =
    DateFormat.getDateInstance(DateFormat.MEDIUM);

  public Date parse(String str) throws ParseException {
    synchronized (Base.class) {
      return format.parse(str);
    }
  }
}

// ...
```

This code example always synchronizes on the Base.class object, even when it is called from a Derived object.

Compliant Solution (Class.forName())

This compliant solution uses the Class.forName() method to synchronize on the Base class's Class object.

```
class Base {
  static DateFormat format =
      DateFormat.getDateInstance(DateFormat.MEDIUM);

  public Date parse(String str) throws ParseException {
    try {
      synchronized (Class.forName("Base")) {
        return format.parse(str);
      }
    } catch (ClassNotFoundException x) {
      // "Base" not found; handle error
    }
    return null;
  }
}

// ...
```

Never accept untrusted inputs as arguments while loading classes using Class. forName(). See rule SEC03-J for more information.

Noncompliant Code Example (getClass() Lock Object, Inner Class)

This noncompliant code example synchronizes on the class object returned by getClass() in the parse() method of class Base. The Base class also has a nested Helper class whose doSomethingAndParse() method incorrectly synchronizes on the value returned by getClass().

```
class Base {
  static DateFormat format =
      DateFormat.getDateInstance(DateFormat.MEDIUM);

  public Date parse(String str) throws ParseException {
    synchronized (getClass()) { // Synchronizes on Base.class
      return format.parse(str);
    }
  }

  public Date doSomething(String str) throws ParseException {
    return new Helper().doSomethingAndParse(str);
  }

  private class Helper {
    public Date doSomethingAndParse(String str) throws ParseException {
      synchronized (getClass()) { // Synchronizes on Helper.class
        // ...
```

```
        return format.parse(str);
      }
    }
  }
}
```

The call to getClass() in the Helper class returns a Helper class object instead of the Base class object. Consequently, a thread that calls Base.parse() locks on a different object than a thread that calls Base.doSomething(). It is easy to overlook concurrency errors in inner classes because they exist within the body of the containing outer class. A reviewer might incorrectly assume that the two classes have the same locking strategy.

Compliant Solution (Class Name Qualification)

This compliant solution synchronizes using a Base class literal in the parse() and doSomethingAndParse() methods.

```
class Base {
  // ...

  public Date parse(String str) throws ParseException {
    synchronized (Base.class) {
      return format.parse(str);
    }
  }

  private class Helper {
    public Date doSomethingAndParse(String str) throws ParseException {
      synchronized (Base.class) { // Synchronizes on Base class literal
        // ...
        return format.parse(str);
      }
    }
  }
}
```

Consequently, both Base and Helper lock on Base's intrinsic lock. Similarly, the Class.forName() method can be used instead of a class literal.

Risk Assessment

Synchronizing on the class object returned by getClass() can result in nondeterministic behavior.

Rule	Severity	Likelihood	Remediation Cost	Priority	Level
LCK02-J	medium	probable	medium	P8	L2

Bibliography

[API 2006]

[Findbugs 2008]

[Pugh 2008]   Synchronization

[Miller 2009]   Locking

■ LCK03-J. Do not synchronize on the intrinsic locks of high-level concurrency objects

Instances of classes that implement either or both of the Lock and Condition interfaces of the java.util.concurrent.locks package are known as high-level concurrency objects. Using the intrinsic locks of such objects is a questionable practice even in cases where the code may appear to function correctly. Consequently, programs that interact with such objects must use only the high-level locking facilities provided by the interfaces; use of the intrinsic locks is prohibited. This problem generally arises when code is refactored from intrinsic locking to the java.util.concurrent dynamic-locking utilities.

Noncompliant Code Example (ReentrantLock)

The doSomething() method in this noncompliant code example synchronizes on the intrinsic lock of an instance of ReentrantLock rather than on the reentrant mutual exclusion Lock encapsulated by ReentrantLock.

```
private final Lock lock = new ReentrantLock();
public void doSomething() {
  synchronized (lock) {
    // ...
  }
}
```

Compliant Solution (lock() and unlock())

This compliant solution uses the lock() and unlock() methods provided by the Lock interface.

```
private final Lock lock = new ReentrantLock();

public void doSomething() {
  lock.lock();
  try {
    // ...
  } finally {
    lock.unlock();
  }
}
```

In the absence of a requirement for the advanced functionality of the `java.util.concurrent` package's dynamic-locking utilities, it is better to use the `Executor` framework or other concurrency primitives such as synchronization and atomic classes.

Risk Assessment

Synchronizing on the intrinsic lock of high-level concurrency utilities can cause nondeterministic behavior resulting from inconsistent locking policies.

Rule	Severity	Likelihood	Remediation Cost	Priority	Level
LCK03-J	medium	probable	medium	P8	L2

Bibliography

[API 2006]

[Findbugs 2008]

[Pugh 2008]   Synchronization

[Miller 2009]   Locking

[Tutorials 2008]   Wrapper Implementations

■ LCK04-J. Do not synchronize on a collection view if the backing collection is accessible

The `java.util.Collections` interface's documentation [API 2006] warns about the consequences of failing to synchronize on an accessible collection object when iterating over its view:

> It is imperative that the user manually synchronize on the returned map when iterating over any of its collection views.... Failure to follow this advice may result in non-deterministic behavior.

Any class that uses a collection view rather than the backing collection as the lock object may end up with two distinct locking strategies. When the backing collection is accessible to multiple threads, the class that locked on the collection view has violated the thread-safety properties and is unsafe. Consequently, programs that both require synchronization while iterating over collection views and have accessible backing collections must synchronize on the backing collection; synchronization on the view is a violation of this rule.

Noncompliant Code Example (Collection View)

This noncompliant code example creates a HashMap object and two view objects: A synchronized view of an empty HashMap encapsulated by the mapView field and a set view of the map's keys encapsulated by the setView field. This example synchronizes on setView [Tutorials 2008].

```
private final Map<Integer, String> mapView =
    Collections.synchronizedMap(new HashMap<Integer, String>());
private final Set<Integer> setView = mapView.keySet();

public Map<Integer, String> getMap() {
  return mapView;
}

public void doSomething() {
  synchronized (setView) {  // Incorrectly synchronizes on setView
    for (Integer k : setView) {
      // ...
    }
  }
}
```

In this example, HashMap provides the backing collection for the synchronized map represented by mapView, which provides the backing collection for setView, as shown in Figure 10–1.

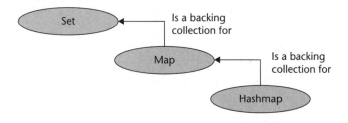

Figure 10-1. Backing collections.

The `HashMap` object is inaccessible, but `mapView` is accessible via the public `getMap()` method. Because the `synchronized` statement uses the intrinsic lock of `setView` rather than of `mapView`, another thread can modify the synchronized map and invalidate the k iterator.

Compliant Solution (Collection Lock Object)

This compliant solution synchronizes on the `mapView` field rather than on the `setView` field.

```java
private final Map<Integer, String> mapView =
    Collections.synchronizedMap(new HashMap<Integer, String>());
private final Set<Integer> setView = mapView.keySet();

public Map<Integer, String> getMap() {
  return mapView;
}

public void doSomething() {
  synchronized (mapView) { // Synchronize on map, rather than set
    for (Integer k : setView) {
      // ...
    }
  }
}
```

This code is compliant because the map's underlying structure cannot be changed during the iteration.

Risk Assessment

Synchronizing on a collection view instead of the collection object can cause nondeterministic behavior.

Rule	Severity	Likelihood	Remediation Cost	Priority	Level
LCK04-J	low	probable	medium	P4	L3

Bibliography

[API 2006]   Class Collections
[Tutorials 2008]   Wrapper Implementations

■ LCK05-J. Synchronize access to static fields that can be modified by untrusted code

Methods that can both modify a static field and be invoked from untrusted code must synchronize access to the static field. Even when client-side locking is a specified requirement of the method, untrusted clients can fail to synchronize (whether inadvertently or maliciously). Because the static field is shared by all clients, untrusted clients may violate the contract by failing to provide suitable locking.

According to Joshua Bloch [Bloch 2008]:

> If a method modifies a static field, you must synchronize access to this field, even if the method is typically used only by a single thread. It is not possible for clients to perform external synchronization on such a method because there can be no guarantee that unrelated clients will do likewise.

Documented design intent is irrelevant when dealing with untrusted code because an attacker can always choose to ignore the documentation.

Noncompliant Code Example

This noncompliant code example fails to synchronize access to the static `counter` field.

```
/* This class is not thread-safe */
public final class CountHits {
  private static int counter;

  public void incrementCounter() {
    counter++;
  }
}
```

This class definition complies with rule VNA02-J, which applies only to classes that promise thread-safety. However, this class has a mutable static `counter` field that is modified by the publicly accessible `incrementCounter()` method. Consequently, this class cannot be used securely by trusted client code because untrusted code can purposely fail to externally synchronize access to the field.

Compliant Solution

This compliant solution uses a static private final lock to protect the `counter` field and consequently lacks any dependence on external synchronization. This solution also complies with rule LCK00-J.

```
/** This class is thread-safe */
public final class CountHits {
  private static int counter;
  private static final Object lock = new Object();

  public void incrementCounter() {
    synchronized (lock) {
      counter++;
    }
  }
}
```

Risk Assessment

Failure to internally synchronize access to static fields that can be modified by untrusted code risks incorrect synchronization because the author of the untrusted code can inadvertently or maliciously ignore the synchronization policy.

Rule	Severity	Likelihood	Remediation Cost	Priority	Level
LCK05-J	low	probable	medium	P4	L3

Related Guidelines

MITRE CWE	CWE-820. Missing synchronization

Bibliography

[API 2006]	
[Bloch 2008]	Item 67. Avoid excessive synchronization

■ LCK06-J. Do not use an instance lock to protect shared static data

Programs must not use instance locks to protect static shared data because instance locks are ineffective when two or more instances of the class are created. Consequently, failure to use a static lock object leaves the shared state unprotected against concurrent access. Lock objects for classes that can interact with untrusted code must also be private and final, as shown in rule LCK00-J.

Noncompliant Code Example (Nonstatic Lock Object for Static Data)

This noncompliant code example attempts to guard access to the static `counter` field using a nonstatic lock object. When two `Runnable` tasks are started, they create two instances of the lock object and lock on each instance separately.

```
public final class CountBoxes implements Runnable {
  private static volatile int counter;
  // ...
  private final Object lock = new Object();

  @Override public void run() {
    synchronized (lock) {
      counter++;
      // ...
    }
  }

  public static void main(String[] args) {
    for (int i = 0; i < 2; i++) {
      new Thread(new CountBoxes()).start();
    }
  }
}
```

This example fails to prevent either thread from observing an inconsistent value of `counter` because the increment operation on volatile fields fails to be atomic in the absence of proper synchronization. (See rule VNA02-J for more information.)

Noncompliant Code Example (Method Synchronization for Static Data)

This noncompliant code example uses method synchronization to protect access to a static class `counter` field.

```
public final class CountBoxes implements Runnable {
  private static volatile int counter;
  // ...

  public synchronized void run() {
    counter++;
    // ...
  }
  // ...
}
```

In this case, the method synchronization uses the intrinsic lock associated with each instance of the class rather than the intrinsic lock associated with the class itself. Consequently, threads constructed using different `Runnable` instances may observe inconsistent values of `counter`.

Compliant Solution (Static Lock Object)

This compliant solution ensures the atomicity of the increment operation by locking on a static object.

```java
public class CountBoxes implements Runnable {
  private static int counter;
  // ...
  private static final Object lock = new Object();

  public void run() {
    synchronized (lock) {
      counter++;
      // ...
    }
  }
  // ...
}
```

It is unnecessary to declare the `counter` variable volatile when using synchronization.

Risk Assessment

Using an instance lock to protect static shared data can result in nondeterministic behavior.

Rule	Severity	Likelihood	Remediation Cost	Priority	Level
LCK06-J	medium	probable	medium	P8	L2

Automated Detection   Some static analysis tools can detect violations of this rule.

Related Guidelines

MITRE CWE   CWE-667, Improper Locking

Bibliography

[API 2006]

■ LCK07-J. Avoid deadlock by requesting and releasing locks in the same order

To avoid data corruption in multithreaded Java programs, shared data must be protected from concurrent modifications and accesses. Locking can be performed at the object level using synchronized methods, synchronized blocks, or the `java.util.concurrent` dynamic lock objects. However, excessive use of locking can result in deadlocks.

Java neither prevents deadlocks nor requires their detection [JLS 2005]. Deadlock can occur when two or more threads request and release locks in different orders. Consequently, programs are required to avoid deadlock by acquiring and releasing locks in the same order.

Additionally, synchronization should be limited to cases where it is absolutely necessary. For example, the `paint()`, `dispose()`, `stop()`, and `destroy()` methods should never be synchronized in an applet because they are always called and used from dedicated threads. Furthermore, the `Thread.stop()` and `Thread.destroy()` methods are deprecated; see rule THI05-J for more information.

This rule also applies to programs that need to work with a limited set of resources. For example, liveness issues can arise when two or more threads are waiting for each other to release resources such as database connections. These issues can be resolved by letting each waiting thread retry the operation at random intervals until they succeed in acquiring the resource successfully.

Noncompliant Code Example (Different Lock Orders)

This noncompliant code example can deadlock because of excessive synchronization. The `balanceAmount` field represents the total balance amount available for a particular Bank-Account object. Users are allowed to initiate an operation that atomically transfers a specified amount from one account to another.

```
final class BankAccount {
  private double balanceAmount;  // Total amount in bank account

  BankAccount(double balance) {
    this.balanceAmount = balance;
  }

  // Deposits the amount from this object instance
  // to BankAccount instance argument ba
  private void depositAmount(BankAccount ba, double amount) {
    synchronized (this) {
      synchronized (ba) {
        if (amount > balanceAmount) {
```

```
            throw new IllegalArgumentException(
                "Transfer cannot be completed"
            );
        }
        ba.balanceAmount += amount;
        this.balanceAmount -= amount;
      }
    }
  }

  public static void initiateTransfer(final BankAccount first,
    final BankAccount second, final double amount) {

    Thread transfer = new Thread(new Runnable() {
        public void run() {
          first.depositAmount(second, amount);
        }
    });
    transfer.start();
  }
}
```

Objects of this class are prone to deadlock. An attacker who has two bank accounts can construct two threads that initiate balance transfers from two different BankAccount object instances a and b. For example, consider the following code:

```
BankAccount a = new BankAccount(5000);
BankAccount b = new BankAccount(6000);
initiateTransfer(a, b, 1000); // starts thread 1
initiateTransfer(b, a, 1000); // starts thread 2
```

Each transfer is performed in its own thread. The first thread atomically transfers the amount from a to b by depositing it in account b and then withdrawing the same amount from a. The second thread performs the reverse operation; that is, it transfers the amount from b to a. When executing depositAmount(), the first thread acquires a lock on object a. The second thread could acquire a lock on object b before the first thread can. Subsequently, the first thread would request a lock on b, which is already held by the second thread. The second thread would request a lock on a, which is already held by the first thread. This constitutes a deadlock condition, because neither thread can proceed.

This noncompliant code example may or may not deadlock, depending on the scheduling details of the platform. Deadlock occurs when (1) two threads request the same two locks in different orders, and (2) each thread obtains a lock that prevents the other thread from completing its transfer. Deadlock is avoided when two threads request the same two locks but one thread completes its transfer before the other thread begins. Similarly, deadlock is avoided if the two threads request the same two locks in the same order (which would happen if they both transfer money from one account to a second account) or if two transfers involving distinct accounts occur concurrently.

Compliant Solution (Private Static Final Lock Object)

This compliant solution avoids deadlock by synchronizing on a private static final lock object before performing any account transfers.

```java
final class BankAccount {
  private double balanceAmount;  // Total amount in bank account
  private static final Object lock = new Object();

  BankAccount(double balance) {
    this.balanceAmount = balance;
  }

  // Deposits the amount from this object instance
  // to BankAccount instance argument ba
  private void depositAmount(BankAccount ba, double amount) {
    synchronized (lock) {
      if (amount > balanceAmount) {
        throw new IllegalArgumentException(
            "Transfer cannot be completed");
      }
      ba.balanceAmount += amount;
      this.balanceAmount -= amount;
    }
  }

  public static void initiateTransfer(final BankAccount first,
      final BankAccount second, final double amount) {

    Thread transfer = new Thread(new Runnable() {
      @Override public void run() {
        first.depositAmount(second, amount);
      }
    });
    transfer.start();
  }
}
```

In this scenario, deadlock cannot occur when two threads with two different Bank-Account objects try to transfer to each other's accounts simultaneously. One thread will acquire the private lock, complete its transfer, and release the lock before the other thread can proceed.

This solution imposes a performance penalty because a private static lock restricts the system to performing transfers sequentially. Two transfers involving four distinct accounts (with distinct target accounts) cannot be performed concurrently. This penalty increases considerably as the number of BankAccount objects increase. Consequently, this solution fails to scale well.

Compliant Solution (Ordered Locks)

This compliant solution ensures that multiple locks are acquired and released in the same order. It requires a consistent ordering over BankAccount objects. Consequently, the BankAccount class implements the java.lang.Comparable interface and overrides the compareTo() method.

```
final class BankAccount implements Comparable<BankAccount> {
  private double balanceAmount;  // Total amount in bank account
  private final Object lock;

  private final long id; // Unique for each BankAccount
  private static long NextID = 0; // Next unused ID

  BankAccount(double balance) {
    this.balanceAmount = balance;
    this.lock = new Object();
    this.id = this.NextID++;
  }

  @Override public int compareTo(BankAccount ba) {
    return (this.id > ba.id) ? 1 : (this.id < ba.id) ? -1 : 0;
  }

  // Deposits the amount from this object instance
  // to BankAccount instance argument ba
  public void depositAmount(BankAccount ba, double amount) {
    BankAccount former, latter;
    if (compareTo(ba) < 0) {
      former = this;
      latter = ba;
    } else {
      former = ba;
      latter = this;
    }
    synchronized (former) {
```

```
      synchronized (latter) {
        if (amount > balanceAmount) {
          throw new IllegalArgumentException(
            "Transfer cannot be completed");
        }
        ba.balanceAmount += amount;
        this.balanceAmount -= amount;
      }
    }
  }

  public static void initiateTransfer(final BankAccount first,
    final BankAccount second, final double amount) {

    Thread transfer = new Thread(new Runnable() {
      @Override public void run() {
        first.depositAmount(second, amount);
      }
    });
    transfer.start();
  }
}
```

Whenever a transfer occurs, the two BankAccount objects are ordered so that the first object's lock is acquired before the second object's lock. When two threads attempt transfers between the same two accounts, they each try to acquire the first account's lock before acquiring the second account's lock. Consequently, one thread acquires both locks, completes the transfer, and releases both locks before the other thread can proceed.

Unlike the previous compliant solution, this solution permits multiple concurrent transfers as long as the transfers involve distinct accounts.

Compliant Solution (ReentrantLock)

In this compliant solution, each BankAccount has a java.util.concurrent.locks.ReentrantLock. This design permits the depositAmount() method to attempt to acquire the locks of both accounts, to release the locks if it fails, and to try again later if necessary.

```
final class BankAccount {
  private double balanceAmount;  // Total amount in bank account
  private final Lock lock = new ReentrantLock();
  private final Random number = new Random(123L);
```

```java
BankAccount(double balance) {
  this.balanceAmount = balance;
}


// Deposits amount from this object instance
// to BankAccount instance argument ba
private void depositAmount(BankAccount ba, double amount)
                          throws InterruptedException {

  while (true) {
    if (this.lock.tryLock()) {
      try {
        if (ba.lock.tryLock()) {
          try {
            if (amount > balanceAmount) {
              throw new IllegalArgumentException(
                  "Transfer cannot be completed");
            }
            ba.balanceAmount += amount;
            this.balanceAmount -= amount;
            break;
          } finally {
            ba.lock.unlock();
          }
        }
      } finally {
        this.lock.unlock();
      }
    }
    int n = number.nextInt(1000);
    int TIME = 1000 + n; // 1 second + random delay to prevent livelock
    Thread.sleep(TIME);
  }
}


public static void initiateTransfer(final BankAccount first,
  final BankAccount second, final double amount) {

  Thread transfer = new Thread(new Runnable() {
      public void run() {
        try {
          first.depositAmount(second, amount);
        } catch (InterruptedException e) {
          Thread.currentThread().interrupt(); // Reset interrupted status
        }
```

```
      }
   });
   transfer.start();
  }
}
```

Deadlock is impossible in this compliant solution because locks are never held indefinitely. If the current object's lock is acquired but the second lock is unavailable, the first lock is released and the thread sleeps for some specified amount of time before attempting to reacquire the lock.

Code that uses this locking strategy has behavior similar to that of synchronized code that uses traditional monitor locks. ReentrantLock also provides several other capabilities. For example, the tryLock() method immediately returns false when another thread already holds the lock. Further, the java.util.concurrent.locks.ReentrantReadWriteLock class has multiple-reader/single-writer semantics and is useful when some threads require a lock to write information while other threads require the lock to concurrently read the information.

Noncompliant Code Example (Different Lock Orders, Recursive)

The following immutable WebRequest class encapsulates a web request received by a server:

```java
// Immutable WebRequest
public final class WebRequest {
  private final long bandwidth;
  private final long responseTime;

  public WebRequest(long bandwidth, long responseTime) {
    this.bandwidth = bandwidth;
    this.responseTime = responseTime;
  }

  public long getBandwidth() {
    return bandwidth;
  }

  public long getResponseTime() {
    return responseTime;
  }
}
```

Each request has a response time associated with it, along with a measurement of the network bandwidth required to fulfill the request.

This noncompliant code example monitors web requests and provides routines for calculating the average bandwidth and response time required to serve incoming requests.

```java
public final class WebRequestAnalyzer {
  private final Vector<WebRequest> requests = new Vector<WebRequest>();

  public boolean addWebRequest(WebRequest request) {
    return requests.add(new WebRequest(request.getBandwidth(),
                        request.getResponseTime()));
  }

  public double getAverageBandwidth() {
    if (requests.size() == 0) {
      throw new IllegalStateException("The vector is empty!");
    }
    return calculateAverageBandwidth(0, 0);
  }

  public double getAverageResponseTime() {
    if (requests.size() == 0) {
      throw new IllegalStateException("The vector is empty!");
    }
    return calculateAverageResponseTime(requests.size() - 1, 0);
  }

  private double calculateAverageBandwidth(int i, long bandwidth) {
    if (i == requests.size()) {
      return bandwidth / requests.size();
    }
    synchronized (requests.elementAt(i)) {
      bandwidth += requests.get(i).getBandwidth();
      // Acquires locks in increasing order
      return calculateAverageBandwidth(++i, bandwidth);
    }
  }

  private double calculateAverageResponseTime(int i, long responseTime) {
    if (i <= -1) {
      return responseTime / requests.size();
    }
    synchronized (requests.elementAt(i)) {
      responseTime += requests.get(i).getResponseTime();
      // Acquires locks in decreasing order
      return calculateAverageResponseTime(--i, responseTime);
    }
  }
}
```

The monitoring application is built around the WebRequestAnalyzer class, which maintains a list of web requests using the requests vector and includes the addWeb-Request() setter method. Any thread can request the average bandwidth or average response time of all web requests by invoking the getAverageBandwidth() and getAverageResponseTime() methods.

These methods use fine-grained locking by holding locks on individual elements (web requests) of the vector. These locks permit new requests to be added while the computations are still underway. Consequently, the statistics reported by the methods are accurate when they return the results.

Unfortunately, this noncompliant code example is prone to deadlock because the recursive calls within the synchronized regions of these methods acquire the intrinsic locks in opposite numerical orders. That is, calculateAverageBandwidth() requests locks from index 0 up to requests.size() - 1, whereas calculateAverageResponse-Time() requests them from index requests.size() - 1 down to 0. Because of recursion, previously acquired locks are never released by either method. Deadlock occurs when two threads call these methods out of order, because one thread calls calculateAverage-Bandwidth(), while the other calls calculateAverageResponseTime() before either method has finished executing.

For example, when there are 20 requests in the vector, and one thread calls getAverage-Bandwidth(), the thread acquires the intrinsic lock of WebRequest 0, the first element in the vector. Meanwhile, if a second thread calls getAverageResponseTime(), it acquires the intrinsic lock of WebRequest 19, the last element in the vector. Consequently, deadlock results because neither thread can acquire all of the locks required to proceed with its calculations.

Note that the addWebRequest() method also has a race condition with calculate-AverageResponseTime(). While iterating over the vector, new elements can be added to the vector, invalidating the results of the previous computation. This race condition can be prevented by locking on the last element of the vector (when it contains at least one element) before inserting the element.

Compliant Solution

In this compliant solution, the two calculation methods acquire and release locks in the same order, beginning with the first web request in the vector.

```
public final class WebRequestAnalyzer {
  private final Vector<WebRequest> requests = new Vector<WebRequest>();

  public boolean addWebRequest(WebRequest request) {
    return requests.add(new WebRequest(request.getBandwidth(),
                        request.getResponseTime()));
  }
```

```java
public double getAverageBandwidth() {
  if (requests.size() == 0) {
    throw new IllegalStateException("The vector is empty!");
  }
  return calculateAverageBandwidth(0, 0);
}

public double getAverageResponseTime() {
  if (requests.size() == 0) {
    throw new IllegalStateException("The vector is empty!");
  }
  return calculateAverageResponseTime(0, 0);
}

private double calculateAverageBandwidth(int i, long bandwidth) {
  if (i == requests.size()) {
    return bandwidth / requests.size();
  }
  synchronized (requests.elementAt(i)) {
    // Acquires locks in increasing order
    bandwidth += requests.get(i).getBandwidth();
    return calculateAverageBandwidth(++i, bandwidth);
  }
}

private double calculateAverageResponseTime(int i, long responseTime) {
  if (i == requests.size()) {
    return responseTime / requests.size();
  }
  synchronized (requests.elementAt(i)) {
    // Acquires locks in increasing order
    responseTime += requests.get(i).getResponseTime();
    return calculateAverageResponseTime(++i, responseTime);
  }
}
}
```

Consequently, while one thread is calculating the average bandwidth or response time, another thread cannot interfere or induce deadlock. Each thread must first synchronize on the first web request, which cannot happen until any prior calculation completes.

Locking on the last element of the vector in `addWebRequest()` is unnecessary for two reasons. First, the locks are acquired in increasing order in all the methods. Second, updates to the vector are reflected in the results of the computations.

Risk Assessment

Acquiring and releasing locks in the wrong order can result in deadlock.

Rule	Severity	Likelihood	Remediation Cost	Priority	Level
LCK07-J	low	likely	high	P3	L3

Automated Detection   Some static analysis tools can detect violations of this rule.

Related Guidelines

CERT C Secure Coding Standard	CON35-C. Avoid deadlock by locking in predefined order
MITRE CWE	CWE-833. Deadlock

Bibliography

[JLS 2005]	Chapter 17, Threads and Locks
[Halloway 2000]	

■ LCK08-J. Ensure actively held locks are released on exceptional conditions

An exceptional condition can circumvent the release of a lock, leading to deadlock. According to the Java API [API 2006]:

> A ReentrantLock is owned by the thread last successfully locking, but not yet unlocking it. A thread invoking lock will return, successfully acquiring the lock, when the lock is not owned by another thread.

Consequently, an unreleased lock in any thread will prevent other threads from acquiring the same lock. Programs must release all actively held locks on exceptional conditions. Intrinsic locks of class objects used for method and block synchronization are automatically released on exceptional conditions (such as abnormal thread termination).

Noncompliant Code Example (Checked Exception)

This noncompliant code example protects a resource using a ReentrantLock but fails to release the lock when an exception occurs while performing operations on the open file. When an exception is thrown, control transfers to the catch block and the call to unlock() fails to execute.

```
public final class Client {
  public void doSomething(File file) {
    final Lock lock = new ReentrantLock();
    InputStream in = null;
    try {
      lock.lock();
      in = new FileInputStream(file);

      // Perform operations on the open file

      lock.unlock();
    } catch (FileNotFoundException x) {
      // Handle exception
    } finally {
      if (in != null) {
        try {
          in.close();
        } catch (IOException x) {
          // Handle exception
        }
      }
    }
  }
}
```

Compliant Solution (`finally` Block)

This compliant solution encapsulates operations that could throw an exception in a `try` block immediately after acquiring the lock. The lock is acquired just before the `try` block, which guarantees that it is held when the `finally` block executes. Invoking `Lock.unlock()` in the `finally` block ensures that the lock is released regardless of whether an exception occurs or not.

```
public final class Client {
  public void doSomething(File file) {
    final Lock lock = new ReentrantLock();
    InputStream in = null;
    lock.lock();
    try {
      in = new FileInputStream(file);
```

```
      // Perform operations on the open file
    } catch (FileNotFoundException fnf) {
      // Forward to handler
    } finally {
      lock.unlock();

      if (in != null) {
        try {
          in.close();
        } catch (IOException e) {
          // Forward to handler
        }
      }
    }
  }
}
```

Compliant Solution (Execute-Around Idiom)

The execute-around idiom provides a generic mechanism to perform resource allocation and cleanup operations so that the client can focus on specifying only the required functionality. This idiom reduces clutter in client code and provides a secure mechanism for resource management.

In this compliant solution, the client's doSomething() method provides only the required functionality by implementing the doSomethingWithFile() method of the Lock-Action interface without having to manage the acquisition and release of locks or the open and close operations of files. The ReentrantLockAction class encapsulates all resource management actions.

```
public interface LockAction {
  void doSomethingWithFile(InputStream in);
}

public final class ReentrantLockAction {
  public static void doSomething(File file, LockAction action) {
    Lock lock = new ReentrantLock();
    InputStream in = null;
    lock.lock();
    try {
```

```
      in = new FileInputStream(file);
      action.doSomethingWithFile(in);
    } catch (FileNotFoundException fnf) {
      // Forward to handler
    } finally {
      lock.unlock();

      if (in != null) {
        try {
          in.close();
        } catch (IOException e) {
          // Forward to handler
        }
      }
    }
  }
}

public final class Client {
  public void doSomething(File file) {
    ReentrantLockAction.doSomething(file, new LockAction() {
        public void doSomethingWithFile(InputStream in) {
          // Perform operations on the open file
        }
    });
  }
}
```

Noncompliant Code Example (Unchecked Exception)

This noncompliant code example uses a ReentrantLock to protect a java.util.Date instance—recall that java.util.Date is thread-unsafe by design.

```
final class DateHandler {

  private final Date date = new Date();

  final Lock lock = new ReentrantLock();
```

```
public void doSomething(String str) {
  lock.lock();
  String dateString = date.toString();
  if (str.equals(dateString)) {
   // ...
  }
  // ...

  lock.unlock();
 }
}
```

A runtime exception can occur because the doSomething() method fails to check whether str is a null reference, preventing the lock from being released.

Compliant Solution (`finally` Block)

This compliant solution encapsulates all operations that can throw an exception in a try block and releases the lock in the associated finally block. Consequently, the lock is released even in the event of a runtime exception.

```
final class DateHandler {

  private final Date date = new Date();

  final Lock lock = new ReentrantLock();

  public void doSomething(String str) {
    lock.lock();
    try {
      String dateString = date.toString();
      if (str != null && str.equals(dateString)) {
       // ...
      }
      // ...

    } finally {
      lock.unlock();
    }
  }
}
```

The `doSomething()` method also avoids throwing a `NullPointerException` by ensuring that the string does not contain a null reference.

Risk Assessment

Failure to release locks on exceptional conditions could lead to thread starvation and deadlock.

Rule	Severity	Likelihood	Remediation Cost	Priority	Level
LCK08-J	low	likely	low	P9	L2

Related Vulnerabilities   The GERONIMO-2234 issue report[1] describes a vulnerability in the Geronimo application server. If the user single-clicks the keystore portlet, the user will lock the default keystore without warning. This causes a crash and stack trace to be produced. Furthermore, the server cannot be restarted because the lock is never cleared.

Related Guidelines

MITRE CWE   CWE-883. Deadlock

Bibliography

[API 2006]   Class `ReentrantLock`

■ LCK09-J. Do not perform operations that can block while holding a lock

Holding locks while performing time-consuming or blocking operations can severely degrade system performance and can result in starvation. Furthermore, deadlock can result if interdependent threads block indefinitely. Blocking operations include network, file, and console I/O (for example, `Console.readLine()`) and object serialization. Deferring a thread indefinitely also constitutes a blocking operation. Consequently, programs must not perform blocking operations while holding a lock.

When the JVM interacts with a file system that operates over an unreliable network, file I/O might incur a large performance penalty. In such cases, avoid file I/O over the network while holding a lock. File operations (such as logging) that could block

---

1. https://issues.apache.org/jira/browse/GERONIMO-2234

waiting for the output stream lock or for I/O to complete could be performed in a dedicated thread to speed up task processing. Logging requests can be added to a queue, assuming that the queue's put() operation incurs little overhead as compared to file I/O [Goetz 2006a].

Noncompliant Code Example (Deferring a Thread)

This noncompliant code example defines a utility method that accepts a time argument.

```java
public synchronized void doSomething(long time)
                        throws InterruptedException {
  // ...
  Thread.sleep(time);
}
```

Because the method is synchronized, when the thread is suspended, other threads cannot use the synchronized methods of the class. The current object's monitor continues to be held because the Thread.sleep() method lacks synchronization semantics.

Compliant Solution (Intrinsic Lock)

This compliant solution defines the doSomething() method with a timeout parameter rather than the time value. Using Object.wait() instead of Thread.sleep() allows setting a timeout period during which a notification may awaken the thread.

```java
public synchronized void doSomething(long timeout)
                          throws InterruptedException {
  // ...
  while (<condition does not hold>) {
    wait(timeout); // Immediately releases the current monitor
  }
}
```

The current object's monitor is immediately released upon entering the wait state. After the timeout period has elapsed, the thread resumes execution after reacquiring the current object's monitor.

According to the Java API class `Object` documentation [API 2006]:

Note that the `wait` method, as it places the current thread into the wait set for this object, unlocks only this object; any other objects on which the current thread may be synchronized remain locked while the thread waits. This method should only be called by a thread that is the owner of this object's monitor.

Programs must ensure that threads that hold locks on other objects release those locks appropriately before entering the wait state. Additional guidance on waiting and notification is available in rules THI03-J and THI02-J.

Noncompliant Code Example (Network I/O)

This noncompliant code example defines a `sendPage()` method that sends a `Page` object from a server to a client. The method is synchronized to protect the `pageBuff` array when multiple threads request concurrent access.

```java
// Class Page is defined separately.
// It stores and returns the Page name via getName()
Page[] pageBuff = new Page[MAX_PAGE_SIZE];

public synchronized boolean sendPage(Socket socket, String pageName)
                                     throws IOException {
  // Get the output stream to write the Page to
  ObjectOutputStream out
    = new ObjectOutputStream(socket.getOutputStream());

  // Find the Page requested by the client
  // (this operation requires synchronization)
  Page targetPage = null;
  for (Page p : pageBuff) {
    if (p.getName().compareTo(pageName) == 0) {
      targetPage = p;
    }
  }

  // Requested Page does not exist
  if (targetPage == null) {
    return false;
  }

  // Send the Page to the client
  // (does not require any synchronization)
  out.writeObject(targetPage);
```

```
    out.flush();
    out.close();
    return true;
  }
```

Calling `writeObject()` within the synchronized `sendPage()` method can result in delays and deadlock-like conditions in high-latency networks or when network connections are inherently *lossy*.

Compliant Solution

This compliant solution separates the process into a sequence of steps:

1. Perform actions on data structures requiring synchronization.

2. Create copies of the objects to be sent.

3. Perform network calls in a separate unsynchronized method.

In this compliant solution, the unsynchronized `sendPage()` method calls the synchronized `getPage()` method to retrieve the requested `Page` in the `pageBuff` array. After the `Page` is retrieved, `sendPage()` calls the unsynchronized `deliverPage()` method to deliver the `Page` to the client.

```
// No synchronization
public boolean sendPage(Socket socket, String pageName) {
  Page targetPage = getPage(pageName);

  if (targetPage == null){
    return false;
  }
  return deliverPage(socket, targetPage);
}

// Requires synchronization
private synchronized Page getPage(String pageName) {
  Page targetPage = null;

  for (Page p : pageBuff) {
    if (p.getName().equals(pageName)) {
      targetPage = p;
    }
  }
  return targetPage;
}
```

```
// Return false if an error occurs, true if successful
public boolean deliverPage(Socket socket, Page page) {
  ObjectOutputStream out = null;
  boolean result = true;
  try {
    // Get the output stream to write the Page to
    out = new ObjectOutputStream(socket.getOutputStream());

    // Send the page to the client
    out.writeObject(page);
    out.flush();
  } catch (IOException io) {
    result = false;
  } finally {
    if (out != null) {
      try {
        out.close();
      } catch (IOException e) {
        result = false;
      }
    }
  }
  return result;
}
```

Exceptions

LCK09-EX0: Classes that provide an appropriate termination mechanism to callers are permitted to violate this rule. See rule THI04-J.

LCK09-EX1: Methods that require multiple locks may hold several locks while waiting for the remaining locks to become available. This constitutes a valid exception, although the programmer must follow other applicable rules, especially rule LCK07-J, to avoid deadlock.

Risk Assessment

Blocking or lengthy operations performed within synchronized regions could result in a deadlocked or unresponsive system.

Rule	Severity	Likelihood	Remediation Cost	Priority	Level
LCK09-J	low	probable	high	P2	L3

Related Guidelines

CERT C Secure Coding Standard	CON36-C. Do not perform operations that can block while holding a lock

Bibliography

[API 2006]	Class Object
[Grosso 2001]	Chapter 10, Serialization
[JLS 2005]	Chapter 17, Threads and Locks
[Rotem 2008]	Fallacies of Distributed Computing Explained

■ LCK10-J. Do not use incorrect forms of the double-checked locking idiom

Lazy initialization defers the construction of a member field or an object referred to by a member field until an instance is actually required rather than computing the field value or constructing the referenced object in the class's constructor. Lazy initialization helps to break harmful circularities in class and instance initialization. It also enables other optimizations [Bloch 2005a].

Lazy initialization uses either a class or an instance method, depending on whether the member object is static. The method checks whether the instance has already been created and, if not, creates it. When the instance already exists, the method simply returns the instance:

```
// Correct single threaded version using lazy initialization
final class Foo {
  private Helper helper = null;

  public Helper getHelper() {
    if (helper == null) {
      helper = new Helper();
    }
    return helper;
  }
  // ...
}
```

Lazy initialization must be synchronized in multithreaded applications to prevent multiple threads from creating extraneous instances of the member object:

```
// Correct multithreaded version using synchronization
final class Foo {
  private Helper helper = null;

  public synchronized Helper getHelper() {
    if (helper == null) {
      helper = new Helper();
    }
    return helper;
  }
  // ...
}
```

The *double-checked locking idiom* improves performance by limiting synchronization to the rare case of computing the field's value or constructing a new instance for the field to reference and by foregoing synchronization during the common case of retrieving an already-created instance or value.

Incorrect forms of the double-checked locking idiom include those that allow publication of an uninitialized or partially initialized object. Consequently, only those forms of the double-checked locking idiom that correctly establish a happens-before relationship both for the `helper` reference and for the complete construction of the `Helper` instance are permitted.

Noncompliant Code Example

The double-checked locking pattern uses block synchronization rather than method synchronization and installs an additional null reference check before attempting synchronization. This noncompliant code example uses an incorrect form of the double-checked locking idiom.

```
// "Double-Checked Locking" idiom
final class Foo {
  private Helper helper = null;
  public Helper getHelper() {
    if (helper == null) {
      synchronized (this) {
        if (helper == null) {
          helper = new Helper();
        }
      }
    }
    return helper;
  }

  // Other methods and members...
}
```

According to Pugh [Pugh 2004]:

> Writes that initialize the Helper object and the write to the helper field can be done or perceived out of order. As a result, a thread which invokes getHelper() could see a non-null reference to a helper object, but see the default values for fields of the helper object, rather than the values set in the constructor.

> Even if the compiler does not reorder those writes, on a multiprocessor, the processor or the memory system may reorder those writes, as perceived by a thread running on another processor.

This code also violates rule TSM03-J.

Compliant Solution (Volatile)

This compliant solution declares the helper field volatile.

```
// Works with acquire/release semantics for volatile
// Broken under JDK 1.4 and earlier
final class Foo {
  private volatile Helper helper = null;

  public Helper getHelper() {
    if (helper == null) {
      synchronized (this) {
        if (helper == null) {
          helper = new Helper();
        }
      }
    }
    return helper;
  }
}
```

When a thread initializes the Helper object, a happens-before relationship is established between this thread and any other thread that retrieves and returns the instance [Pugh 2004, Manson 2004].

Compliant Solution (Static Initialization)

This compliant solution initializes the helper field in the declaration of the static variable [Manson 2006].

```
final class Foo {
  private static final Helper helper = new Helper();

  public static Helper getHelper() {
    return helper;
  }
}
```

Variables that are declared static and initialized at declaration or from a static initializer are guaranteed to be fully constructed before being made visible to other threads. However, this solution forgoes the benefits of lazy initialization.

Compliant Solution (Initialize-on-Demand Holder Class Idiom)

This compliant solution uses the initialize-on-demand holder class idiom that implicitly incorporates lazy initialization by declaring a static variable within a static Holder inner class.

```
final class Foo {
  // Lazy initialization
  private static class Holder {
    static Helper helper = new Helper();
  }

  public static Helper getInstance() {
    return Holder.helper;
  }
}
```

Initialization of the static helper field is deferred until the getInstance() method is called. The necessary happens-before relationships are created by the combination of the class loader's actions loading and initializing the Holder instance and the guarantees provided by the Java memory model. This idiom is a better choice than the double-checked locking idiom for lazily initializing static fields [Bloch 2008]. However, this idiom cannot be used to lazily initialize instance fields [Bloch 2001].

Compliant Solution (ThreadLocal Storage)

This compliant solution (originally suggested by Alexander Terekhov [Pugh 2004]) uses a ThreadLocal object to track whether each individual thread has participated in the synchronization that creates the needed happens-before relationships. Each thread stores a non-null value into its thread-local `perThreadInstance` only inside the synchronized `createHelper()` method; consequently, any thread that sees a null value must establish the necessary happens-before relationships by invoking `createHelper()`.

```java
final class Foo {
  private final ThreadLocal<Foo> perThreadInstance =
      new ThreadLocal<Foo>();
  private Helper helper = null;

  public Helper getHelper() {
    if (perThreadInstance.get() == null) {
      createHelper();
    }
    return helper;
  }

  private synchronized void createHelper() {
    if (helper == null) {
      helper = new Helper();
    }
    // Any non-null value can be used as an argument to set()
    perThreadInstance.set(this);
  }
}
```

Compliant Solution (Immutable)

In this compliant solution, suppose that the `Helper` class is immutable. The Java Memory Model (JMM) guarantees that immutable objects are fully constructed before they become visible to any other thread. Additionally, the block synchronization in the `getHelper()` method suffices to ensure that all methods that can see a non-null value of the `helper` field have a proper happens-before relationship for the update to the `helper` reference. This synchronization and the aforementioned JMM guarantee combine to ensure that only fully initialized `Helper` objects are visible to threads that see non-null values. Consequently, this compliant solution correctly creates both of the needed happens-before relationships.

```java
public final class Helper {
  private final int n;

  public Helper(int n) {
    this.n = n;
  }
```

```
  // Other fields and methods, all fields are final
}

final class Foo {
  private Helper helper = null;

  public Helper getHelper() {
    if (helper == null) {
      synchronized (this) {
        if (helper == null) {
          helper = new Helper();
        }
      }
    }
    return helper;
  }
}
```

Exceptions

LCK10-EX0: Use of the noncompliant form of the double-checked locking idiom is permitted for 32-bit primitive values (for example, `int` or `float`) [Pugh 2004], although this usage is discouraged. The noncompliant form establishes the necessary happens-before relationship between threads that see an initialized version of the primitive value. The second happens-before relationship (for the initialization of the fields of the referent) is of no practical value because unsynchronized reads and writes of primitive values up to 32-bits are guaranteed to be atomic. Consequently, the noncompliant form establishes the only needed happens-before relationship in this case. Note, however, that the noncompliant form fails for `long` or `double` because unsynchronized reads or writes of 64-bit primitives lack a guarantee of atomicity and consequently require a second happens-before relationship to guarantee that all threads see only fully assigned 64-bit values. (See rule VNA05-J.)

Risk Assessment

Using incorrect forms of the double-checked locking idiom can lead to synchronization problems and can expose partially initialized objects.

Rule	Severity	Likelihood	Remediation Cost	Priority	Level
LCK10-J	low	probable	medium	P4	L3

Related Guidelines

MITRE CWE   CWE-609. Double-checked locking

Bibliography

[API 2006]

[Bloch 2001]   Item 48. Synchronize access to shared mutable data

[Bloch 2008]   Item 71. Use lazy initialization judiciously

[JLS 2005]   §12.4, Initialization of Classes and Interfaces

[Pugh 2004]

■ LCK11-J. Avoid client-side locking when using classes that do not commit to their locking strategy

According to Goetz and colleagues [Goetz 2006a]:

> Client-side locking entails guarding client code that uses some object X with the lock X uses to guard its own state. In order to use client-side locking, you must know what lock X uses.

While client-side locking is acceptable when the thread-safe class commits to and clearly documents its locking strategy, Goetz and colleagues caution against its misuse [Goetz 2006a]:

> If extending a class to add another atomic operation is fragile because it distributes the locking code for a class over multiple classes in an object hierarchy, client-side locking is even more fragile because it entails putting locking code for class C into classes that are totally unrelated to C. Exercise care when using client-side locking on classes that do not commit to their locking strategy.

The documentation of a class that supports client-side locking should explicitly state its applicability. For example, the class `java.util.concurrent.ConcurrentHashMap <K,V>` should not be used for client-side locking because its documentation [API 2006] states that:

> However, even though all operations are thread-safe, retrieval operations do not entail locking, and there is not any support for locking the entire table in a way that prevents all access. This class is fully interoperable with `Hashtable` in programs that rely on its thread safety but not on its synchronization details.

Use of client-side locking is permitted only when the documentation of the class recommends it. For example, the documentation of the `synchronizedList()` wrapper method of `java.util.Collections` class [API 2006] states:

> In order to guarantee serial access, it is critical that all access to the backing list is accomplished through the returned list. It is imperative that the user manually synchronize on the returned list when iterating over it. Failure to follow this advice may result in non-deterministic behavior.

When the backing list is inaccessible to an untrusted client, this advice is consistent with rule LCK04-J.

Noncompliant Code Example (Intrinsic Lock)

This noncompliant code example uses a thread-safe `Book` class that cannot be refactored. Refactoring might be impossible, for example, when the source code is unavailable for review or when the class is part of a general library that cannot be extended.

```
final class Book {
  // Could change its locking policy in the future
  // to use private final locks
  private final String title;
  private Calendar dateIssued;
  private Calendar dateDue;

  Book(String title) {
    this.title = title;
  }

  public synchronized void issue(int days) {
    dateIssued = Calendar.getInstance();
    dateDue = Calendar.getInstance();
    dateDue.add(dateIssued.DATE, days);
  }

  public synchronized Calendar getDueDate() {
    return dateDue;
  }
}
```

This class fails to commit to its locking strategy (that is, it reserves the right to change its locking strategy without notice). Furthermore, it fails to document that callers can safely use client-side locking. The `BookWrapper` client class uses client-side locking in the `renew()` method by synchronizing on a `Book` instance.

```
// Client
public class BookWrapper {
  private final Book book;

  BookWrapper(Book book) {
    this.book = book;
  }

  public void issue(int days) {
    book.issue(days);
  }

  public Calendar getDueDate() {
    return book.getDueDate();
  }

  public void renew() {
    synchronized (book) {
      if (book.getDueDate().before(Calendar.getInstance())) {
        throw new IllegalStateException("Book overdue");
      } else {
        book.issue(14); // Issue book for 14 days
      }
    }
  }
}
```

If the Book class were to change its synchronization policy in the future, the Book-Wrapper class's locking strategy might silently break. For instance, the BookWrapper class's locking strategy would break if Book were modified to use a private final lock object, as recommended by rule LCK00-J. This is because threads that call BookWrapper. getDueDate() would perform operations on the thread-safe Book using its new locking policy. However, threads that call the renew() method would always synchronize on the intrinsic lock of the Book instance. Consequently, the implementation would use two different locks.

Compliant Solution (Private Final Lock Object)

This compliant solution uses a private final lock object and synchronizes the methods of the BookWrapper class using this lock.

```java
public final class BookWrapper {
  private final Book book;
  private final Object lock = new Object();

  BookWrapper(Book book) {
    this.book = book;
  }

  public void issue(int days) {
    synchronized (lock) {
      book.issue(days);
    }
  }

  public Calendar getDueDate() {
    synchronized (lock) {
      return book.getDueDate();
    }
  }

  public void renew() {
    synchronized (lock) {
      if (book.getDueDate().before(Calendar.getInstance())) {
        throw new IllegalStateException("Book overdue");
      } else {
        book.issue(14); // Issue book for 14 days
      }
    }
  }
}
```

The BookWrapper class's locking strategy is now independent of the locking policy of the Book instance.

Noncompliant Code Example (Class Extension and Accessible Member Lock)

Goetz and colleagues describe the fragility of class extension for adding functionality to thread-safe classes [Goetz 2006a]:

> Extension is more fragile than adding code directly to a class, because the implementation of the synchronization policy is now distributed over multiple, separately maintained source files. If the underlying class were to change its synchronization policy by choosing a different lock to guard its state variables, the subclass would subtly and silently break because it no longer used the right lock to control concurrent access to the base class's state.

In this noncompliant code example, the PrintableIPAddressList class extends the thread-safe IPAddressList class. PrintableIPAddressList locks on IPAddressList.ips in the addAndPrintIPAddresses() method. This is another example of client-side locking because a subclass is using an object owned and locked by its superclass.

```java
// This class could change its locking policy in the future,
// for example, if new non-atomic methods are added
class IPAddressList {
  private final List<InetAddress> ips =
    Collections.synchronizedList(new ArrayList<InetAddress>());

  public List<InetAddress> getList() {
    return ips; // No defensive copies required
                // as visibility is package-private
  }

  public void addIPAddress(InetAddress address) {
    ips.add(address);
  }
}

class PrintableIPAddressList extends IPAddressList {
  public void addAndPrintIPAddresses(InetAddress address) {
    synchronized (getList()) {
      addIPAddress(address);
      InetAddress[] ia =
        (InetAddress[]) getList().toArray(new InetAddress[0]);
      // ...
    }
  }
}
```

If the IPAddressList class were modified to use block synchronization on a private final lock object, as recommended by rule LCK00-J, the PrintableIPAddressList subclass would silently break. Moreover, if a wrapper such as Collections.synchronizedList() were used, it would be difficult for a client to determine the type of the class being wrapped to extend it [Goetz 2006a].

Compliant Solution (Composition)

This compliant solution wraps an object of the IPAddressList class and provides synchronized accessors to manipulate the state of the object.

Composition offers encapsulation benefits, usually with minimal overhead. Refer to rule OBJ02-J for more information on composition.

```
// Class IPAddressList remains unchanged
class PrintableIPAddressList {
  private final IPAddressList ips;

  public PrintableIPAddressList(IPAddressList list) {
    this.ips = list;
  }

  public synchronized void addIPAddress(InetAddress address) {
    ips.addIPAddress(address);
  }

  public synchronized void addAndPrintIPAddresses(InetAddress address) {
    addIPAddress(address);
    InetAddress[] ia =
        (InetAddress[]) ips.getList().toArray(new InetAddress[0]);
    // ...
  }
}
```

In this case, composition allows the `PrintableIPAddressList` class to use its own intrinsic lock independent of the underlying list class's lock. The underlying collection lacks a requirement for thread-safety because the `PrintableIPAddressList` wrapper prevents direct access to its methods by publishing its own synchronized equivalents. This approach provides consistent locking even when the underlying class changes its locking policy in the future [Goetz 2006a].

Risk Assessment

Using client-side locking when the thread-safe class fails to commit to its locking strategy can cause data inconsistencies and deadlock.

Rule	Severity	Likelihood	Remediation Cost	Priority	Level
LCK11-J	low	probable	medium	P4	L3

Bibliography

[API 2006]	Class `Vector`, Class `WeakReference`, Class `ConcurrentHashMap<K,V>`
[JavaThreads 2004]	8.2, Synchronization and Collection Classes
[Goetz 2006a]	4.4.1, Client-side Locking; 4.4.2, Composition; and 5.2.1, `ConcurrentHashMap`
[Lee 2009]	Map & Compound Operation

Chapter 11

Thread APIs (THI)

▪ Rules

▪ Risk Assessment Summary

Rule	Severity	Likelihood	Remediation Cost	Priority	Level
THI00-J	low	probable	medium	P4	L3
THI01-J	low	probable	medium	P4	L3
THI02-J	low	unlikely	medium	P2	L3
THI03-J	low	unlikely	medium	P2	L3
THI04-J	low	probable	medium	P4	L3
THI05-J	low	probable	medium	P4	L3

■ THI00-J. Do not invoke Thread.run()

Thread startup can be misleading because the code can appear to be performing its function correctly when it is actually being executed by the wrong thread. Invoking the Thread.start() method instructs the Java runtime to start executing the thread's run() method using the started thread. Invoking a Thread object's run() method directly is incorrect. When a Thread object's run() method is invoked directly, the statements in the run() method are executed by the current thread rather than by the newly created thread. Furthermore, if the Thread object was constructed by instantiating a subclass of Thread that fails to override the run() method rather than constructed from a Runnable object, any calls to the subclass's run() method would invoke Thread.run(), which does nothing. Consequently, programs must not directly invoke a Thread object's run() method.

Noncompliant Code Example

This noncompliant code example explicitly invokes run() in the context of the current thread.

```java
public final class Foo implements Runnable {
  @Override public void run() {
    // ...
  }

  public static void main(String[] args) {
    Foo foo = new Foo();
    new Thread(foo).run();
  }
}
```

The newly created thread is never started because of the incorrect assumption that run() starts the new thread. Consequently, the statements in the run() method are executed by the current thread rather than by the new thread.

Compliant Solution

This compliant solution correctly uses the start() method to tell the Java runtimes to start a new thread.

```
public final class Foo implements Runnable {
  @Override public void run() {
   // ...
  }

  public static void main(String[] args) {
    Foo foo = new Foo();
    new Thread(foo).start();
  }
}
```

Exceptions

THI00-EX0: The run() method may be directly invoked during unit testing. Note that this method cannot be used to test a class for multithreaded use.

Given a Thread object that has been constructed with a runnable argument, when invoking the Thread.run() method, the Thread object may be cast to Runnable to eliminate analyzer diagnostics.

```
public void sampleRunTest() {

  Thread thread = new Thread(new Runnable() {
     @Override public void run() {
      // ...
     }
  });

  ((Runnable) thread).run();  // THI00-EX0: Does not start a new thread

}
```

Casting a thread to Runnable before calling the run() method documents that the explicit call to Thread.run() is intentional. Adding an explanatory comment alongside the invocation is highly recommended.

THI00-EX1: Runtime system code involved in starting new threads is permitted to invoke a Thread object's run() method directly; this is an obvious necessity for a working Java runtime system. Note that the likelihood that this exception applies to user-written code is vanishingly small.

Risk Assessment

Failure to start threads correctly can cause unexpected behavior.

Rule	Severity	Likelihood	Remediation Cost	Priority	Level
THI00-J	low	probable	medium	P4	L3

Automated Detection Automated detection of direct invocations of `Thread.run()` methods is straightforward. Sound automated determination of which specific invocations are permitted may be infeasible. Heuristic approaches may be useful.

Related Guidelines

MITRE CWE   CWE-572. Call to `Thread run()` instead of `start()`

Bibliography

[API 2006]   Interface `Runnable` and class `Thread`

▪ THI01-J. Do not invoke ThreadGroup methods

Each thread in Java is assigned to a thread group upon the thread's creation. These groups are implemented by the `java.lang.ThreadGroup` class. When the thread group name is not specified explicitly, the `main` default group is assigned by the Java Virtual Machine (JVM) [Tutorials 2008]. The convenience methods of the `ThreadGroup` class can be used to operate on all threads belonging to a thread group at once. For instance, the `ThreadGroup.interrupt()` method interrupts all threads in the thread group. Thread groups also help reinforce layered security by confining threads into groups so that they avoid interference with threads in other groups [JavaThreads 2004].

Even though thread groups are useful for keeping threads organized, programmers seldom benefit from their use because many of the methods of the `ThreadGroup` class are deprecated (for example, `allowThreadSuspension()`, `resume()`, `stop()`, and `suspend()`). Furthermore, many nondeprecated methods are obsolete in that they offer little desirable functionality. Ironically, a few `ThreadGroup` methods are not even thread-safe [Bloch 2001].

Insecure yet nondeprecated methods include

- `ThreadGroup.activeCount()`
  According to the Java API, the `activeCount()` method [API 2006]:

  returns an estimate of the number of active threads in this thread group.

This method is often used as a precursor to thread enumeration. Threads that have never started nevertheless reside in the thread group and are considered to be active. The active count is also affected by the presence of certain system threads [API 2006]. Consequently, the activeCount() method might fail to reflect the actual number of running tasks in the thread group.

- ThreadGroup.enumerate()
  According to the Java API, ThreadGroup class documentation [API 2006]:

  [The enumerate() method] copies into the specified array every active thread in this thread group and its subgroups. An application should use the activeCount method to get an estimate of how big the array should be. If the array is too short to hold all the threads, the extra threads are silently ignored.

Using the ThreadGroup APIs to shut down threads also has pitfalls. Because the stop() method is deprecated, programs require alternative methods to stop threads. According to *The Java Programming Language* [JPL 2006]:

One way is for the thread initiating the termination to join the other threads and so know when those threads have terminated. However, an application may have to maintain its own list of the threads it creates because simply inspecting the ThreadGroup may return library threads that do not terminate and for which join will not return.

The Executor framework provides a better API for managing a logical grouping of threads and offers secure facilities for handling shutdown and thread exceptions [Bloch 2008]. Consequently, programs must not invoke ThreadGroup methods.

Noncompliant Code Example

This noncompliant code example contains a NetworkHandler class that maintains a controller thread. The controller thread delegates each new request to a worker thread. To demonstrate the race condition in this example, the controller thread serves three requests by starting three threads in succession from its run() method. All threads are defined to belong to the Chief thread group.

```
final class HandleRequest implements Runnable {
  public void run() {
    // Do something
  }
}
```

```java
public final class NetworkHandler implements Runnable {
  private static ThreadGroup tg = new ThreadGroup("Chief");

  @Override public void run() {
    new Thread(tg, new HandleRequest(), "thread1").start();
    new Thread(tg, new HandleRequest(), "thread2").start();
    new Thread(tg, new HandleRequest(), "thread3").start();
  }

  public static void printActiveCount(int point) {
    System.out.println("Active Threads in Thread Group " + tg.getName() +
        " at point(" + point + "):" + " " + tg.activeCount());
  }

  public static void printEnumeratedThreads(Thread[] ta, int len) {
    System.out.println("Enumerating all threads...");
    for (int i = 0; i < len; i++) {
      System.out.println("Thread " + i + " = " + ta[i].getName());
    }
  }

  public static void main(String[] args) throws InterruptedException {
    // Start thread controller
    Thread thread = new Thread(tg, new NetworkHandler(), "controller");
    thread.start();

    // Gets the active count (insecure)
    Thread[] ta = new Thread[tg.activeCount()];

    printActiveCount(1); // P1
    // Delay to demonstrate TOCTOU condition (race window)
    Thread.sleep(1000);
    // P2: the thread count changes as new threads are initiated
    printActiveCount(2);
    // Incorrectly uses the (now stale) thread count obtained at P1
    int n = tg.enumerate(ta);
    // Silently ignores newly initiated threads
    printEnumeratedThreads(ta, n);
                                    // (between P1 and P2)

    // This code destroys the thread group if it does
    // not have any live threads
    for (Thread thr : ta) {
      thr.interrupt();
      while(thr.isAlive());
    }
    tg.destroy();
  }
}
```

This implementation contains a time-of-check, time-of-use (TOCTOU) vulnerability because it obtains the count and enumerates the list without ensuring atomicity. If one or more new requests were to occur after the call to `activeCount()` and before the call to `enumerate()` in the `main()` method, the total number of threads in the group would increase, but the enumerated list `ta` would contain only the initial number, that is, two thread references: `main` and `controller`. Consequently, the program would fail to account for the newly started threads in the `Chief` thread group.

Any subsequent use of the `ta` array would be insecure. For example, calling the `destroy()` method to destroy the thread group and its subgroups would not work as expected. The precondition to calling `destroy()` is that the thread group must be empty with no executing threads. The code attempts to comply with the precondition by interrupting every thread in the thread group. However, the thread group would not be empty when the `destroy()` method was called, causing a `java.lang.IllegalThreadStateException` to be thrown.

Compliant Solution

This compliant solution uses a fixed thread pool rather than a `ThreadGroup` to group its three tasks. The `java.util.concurrent.ExecutorService` interface provides methods to manage the thread pool. Although the interface lacks methods for finding the number of actively executing threads or for enumerating the threads, the logical grouping can help control the behavior of the group as a whole. For instance, invoking the `shutdownPool()` method terminates all threads belonging to a particular thread pool.

```java
public final class NetworkHandler {
  private final ExecutorService executor;

  NetworkHandler(int poolSize) {
    this.executor = Executors.newFixedThreadPool(poolSize);
  }

  public void startThreads() {
    for (int i = 0; i < 3; i++) {
      executor.execute(new HandleRequest());
    }
  }

  public void shutdownPool() {
    executor.shutdown();
  }

  public static void main(String[] args) {
    NetworkHandler nh = new NetworkHandler(3);
    nh.startThreads();
    nh.shutdownPool();
  }
}
```

Before Java SE 5.0, applications that needed to catch an uncaught exception in a separate thread had to extend the `ThreadGroup` class because this was the only direct approach to provide the required functionality. Specifically, an application's `UncaughtException-Handler` could only be controlled by subclassing `ThreadGroup`. In more recent versions of Java, `UncaughtExceptionHandler` is maintained on a per-thread basis using an interface enclosed by the `Thread` class. Consequently, the `ThreadGroup` class provides little unique functionality [Goetz 2006a], [Bloch 2008].

Refer to TPS03-J for more information on using uncaught exception handlers in thread pools.

Risk Assessment

Use of the `ThreadGroup` APIs may result in race conditions, memory leaks, and inconsistent object state.

Rule	Severity	Likelihood	Remediation Cost	Priority	Level
THI01-J	low	probable	medium	P4	L3

Bibliography

[API 2006]	Methods `activeCount` and `enumerate`; Classes `ThreadGroup` and `Thread`
[Bloch 2001]	Item 53. Avoid thread groups
[Bloch 2008]	Item 73. Avoid thread groups
[Goetz 2006a]	Section 7.3.1, Uncaught Exception Handlers
[JavaThreads 2004]	13.1, `ThreadGroups`
[JPL 2006]	23.3.3, Shutdown Strategies
[SDN 2006]	Bug ID 4089701 and 4229558
[Tutorials 2008]	

▪ THI02-J. Notify all waiting threads rather than a single thread

Threads that invoke `Object.wait()` expect to wake up and resume execution when their condition predicate becomes true. To be compliant with THI03-J, waiting threads must test their condition predicates upon receiving notifications and must resume waiting if the predicates are false.

The notify() and notifyAll() methods of package java.lang.Object are used to wake up a waiting thread or threads, respectively. These methods must be invoked from a thread that holds the same object lock as the waiting thread(s); these methods throw an IllegalMonitorStateException when invoked from any other thread. The notifyAll() method wakes up all threads waiting on an object lock and allows threads whose condition predicate is true to resume execution. Furthermore, if all the threads whose condition predicate evaluates to true previously held a specific lock before going into the wait state, only one of them will reacquire the lock upon being notified. Presumably, the other threads will resume waiting. The notify() method wakes up only one thread, with no guarantee regarding which specific thread is notified. The chosen thread is permitted to resume waiting if its condition predicate is unsatisfied; this often defeats the purpose of the notification.

Consequently, invoking the notify() method is permitted only when *all* of the following conditions are met:

- All waiting threads have identical condition predicates.
- All threads perform the same set of operations after waking up. That is, any one thread can be selected to wake up and resume for a single invocation of notify().
- Only one thread is required to wake upon the notification.

These conditions are satisfied by threads that are identical and provide a stateless service or utility.

The java.util.concurrent.locks utilities provide the Condition.signal() and Condition.signalAll() methods to awaken threads that are blocked on a Condition. await() call. Condition objects are required when using java.util.concurrent.locks. Lock objects. Although Lock objects allow the use of Object.wait(), Object.notify(), and Object.notifyAll() methods, such uses are prohibited by rule LCK03-J. Code that synchronizes using a Lock object uses one or more Condition objects associated with the Lock object rather than using its own intrinsic lock. These objects interact directly with the locking policy enforced by the Lock object. Consequently, the await(), signal(), and signalAll() methods are used in place of the wait(), notify(), and notifyAll() methods.

The signal() method must not be used unless all of these conditions are met:

- The Condition object is identical for each waiting thread.
- All threads must perform the same set of operations after waking up. This means that any one thread can be selected to wake up and resume for a single invocation of signal().
- Only one thread is required to wake upon receiving the signal.

or all of these conditions are met:

- Each thread uses a unique `Condition` object.
- Each `Condition` object is associated with the same `Lock` object.

When used securely, the `signal()` method has better performance than `signalAll()`.

Noncompliant Code Example (`notify()`)

This noncompliant code example shows a complex, multistep process being undertaken by several threads. Each thread executes the step identified by the `time` field. Each thread waits for the `time` field to indicate that it is time to perform the corresponding thread's step. After performing the step, each thread first increments `time` and then notifies the thread that is responsible for the next step.

```java
public final class ProcessStep implements Runnable {
  private static final Object lock = new Object();
  private static int time = 0;
  private final int step; // Perform operations when field time
                          // reaches this value
  public ProcessStep(int step) {
    this.step = step;
  }

  @Override public void run() {
    try {
      synchronized (lock) {
        while (time != step) {
          lock.wait();
        }

        // Perform operations

        time++;
        lock.notify();
      }
    } catch (InterruptedException ie) {
      Thread.currentThread().interrupt(); // Reset interrupted status
    }
  }

  public static void main(String[] args) {
    for (int i = 4; i >= 0; i--) {
      new Thread(new ProcessStep(i)).start();
    }
  }
}
```

This noncompliant code example violates the liveness property. Each thread has a different condition predicate because each requires step to have a different value before proceeding. The Object.notify() method wakes only one thread at a time. Unless it happens to wake the thread that is required to perform the next step, the program will deadlock.

Compliant Solution (notifyAll())

In this compliant solution, each thread completes its step and then calls notifyAll() to notify the waiting threads. The thread that is ready can then perform its task while all the threads whose condition predicates are false (loop condition expression is true) promptly resume waiting.

Only the run() method from the noncompliant code example is modified, as follows:

```java
public final class ProcessStep implements Runnable {
  private static final Object lock = new Object();
  private static int time = 0;
  private final int step; // Perform operations when field time
                          // reaches this value
  public ProcessStep(int step) {
    this.step = step;
  }

  @Override public void run() {
    try {
      synchronized (lock) {
        while (time != step) {
          lock.wait();
        }

        // Perform operations

        time++;
        lock.notifyAll(); // Use notifyAll() instead of notify()
      }
    } catch (InterruptedException ie) {
      Thread.currentThread().interrupt(); // Reset interrupted status
    }
  }
}
```

Noncompliant Code Example (Condition Interface)

This noncompliant code example is similar to the noncompliant code example for notify() but uses the Condition interface for waiting and notification.

```java
public class ProcessStep implements Runnable {
  private static final Lock lock = new ReentrantLock();
  private static final Condition condition = lock.newCondition();
  private static int time = 0;
  private final int step; // Perform operations when field time
                          // reaches this value
  public ProcessStep(int step) {
    this.step = step;
  }

  @Override public void run() {
    lock.lock();
    try {
      while (time != step) {
        condition.await();
      }

      // Perform operations

      time++;
      condition.signal();
    } catch (InterruptedException ie) {
      Thread.currentThread().interrupt(); // Reset interrupted status
    } finally {
      lock.unlock();
    }
  }

  public static void main(String[] args) {
    for (int i = 4; i >= 0; i--) {
      new Thread(new ProcessStep(i)).start();
    }
  }
}
```

As with `Object.notify()`, the `signal()` method may awaken an arbitrary thread.

Compliant Solution (`signalAll()`)

This compliant solution uses the `signalAll()` method to notify all waiting threads. Before `await()` returns, the current thread reacquires the lock associated with this condition. When the thread returns, it is guaranteed to hold this lock [API 2006]. The thread that is ready can perform its task while all the threads whose condition predicates are false resume waiting.

Only the run() method from the noncompliant code example is modified, as follows:

```java
public class ProcessStep implements Runnable {
  private static final Lock lock = new ReentrantLock();
  private static final Condition condition = lock.newCondition();
  private static int time = 0;
  private final int step; // Perform operations when field time
                          // reaches this value
  public ProcessStep(int step) {
    this.step = step;
  }

  @Override public void run() {
    lock.lock();
    try {
      while (time != step) {
        condition.await();
      }

      // Perform operations

      time++;
      condition.signalAll();
    } catch (InterruptedException ie) {
      Thread.currentThread().interrupt(); // Reset interrupted status
    } finally {
      lock.unlock();
    }
  }

}
```

Compliant Solution (Unique Condition per Thread)

This compliant solution assigns each thread its own condition. All the Condition objects are accessible to all the threads.

```java
// Declare class as final because its constructor throws an exception
public final class ProcessStep implements Runnable {
  private static final Lock lock = new ReentrantLock();
  private static int time = 0;
  private final int step; // Perform operations when field time
                          // reaches this value
  private static final int MAX_STEPS = 5;
  private static final Condition[] conditions = new Condition[MAX_STEPS];
```

```
public ProcessStep(int step) {
  if (step <= MAX_STEPS) {
    this.step = step;
    conditions[step] = lock.newCondition();
  } else {
    throw new IllegalArgumentException("Too many threads");
  }
}

@Override public void run() {
  lock.lock();
  try {
    while (time != step) {
      conditions[step].await();
    }

    // Perform operations

    time++;
    if (step + 1 < conditions.length) {
      conditions[step + 1].signal();
    }
  } catch (InterruptedException ie) {
    Thread.currentThread().interrupt(); // Reset interrupted status
  } finally {
    lock.unlock();
  }
}

public static void main(String[] args) {
  for (int i = MAX_STEPS - 1; i >= 0; i--) {
    ProcessStep ps = new ProcessStep(i);
    new Thread(ps).start();
  }
}
}
```

Even though the signal() method is used, only the thread whose condition predicate corresponds to the unique Condition variable will awaken.

This compliant solution is safe only when untrusted code cannot create a thread with an instance of this class.

Risk Assessment

Notifying a single thread rather than all waiting threads can violate the liveness property of the system.

Rule	Severity	Likelihood	Remediation Cost	Priority	Level
THI02-J	low	unlikely	medium	P2	L3

Related Guidelines

CERT C Secure Coding Standard	CON38-C. Notify all threads waiting on a condition variable instead of a single thread

Bibliography

[API 2006]	`java.util.concurrent.locks.Condition` interface
[JLS 2005]	Chapter 17, Threads and Locks
[Goetz 2006a]	Section 14.2.4, Notification
[Bloch 2001]	Item 50. Never invoke wait outside a loop

■ THI03-J. Always invoke `wait()` and `await()` methods inside a loop

The `Object.wait()` method temporarily cedes possession of a lock so that other threads that may be requesting the lock can proceed. `Object.wait()` must always be called from a synchronized block or method. The waiting thread resumes execution only after it has been notified, generally as a result of the invocation of the `notify()` or `notifyAll()` method by some other thread. The `wait()` method must be invoked from a loop that checks whether a condition predicate holds. Note that a condition predicate is the negation of the condition expression in the loop. For example, the condition predicate for removing an element from a vector is `!isEmpty()`, whereas the condition expression for the `while` loop condition is `isEmpty()`. Following is the correct way to invoke the `wait()` method when the vector is empty:

```java
private Vector vector;
//...

public void consumeElement() throws InterruptedException {
  synchronized (vector) {
    while (vector.isEmpty()) {
      vector.wait();
    }

    // Resume when condition holds
  }
}
```

The notification mechanism notifies the waiting thread and allows it to check its condition predicate. The invocation of `notify()` or `notifyAll()` in another thread cannot precisely determine which waiting thread will be resumed. Condition predicate statements allow notified threads to determine whether they should resume upon receiving the notification. Condition predicates are also useful when a thread is required to block until a condition becomes true, for example, when waiting for data to arrive on an input stream before reading the data.

Both safety and liveness are concerns when using the wait/notify mechanism. The safety property requires that all objects maintain consistent states in a multithreaded environment [Lea 2000a]. The liveness property requires that every operation or method invocation execute to completion without interruption.

To guarantee liveness, programs must test the `while` loop condition before invoking the `wait()` method. This early test checks whether another thread has already satisfied the condition predicate and sent a notification. Invoking the `wait()` method after the notification has been sent results in indefinite blocking.

To guarantee safety, programs must test the `while` loop condition after returning from the `wait()` method. Although `wait()` is intended to block indefinitely until a notification is received, it must still be encased within a loop to prevent the following vulnerabilities [Bloch 2001]:

- Thread in the middle—A third thread can acquire the lock on the shared object during the interval between a notification being sent and the receiving thread resuming execution. This third thread can change the state of the object, leaving it inconsistent. This is a TOCTOU race condition.

- Malicious notification—A random or malicious notification can be received when the condition predicate is false. Such a notification would cancel the `wait()`.

- Misdelivered notification—The order in which threads execute after receipt of a `notifyAll()` signal is unspecified. Consequently, an unrelated thread could start executing and discover that its condition predicate is satisfied. Consequently, it could resume execution, although it was required to remain dormant.

- Spurious wakeups—Certain JVM implementations are vulnerable to spurious wakeups that result in waiting threads waking up even without a notification [API 2006].

For these reasons, programs must check the condition predicate after the `wait()` method returns. A `while` loop is the best choice for checking the condition predicate both before and after invoking `wait()`.

Similarly, the await() method of the Condition interface must also be invoked inside a loop. According to the Java API [API 2006], Interface Condition:

> When waiting upon a Condition, a "spurious wakeup" is permitted to occur, in general, as a concession to the underlying platform semantics. This has little practical impact on most application programs as a Condition should always be waited upon in a loop, testing the state predicate that is being waited for. An implementation is free to remove the possibility of spurious wakeups, but it is recommended that applications programmers always assume that they can occur and so always wait in a loop.

New code should use the java.util.concurrent.locks concurrency utilities in place of the wait/notify mechanism. However, legacy code that complies with the other requirements of this rule is permitted to depend on the wait/notify mechanism.

Noncompliant Code Example

This noncompliant code example invokes the wait() method inside a traditional if block and fails to check the postcondition after the notification is received. If the notification were accidental or malicious, the thread could wake up prematurely.

```
synchronized (object) {
  if (<condition does not hold>) {
    object.wait();
  }
  // Proceed when condition holds
}
```

Compliant Solution

This compliant solution calls the wait() method from within a while loop to check the condition both before and after the call to wait().

```
synchronized (object) {
  while (<condition does not hold>) {
    object.wait();
  }
  // Proceed when condition holds
}
```

Invocations of the java.util.concurrent.locks.Condition.await() method must also be enclosed in a similar loop.

Risk Assessment

Failure to encase the wait() or await() methods inside a while loop can lead to indefinite blocking and denial of service (DoS).

Rule	Severity	Likelihood	Remediation Cost	Priority	Level
THI03-J	low	unlikely	medium	P2	L3

Bibliography

[API 2006]	Class Object
[Bloch 2001]	Item 50. Never invoke wait outside a loop
[Lea 2000a]	3.2.2, Monitor Mechanics; 1.3.2, Liveness
[Goetz 2006a]	Section 14.2, Using Condition Queues

▪ THI04-J. Ensure that threads performing blocking operations can be terminated

Threads and tasks that block on operations involving network or file I/O must provide callers with an explicit termination mechanism to prevent DoS vulnerabilities.

Noncompliant Code Example (Blocking I/O, Volatile Flag)

This noncompliant code example uses a volatile done flag to indicate that it is safe to shut down the thread, as suggested in rule THI05-J. However, when the thread is blocked on network I/O as a consequence of invoking the readLine() method, it cannot respond to the newly set flag until the network I/O is complete. Consequently, thread termination may be indefinitely delayed.

```
// Thread-safe class
public final class SocketReader implements Runnable {
  private final Socket socket;
  private final BufferedReader in;
  private volatile boolean done = false;
  private final Object lock = new Object();

  public SocketReader(String host, int port) throws IOException {
    this.socket = new Socket(host, port);
    this.in = new BufferedReader(
        new InputStreamReader(this.socket.getInputStream())
    );
  }
}
```

```
// Only one thread can use the socket at a particular time
@Override public void run() {
  try {
    synchronized (lock) {
      readData();
    }
  } catch (IOException ie) {
    // Forward to handler
  }
}

public void readData() throws IOException {
  String string;
  while (!done && (string = in.readLine()) != null) {
    // Blocks until end of stream (null)
  }
}

public void shutdown() {
  done = true;
}

public static void main(String[] args)
                    throws IOException, InterruptedException {
  SocketReader reader = new SocketReader("somehost", 25);
  Thread thread = new Thread(reader);
  thread.start();
  Thread.sleep(1000);
  reader.shutdown(); // Shutdown the thread
}
}
```

Noncompliant Code Example (Blocking I/O, Interruptible)

This noncompliant code example is similar to the preceding example but uses thread interruption to shut down the thread. Network I/O on a `java.net.Socket` is unresponsive to thread interruption.

```
// Thread-safe class
public final class SocketReader implements Runnable {
  // other methods...

  public void readData() throws IOException {
    String string;
    while (!Thread.interrupted() && (string = in.readLine()) != null) {
```

```
      // Blocks until end of stream (null)
    }
  }

  public static void main(String[] args)
                    throws IOException, InterruptedException {
    SocketReader reader = new SocketReader("somehost", 25);
    Thread thread = new Thread(reader);
    thread.start();
    Thread.sleep(1000);
    thread.interrupt(); // Interrupt the thread
  }
}
```

Compliant Solution (Close Socket Connection)

This compliant solution terminates the blocking network I/O by closing the socket in the shutdown() method. The readLine() method throws a SocketException when the socket is closed, consequently allowing the thread to proceed. Note that it is impossible to keep the connection alive while simultaneously halting the thread both cleanly and immediately.

```
public final class SocketReader implements Runnable {
  // other methods...

  public void readData() throws IOException {
    String string;
    try {
      while ((string = in.readLine()) != null) {
        // Blocks until end of stream (null)
      }
    } finally {
      shutdown();
    }
  }

  public void shutdown() throws IOException {
    socket.close();
  }

  public static void main(String[] args)
                    throws IOException, InterruptedException {
    SocketReader reader = new SocketReader("somehost", 25);
```

```
      Thread thread = new Thread(reader);
      thread.start();
      Thread.sleep(1000);
      reader.shutdown();
    }
  }
```

After the `shutdown()` method is called from `main()`, the `finally` block in `readData()` executes and calls `shutdown()` again, closing the socket for a second time. However, when the socket has already been closed, this second call does nothing.

When performing asynchronous I/O, a `java.nio.channels.Selector` can be unblocked by invoking either its `close()` or its `wakeup()` method.

When additional operations must be performed after emerging from the blocked state, use a `boolean` flag to indicate pending termination. When supplementing the code with such a flag, the `shutdown()` method should also set the flag to `false` so that the thread can cleanly exit from the while loop.

Compliant Solution (Interruptible Channel)

This compliant solution uses an interruptible channel, `java.nio.channels.Socket-Channel`, instead of a `Socket` connection. If the thread performing the network I/O is interrupted using the `Thread.interrupt()` method while it is reading the data, the thread receives a `ClosedByInterruptException`, and the channel is closed immediately. The thread's interrupted status is also set.

```
public final class SocketReader implements Runnable {
  private final SocketChannel sc;
  private final Object lock = new Object();

  public SocketReader(String host, int port) throws IOException {
    sc = SocketChannel.open(new InetSocketAddress(host, port));
  }

  @Override public void run() {
    ByteBuffer buf = ByteBuffer.allocate(1024);
    try {
      synchronized (lock) {
        while (!Thread.interrupted()) {
          sc.read(buf);
          // ...
        }
      }
```

```
    } catch (IOException ie) {
      // Forward to handler
    }
  }

  public static void main(String[] args)
                      throws IOException, InterruptedException {
    SocketReader reader = new SocketReader("somehost", 25);
    Thread thread = new Thread(reader);
    thread.start();
    Thread.sleep(1000);
    thread.interrupt();
  }
}
```

This technique interrupts the current thread. However, it stops the thread only because the code polls the thread's interrupted status with the `Thread.interrupted()` method and terminates the thread when it is interrupted. Using a `SocketChannel` ensures that the condition in the while loop is tested as soon as an interruption is received, even though the read is normally a blocking operation. Similarly, invoking the `interrupt()` method of a thread blocked on a `java.nio.channels.Selector` also causes that thread to awaken.

Noncompliant Code Example (Database Connection)

This noncompliant code example shows a thread-safe `DBConnector` class that creates one JDBC connection per thread. Each connection belongs to one thread and is not shared by other threads. This is a common use case because JDBC connections are intended to be single-threaded.

```
public final class DBConnector implements Runnable {
  private final String query;

  DBConnector(String query) {
    this.query = query;
  }

  @Override public void run() {
    Connection connection;
    try {
      // Username and password are hard coded for brevity
      connection = DriverManager.getConnection(
```

```
            "jdbc:driver:name",
            "username",
            "password"
      );
      Statement stmt = connection.createStatement();
      ResultSet rs = stmt.executeQuery(query);
      // ...
    } catch (SQLException e) {
      // Forward to handler
    }
    // ...
  }

  public static void main(String[] args) throws InterruptedException {
    DBConnector connector = new DBConnector("suitable query");
    Thread thread = new Thread(connector);
    thread.start();
    Thread.sleep(5000);
    thread.interrupt();
  }
}
```

Database connections, like sockets, lack inherent interruptibility. Consequently, this design fails to support the client's attempts to cancel a task by closing the resource when the corresponding thread is blocked on a long-running query, such as a join.

Compliant Solution (`Statement.cancel()`)

This compliant solution uses a ThreadLocal wrapper around the connection so that a thread calling the initialValue() method obtains a unique connection instance. This approach allows provision of a cancelStatement() so that other threads or clients can interrupt a long-running query when required. The cancelStatement() method invokes the Statement.cancel() method.

```
public final class DBConnector implements Runnable {
  private final String query;
  private volatile Statement stmt;

  DBConnector(String query) {
    this.query = query;
    if (getConnection() != null) {
      try {
```

```
        stmt = getConnection().createStatement();
      } catch (SQLException e) {
        // Forward to handler
      }
    }
  }

  private static final ThreadLocal<Connection> connectionHolder =
                                    new ThreadLocal<Connection>() {
    Connection connection = null;

    @Override public Connection initialValue() {
      try {
        // ...
        connection = DriverManager.getConnection(
          "jdbc:driver:name",
          "username",
          "password"
        );
      } catch (SQLException e) {
        // Forward to handler
      }
      return connection;
    }
  };

  public Connection getConnection() {
    return connectionHolder.get();
  }

  public boolean cancelStatement() { // Allows client to cancel statement
    if (stmt != null) {
      try {
        stmt.cancel();
        return true;
      } catch (SQLException e) {
        // Forward to handler
      }
    }
    return false;
  }

  @Override public void run() {
    try {
      if (stmt == null || (stmt.getConnection() != getConnection())) {
        throw new IllegalStateException();
      }
```

```
      ResultSet rs = stmt.executeQuery(query);
      // ...
    } catch (SQLException e) {
      // Forward to handler
    }
    // ...
  }

  public static void main(String[] args) throws InterruptedException {
    DBConnector connector = new DBConnector("suitable query");
    Thread thread = new Thread(connector);
    thread.start();
    Thread.sleep(5000);
    connector.cancelStatement();
  }
}
```

The `Statement.cancel()` method cancels the query, provided the database management system (DBMS) and driver both support cancellation. It is impossible to cancel the query if either the DBMS or the driver fail to support cancellation.

According to the Java API, interface `Statement` documentation [API 2006]:

> By default, only one `ResultSet` object per `Statement` object can be open at the same time. As a result, if the reading of one `ResultSet` object is interleaved with the reading of another, each must have been generated by different `Statement` objects.

This compliant solution ensures that only one `ResultSet` is associated with the `Statement` belonging to an instance, and consequently, only one thread can access the query results.

Risk Assessment

Failure to provide facilities for thread termination can cause nonresponsiveness and DoS.

Rule	Severity	Likelihood	Remediation Cost	Priority	Level
THI04-J	low	probable	medium	P4	L3

Bibliography

[API 2006]	Class `Thread`, method `stop`, interface `ExecutorService`
[Darwin 2004]	24.3, Stopping a Thread
[JDK7 2008]	Java Thread Primitive Deprecation

[JPL 2006]	14.12.1, Don't stop; 23.3.3, Shutdown Strategies
[JavaThreads 2004]	2.4, Two Approaches to Stopping a Thread
[Goetz 2006a]	Chapter 7, Cancellation and Shutdown

■ THI05-J. Do not use Thread.stop() to terminate threads

Threads preserve class invariants when they are allowed to exit normally. Programmers often attempt to terminate threads abruptly when they believe the task is complete, the request has been canceled, or the program or JVM must shut down expeditiously.

Certain thread APIs were introduced to facilitate thread suspension, resumption, and termination but were later deprecated because of inherent design weaknesses. For example, the Thread.stop() method causes the thread to immediately throw a ThreadDeath exception, which usually stops the thread. More information about deprecated methods is available in rule MET02-J.

Invoking Thread.stop() results in the release of all locks a thread has acquired, potentially exposing the objects protected by those locks when those objects are in an inconsistent state. The thread might catch the ThreadDeath exception and use a finally block in an attempt to repair the inconsistent object or objects. However, this requires careful inspection of all synchronized methods and blocks because a ThreadDeath exception can be thrown at any point during the thread's execution. Furthermore, code must be protected from ThreadDeath exceptions that might occur while executing catch or finally blocks [Sun 1999]. Consequently, programs must not invoke Thread.stop().

Removing the java.lang.RuntimePermission stopThread permission from the security policy file prevents threads from being stopped using the Thread.stop() method. Although this approach guarantees that the program cannot use the Thread.stop() method, it is nevertheless strongly discouraged. Existing trusted, custom-developed code that uses the Thread.stop() method presumably depends on the ability of the system to perform this action. Furthermore, the system might fail to correctly handle the resulting security exception. Additionally, third-party libraries may also depend on use of the Thread.stop() method.

Refer to rule ERR09-J for information on preventing data corruption when the JVM is abruptly shut down.

Noncompliant Code Example (Deprecated Thread.stop())

This noncompliant code example shows a thread that fills a vector with pseudorandom numbers. The thread is forcefully stopped after a given amount of time.

```
public final class Container implements Runnable {
  private final Vector<Integer> vector = new Vector<Integer>(1000);

  public Vector<Integer> getVector() {
    return vector;
  }

  @Override public synchronized void run() {
    Random number = new Random(123L);
    int i = vector.capacity();
    while (i > 0) {
      vector.add(number.nextInt(100));
      i--;
    }
  }

  public static void main(String[] args) throws InterruptedException {
    Thread thread = new Thread(new Container());
    thread.start();
    Thread.sleep(5000);
    thread.stop();
  }
}
```

Because the Vector class is thread-safe, operations performed by multiple threads on its shared instance are expected to leave it in a consistent state. For instance, the Vector. size() method always returns the correct number of elements in the vector, even after concurrent changes to the vector, because the vector instance uses its own intrinsic lock to prevent other threads from accessing it while its state is temporarily inconsistent.

However, the Thread.stop() method causes the thread to stop what it is doing and throw a ThreadDeath exception. All acquired locks are subsequently released [API 2006]. If the thread were in the process of adding a new integer to the vector when it was stopped, the vector would become accessible while it is in an inconsistent state. For example, this could result in Vector.size() returning an incorrect element count because the element count is incremented after adding the element.

Compliant Solution (Volatile flag)

This compliant solution uses a volatile flag to request thread termination. The shutdown() accessor method is used to set the flag to true. The thread's run() method polls the done flag and terminates when it is set.

```
public final class Container implements Runnable {
  private final Vector<Integer> vector = new Vector<Integer>(1000);
  private volatile boolean done = false;

  public Vector<Integer> getVector() {
    return vector;
  }

  public void shutdown() {
    done = true;
  }

  @Override public synchronized void run() {
    Random number = new Random(123L);
    int i = vector.capacity();
    while (!done && i > 0) {
      vector.add(number.nextInt(100));
      i--;
    }
  }

  public static void main(String[] args) throws InterruptedException {
    Container container = new Container();
    Thread thread = new Thread(container);
    thread.start();
    Thread.sleep(5000);
    container.shutdown();
  }
}
```

Compliant Solution (Interruptible)

In this compliant solution, the Thread.interrupt() method is called from main() to terminate the thread. Invoking Thread.interrupt() sets an internal interrupt status flag. The
thread polls that flag using the Thread.interrupted() method, which both returns true if
the current thread has been interrupted and clears the interrupt status flag.

```
public final class Container implements Runnable {
  private final Vector<Integer> vector = new Vector<Integer>(1000);

  public Vector<Integer> getVector() {
    return vector;
  }

  @Override public synchronized void run() {
    Random number = new Random(123L);
    int i = vector.capacity();
    while (!Thread.interrupted() && i > 0) {
```

```
    vector.add(number.nextInt(100));
    i--;
  }
}
public static void main(String[] args) throws InterruptedException {
  Container c = new Container();
  Thread thread = new Thread(c);
  thread.start();
  Thread.sleep(5000);
  thread.interrupt();
}
}
```

A thread may use interruption for performing tasks other than cancellation and shutdown. Consequently, a thread should be interrupted only when its interruption policy is known in advance. Failure to do so can result in failed interruption requests.

Risk Assessment

Forcing a thread to stop can result in inconsistent object state. Critical resources could also leak if cleanup operations are not carried out as required.

Rule	Severity	Likelihood	Remediation Cost	Priority	Level
THI05-J	low	probable	medium	P4	L3

Related Guidelines

CERT C Secure Coding Standard	POS47-C. Do not use threads that can be canceled asynchronously
MITRE CWE	CWE-705. Incorrect Control Flow Scoping

Bibliography

[API 2006]	Class `Thread`, method `stop`, interface `ExecutorService`
[Sun 1999]	
[Darwin 2004]	24.3, Stopping a Thread
[JDK7 2008]	Concurrency Utilities, More information: Java Thread Primitive Deprecation
[JPL 2006]	14.12.1, Don't Stop; 23.3.3, Shutdown Strategies
[JavaThreads 2004]	2.4, Two Approaches to Stopping a Thread
[Goetz 2006a]	Chapter 7, Cancellation and Shutdown

Chapter | 12

Thread Pools (TPS)

■ Rules

■ Risk Assessment Summary

Rule	Severity	Likelihood	Remediation Cost	Priority	Level
TPS00-J	low	probable	high	P2	L3
TPS01-J	low	probable	medium	P4	L3
TPS02-J	low	probable	medium	P4	L3
TPS03-J	low	probable	medium	P4	L3
TPS04-J	medium	probable	high	P4	L3

■ TPS00-J. Use thread pools to enable graceful degradation of service during traffic bursts

Many programs must address the problem of handling a series of incoming requests. One simple concurrency strategy is the thread-per-message design pattern, which uses a new thread for each request [Lea 2000a]. This pattern is generally preferred over sequential executions of time-consuming, I/O-bound, session-based, or isolated tasks.

However, the pattern also introduces overheads not seen in sequential execution, including the time and resources required for thread creation and scheduling, for task processing, for resource allocation and deallocation, and for frequent context switching [Lea 2000a]. Furthermore, an attacker can cause a denial of service (DoS) by overwhelming the system with too many requests all at once, causing the system to become unresponsive rather than degrading gracefully. From a safety perspective, one component can exhaust all resources because of an intermittent error, consequently starving all other components.

Thread pools allow a system to limit the maximum number of simultaneous requests that it processes to a number that it can comfortably serve rather than terminating all services when presented with a deluge of requests. Thread pools overcome these issues by controlling the maximum number of worker threads that can execute concurrently. Each object that supports thread pools accepts a `Runnable` or `Callable<T>` task and stores it in a temporary queue until resources become available. Additionally, thread life-cycle management overhead is minimized because the threads in a thread pool can be reused and can be efficiently added to or removed from the pool.

Programs that use multiple threads to service requests should—and programs that may be subjected to DoS attacks *must*—ensure graceful degradation of service during traffic bursts. Use of thread pools is one acceptable approach to meeting this requirement.

Noncompliant Code Example (Thread-Per-Message)

This noncompliant code example demonstrates the thread-per-message design pattern. The `RequestHandler` class provides a public static factory method so that callers can obtain a `RequestHandler` instance. The `handleRequest()` method is subsequently invoked to handle each request in its own thread.

```
class Helper {
  public void handle(Socket socket) {
    //...
  }
}

final class RequestHandler {
  private final Helper helper = new Helper();
  private final ServerSocket server;
```

```
    private RequestHandler(int port) throws IOException {
      server = new ServerSocket(port);
    }

    public static RequestHandler newInstance() throws IOException {
      return new RequestHandler(0); // Selects next available port
    }

    public void handleRequest() {
      new Thread(new Runnable() {
        public void run() {
          try {
            helper.handle(server.accept());
          } catch (IOException e) {
            // Forward to handler
          }
        }
      }).start();
    }
  }
```

The thread-per-message strategy fails to provide graceful degradation of service. As threads are created, processing continues normally until some scarce resource is exhausted. For example, a system may allow only a limited number of open file descriptors even though additional threads can be created to serve requests. When the scarce resource is memory, the system may fail abruptly, resulting in a DoS.

Compliant Solution (Thread Pool)

This compliant solution uses a fixed thread pool that places a strict limit on the number of concurrently executing threads. Tasks submitted to the pool are stored in an internal queue. This prevents the system from being overwhelmed when attempting to respond to all incoming requests and allows it to degrade gracefully by serving a fixed maximum number of simultaneous clients [Tutorials 2008].

```
  // class Helper remains unchanged
  final class RequestHandler {
    private final Helper helper = new Helper();
    private final ServerSocket server;
    private final ExecutorService exec;

    private RequestHandler(int port, int poolSize) throws IOException {
      server = new ServerSocket(port);
      exec = Executors.newFixedThreadPool(poolSize);
    }
```

```
    public static RequestHandler newInstance(int poolSize)
                                             throws IOException {
      return new RequestHandler(0, poolSize);
    }

    public void handleRequest() {
      Future<?> future = exec.submit(new Runnable() {
        @Override public void run() {
          try {
            helper.handle(server.accept());
          } catch (IOException e) {
            // Forward to handler
          }
        }
      });
    }
    // ... other methods such as shutting down the thread pool
    // and task cancellation ...
}
```

According to the Java API documentation for the `Executor` interface [API 2006]:

[The interface `Executor` is] an object that executes submitted `Runnable` tasks. This interface provides a way of decoupling task submission from the mechanics of how each task will be run, including details of thread use, scheduling, etc. An `Executor` is normally used instead of explicitly creating threads.

The `ExecutorService` interface used in this compliant solution derives from the `java.util.concurrent.Executor` interface. The `ExecutorService.submit()` method allows callers to obtain a `Future<V>` object. This object both encapsulates the as-yet unknown result of an asynchronous computation and also enables callers to perform additional functions such as task cancellation.

The choice of `newFixedThreadPool` is not always appropriate. Refer to the Java API documentation for guidance on choosing among the following methods to meet specific design requirements [API 2006]:

■ newFixedThreadPool()

■ newCachedThreadPool()

■ newSingleThreadExecutor()

■ newScheduledThreadPool()

Risk Assessment

Using simplistic concurrency primitives to process an unbounded number of requests could result in severe performance degradation, deadlock, or system resource exhaustion and DoS.

Rule	Severity	Likelihood	Remediation Cost	Priority	Level
TPS00-J	low	probable	high	P2	L3

Related Guidelines

MITRE CWE	CWE-405. Asymmetric resource consumption (amplification)
	CWE-410. Insufficient resource pool

Bibliography

[API 2006]	Interface Executor
[Lea 2000a]	4.1.3, Thread-Per-Message; 4.1.4, Worker Threads
[Tutorials 2008]	Thread Pools
[Goetz 2006a]	Chapter 8, Applying Thread Pools

■ TPS01-J. Do not execute interdependent tasks in a bounded thread pool

Bounded thread pools allow the programmer to specify an upper limit on the number of threads that can concurrently execute in a thread pool. Programs must not use threads from a bounded thread pool to execute tasks that depend on the completion of other tasks in the pool.

A form of deadlock called *thread-starvation deadlock* arises when all the threads executing in the pool are blocked on tasks that are waiting on an internal queue for an available thread in which to execute. Thread-starvation deadlock occurs when currently executing tasks submit other tasks to a thread pool and wait for them to complete and the thread pool lacks the capacity to accommodate all the tasks at once.

This problem can be confusing because the program can function correctly when fewer threads are needed. The issue can be mitigated, in some cases, by choosing a larger pool size. However, determining a suitable size may be difficult or even impossible.

Similarly, threads in a thread pool may fail to be recycled when two executing tasks each require the other to complete before they can terminate. A blocking operation within a subtask can also lead to unbounded queue growth [Goetz 2006a].

Noncompliant Code Example (Interdependent Subtasks)

This noncompliant code example is vulnerable to thread-starvation deadlock. It consists of the ValidationService class, which performs various input validation tasks such as checking whether a user-supplied field exists in a back-end database.

The fieldAggregator() method accepts a variable number of String arguments and creates a task corresponding to each argument to enable concurrent processing. The task performs input validation using the ValidateInput class.

In turn, the ValidateInput class attempts to sanitize the input by creating a subtask for each request using the SanitizeInput class. All tasks are executed in the same thread pool. The fieldAggregator() method blocks until all the tasks have finished executing and, when all results are available, returns the aggregated results as a StringBuilder object to the caller.

```java
public final class ValidationService {
  private final ExecutorService pool;

  public ValidationService(int poolSize) {
    pool = Executors.newFixedThreadPool(poolSize);
  }

  public void shutdown() {
    pool.shutdown();
  }

  public StringBuilder fieldAggregator(String... inputs)
      throws InterruptedException, ExecutionException {

    StringBuilder sb = new StringBuilder();
    // Stores the results
    Future<String>[] results = new Future[inputs.length];

    // Submits the tasks to thread pool
    for (int i = 0; i < inputs.length; i++) {
      results[i] = pool.submit(
        new ValidateInput<String>(inputs[i], pool));
    }

    for (int i = 0; i < inputs.length; i++) { // Aggregates the results
      sb.append(results[i].get());
    }
    return sb;
  }
}
```

```
public final class ValidateInput<V> implements Callable<V> {
  private final V input;
  private final ExecutorService pool;

  ValidateInput(V input, ExecutorService pool) {
    this.input = input;
    this.pool = pool;
  }

  @Override public V call() throws Exception {
    // If validation fails, throw an exception here
    // Subtask
    Future<V> future = pool.submit(new SanitizeInput<V>(input));
    return (V) future.get();
  }
}

public final class SanitizeInput<V> implements Callable<V> {
  private final V input;

  SanitizeInput(V input) {
    this.input = input;
  }

  @Override public V call() throws Exception {
    // Sanitize input and return
    return (V) input;
  }
}
```

Assume, for example, that the pool size is set to six. The ValidationService.fieldAggregator() method is invoked to validate six arguments; consequently, it submits six tasks to the thread pool. Each task submits a corresponding subtask to sanitize the input. The SanitizeInput subtasks must execute before the original six tasks can return their results. However, this is impossible because all six threads in the thread pool are blocked. Furthermore, the shutdown() method cannot shut down the thread pool when it contains active tasks.

Thread-starvation deadlock can also occur when a single-threaded Executor is used, for example, when the caller creates several subtasks and waits for the results.

Compliant Solution (No Interdependent Tasks)

This compliant solution modifies the ValidateInput<V> class so that the SanitizeInput tasks are executed in the same threads as the ValidateInput tasks rather than in separate threads. Consequently, the ValidateInput and SanitizeInput tasks are independent; this eliminates their need to wait for each other to complete. The SanitizeInput class has also been modified to omit implementation of the Callable interface.

```
public final class ValidationService {
  // ...
  public StringBuilder fieldAggregator(String... inputs)
      throws InterruptedException, ExecutionException {
    // ...
    for (int i = 0; i < inputs.length; i++) {
      // Don't pass-in thread pool
      results[i] = pool.submit(new ValidateInput<String>(inputs[i]));
    }
    // ...
  }
}

// Does not use same thread pool
public final class ValidateInput<V> implements Callable<V> {
  private final V input;

  ValidateInput(V input) {
    this.input = input;
  }

  @Override public V call() throws Exception {
    // If validation fails, throw an exception here
    return (V) new SanitizeInput().sanitize(input);
  }
}

public final class SanitizeInput<V> {  // No longer a Callable task
  public SanitizeInput() {}

  public V sanitize(V input) {
    // Sanitize input and return
    return input;
  }
}
```

Thread-starvation issues can be partially mitigated by choosing a large thread pool size. However, an untrusted caller can still overwhelm the system by supplying more inputs. (See rule TPS00-J.)

Note that operations that have further constraints, such as the total number of database connections or total ResultSet objects open at a particular time, impose an upper bound on the usable thread pool size as each thread continues to block until the resource becomes available.

Private static ThreadLocal variables may be used to maintain local state in each thread. When using thread pools, the lifetime of ThreadLocal variables should be bounded by the corresponding task [Goetz 2006a]. Furthermore, programs must not use these variables to communicate between tasks. There are additional constraints in the use of ThreadLocal variables in thread pools; see rule TPS04-J for more information.

Noncompliant Code Example (Subtasks)

This noncompliant code example contains a series of subtasks that execute in a shared thread pool [Gafter 2006]. The BrowserManager class calls perUser(), which starts tasks that invoke perProfile(). The perProfile() method starts tasks that invoke perTab(), and in turn, perTab starts tasks that invoke doSomething(). BrowserManager then waits for the tasks to finish. The threads are allowed to invoke doSomething() in any order, provided that count correctly records the number of methods executed.

```
public final class BrowserManager {
  private final ExecutorService pool = Executors.newFixedThreadPool(10);
  private final int numberOfTimes;
  private static AtomicInteger count = new AtomicInteger(); // count = 0

  public BrowserManager(int n) {
    numberOfTimes = n;
  }

  public void perUser() {
    methodInvoker(numberOfTimes, "perProfile");
    pool.shutdown();
  }

  public void perProfile() {
    methodInvoker(numberOfTimes, "perTab");
  }

  public void perTab() {
    methodInvoker(numberOfTimes, "doSomething");
  }

  public void doSomething() {
    System.out.println(count.getAndIncrement());
  }

  public void methodInvoker(int n, final String method) {
    final BrowserManager manager = this;
    Callable<Object> callable = new Callable<Object>() {
      @Override public Object call() throws Exception {
        Method meth = manager.getClass().getMethod(method);
        return meth.invoke(manager);
      }
    };

    Collection<Callable<Object>> collection =
      Collections.nCopies(n, callable);
```

```
   try {
     Collection<Future<Object>> futures = pool.invokeAll(collection);
   } catch (InterruptedException e) {
     // Forward to handler
     Thread.currentThread().interrupt(); // Reset interrupted status
   }
   // ...
 }

 public static void main(String[] args) {
   BrowserManager manager = new BrowserManager(5);
   manager.perUser();
 }
}
```

Unfortunately, this program is susceptible to a thread-starvation deadlock. For example, if each of the five perUser tasks spawns five perProfile tasks, where each perProfile task spawns a perTab task, the thread pool will be exhausted, and perTab() will be unable to allocate any additional threads to invoke the doSomething() method.

Compliant Solution (`CallerRunsPolicy`)

This compliant solution selects and schedules tasks for execution, avoiding thread-starvation deadlock. It sets the CallerRunsPolicy on a ThreadPoolExecutor and uses a SynchronousQueue [Gafter 2006]. The policy dictates that when the thread pool runs out of available threads, any subsequent tasks will run in the thread that submitted the tasks.

```
public final class BrowserManager {
  private final static ThreadPoolExecutor pool =
      new ThreadPoolExecutor(0, 10, 60L, TimeUnit.SECONDS,
                             new SynchronousQueue<Runnable>());
  private final int numberOfTimes;
  private static AtomicInteger count = new AtomicInteger(); // count = 0

  static {
    pool.setRejectedExecutionHandler(
    new ThreadPoolExecutor.CallerRunsPolicy());
  }

  // ...
}
```

According to Goetz and colleagues [Goetz 2006a]:

A SynchronousQueue is not really a queue at all, but a mechanism for managing handoffs between threads. In order to put an element on the SynchronousQueue, another thread must already be waiting to accept the handoff. If no thread is waiting, but the current pool size is less than the maximum, ThreadPoolExecutor creates a new thread; otherwise, the task is rejected according to the saturation policy.

According to the Java API [API 2006], the CallerRunsPolicy class is:

A handler for rejected tasks that runs the rejected task directly in the calling thread of the execute method, unless the executor has been shut down, in which case, the task is discarded.

In this compliant solution, tasks that have other tasks waiting to accept the handoff are added to the SynchronousQueue when the thread pool is full. For example, tasks corresponding to perTab() are added to the SynchronousQueue because the tasks corresponding to perProfile() are waiting to receive the handoff. Once the pool is full, additional tasks are rejected according to the saturation policy in effect. Because the CallerRunsPolicy is used to handle these rejected tasks, all the rejected tasks are executed in the main thread that started the initial tasks. When all the threads corresponding to perTab() have finished executing, the next set of tasks corresponding to perProfile() are added to the SynchronousQueue because the handoff is subsequently used by perUser() tasks.

The CallerRunsPolicy allows graceful degradation of service when faced with many requests by distributing the workload from the thread pool to the work queue. Because the submitted tasks cannot block for any reason other than waiting for other tasks to complete, the policy guarantees that the current thread can handle multiple tasks sequentially. The policy would fail to prevent thread-starvation deadlock if the tasks were to block for some other reason, such as network I/O. Furthermore, this approach avoids unbounded queue growth because SynchronousQueue avoids storing tasks indefinitely for future execution, and all tasks are handled either by the current thread or by a thread in the thread pool.

This compliant solution is subject to the vagaries of the thread scheduler, which might schedule the tasks suboptimally. However, it avoids thread-starvation deadlock.

Risk Assessment

Executing interdependent tasks in a thread pool can lead to denial of service.

Rule	Severity	Likelihood	Remediation Cost	Priority	Level
TPS01-J	low	probable	medium	P4	L3

Bibliography

[API 2006]

[Gafter 2006]   A Thread Pool Puzzler

[Goetz 2006a]   8.3.2, Managing queued tasks; 8.3.3, Saturation Policies; 5.3.3, Dequeues and work stealing

■ TPS02-J. Ensure that tasks submitted to a thread pool are interruptible

Programs may submit *only* tasks that support interruption using `Thread.interrupt()` to thread pools that require the ability to shut down the thread pool or to cancel individual tasks within the pool. Programs must not submit tasks that lack interruption support to such thread pools. According to the Java API interface [API 2006], the `java.util.concurrent.ExecutorService.shutdownNow()` method:

> … attempts to stop all actively executing tasks, halts the processing of waiting tasks, and returns a list of the tasks that were awaiting execution. There are no guarantees beyond best-effort attempts to stop processing actively executing tasks. For example, typical implementations will cancel via `Thread.interrupt()`, so any task that fails to respond to interrupts may never terminate.

Noncompliant Code Example (Shutting Down Thread Pools)

This noncompliant code example submits the `SocketReader` class as a task to the thread pool declared in `PoolService`.

```
public final class SocketReader implements Runnable { // Thread-safe class
  private final Socket socket;
  private final BufferedReader in;
  private final Object lock = new Object();

  public SocketReader(String host, int port) throws IOException {
    this.socket = new Socket(host, port);
    this.in = new BufferedReader(
      new InputStreamReader(this.socket.getInputStream())
    );
  }

  // Only one thread can use the socket at a particular time
  @Override public void run() {
```

```java
      try {
        synchronized (lock) {
          readData();
        }
      } catch (IOException ie) {
        // Forward to handler
      }
    }

    public void readData() throws IOException {
      String string;
      try {
        while ((string = in.readLine()) != null) {
          // Blocks until end of stream (null)
        }
      } finally {
        shutdown();
      }
    }

    public void shutdown() throws IOException {
      socket.close();
    }
  }

public final class PoolService {
  private final ExecutorService pool;

  public PoolService(int poolSize) {
    pool = Executors.newFixedThreadPool(poolSize);
  }

  public void doSomething() throws InterruptedException, IOException {
    pool.submit(new SocketReader("somehost", 8080));
    // ...
    List<Runnable> awaitingTasks = pool.shutdownNow();
  }

  public static void main(String[] args)
                          throws InterruptedException, IOException {
    PoolService service = new PoolService(5);
    service.doSomething();
  }
}
```

The shutdownNow() method may fail to shut down the thread pool because the task lacks support for interruption using the Thread.interrupt() method, and because the shutdown() method must wait until all executing tasks have finished.

Similarly, tasks that use some mechanism other than Thread.interrupted() to determine when to shut down will be unresponsive to shutdown() or shutdownNow(). For instance, tasks that check a volatile flag to determine whether it is safe to shut down are unresponsive to these methods. Rule THI05-J provides more information on using a flag to terminate threads.

Compliant Solution (Submit Interruptible Tasks)

This compliant solution defines an interruptible version of the SocketReader class, which is instantiated and submitted to the thread pool.

```java
public final class SocketReader implements Runnable {
  private final SocketChannel sc;
  private final Object lock = new Object();

  public SocketReader(String host, int port) throws IOException {
    sc = SocketChannel.open(new InetSocketAddress(host, port));
  }

  @Override public void run() {
    ByteBuffer buf = ByteBuffer.allocate(1024);
    try {
      synchronized (lock) {
        while (!Thread.interrupted()) {
          sc.read(buf);
          // ...
        }
      }
    } catch (IOException ie) {
      // Forward to handler
    }
  }
}

public final class PoolService {
  // ...
}
```

Exceptions

TPS02-EX0: Short-running tasks that execute without blocking are exempt from this rule.

Risk Assessment

Submitting tasks that are uninterruptible may prevent a thread pool from shutting down and consequently may cause DoS.

Rule	Severity	Likelihood	Remediation Cost	Priority	Level
TPS02-J	low	probable	medium	P4	L3

Bibliography

[API 2006]   Interface `ExecutorService`

[Goetz 2006a]   Chapter 7, Cancellation and Shutdown

■ TPS03-J. Ensure that tasks executing in a thread pool do not fail silently

All tasks in a thread pool must provide a mechanism for notifying the application if they terminate abnormally. Failure to do so cannot cause resource leaks because the threads in the pool are still recycled, but it makes failure diagnosis extremely difficult or impossible.

The best way to handle exceptions at the application level is to use an exception handler. The handler can perform diagnostic actions, clean up and shut down the JVM, or simply log the details of the failure.

Noncompliant Code Example (Abnormal Task Termination)

This noncompliant code example consists of the `PoolService` class that encapsulates a thread pool and a runnable `Task` class. The `Task.run()` method can throw runtime exceptions, such as `NullPointerException`.

```
final class PoolService {
  private final ExecutorService pool = Executors.newFixedThreadPool(10);

  public void doSomething() {
    pool.execute(new Task());
  }
}

final class Task implements Runnable {
  @Override public void run() {
```

```
    // ...
    throw new NullPointerException();
    // ...
  }
 }
}
```

The task fails to notify the application when it terminates unexpectedly as a result of the runtime exception. Moreover, it lacks a recovery mechanism. Consequently, if Task were to throw a NullPointerException, the exception would be ignored.

Compliant Solution (ThreadPoolExecutor Hooks)

Task-specific recovery or cleanup actions can be performed by overriding the after-Execute() hook of the java.util.concurrent.ThreadPoolExecutor class. This hook is called either when a task concludes successfully by executing all statements in its run() method or when the task halts because of an exception. Some implementations may fail to catch java.lang.Error. (See Bug ID 6450211[1] for more information [SDN 2008].) When using this approach, substitute the executor service with a custom ThreadPoolExecutor that overrides the afterExecute() hook:

```
final class PoolService {
  // The values have been hard coded for brevity
  ExecutorService pool = new CustomThreadPoolExecutor(
      10, 10, 10, TimeUnit.SECONDS, new ArrayBlockingQueue<Runnable>(10));
  // ...
}

class CustomThreadPoolExecutor extends ThreadPoolExecutor {
  // ... Constructor ...
  public CustomThreadPoolExecutor(
      int corePoolSize, int maximumPoolSize, long keepAliveTime,
      TimeUnit unit, BlockingQueue<Runnable> workQueue) {
    super(corePoolSize, maximumPoolSize, keepAliveTime, unit, workQueue);
  }

  @Override
  public void afterExecute(Runnable r, Throwable t) {
    super.afterExecute(r, t);
    if (t != null) {
      // Exception occurred, forward to handler
    }
```

---

1. http://bugs.sun.com/bugdatabase/view_bug.do?bug_id=6450211

```
    // ... Perform task-specific clean-up actions
  }

  @Override
  public void terminated() {
    super.terminated();
    // ... Perform final clean-up actions
  }
}
```

The terminated() hook is called after all the tasks have finished executing and the Executor has terminated cleanly. This hook can be overridden to release resources acquired by the thread pool, much like a finally block.

Compliant Solution (Uncaught Exception Handler)

This compliant solution sets an uncaught exception handler on behalf of the thread pool. A ThreadFactory argument is passed to the thread pool during construction. The factory is responsible for creating new threads and setting the uncaught exception handler on their behalf. The Task class is unchanged from the noncompliant code example.

```
final class PoolService {
  private static final ThreadFactory factory =
    new ExceptionThreadFactory(new MyExceptionHandler());
  private static final ExecutorService pool =
    Executors.newFixedThreadPool(10, factory);

  public void doSomething() {
    pool.execute(new Task()); // Task is a runnable class
  }

  public static class ExceptionThreadFactory implements ThreadFactory {
    private static final ThreadFactory defaultFactory =
      Executors.defaultThreadFactory();
    private final Thread.UncaughtExceptionHandler handler;

    public ExceptionThreadFactory(
      Thread.UncaughtExceptionHandler handler) {
      this.handler = handler;
    }
```

```
    @Override public Thread newThread(Runnable run) {
      Thread thread = defaultFactory.newThread(run);
      thread.setUncaughtExceptionHandler(handler);
      return thread;
    }
  }

  public static class MyExceptionHandler extends ExceptionReporter
      implements Thread.UncaughtExceptionHandler {
    // ...

    @Override public void uncaughtException(Thread thread, Throwable t) {
      // Recovery or logging code
    }
  }
}
```

The `ExecutorService.submit()` method can be used (in place of the `execute()` method) to submit a task to a thread pool and obtain a `Future` object. When the task is submitted via `ExecutorService.submit()`, thrown exceptions never reach the uncaught exception handler because the thrown exception is considered to be part of the return status and is consequently wrapped in an `ExecutionException` and rethrown by `Future.get()` [Goetz 2006a].

Compliant Solution (`Future<V>` and `submit()`)

This compliant solution invokes the `ExecutorService.submit()` method to submit the task so that a `Future` object can be obtained. It uses the `Future` object to let the task rethrow the exception so that it can be handled locally.

```
final class PoolService {
  private final ExecutorService pool = Executors.newFixedThreadPool(10);

  public void doSomething() {
    Future<?> future = pool.submit(new Task());

    // ...

    try {
      future.get();
```

```
    } catch (InterruptedException e) {
      Thread.currentThread().interrupt(); // Reset interrupted status
    } catch (ExecutionException e) {
      Throwable exception = e.getCause();
      // Forward to exception reporter
    }
  }
}
```

Furthermore, any exception that prevents doSomething() from obtaining the Future value can be handled as required.

Exceptions

TPS03-EX0: This rule may be violated only when the code for all runnable and callable tasks has been audited to ensure that exceptional conditions are impossible. Nonetheless, it remains good practice to install a task-specific or global exception handler to initiate recovery or log any exceptional conditions.

Risk Assessment

Failure to provide a mechanism for reporting that tasks in a thread pool failed as a result of an exceptional condition can make it difficult or impossible to diagnose the problem.

Rule	Severity	Likelihood	Remediation Cost	Priority	Level
TPS03-J	low	probable	medium	P4	L3

Related Guidelines

MITRE CWE   CWE-392. Missing report of error condition

Bibliography

[API 2006]   Interfaces ExecutorService, ThreadFactory; class Thread
[Goetz 2006a]   Chapter 7.3, Handling Abnormal Thread Termination

■ TPS04-J. Ensure ThreadLocal variables are reinitialized when using thread pools

The java.lang.ThreadLocal<T> class provides thread-local variables. According to the Java API [API 2006]:

> These variables differ from their normal counterparts in that each thread that accesses one (via its get or set method) has its own, independently initialized copy of the variable. ThreadLocal instances are typically private static fields in classes that wish to associate state with a thread (for example, a user ID or transaction ID).

The use of ThreadLocal objects requires care in classes whose objects are required to be executed by multiple threads in a thread pool. The technique of thread pooling allows threads to be reused to reduce thread creation overhead or when creating an unbounded number of threads can diminish the reliability of the system. Each task that enters the pool expects to see ThreadLocal objects in their initial, default state. However, when Thread-Local objects are modified on a thread that is subsequently made available for reuse, the next task executing on the reused thread sees the state of the ThreadLocal objects as modified by the previous task that executed on that thread [JPL 2006].

Programs must ensure that each task that executes on a thread from a thread pool sees only correctly initialized instances of ThreadLocal objects.

Noncompliant Code Example

This noncompliant code example consists of an enumeration of days (Day) and two classes (Diary and DiaryPool). The Diary class uses a ThreadLocal variable to store thread-specific information, such as each task's current day. The initial value of the current day is Monday; this can be changed later by invoking the setDay() method. The class also contains a threadSpecificTask() instance method that performs a thread-specific task.

The DiaryPool class consists of the doSomething1() and doSomething2() methods that each start a thread. The doSomething1() method changes the initial (default) value of the day to Friday and invokes threadSpecificTask(). On the other hand, doSomething2() relies on the initial value of the day (Monday) and invokes threadSpecificTask(). The main() method creates one thread using doSomething1() and two more using doSomething2().

```
public enum Day {
  MONDAY, TUESDAY, WEDNESDAY, THURSDAY, FRIDAY, SATURDAY, SUNDAY;
}

public final class Diary {
  private static final ThreadLocal<Day> days =
    new ThreadLocal<Day>() {
```

```
  // Initialize to Monday
  protected Day initialValue() {
    return Day.MONDAY;
  }
};

private static Day currentDay() {
  return days.get();
}

public static void setDay(Day newDay) {
  days.set(newDay);
}

// Performs some thread-specific task
public void threadSpecificTask() {
  // Do task ...
}
}

public final class DiaryPool {
  final int numOfThreads = 2; // Maximum number of threads allowed in pool
  final Executor exec;
  final Diary diary;

  DiaryPool() {
    exec = (Executor) Executors.newFixedThreadPool(numOfThreads);
    diary = new Diary();
  }

  public void doSomething1() {
    exec.execute(new Runnable() {
      @Override public void run() {
        diary.setDay(Day.FRIDAY);
        diary.threadSpecificTask();
      }
    });
  }

  public void doSomething2() {
    exec.execute(new Runnable() {
      @Override public void run() {
        diary.threadSpecificTask();
      }
    });
  }
```

```
public static void main(String[] args) {
  DiaryPool dp = new DiaryPool();
  dp.doSomething1(); // Thread 1, requires current day as Friday
  dp.doSomething2(); // Thread 2, requires current day as Monday
  dp.doSomething2(); // Thread 3, requires current day as Monday
  }
}
```

The `DiaryPool` class creates a thread pool that reuses a fixed number of threads operating off a shared, unbounded queue. At any point, no more than `numOfThreads` threads are actively processing tasks. If additional tasks are submitted when all threads are active, they wait in the queue until a thread is available. The thread-local state of the thread persists when a thread is recycled.

The following table shows a possible execution order:

Time	Task	Pool Thread	Submitted by Method	Day
1	t_1	1	doSomething1()	Friday
2	t_2	2	doSomething2()	Monday
3	t_3	1	doSomething2()	Friday

In this execution order, it is expected that the two tasks (t_2 and t_3) started from doSomething2() would observe the current day as Monday. However, because pool thread 1 is reused, t_3 observes the day to be Friday.

Noncompliant Code Example (Increase Thread Pool Size)

This noncompliant code example increases the size of the thread pool from two to three in an attempt to mitigate the issue.

```
public final class DiaryPool {
  final int numOfthreads = 3;
  // ...
}
```

Although increasing the size of the thread pool resolves the problem for this example, it fails to scale because changing the thread pool size is insufficient if additional tasks can be submitted to the pool.

Compliant Solution (`try-finally` Clause)

This compliant solution adds the `removeDay()` method to the `Diary` class and wraps the statements in the `doSomething1()` method of class `DiaryPool` in a `try-finally` block. The `finally` block restores the initial state of the thread-local days object by removing the current thread's value from it.

```java
public final class Diary {
  // ...
  public static void removeDay() {
    days.remove();
  }
}

public final class DiaryPool {
  // ...

  public void doSomething1() {
      exec.execute(new Runnable() {
        @Override public void run() {
          try {
            Diary.setDay(Day.FRIDAY);
            diary.threadSpecificTask();
          } finally {
            Diary.removeDay(); // Diary.setDay(Day.MONDAY)
                               // can also be used
          }
        }
     });
  }

  // ...
}
```

If the thread-local variable is read by the same thread again, it is reinitialized using the `initialValue()` method unless the task has already set the variable's value explicitly [API 2006]. This solution transfers the responsibility for maintenance to the client (`DiaryPool`) but is a good option when the `Diary` class cannot be modified.

Compliant Solution (`beforeExecute()`)

This compliant solution uses a custom `ThreadPoolExecutor` that extends `ThreadPool-Executor` and overrides the `beforeExecute()` method. The `beforeExecute()` method is invoked before the `Runnable` task is executed in the specified thread. The method reinitializes the thread-local variable before task r is executed by thread t.

```
class CustomThreadPoolExecutor extends ThreadPoolExecutor {
  public CustomThreadPoolExecutor(int corePoolSize,
      int maximumPoolSize, long keepAliveTime,
      TimeUnit unit, BlockingQueue<Runnable> workQueue) {
    super(corePoolSize, maximumPoolSize, keepAliveTime,
          unit, workQueue);
  }

  @Override
  public void beforeExecute(Thread t, Runnable r) {
    if (t == null || r == null) {
      throw new NullPointerException();
    }
    Diary.setDay(Day.MONDAY);
    super.beforeExecute(t, r);
  }
}
public final class DiaryPool {
  // ...
  DiaryPool() {
    exec = new CustomThreadPoolExecutor(NumOfthreads, NumOfthreads,
            10, TimeUnit.SECONDS, new ArrayBlockingQueue<Runnable>(10));
    diary = new Diary();
  }
  // ...
}
```

Exceptions

TPS04-EX0: It is unnecessary to reinitialize a `ThreadLocal` object that does not change state after initialization. For example, there may be only one type of database connection represented by the initial value of the `ThreadLocal` object.

Risk Assessment

Objects using `ThreadLocal` data and executed by different tasks in a thread pool without reinitialization might be in an unexpected state when reused.

Rule	Severity	Likelihood	Remediation Cost	Priority	Level
TPS04-J	medium	probable	high	P4	L3

Bibliography

[API 2006]	Class `java.lang.ThreadLocal<T>`
[JPL 2006]	14.13, `ThreadLocal` Variables

Chapter 13

Thread-Safety Miscellaneous (TSM)

■ Rules

■ Risk Assessment Summary

Rule	Severity	Likelihood	Remediation Cost	Priority	Level
TSM00-J	low	probable	medium	P4	L3
TSM01-J	medium	probable	high	P4	L3
TSM02-J	low	probable	high	P2	L3
TSM03-J	medium	probable	medium	P8	L2

■ TSM00-J. Do not override thread-safe methods with methods that are not thread-safe

Overriding thread-safe methods with methods that are unsafe for concurrent use can result in improper synchronization when a client that depends on the thread-safety promised by the parent inadvertently operates on an instance of the subclass. For example, an overridden synchronized method's contract can be violated when a subclass provides an implementation that is unsafe for concurrent use. Such overriding can easily result in errors that are difficult to diagnose. Consequently, programs must not override thread-safe methods with methods that are unsafe for concurrent use.

The locking strategy of classes designed for inheritance should always be documented. This information can subsequently be used to determine an appropriate locking strategy for subclasses (see rules LCK00-J and LCK11-J).

Noncompliant Code Example (Synchronized Method)

This noncompliant code example overrides the synchronized doSomething() method in the Base class with an unsynchronized method in the Derived class.

```
class Base {
  public synchronized void doSomething() {
    // ...
  }
}

class Derived extends Base {
  @Override public void doSomething() {
    // ...
  }
}
```

The doSomething() method of the Base class can be safely used by multiple threads, but instances of the Derived subclass cannot.

This programming error can be difficult to diagnose because threads that accept instances of Base can also accept instances of its subclasses. Consequently, clients could be unaware that they are operating on a thread-unsafe instance of a subclass of a thread-safe class.

Compliant Solution (Synchronized Method)

This compliant solution synchronizes the doSomething() method of the subclass.

```
class Base {
  public synchronized void doSomething() {
    // ...
  }
}

class Derived extends Base {
  @Override public synchronized void doSomething() {
    // ...
  }
}
```

This solution also complies with rule LCK00-J because the accessibility of the class is package-private. Package-private accessibility is permitted when untrusted code cannot infiltrate the package.

Compliant Solution (Private Final Lock Object)

This compliant solution ensures that the `Derived` class is thread-safe by overriding the synchronized `doSomething()` method of the `Base` class with a method that synchronizes on a private final lock object.

```
class Base {

  public synchronized void doSomething() {
    // ...
  }
}

class Derived extends Base {
  private final Object lock = new Object();

  @Override public void doSomething() {
    synchronized (lock) {
      // ...
    }
  }
}
```

This is an acceptable solution, provided the locking policy of the `Derived` class is consistent with that of the `Base` class.

Noncompliant Code Example (Private Lock)

This noncompliant code example defines a doSomething() method in the Base class that uses a private final lock in accordance with rule LCK00-J.

```
class Base {
  private final Object lock = new Object();

  public void doSomething() {
    synchronized (lock) {
      // ...
    }
  }
}

class Derived extends Base {
  @Override public void doSomething() {
    try {
      super.doSomething();
    } finally {
      logger.log(Level.FINE, "Did something");
    }
  }
}
```

It is possible for multiple threads to cause the entries to be logged in an order that differs from the order in which the tasks are performed. Consequently, the doSomething() method of the Derived class cannot be used safely by multiple threads because it is not thread-safe.

Compliant Solution (Private Lock)

This compliant solution synchronizes the doSomething() method of the subclass using its own private final lock object.

```
class Base {
  private final Object lock = new Object();

  public void doSomething() {
    synchronized (lock) {
      // ...
```

```
      }
    }
  }

class Derived extends Base {
  private final Object lock = new Object();

  @Override public void doSomething() {
    synchronized (lock) {
      try {
        super.doSomething();
      } finally {
        logger.log(Level.FINE, "Did something");
      }
    }
  }
}
```

Note that the `Base` and `Derived` objects maintain distinct locks that are inaccessible from each other's classes. Consequently, `Derived` can provide thread-safety guarantees independent of `Base`.

Risk Assessment

Overriding thread-safe methods with methods that are unsafe for concurrent access can result in unexpected behavior.

Rule	Severity	Likelihood	Remediation Cost	Priority	Level
TSM00-J	low	probable	medium	P4	L3

Bibliography

[API 2006]
[SDN 2008]   Sun bug database, Bug ID 4294756

■ TSM01-J. Do not let the `this` reference escape during object construction

According to the *Java Language Specification*, §15.8.3, `this` [JLS 2005]:

> When used as a primary expression, the keyword `this` denotes a value that is a reference to the object for which the instance method was invoked (§15.12), or to the

object being constructed. The type of this is the class C within which the keyword this occurs. At run time, the class of the actual object referred to may be the class C or any subclass of C.

The this reference is said to have escaped when it is made available beyond its current scope. Following are common ways by which the this reference can escape:

- Returning this from a nonprivate, overridable method that is invoked from the constructor of a class whose object is being constructed. (For more information, see rule MET05-J.)

- Returning this from a nonprivate method of a mutable class, which allows the caller to manipulate the object's state indirectly. This commonly occurs in method-chaining implementations; see rule VNA04-J for more information.

- Passing this as an argument to an *alien method* invoked from the constructor of a class whose object is being constructed.

- Using inner classes. An inner class implicitly holds a reference to the instance of its outer class unless the inner class is declared static.

- Publishing by assigning this to a public static variable from the constructor of a class whose object is being constructed.

- Throwing an exception from a constructor. Doing so may cause code to be vulnerable to a finalizer attack; see rule OBJ11-J for more information.

- Passing internal object state to an alien method. This enables the method to retrieve the this reference of the internal member object.

This rule describes the potential consequences of allowing the this reference to escape during object construction, including race conditions and improper initialization. For example, declaring a field final ordinarily ensures that all threads see the field in a fully initialized state; however, allowing the this reference to escape during object construction can expose the field to other threads in an uninitialized or partially initialized state. Rule TSM03-J, which describes the guarantees provided by various mechanisms for safe publication, relies on conformance to this rule. Consequently, programs must not allow the this reference to escape during object construction.

In general, it is important to detect cases in which the this reference can leak out beyond the scope of the current context. In particular, public variables and methods should be carefully scrutinized.

Noncompliant Code Example (Publish before Initialization)

This noncompliant code example publishes the this reference before initialization has concluded by storing it in a public static volatile class field. Consequently, other threads can obtain a partially initialized Publisher instance.

```
final class Publisher {
  public static volatile Publisher published;
  int num;

  Publisher(int number) {
    published = this;
    // Initialization
    this.num = number;
    // ...
  }
}
```

If an object's initialization (and consequently, its construction) depends on a security check within the constructor, the security check can be bypassed when an untrusted caller obtains the partially initialized instance. For more information, see rule OBJ11-J.

Noncompliant Code Example (Nonvolatile Public Static Field)

This noncompliant code example publishes the this reference in the last statement of the constructor. It remains vulnerable because the published field has public accessibility and the programmer has failed to declare it as volatile.

```
final class Publisher {
  public static Publisher published;
  int num;

  Publisher(int number) {
    // Initialization
    this.num = number;
    // ...
    published = this;
  }
}
```

Because the field is nonvolatile and nonfinal, the statements within the constructor can be reordered by the compiler in such a way that the this reference is published before the initialization statements have executed.

Compliant Solution (Volatile Field and Publish after Initialization)

This compliant solution both declares the published field volatile and reduces its accessibility to package-private so that callers outside the current package scope cannot obtain the this reference.

```
final class Publisher {
  static volatile Publisher published;
  int num;

  Publisher(int number) {
    // Initialization
    this.num = number;
    // ...
    published = this;
  }
}
```

The constructor publishes the `this` reference after initialization has concluded. However, the caller that instantiates `Publisher` must ensure that it cannot see the default value of the `num` field before it is initialized; to do otherwise would violate rule TSM03-J. Consequently, the field that holds the reference to `Publisher` might need to be declared volatile in the caller.

Initialization statements may be reordered when the `published` field is not declared volatile. The Java compiler, however, forbids declaring fields as both volatile and final.

The class `Publisher` must also be final; otherwise, a subclass can call its constructor and publish the `this` reference before the subclass's initialization has concluded.

Compliant Solution (Public Static Factory Method)

This compliant solution eliminates the internal member field and provides a `newInstance()` factory method that creates and returns a `Publisher` instance.

```
final class Publisher {
  final int num;

  private Publisher(int number) {
    // Initialization
    this.num = number;
  }

  public static Publisher newInstance(int number) {
    Publisher published = new Publisher(number);
    return published;
  }
}
```

This approach ensures that threads cannot see an inconsistent Publisher instance. The num field is also declared final, making the class immutable and consequently eliminating the possibility of obtaining a partially initialized object.

Noncompliant Code Example (Handlers)

This noncompliant code example defines the ExceptionReporter interface:

```
public interface ExceptionReporter {
  public void setExceptionReporter(ExceptionReporter er);
  public void report(Throwable exception);
}
```

This interface is implemented by the DefaultExceptionReporter class, which reports exceptions after filtering out any sensitive information. See rule ERR00-J for more information.

The DefaultExceptionReporter constructor prematurely publishes the this reference before construction of the object has concluded. This occurs in the last statement of the constructor (er.setExceptionReporter(this)), which sets the exception reporter. Because it is the last statement of the constructor, this may be misconstrued as benign.

```
// Class DefaultExceptionReporter
public class DefaultExceptionReporter implements ExceptionReporter {
  public DefaultExceptionReporter(ExceptionReporter er) {
    // Carry out initialization
    // Incorrectly publishes the "this" reference
    er.setExceptionReporter(this);
  }

  // Implementation of setExceptionReporter() and report()
}
```

The MyExceptionReporter class subclasses DefaultExceptionReporter with the intent of adding a logging mechanism that logs critical messages before reporting an exception.

```
// Class MyExceptionReporter derives from DefaultExceptionReporter
public class MyExceptionReporter extends DefaultExceptionReporter {
  private final Logger logger;
```

```
public MyExceptionReporter(ExceptionReporter er) {
  super(er); // Calls superclass's constructor
  // Obtain the default logger
  logger = Logger.getLogger("com.organization.Log");
}

public void report(Throwable t) {
  logger.log(Level.FINEST,"Loggable exception occurred", t);
}
}
```

The `MyExceptionReporter` constructor invokes the `DefaultExceptionReporter` superclass's constructor (a mandatory first step), which publishes the exception reporter before the initialization of the subclass has concluded. Note that the subclass initialization consists of obtaining an instance of the default logger. Publishing the exception reporter is equivalent to setting it to receive and handle exceptions from that point on.

Logging will fail when an exception occurs before the call to `Logger.getLogger()` in the `MyExceptionReporter` subclass because dereferencing the uninitialized `logger` field generates a `NullPointerException`, which could itself be consumed by the reporting mechanism without being logged.

This erroneous behavior results from the race condition between an oncoming exception and the initialization of `MyExceptionReporter`. If the exception arrives too soon, it will find the `MyExceptionReporter` object in an inconsistent state. This behavior is especially counterintuitive because `logger` has been declared final, so observing an uninitialized value would be unexpected.

Premature publication of an event listener causes a similar problem; the listener can receive event notifications before the subclass's initialization has finished.

Compliant Solution

Rather than publishing the `this` reference from the `DefaultExceptionReporter` constructor, this compliant solution adds a `publishExceptionReporter()` method to `DefaultExceptionReporter` to permit setting the exception reporter. This method can be invoked on a subclass instance after the subclass's initialization has concluded.

```
public class DefaultExceptionReporter implements ExceptionReporter {
  public DefaultExceptionReporter(ExceptionReporter er) {
    // ...
  }
```

```
  // Should be called after subclass's initialization is over
  public void publishExceptionReporter() {
    setExceptionReporter(this); // Registers this exception reporter
  }

  // Implementation of setExceptionReporter() and report()
}
```

The `MyExceptionReporter` subclass inherits the `publishExceptionReporter()` method. Callers that instantiate `MyExceptionReporter` can use the resulting instance to set the exception reporter after initialization is complete.

```
// Class MyExceptionReporter derives from DefaultExceptionReporter
public class MyExceptionReporter extends DefaultExceptionReporter {
  private final Logger logger;

  public MyExceptionReporter(ExceptionReporter er) {
    super(er); // Calls superclass's constructor
    logger = Logger.getLogger("com.organization.Log");
  }
  // Implementations of publishExceptionReporter(),
  // setExceptionReporter() and report()
  // are inherited
}
```

This approach ensures that the reporter cannot be set before the constructor has fully initialized the subclass and enabled logging.

Noncompliant Code Example (Inner Class)

Inner classes maintain a copy of the `this` reference of the outer object. Consequently, the `this` reference could leak outside the scope [Goetz 2002]. This noncompliant code example uses a different implementation of the `DefaultExceptionReporter` class. The constructor uses an anonymous inner class to publish an exception reporter that invokes a `filter()` method.

```
public class DefaultExceptionReporter implements ExceptionReporter {
  public DefaultExceptionReporter(ExceptionReporter er) {
    er.setExceptionReporter(new DefaultExceptionReporter(er) {
      public void report(Throwable t) {
```

```
        filter(t);
      }
    });
  }
  // Default implementations of setExceptionReporter() and report()
}
```

Other threads can see the this reference of the outer class because it is published by the inner class. Furthermore, the issue described in the noncompliant code example for handlers will resurface if the class is subclassed.

Compliant Solution

Use a private constructor and a public static factory method to safely publish the exception reporter that invokes a filter() method from within the constructor [Goetz 2006a].

```
public class DefaultExceptionReporter implements ExceptionReporter {
  private final DefaultExceptionReporter defaultER;

  private DefaultExceptionReporter(ExceptionReporter excr) {
    defaultER = new DefaultExceptionReporter(excr) {
      public void report(Throwable t) {
        filter(t);
      }
    };
  }

  public static DefaultExceptionReporter newInstance(
              ExceptionReporter excr) {
    DefaultExceptionReporter der = new DefaultExceptionReporter(excr);
    excr.setExceptionReporter(der.defaultER);
    return der;
  }
  // Default implementations of setExceptionReporter() and report()
}
```

Because the constructor is private, untrusted code cannot create instances of the class; consequently, the this reference cannot escape. Using a public static factory method to create new instances also protects against untrusted manipulation of internal object state and publication of partially initialized objects. See rule TSM03-J for additional information.

Noncompliant Code Example (Thread)

This noncompliant code example starts a thread inside the constructor.

```
final class ThreadStarter implements Runnable {
  public ThreadStarter() {
    Thread thread = new Thread(this);
    thread.start();
  }

  @Override public void run() {
    // ...
  }
}
```

The new thread can access the `this` reference of the current object [Goetz 2002], [Goetz 2006a]. Notably, the `Thread()` constructor is alien to the `ThreadStarter` class.

Compliant Solution (Thread)

This compliant solution creates and starts the thread in a method rather than in the constructor.

```
final class ThreadStarter implements Runnable {
  public void startThread() {
    Thread thread = new Thread(this);
    thread.start();
  }

  @Override public void run() {
    // ...
  }
}
```

Exceptions

TSM01-EX0: It is safe to create a thread in the constructor, provided the thread is not started until *after* object construction is complete, because a call to `start()` on a thread happens-before any actions in the started thread [JLS 2005].

Even though this code example creates a thread that references `this` in the constructor, the thread is started only when its `start()` method is called from the `startThread()` method [Goetz 2002], [Goetz 2006a].

```java
final class ThreadStarter implements Runnable {
  Thread thread;

  public ThreadStarter() {
    thread = new Thread(this);
  }

  public void startThread() {
    thread.start();
  }

  @Override public void run() {
    // ...
  }
}
```

TSM01-EX1: Use of the `ObjectPreserver` pattern [Grand 2002] described in rule TSM02-J is safe and is permitted.

Risk Assessment

Allowing the `this` reference to escape can result in improper initialization and runtime exceptions.

Rule	Severity	Likelihood	Remediation Cost	Priority	Level
TSM01-J	medium	probable	High	P4	L3

Bibliography

[JLS 2005]	Keyword `this`
[Goetz 2002]	
[Goetz 2006a]	Section 3.2, Publication and Escape
[Grand 2002]	Chapter 5, Creational Patterns, Singleton

■ TSM02-J. Do not use background threads during class initialization

Starting and using background threads during class initialization can result in class initialization cycles and deadlock. For example, the main thread responsible for performing class initialization can block waiting for the background thread, which in turn will wait for the main thread to finish class initialization. This issue can arise, for example, when a database connection is established in a background thread during class initialization [Bloch 2005b]. Consequently, programs must ensure that class initialization is complete before starting any threads.

Noncompliant Code Example (Background Thread)

In this noncompliant code example, the static initializer starts a background thread as part of class initialization. The background thread attempts to initialize a database connection but should wait until all members of the ConnectionFactory class, including dbConnection, are initialized.

```java
public final class ConnectionFactory {
  private static Connection dbConnection;
  // Other fields ...

  static {
    Thread dbInitializerThread = new Thread(new Runnable() {
        @Override public void run() {
          // Initialize the database connection
          try {
            dbConnection = DriverManager.getConnection("connection string");
          } catch (SQLException e) {
            dbConnection = null;
          }
        }
    });
    // Other initialization, for example, start other threads

    dbInitializerThread.start();
    try {
      dbInitializerThread.join();
    } catch (InterruptedException ie) {
      throw new AssertionError(ie);
    }
  }

  public static Connection getConnection() {
    if (dbConnection == null) {
      throw new IllegalStateException("Error initializing connection");
    }
    return dbConnection;
  }
}
```

```
public static void main(String[] args) {
  // ...
  Connection connection = getConnection();
  }
}
```

Statically initialized fields are guaranteed to be fully constructed before they are made visible to other threads (see rule TSM03-J for more information). Consequently, the background thread must wait for the main (or foreground) thread to finish initialization before it can proceed. However, the `ConnectionFactory` class's main thread invokes the `join()` method, which waits for the background thread to finish. This interdependency causes a class initialization cycle that results in a deadlock situation [Bloch 2005b].

Similarly, it is inappropriate to start threads from constructors (see rule TSM01-J for more information). Creating timers that perform recurring tasks and starting those timers from within code responsible for initialization also introduces liveness issues.

Compliant Solution (Static Initializer, No Background Threads)

This compliant solution initializes all fields on the main thread rather than spawning background threads from the static initializer.

```
public final class ConnectionFactory {
  private static Connection dbConnection;
  // Other fields ...

  static {
    // Initialize a database connection
    try {
      dbConnection = DriverManager.getConnection("connection string");
    } catch (SQLException e) {
      dbConnection = null;
    }
    // Other initialization (do not start any threads)
  }

  // ...
}
```

Compliant Solution (`ThreadLocal`)

This compliant solution initializes the database connection from a `ThreadLocal` object so that each thread can obtain its own unique instance of the connection.

```
public final class ConnectionFactory {
  private static final ThreadLocal<Connection> connectionHolder
                    = new ThreadLocal<Connection>() {
    @Override public Connection initialValue() {
      try {
        Connection dbConnection =
          DriverManager.getConnection("connection string");
        return dbConnection;
      } catch (SQLException e) {
        return null;
      }
    }
  };
  // Other fields ...

  static {
    // Other initialization (do not start any threads)
  }

  public static Connection getConnection() {
    Connection connection = connectionHolder.get();
    if (connection == null) {
      throw new IllegalStateException("Error initializing connection");
    }
    return connection;
  }

  public static void main(String[] args) {
    // ...
    Connection connection = getConnection();
  }
}
```

The static initializer can be used to initialize any shared class field. Alternatively, the fields can be initialized from the initialValue() method.

Exceptions

TSM02-EX0: Programs are permitted to start a background thread (or threads) during class initialization, provided the thread cannot access any fields. For example, the following ObjectPreserver class (based on [Grand 2002]) provides a mechanism for storing object references, which prevents an object from being garbage-collected even when the object is never again dereferenced.

```java
public final class ObjectPreserver implements Runnable {
  private static final ObjectPreserver lifeLine = new ObjectPreserver();

  private ObjectPreserver() {
    Thread thread = new Thread(this);
    thread.setDaemon(true);
    thread.start(); // Keep this object alive
  }

  // Neither this class nor HashMap will be garbage-collected.
  // References from HashMap to other objects
  // will also exhibit this property
  private static final ConcurrentHashMap<Integer,Object> protectedMap
    = new ConcurrentHashMap<Integer,Object>();

  public synchronized void run() {
    try {
      wait();
    } catch (InterruptedException e) {
      Thread.currentThread().interrupt(); // Reset interrupted status
    }
  }

  // Objects passed to this method will be preserved until
  // the unpreserveObject() method is called
  public static void preserveObject(Object obj) {
    protectedMap.put(0, obj);
  }

  // Returns the same instance every time
  public static Object getObject() {
    return protectedMap.get(0);
  }

  // Unprotect the objects so that they can be garbage-collected
  public static void unpreserveObject() {
    protectedMap.remove(0);
  }
}
```

This is a singleton class (see rule MSC07-J for more information on how to defensively code singleton classes). The initialization involves creating a background thread using the current instance of the class. The thread waits indefinitely by invoking Object.wait().

Consequently, this object persists for the remainder of the Java Virtual Machine's (JVM's) lifetime. Because the object is managed by a daemon thread, the thread cannot interfere with normal shutdown of the JVM.

Although the initialization involves a background thread, that thread neither accesses fields nor creates any liveness or safety issues. Consequently, this code is a safe and useful exception to this rule.

Risk Assessment

Starting and using background threads during class initialization can result in deadlock.

Rule	Severity	Likelihood	Remediation Cost	Priority	Level
TSM02-J	low	probable	High	P2	L3

Bibliography

[Bloch 2005b]   8, Lazy Initialization
[Grand 2002]   Chapter 5, Creational Patterns, Singleton

■ TSM03-J. Do not publish partially initialized objects

During initialization of a shared object, the object must be accessible only to the thread constructing it. However, the object can be published safely (that is, made visible to other threads) once its initialization is complete. The Java Memory Model (JMM) allows multiple threads to observe the object after its initialization has begun but before it has concluded. Consequently, programs must prevent publication of partially initialized objects.

This rule prohibits publishing a reference to a partially initialized member object instance before initialization has concluded. It specifically applies to safety in multithreaded code. Rule TSM01-J prohibits the `this` reference of the current object from escaping its constructor. Rule OBJ11-J describes the consequences of publishing partially initialized objects even in single-threaded programs.

Noncompliant Code Example

This noncompliant code example constructs a `Helper` object in the `initialize()` method of the `Foo` class. The `Helper` object's fields are initialized by its constructor.

```
class Foo {
  private Helper helper;

  public Helper getHelper() {
    return helper;
  }

  public void initialize() {
    helper = new Helper(42);
  }
}

public class Helper {
  private int n;

  public Helper(int n) {
    this.n = n;
  }
  // ...
}
```

If a thread were to access helper using the getHelper() method before the initialize() method executed, the thread would observe an uninitialized helper field. Later, if one thread calls initialize() and another calls getHelper(), the second thread could observe one of the following:

■ The helper reference as null

■ A fully initialized Helper object with the n field set to 42

■ A partially initialized Helper object with an uninitialized n, which contains the default value 0

In particular, the JMM permits compilers to allocate memory for the new Helper object and to assign a reference to that memory to the helper field before initializing the new Helper object. In other words, the compiler can reorder the write to the helper instance field and the write that initializes the Helper object (that is, this.n = n) so that the former occurs first. This can expose a race window during which other threads can observe a partially initialized Helper object instance.

There is a separate issue: If more than one thread were to call initialize(), multiple Helper objects would be created. This is merely a performance issue—correctness would be preserved. The n field of each object would be properly initialized, and the unused Helper object (or objects) would eventually be garbage-collected.

Compliant Solution (Synchronization)

Appropriate use of method synchronization can prevent publication of references to partially initialized objects, as shown in this compliant solution.

```
class Foo {
  private Helper helper;

  public synchronized Helper getHelper() {
    return helper;
  }

  public synchronized void initialize() {
    helper = new Helper(42);
  }
}
```

Synchronizing both methods guarantees that they cannot execute concurrently. If one thread were to call `initialize()` just before another thread called `getHelper()`, the synchronized `initialize()` method would always finish first. The `synchronized` keywords establish a happens-before relationship between the two threads. Consequently, the thread calling `getHelper()` would see either the fully initialized `Helper` object or an absent `Helper` object (that is, `helper` would contain a `null` reference). This approach guarantees proper publication both for immutable and mutable members.

Compliant Solution (Final Field)

The JMM guarantees that the fully initialized values of fields that are declared final are safely published to every thread that reads those values at some point no later than the end of the object's constructor.

```
class Foo {
  private final Helper helper;

  public Helper getHelper() {
    return helper;
  }
  public Foo() {
    // Point 1
    helper = new Helper(42);
    // Point 2
  }
}
```

However, this solution requires the assignment of a new `Helper` instance to `helper` from `Foo`'s constructor. According to the *Java Language Specification*, §17.5.2, "Reading Final Fields During Construction" [JLS 2005]:

A read of a final field of an object within the thread that constructs that object is ordered with respect to the initialization of that field within the constructor by the usual happens-before rules. If the read occurs after the field is set in the constructor, it sees the value the final field is assigned; otherwise, it sees the default value.

Consequently, the reference to the `helper` instance should remain unpublished until the `Foo` class's constructor has completed. See rule TSM01-J for additional information.

Compliant Solution (Final Field and Thread-Safe Composition)

Some collection classes provide thread-safe access to contained elements. When a `Helper` object is inserted into such a collection, it is guaranteed to be fully initialized before its reference is made visible. This compliant solution encapsulates the `helper` field in a `Vector<Helper>`.

```
class Foo {
  private final Vector<Helper> helper;

  public Foo() {
    helper = new Vector<Helper>();
  }

  public Helper getHelper() {
    if (helper.isEmpty()) {
      initialize();
    }
    return helper.elementAt(0);
  }

  public synchronized void initialize() {
    if (helper.isEmpty()) {
      helper.add(new Helper(42));
    }
  }
}
```

The `helper` field is declared final to guarantee that the vector is always created before any accesses take place. It can be initialized safely by invoking the synchronized `initialize()` method, which ensures that only one `Helper` object is ever added to the vector.

If invoked before `initialize()`, the `getHelper()` avoids the possibility of a null-pointer dereference by conditionally invoking `initialize()`. Although the `isEmpty()` call in `getHelper()` is made from an unsynchronized context (which permits multiple threads to decide that they must invoke `initialize`), race conditions that could result in addition of a second object to the vector are nevertheless impossible. The synchronized `initialize()` method also checks whether `helper` is empty before adding a new `Helper` object, and at most one thread can execute `initialize()` at any time. Consequently, only the first thread to execute `initialize()` can ever see an empty vector and the `getHelper()` method can safely omit any synchronization of its own.

Compliant Solution (Static Initialization)

In this compliant solution, the `helper` field is initialized statically, ensuring that the object referenced by the field is fully initialized before its reference becomes visible.

```
// Immutable Foo
final class Foo {
  private static final Helper helper = new Helper(42);

  public static Helper getHelper() {
    return helper;
  }
}
```

The `helper` field should be declared final to document the class's immutability. According to JSR-133, § 9.2.3, "Static Final Fields" [JSR-133 2004]:

> The rules for class initialization ensure that any thread that reads a *static* field will be synchronized with the static initialization of that class, which is the only place where static final fields can be set. Thus, no special rules in the JMM are needed for static final fields.

Compliant Solution (Immutable Object—Final Fields, Volatile Reference)

The JMM guarantees that any final fields of an object are fully initialized before a published object becomes visible [Goetz 2006a]. By declaring n final, the `Helper` class is made immutable. Furthermore, if the `helper` field is declared volatile in compliance with rule VNA01-J, `Helper`'s reference is guaranteed to be made visible to any thread that calls `getHelper()` only after `Helper` has been fully initialized.

```
class Foo {
  private volatile Helper helper;

  public Helper getHelper() {
    return helper;
  }

  public void initialize() {
    helper = new Helper(42);
  }
}
// Immutable Helper
public final class Helper {
  private final int n;

  public Helper(int n) {
    this.n = n;
  }
  // ...
}
```

This compliant solution requires that `helper` be declared volatile and that class `Helper` is immutable. If the `helper` field were not volatile, it would violate rule VNA01-J.

Providing a public static factory method that returns a new instance of `Helper` is both permitted and encouraged. This approach allows the `Helper` instance to be created in a private constructor.

Compliant Solution (Mutable Thread-Safe Object, Volatile Reference)

When `Helper` is mutable but thread-safe, it can be published safely by declaring the `helper` field in the `Foo` class volatile.

```
class Foo {
  private volatile Helper helper;

  public Helper getHelper() {
    return helper;
  }

  public void initialize() {
    helper = new Helper(42);
  }
}
```

```
// Mutable but thread-safe Helper
public class Helper {
  private volatile int n;
  private final Object lock = new Object();

  public Helper(int n) {
    this.n = n;
  }

  public void setN(int value) {
    synchronized (lock) {
      n = value;
    }
  }
}
```

Synchronization is required to ensure the visibility of mutable members after initial publication because the Helper object can change state after its construction. This compliant solution synchronizes the setN() method to guarantee the visibility of the n field.

If the Helper class were synchronized incorrectly, declaring helper volatile in the Foo class would guarantee only the visibility of the initial publication of Helper; the visibility guarantee would exclude visibility of subsequent state changes. Consequently, volatile references alone are inadequate for publishing objects that are not thread-safe.

If the helper field in the Foo class is not declared volatile, the n field must be declared volatile to establish a happens-before relationship between the initialization of n and the write of Helper to the helper field. This is required only when the caller (class Foo) cannot be trusted to declare helper volatile.

Because the Helper class is declared public, it uses a private lock to handle synchronization in conformance with rule LCK00-J.

Exceptions

TSM03-EX0: Classes that prevent partially initialized objects from being used may publish partially initialized objects. This could be implemented, for example, by setting a volatile Boolean flag in the last statement of the initializing code and checking whether the flag is set before allowing class methods to execute.

The following compliant solution shows this technique:

```java
public class Helper {
  private int n;
  private volatile boolean initialized; // Defaults to false

  public Helper(int n) {
    this.n = n;
    this.initialized = true;
  }

  public void doSomething() {
    if (!initialized) {
      throw new SecurityException(
          "Cannot use partially initialized instance");
    }
    // ...
  }
  // ...
}
```

This technique ensures that if a reference to the Helper object instance were published before its initialization was complete, the instance would be unusable because each method within Helper checks the flag to determine whether the initialization has finished.

Risk Assessment

Failure to synchronize access to shared mutable data can cause different threads to observe different states of the object or to observe a partially initialized object.

Rule	Severity	Likelihood	Remediation Cost	Priority	Level
TSM03-J	medium	probable	medium	P8	L2

Bibliography

[API 2006]
[Bloch 2001]   Item 48. Synchronize access to shared mutable data
[Goetz 2006a]   Section 3.5.3, Safe Publication Idioms
[Goetz 2007]   Pattern #2, One-Time Safe Publication
[JPL 2006]   14.10.2, Final Fields and Security
[Pugh 2004]

Chapter 14

Input Output (FIO)

■ Rules

■ Risk Assessment Summary

Rule	Severity	Likelihood	Remediation Cost	Priority	Level
FIO00-J	medium	unlikely	medium	P4	L3
FIO01-J	medium	probable	high	P4	L3
FIO02-J	medium	probable	high	P4	L3
FIO03-J	medium	probable	medium	P8	L2
FIO04-J	low	probable	medium	P4	L3
FIO05-J	medium	likely	low	P18	L1
FIO06-J	low	unlikely	medium	P2	L3
FIO07-J	low	probable	medium	P4	L3
FIO08-J	high	probable	medium	P12	L1
FIO09-J	low	unlikely	medium	P2	L3
FIO10-J	low	unlikely	medium	P2	L3
FIO11-J	low	unlikely	medium	P2	L3
FIO12-J	low	unlikely	low	P3	L3
FIO13-J	medium	probable	high	P4	L3
FIO14-J	medium	likely	medium	P12	L1

■ FIO00-J. Do not operate on files in shared directories

Multiuser systems allow multiple users with different privileges to share a file system. Each user in such an environment must be able to determine which files are shared and which are private, and each user must be able to enforce these decisions.

Unfortunately, a wide variety of file system vulnerabilities can be exploited by an attacker to gain access to files for which they lack sufficient privileges, particularly when operating on files that reside in shared directories in which multiple users may create, move, or delete files. Privilege escalation is also possible when these programs run with elevated privileges. A number of file system properties and capabilities can be exploited by an attacker, including *file links*, *device files*, and *shared file access*. To prevent vulnerabilities, a program must operate only on files in *secure directories*.

A directory is secure with respect to a particular user if only the user and the system administrator are allowed to create, move or delete files inside the directory. Furthermore, each parent directory must itself be a secure directory up to and including the root directory. On most systems, home or user directories are secure by default and only shared directories are insecure.

File Links

Many operating systems support *file links*, including symbolic (soft) links, hard links, shortcuts, shadows, aliases, and junctions. Symbolic links can be created in POSIX using the ln -s command and hard links using the ln command. Hard links are indistinguishable from normal files on POSIX systems.

Three file link types are supported in Windows NTFS (New Technology File System): hard links, junctions, and symbolic links. Symbolic links are available in NTFS starting with Windows Vista.

File links can create security issues for programs that fail to consider the possibility that the file being opened may actually be a link to a different file. This is especially dangerous when the vulnerable program is running with elevated privileges. When creating new files, an application running with elevated privileges may erroneously overwrite an existing file that resides outside the shared directory.

Device Files

File names on many operating systems may be used to access *device files*. Device files are used to access hardware and peripherals. Reserved MS-DOS device names include AUX, CON, PRN, COM1, and LPT1. Character special files and block special files are POSIX device files that direct operations on the files to the appropriate device drivers.

Performing operations on device files intended only for ordinary character or binary files can result in crashes and denial-of-service (DoS) attacks. For example, when Windows attempts to interpret the device name as a file resource, it performs an invalid resource access that usually results in a crash [Howard 2002].

Device files in POSIX can be a security risk when an attacker can access them in an unauthorized way. For instance, if malicious programs can read or write to the /dev/ kmem device, they may be able to alter their own priority, user ID, or other attributes of their process or they may simply crash the system. Similarly, access to disk devices, tape devices, network devices, and terminals being used by other processes can also lead to problems [Garfinkel 1996].

On Linux, it is possible to lock certain applications by attempting to read or write data on devices rather than files. Consider the following device path names:

```
/dev/mouse
/dev/console
/dev/tty0
/dev/zero
```

A Web browser that failed to check for these devices would allow an attacker to create a website with image tags such as <IMG src="file:///dev/mouse"> that would lock the user's mouse.

Shared File Access

On many systems, files can be simultaneously accessed by concurrent processes. Exclusive access grants unrestricted file access to the locking process while denying access to all other processes, eliminating the potential for a race condition on the locked region. The `java.nio.channels.FileLock` class may be used for file locking. According to the Java API [API 2006] documentation:

> A file lock is either exclusive or shared. A shared lock prevents other concurrently running programs from acquiring an overlapping exclusive lock but does allow them to acquire overlapping shared locks. An exclusive lock prevents other programs from acquiring an overlapping lock of either type. Once it is released, a lock has no further effect on the locks that may be acquired by other programs.

Shared locks support concurrent read access from multiple processes; *exclusive locks* support exclusive write access. File locks provide protection across processes, but they do not provide protection from multiple threads within a single process. Both shared locks and exclusive locks eliminate the potential for a cross-process race condition on the locked region. Exclusive locks provide mutual exclusion; shared locks prevent alteration of the state of the locked file region (one of the required properties for a data race).

The Java API [API 2006] documentation states that "whether or not a lock actually prevents another program from accessing the content of the locked region is system-dependent and consequently unspecified."

Microsoft Windows uses a mandatory file-locking mechanism that prevents processes from accessing a locked file region.

Linux implements both mandatory locks and advisory locks. Advisory locks are not enforced by the operating system, which diminishes their value from a security perspective. Unfortunately, the mandatory file lock in Linux is generally impractical because

- mandatory locking is supported only by certain network file systems.
- file systems must be mounted with support for mandatory locking, which is disabled by default.
- locking relies on the group ID bit, which can be turned off by another process (thereby defeating the lock).
- the lock is implicitly dropped if the holding process closes any descriptor of the file.

Noncompliant Code Example

In this noncompliant code example, an attacker could specify the name of a locked device or a first in, first out (FIFO) file, causing the program to hang when opening the file.

```
String file = /* provided by user */;
InputStream in = null;
try {
  in = new FileInputStream(file);
  // ...
} finally {
  try {
    if (in != null) {
    in.close();}
  } catch (IOException x) {
    // handle error
  }
}
```

Noncompliant Code Example (Java SE 7)

This noncompliant code example uses the *try-with-resources* statement from Java SE 7 to open the file. While this guarantees the file's successful closure if an exception is thrown, it is subject to the same vulnerabilities as the previous example.

```
String filename = /* provided by user */;
Path path = new File(filename).toPath();
try (InputStream in = Files.newInputStream(path)) {
  // read file
} catch (IOException x) {
  // handle error
}
```

Noncompliant Code Example (Java SE 7: `isRegularFile()`)

This noncompliant code example first checks that the file is a regular file (using the new Java SE 7 NIO2 APIs) before opening it.

```
String filename = /* provided by user */;
Path path = new File(filename).toPath();
try {
  BasicFileAttributes attr =
      Files.readAttributes(path, BasicFileAttributes.class);

  // Check
  if (!attr.isRegularFile()) {
    System.out.println("Not a regular file");
```

```
    return;
  }
  // other necessary checks

  // Use
  try (InputStream in = Files.newInputStream(path)) {
    // read file
  }
} catch (IOException x) {
  // handle error
}
```

This test can still be circumvented by a symbolic link. By default, the `readAttri-butes()` method follows symbolic links and reads the file attributes of the final target of the link. The result is that the program may reference a file other than the one intended.

Noncompliant Code Example (Java SE 7: `NOFOLLOW_LINKS`)

This noncompliant code example checks the file by calling the `readAttributes()` method with the `NOFOLLOW_LINKS` link option to prevent the method from following symbolic links. This allows the detection of symbolic links because the `isRegularFile()` check is carried out on the symbolic link file and not on the final target of the link.

```
String filename = /* provided by user */;
Path path = new File(filename).toPath();
try {
  BasicFileAttributes attr = Files.readAttributes(
      path, BasicFileAttributes.class, LinkOption.NOFOLLOW_LINKS);

  // Check
  if (!attr.isRegularFile()) {
    System.out.println("Not a regular file");
    return;
  }
  // other necessary checks

  // Use
  try (InputStream in = Files.newInputStream(path)) {
    // read file
  };
} catch (IOException x) {
  // handle error
}
```

This code is still vulnerable to a time-of-check, time-of-use (TOCTOU) race condition. For example, an attacker can replace the regular file with a file link or device file after the code has completed its checks but before it opens the file.

Noncompliant Code Example (Java SE 7: Check-Use-Check)

This noncompliant code example performs the necessary checks and then opens the file. After opening the file, it performs a second check to make sure that the file has not been moved and that the file opened is the same file that was checked. This reduces the chance that an attacker has changed the file between checking and then opening the file. In both checks, the file's `fileKey` attribute is examined. This serves as a unique key for identifying files and is a more reliable indicator of the file's identity than its path name.

The SE 7 Documentation [J2SE 2011] describes the `fileKey` attribute:

Returns an object that uniquely identifies the given file, or null if a file key is not available. On some platforms or file systems it is possible to use an identifier, or a combination of identifiers to uniquely identify a file. Such identifiers are important for operations such as file tree traversal in file systems that support symbolic links or file systems that allow a file to be an entry in more than one directory. On UNIX file systems, for example, the device ID and inode are commonly used for such purposes.

The file key returned by this method can only be guaranteed to be unique if the file system and files remain static. Whether a file system re-uses identifiers after a file is deleted is implementation dependent and consequently unspecified.

File keys returned by this method can be compared for equality and are suitable for use in collections. If the file system and files remain static, and two files are the same with non-null file keys, then their file keys are equal.

```
String filename = /* provided by user */;
Path path = new File(filename).toPath();
try {
  BasicFileAttributes attr = Files.readAttributes(
      path, BasicFileAttributes.class, LinkOption.NOFOLLOW_LINKS);
  Object fileKey = attr.fileKey();

  // Check
  if (!attr.isRegularFile()) {
    System.out.println("Not a regular file");
    return;
  }
  // other necessary checks
```

```
  // Use
  try (InputStream in = Files.newInputStream(path)) {

    // Check
    BasicFileAttributes attr2 = Files.readAttributes(
        path, BasicFileAttributes.class, LinkOption.NOFOLLOW_LINKS
    );
    Object fileKey2 = attr2.fileKey();
    if (fileKey != fileKey2) {
      System.out.println("File has been tampered with");
    }

    // read file
  };
} catch (IOException x) {
  // handle error
}
```

While this code goes to great lengths to prevent an attacker from successfully tricking it into opening the wrong file, it still has several vulnerabilities:

■ The TOCTOU race condition still exists between the first check and open. During this race window, an attacker can replace the regular file with a symbolic link or other nonregular file. The second check detects this race condition but does not eliminate it.

■ An attacker could subvert this code by letting the check operate on a regular file, substituting the nonregular file for the open, and then resubstituting the regular file to circumvent the second check. This vulnerability exists because Java lacks any mechanism to obtain file attributes from a file by any means other than the file name, and the binding of the file name to a file object is reasserted every time the file name is used in an operation. Consequently, an attacker can still swap a benign file for a nefarious file, such as a symbolic link.

■ A system with hard links allows an attacker to construct a malicious file that is a hard link to a protected file. Hard links cannot be reliably detected by a program and can foil any canonicalization attempts, which are prescribed by rule IDS02-J.

Compliant Solution (POSIX, Java SE 7: Secure Directory)

Because of the potential for race conditions and the inherent accessibility of shared directories, files must be operated on only in secure directories. Because programs may run with reduced privileges and lack the facilities to construct a secure directory, a program may need to throw an exception if it determines that a given path name is not in a secure directory.

Following is a POSIX-specific implementation of an `isInSecureDir()` method. This method ensures that the supplied file and all directories above it are owned by either the user or the system administrator, that each directory lacks write access for any other users, and that directories above the given file may not be deleted or renamed by any other users (except the system administrator).

```
public static boolean isInSecureDir(Path file) {
  return isInSecureDir(file, null);
public static boolean isInSecureDir(Path file, UserPrincipal user) {
  return isInSecureDir(file, null, 5);
}

/**
 * Indicates whether file lives in a secure directory relative
 * to the program's user
 * @param file Path to test
 * @param user User to test. If null, defaults to current user
 * @param symlinkDepth Number of symbolic links allowed
 * @return true if file's directory is secure
 */
public static boolean isInSecureDir(Path file, UserPrincipal user,
                                    int symlinkDepth) {
  if (!file.isAbsolute()) {
    file = file.toAbsolutePath();
  if (symlinkDepth <= 0) {
    // Too many levels of symbolic links
    return false;
  }

  // Get UserPincipal for specified user and superuser
  FileSystem fileSystem =
      Paths.get(file.getRoot().toString()).getFileSystem();
  UserPrincipalLookupService upls =
      fileSystem.getUserPrincipalLookupService();
  UserPrincipal root = null;
  try {
    root = upls.lookupPrincipalByName("root");
    if (user == null) {
      user = upls.lookupPrincipalByName(System.getProperty("user.name"));
    }
    if (root == null || user == null) {
      return false;
    }
  } catch (IOException x) {
    return false;
  }
```

```
    // If any parent dirs (from root on down) are not secure,
    // dir is not secure
    for (int i = 1; i <= file.getNameCount(); i++) {
      Path partialPath = Paths.get(file.getRoot().toString(),
                                    file.subpath(0, i).toString());

      try {
        if (Files.isSymbolicLink(partialPath)) {
          if (!isInSecureDir(Files.readSymbolicLink(partialPath),
                             user, symlinkDepth - 1))) {
            // Symbolic link, linked-to dir not secure
            return false;
          }
        } else {
          UserPrincipal owner = Files.getOwner(partialPath);
          if (!user.equals(owner) && !root.equals(owner)) {
            // dir owned by someone else, not secure
            return false;
          }
          PosixFileAttributes attr =
              Files.readAttributes(partialPath, PosixFileAttributes.class);
          Set<PosixFilePermission> perms = attr.permissions();
          if (perms.contains(PosixFilePermission.GROUP_WRITE) ||
              perms.contains(PosixFilePermission.OTHERS_WRITE)) {
            // someone else can write files, not secure
            return false;
          }
        }
      } catch (IOException x) {
        return false;
      }
    }

    return true;
  }
```

When checking directories, it is important to traverse from the root directory to the leaf directory to avoid a dangerous race condition whereby an attacker who has privileges to at least one of the directories can rename and re-create a directory after the privilege verification of subdirectories but before the verification of the tampered directory.

If the path contains any symbolic links, this method will recursively invoke itself on the linked-to directory and ensure it is also secure. A symlinked directory may be secure if both its source and linked-to directory are secure. The method checks every directory in the path, ensuring that every directory is owned by the current user or the system administrator and that all directories in the path prevent other users from creating, deleting or renaming files.

On POSIX systems, disabling group and world write access to a directory prevents modification by anyone other than the owner of the directory and the system administrator.

Note that this method is effective only on file systems that are fully compatible with POSIX file access permissions; it may behave incorrectly for file systems with other permission mechanisms.

The following compliant solution uses the isInSecureDir() method to ensure that an attacker cannot tamper with the file to be opened and subsequently removed. Note that once the path name of a directory has been checked using isInSecureDir(), all further file operations on that directory must be performed using the same path. This compliant solution also performs the same checks performed by the previous examples, such as making sure the requested file is a regular file, and not a symbolic link, device file, or other special file.

```
String filename = /* provided by user */;
Path path = new File(filename).toPath();
try {
  if (!isInSecureDir(path)) {
    System.out.println("File not in secure directory");
    return;
  }

  BasicFileAttributes attr = Files.readAttributes(
      path, BasicFileAttributes.class, LinkOption.NOFOLLOW_LINKS);

  // Check
  if (!attr.isRegularFile()) {
    System.out.println("Not a regular file");
    return;
  }
  // other necessary checks

  try (InputStream in = Files.newInputStream(path)) {
    // read file
  }
} catch (IOException x) {
  // handle error
}
```

Programs with elevated privileges may need to write files to directories owned by unprivileged users. One example would be a mail daemon that reads a mail message from one user and places it in a directory owned by another user. In such cases, the mail daemon should assume the privileges of a user when reading or writing files on behalf of that user, in which case all file access should occur in secure directories relative to that user. When a program with elevated privileges must write files on its own behalf, these files should be in secure directories relative to the privileges of the program (such as directories accessible only by the system administrator).

Exceptions

FIO00-EX0: Programs that operate on single-user systems or on systems that have no shared directories or no possibility of file system vulnerabilities do not need to ensure that files are maintained in secure directories before operating on them.

Risk Assessment

Performing operations on files in shared directories can result in DoS attacks. If the program has elevated privileges, privilege escalation exploits are possible.

Rule	Severity	Likelihood	Remediation Cost	Priority	Level
FIO00-J	medium	unlikely	medium	P4	L3

Related Guidelines

CERT C Secure Coding Standard	FIO32-C. Do not perform operations on devices that are only appropriate for files
CERT C++ Secure Coding Standard	FIO32-CPP. Do not perform operations on devices that are only appropriate for files
MITRE CWE	CWE-67. Improper handling of windows device names

Bibliography

[API 2006]	Class `File`, methods `createTempFile`, `delete`, `deleteOnExit`
[CVE 2011]	CVE-2008-5354
[Darwin 2004]	11.5, Creating a Transient File
[Garfinkel 1996]	Section 5.6, Device Files
[Howard 2002]	Chapter 11, Canonical Representation Issues
[J2SE 2011]	The try-with-resources Statement
[Open Group 2004]	`open()`
[SDN 2008]	Bug IDs 4171239, 4405521, 4635827, 4631820
[Secunia 2008]	Secunia Advisory 20132

■ FIO01-J. Create files with appropriate access permissions

Files on multiuser systems are generally owned by a particular user. The owner of the file can specify which other users on the system should be allowed to access the contents of these files.

These file systems use a privileges and permissions model to protect file access. When a file is created, the file access permissions dictate who may access or operate on the file. When a program creates a file with insufficiently restrictive access permissions, an attacker may read or modify the file before the program can modify the permissions. Consequently, files must be created with access permissions that prevent unauthorized file access.

Noncompliant Code Example

The constructors for `FileOutputStream` and `FileWriter` do not allow the programmer to explicitly specify file access permissions.

In this noncompliant code example, the access permissions of any file created are implementation-defined and may not prevent unauthorized access.

```
Writer out = new FileWriter("file");
```

Compliant Solution (Java 1.6 and Earlier)

Java 1.6 and earlier lack a mechanism for specifying default permissions upon file creation. Consequently, the problem must be avoided or solved using some mechanism external to Java, such as by using native code and the Java Native Interface (JNI).

Compliant Solution (Java SE 7, POSIX)

The Java SE 7 new I/O facility (`java.nio`) provides classes for managing file access permissions. Additionally, many of the methods and constructors that create files accept an argument allowing the program to specify the initial file permissions.

The `Files.newByteChannel()` method allows a file to be created with specific permissions. This method is platform-independent, but the actual permissions are platform-specific. This compliant solution defines sufficiently restrictive permissions for POSIX platforms.

```
Path file = new File("file").toPath();

// Throw exception rather than overwrite existing file
Set<OpenOption> options = new HashSet<OpenOption>();
options.add(StandardOpenOption.CREATE_NEW);
options.add(StandardOpenOption.APPEND);
```

```
// File permissions should be such that only user may read/write file
Set<PosixFilePermission> perms =
    PosixFilePermissions.fromString("rw-------");
FileAttribute<Set<PosixFilePermission>> attr =
  PosixFilePermissions.asFileAttribute(perms);

try (SeekableByteChannel sbc =
        Files.newByteChannel(file, options, attr)) {
  // write data
};
```

Exceptions

FIO01-EX0: When a file is created inside a directory that is both secure and unreadable by untrusted users, that file may be created with the default access permissions. This could be the case if, for example, the entire file system is trusted or is accessible only to trusted users. See rule FIO00-J for the definition of a secure directory.

FIO01-EX1: Files that do not contain privileged information need not be created with specific access permissions.

Risk Assessment

Files created with insufficiently restrictive access permissions can result in information disclosure.

Rule	Severity	Likelihood	Remediation Cost	Priority	Level
FIO01-J	medium	probable	high	P4	L3

Related Guidelines

CERT C++ Secure Coding Standard	FIO06-CPP. Create files with appropriate access permissions
CERT C Secure Coding Standard	FIO06-C. Create files with appropriate access permissions
ISO/IEC TR 24772:2010	Missing or Inconsistent Access Control [XZN]
MITRE CWE	CWE-279. Incorrect execution-assigned permissions
	CWE-276. Incorrect default permissions
	CWE-732. Incorrect permission assignment for critical resource

Bibliography

[API 2006]

[CVE]

[Dowd 2006]   Chapter 9, UNIX 1: Privileges and Files

[J2SE 2011]

[OpenBSD]

[Open Group 2004]   The open Function and The umask Function

[Viega 2003]   Section 2.7, Restricting Access Permissions for New Files on UNIX

■ FIO02-J. Detect and handle file-related errors

Java's file manipulation methods often indicate failure with a return value instead of throwing an exception. The Java Tutorials for Java 7 [Tutorials 2008] note:

> Prior to the Java SE 7 release, the java.io.File class was the mechanism used for file I/O, but it had several drawbacks.

One of these drawbacks is that:

> Many methods didn't throw exceptions when they failed, so it was impossible to obtain a useful error message. For example, if a file deletion failed, the program would receive a "delete fail" but wouldn't know if it was because the file didn't exist, the user didn't have permissions, or there was some other problem.

Consequently, programs that ignore the return values from file operations often fail to detect that those operations have failed. Java programs must check the return values of methods that perform file I/O (this is a specific instance of rule EXP00-J).

Noncompliant Code Example (delete())

This noncompliant code example attempts to delete a specified file but gives no indication of its success. The Java Platform, Standard Edition 6 API Specification [API 2006] requires File.delete() to throw a SecurityException only when the program lacks authorization to delete the file. No other exceptions are thrown, so the deletion can silently fail.

```
File file = new File(args[0]);
file.delete();
```

Compliant Solution

This compliant solution checks the return value of `delete()`.

```java
File file = new File(args[0]);
if (!file.delete()) {
  System.out.println("Deletion failed");
}
```

Compliant Solution (Java SE 7)

This compliant solution uses the `java.nio.file.Files.delete()` method from Java SE 7 to delete the file.

```java
Path file = new File(args[0]).toPath();
try {
  Files.delete(file);
} catch (IOException x) {
  System.out.println("Deletion failed");
  // handle error
}
```

The Java SE 7 Documentation [J2SE 2011] defines `Files.delete()` to throw the following exceptions:

Exception	Reason
NoSuchFileException	File does not exist
DirectoryNotEmptyException	File is a directory and could not otherwise be deleted because the directory is not empty
IOException	An I/O error occurs
SecurityException	In the case of the default provider and a security manager is installed, the `SecurityManager.checkDelete(String)` method is invoked to check delete access to the file

Risk Assessment

Failure to check the return values of methods that perform file I/O can result in unexpected behavior.

Rule	Severity	Likelihood	Remediation Cost	Priority	Level
FIO02-J	medium	probable	high	P4	L3

Related Guidelines

CERT C Secure Coding Standard	FIO04-C. Detect and handle input and output errors
CERT C++ Secure Coding Standard	FIO04-CPP. Detect and handle input and output errors

Bibliography

[API 2006]	`File.delete()`
[J2SE 2011]	`Files.delete()`
[Seacord 2005]	Chapter 7, File I/O

■ FIO03-J. Remove temporary files before termination

Temporary files can be used to

- share data between processes.
- store auxiliary program data (for example, to preserve memory).
- construct and/or load classes, JAR files, and native libraries dynamically.

Programmers frequently create temporary files in directories that are writable by everyone; examples include /tmp and /var/tmp on POSIX and C:\TEMP on Windows. Files in such directories may be purged regularly, such as every night or during reboot. However, an attacker who has access to the local file system can exploit operations on files in shared directories when those files are created insecurely or remain accessible after use. For example, an attacker who can both predict the name of a temporary file and change or replace that file can exploit a TOCTOU race condition to cause a failure in creating the temporary file from within program code or to cause the program to operate on a file determined by the attacker. This exploit is particularly dangerous when the vulnerable process is running with elevated privileges because the attacker can operate on any file accessible by the vulnerable process. On multiuser systems, a user can also be tricked by an attacker into unintentionally operating on his or her own files. Consequently, temporary file management must comply with rule FIO00-J.

Many programs that create temporary files attempt to give them unique and unpredictable file names. This is a common attempt at mitigating the risk of creating a file in an insecure or shared directory. If the file name is predictable, an attacker could guess or predict the name of the file to be created and could create a link with the same name to a normally inaccessible file. However, when temporary files are created in a secure directory, an attacker cannot tamper with them. Consequently, the need for unpredictable names is eliminated.

Temporary files are *files* and consequently must conform to the requirements specified by other rules governing operations on files, including rules FIO00-J and FIO01-J. Furthermore, temporary files have the additional requirement that they must be removed before program termination.

Removing temporary files when they are no longer required allows file names and other resources (such as secondary storage) to be recycled. Each program is responsible for ensuring that temporary files are removed during normal operation. There is no surefire method that can guarantee the removal of orphaned files in the case of abnormal termination, even in the presence of a `finally` block, because the `finally` block may fail to execute. For this reason, many systems employ temporary file cleaner utilities to sweep temporary directories and remove old files. Such utilities can be invoked manually by a system administrator or can be periodically invoked by a system process. However, these utilities are themselves frequently vulnerable to file-based exploits.

Noncompliant Code Example

For this and subsequent code examples assume that files are created in a secure directory in compliance with rule FIO00-J and are created with proper access permissions in compliance with rule FIO01-J. Both requirements may be managed outside the JVM.

This noncompliant code example fails to remove the file upon completion.

```java
class TempFile {
  public static void main(String[] args) throws IOException{
    File f = new File("tempnam.tmp");
    if (f.exists()) {
      System.out.println("This file already exists");
      return;
    }

    FileOutputStream fop = null;
    try {
      fop = new FileOutputStream(f);
      String str = "Data";
      fop.write(str.getBytes());
    } finally {
      if (fop != null) {
        try {
          fop.close();
        } catch (IOException x) {
          // handle error
        }
      }
    }
  }
}
```

Noncompliant Code Example (`createTempFile()`, `deleteOnExit()`)

This noncompliant code example invokes the `File.createTempFile()` method, which generates a unique temporary file name based on two parameters, a prefix and an extension. This is the only method currently designed and provided for producing unique file names, although the names produced can be easily predicted. A random number generator can be used to produce the prefix if a random file name is required.

This example also uses the `deleteOnExit()` method to ensure that the temporary file is deleted when the Java Virtual Machine (JVM) terminates. However, according to the Java API [API 2006] Class `File`, method `deleteOnExit()` documentation:

> Deletion will be attempted only for normal termination of the virtual machine, as defined by the Java Language Specification. Once deletion has been requested, it is not possible to cancel the request. This method should consequently be used with care. Note: This method should not be used for file-locking, as the resulting protocol cannot be made to work reliably.

Consequently, the file is not deleted if the JVM terminates unexpectedly. A longstanding bug on Windows-based systems reported as Bug ID: 4171239 [SDN 2008] causes JVMs to fail to delete a file when `deleteOnExit()` is invoked before the associated stream or `RandomAccessFile` is closed.

```
class TempFile {
  public static void main(String[] args) throws IOException{
    File f = File.createTempFile("tempnam",".tmp");
    FileOutputStream fop = null;
    try {
      fop = new FileOutputStream(f);
      String str = "Data";
      fop.write(str.getBytes());
      fop.flush();
    } finally {
      // Stream/file still open; file will
      // not be deleted on Windows systems
      // Delete the file when the JVM terminates
      f.deleteOnExit();

      if (fop != null) {
        try {
```

```
        fop.close();
      } catch (IOException x) {
      // handle error
      }
    }
   }
  }
 }
```

Compliant Solution (Java SE 7: `delete_on_close`)

This compliant solution creates a temporary file using several methods from Java SE 7's NIO2 package. It uses the `createTempFile()` method, which creates an unpredictable name. (The actual method by which the name is created is implementation-defined and undocumented.) The file is opened using the try-with-resources construct, which automatically closes the file regardless of whether an exception occurs. Finally, the file is opened with the Java SE 7 `DELETE_ON_CLOSE` option, which removes the file automatically when it is closed.

```
class TempFile {
  public static void main(String[] args) {
    Path tempFile = null;
    try {
      tempFile = Files.createTempFile("tempnam", ".tmp");
      try (BufferedWriter writer =
        Files.newBufferedWriter(tempFile, Charset.forName("UTF8"),
                            StandardOpenOption.DELETE_ON_CLOSE)) {
        // write to file
      }
      System.out.println("Temporary file write done, file erased");
    } catch (FileAlreadyExistsException x) {
      System.err.println("File exists: " + tempFile);
    } catch (IOException x) {
      // Some other sort of failure, such as permissions.
      System.err.println("Error creating temporary file: " + x);
    }
  }
}
```

Compliant Solution

When a secure directory for storing temporary files is not available, the vulnerabilities that result from using temporary files in insecure directories can be avoided by using alternative mechanisms, including

- other IPC mechanisms such as sockets and remote procedure calls.
- the low-level JNI.
- memory-mapped files.
- threads to share heap data within the same JVM (applies to data sharing between Java processes only).

Risk Assessment

Failure to remove temporary files before termination can result in information leakage and resource exhaustion.

Rule	Severity	Likelihood	Remediation Cost	Priority	Level
FIO03-J	medium	probable	medium	P8	L2

Related Guidelines

CERT C Secure Coding Standard	FIO43-C. Do not create temporary files in shared directories
CERT C++ Secure Coding Standard	FIO43-CPP. Do not create temporary files in shared directories
MITRE CWE	CWE-377. Insecure temporary file
	CWE-459.Incomplete cleanup

Bibliography

[API 2006]	Class `File`, methods `createTempFile`, `delete`, `deleteOnExit`
[Darwin 2004]	11.5, Creating a Transient File
[J2SE 2011]	
[SDN 2008]	Bug IDs 4171239, 4405521, 4635827, 4631820
[Secunia 2008]	Secunia Advisory 20132

■ FIO04-J. Close resources when they are no longer needed

The Java garbage collector is called to free unreferenced but as-yet unreleased memory. However, the garbage collector cannot free nonmemory resources such as open file descriptors and database connections. Consequently, failing to release such resources can lead to resource exhaustion attacks. In addition, programs can experience resource starvation while waiting for `finalize()` to release resources such as `Lock` or `Semaphore` objects. This can occur because Java lacks any temporal guarantee of *when* `finalize()` methods execute, other than "sometime before program termination." Finally, output streams may cache object references; such cached objects are not garbage-collected until after the output stream is closed. Consequently, output streams should be closed promptly after use.

A program may leak resources when it relies on `finalize()` to release system resources or when there is confusion over which part of the program is responsible for releasing system resources. In a busy system, the delay before the `finalize()` method is called for an object provides a window of vulnerability during which an attacker could induce a DoS attack. Consequently, resources other than raw memory must be explicitly freed in nonfinalizer methods because of the unsuitability of using finalizers. See rule MET12-J for additional reasons to avoid the use of finalizers.

Note that on Windows systems, attempts to delete open files fail silently. See rule FIO03-J for more information.

Noncompliant Code Example (File Handle)

This noncompliant code example opens a file and uses it but fails to explicitly close the file.

```
public int processFile(String fileName)
                    throws IOException, FileNotFoundException {
  FileInputStream stream = new FileInputStream(fileName);
  BufferedReader bufRead =
      new BufferedReader(new InputStreamReader(stream));
  String line;
  while ((line = bufRead.readLine()) != null) {
    sendLine(line);
  }
  return 1;
}
```

Compliant Solution

This compliant solution releases all acquired resources, regardless of any exceptions that might occur. Even though dereferencing `bufRead` might result in an exception, the `FileInputStream` object is closed as required.

```
try {
  final FileInputStream stream = new FileInputStream(fileName);
  try {
    final BufferedReader bufRead =
        new BufferedReader(new InputStreamReader(stream));
```

```
    String line;
    while ((line = bufRead.readLine()) != null) {
      sendLine(line);
    }
  } finally {
    if (stream != null) {
      try {
        stream.close();
      } catch (IOException e) {
        // forward to handler
      }
    }
  }
} catch (IOException e) {
  // forward to handler
}
```

Compliant Solution (Java SE 7: try-with-resources)

This compliant solution uses the try-with-resources statement, introduced in Java SE 7, to release all acquired resources, regardless of any exceptions that might occur.

```
try (FileInputStream stream = new FileInputStream(fileName);
    BufferedReader bufRead =
        new BufferedReader(new InputStreamReader(stream))) {
  String line;
  while ((line = bufRead.readLine()) != null) {
    sendLine(line);
  }
} catch (IOException e) {
  // forward to handler
}
```

The try-with-resources construct sends any IOException to the catch clause, where it is forwarded to an exception handler. This includes exceptions generated during the allocation of resources (that is, the creation of the FileInputStream or BufferedReader). It also includes any IOException thrown during execution of the while loop. Finally, it includes any IOException generated by closing bufRead or stream.

Noncompliant Code Example (SQL Connection)

The problem of resource pool exhaustion is exacerbated in the case of database connections. Many database servers allow only a fixed number of connections, depending on configuration and licensing. Consequently, failure to release database connections can result in rapid exhaustion of available connections. This noncompliant code example fails to close the connection when an error occurs during execution of the SQL statement or during processing of the results.

```java
public void getResults(String sqlQuery) {
  try {
    Connection conn = getConnection();
    Statement stmt = conn.createStatement();
    ResultSet rs = stmt.executeQuery(sqlQuery);
    processResults(rs);
    stmt.close();
    conn.close();
  } catch (SQLException e) { /* forward to handler */ }
}
```

Noncompliant Code Example

This noncompliant code example attempts to address exhaustion of database connections by adding cleanup code in a `finally` block. However, `rs`, `stmt`, or `conn` could be `null`, causing the code in the `finally` block to throw a `NullPointerException`.

```java
Statement stmt = null;
ResultSet rs = null;
Connection conn = getConnection();
try {
  stmt = conn.createStatement();
  rs = stmt.executeQuery(sqlQuery);
  processResults(rs);
} catch(SQLException e) {
  // forward to handler
} finally {
  rs.close();
  stmt.close();
  conn.close();
}
```

Noncompliant Code Example

In this noncompliant code example, the call to `rs.close()` or the call to `stmt.close()` might throw a `SQLException`. Consequently, `conn.close()` is never called. This is a violation of rule ERR05-J.

```
Statement stmt = null;
ResultSet rs = null;
Connection conn = getConnection();
try {
  stmt = conn.createStatement();
  rs = stmt.executeQuery(sqlQuery);
  processResults(rs);
} catch (SQLException e) {
 // forward to handler
} finally {
  if (rs != null) {
    rs.close();
  }
  if (stmt != null) {
    stmt.close();
  if (conn != null) {
    conn.close();
  }
}
```

Compliant Solution

This compliant solution ensures that resources are released as required.

```
Statement stmt = null;
ResultSet rs = null;
Connection conn = getConnection();
try {
  stmt = conn.createStatement();
  rs = stmt.executeQuery(sqlQuery);
  processResults(rs);
} catch (SQLException e) {
  // forward to handler
} finally {
  try {
    if (rs != null) {rs.close();}
  } catch (SQLException e) {
    // forward to handler
  } finally {
    try {
      if (stmt != null) {stmt.close();}
    } catch (SQLException e) {
      // forward to handler
    } finally {
```

```
    try {
      if (conn != null) {conn.close();}
    } catch (SQLException e) {
      // forward to handler
    }
  }
 }
}
```

Compliant Solution (Java SE 7: try-with-resources)

This compliant solution uses the try-with-resources construct, introduced in Java SE 7, to ensure that resources are released as required.

```
try (Connection conn = getConnection();
     Statement stmt = conn.createStatement();
     ResultSet rs = stmt.executeQuery(sqlQuery)) {
  processResults(rs);
} catch (SQLException e) {
  // forward to handler
}
```

The try-with-resources construct sends any `SQLException` to the `catch` clause, where it is forwarded to an exception handler. This includes exceptions generated during the allocation of resources (that is, the creation of the `Connection`, `Statement`, or `ResultSet`). It also includes any `SQLException` thrown by `processResults()`. Finally, it includes any `SQLException` generated by closing `rs`, `stmt`, or `conn`.

Risk Assessment

Failure to explicitly release nonmemory system resources when they are no longer needed can result in resource exhaustion.

Rule	Severity	Likelihood	Remediation Cost	Priority	Level
FIO04-J	low	probable	medium	P4	L3

Automated Detection Although sound automated detection of this vulnerability is not feasible in the general case, many interesting cases can be soundly detected. Some static analysis tools can detect cases where there is leak of a socket resource or leak of a stream representing a file or other system resources.

Related Guidelines

CERT C Secure Coding Standard	FIO42-C. Ensure files are properly closed when they are no longer needed
CERT C++ Secure Coding Standard	FIO42-CPP. Ensure files are properly closed when they are no longer needed
MITRE CWE	CWE-404. Improper resource shutdown or release
	CWE-459. Incomplete cleanup
	CWE-770. Allocation of resources without limits or throttling
	CWE-405. Asymmetric resource consumption (amplification)

Bibliography

[API 2006]	Class `Object`
[Goetz 2006b]	
[J2SE 2011]	The try-with-resources Statement

■ FIO05-J. Do not expose buffers created using the `wrap()` or `duplicate()` methods to untrusted code

Buffer classes defined in the `java.nio` package, such as `IntBuffer`, `CharBuffer`, and `ByteBuffer`, define a variety of `wrap()` methods that wrap an array of the corresponding primitive data type into a buffer and return the buffer as a `Buffer` object. Although these methods create a new `Buffer` object, the new `Buffer` is backed by the given input array. According to the Java API for these methods [API 2006]:

> The new buffer will be backed by the given character array; that is, modifications to the buffer will cause the array to be modified and vice versa.

> Exposing these buffers to untrusted code exposes the backing array to malicious modification. Likewise, the `duplicate()` methods create additional buffers that are backed by the original buffer's backing array; exposing such additional buffers to untrusted code affords the same opportunity for malicious modification.

Noncompliant Code Example (`wrap()`)

This noncompliant code example declares a char array, wraps it within a `Buffer`, and exposes that `Buffer` to untrusted code via the `getBufferCopy()` method.

```
final class Wrap {
  private char[] dataArray;

  public Wrap() {
    dataArray = new char[10];
    // Initialize
  }

  public CharBuffer getBufferCopy() {
    return CharBuffer.wrap(dataArray);
  }
}
```

Compliant Solution (`asReadOnlyBuffer()`)

This compliant solution returns a read-only view of the char array in the form of a read-only CharBuffer. The standard library implementation of CharBuffer guarantees that attempts to modify the elements of a read-only CharBuffer will result in a java.nio.ReadOnlyBufferException.

```
final class Wrap {
  private char[] dataArray;

  public Wrap() {
    dataArray = new char[10];
    // Initialize
  }

  public CharBuffer getBufferCopy() {
    return CharBuffer.wrap(dataArray).asReadOnlyBuffer();
  }
}
```

Compliant Solution (Copy)

This compliant solution allocates a new CharBuffer and explicitly copies the contents of the char array into it before returning the copy. Consequently, malicious callers can modify the copy of the array but cannot modify the original.

```
final class Wrap {
  private char[] dataArray;
  public Wrap() {
```

```
    dataArray = new char[10];
    // Initialize
  }

  public CharBuffer getBufferCopy() {
    CharBuffer cb = CharBuffer.allocate(dataArray.length);
    cb.put(dataArray);
    return cb;
  }
}
```

Noncompliant Code Example (duplicate())

This noncompliant code example invokes the duplicate() method to create and return a copy of the CharBuffer. As stated in the contract for the duplicate() method, the returned buffer is backed by the same array as is the original buffer. Consequently, if a caller were to modify the elements of the backing array, these modifications would also affect the original buffer.

```
final class Dup {
  CharBuffer cb;

  public Dup() {
    cb = CharBuffer.allocate(10);
    // Initialize
  }

  public CharBuffer getBufferCopy() {
    return cb.duplicate();
  }
}
```

Compliant Solution (asReadOnlyBuffer())

This compliant solution exposes a read-only view of the CharBuffer to untrusted code.

```
final class Dup {
  CharBuffer cb;

  public Dup() {
    cb = CharBuffer.allocate(10);
```

```
    // Initialize
  }

  public CharBuffer getBufferCopy() {
    return cb.asReadOnlyBuffer();
  }
}
```

Risk Assessment

Exposing buffers created using the `wrap()` or `duplicate()` methods may allow an untrusted caller to alter the contents of the original data.

Rule	Severity	Likelihood	Remediation Cost	Priority	Level
FIO05-J	medium	likely	low	P18	L1

Automated Detection   Sound automated detection of this vulnerability is not feasible. Heuristic approaches may be useful.

Bibliography

[API 2006]   Class `CharBuffer`
[Hitchens 2002]   2.3 Duplicating Buffers

■ FIO06-J. Do not create multiple buffered wrappers on a single `InputStream`

Java input classes such as `Scanner` and `BufferedInputStream` facilitate fast, nonblocking I/O by buffering an underlying input stream. Programs can create multiple wrappers on an `InputStream`. Programs that use multiple wrappers around a single input stream, however, can behave unpredictably depending on whether the wrappers allow look-ahead. An attacker can exploit this difference in behavior by, for example, redirecting `System.in` (from a file) or by using the `System.setIn()` method to redirect `System.in`. In general, any input stream that supports nonblocking buffered I/O is susceptible to this form of misuse.

An input stream must not have more than one buffered wrapper. Instead, create and use only one wrapper per input stream, either by passing it as an argument to the methods that need it or by declaring it as a class variable.

Noncompliant Code Example

This noncompliant code example creates multiple BufferedInputStream wrappers on System.in, even though there is only one declaration of a BufferedInputStream. The getChar() method creates a new BufferedInputStream each time it is called. Data that is read from the underlying stream and placed in the buffer during execution of one call cannot be replaced in the underlying stream so that a second call has access to it. Consequently, data that remains in the buffer at the end of a particular execution of getChar() is lost. Although this noncompliant code example uses a BufferedInputStream, any buffered wrapper is unsafe; this condition is also exploitable when using a Scanner, for example.

```java
public final class InputLibrary {
  public static char getChar() throws EOFException, IOException {
    // wrapper
    BufferedInputStream in = new BufferedInputStream(System.in);
    int input = in.read();
    if (input == -1) {
      throw new EOFException();
    }
    // Down casting is permitted because InputStream
    // guarantees read() in range
    // 0..255 if it is not -1
    return (char) input;
  }

  public static void main(String[] args) {
    try {
      // Either redirect input from the console or use
      // System.setIn(new FileInputStream("input.dat"));
      System.out.print("Enter first initial: ");
      char first = getChar();
      System.out.println("Your first initial is " + first);
      System.out.print("Enter last initial: ");
      char last = getChar();
      System.out.println("Your last initial is " + last);
    } catch (EOFException e) {
      System.err.println("ERROR");
      // Forward to handler
    } catch (IOException e) {
      System.err.println("ERROR");
      // Forward to handler
    }
  }
}
```

Implementation Details (POSIX) When compiled under Java 1.6.0 and run from the command line, this program successfully takes two characters as input and prints them out. However, when run with a file redirected to standard input, the program throws EOFException because the second call to getChar() finds no characters to read upon encountering the end of the stream.

It may appear that the mark() and reset() methods of BufferedInputStream could be used to *replace* the read bytes. However, these methods provide look-ahead by operating on the internal buffers of the BufferedInputStream rather than by operating directly on the underlying stream. Because the example code creates a new BufferedInputStream on each call to getchar(), the internal buffers of the previous BufferedInputStream are lost.

Compliant Solution (Class Variable)

Create and use only a single BufferedInputStream on System.in. This compliant solution ensures that all methods can access the BufferedInputStream by declaring it as a class variable.

```
public final class InputLibrary {
  private static BufferedInputStream in =
    new BufferedInputStream(System.in);

  public static char getChar() throws EOFException, IOException {
    int input = in.read();
    if (input == -1) {
      throw new EOFException();
    }
    in.skip(1); // This statement is to advance to the next line
                // The noncompliant code example deceptively
                // appeared to work without it (in some cases)
    return (char) input;
  }

  public static void main(String[] args) {
    try {
      System.out.print("Enter first initial: ");
      char first = getChar();
      System.out.println("Your first initial is " + first);
      System.out.print("Enter last initial: ");
      char last = getChar();
      System.out.println("Your last initial is " + last);
    } catch (EOFException e) {
      System.err.println("ERROR");
      // Forward to handler
```

```
      } catch (IOException e) {
        System.err.println("ERROR");
        // Forward to handler
      }
    }
  }
}
```

Implementation Details (POSIX)   When compiled under Java 1.6.0 and run from the command line, this program successfully takes two characters as input and prints them out. Unlike the noncompliant code example, this program also produces correct output when run with a file redirected to standard input.

Compliant Solution (Accessible Class Variable)

This compliant solution uses both System.in and the InputLibrary class, which creates a buffered wrapper around System.in. Because the InputLibrary class and the remainder of the program must share a single buffered wrapper, the InputLibrary class must export a reference to that wrapper. Code outside the InputLibrary class must use the exported wrapper rather than creating and using its own additional buffered wrapper around System.in.

```
public final class InputLibrary {
  private static BufferedInputStream in =
    new BufferedInputStream(System.in);

  static BufferedInputStream getBufferedWrapper() {
    return in;
  }

  // ...other methods
}

// Some code that requires user input from System.in
class AppCode {
  private static BufferedInputStream in;

  AppCode() {
    in = InputLibrary.getBufferedWrapper();
  }

  // ...other methods
}
```

Note that reading from a stream is not a thread-safe operation by default; consequently, this compliant solution may be inappropriate in multithreaded environments. In such cases, explicit synchronization is required.

Risk Assessment

Creating multiple buffered wrappers around an `InputStream` can cause unexpected program behavior when the `InputStream` is redirected.

Rule	Severity	Likelihood	Remediation Cost	Priority	Level
FIO06-J	low	unlikely	medium	P2	L3

Automated Detection   Sound automated detection of this vulnerability is not feasible in the general case. Heuristic approaches may be useful.

Bibliography

[API 2006]   Method read

[API 2006]   Class BufferedInputStream

■ FIO07-J. Do not let external processes block on input and output streams

The `exec()` method of the `java.lang.Runtime` class and the related `ProcessBuilder.start()` method can be used to invoke external programs. While running, these programs are represented by a `java.lang.Process` object. This process contains an input stream, output stream, and error stream. Because the `Process` object allows a Java program to communicate with its external program, the process's input stream is an `OutputStream` object, accessible by the `Process.getOutputStream()` method. Likewise, the process's output stream and error streams are both represented by `InputStream` objects, accessible by the `Process.getInputStream()` and `Process.getErrorStream()` methods.

These processes may require input to be sent to their input stream, and they may also produce output on their output stream, their error stream, or both. Incorrect handling of such external programs can cause unexpected exceptions, DoS, and other security problems.

A process that tries to read input on an empty input stream will block until input is supplied. Consequently, input must be supplied when invoking such a process.

Output from an external process can exhaust the available buffer reserved for its output or error stream. When this occurs, the Java program can block the external process as well, preventing any forward progress for both the Java program and the external process. Note that many platforms limit the buffer size available for output streams. Consequently, when invoking an external process, if the process sends any data to its output stream, the output stream must be emptied. Similarly, if the process sends any data to its error stream, the error stream must also be emptied.

Noncompliant Code Example (`exitValue()`)

This noncompliant code example invokes a hypothetical cross-platform notepad application using the external command `notemaker`. The `notemaker` application does not read its input stream but sends output to both its output stream and error stream.

This noncompliant code example invokes `notemaker` using the `exec()` method, which returns a `Process` object. The `exitValue()` method returns the exit value for processes that have terminated, but it throws an `IllegalThreadStateException` when invoked on an active process. Because this noncompliant example program fails to wait for the `notemaker` process to terminate, the call to `exitValue()` is likely to throw an `IllegalThreadStateException`.

```
public class Exec {
  public static void main(String args[]) throws IOException {
    Runtime rt = Runtime.getRuntime();
    Process proc = rt.exec("notemaker");
    int exitVal = proc.exitValue();
  }
}
```

Noncompliant Code Example (`waitFor()`)

In this noncompliant code example, the `waitFor()` method blocks the calling thread until the `notemaker` process terminates. This prevents the `IllegalThreadStateException` from the previous example. However, the example program may experience an arbitrary delay before termination. Output from the `notemaker` process can exhaust the available buffer for the output or error stream because neither stream is read while waiting for the process to complete. If either buffer becomes full, it can block the `notemaker` process as well, preventing all progress for both the `notemaker` process and the Java program.

```
public class Exec {
  public static void main(String args[])
                        throws IOException, InterruptedException {
    Runtime rt = Runtime.getRuntime();
    Process proc = rt.exec("notemaker");
    int exitVal = proc.waitFor();
  }
}
```

Noncompliant Code Example (Process Output Stream)

This noncompliant code example properly empties the process's output stream, thereby preventing the output stream buffer from becoming full and blocking. However, it ignores the process's error stream, which can also fill and cause the process to block.

```
public class Exec {
  public static void main(String args[])
                    throws IOException, InterruptedException {
    Runtime rt = Runtime.getRuntime();
    Process proc = rt.exec("notemaker");
    InputStream is = proc.getInputStream();
    int c;
    while ((c = is.read()) != -1) {
      System.out.print((char) c);
    }
    int exitVal = proc.waitFor();
  }
}
```

Compliant Solution (`redirectErrorStream()`)

This compliant solution redirects the process's error stream to its output stream. Consequently, the program can empty the single output stream without fear of blockage.

```
public class Exec {
  public static void main(String args[])
                    throws IOException, InterruptedException {
    ProcessBuilder pb = new ProcessBuilder("notemaker");
    pb = pb.redirectErrorStream(true);
    Process proc = pb.start();
    InputStream is = proc.getInputStream();
    int c;
    while ((c = is.read()) != -1) {
      System.out.print((char) c);
    }
    int exitVal = proc.waitFor();
  }
}
```

Compliant Solution (Process Output Stream and Error Stream)

This compliant solution spawns two threads to consume the process's output stream and error stream. Consequently, the process cannot block indefinitely on those streams.

When the output and error streams are handled separately, they must be emptied independently. Failure to do so can cause the program to block indefinitely.

```java
class StreamGobbler extends Thread {
  InputStream is;
  PrintStream os;

  StreamGobbler(InputStream is, PrintStream os) {
    this.is = is;
    this.os = os;
  }

  public void run() {
    try {
      int c;
      while ((c = is.read()) != -1)
        os.print((char) c);
    } catch (IOException x) {
      // handle error
    }
  }
}

public class Exec {
  public static void main(String[] args)
    throws IOException, InterruptedException {
    Runtime rt = Runtime.getRuntime();
    Process proc = rt.exec("notemaker");

    // Any error message?
    StreamGobbler errorGobbler =
        new StreamGobbler(proc.getErrorStream(), System.err);

    // Any output?
    StreamGobbler outputGobbler =
        new StreamGobbler(proc.getInputStream(), System.out);

    errorGobbler.start();
    outputGobbler.start();

    // Any error?
    int exitVal = proc.waitFor();
    errorGobbler.join();   // Handle condition where the
    outputGobbler.join();  // process ends before the threads finish
  }
}
```

Exceptions

FIO07-EX0: Failure to supply input to a process that never reads input from its input stream is harmless and can be beneficial. Failure to empty the output or error streams of a process that never sends output to its output or error streams is similarly harmless or even beneficial. Consequently, programs are permitted to ignore the input, output, or error streams of processes that are *guaranteed* not to use those streams.

Risk Assessment

Failure to properly manage the I/O streams of external processes can result in runtime exceptions and DoS vulnerabilities.

Rule	Severity	Likelihood	Remediation Cost	Priority	Level
FIO07-J	low	probable	medium	P4	L3

Related Vulnerabilities   GROOVY-3275

Bibliography

[API 2006]	Method `exec()`
[Daconta 2000]	
[Daconta 2003]	Pitfall 1

■ FIO08-J. Use an `int` to capture the return value of methods that read a character or byte

The abstract `InputStream.read()` method reads a single byte from an input source and returns its value as an `int` in the range 0 to 255. It will return –1 only when the end of the input stream has been reached. The similar `Reader.read()` method reads a single character and returns its value as an `int` in the range 0 to 65,535. It also returns –1 only when the end of the stream has been reached. Both methods are meant to be overridden by subclasses.

These methods are often used to read a byte or character from a stream. Unfortunately, many programmers prematurely convert the resulting `int` back to a `byte` or `char` before checking whether they have reached the end of the stream (indicated by a return value of –1). Programs must check for the end of stream (e.g., –1) before narrowing the return value to a `byte` or `char`.

This rule applies to any `InputStream` or `Reader` subclass that provides an implementation of the `read()` method. This rule is a specific instance of rule NUM12-J.

Noncompliant Code Example (byte)

This noncompliant code example casts the value returned by the read() method directly to a value of type byte and then compares this value with –1 in an attempt to detect the end of the stream. This conversion leaves the value of c as 0xFFFF (e.g., Character.MAX_VALUE) instead of –1. Consequently, the test for the end of stream never evaluates to true (because the char type is unsigned and the value of c is 0-extended to 0x0000FFFF).

```
FileInputStream in;
// initialize stream
byte data;
while ((data = (byte) in.read()) != -1) {
  // ...
}
```

When the read() method in this noncompliant code example returns the byte value 0xFF, the returned byte value is indistinguishable from the –1 value used to indicate the end of stream, because the byte value is promoted and sign-extended to an int before being compared with –1.

Compliant Solution (byte)

Use a variable of type int to capture the return value of the byte input method. When the value returned by read() is not –1, it can be safely cast to type byte. When read() returns 0XFF, the comparison will test 0x000000FF against 0xFFFFFFFF and fail.

```
FileInputStream in;
// initialize stream
int inbuff;
byte data;
while ((inbuff = in.read()) != -1) {
  data = (byte) inbuff;
  // ...
}
```

Noncompliant Code Example (char)

This noncompliant code example casts the value of type int returned by the read() method directly to a value of type char, which is then compared with –1 in an attempt to detect the end of stream. This conversion leaves the value of c as 0xFFFF (that is, Character.MAX_VALUE) instead of –1. Consequently, the test for the end of stream never evaluates to true.

```
FileReader in;
// initialize stream
char c;
while ((c = (char) in.read()) != -1) {
  // ...
}
```

Compliant Solution (char)

Use a variable of type int to capture the return value of the character input method. When the value returned by read() is not –1, it can be safely cast to type char.

```
FileReader in;
// initialize stream
int inbuff;
char data;
while ((inbuff = in.read()) != -1) {
  data = (char) inbuff;
  // ...
}
```

Risk Assessment

Historically, using a narrow type to capture the return value of a byte input method has resulted in significant vulnerabilities, including command injection attacks; see CA-1996-22 advisory.[1] Consequently, the severity of this error is high.

Rule	Severity	Likelihood	Remediation Cost	Priority	Level
FIO08-J	high	probable	medium	P12	L1

Automated Detection Some static analysis tools can detect violations of this rule.

Related Guidelines

CERT C Secure Coding Standard	FIO34-C. Use int to capture the return value of character IO functions
CERT C++ Secure Coding Standard	FIO34-CPP. Use int to capture the return value of character IO functions

---

1. http://www.cert.org/advisories/CA-1996-22.html

Bibliography

[API 2006]   .Class `InputStream`

[JLS 2005]   §4.2 Primitive Types and Values

[Pugh 2008]   Waiting for the End

■ FIO09-J. Do not rely on the `write()` method to output integers outside the range 0 to 255

The `write()` method, defined in the class `java.io.OutputStream`, takes an argument of type `int` the value of which must be in the range 0 to 255. Because a value of type `int` could be outside this range, failure to range check can result in the truncation of the higher-order bits of the argument.

The general contract for the `write()` method says that it writes one byte to the output stream. The byte to be written constitutes the eight lower-order bits of the argument b, passed to the `write()` method; the 24 high-order bits of b are ignored (see [API 2006] `java.io.OutputStream.write()` for more information).

Noncompliant Code Example

This noncompliant code example accepts a value from the user without validating it. Any value that is not in the range of 0 to 255 is truncated. For instance, `write(303)` prints / on ASCII-based systems because the lower-order 8 bits of 303 are used while the 24 high-order bits are ignored (303 % 256 = 47, which is the ASCII code for /). That is, the result is the remainder of the input divided by 256.

```
class ConsoleWrite {
  public static void main(String[] args) {
    // Any input value > 255 will result in unexpected output
    System.out.write(Integer.valueOf(args[0]));
    System.out.flush();
  }
}
```

Compliant Solution (Range-Check Inputs)

This compliant solution prints the corresponding character only if the input integer is in the proper range. If the input is outside the representable range of an `int`, the `Integer.valueOf()` method throws a `NumberFormatException`. If the input can be represented by an `int` but is outside the range required by `write()`, this code throws an `ArithmeticException`.

```
class FileWrite {
  public static void main(String[] args)
                       throws NumberFormatException, IOException {
    // Perform range checking
    int value = Integer.valueOf(args[0]);
    if (value < 0 || value > 255) {
      throw new ArithmeticException("Value is out of range");
    }

    System.out.write(value);
    System.out.flush();
  }
}
```

Compliant Solution (`writeInt()`)

This compliant solution uses the `writeInt()` method of the `DataOutputStream` class, which can output the entire range of values representable as an `int`.

```
class FileWrite {
  public static void main(String[] args)
                       throws NumberFormatException, IOException {
    DataOutputStream dos = new DataOutputStream(System.out);
    dos.writeInt(Integer.valueOf(args[0].toString()));
    System.out.flush();
  }
}
```

Risk Assessment

Using the `write()` method to output integers outside the range 0 to 255 will result in truncation.

Rule	Severity	Likelihood	Remediation Cost	Priority	Level
FIO09-J	low	unlikely	medium	P2	L3

Automated Detection Automated detection of all uses of the `write()` method is straightforward. Sound determination of whether the truncating behavior is correct is not feasible in the general case. Heuristic checks could be useful.

Related Guidelines

MITRE CWE   CWE-252. Unchecked return value

Bibliography

[API 2006]   Method `write()`
[Harold 1999]

■ FIO10-J. Ensure the array is filled when using read() to fill an array

The contracts of the read methods for the `InputStream` and `Reader` classes and their sub-classes are complicated with regard to filling byte or character arrays. According to the Java API [API 2006] for the class `InputStream`, the `read(byte[] b, int off, int len)` method provides the following behavior:

> The default implementation of this method blocks until the requested amount of input data `len` has been read, end of file is detected, or an exception is thrown. Subclasses are encouraged to provide a more efficient implementation of this method.

However, the `read(byte[] b)` method:

> reads some number of bytes from the input stream and stores them into the buffer array `b`. The number of bytes actually read is returned as an integer. The number of bytes read is, at most, equal to the length of `b`.

The `read()` methods return as soon as they find available input data. As a result, these methods can stop reading data before the array is filled because the available data may be insufficient to fill the array.

Ignoring the result returned by the `read()` methods is a violation of rule EXP00-J. Security issues can arise even when return values are considered because the default behavior of the `read()` methods lacks any guarantee that the entire buffer array is filled. Consequently, when using `read()` to fill an array, the program must check the return value of `read()` and must handle the case where the array is only partially filled. In such cases, the program may try to fill the rest of the array, or work only with the subset of the array that was filled, or throw an exception.

This rule applies only to `read()` methods that take an array argument. To read a single byte, use the `InputStream.read()` method that takes no arguments and returns an `int`. To read a single character, use a `Reader.read()` method that takes no arguments and returns the character read as an `int`.

Noncompliant Code Example (read())

This noncompliant code example attempts to read 1024 bytes encoded in UTF-8 from an InputStream and return them as a String. It explicitly specifies the character encoding used to build the string, in compliance with rule IDS13-J.

```
public static String readBytes(InputStream in) throws IOException {
  byte[] data = new byte[1024];
  if (in.read(data) == -1) {
    throw new EOFException();
  }
  return new String(data, "UTF-8");
}
```

The programmer's misunderstanding of the general contract of the read() method can result in failure to read the intended data in full. It is possible that the data is less than 1024 bytes long and that additional data is available from the input stream.

Compliant Solution (Multiple Calls to read())

This compliant solution reads all the desired bytes into its buffer, accounting for the total number of bytes read and adjusting the remaining bytes' offset, consequently ensuring that the required data is read in full. It also avoids splitting multibyte encoded characters across buffers by deferring construction of the result string until the data has been fully read. (See rule IDS10-J for more information.)

```
public static String readBytes(InputStream in) throws IOException {
  int offset = 0;
  int bytesRead = 0;
  byte[] data = new byte[1024];
  while ((bytesRead = in.read(data, offset, data.length - offset))
    != -1) {
    offset += bytesRead;
    if (offset >= data.length) {
      break;
    }
  }
  String str = new String(data, "UTF-8");
  return str;
}
```

Compliant Solution (`readFully()`)

The no-argument and one-argument `readFully()` methods of the `DataInputStream` class guarantee that either all of the requested data is read or an exception is thrown. These methods throw `EOFException` if they detect the end of input before the required number of bytes have been read; they throw `IOException` if some other I/O error occurs.

```java
public static String readBytes(FileInputStream fis)
                              throws IOException {
  byte[] data = new byte[1024];
  DataInputStream dis = new DataInputStream(fis);
  dis.readFully(data);
  String str = new String(data, "UTF-8");
  return str;
}
```

Risk Assessment

Incorrect use of the `read()` method can result in the wrong number of bytes being read or character sequences being interpreted incorrectly.

Rule	Severity	Likelihood	Remediation Cost	Priority	Level
FIO10-J	low	unlikely	medium	P2	L3

Related Guidelines

MITRE CWE   CWE-135. Incorrect calculation of multi-byte string length

Bibliography

[API 2006]   Class `InputStream`, `DataInputStream`

[Chess 2007]   8.1, Handling Errors with Return Codes

[Harold 1999]   Chapter 7, Data Streams, Reading Byte Arrays

[Phillips 2005]

■ FIO11-J. Do not attempt to read raw binary data as character data

In Java, byte arrays are often used to transmit raw binary data as well as character-encoded data. Attempts to read raw binary data as if it were character-encoded data often fail because some of the bytes fall outside the default or specified encoding scheme and for that reason fail to denote valid characters. For example, converting a cryptographic key containing nonrepresentable bytes to character-encoded data for transmission may result in an error.

Noncompliant Code Example

This noncompliant code example attempts to convert the byte array representing a `BigInteger` into a `String`. Because some of the bytes do not denote valid characters, the resulting `String` representation loses information. Converting the `String` back to a `BigInteger` produces a different value.

```
BigInteger x = new BigInteger("530500452766");
// convert x to a String
byte[] byteArray = x.toByteArray();
String s = new String(byteArray);
// convert s back to a BigInteger
byteArray = s.getBytes();
x = new BigInteger(byteArray);
```

When this program was run on a Linux platform where the default character encoding is US-ASCII, the string s got the value {?J??, because some of the characters were unprintable. When converted back to a `BigInteger`, x got the value 149830058370101340468658109.

Compliant Solution

This compliant solution first produces a `String` representation of the `BigInteger` object and then converts the `String` object to a byte array. This process is reversed on input. Because the textual representation in the `String` object was generated by the `BigInteger` class, it contains valid characters.

```
BigInteger x = new BigInteger("530500452766");
String s = x.toString();  // valid character data
try {
  byte[] byteArray = s.getBytes("UTF8");
  // ns prints as "530500452766"
  String ns = new String(byteArray, "UTF8");
  // construct the original BigInteger
  BigInteger x1 = new BigInteger(ns);
} catch (UnsupportedEncodingException ex) {
  // handle error
}
```

Do not try to convert the `String` object to a byte array to obtain the original `BigInteger`. Character-encoded data may yield a byte array that, when converted to a `BigInteger`, results in a completely different value.

Exceptions

FIO11-EX0: Binary data that is expected to be a valid string may be read and converted to a string. How to perform this operation securely is explained in rule IDS13-J. Also see rule IDS10-J.

Risk Assessment

Attempting to read a byte array containing binary data as if it were character data can produce erroneous results.

Rule	Severity	Likelihood	Remediation Cost	Priority	Level
FIO11-J	low	unlikely	medium	P2	L3

Bibliography

[API 2006]   Class String

■ FIO12-J. Provide methods to read and write little-endian data

In Java, data is stored in big-endian format (also called network order). That is, all data is represented sequentially starting from the most significant bit to the least significant. JDK versions prior to JDK 1.4 required definition of custom methods that manage reversing byte order to maintain compatibility with little-endian systems. Correct handling of byte order–related issues is critical when exchanging data in a networked environment that includes both big-endian and little-endian machines or when working with other languages using JNI. Failure to handle byte-ordering issues can cause unexpected program behavior.

Noncompliant Code Example

The read methods (readByte(), readShort(), readInt(), readLong(), readFloat(), and readDouble()) and the corresponding write methods defined by class java.io.DataInput Stream and class java.io.DataOutputStream operate only on big-endian data. Use of these methods while interoperating with traditional languages, such as C or C++, is insecure because such languages lack any guarantees about endianness. This noncompliant code example shows such a discrepancy.

```
try {
  DataInputStream dis = null;
  try {
    dis = new DataInputStream(new FileInputStream("data"));
```

```
      // Little-endian data might be read as big-endian
      int serialNumber = dis.readInt();
  } catch (IOException x) {
    // handle error
  } finally {
    if (dis != null) {
      try {
        dis.close();
      } catch (IOException e) {
        // handle error
      }
    }
  }
```

Compliant Solution (`ByteBuffer`)

This compliant solution uses methods provided by class `ByteBuffer` (see [API 2006] Byte-Buffer) to correctly extract an `int` from the original input value. It wraps the input byte array with a `ByteBuffer`, sets the byte order to little-endian, and extracts the `int`. The result is stored in the integer `serialNumber`. Class `ByteBuffer` provides analogous get and put methods for other numeric types.

```
try {
  DataInputStream dis = null;
  try {
    dis = new DataInputStream( new FileInputStream("data"));
    byte[] buffer = new byte[4];
    int bytesRead = dis.read(buffer);  // Bytes are read into buffer
    if (bytesRead != 4) {
      throw new IOException("Unexpected End of Stream");
    }
    int serialNumber =
        ByteBuffer.wrap(buffer).order(ByteOrder.LITTLE_ENDIAN).getInt();
  } finally {
    if (dis != null)
      try {
        dis.close();
      } catch (IOException x) {
        // handle error
      }
  }
} catch (IOException x) {
  // handle error
}
```

Compliant Solution (Define Special-Purpose Methods)

An alternative compliant solution is to define read and write methods that support the necessary byte-swapping while reading from or writing to the file. In this example, the `readLittleEndianInteger()` method reads four bytes into a byte buffer and then pieces together the integer in the correct order. The `writeLittleEndianInteger()` method obtains bytes by repeatedly casting the integer so that the least significant byte is extracted on successive right shifts. Long values can be handled by defining a byte buffer of size 8.

```java
// Read method
public static int readLittleEndianInteger(InputStream ips)
                                          throws IOException {
  byte[] buffer = new byte[4];
  int check = ips.read(buffer);

  if (check != 4) {
    throw new IOException("Unexpected End of Stream");
  }

  int result = (buffer[3] << 24) | (buffer[2] << 16) |
               (buffer[1] << 8)  | buffer[0];
  return result;
}

// Write method
public static void writeLittleEndianInteger(int i, OutputStream ops)
  throws IOException {
  byte[] buffer = new byte[4];
  buffer[0] = (byte) i;
  buffer[1] = (byte) (i >> 8);
  buffer[2] = (byte) (i >> 16);
  buffer[3] = (byte) (i >> 24);
  ops.write(buffer);
}
```

Compliant Solution (reverseBytes())

When programming for JDK 1.5+, use the `reverseBytes()` method defined in the classes `Character`, `Short`, `Integer`, and `Long` to reverse the order of the integral value's bytes. Note that classes `Float` and `Double` lack such a method.

```java
public static int reverse(int i) {
  return Integer.reverseBytes(i);
}
```

Risk Assessment

Reading and writing data without considering endianness can lead to misinterpretations of both the magnitude and sign of the data.

Rule	Severity	Likelihood	Remediation Cost	Priority	Level
FIO12-J	low	unlikely	low	P3	L3

Automated Detection   Automated detection is infeasible in the general case.

Related Guidelines

MITRE CWE CWE-198.   Use of incorrect byte ordering

Bibliography

[API 2006]	Class `ByteBuffer`: Methods `wrap` and `order`. Class `Integer`: method `reverseBytes`
[Cohen 1981]	On Holy Wars and a Plea for Peace
[Harold 1997]	Chapter 2, Primitive Data Types, Cross-Platform Issues

▪ FIO13-J. Do not log sensitive information outside a trust boundary

Logging is essential for debugging, incident response, and collecting forensic evidence. Nevertheless, logging sensitive data raises many concerns, including the privacy of the stakeholders, limitations imposed by the law on the collection of personal information, and the potential for data exposure by insiders. Sensitive information includes, but is not limited to, IP addresses, user names and passwords, email addresses, credit card numbers, and any personally identifiable information such as social security numbers. Many countries prohibit or restrict collection of personal data; others permit retention of personal data only when held in an anonymized form. Consequently, logs must not contain sensitive data, particularly when prohibited by law.

Unfortunately, violations of this rule are common. For example, prior to version 0.8.1, the LineControl Java client logged sensitive information, including the local user's password, as documented by CVE-2005-2990.[2]

The `java.util.logging` class provides a basic logging framework for JDK versions 1.4 and higher. Other logging frameworks exist, but the basic principles apply regardless of the particular logging framework chosen.

---

2. http://cve.mitre.org/cgi-bin/cvename.cgi?name=CVE-2005-2990

Programs typically support varying levels of protection. Some information, such as access times, can be safely logged. Some information can be logged, but the log file must be restricted from everyone but particular administrators. Other information, such as credit card numbers, can be included in logs only in encrypted form. Information, such as passwords, should not be logged at all.

For the following code examples, the log lies outside the trust boundary of the information being recorded. Also, normal log messages should include additional parameters such as date, time, source event, and so forth. This information has been omitted from the following code examples for brevity.

Noncompliant Code Example

In this noncompliant code example, a server logs the IP address of the remote client in the event of a security exception. This data can be misused, for example, to build a profile of a user's browsing habits. Such logging may violate legal restrictions in many countries.

When the log cannot contain IP addresses, it should not contain any information about a `SecurityException`, because it might leak an IP address. When an exception contains sensitive information, the custom `MyExceptionReporter` class should extract or cleanse it before returning control to the next statement in the `catch` block (see rule ERR00-J).

```java
public void logRemoteIPAddress(String name) {
  Logger logger = Logger.getLogger("com.organization.Log");
  InetAddress machine = null;
  try {
    machine = InetAddress.getByName(name);
  } catch (UnknownHostException e) {
    Exception e = MyExceptionReporter.handle(e);
  } catch (SecurityException e) {
    Exception e = MyExceptionReporter.handle(e);
    logger.severe(name + "," + machine.getHostAddress() + "," +
                e.toString());
  }
}
```

Compliant Solution

This compliant solution does not log security exceptions except for the logging implicitly performed by `MyExceptionReporter`.

```java
// ...
catch (SecurityException e) {
  Exception e = MyExceptionReporter.handle(e);
}
```

Noncompliant Code Example

Log messages with sensitive information should not be printed to the console display for security reasons (a possible example of sensitive information is passenger age). The `java.util.logging.Logger` class supports different logging levels that can be used for classifying such information. These are FINEST, FINER, FINE, CONFIG, INFO, WARNING, and SEVERE. By default, the INFO, WARNING, and SEVERE levels print the message to the console, which is accessible by end users and system administrators.

If we assume that the passenger age can appear in log files on the current system but not on the console display, this code example is noncompliant.

```
logger.info("Age: " + passengerAge);
```

Compliant Solution

This compliant solution logs the passenger age at the FINEST level to prevent this information from displaying on the console. As noted previously, we are assuming the age may appear in system log files but not on the console.

```
// make sure that all handlers only print
// log messages rated INFO or higher
Handler handlers[] = logger.getHandlers();
for (int i = 0; i < handlers.length; i++) {
  handlers[i].setLevel(Level.INFO);
}
// ...
logger.finest("Age: " + passengerAge);
```

Risk Assessment

Logging sensitive information can violate system security policies and can violate user privacy when the logging level is incorrect or when the log files are insecure.

Rule	Severity	Likelihood	Remediation Cost	Priority	Level
FIO13-J	medium	probable	high	P4	L3

Related Guidelines

MITRE CWE	CWE-532. Information exposure through log files
	CWE-533. Information exposure through server log files
	CWE-359. Privacy violation
	CWE-542. Information exposure through cleanup log files

Bibliography

[API 2006]   Class `java.util.logging.Logger`
[Chess 2007]   11.1, Privacy and Regulation: Handling Private Information
[CVE 2011]   CVE-2005-2990
[Sun 2006]   Java Logging Overview

■ FIO14-J. Perform proper cleanup at program termination

When certain kinds of errors are detected, such as irrecoverable logic errors, rather than risk data corruption by continuing to execute in an indeterminate state, the appropriate strategy may be for the system to quickly shut down, allowing the operator to start it afresh in a determinate state.

Section 6.46, "Termination Strategy [REU]," of [ISO/IEC TR 24772:2010] says:

> When a fault is detected, there are many ways in which a system can react. The quickest and most noticeable way is to fail hard, also known as fail fast or fail stop. The reaction to a detected fault is to immediately halt the system. Alternatively, the reaction to a detected fault could be to fail soft. The system would keep working with the faults present, but the performance of the system would be degraded. Systems used in a high availability environment such as telephone switching centers, e-commerce, or other "always available" applications would likely use a fail soft approach. What is actually done in a fail soft approach can vary depending on whether the system is used for safety critical or security critical purposes. For fail-safe systems, such as flight controllers, traffic signals, or medical monitoring systems, there would be no effort to meet normal operational requirements, but rather to limit the damage or danger caused by the fault. A system that fails securely, such as cryptologic systems, would maintain maximum security when a fault is detected, possibly through a denial of service.

And:

> The reaction to a fault in a system can depend on the criticality of the part in which the fault originates. When a program consists of several tasks, each task may be critical, or not. If a task is critical, it may or may not be restartable by the rest of the program. Ideally, a task that detects a fault within itself should be able to halt leaving its resources available for use by the rest of the program, halt clearing away its resources, or halt the entire program. The latency of task termination and whether tasks can ignore termination signals should be clearly specified. Having inconsistent reactions to a fault can potentially be a vulnerability.

Java provides two options for program termination: `Runtime.exit()` (this is equivalent to `System.exit()`) and `Runtime.halt()`.

Runtime.exit()

`Runtime.exit()` is the typical way of exiting a program. According to the Java API [API 06], `Runtime.exit()`

terminates the currently running Java virtual machine by initiating its shutdown sequence. This method never returns normally. The argument serves as a status code; by convention, a nonzero status code indicates abnormal termination.

The virtual machine's shutdown sequence consists of two phases. In the first phase all registered shutdown hooks, if any, are started in some unspecified order and allowed to run concurrently until they finish. In the second phase all uninvoked finalizers are run if finalization-on-exit has been enabled. Once this is performed the virtual machine halts.

If this method is invoked after the virtual machine has begun its shutdown sequence, then if shutdown hooks are being run, this method will block indefinitely. If shutdown hooks have already been run and on-exit finalization has been enabled, then this method halts the virtual machine with the given status code if the status is nonzero; otherwise, it blocks indefinitely.

The `System.exit()` method is the conventional and convenient means of invoking this method.

The `Runtime.addShutdownHook()` method can be used to customize `Runtime.exit()` to perform additional actions at program termination.

This method uses a `Thread`, which must be initialized but unstarted. The thread starts when the JVM begins to shut down. Because the JVM usually has a fixed time to shut down, these threads should not be long-running and should not attempt user interaction.

Runtime.halt()

`Runtime.halt()` is similar to `Runtime.exit()` but does *not* run shutdown hooks or finalizers. According to the Java API [API 06], `Runtime.halt()`

forcibly terminates the currently running Java virtual machine. This method never returns normally.

This method should be used with extreme caution. Unlike the exit method, this method does not cause shutdown hooks to be started and does not run uninvoked finalizers if finalization-on-exit has been enabled. If the shutdown sequence has already been initiated, then this method does not wait for any running shutdown hooks or finalizers to finish their work.

Java programs do not flush unwritten buffered data or close open files when they exit, so programs must perform these operations manually. Programs must also perform any other cleanup that involves external resources, such as releasing shared locks.

Noncompliant Code Example

This example creates a new file, outputs some text to it, and abruptly exits using `Runtime.exit()`. Consequently, the file may be closed without the text actually being written.

```
public class CreateFile {
  public static void main(String[] args)
                        throws FileNotFoundException {
    final PrintStream out =
        new PrintStream(new BufferedOutputStream(
                        new FileOutputStream("foo.txt")));
    out.println("hello");
    Runtime.getRuntime().exit(1);
  }
}
```

Compliant Solution (`close()`)

This solution explicitly closes the file before exiting.

```
public class CreateFile {
  public static void main(String[] args)
                        throws FileNotFoundException {
    final PrintStream out =
    new PrintStream(new BufferedOutputStream(
      new FileOutputStream("foo.txt")));
    try {
      out.println("hello");
    } finally {
      try {
        out.close();
      } catch (IOException x) {
        // handle error
      }
    }
    Runtime.getRuntime().exit(1);
  }
}
```

Compliant Solution (Shutdown Hook)

This compliant solution adds a shutdown hook to close the file. This hook is invoked by `Runtime.exit()` and is called before the JVM is halted.

```java
public class CreateFile {
  public static void main(String[] args)
                         throws FileNotFoundException {
    final PrintStream out =
      new PrintStream(new BufferedOutputStream(
                      new FileOutputStream("foo.txt")));
    Runtime.getRuntime().addShutdownHook(new Thread(new Runnable() {
      public void run() {
        out.close();
      }
    }));
    out.println("hello");
    Runtime.getRuntime().exit(1);
  }
}
```

Noncompliant Code Example (`Runtime.halt()`)

This noncompliant code example calls `Runtime.halt()` instead of `Runtime.exit()`. The `Runtime.halt()` method stops the JVM without invoking any shutdown hooks; consequently the file is not properly written to or closed.

```java
public class CreateFile {
  public static void main(String[] args)
                         throws FileNotFoundException {
    final PrintStream out =
        new PrintStream(new BufferedOutputStream(
                        new FileOutputStream("foo.txt")));
    Runtime.getRuntime().addShutdownHook(new Thread(new Runnable() {
      public void run() {
        out.close();
      }
    }));
    out.println("hello");
    Runtime.getRuntime().halt(1);
  }
}
```

Noncompliant Code Example (Signal)

When a user forcefully exits a program, for example by pressing the ctrl + c keys or by using the kill command, the JVM terminates abruptly. Although this event cannot be captured, the program should nevertheless perform any mandatory cleanup operations before exiting. This noncompliant code example fails to do so.

```java
public class InterceptExit {
  public static void main(String[] args)
                        throws FileNotFoundException {
    InputStream in = null;
    try {
      in = new FileInputStream("file");
      System.out.println("Regular code block");
      // Abrupt exit such as ctrl + c key pressed
      System.out.println("This never executes");
    } finally {
      if (in != null) {
        try {
          in.close();  // this never executes either
        } catch (IOException x) {
          // handle error
        }
      }
    }
  }
}
```

Compliant Solution (addShutdownHook())

Use the addShutdownHook() method of java.lang.Runtime to assist with performing cleanup operations in the event of abrupt termination. The JVM starts the shutdown hook thread when abrupt termination is initiated; the shutdown hook runs concurrently with other JVM threads.

According to the Java API [API 2006], Class Runtime, method addShutdownHook():

A shutdown hook is simply an initialized but unstarted thread. When the virtual machine begins its shutdown sequence it will start all registered shutdown hooks in some unspecified order and let them run concurrently. When all the hooks have finished it will then run all uninvoked finalizers if finalization-on-exit has been enabled. Finally, the virtual machine will halt. Once the shutdown sequence has begun it can be stopped only by invoking the halt method, which forcibly terminates the virtual machine. Once the shutdown sequence has begun it is impossible to register a new shutdown hook or de-register a previously registered hook.

Some precautions must be taken because the JVM might be in a sensitive state during shutdown. Shutdown hook threads should

- be lightweight and simple.
- be thread-safe.
- hold locks when accessing data and release those locks when done.
- avoid relying on system services, because the services themselves may be shutting down (for example, the logger may shut down from another hook).

To avoid race conditions or deadlock between shutdown actions, it may be better to run a series of shutdown tasks from one thread by using a single shutdown hook [Goetz 2006a]. This compliant solution shows the standard method to install a hook.

```java
public class Hook {
  public static void main(String[] args) {
    try {
      final InputStream in = new FileInputStream("file");
      Runtime.getRuntime().addShutdownHook(new Thread() {
        public void run() {
          // Log shutdown and close all resources
          in.close();
        }
      });

      // ...
    } catch (IOException x) {
      // handle error
    } catch (FileNotFoundException x) {
      // handle error
    }
  }
}
```

The JVM can abort for external reasons, such as an external `SIGKILL` signal (POSIX) or the `TerminateProcess()` call (Windows), or memory corruption caused by native methods. Shutdown hooks may fail to execute as expected in such cases because the JVM cannot guarantee that they will be executed as intended.

Risk Assessment

Failure to perform necessary cleanup at program termination may leave the system in an inconsistent state.

Rule	Severity	Likelihood	Remediation Cost	Priority	Level
FIO14-J	medium	likely	medium	P12	L1

Related Guidelines

The CERT C Secure Coding Standard	ERR04-C. Choose an appropriate termination strategy
The CERT C++ Secure Coding Standard	ERR04-CPP. Choose an appropriate termination strategy
ISO/IEC TR 24772:2010	Termination Strategy [REU]
MITRE CWE	CWE-705. Incorrect control flow scoping

Bibliography

[API 2006]	Class `Runtime`
[ISO/IEC TR 24772:2010]	Section 6.46, Termination Strategy [REU]

15

Serialization (SER)

■ Rules

■ Risk Assessment Summary

Rule	Severity	Likelihood	Remediation Cost	Priority	Level
SER00-J	low	probable	high	P2	L3
SER01-J	high	likely	low	P27	L1
SER02-J	medium	probable	high	P4	L3
SER03-J	medium	likely	high	P6	L2
SER04-J	high	probable	high	P6	L2
SER05-J	medium	likely	medium	P12	L1
SER06-J	low	probable	medium	P4	L3
SER07-J	medium	probable	high	P4	L3
SER08-J	high	likely	medium	P18	L1
SER09-J	low	probable	medium	P4	L3
SER10-J	low	unlikely	low	P3	L3
SER11-J	low	probable	low	P6	L2

■ SER00-J. Maintain serialization compatibility during class evolution

Once an object of a particular class has been serialized, future refactoring of the class's code often becomes problematic. Specifically, existing serialized forms (encoded representations) become part of the object's published API and must be supported for an indefinite period. This can be troublesome from a security perspective; not only does it promote dead code, it also forces the provider to maintain a compatible code base for the lifetime of their products.

Classes that implement `Serializable` without overriding its functionality are said to be using the *default* serialized form. In the event the class changes, byte streams produced by users of old versions of the class become incompatible with the new implementation. Programs must maintain serialization compatibility during class evolution. An acceptable approach is the use of a *custom* serialized form, which relieves the implementer of the necessity to maintain the original serialized form and the corresponding version of the class in addition to the newly evolved version.

Noncompliant Code Example

This noncompliant code example implements a `GameWeapon` class with a serializable field called `numOfWeapons` and uses the default serialization form. Any changes to the internal representation of the class can break the existing serialized form.

```
class GameWeapon implements Serializable {
  int numOfWeapons = 10;

  public String toString() {
    return String.valueOf(numOfWeapons);
  }
}
```

Because this class does not provide a `serialVersionUID`, the Java Virtual Machine (JVM) assigns it one using implementation-defined methods. If the class definition changes, the `serialVersionUID` is also likely to change. Consequently, the JVM will refuse to associate the serialized form of an object with the class definition when the version IDs are different.

Compliant Solution (`serialVersionUID`)

In this solution, the class has an explicit `serialVersionUID` that contains a number unique to this version of the class. The JVM will make a good-faith effort to deserialize any serialized object with the same class name and version ID.

```
class GameWeapon implements Serializable {
  private static final long serialVersionUID = 24L;

  int numOfWeapons = 10;

  public String toString() {
    return String.valueOf(numOfWeapons);
  }
}
```

Compliant Solution (`serialPersistentFields`)

Ideally, `Serializable` should only be implemented for stable classes. One way to maintain the original serialized form and allow the class to evolve is to use custom serialization with the help of `serialPersistentFields`. The `static` and `transient` qualifiers specify which fields should *not* be serialized, whereas the `serialPersistentFields` field specifies which fields should be serialized. It also relieves the class from defining the serializable field within the class implementation, decoupling the current implementation from the overall logic. New fields can easily be added without breaking compatibility across releases.

```java
class WeaponStore implements Serializable {
  int numOfWeapons = 10; // Total number of weapons
}

public class GameWeapon implements Serializable {
  WeaponStore ws = new WeaponStore();
  private static final ObjectStreamField[] serialPersistentFields
    = {new ObjectStreamField("ws", WeaponStore.class)};

  private void readObject(ObjectInputStream ois) throws IOException {
    try {
      ObjectInputStream.GetField gf = ois.readFields();
      this.ws = (WeaponStore) gf.get("ws", ws);
    } catch (ClassNotFoundException e) { /* Forward to handler */ }
  }

  private void writeObject(ObjectOutputStream oos) throws IOException {
    ObjectOutputStream.PutField pf = oos.putFields();
    pf.put("ws", ws);
    oos.writeFields();
  }

  public String toString() {
    return String.valueOf(ws);
  }
}
```

Risk Assessment

Failure to provide a consistent serialization mechanism across releases can limit the extensibility of classes. If classes are extended, compatibility issues may result.

Rule	Severity	Likelihood	Remediation Cost	Priority	Level
SER00-J	low	probable	high	P2	L3

Automated Detection   Automated detection of classes that use the default serialized form is straightforward.

Related Guidelines

MITRE CWE   CWE-589. Call to non-ubiquitous API

Bibliography

[API 2006]

[Bloch 2008]   Item 74. Implement serialization judiciously

[Harold 2006]   13.7.5, serialPersistentFields

[Sun 2006]   Serialization Specification, 1.5, Defining Serializable Fields for a Class, and 1.7, Accessing Serializable Fields of a Class

■ SER01-J. Do not deviate from the proper signatures of serialization methods

Classes that require special handling during object serialization and deserialization must implement special methods with exactly the following signatures [API 2006]:

```
private void writeObject(java.io.ObjectOutputStream out)
    throws IOException;
private void readObject(java.io.ObjectInputStream in)
    throws IOException, ClassNotFoundException;
private void readObjectNoData() throws ObjectStreamException;
```

Note that these methods must be declared private for any serializable class. Serializable classes may also implement the readResolve() and writeReplace() methods. According to the Serialization Specification [Sun 2006], readResolve() and writeReplace() method documentation:

For Serializable and Externalizable classes, the readResolve method allows a class to replace/resolve the object read from the stream before it is returned to the caller. By implementing the readResolve method, a class can directly control the types and instances of its own instances being deserialized.

For Serializable and Externalizable classes, the writeReplace method allows a class of an object to nominate its own replacement in the stream before the object is written. By implementing the writeReplace method, a class can directly control the types and instances of its own instances being serialized.

It is possible to add any access-specifier to the readResolve() and writeReplace() methods. However, if these methods are declared private, extending classes cannot invoke or override them. Similarly, if these methods are declared static, extending classes cannot override these methods; they can only hide them.

Deviating from these method signatures produces a method that is not invoked during object serialization or deserialization. Such methods, especially if declared public, might be accessible to untrusted code.

Unlike most interfaces, `Serializable` does not define the method signatures it requires. Interfaces allow only public fields and methods, whereas `readObject()`, `readObject-NoData`, and `writeObject()` must be declared private. Similarly, the `Serializable` interface does not prevent `readResolve()` and `writeReplace()` methods from being declared static, public, or private. Consequently, the Java serialization mechanism fails to let the compiler identify an incorrect method signature for any of these methods.

Noncompliant Code Example (`readObject()`, `writeObject()`)

This noncompliant code example shows a class `Ser` with a private constructor, indicating that code external to the class should be unable to create instances of it. The class implements `java.io.Serializable` and defines public `readObject()` and `writeObject()` methods. Consequently, untrusted code can obtain the reconstituted objects by using `readObject()` and can write to the stream by using `writeObject()`.

```
public class Ser implements Serializable {
  private final long serialVersionUID = 123456789;
  private Ser() {
    // initialize
  }
  public static void writeObject(final ObjectOutputStream stream)
    throws IOException {
    stream.defaultWriteObject();
  }
  public static void readObject(final ObjectInputStream stream)
      throws IOException, ClassNotFoundException {
    stream.defaultReadObject();
  }
}
```

Similarly, omitting the `static` keyword is insufficient to make this example secure; the JVM will not detect the two methods, resulting in failure to use the custom serialized form.

Compliant Solution (`readObject()`, `writeObject()`)

This compliant solution declares the `readObject()` and `writeObject()` methods private and nonstatic to limit their accessibility.

```
private void writeObject(final ObjectOutputStream stream)
  throws IOException {
  stream.defaultWriteObject();
}
```

```
private void readObject(final ObjectInputStream stream)
    throws IOException, ClassNotFoundException {
  stream.defaultReadObject();
}
```

Reducing the accessibility also prevents malicious overriding of the two methods.

Noncompliant Code Example (`readResolve()`, `writeReplace()`)

This noncompliant code example declares the `readResolve()` and `writeReplace()` methods as private.

```
class Extendable implements Serializable {
  private Object readResolve() {
    // ...
  }

  private Object writeReplace() {
    // ...
  }
}
```

Noncompliant Code Example (`readResolve()`, `writeReplace()`)

This noncompliant code example declares the `readResolve()` and `writeReplace()` methods as static.

```
class Extendable implements Serializable {
  protected static Object readResolve() {
    // ...
  }

  protected static Object writeReplace() {
    // ...
  }
}
```

Compliant Solution (`readResolve()`, `writeReplace()`)

This compliant solution declares the two methods protected while eliminating the static keyword so that subclasses can inherit them.

```
class Extendable implements Serializable {
  protected Object readResolve() {
   // ...
  }

  protected Object writeReplace() {
   // ...
  }
}
```

Risk Assessment

Deviating from the proper signatures of serialization methods can lead to unexpected behavior. Failure to limit the accessibility of the `readObject()` and `writeObject()` methods can leave code vulnerable to untrusted invocations. Declaring `readResolve()` and `writeReplace()` methods to be static or private can force subclasses to silently ignore them, while declaring them public allows them to be invoked by untrusted code.

Rule	Severity	Likelihood	Remediation Cost	Priority	Level
SER01-J	high	likely	low	P27	L1

Related Guidelines

MITRE CWE   CWE-502. Deserialization of untrusted data

Bibliography

[API 2006]   `Serializable`
[Sun 2006]   Serialization Specification
[Ware 2008]

■ SER02-J. Sign then seal sensitive objects before sending them across a trust boundary

Sensitive data must be protected from eavesdropping and malicious tampering. An obfuscated transfer object [Steel 2005] that is strongly encrypted can protect data. This approach is known as *sealing* the object. To guarantee object integrity, apply a digital signature to the sealed object.

Sealing and signing objects is the preferred mechanism to secure data when

- serializing or transporting sensitive data.
- a secure communication channel such as SSL (Secure Sockets Layer) is absent or is too costly for limited transactions.
- sensitive data must persist over an extended period of time (for example, on a hard drive).

Avoid using home-brewed cryptographic algorithms; such algorithms will almost certainly introduce unnecessary vulnerabilities. Applications that apply home-brewed "cryptography" in the readObject() and writeObject() methods are prime examples of *anti-patterns*.

This rule applies to the intentional serialization of sensitive information. Rule SER03-J is meant to prevent the unintentional serialization of sensitive information.

Noncompliant Code Example

The code examples for this rule are all based on the following code example.

```
class SerializableMap<K,V> implements Serializable {
  final static long serialVersionUID = -2648720192864531932L;
  private Map<K,V> map;

  public SerializableMap() {
    map = new HashMap<K,V>();
  }

  public Object getData(K key)  {
    return map.get(key);
  }

  public void setData(K key, V data)  {
    map.put(key, data);
  }
}

public class MapSerializer {
  public static SerializableMap<String, Integer> buildMap() {
    SerializableMap<String, Integer> map =
        new SerializableMap<String, Integer>();
    map.setData("John Doe", new Integer(123456789));
    map.setData("Richard Roe", new Integer(246813579));
    return map;
  }

  public static void InspectMap(SerializableMap<String, Integer> map) {
    System.out.println("John Doe's number is " + map.getData("John Doe"));
    System.out.println("Richard Roe's number is " +
                       map.getData("Richard Roe"));
  }
```

```
public static void main(String[] args) {
  // ...
}
}
```

This code sample defines a serializable map, a method to populate the map with values, and a method to check the map for those values.

This noncompliant code example simply serializes then deserializes the map. Consequently, the map can be serialized and transferred across different business tiers. Unfortunately, the example lacks any safeguards against byte stream manipulation attacks while the binary data is in transit. Likewise, anyone can reverse-engineer the serialized stream data to recover the data in the HashMap.

```
public static void main(String[] args)
                    throws IOException, ClassNotFoundException {
  // Build map
  SerializableMap<String, Integer> map = buildMap();

  // Serialize map
  ObjectOutputStream out =
      new ObjectOutputStream(new FileOutputStream("data"));
  out.writeObject(map);
  out.close();

  // Deserialize map
  ObjectInputStream in =
      new ObjectInputStream(new FileInputStream("data"));
  map = (SerializableMap<String, Integer>) in.readObject();
  in.close();

  // Inspect map
  InspectMap(map);
}
```

If the data in the map were sensitive, this example would also violate rule SER03-J.

Noncompliant Code Example (Seal)

This noncompliant code example uses the javax.crypto.SealedObject class to provide message confidentiality. This class encapsulates a serialized object and encrypts (or seals) it. A strong cryptographic algorithm that uses a secure cryptographic key and padding scheme must be employed to initialize the Cipher object parameter. The seal() and unseal() utility methods provide the encryption and decryption facilities respectively.

This noncompliant code example encrypts the map into a `SealedObject`, rendering the data inaccessible to prying eyes. However, the program fails to sign the data, rendering it impossible to authenticate.

```
public static void main(String[] args)
                        throws IOException, GeneralSecurityException,
                               ClassNotFoundException {
  // Build map
  SerializableMap<String, Integer> map = buildMap();

  // Generate sealing key & seal map
  KeyGenerator generator;
  generator = KeyGenerator.getInstance("AES");
  generator.init(new SecureRandom());
  Key key = generator.generateKey();
  Cipher cipher = Cipher.getInstance("AES");
  cipher.init(Cipher.ENCRYPT_MODE, key);
  SealedObject sealedMap = new SealedObject(map, cipher);

  // Serialize map
  ObjectOutputStream out =
      new ObjectOutputStream(new FileOutputStream("data"));
  out.writeObject(sealedMap);
  out.close();

  // Deserialize map
  ObjectInputStream in =
      new ObjectInputStream(new FileInputStream("data"));
  sealedMap = (SealedObject) in.readObject();
  in.close();

  // Unseal map
  cipher = Cipher.getInstance("AES");
  cipher.init(Cipher.DECRYPT_MODE, key);
  map = (SerializableMap<String, Integer>) sealedMap.getObject(cipher);

  // Inspect map
  InspectMap(map);
}
```

Noncompliant Code Example (Seal Then Sign)

This noncompliant code example uses the `java.security.SignedObject` class to sign an object when the integrity of the object must be ensured. The two new arguments passed in to the `SignedObject()` method to sign the object are `Signature` and a private key derived from a KeyPair object. To verify the signature, a PublicKey as well as a Signature argument is passed to the SignedObject.verify() method.

This noncompliant code example signs the object as well as seals it. According to Abadi and Needham [Abadi 1996]:

> When a principal signs material that has already been encrypted, it should not be inferred that the principal knows the content of the message. On the other hand, it is proper to infer that the principal that signs a message and then encrypts it for privacy knows the content of the message.

Any malicious party can intercept the originally signed encrypted message from the originator, strip the signature, and add its own signature to the encrypted message. Both the malicious party and the receiver have no information about the contents of the original message as it is encrypted and then signed (it can be decrypted only after verifying the signature). The receiver has no way of confirming the sender's identity unless the legitimate sender's public key is obtained over a secure channel. One of the three Internal Telegraph and Telephone Consultative Committee (CCITT) X.509 standard protocols was susceptible to such an attack [CCITT 1988].

Because the signing occurs after the sealing, it cannot be assumed that the signer is the true originator of the object.

```
public static void main(String[] args)
                        throws IOException, GeneralSecurityException,
                               ClassNotFoundException {
    // Build map
    SerializableMap<String, Integer> map = buildMap();

    // Generate sealing key & seal map
    KeyGenerator generator;
    generator = KeyGenerator.getInstance("AES");
    generator.init(new SecureRandom());
    Key key = generator.generateKey();
    Cipher cipher = Cipher.getInstance("AES");
    cipher.init(Cipher.ENCRYPT_MODE, key);
    SealedObject sealedMap = new SealedObject(map, cipher);

    // Generate signing public/private key pair & sign map
    KeyPairGenerator kpg = KeyPairGenerator.getInstance("DSA");
    KeyPair kp = kpg.generateKeyPair();
    Signature sig = Signature.getInstance("SHA1withDSA");
    SignedObject signedMap =
        new SignedObject(sealedMap, kp.getPrivate(), sig);
```

```
    // Serialize map
    ObjectOutputStream out =
        new ObjectOutputStream(new FileOutputStream("data"));
    out.writeObject(signedMap);
    out.close();

    // Deserialize map
    ObjectInputStream in =
        new ObjectInputStream(new FileInputStream("data"));
    signedMap = (SignedObject) in.readObject();
    in.close();

    // Verify signature and retrieve map
    if (!signedMap.verify(kp.getPublic(), sig)) {
      throw new GeneralSecurityException("Map failed verification");
    }
    sealedMap = (SealedObject) signedMap.getObject();

    // Unseal map
    cipher = Cipher.getInstance("AES");
    cipher.init(Cipher.DECRYPT_MODE, key);
    map = (SerializableMap<String, Integer>) sealedMap.getObject(cipher);
    // Inspect map
    InspectMap(map);
}
```

Compliant Solution (Sign Then Seal)

This compliant solution correctly signs the object before sealing it. This provides a guarantee of authenticity to the object in addition to protection from man-in-the-middle attacks.

```
public static void main(String[] args)
                    throws IOException, GeneralSecurityException,
                        ClassNotFoundException {
    // Build map
    SerializableMap<String, Integer> map = buildMap();

    // Generate signing public/private key pair & sign map
    KeyPairGenerator kpg = KeyPairGenerator.getInstance("DSA");
    KeyPair kp = kpg.generateKeyPair();
    Signature sig = Signature.getInstance("SHA1withDSA");
    SignedObject signedMap = new SignedObject(map, kp.getPrivate(), sig);
```

```
// Generate sealing key & seal map
KeyGenerator generator;
generator = KeyGenerator.getInstance("AES");
generator.init(new SecureRandom());
Key key = generator.generateKey();
Cipher cipher = Cipher.getInstance("AES");
cipher.init(Cipher.ENCRYPT_MODE, key);
SealedObject sealedMap = new SealedObject(signedMap, cipher);

// Serialize map
ObjectOutputStream out =
    new ObjectOutputStream(new FileOutputStream("data"));
out.writeObject(sealedMap);
out.close();

// Deserialize map
ObjectInputStream in =
    new ObjectInputStream(new FileInputStream("data"));
sealedMap = (SealedObject) in.readObject();
in.close();

// Unseal map
cipher = Cipher.getInstance("AES");
cipher.init(Cipher.DECRYPT_MODE, key);
signedMap = (SignedObject) sealedMap.getObject(cipher);

// Verify signature and retrieve map
if (!signedMap.verify(kp.getPublic(), sig)) {
  throw new GeneralSecurityException("Map failed verification");
}
map = (SerializableMap<String, Integer>) signedMap.getObject();

// Inspect map
InspectMap(map);
}
```

Exceptions

SER02-EX0: A reasonable use for signing a sealed object is to certify the authenticity of a sealed object passed from elsewhere. This represents a commitment *about the sealed object itself* rather than about its content [Abadi 1996].

SER02-EX1: Signing and sealing is required only for objects that must cross a trust boundary. Objects that never leave the trust boundary need not be signed or sealed. For instance, when an entire network is contained within a trust boundary, objects that never leave that network need not be signed or sealed.

Risk Assessment

Failure to sign and then seal objects during transit can lead to loss of object integrity or confidentiality.

Rule	Severity	Likelihood	Remediation Cost	Priority	Level
SER02-J	medium	probable	high	P4	L3

Automated Detection   This rule is not amenable to static analysis in the general case.

Related Guidelines

MITRE CWE   CWE-319. Cleartext transmission of sensitive information

Bibliography

[API 2006]

[Gong 2003]   9.10, Sealing Objects

[Harold 1999]   Chapter 11, Object serialization, sealed objects

[Neward 2004]   Item 64. Use `SignedObject` to provide integrity of serialized objects

Item 65. Use `SealedObject` to provide confidentiality of serializable objects

[Steel 2005]   Chapter 10, Securing the Business Tier, Obfuscated Transfer Object

■ SER03-J. Do not serialize unencrypted, sensitive data

While serialization allows an object's state to be saved as a sequence of bytes and then reconstituted at a later time, it provides no mechanism to protect the serialized data. An attacker who gains access to the serialized data can use it to discover sensitive information and to determine implementation details of the objects. An attacker can also modify the serialized data in an attempt to compromise the system when the malicious data is deserialized. Consequently, sensitive data that is serialized is potentially exposed, without regard to the access qualifiers (such as the `private` keyword) that were used in the original code. Moreover, the security manager cannot guarantee the integrity of the deserialized data.

Examples of sensitive data that should never be serialized include cryptographic keys, digital certificates, and classes that may hold references to sensitive data at the time of serialization.

This rule is meant to prevent the unintentional serialization of sensitive information. Rule SER02-J applies to the intentional serialization of sensitive information.

Noncompliant Code Example

The data members of class `Point` are private. Assuming the coordinates are sensitive, their presence in the data stream would expose them to malicious tampering.

```java
public class Point {
  private double x;
  private double y;

  public Point(double x, double y) {
    this.x = x;
    this.y = y;
  }

  public Point() {
    // no-argument constructor
  }
}

public class Coordinates extends Point implements Serializable {
  public static void main(String[] args) {
    FileOutputStream fout = null;
    try {
      Point p = new Point(5, 2);
      fout = new FileOutputStream("point.ser");
      ObjectOutputStream oout = new ObjectOutputStream(fout);
      oout.writeObject(p);
    } catch (Throwable t) {
      // Forward to handler
    } finally {
      if (fout != null) {
        try {
          fout.close();
        } catch (IOException x) {
          // handle error
        }
      }
    }
  }
}
```

In the absence of sensitive data, classes can be serialized by simply implementing the `java.io.Serializable` interface. By doing so, the class indicates that no security issues may result from the object's serialization. Note that any derived subclasses also inherit this interface and are consequently serializable. This approach is inappropriate for any class that contains sensitive data.

Compliant Solution

When serializing a class that contains sensitive data, programs must ensure that sensitive data is omitted from the serialized form. This includes suppressing both serialization of data members that contain sensitive data and serialization of references to nonserializable or sensitive objects.

This compliant solution both avoids the possibility of incorrect serialization and protects sensitive data members from accidental serialization by declaring the relevant members as transient so that they are omitted from the list of fields to be serialized by the default serialization mechanism.

```java
public class Point {
  private transient double x; // declared transient
  private transient double y; // declared transient
  public Point(double x, double y) {
    this.x = x;
    this.y = y;
  }
  public Point() {
    // no-argument constructor
  }
}

public class Coordinates extends Point implements Serializable {
  public static void main(String[] args) {
    try {
      Point p = new Point(5,2);
      FileOutputStream fout = new FileOutputStream("point.ser");
      ObjectOutputStream oout = new ObjectOutputStream(fout);
      oout.writeObject(p);
      oout.close();
    } catch (Exception e) {
      // Forward to handler
    } finally {
      if (fout != null) {
        try {
          fout.close();
        } catch (IOException x) {
          // handle error
        }
      }
    }
  }
}
```

Other compliant solutions include:

■ developing custom implementations of the `writeObject()`, `writeReplace()`, and `writeExternal()` methods that prevent sensitive fields from being written to the serialized stream.

■ defining the `serialPersistentFields` array field and ensuring that sensitive fields are omitted from the array. (See rule SER00-J.)

Noncompliant Code Example

Serialization can be used maliciously, for example, to return multiple instances of a single-ton class object. In this noncompliant code example (based on [Bloch 2005a]), a subclass `SensitiveClass` inadvertently becomes serializable because it extends the `java.lang.Number` class, which implements `Serializable`.

```java
public class SensitiveClass extends Number {
  // ..implement abstract methods, such as Number.doubleValue()...

  private static final SensitiveClass INSTANCE = new SensitiveClass();
  public static SensitiveClass getInstance() {
    return INSTANCE;
  }

  private SensitiveClass() {
    // Perform security checks and parameter validation
  }

  protected int getBalance() {
    int balance = 1000;
    return balance;
  }
}

class Malicious {
  public static void main(String[] args) {
    SensitiveClass sc =
        (SensitiveClass) deepCopy(SensitiveClass.getInstance());
    // Prints false; indicates new instance
    System.out.println(sc == SensitiveClass.getInstance());
    System.out.println("Balance = " + sc.getBalance());
  }

  // This method should not be used in production code
  static public Object deepCopy(Object obj) {
```

```
   try {
     ByteArrayOutputStream bos = new ByteArrayOutputStream();
     new ObjectOutputStream(bos).writeObject(obj);
     ByteArrayInputStream bin =
         new ByteArrayInputStream(bos.toByteArray());
     return new ObjectInputStream(bin).readObject();
   } catch (Exception e) {
     throw new IllegalArgumentException(e);
   }
  }
}
```

See rule MSC07-J for more information about singleton classes.

Compliant Solution

Extending a class or interface that implements Serializable should be avoided whenever possible. When extension of such a class is necessary, inappropriate serialization of the subclass can be prohibited by throwing NotSerializableException from a custom writeObject() or readResolve() method, defined in the subclass SensitiveClass. Note that the custom writeObject() or readResolve() methods must be declared final to prevent a malicious subclass from overriding them.

```
class SensitiveClass extends Number {
  // ...

  private final Object readResolve() throws NotSerializableException {
    throw new NotSerializableException();
  }
}
```

Exceptions

SER03-EX0: Sensitive data that has been properly encrypted may be serialized.

Risk Assessment

If sensitive data can be serialized, it may be transmitted over an insecure connection, stored in an insecure location, or disclosed inappropriately.

Rule	Severity	Likelihood	Remediation Cost	Priority	Level
SER03-J	medium	likely	high	P6	L2

Related Guidelines

MITRE CWE

CWE-499. Serializable class containing sensitive data

CWE-502. Deserialization of untrusted data

Secure Coding Guidelines for the Java Programming Language, Version 3.0

Guideline 5-2. Guard sensitive data during serialization

Bibliography

[Bloch 2005a]   Puzzle 83. Dyslexic monotheism
[Bloch 2001]   Item 1. Enforce the singleton property with a private constructor
[Greanier 2000]   Discover the Secrets of the Java Serialization API
[Harold 1999]
[JLS 2005]   Transient Modifier
[Long 2005]   Section 2.4, Serialization
[Sun 2006]   Serialization Specification, A.4, Preventing Serialization of Sensitive Data

■ SER04-J. Do not allow serialization and deserialization to bypass the security manager

Serialization and deserialization features can be exploited to bypass security manager checks. A serializable class may contain security manager checks in its constructors for various reasons, including preventing untrusted code from modifying the internal state of the class. Such security manager checks must be replicated anywhere a class instance can be constructed. For example, if a class enables a caller to retrieve sensitive internal state contingent upon security checks, those checks must be replicated during deserialization. This ensures that an attacker cannot extract sensitive information by deserializing the object.

Noncompliant Code Example

In this noncompliant code example, security manager checks are used within the constructor but are omitted from the `writeObject()` and `readObject()` methods that are used in the serialization-deserialization process. This omission allows untrusted code to maliciously create instances of the class.

```
public final class Hometown implements Serializable {
  // Private internal state
  private String town;
  private static final String UNKNOWN = "UNKNOWN";
```

```
void performSecurityManagerCheck() throws AccessDeniedException {
  // ...
}

void validateInput(String newCC) throws InvalidInputException {
  // ...
}

public Hometown() {
  performSecurityManagerCheck();

  // Initialize town to default value
  town = UNKNOWN;
}

// Allows callers to retrieve internal state
String getValue() {
  performSecurityManagerCheck();
  return town;
}

// Allows callers to modify (private) internal state
public void changeTown(String newTown) {
  if (town.equals(newTown)) {
    // No change
    return;
  } else {
    performSecurityManagerCheck();
    validateInput(newTown);
    town = newTown;
  }
}

private void writeObject(ObjectOutputStream out) throws IOException {
  out.writeObject(town);
}

private void readObject(ObjectInputStream in) throws IOException {
  in.defaultReadObject();
  // If the deserialized name does not match
  // the default value normally
  // created at construction time, duplicate the checks
  if (!UNKNOWN.equals(town)) {
    validateInput(town);
  }
}
}
```

Despite the security manager checks, the data in this example is not sensitive. Serializing unencrypted, sensitive data violates rule SER03-J.

`AccessDeniedException` and `InvalidInputException` are both security exceptions that can be thrown by any method without requiring a `throws` declaration.

Compliant Solution

This compliant solution implements the required security manager checks in all constructors and methods that can either modify or retrieve internal state. Consequently, an attacker cannot create a modified instance of the object (using deserialization) or read the serialized byte stream to reveal serialized data.

```
public final class Hometown implements Serializable {
  // ... all methods the same except the following:

  // writeObject() correctly enforces checks during serialization
  private void writeObject(ObjectOutputStream out) throws IOException {
    performSecurityManagerCheck();
    out.writeObject(town);
  }

  // readObject() correctly enforces checks during deserialization
  private void readObject(ObjectInputStream in) throws IOException {
    in.defaultReadObject();
    // If the deserialized name does not match
    // the default value normally
    // created at construction time, duplicate the checks
    if (!UNKNOWN.equals(town)) {
      performSecurityManagerCheck();
      validateInput(town);
    }
  }
}
```

Refer to rule SEC04-J for information about implementing the `performSecurityManagerCheck()` method, which is important for protection against finalizer attacks.

The `ObjectInputStream.defaultReadObject()` fills the object's fields with data from the input stream. Because each field is deserialized recursively, it is possible for the `this` reference to escape from control of the deserialization routines. This can happen if a referenced object publishes the `this` reference in its constructors or field initializers. See rule TSM01-J for more information. To be compliant, recursively deserialized subobjects must not publish the `this` object reference.

Risk Assessment

Allowing serialization or deserialization to bypass the security manager may result in classes being constructed without required security checks.

Rule	Severity	Likelihood	Remediation Cost	Priority	Level
SER04-J	high	probable	high	P6	L2

Related Guidelines

Secure Coding Guidelines for the Java Programming Language, Version 3.0	Guideline 5-4. Duplicate the `SecurityManager` checks enforced in a class during serialization and deserialization

Bibliography

[Long 2005]   Section 2.4, Serialization

■ SER05-J. Do not serialize instances of inner classes

"An inner class is a nested class that is not explicitly or implicitly declared static" [JLS 2005]. Serialization of inner classes (including local and anonymous classes) is error prone. According to the Serialization Specification [Sun 2006]:

- Serializing an inner class declared in a non-static context that contains implicit non-transient references to enclosing class instances results in serialization of its associated outer class instance.

- Synthetic fields generated by Java compilers to implement inner classes are implementation dependent and may vary between compilers; differences in such fields can disrupt compatibility as well as result in conflicting default `serialVersionUID` values. The names assigned to local and anonymous inner classes are also implementation dependent and may differ between compilers.

- Because inner classes cannot declare static members other than compile-time constant fields, they cannot use the `serialPersistentFields` mechanism to designate serializable fields.

- Because inner classes associated with outer instances do not have zero-argument constructors (constructors of such inner classes implicitly accept the enclosing instance as a prepended parameter), they cannot implement `Externalizable`. The `Externalizable` interface requires the implementing object to manually save and restore its state using the `writeExternal()` and `readExternal()` methods.

Consequently, programs must not serialize inner classes.

Because none of these issues apply to static member classes, serialization of static member classes is permitted.

Noncompliant Code Example

In this noncompliant code example, the fields contained within the outer class are serialized when the inner class is serialized.

```
public class OuterSer implements Serializable {
  private int rank;
  class InnerSer implements Serializable {
    protected String name;
    //...
  }
}
```

Compliant Solution

The `InnerSer` class of this compliant solution deliberately fails to implement the `Serializable` interface.

```
public class OuterSer implements Serializable {
  private int rank;
  class InnerSer {
    protected String name;
    //...
  }
}
```

Compliant Solution

The inner class may be declared static to prevent its serialization. A static inner class may also implement `Serializable`.

```
public class OuterSer implements Serializable {
  private int rank;
  static class InnerSer implements Serializable {
    protected String name;
    //...
  }
}
```

Risk Assessment

Serialization of inner classes can introduce platform dependencies and can cause serialization of instances of the outer class.

Rule	Severity	Likelihood	Remediation Cost	Priority	Level
SER05-J	medium	likely	medium	P12	L1

■ SER06-J. Make defensive copies of private mutable components during deserialization

Every serializable class that has private mutable instance variables must defensively copy them in the `readObject()` method. An attacker can tamper with the serialized form of such a class, appending extra references to the byte stream. When deserialized, this byte stream could allow the creation of a class instance whose internal variable references are controlled by the attacker. Consequently, the class instance can mutate and violate its class invariants.

This rule is an instance of rule OBJ06-J, which applies to constructors and to other methods that accept untrusted mutable arguments. This rule applies the same principle to deserialized mutable fields.

Noncompliant Code Example

This noncompliant code example fails to defensively copy the mutable `Date` object `date`. An attacker might be able to create an instance of `MutableSer` whose `date` object contains a nefarious subclass of `Date` and whose methods can perform actions specified by an attacker. Any code that depends on the immutability of the subobject is vulnerable.

```
class MutableSer implements Serializable {
  private static final Date epoch = new Date(0);
  private Date date = null; // Mutable component

  public MutableSer(Date d){
    // Constructor performs defensive copying
    date = new Date(d.getTime());
  }

  private void readObject(ObjectInputStream ois)
      throws IOException, ClassNotFoundException {
    ois.defaultReadObject();
    // Perform validation if necessary
  }
}
```

Compliant Solution

This compliant solution creates a defensive copy of the mutable `Date` object `date` in the `readObject()` method. Note the use of field-by-field input and validation of incoming fields. Additionally, note that this compliant solution is insufficient to protect sensitive data (see rule SER03-J for additional information).

```
private void readObject(ObjectInputStream ois)
  throws IOException, ClassNotFoundException {
  ObjectInputStream.GetField fields = ois.readFields();
  Date inDate = (Date) fields.getField("date", epoch);
  // Defensively copy the mutable component
  date = new Date(inDate.getTime());
  // Perform validation if necessary
}
```

There is no need to copy immutable subobjects. Also, avoid using the subobject's `clone()` method because it can be overridden when the subobject's class is not final and produces only a shallow copy. The references to the subobjects themselves must be nonfinal so that defensive copying can occur. It is also inadvisable to use the `writeUnshared()` and `readUnshared()` methods as an alternative [Bloch 2008].

Risk Assessment

Failure to defensively copy mutable components during deserialization can violate the immutability contract of an object.

Rule	Severity	Likelihood	Remediation Cost	Priority	Level
SER06-J	low	probable	medium	P4	L3

Related Guidelines

MITRE CWE   CWE-502. Deserialization of untrusted data

Bibliography

[API 2006]

[Bloch 2008]   Item 76. Write `readObject` methods defensively

[Sun 2006]   Serialization Specification, A.6, Guarding Unshared Deserialized Objects

■ SER07-J. Do not use the default serialized form for implementation-defined invariants

Serialization can be used maliciously, for example, to violate the intended invariants of a class. Deserialization is equivalent to object construction; consequently, all invariants enforced during object construction must also be enforced during deserialization. The default serialized form lacks any enforcement of class invariants; consequently, programs must not use the default serialized form for any class with implementation-defined invariants.

The deserialization process creates a new instance of the class without invoking any of the class's constructors. Consequently, any input validation checks in constructors are bypassed. Moreover, transient and static fields may fail to reflect their true values because such fields are bypassed during the serialization procedure and consequently cannot be restored from the object stream. As a result, any class that has transient fields or that performs validation checks in its constructors must also perform similar validation checks when being deserialized.

Validating deserialized objects establishes that the object state is within defined limits and ensures that all transient and static fields have their default *secure* values. However, fields that are declared final and contain a constant value will contain the proper value rather than the default value after deserialization. For example, the value of the field `private transient final n = 42` will be 42 after deserialization rather than 0. Deserialization produces default values for all other cases.

Noncompliant Code Example (Singleton)

In this noncompliant code example [Bloch 2005a], a class with singleton semantics uses the default serialized form, which fails to enforce any implementation-defined invariants. Consequently, malicious code can create a second instance even though the class should have only a single instance. For purposes of this example, we assume that the class contains only nonsensitive data.

```
public class NumberData extends Number {
  // ...implement abstract Number methods, like Number.doubleValue()...

  private static final NumberData INSTANCE = new NumberData ();
  public static NumberData getInstance() {
    return INSTANCE;
  }
}
```

```
   private NumberData() {
     // Perform security checks and parameter validation
   }

   protected int printData() {
     int data = 1000;
     // print data
     return data;
   }
 }

class Malicious {
  public static void main(String[] args) {
    NumberData sc = (NumberData) deepCopy(NumberData.getInstance());
    // Prints false; indicates new instance
    System.out.println(sc == NumberData.getInstance());
    System.out.println("Balance = " + sc.printData());
  }

  // This method should not be used in production code
  public static Object deepCopy(Object obj) {
    try {
      ByteArrayOutputStream bos = new ByteArrayOutputStream();
      new ObjectOutputStream(bos).writeObject(obj);
      ByteArrayInputStream bin =
          new ByteArrayInputStream(bos.toByteArray());
      return new ObjectInputStream(bin).readObject();
    } catch (Exception e) {
      throw new IllegalArgumentException(e);
    }
  }
}
```

Compliant Solution

This compliant solution uses an `enum` and adds a custom `readResolve()` method that replaces the deserialized instance with a reference to the appropriate singleton from the current execution. More complicated cases may also require custom `writeObject()` or `readObject()` methods in addition to (or instead of) the custom `readResolve()` method.

```
public enum NumberEnum {
  INSTANCE;
  NumberData number = new NumberData();
  // ...
```

```
    protected final Object readResolve() throws NotSerializableException {
      return INSTANCE;
    }
  }

  public class NumberData extends Number {
    // ...
  }
```

This compliant solution uses composition rather than extension of the Number class. More information on singleton classes is available in rule MSC07-J.

Noncompliant Code Example

This noncompliant code example uses a custom-defined readObject() method but fails to perform input validation after deserialization. The design of the system requires the maximum ticket number of any lottery ticket to be 20,000. However, an attacker can manipulate the serialized array to generate a different number on deserialization.

```
public class Lottery implements Serializable {
  private int ticket = 1;
  private SecureRandom draw = new SecureRandom();

  public Lottery(int ticket) {
    this.ticket = (int) (Math.abs(ticket % 20000) + 1);
  }

  public int getTicket() {
    return this.ticket;
  }

  public int roll() {
    this.ticket = (int) ((Math.abs(draw.nextInt()) % 20000) + 1);
    return this.ticket;
  }

  public static void main(String[] args) {
    Lottery l = new Lottery(2);
    for (int i = 0; i < 10; i++) {
      l.roll();
      System.out.println(l.getTicket());
    }
  }
}
```

```
    private void readObject(ObjectInputStream in)
      throws IOException, ClassNotFoundException {
      in.defaultReadObject();
    }
  }
```

Compliant Solution

Any input validation performed in the constructors must also be implemented wherever an object can be deserialized. This compliant solution performs field-by-field validation by reading all fields of the object using the `readFields()` method and `ObjectInputStream.GetField()` constructor. The value for each field must be fully validated *before* it is assigned to the object under construction. For more complicated invariants, this may require reading multiple field values into local variables to enable checks that depend on combinations of field values.

```
  public final class Lottery implements Serializable {
    // ...
    private synchronized void readObject(java.io.ObjectInputStream s)
                        throws IOException, ClassNotFoundException {
      ObjectInputStream.GetField fields = s.readFields();
      int ticket = fields.get("ticket", 0);
      if (ticket > 20000 || ticket <= 0) {
        throw new InvalidObjectException("Not in range!");
      }
      // Validate draw
      this.ticket = ticket;
    }
  }
```

Note that the class must be declared final to prevent a malicious subclass from carrying out a finalizer attack. (See rule OBJ11-J for information about finalizer attacks.) For extendable classes, an acceptable alternative is to use a flag that indicates whether the instance is safe for use. The flag can be set after validation and must be checked in every method before any operation is performed. Additionally, any transient or static fields must be explicitly set to an appropriate value within `readObject()`.

Note that this compliant solution is insufficient to protect sensitive data. See rule SER03-J for additional information.

Compliant Solution (Transient)

This compliant solution marks the fields as transient, so they are not serialized. The read-Object() method initializes them using the roll() method. This class need not be final, as its fields are private and cannot be tampered with by subclasses.

```java
public class Lottery implements Serializable {
  private transient int ticket = 1;
  private transient SecureRandom draw = new SecureRandom();

  public Lottery(int ticket) {
    this.ticket = (int) (Math.abs(ticket % 20000) + 1);
  }

  public int getTicket() {
    return this.ticket;
  }

  public int roll() {
    this.ticket = (int) ((Math.abs(draw.nextInt()) % 20000) + 1);
    return this.ticket;
  }

  public static void main(String[] args) {
    Lottery l = new Lottery(2);
    for (int i = 0; i < 10; i++) {
      l.roll();
      System.out.println(l.getTicket());
    }
  }

  private void readObject(ObjectInputStream in)
          throws IOException, ClassNotFoundException {
    in.defaultReadObject();
    this.draw = new SecureRandom();
    roll();
  }
}
```

Compliant Solution (Nonserializable)

This compliant solution simply does not mark the Lottery class serializable.

```
public final class Lottery {
  // ...
}
```

Risk Assessment

Using the default serialized form for any class with implementation-defined invariants may result in the malicious tampering of class invariants.

Rule	Severity	Likelihood	Remediation Cost	Priority	Level
SER07-J	medium	probable	high	P4	L3

Related Guidelines

MITRE CWE	CWE-502. Deserialization of untrusted data
Secure Coding Guidelines for the Java Programming Language, Version 3.0	Guideline 5-3. View deserialization the same as object construction

Bibliography

[API 2006]	Class `Object`, Class `Hashtable`
[Bloch 2008]	Item 75. Consider using a custom serialized form
[Greanier 2000]	
[Harold 1999]	Chapter 11, Object Serialization, Validation
[Hawtin 2008]	Antipattern 8. Believing deserialisation is unrelated to construction

■ SER08-J. Minimize privileges before deserializing from a privileged context

Unrestricted deserializing from a privileged context allows an attacker to supply crafted input which, upon deserialization, can yield objects that the attacker would otherwise lack permissions to construct. One example is the construction of a sensitive object such as a custom class loader. Consequently, avoid deserializing from a privileged context. When deserializing requires privileges, programs must strip all permissions other than the minimum set required for the intended usage.

Noncompliant Code Example (CVE-2008-5353: ZoneInfo)

CVE-2008-5353 describes a Java vulnerability discovered in August 2008 by Sami Koivu [CVE 2011]. Julien Tinnes subsequently wrote an exploit that allowed arbitrary code execution on multiple platforms running vulnerable versions of Java. The problem resulted from deserializing untrusted input from within a privileged context. The vulnerability involves the `sun.util.Calendar.ZoneInfo` class, which, being serializable, is deserialized by the `readObject()` method of the `ObjectInputStream` class.

The default security model of an applet does not allow access to `sun.util.calendar.ZoneInfo` because applets cannot be permitted to invoke any method from any class within the `sun` package. As a result, prior to JDK 1.6 u11, the acceptable method for an unsigned applet to deserialize a `ZoneInfo` object was to execute the call from a privileged context, such as a `doPrivileged()` block. This constitutes a vulnerability because there is no guaranteed method of knowing whether the serialized stream contains a bona fide `ZoneInfo` object rather than a malicious serializable class. The vulnerable code casts the malicious object to the `ZoneInfo` type, which typically causes a `ClassCastException` if the actual deserialized class is not a `ZoneInfo` object. This exception, however, is of little consequence because it is possible to store a reference to the newly created object in a static context so that the garbage collector cannot act upon it.

A nonserializable class can be extended and its subclass can be made serializable. Also, a subclass automatically becomes serializable if it derives from a serializable class. During deserialization of the subclass, the JVM calls the no-argument constructor of the most derived superclass that *does not* implement `java.io.Serializable` either directly or indirectly. This allows it to fix the state of this superclass. In the following code snippet, class A's no-argument constructor is called when C is deserialized because A does not implement `Serializable`. Subsequently, `Object`'s constructor is invoked. This procedure cannot be carried out programmatically, so the JVM generates the equivalent bytecode at runtime. Typically, when the superclass's constructor is called by a subclass, the subclass remains on the stack. However, in deserialization this does not happen. Only the unvalidated bytecode is present. This allows any security checks within the superclass's constructor to be bypassed in that the complete execution chain is not scrutinized.

```
class A { // has Object as superclass
  A(int x) { }
  A() { }
}

class B extends A implements Serializable {
  B(int x) { super(x); }
}

class C extends class B {
  C(int x) { super(x); }
}
```

At this point, there is no subclass code on the stack and the superclass's constructor is executed with no restrictions because `doPrivileged()` allows the immediate caller to exert its full privileges. Because the immediate caller java.util.Calendar is trusted, it exhibits full system privileges.

A custom class loader can be used to exploit this vulnerability. Instantiating a class loader object requires special permissions that are made available by the security policy that is enforced by the SecurityManager. An unsigned applet cannot carry out this step by default. However, if an unsigned applet can execute a custom class loader's constructor, it can effectively bypass all the security checks (it has the requisite privileges as a direct consequence of the vulnerability). A custom class loader can be designed to extend the system class loader, undermine security, and carry out prohibited actions such as reading or deleting files on the user's file system. Moreover, legitimate security checks in the constructor are meaningless because the code is granted all privileges. The following noncompliant code example illustrates the vulnerability.

```
try {
  ZoneInfo zi = (ZoneInfo) AccessController.doPrivileged(
    new PrivilegedExceptionAction() {
      public Object run() throws Exception {
        return input.readObject();
      }
  });
  if (zi != null) {
    zone = zi;
  }
} catch (Exception e)
{
  // handle error
}
```

Compliant Solution (CVE-2008-5353: Zoneinfo)

This vulnerability was fixed in JDK v1.6 u11 by defining a new AccessControlContext INSTANCE, with a new ProtectionDomain. The ProtectionDomain encapsulated a RuntimePermission called accessClassInPackage.sun.util.calendar. Consequently, the code was granted the minimal set of permissions required to access the sun.util.calendar class. This whitelisting approach guaranteed that a security exception would be thrown in all other cases of invalid access. The code also uses the two-argument form of doPrivileged(), which strips all permissions other than the ones specified in the ProtectionDomain.

```
private static class CalendarAccessControlContext {
  private static final AccessControlContext INSTANCE;
    static {
```

```
      RuntimePermission perm =
          new RuntimePermission("accessClassInPackage.sun.util.
                             calendar");
      PermissionCollection perms = perm.newPermissionCollection();
      perms.add(perm);
      INSTANCE = new AccessControlContext(new ProtectionDomain[] {
          new ProtectionDomain(null, perms)
      });
    }
  }

// ...
try {
  zi = AccessController.doPrivileged(
      new PrivilegedExceptionAction<ZoneInfo>() {
        public ZoneInfo run() throws Exception {
          return (ZoneInfo) input.readObject();
        }
      }, CalendarAccessControlContext.INSTANCE);
} catch (PrivilegedActionException pae) { /* ... */ }
if (zi != null) {
  zone = zi;
}
```

Risk Assessment

Deserializing objects from an unrestricted privileged context can result in arbitrary code execution.

Rule	Severity	Likelihood	Remediation Cost	Priority	Level
SER08-J	high	likely	medium	P18	L1

Related Guidelines

MITRE CWE   CWE-250. Execution with unnecessary privileges

Bibliography

[API 2006]

[CVE 2011]   CVE-2008-5353

■ SER09-J. Do not invoke overridable methods from the `readObject()` method

Invoking overridable methods from the `readObject()` method can allow the overriding method to read the state of the subclass before it is fully constructed because the base class is deserialized first, followed by the subclass. As a result, `readObject()` must not call any overridable methods.

Also see the related rule MET06-J.

Noncompliant Code Example

This noncompliant code example invokes an overridable method from the `readObject()` method.

```
private void readObject(final ObjectInputStream stream)
                    throws IOException, ClassNotFoundException {
  overridableMethod();
  stream.defaultReadObject();
}

public void overridableMethod() {
  // ...
}
```

Compliant Solution

This compliant solution removes the call to the overridable method. When removing such calls is infeasible, declare the method private or final.

```
private void readObject(final ObjectInputStream stream)
                    throws IOException, ClassNotFoundException {
  stream.defaultReadObject();
}
```

Exceptions

SER09-EX0: The `readObject()` method may invoke the overridable methods `default-ReadObject()` and `readFields()` in class `java.io.ObjectInputStream` [SCG 2009].

Risk Assessment

Invoking overridable methods from the `readObject()` method can lead to initialization errors.

Rule	Severity	Likelihood	Remediation Cost	Priority	Level
SER09-J	low	probable	medium	P4	L3

Related Guidelines

Secure Coding Guidelines for the Java Programming Language, Version 3.0

Guideline 4-4. Prevent constructors from calling methods that can be overridden

Bibliography

[API 2006]

[Bloch 2008]   Item 17. Design and document for inheritance or else prohibit it

■ SER10-J. Avoid memory and resource leaks during serialization

Serialization can extend the lifetime of objects, preventing their garbage collection. The `ObjectOutputStream` ensures that each object is written to the stream only once by retaining a reference (or handle) to each object written to the stream. When a previously written object is subsequently written to the stream again, it is replaced with a reference to the originally written data in the stream. Note that this substitution takes place without regard to whether the object's *contents* have changed in the interim. This requires a table of references to be maintained to keep track of previously serialized objects. This table of references prevents garbage collection of the previously serialized objects because the garbage collector cannot collect object instances referred to by live references.

This behavior is both desirable and correct for data that may contain arbitrary object graphs, especially when the graphs are fully allocated and constructed prior to serialization. However, it can lead to memory exhaustion when serializing data that lacks references to other objects being serialized and can be allocated in part or in full after serialization has begun. One such example is serializing a data stream from an external sensor. In such cases, programs must take additional action to avoid memory exhaustion. That is, programs reading in independent serialized data must reset the table of references between reads to prevent memory exhaustion.

This rule is a specific instance of the more general rule MSC05-J.

Noncompliant Code Example

This noncompliant code example reads and serializes data from an external sensor. Each invocation of the readSensorData() method returns a newly created SensorData instance, each containing one megabyte of data. SensorData instances are pure data streams, containing data and arrays but lacking references to other SensorData objects.

As already described, the ObjectOutputStream maintains a cache of previously written objects. Consequently, all SensorData objects remain alive until the cache itself becomes garbage-collected. This can result in an OutOfMemoryError because the stream remains open while new objects are being written to it.

```java
class SensorData implements Serializable {
  // 1 MB of data per instance!
  ...
  public static SensorData readSensorData() {...}
  public static boolean isAvailable() {...}
}

class SerializeSensorData {
  public static void main(String[] args) throws IOException {
    ObjectOutputStream out = null;
    try {
      out = new ObjectOutputStream(
          new BufferedOutputStream(new FileOutputStream("ser.dat")));
      while (SensorData.isAvailable()) {
        // note that each SensorData object is 1 MB in size
        SensorData sd = SensorData.readSensorData();
        out.writeObject(sd);
      }
    } finally {
      if (out != null) {
        out.close();
      }
    }
  }
}
```

Compliant Solution

This compliant solution takes advantage of the known properties of the sensor data by resetting the output stream after each write. The reset clears the output stream's internal object cache; consequently, the cache no longer maintains references to previously written Sensor-Data objects. The garbage collector can collect SensorData instances that are no longer needed.

```
class SerializeSensorData {
  public static void main(String[] args) throws IOException {
    ObjectOutputStream out = null;
    try {
      out = new ObjectOutputStream(
          new BufferedOutputStream(new FileOutputStream("ser.dat")));
      while (SensorData.isAvailable()) {
        // note that each SensorData object is 1 MB in size
        SensorData sd = SensorData.readSensorData();
        out.writeObject(sd);
        out.reset(); // reset the stream
      }
    } finally {
      if (out != null) {
        out.close();
      }
    }
  }
}
```

Risk Assessment

Memory and resource leaks during serialization can result in a resource exhaustion attack or crash the JVM.

Rule	Severity	Likelihood	Remediation Cost	Priority	Level
SER10-J	low	unlikely	low	P3	L3

Related Guidelines

MITRE CWE	CWE-400. Uncontrolled resource consumption (aka "resource exhaustion")
	CWE-770. Allocation of resources without limits or throttling

Bibliography

[API 2006]

[Harold 2006]   13.4, Performance

[Sun 2006]   Serialization Specification

■ SER11-J. Prevent overwriting of externalizable objects

Classes that implement the `Externalizable` interface must provide the `readExternal()` and `writeExternal()` methods. These methods have package-private or public access, and so they can be called by trusted and untrusted code alike. Consequently, programs must ensure that these methods execute only when intended and that they cannot overwrite the internal state of objects at arbitrary points during program execution.

Noncompliant Code Example

This noncompliant code example allows any caller to reset the value of the object at any time because the `readExternal()` method is necessarily declared to be public and lacks protection against hostile callers.

```
public void readExternal(ObjectInput in)
                         throws IOException, ClassNotFoundException {
  // Read instance fields
  this.name = (String) in.readObject();
  this.UID = in.readInt();
  //...
}
```

Compliant Solution

This compliant solution protects against multiple initialization through the use of a Boolean flag that is set after the instance fields have been populated. It also protects against race conditions by synchronizing on a private lock object (see rule LCK00-J).

```
private final Object lock = new Object();
private boolean initialized = false;

public void readExternal(ObjectInput in)
                         throws IOException, ClassNotFoundException {
  synchronized (lock) {
    if (!initialized) {
      // Read instance fields
      this.name = (String) in.readObject();
      this.UID = in.readInt();
      //...
      initialized = true;
    } else {
```

```
      throw new IllegalStateException();
    }
  }
}
```

Note that this compliant solution is inadequate to protect sensitive data.

Risk Assessment

Failure to prevent the overwriting of an externalizable object can corrupt the state of the object.

Rule	Severity	Likelihood	Remediation Cost	Priority	Level
SER11-J	low	probable	low	P6	L2

Bibliography

[API 2006]

[Sun 2006]   Serialization Specification, A.7, Preventing Overwriting of Externalizable Objects

Chapter 16

Platform Security (SEC)

■ Risk Assessment Summary

Rule	Severity	Likelihood	Remediation Cost	Priority	Level
SEC00-J	Medium	likely	high	P6	L2
SEC01-J	High	likely	low	P27	L1
SEC02-J	High	probable	medium	P12	L1
SEC03-J	High	probable	medium	P12	L1
SEC04-J	High	probable	medium	P12	L1
SEC05-J	High	probable	medium	P12	L1
SEC06-J	High	probable	medium	P12	L1
SEC07-J	High	probable	low	P18	L1
SEC08-J	Medium	probable	high	P4	L3

■ SEC00-J. Do not allow privileged blocks to leak sensitive information across a trust boundary

The `java.security.AccessController` class is part of Java's security mechanism; it is responsible for enforcing the applicable security policy. This class's static `doPrivileged()` method executes a code block with a relaxed security policy. The `doPrivileged()` method stops permissions from being checked further down the call chain. Consequently, any method that invokes `doPrivileged()` must assume responsibility for enforcing its own security on the code block supplied to `doPrivileged()`. Likewise, code in the `doPrivileged()` method must not leak sensitive information or capabilities.

For example, suppose that a web application must maintain a sensitive password file for a web service and also run untrusted code. The application could then enforce a security policy preventing the majority of its own code—as well as all untrusted code—from accessing the sensitive file. Because it must also provide mechanisms for adding and changing passwords, it can call the `doPrivileged()` method to temporarily allow untrusted code to access the sensitive file for the purpose of managing passwords. In this case, any privileged block must prevent any information about passwords from being accessible to untrusted code.

Noncompliant Code Example

In this noncompliant code example, the `doPrivileged()` method is called from the `open-PasswordFile()` method. The `openPasswordFile()` method is privileged and returns a

FileInputStream for the sensitive password file to its caller. Because the method is public, it could be invoked by an untrusted caller.

```java
public class PasswordManager {

  public static void changePassword() throws FileNotFoundException {
    FileInputStream fin = openPasswordFile();

    // test old password with password in file contents; change password
    // then close the password file

  }

  public static FileInputStream openPasswordFile()
      throws FileNotFoundException {
    final String password_file = "password";
    FileInputStream fin = null;
    try {
      fin = AccessController.doPrivileged(
        new PrivilegedExceptionAction<FileInputStream>() {
          public FileInputStream run() throws FileNotFoundException {
            // Sensitive action; can't be done outside privileged block
            FileInputStream in = new FileInputStream(password_file);
            return in;
          }
      });
    } catch (PrivilegedActionException x) {
      Exception cause = x.getException();
      if (cause instanceof FileNotFoundException) {
        throw (FileNotFoundException) cause;
      } else {
        throw new Error("Unexpected exception type", cause);
      }
    }
    return fin;
  }
}
```

Compliant Solution

In general, when any method containing a privileged block exposes a field (such as an object reference) beyond its own boundary, it becomes trivial for untrusted callers to exploit the program.

This compliant solution mitigates the vulnerability by declaring openPasswordFile() to be private. Consequently, an untrusted caller can call changePassword() but cannot directly invoke the openPasswordFile() method.

```
public class PasswordManager {
  public static void changePassword() throws FileNotFoundException {
    // ...
  }

  private static FileInputStream openPasswordFile()
      throws FileNotFoundException {
    // ...
  }
}
```

Compliant Solution (Hiding Exceptions)

Both the previous noncompliant code example and the previous compliant solution throw a `FileNotFoundException` when the password file is missing. If the existence of the password file is itself considered sensitive information, this exception must also not be allowed to leak outside the trusted code.

This compliant solution suppresses the exception, leaving the array to contain a single null value to indicate that the file does not exist. It uses the simpler `PrivilegedAction` class rather than `PrivilegedExceptionAction` to prevent exceptions from propagating out of the `doPrivileged()` block. The `Void` return type is recommended for privileged actions that do not return any value.

```
class PasswordManager {

  public static void changePassword() {
    FileInputStream fin = openPasswordFile();
    if (fin == null) {
      // no password file; handle error
    }

    // test old password with password in file contents; change password
  }

  private static FileInputStream openPasswordFile() {
    final String password_file = "password";
    final FileInputStream fin[] = { null };
    AccessController.doPrivileged(new PrivilegedAction<Void>() {
        public Void run() {
          try {
            // Sensitive action; can't be done outside
            // doPrivileged() block
```

```
            fin[0] = new FileInputStream(password_file);
        } catch (FileNotFoundException x) {
          // report to handler
        }
        return null;
      }
  });
  return fin[0];
  }
}
```

Risk Assessment

Returning references to sensitive resources from within a doPrivileged() block can break encapsulation and confinement and leak capabilities. Any caller who can invoke the privileged code directly and obtain a reference to a sensitive resource or field can maliciously modify its elements.

Rule	Severity	Likelihood	Remediation Cost	Priority	Level
SEC00-J	medium	likely	high	P6	L2

Automated Detection Identifying sensitive information requires assistance from the programmer; fully automated identification of sensitive information is beyond the current state of the art.

Assuming user-provided tagging of sensitive information, escape analysis could be performed on the doPrivileged() blocks to prove that nothing sensitive leaks out from them. Methods similar to those used in thread-role analysis could be used to identify the methods that must, or must not, be called from doPrivileged() blocks.

Related Guidelines

MITRE CWE	CWE-266. Incorrect privilege assignment
	CWE-272. Least privilege violation
Secure Coding Guidelines for the Java Programming Language, Version 3.0	Guideline 6-2. Safely invoke java.security.AccessController.doPrivileged()

Bibliography

[API 2006]   Method doPrivileged()

[Gong 2003]   Sections 6.4, AccessController, and 9.5, Privileged Code

■ SEC01-J. Do not allow tainted variables in privileged blocks

Do not operate on unvalidated or untrusted data (also known as *tainted* data) in a privileged block. An attacker can supply malicious input that could result in privilege escalation attacks. Appropriate mitigations include hard-coding values rather than accepting arguments (when appropriate) and validating or sanitizing data before performing privileged operations (see rule IDS00-J).

Noncompliant Code Example

This noncompliant code example accepts a tainted path or file name as an argument. An attacker can access a protected file by supplying its path name as an argument to this method.

```
private void privilegedMethod(final String filename)
                              throws FileNotFoundException {
  try {
    FileInputStream fis =
      (FileInputStream) AccessController.doPrivileged(
        new PrivilegedExceptionAction() {
        public FileInputStream run() throws FileNotFoundException {
          return new FileInputStream(filename);
        }
      }
    );
    // do something with the file and then close it
  } catch (PrivilegedActionException e) {
    // forward to handler
  }
}
```

Compliant Solution (Input Validation)

This compliant solution invokes the `cleanAFilenameAndPath()` method to sanitize malicious inputs. Successful completion of the sanitization method indicates that the input is acceptable and the `doPrivileged()` block can be executed.

```
private void privilegedMethod(final String filename)
                              throws FileNotFoundException {
  final String cleanFilename;
  try {
    cleanFilename = cleanAFilenameAndPath(filename);
```

```
    } catch (/* exception as per spec of cleanAFileNameAndPath */) {
      // log or forward to handler as appropriate based on specification
      // of cleanAFilenameAndPath
    }
    try {
      FileInputStream fis =
          (FileInputStream) AccessController.doPrivileged(
            new PrivilegedExceptionAction() {
            public FileInputStream run() throws FileNotFoundException {
              return new FileInputStream(cleanFilename);
            }
          }
      );
      // do something with the file and then close it
    } catch (PrivilegedActionException e) {
      // forward to handler
    }
  }
}
```

One potential drawback of this approach is that effective sanitization methods can be difficult to write. A benefit of this approach is that it works well in combination with *taint analysis* (see the Automated Detection section for this rule). For more information on how to perform secure file operations, see rule FIO00-J.

Compliant Solution (Built-in File Name and Path)

Sanitization of tainted inputs always carries the risk that the data is not fully sanitized. Both file and path name equivalence and directory traversal are common examples of vulnerabilities arising from the improper sanitization of path and file name inputs (see rule IDS02-J). A design that requires an unprivileged user to access an arbitrary, protected file (or other resource) is always suspect. Consider alternatives such as using a hard-coded resource name or permitting the user to select only from a list of options that are indirectly mapped to the resource names.

This compliant solution both explicitly hard-codes the name of the file and confines the variables used in the privileged block to the same method. This ensures that no malicious file can be loaded by exploiting the privileged method.

```
static final String FILEPATH = "/path/to/protected/file/fn.ext";

private void privilegedMethod() throws FileNotFoundException {
  try {
    FileInputStream fis =
```

```
        (FileInputStream) AccessController.doPrivileged(
          new PrivilegedExceptionAction() {
          public FileInputStream run() throws FileNotFoundException {
            return new FileInputStream(FILEPATH);
          }
        }
      );
      // do something with the file and then close it
    } catch (PrivilegedActionException e) {
      // forward to handler and log
    }
  }
```

Risk Assessment

Allowing tainted inputs in privileged operations can result in privilege escalation attacks.

Rule	Severity	Likelihood	Remediation Cost	Priority	Level
SEC01-J	high	likely	low	P27	L1

Automated Detection   Tools that support *taint analysis* enable assurance of code usage that is substantially similar to the first compliant solution. Typical taint analyses assume that one or more methods exist that can *sanitize* potentially tainted inputs, providing untainted outputs (or appropriate errors). The taint analysis then ensures that only untainted data is used inside the doPrivileged() block. Note that the static analyses must necessarily assume that the sanitization methods are always successful, while in reality, this may not be the case.

Related Guidelines

MITRE CWE	CWE-266. Incorrect privilege assignment
	CWE-272. Least privilege violation
	CWE-732. Incorrect permission assignment for critical resource
Secure Coding Guidelines for the Java Programming Language, Version 3.0	Guideline 6-2. Safely invoke java.security.AccessController.doPrivileged

Bibliography

[API 2006]	Method doPrivileged()
[Gong 2003]	Sections 6.4, AccessController, and 9.5, Privileged Code
[Jovanovic 2006]	Pixy: A Static Analysis Tool for Detecting Web Application Vulnerabilities

■ SEC02-J. Do not base security checks on untrusted sources

Security checks based on untrusted sources can be bypassed. Any untrusted object or argument must be defensively copied before a security check is performed. The copy operation must be a deep copy; the implementation of the `clone()` method may produce a shallow copy, which can still be compromised. In addition, the implementation of the `clone()` method can be provided by the attacker. See rule OBJ06-J for more information.

Noncompliant Code Example

This noncompliant code example describes a security vulnerability from the Java 1.5 `java.io` package. In this release, `java.io.File` is nonfinal, allowing an attacker to supply an untrusted argument constructed by extending the legitimate `File` class. In this manner, the `getPath()` method can be overridden so that the security check passes the first time it is called but the value changes the second time to refer to a sensitive file such as `/etc/passwd`. This is an example of a time-of-check, time-of-use (TOCTOU) vulnerability.

```
public RandomAccessFile openFile(final java.io.File f) {
  askUserPermission(f.getPath());
  // ...
  return (RandomAccessFile) AccessController.doPrivileged() {
    public Object run() {
      return new RandomAccessFile(f.getPath());
    }
  }
}
```

The attacker could extend `java.io.File` as follows:

```
public class BadFile extends java.io.File {
  private int count;
  public String getPath() {
    return (++count == 1) ? "/tmp/foo" : "/etc/passwd";
  }
}
```

Compliant Solution (Final)

This vulnerability can be mitigated by declaring `java.io.File` final.

Compliant Solution (Copy)

This compliant solution ensures that the `java.io.File` object can be trusted despite not being final. The solution creates a new `File` object using the standard constructor. This ensures that any methods invoked on the `File` object are the standard library methods and not overriding methods that have been provided by the attacker.

```
public RandomAccessFile openFile(java.io.File f) {
  final java.io.File copy = new java.io.File(f.getPath());
  askUserPermission(copy.getPath());
  // ...
  return (RandomAccessFile) AccessController.doPrivileged() {
    public Object run() {
      return new RandomAccessFile(copy.getPath());
    }
  }
}
```

Note that using the `clone()` method instead of the `openFile()` method would copy the attacker's class, which is not desirable. (Refer to rule OBJ06-J.)

Risk Assessment

Basing security checks on untrusted sources can result in the check being bypassed.

Rule	Severity	Likelihood	Remediation Cost	Priority	Level
SEC02-J	high	probable	medium	P12	L1

Related Guidelines

ISO/IEC TR 24772:2010	Authentication Logic Error [XZO]
MITRE CWE	CWE-302. Authentication bypass by assumed-immutable data
	CWE-470. Use of externally-controlled input to select classes or code ("unsafe reflection")

Bibliography

[Sterbenz 2006]

■ SEC03-J. Do not load trusted classes after allowing untrusted code to load arbitrary classes

The Java classes used by a program are not necessarily loaded upon program startup. Many Java Virtual Machines (JVMs) load classes only when they need them.

If untrusted code is permitted to load classes, it may possess the ability to load sensitive classes required by trusted code. If the trusted code has not already loaded these classes, subsequent attempts may result in untrusted classes being substituted for the sensitive classes. As a result, if a program permits untrusted code to load classes, it must first *preload* any sensitive classes it needs. Once properly loaded, these sensitive classes cannot be replaced by untrusted code.

Noncompliant Code Example (Tomcat)

This noncompliant code example shows a vulnerability present in several versions of the Tomcat HTTP web server (fixed in version 6.0.20) that allows untrusted web applications to override the default XML parser used by the system to process `web.xml`, `context.xml` and tag library descriptor (TLD) files of other web applications deployed on the Tomcat instance. Consequently, untrusted web applications that install a parser could view and/or alter these files under certain circumstances.

The noncompliant code example shows the code associated with initialization of a new `Digester` instance in the `org.apache.catalina.startup.ContextConfig` class. "A `Digester` processes an XML input stream by matching a series of element nesting patterns to execute Rules that have been added prior to the start of parsing" [Tomcat 2009]. The code to initialize the `Digester` follows:

```
protected static Digester webDigester = null;

if (webDigester == null) {
  webDigester = createWebDigester();
}
```

The `createWebDigester()` method is responsible for creating the `Digester`. This method calls `createWebXMLDigester()`, which invokes the method `DigesterFactory.newDigester()`. This method creates the new digester instance and sets a `boolean` flag `useContextClassLoader` to `true`.

```
// This method exists in the class DigesterFactory and is called by
// ContextConfig.createWebXmlDigester()
// which is in turn called by ContextConfig.createWebDigester().
// webDigester finally contains the value of digester defined
// in this method.
public static Digester newDigester(boolean xmlValidation,
                                   boolean xmlNamespaceAware,
                                   RuleSet rule) {
  Digester digester = new Digester();
  // ...
  digester.setUseContextClassLoader(true);
  // ...
  return digester;
}
```

The useContextClassLoader flag is used by Digester to decide which ClassLoader to use when loading new classes. When true, it uses the WebappClassLoader, which is untrusted because it loads whatever classes are requested by various web applications.

```
public ClassLoader getClassLoader() {
  // ...
  if (this.useContextClassLoader) {
    // Uses the context class loader which was previously set
    // to the WebappClassLoader
    ClassLoader classLoader =
        Thread.currentThread().getContextClassLoader();
  }
  return classloader;
}
```

The Digester.getParser() method is subsequently called by Tomcat to process web.xml and other files:

```
// Digester.getParser() calls this method.
// It is defined in class Digester
public SAXParserFactory getFactory() {
  if (factory == null) {
    // Uses WebappClassLoader
    factory = SAXParserFactory.newInstance();
```

```
  // ...
  }
  return (factory);
}
```

The underlying problem is that the newInstance() method is being invoked on behalf of a web application's class loader, the WebappClassLoader, and it loads classes before Tomcat has loaded all the classes it needs. If a web application has loaded its own Trojan javax.xml.parsers.SAXParserFactory, when Tomcat tries to access a SAXParserFactory, it accesses the Trojan SaxParserFactory installed by the web application rather than the standard Java SAXParserFactory that Tomcat depends on.

Compliant Solution (Tomcat)

In this compliant solution, Tomcat initializes the SAXParserFactory when it creates the Digester. This guarantees that the SAXParserFactory is constructed using the container's class loader rather than the WebappClassLoader.

The webDigester is also declared final. This prevents any subclasses from assigning a new object reference to webDigester. (See rule OBJ10-J for more information.) It also prevents a race condition where another thread could access webDigester before it is fully initialized. (See rule OBJ11-J for more information.)

```
protected static final Digester webDigester = init();

protected Digester init() {
  Digester digester = createWebDigester();
  // Does not use the context Classloader at initialization
  digester.getParser();
  return digester;
}
```

Even if the Tomcat server continues to use the WebappClassLoader to create the parser instance when attempting to process the web.xml and other files, the explicit call to get-Parser() in init() ensures that the default parser has been set during prior initialization and cannot be replaced. Because this is a one-time setting, future attempts to change the parser are futile.

Note that the Class.newInstance() method requires the class to contain a no-argument constructor. If this requirement is not satisfied, a runtime exception results, which indirectly prevents a security breach.

Risk Assessment

Allowing untrusted code to load classes enables untrusted code to replace benign classes with Trojan classes.

Rule	Severity	Likelihood	Remediation Cost	Priority	Level
SEC03-J	high	probable	medium	P12	L1

Related Guidelines

Secure Coding Guidelines for the Java Programming Language, Version 3.0

Guideline 6-3. Safely invoke standard APIs that bypass `SecurityManager` checks depending on the immediate caller's class loader

Bibliography

[CVE 2011]   CVE-2009-0783

[Gong 2003]   Section 4.3.2, Class Loader Delegation Hierarchy

[JLS 2005]   §4.3.2, The Class `Object`

[Tomcat 2009]   Bug ID 29936, API Class `org.apache.tomcat.util.digester.Digester`, Security fix in v 6.0.20

▪ SEC04-J. Protect sensitive operations with security manager checks

Sensitive operations must be protected by security manager checks.

Noncompliant Code Example

This noncompliant code example instantiates a `Hashtable` and defines a `removeEntry()` method to allow the removal of its entries. This method is considered sensitive, perhaps because the hash table contains sensitive information. However, the method is public and nonfinal, which leaves it exposed to malicious callers.

```
class SensitiveHash {
  Hashtable<Integer,String> ht = new Hashtable<Integer,String>();

  public void removeEntry(Object key) {
    ht.remove(key);
  }
}
```

Compliant Solution

This compliant solution installs a security check to protect entries from being maliciously removed from the Hashtable instance. A SecurityException is thrown if the caller lacks the java.security.SecurityPermission removeKeyPermission.

```java
class SensitiveHash {
  Hashtable<Integer,String> ht = new Hashtable<Integer,String>();

  void removeEntry(Object key) {
    check("removeKeyPermission");
    ht.remove(key);
  }

  private void check(String directive) {
    SecurityManager sm = System.getSecurityManager();
    if (sm != null) {
      sm.checkSecurityAccess(directive);
    }
  }
}
```

The SecurityManager.checkSecurityAccess() method determines whether the action controlled by the particular permission is allowed or not.

Noncompliant Code Example (check*())

This noncompliant code example uses the SecurityManager.checkRead() method to check whether the file schema.dtd can be read from the file system. The check*() methods lack support for fine-grained access control. For example, the check*() methods are inadequate to enforce a policy permitting read access to all files with the dtd extension and forbidding read access to all other files. Non-JDK code must not use the check*() methods because the default implementations of the Java libraries already use these methods to protect sensitive operations.

```java
SecurityManager sm = System.getSecurityManager();

if (sm != null) {  // check whether file may be read
  sm.checkRead("/local/schema.dtd");
}
```

Compliant Solution (`checkPermission()`)

Java SE 1.2 added two methods—checkPermission(Permission perm) and checkPermission(Permission perm, Object context)—to the SecurityManager class. The motivations for this change included

- eliminating the need to hard code names of checks in method names.
- encapsulating the complicated algorithms and code for examining the Java runtime in a single checkPermission() method.
- supporting introduction of additional permissions by subclassing the Permission class.

The single argument checkPermission() method uses the context of the currently executing thread environment to perform the checks. If the context has the permissions defined in the local policy file, the check succeeds; otherwise, a SecurityException is thrown.

This compliant solution shows the single argument checkPermission() method and allows files in the local directory with the dtd extension to be read. DTDPermission is a custom permission that enforces this level of access. Even if the java.io.FilePermission is granted to the application with the action read, DTD files are subject to additional access control.

```
SecurityManager sm = System.getSecurityManager();

if (sm != null) { //check whether file can be read or not
  DTDPermission perm = new DTDPermission("/local/", "readDTD");
  sm.checkPermission(perm);
}
```

Compliant Solution (Multiple Threads)

Occasionally, the security check code exists in one context (such as a worker thread), while the check must be conducted on a different context, such as another thread. The two-argument checkPermission() method is used in this case. It accepts an AccessControl-Context instance as the context argument. The effective permissions are those of the context argument only rather than the intersection of the permissions of the two contexts.

Both the single- and double-argument checkPermission() methods defer to the single-argument java.security.AccessController.checkPermission(Permission perm) method. When invoked directly, this method operates only on the current execution context and, as a result, does not supersede the security manager's two argument version.

A cleaner approach to making a security check from a different context is to take a *snapshot* of the execution context in which the check must be performed, using the `java.security.AccessController.getContext()` method that returns an `AccessControl-Context` object. The `AccessControlContext` class itself defines a `checkPermission()` method that encapsulates a context instead of accepting the current executing context as an argument. This allows the check to be performed at a later time, as shown in the following example.

```
// Take the snapshot of the required context,
// store in acc and pass it to another context
AccessControlContext acc = AccessController.getContext();

// Accept acc in another context and invoke checkPermission() on it
acc.checkPermission(perm);
```

Risk Assessment

Failure to enforce security checks in code that performs sensitive operations can lead to malicious tampering of sensitive data.

Rule	Severity	Likelihood	Remediation Cost	Priority	Level
SEC04-J	high	probable	medium	P12	L1

Automated Detection Identifying sensitive operations requires assistance from the programmer; fully automated identification of sensitive operations is beyond the current state of the art.

Given knowledge of which operations are sensitive, as well as which specific security checks must be enforced for each operation, an automated tool could reasonably enforce the invariant that the sensitive operations are invoked *only* from contexts where the required security checks have been performed.

Bibliography

[API 2006]

■ SEC05-J. Do not use reflection to increase accessibility of classes, methods, or fields

Reflection enables a Java program to analyze and modify itself. In particular, a program can discover the values of field variables and change them [Forman 2005], [Sun 2002]. The Java reflection API includes a method that enables fields that are normally inaccessible to be accessed under reflection. The following code prints out the names and values of all fields of an object someObject of class SomeClass:

```
Field fields[] = SomeClass.getDeclaredFields();
for (Field field : fields) {
  if (!Modifier.isPublic(field.getModifiers())) {
    field.setAccessible(true);
  }
  System.out.print("Field: " + field.getName());
  System.out.println(", value: " + field.get(someObject));
}
```

A field could be set to a new value as follows:

```
String newValue = reader.readLine();
field.set(someObject, returnValue(newValue, field.getType()));
```

When the default security manager is used, it prevents fields that are normally inaccessible from being accessed under reflection. The default security manager throws a java.security.AccessControlException in these circumstances. However, java.lang.reflect.ReflectPermission can be granted with action suppressAccessChecks to override this default behavior.

For example, although an object is ordinarily prevented from accessing private members or invoking private methods of another class, the APIs belonging to the java.lang.reflect package allow an object to do so contingent upon performing the language-defined access checks. It is important to note, however, that these access checks consider only the language-level visibility of the immediate caller. Consequently, unwary programmers can create an opportunity for a privilege escalation attack by untrusted callers.

The following table lists the APIs that should be used with care [SCG 2009].

APIs that Mirror Language Checks

java.lang.Class.newInstance()

java.lang.reflect.Constructor.newInstance()

java.lang.reflect.Field.get*()

java.lang.reflect.Field.set*()

java.lang.reflect.Method.invoke()

java.util.concurrent.atomic.AtomicIntegerFieldUpdater.newUpdater()

java.util.concurrent.atomic.AtomicLongFieldUpdater.newUpdater()

java.util.concurrent.atomic.AtomicReferenceFieldUpdater.newUpdater()

Because the setAccessible() and getAccessible() methods of class java.lang.reflect.Field are used to instruct the JVM to override the language access checks, they perform standard (and more restrictive) security manager checks and consequently lack the vulnerability discussed in this rule. Nevertheless, these methods should be used only with extreme caution. The remaining `set*()` and `get*()` field reflection methods perform only the language access checks and are vulnerable.

Use of reflection complicates security analysis and can easily introduce security vulnerabilities. Consequently, programmers should avoid using the reflection APIs when it is feasible to do so. Exercise extreme caution when the use of reflection is necessary. In particular, reflection must not be used to provide access to classes, methods, and fields unless these items are already accessible without the use of reflection. For example, the use of reflection to access or modify fields is not allowed unless those fields are already accessible and modifiable by other means, such as through getter and setter methods.

This rule is similar to rule MET04-J, but it warns against using reflection, rather than inheritance, to subvert accessibility.

Noncompliant Code Example

In this noncompliant code example, the private fields i and j can be modified using reflection via a `Field` object. Furthermore, any class can modify these fields using reflection via the `zeroField()` method. However, only class `FieldExample` can modify these fields without the use of reflection.

Allowing hostile code to pass arbitrary field names to the `zeroField()` method can

- leak information about field names by throwing an exception for invalid or inaccessible field names. See rule ERR01-J, for additional information. This example complies with rule ERR01-J by catching the relevant exceptions at the end of the method.
- access potentially sensitive data that is visible to `zeroField()` but is hidden from the attacking method. This privilege escalation attack can be difficult to find during code review because the specific field(s) being accessed are controlled by strings in the attacker's code rather than by locally visible source code.

```
class FieldExample {
  private int i = 3;
  private int j = 4;

  public String toString() {
    return "FieldExample: i=" + i + ", j=" + j;
  }

  public void zeroI() {
    this.i = 0;
  }
}
```

```
    public void zeroField(String fieldName) {
      try {
        Field f = this.getClass().getDeclaredField(fieldName);
        // Subsequent access to field f passes language access checks
        // because zeroField() could have accessed the field via
        // ordinary field references
        f.setInt(this, 0);
        // log appropriately or throw sanitized exception; see EXC06-J
      } catch (NoSuchFieldException ex) {
        // report to handler
      } catch (IllegalAccessException ex) {
        // report to handler
      }
    }

    public static void main(String[] args) {
      FieldExample fe = new FieldExample();
      System.out.println(fe.toString());
      for (String arg : args) {
        fe.zeroField(arg);
        System.out.println(fe.toString());
      }
    }
  }
```

Compliant Solution (Private)

When you must use reflection, make sure that the immediate caller (method) is isolated from hostile code by declaring it private or final, as in this compliant solution.

```
class FieldExample {
  // ...

  private void zeroField(String fieldName) {
    // ...
  }
}
```

Note that when language access checks are overridden through use of `java.lang.reflect.Field.setAccessible()`, the immediate caller gains access even to the private fields of other classes. Consequently, never grant the permission `ReflectPermission` with action `suppressAccessChecks`; this ensures that the security manager will block attempts to access private fields of other classes.

Compliant Solution (Nonreflection)

When a class must use reflection to provide access to fields, it must also provide the same access using a nonreflection interface. This compliant solution provides limited setter methods that grant all callers the ability to zero out its fields without using reflection. If these setter methods comply with all other rules or security policies, the use of reflection also complies with this rule.

```
class FieldExample {
  // ...

  public void zeroField(String fieldName) {
    // ...
  }

  public void zeroI() {
    this.i = 0;
  }

  public void zeroJ() {
    this.i = 0;
  }
}
```

Noncompliant Code Example

In this noncompliant code example, the programmer intends that code outside the `Safe` package should be prevented from creating a new instance of an arbitrary class. Consequently, the `Trusted` class uses a package-private constructor. However, because the API is public, an attacker can pass `Trusted.class` itself as an argument to the `create()` method and bypass the language access checks that prevent code outside the package from invoking the package-private constructor. The `create()` method returns an unauthorized instance of the `Trusted` class.

```
package Safe;
public class Trusted {
  Trusted() { } // package private constructor
```

```
  public static <T> T create(Class<T> c)
      throws InstantiationException, IllegalAccessException {
    return c.newInstance();
  }
}

package Attacker;
import Safe.Trusted;

public class Attack {
  public static void main(String[] args)
      throws InstantiationException, IllegalAccessException {
    System.out.println(Trusted.create(Trusted.class)); // succeeds
  }
}
```

In the presence of a security manager s, the `Class.newInstance()` method throws a security exception when (a) `s.checkMemberAccess(this, Member.PUBLIC)` denies creation of new instances of this class or (b) the caller's class loader is not the same or an ancestor of the class loader for the current class and invocation of `s.checkPackageAccess()` denies access to the package of this class.

The `checkMemberAccess()` method allows access to public members and classes that have the same class loader as the caller. However, the class loader comparison is often insufficient; for example, all applets share the same class loader by convention, consequently allowing a malicious applet to pass the security check in this case.

Compliant Solution (Access Reduction)

This compliant solution reduces the access of the `create()` method to package-private, preventing a caller from outside the package from using that method to bypass the language access checks to create an instance of the `Trusted` class. A caller that can create a `Trusted` class instance using reflection can simply call the `Trusted()` constructor instead.

```
package Safe;
public class Trusted {
  Trusted() { } // package private constructor
  static <T> T create(Class<T> c)
      throws InstantiationException, IllegalAccessException {
    return c.newInstance();
  }
}
```

Compliant Solution (Security Manager Check)

This compliant solution uses the getConstructors() method to check whether the class provided as an argument has public constructors. The security issue is irrelevant when public constructors are present because such constructors are already accessible even to malicious code. When public constructors are absent, the create() method uses the security manager's checkPackageAccess() method to ensure that all callers in the execution chain have sufficient permissions to access classes and their respective members defined in package Safe.

```
import java.beans.Beans;
import java.io.IOException;
package Safe;

public class Trusted  {
  Trusted() { }

  public static <T> T create(Class<T> c)
      throws InstantiationException, IllegalAccessException {

    if (c.getConstructors().length == 0) {  // No public constructors
      SecurityManager sm = System.getSecurityManager();
      if (sm != null) {
        // throws an exception when access is not allowed
        sm.checkPackageAccess("Safe");
      }
    }
    return c.newInstance(); // Safe to return
  }
}
```

The disadvantage of this compliant solution is that the class must be granted reflection permissions to permit the call to getConstructors().

Compliant Solution (`java.beans` Package)

This compliant solution uses the java.beans.Beans API to check whether the Class object being received has any public constructors.

```
public class Trusted {
  Trusted() { }

  public static <T> T create(Class<T> c)
      throws IOException, ClassNotFoundException {
```

```
    // Executes without exception only if there are public constructors
    ClassLoader cl = new SafeClassLoader();
    Object b = Beans.instantiate(cl, c.getName());
    return c.cast(b);
  }
}
```

The `Beans.instantiate()` method succeeds only when the class being instantiated has a public constructor; otherwise, it throws an `IllegalAccessException`. The method uses a class loader argument along with the name of the class to instantiate. Unlike the previous compliant solution, this approach avoids the need for any reflection permissions.

Risk Assessment

Misuse of APIs that perform language access checks only against the immediate caller can break data encapsulation, leak sensitive information, or permit privilege escalation attacks.

Rule	Severity	Likelihood	Remediation Cost	Priority	Level
SEC05-J	high	probable	medium	P12	L1

Related Guidelines

Secure Coding Guidelines for the Java Programming Language, Version 3.0	Guideline 6-5. Be aware of standard APIs that perform Java language access checks against the immediate caller

Bibliography

[Chan 1999]	`java.lang.reflect AccessibleObject`

■ SEC06-J. Do not rely on the default automatic signature verification provided by `URLClassLoader` and `java.util.jar`

Code should only be signed when it requires elevated privileges to perform one or more tasks. See rule ENV00-J for more information.

For example, applets are denied the privilege of making HTTP connections to any hosts except the host from which they came. When an applet requires an HTTP connection with an external host to download plug-ins or extensions, its vendor may provide signed code rather than forcing the user to arbitrarily assign the permissions it requires. Because executing privilege-elevated signed code can be extremely dangerous, verifying the authenticity of its origin is of utmost importance.

Java-based technologies typically use the Java Archive (JAR) feature to package files for platform-independent deployment. JAR files are the preferred means of distribution for Enterprise JavaBeans (EJB), MIDlets (J2ME), and Weblogic Server J2EE applications, for example. The point-and-click installation provided by Java Web Start also relies on the JAR file format for packaging. Vendors sign their JAR files when required. This certifies the *authenticity* of the code, but it cannot guarantee the security of the code.

According to the Java Tutorials [Tutorials 2008]:

> If you are creating applet code that you will sign, it needs to be placed in a JAR file. The same is true if you are creating application code that may be similarly restricted by running it with a security manager. The reason you need the JAR file is that when a policy file specifies that code signed by a particular entity is permitted one or more operations, such as specific file reads or writes, the code is expected to come from a signed JAR file. (The term "signed code" is an abbreviated way of saying "code in a class file that appears in a JAR file that was signed.")

Client code may lack programmatic checks of code signatures. For example, instances of URLClassLoader and its subclasses and java.util.jar automatically verify signatures of signed JAR files. Developer-implemented custom class loaders may lack this check. Moreover, even in the URLClassLoader case, the automatic verification performs an integrity check; it fails to authenticate the loaded class because the check uses the public key contained within the JAR without validating that public key. The legitimate JAR file may be replaced with a malicious JAR file containing a different public key along with appropriately modified digest values.

The default automatic signature verification process may still be used but is not sufficient. Systems that use the default automatic signature verification process must perform additional checks to ensure that the signature is correct (such as comparing it against a known trusted signature).

Noncompliant Code Example

This noncompliant code example demonstrates the JarRunner application, which can be used to dynamically execute a particular class residing within a JAR file (abridged version of the class in *The Java Tutorials* [Tutorials 2008]). It creates a JarClassLoader that loads an application update, plug-in, or patch over an untrusted network such as the Internet. The URL to fetch the code is specified as the first argument (for example, http://www.securecoding. cert.org/software-updates.jar); any other arguments specify the arguments that are to be passed to the class that is loaded. JarRunner uses reflection to invoke the main() method of the loaded class. Unfortunately, by default, JarClassLoader verifies the signature using the public key contained within the JAR file.

```
public class JarRunner {
  public static void main(String[] args)
      throws IOException, ClassNotFoundException,
            NoSuchMethodException, InvocationTargetException {

    URL url = new URL(args[0]);

    // Create the class loader for the application jar file
    JarClassLoader cl = new JarClassLoader(url);

    // Get the application's main class name
    String name = cl.getMainClassName();

    // Get arguments for the application
    String[] newArgs = new String[args.length - 1];
    System.arraycopy(args, 1, newArgs, 0, newArgs.length);

    // Invoke application's main class
    cl.invokeClass(name, newArgs);
  }
}

final class JarClassLoader extends URLClassLoader {
  private URL url;

  public JarClassLoader(URL url) {
    super(new URL[] { url });
    this.url = url;
  }

  public String getMainClassName() throws IOException {
    URL u = new URL("jar", "", url + "!/");
    JarURLConnection uc = (JarURLConnection) u.openConnection();
    Attributes attr = uc.getMainAttributes();
    return attr != null ?
      attr.getValue(Attributes.Name.MAIN_CLASS) : null;
  }

  public void invokeClass(String name, String[] args)
      throws ClassNotFoundException, NoSuchMethodException,
            InvocationTargetException {
    Class c = loadClass(name);
    Method m = c.getMethod("main", new Class[] { args.getClass() });
    m.setAccessible(true);
    int mods = m.getModifiers();
    if (m.getReturnType() != void.class || !Modifier.isStatic(mods) ||
        !Modifier.isPublic(mods)) {
```

```
      throw new NoSuchMethodException("main");
    }
    try {
      m.invoke(null, new Object[] { args });
    } catch (IllegalAccessException e) {
      System.out.println("Access denied");
    }
  }
}
```

Compliant Solution (`jarsigner`)

Users can—but usually do not—explicitly check JAR file signatures at the command line. This may be an adequate solution for programs that require manual installation of JAR files. Any malicious tampering results in a `SecurityException` when the `jarsigner` tool is invoked with the `-verify` option.

```
jarsigner -verify signed-updates-jar-file.jar
```

Compliant Solution (Certificate Chain)

When the local system cannot reliably verify the signature, the invoking program must verify the signature programmatically by obtaining the chain of certificates from the `Code-Source` of the class being loaded and checking whether any of the certificates belong to a trusted signer whose certificate has been securely obtained beforehand and stored in a local keystore. This compliant solution demonstrates the necessary modifications to the `invoke-Class()` method.

```
public void invokeClass(String name, String[] args)
    throws ClassNotFoundException, NoSuchMethodException,
           InvocationTargetException, GeneralSecurityException,
           IOException {
  Class c = loadClass(name);
  Certificate[] certs =
      c.getProtectionDomain().getCodeSource().getCertificates();
  if (certs == null) {
    // return, do not execute if unsigned
```

```
    System.out.println("No signature!");
    return;
}

KeyStore ks = KeyStore.getInstance("JKS");
ks.load(new FileInputStream(System.getProperty(
    "user.home"+ File.separator + "keystore.jks")),
    "loadkeystorepassword".toCharArray());
// user is the alias
Certificate pubCert = ks.getCertificate("user");
// check with the trusted public key, else throws exception
certs[0].verify(pubCert.getPublicKey());
}
```

Because the `invokeClass()` method now has two additional exceptions in its `throws` clause, the `catch` block in the `main()` method must be altered accordingly.

The `URLClassLoader` and all its subclasses are given by default only enough permissions to interact with the URL that was specified when the `URLClassLoader` object was created. This means that the loaded code can interact only with the specified host. This fails to mitigate the risk completely, however, because the loaded code may have been granted privileges that permit other sensitive operations such as updating an existing local JAR file.

Risk Assessment

Failure to verify a digital signature, whether manually or programmatically, can result in the execution of malicious code.

Rule	Severity	Likelihood	Remediation Cost	Priority	Level
SEC06-J	high	probable	medium	P12	L1

Automated Detection Automated detection is not feasible in the fully general case. However, an approach similar to Design Fragments [Fairbanks 07] could assist both programmers and static analysis tools.

Related Guidelines

ISO/IEC TR 24772:2010	Improperly Verified Signature [XZR]
MITRE CWE	CWE-300. Channel accessible by non-endpoint (aka "man-in-the-middle")

CWE-319. Cleartext transmission of sensitive information

CWE-494. Download of code without integrity check

CWE-347. Improper verification of cryptographic signature

Bibliography

[API 2006]

[Bea 2008]

[Eclipse 2008]   JAR Signing and Signed Bundles and Protecting against Malicious Code

[Fairbanks 2007]

[Flanagan 2005]   Chapter 24, The `java.util.jar` Package

[Gong 2003]   12.8.3, `jarsigner`

[Halloway 2001]

[JarSpec 2008]   Signature Validation

[Oaks 2001]   Chapter 12, Digital Signatures, Signed Classes

[Muchow 2001]

[Tutorials 2008]   The `JarRunner` Class, Lesson: API and Tools Use for Secure Code and File
                      Exchanges and Verifying Signed JAR Files

▪ SEC07-J. Call the superclass's `getPermissions()` method when writing a custom class loader

When a custom class loader must override the `getPermissions()` method, the implementation must consult the default system policy by explicitly invoking the superclass's `getPermissions()` method before assigning arbitrary permissions to the code source. A custom class loader that ignores the superclass's `getPermissions()` could load untrusted classes with elevated privileges.

Noncompliant Code Example

This noncompliant code example shows a fragment of a custom class loader that extends the class `URLClassLoader`. It overrides the `getPermissions()` method but does not call its superclass's more restrictive `getPermissions()` method. Consequently, a class defined using this custom class loader has permissions that are completely independent of those specified in the systemwide policy file. In effect, the class's permissions override them.

```
protected PermissionCollection getPermissions(CodeSource cs) {
  PermissionCollection pc = new Permissions();
  // allow exit from the VM anytime
  pc.add(new RuntimePermission("exitVM"));
  return pc;
}
```

Compliant Solution

In this compliant solution, the getPermissions() method calls super.getPermissions().
As a result, the default systemwide security policy is applied, in addition to the custom
policy.

```
protected PermissionCollection getPermissions(CodeSource cs) {
  PermissionCollection pc = super.getPermissions(cs);
  // allow exit from the VM anytime
  pc.add(new RuntimePermission("exitVM"));
  return pc;
}
```

Risk Assessment

Failure to consult the default system policy while defining a custom class loader violates the
tenets of defensive programming and can result in classes defined with unintended
permissions.

Rule	Severity	Likelihood	Remediation Cost	Priority	Level
SEC07-J	high	probable	low	P18	L1

Automated Detection   Violations of this rule can be discovered with a heuristic checker in
the style of FindBugs. As with all heuristic checks, achieving a low false-positive rate is
essential.

Bibliography

[API 2006]   Class ClassLoader
[Oaks 2001]
[Security 2006]

■ SEC08-J. Define wrappers around native methods

Native methods are defined in Java and written in languages such as C and C++ [JNI 2006]. The added extensibility comes at the cost of flexibility and portability because the code no longer conforms to the policies enforced by Java. Native methods have been used for performing platform-specific operations, interfacing with legacy library code, and improving program performance [Bloch 2008].

Defining a wrapper method facilitates installing appropriate security manager checks, validating arguments passed to native code, validating return values, defensively copying mutable inputs, and sanitizing untrusted data. Consequently, every native method must be private and must be invoked only by a wrapper method.

Noncompliant Code Example

In this noncompliant code example, the nativeOperation() method is both native and public; therefore, untrusted callers may invoke it. Native method invocations bypass security manager checks.

This example includes the doOperation() wrapper method, which invokes the nativeOperation() native method but fails to provide input validation or security checks.

```
public final class NativeMethod {

  // public native method
  public native void nativeOperation(byte[] data, int offset, int len);

  // wrapper method that lacks security checks and input validation
  public void doOperation(byte[] data, int offset, int len) {
    nativeOperation(data, offset, len);
  }

  static {
    // load native library in static initializer of class
    System.loadLibrary("NativeMethodLib");
  }
}
```

Compliant Solution

This compliant solution declares the native method private. The doOperation() wrapper method checks permissions, creates a defensive copy of the mutable input array data, and checks the ranges of the arguments. The nativeOperation() method is consequently called with secure inputs. Note that the validation checks must produce outputs that conform to the input requirements of the native methods.

```
public final class NativeMethodWrapper {

  // private native method
  private native void nativeOperation(byte[] data, int offset, int len);

  // wrapper method performs SecurityManager and input validation checks
  public void doOperation(byte[] data, int offset, int len) {
    // permission needed to invoke native method
    securityManagerCheck();

    if (data == null) {
      throw new NullPointerException();
    }

    // copy mutable input
    data = data.clone();

    // validate input
    if ((offset < 0) || (len < 0) || (offset > (data.length - len))) {
      throw new IllegalArgumentException();
    }

    nativeOperation(data, offset, len);
  }

  static {
    // load native library in static initializer of class
    System.loadLibrary("NativeMethodLib");
  }
}
```

Exceptions

SEC08-EX0: Native methods that do not require security manager checks, validation of arguments or return values, or defensive copying of mutable inputs (for example, the standard C function int rand(void)) do not need to be wrapped.

Risk Assessment

Failure to define wrappers around native methods can allow unprivileged callers to invoke them and exploit inherent vulnerabilities such as buffer overflows in native libraries.

Rule	Severity	Likelihood	Remediation Cost	Priority	Level
SEC08-J	medium	probable	high	P4	L3

Automated Detection   Automated detection is not feasible in the fully general case. However, an approach similar to Design Fragments [Fairbanks 07] could assist both programmers and static analysis tools.

Related Guidelines

MITRE CWE

Secure Coding Guidelines for the Java Programming Language, Version 3.0

CWE-111. Direct use of unsafe JNI

Guideline 3-3. Define wrappers around native methods

Bibliography

[Fairbanks 2007]

[JNI 2006]

[Liang 1997]

[Macgregor 1998]   Section 2.2.3, Interfaces and Architectures

Chapter 17

Runtime Environment (ENV)

■ Rules

■ Risk Assessment Summary

Rule	Severity	Likelihood	Remediation Cost	Priority	Level
ENV00-J	high	probable	medium	P12	L1
ENV01-J	high	probable	medium	P12	L1
ENV02-J	low	likely	low	P9	L2
ENV03-J	high	likely	low	P27	L1

(continued)

Rule	Severity	Likelihood	Remediation Cost	Priority	Level
ENV04-J	high	likely	low	P27	L1
ENV05-J	high	probable	low	P18	L1

■ ENV00-J. Do not sign code that performs only unprivileged operations

Java uses code signing as a requirement for granting elevated privileges to code. Many security policies permit signed code to operate with elevated privileges. For example, Java applets can escape the default sandbox restrictions when signed. Consequently, users can grant explicit permissions either to a particular code base or to all code signed by a particular signer. This approach places control of security in the hands of the user, who can choose whether to run an application with full or restricted permissions.

Signing code, however, has its own problems. According to Schneier [Schneier 2000]:

> First, users have no idea how to decide if a particular signer is trusted or not. Second, just because a component is signed doesn't mean that it is safe. Third, just because two components are individually signed does not mean that using them together is safe; lots of accidental harmful interactions can be exploited. Fourth, "safe" is not an all-or-nothing thing; there are degrees of safety. And fifth, the fact that the evidence of attack (the signature on the code) is stored on the computer under attack is mostly useless: The attacker could delete or modify the signature during the attack, or simply reformat the drive where the signature is stored.

Code signing is designed to authenticate the origin of the code as well as to verify the integrity of the code. It relies on a certification authority (CA) to confirm the identity of the principal signer. Naive users should not be expected to understand how certificates and the public key infrastructure (PKI) work.

Users commonly associate digital signatures with safety of code execution, trusting the code to cause them no harm. The problem arises when a vulnerability is discovered in signed code. Because many systems are configured to permanently trust certain signing organizations, those systems fail to notify their users when downloading content signed by the trusted organization, even when that content contains vulnerabilities. An attacker can offer the users legitimately signed vulnerable content with the intention of exploiting that content.

Consider, for example, signed Java applets. When a certificate is verified, on widely used platforms, the user is presented with a security dialog in which the option "Always trust the content from the publisher" is selected by default. The dialog primarily asks whether or not the signed code should be executed. Unfortunately, if the user confirms the dialog with the check box selected, the "Always trust…" setting overrides any future warning dialogs. An attacker can take advantage of this mechanism by exploiting vulnerable code signed by the trusted organization. In this case, the code will execute with the user's implied permission and can be freely exploited.

An organization that signs its own code should not vouch for code acquired from a third party without carefully auditing the third-party code. When signing privileged code, ensure that all of the signed code is confined to a single JAR file (see rule ENV01-J for more information) and also that any code invoked from the privileged code is also contained in that JAR file. Nonprivileged code must be left unsigned, restricting it to the sandbox. For example, unsigned applets and Java Network Launching Protocol (JNLP) applications are granted the minimum set of privileges and are restricted to the sandbox. Finally, never sign any code that is incomprehensible or unaudited.

Exceptions

ENV00-EX1: An organization that has an internal PKI and uses code signing for internal development activities (such as facilitating code check-in and tracking developer activity) may sign unprivileged code. This code base should not be carried forward to a production environment. The keys used for internal signing must be distinct from those used to sign externally available code.

Risk Assessment

Signing unprivileged code violates the principle of least privilege because it can circumvent security restrictions defined by the security policies of applets and JNLP applications, for example.

Rule	Severity	Likelihood	Remediation Cost	Priority	Level
ENV00-J	high	probable	medium	P12	L1

Automated Detection   Detecting code that should be considered privileged or sensitive requires programmer assistance. Given identified privileged code as a starting point, automated tools could compute the closure of all code that can be invoked from that point. Such a tool could plausibly determine whether a body of signed code both includes that entire closure and excludes all other code.

Related Guidelines

ISO/IEC TR 24772:2010   Adherence to Least Privilege [XYN]

Bibliography

[Dormann 2008]

[McGraw 1999]   Appendix C, Sign Only Privileged Code

[Schneier 2000]

■ ENV01-J. Place all security-sensitive code in a single jar and sign and seal it

In Java SE 6 and Java SE 7, privileged code must either use the `AccessController` mechanism or be signed by an owner (or provider) whom the user trusts. Attackers could link privileged code with malicious code if the privileged code directly or indirectly invokes code from another package. Trusted JAR files often contain code that requires no elevated privileges itself, but that depends on privileged code; such code is known as security-sensitive code. If an attacker can link security-sensitive code with malicious code, he or she can indirectly cause incorrect behavior. This is called a *mix-and-match* attack.

Execution of untrusted code causes loss of privileges. When trusted code calls untrusted code that attempts to perform some action requiring permissions withheld by the security policy, that action is not allowed. However, privileged code may use a class that exists in an untrusted container and performs only unprivileged operations. If the attacker were to replace the class in the untrusted container with a malicious implementation, the trusted code might retrieve incorrect results and cause the privileged code to misbehave at the attacker's discretion.

According to the Java API [EMA 2008]:

> A package sealed within a JAR specifies that all classes defined in that package must originate from the same JAR. Otherwise, a `SecurityException` is thrown.

Sealing a JAR file automatically enforces the requirement of keeping privileged code together. In addition, it is important to minimize the accessibility of classes and their members (see rule OBJ02-J).

Noncompliant Code Example (Privileged Code)

This noncompliant code example includes a `doPrivileged()` block and calls a method defined in a class in a different, untrusted JAR file.

```
package trusted;
import untrusted.RetValue;
public class MixMatch {
  private void privilegedMethod() throws IOException {
```

```
    try {
      AccessController.doPrivileged(
        new PrivilegedExceptionAction<FileInputStream>() {
          public FileInputStream run() throws FileNotFoundException {
            final FileInputStream fis = new FileInputStream("file.txt");
            try {
              RetValue rt = new RetValue();

              if (rt.getValue() == 1) {
                // do something with sensitive file
              }
            } finally {
              fis.close();
            }
          }
        }
      );
    } catch (PrivilegedActionException e) {
      // forward to handler and log
    }
  }

  public static void main(String[] args) throws IOException {
    MixMatch mm = new MixMatch();
    mm.privilegedMethod();
  }
}

// In another JAR file:
package untrusted;

class RetValue {
  public int getValue() {
    return 1;
  }
}
```

An attacker can provide an implementation of class RetValue so that the privileged code uses an incorrect return value. Even though class MixMatch consists only of trusted, signed code, an attacker can still cause this behavior by maliciously deploying a valid signed JAR file containing the untrusted RetValue class.

This example almost violates rule SEC01-J but does not do so. It instead allows potentially tainted code in its doPrivileged() block, which is a similar issue.

Noncompliant Code Example (Security-Sensitive Code)

This noncompliant code example improves upon the previous example by moving the use of the RetValue class outside the doPrivileged() block.

```
package trusted;
import untrusted.RetValue;

public class MixMatch {
  private void privilegedMethod() throws IOException {
    try {
      final FileInputStream fis = AccessController.doPrivileged(
        new PrivilegedExceptionAction<FileInputStream>() {
          public FileInputStream run() throws FileNotFoundException {
            return new FileInputStream("file.txt");
          }
        }
      );
      try {
        RetValue rt = new RetValue();

        if (rt.getValue() == 1) {
          // do something with sensitive file
        }
      } finally {
        fis.close();
      }
    } catch (PrivilegedActionException e) {
      // forward to handler and log
    }
  }

  public static void main(String[] args) throws IOException {
    MixMatch mm = new MixMatch();
    mm.privilegedMethod();
  }
}

// In another JAR file:
package untrusted;

class RetValue {
  public int getValue() {
    return 1;
  }
}
```

Although the RetValue class is used only outside the doPrivileged() block, the behavior of RetValue.getValue() affects the behavior of security-sensitive code that operates on the file opened within the doPrivileged() block. Consequently, an attacker can still exploit the security-sensitive code with a malicious implementation of RetValue.

Compliant Solution

This compliant solution combines all security-sensitive code into the same package and the same JAR file. It also reduces the accessibility of the getValue() method to package-private. Sealing the package is necessary to prevent attackers from inserting any rogue classes.

```
package trusted;

public class MixMatch {
  // ...
}

// In the same signed & sealed JAR file:
package trusted;

class RetValue {
  int getValue() {
    return 1;
  }
}
```

To seal a package, use the sealed attribute in the JAR file's manifest file header, as follows.

```
Name: trusted/ // package name
Sealed: true   // sealed attribute
```

Exceptions

ENV01-EX0: Independent groups of privileged code and associated security-sensitive code (a "group" hereafter) may be placed in separate sealed packages and even in separate JAR files, subject to the following enabling conditions:

■ The code in any one of these independent groups must lack any dynamic or static dependency on any of the code in any of the other groups. This means that code from one such group cannot invoke code from any of the others, whether directly or transitively.

- All code from any single group is contained within one or more sealed packages.

- All code from any single group is contained within a single signed JAR file.

Risk Assessment

Failure to place all privileged code together in one package and seal the package can lead to mix-and-match attacks.

Rule	Severity	Likelihood	Remediation Cost	Priority	Level
ENV01-J	high	probable	medium	P12	L1

Automated Detection   Detecting code that should be considered privileged or sensitive requires programmer assistance. Given identified privileged code as a starting point, automated tools could compute the closure of all code that can be invoked from that point. Such a tool could plausibly determine whether all code in that closure exists within a single package. A further check of whether the package is sealed is feasible.

Related Guidelines

MITRE CWE	CWE-349. Acceptance of extraneous untrusted data with trusted data

Bibliography

[API 2006]

[McGraw 1999]   Rule 7. If you must sign your code, put it all in one archive file

[Ware 2008]

■ ENV02-J. Do not trust the values of environment variables

Both environment variables and system properties provide user-defined mappings between keys and their corresponding values and can be used to communicate those values from the environment to a process. According to the Java API [API 2006] `java.lang.System` class documentation:

> Environment variables have a more global effect because they are visible to all descendants of the process which defines them, not just the immediate Java subprocess. They can have subtly different semantics, such as case insensitivity, on different operating systems. For these reasons, environment variables are more likely to have unintended side effects. It is best to use system properties where possible. Environment variables should be used when a global effect is desired, or when an external system interface requires an environment variable (such as `PATH`).

Programs that execute in a more trusted domain than their environment must assume that the values of environment variables are untrusted and must sanitize and validate any environment variable values before use.

The default values of system properties are set by the Java Virtual Machine (JVM) upon startup and can be considered trusted. However, they may be overridden by properties from untrusted sources, such as a configuration file. System properties from untrusted sources must be sanitized and validated before use.

The Java Tutorial [Campione 1996] states:

> To maximize portability, never refer to an environment variable when the same value is available in a system property. For example, if the operating system provides a user name, it will always be available in the system property `user.name`.

Actually, relying on environment variables is more than a portability issue. An attacker can essentially control all environment variables that enter a program using a mechanism such as the `java.lang.ProcessBuilder` class.

Consequently, when an environment variable contains information that is available by other means, including system properties, that environment variable must not be used. Finally, environment variables must not be used without appropriate validation.

Noncompliant Code Example

This noncompliant code example tries to get the user name, using an environment variable.

```
String username = System.getenv("USER");
```

First, this is a portability issue. *The Java Tutorial* [Campione 1996] further suggests:

> The way environment variables are used also varies. For example, Windows provides the user name in an environment variable called `USERNAME`, while UNIX implementations might provide the user name in `USER`, `LOGNAME`, or both.

Second, an attacker can execute this program with the `USER` environment variable set to any value he or she chooses. The following code example does just that on a POSIX platform:

```
public static void main(String args[]) {
  if (args.length != 1) {
    System.err.println("Please supply a user name as the argument");
    return;
  }
```

```
String user = args[0];
ProcessBuilder pb = new ProcessBuilder();
pb.command("/usr/bin/printenv");
Map<String,String> environment = pb.environment();
environment.put("USER", user);
pb.redirectErrorStream(true);
try {
  Process process = pb.start();
  InputStream in = process.getInputStream();
  int c;
  while ((c = in.read()) != -1) {
    System.out.print((char) c);
  }
  int exitVal = process.waitFor();
} catch (IOException x) {
  // forward to handler
} catch (InterruptedException x) {
  // forward to handler
}
}
```

This program runs the POSIX/usr/bin/printenv command, which prints out all environment variables and their values. It takes a single argument string and sets the USER environment variable to that string. The subsequent output of the printenv program will indicate that the USER environment variable is set to the string requested.

Compliant Solution

This compliant solution obtains the user name using the user.name system property. The Java Virtual Machine (JVM), upon initialization sets this system property to the correct user name, even if the USER environment variable has been set to an incorrect value or is missing.

```
String username = System.getProperty("user.name");
```

Risk Assessment

Untrusted environment variables can provide data for injection and other attacks if not properly sanitized.

Rule	Severity	Likelihood	Remediation Cost	Priority	Level
ENV02-J	low	likely	low	P9	L2

Bibliography

[API 2006]

[Campione 1996]

■ ENV03-J. Do not grant dangerous combinations of permissions

Certain combinations of permissions can produce significant capability increases and should not be granted. Other permissions should be granted only to special code.

AllPermission

The permission `java.security.AllPermission` grants all possible permissions to code. This facility was included to reduce the burden of managing a multitude of permissions during routine testing as well as when a body of code is completely trusted. Code is typically granted `AllPermission` via the security policy file; it is also possible to programmatically associate `AllPermission` with a `ProtectionDomain`. This permission is dangerous in production environments. Never grant `AllPermission` to untrusted code.

ReflectPermission, suppressAccessChecks

Granting `ReflectPermission` on the target `suppressAccessChecks` suppresses all standard Java language access checks when the permitted class attempts to operate on package-private, protected, or private members of another class. Consequently, the permitted class can obtain permissions to examine any field or invoke any method belonging to an arbitrary class [Reflect 2006]. As a result, `ReflectPermission` must never be granted with target `suppressAccessChecks`.

According to the technical note *Permissions in the Java SE 6 Development Kit* [Permissions 2008], Section ReflectPermission, target `suppressAccessChecks`:

> **Warning:** *Extreme caution should be taken before granting this permission to code*, for it provides the ability to access fields and invoke methods in a class. This includes not only public, but protected and private fields and methods as well.

RuntimePermission, createClassLoader

The permission `java.lang.RuntimePermission` applied to target `createClassLoader` grants code the permission to create a `ClassLoader` object. This is extremely dangerous because malicious code can create its own custom class loader and load classes by assigning them arbitrary permissions. A custom class loader can define a class (or ProtectionDomain) with permissions that override any restrictions specified in the systemwide security policy file.

Permissions in the Java™ SE 6 Development Kit (JDK) [Permissions 2008] states:

> This is an extremely dangerous permission to grant. Malicious applications that can instantiate their own class loaders could then load their own rogue classes into the system. These newly loaded classes could be placed into any protection domain by the class loader, thereby automatically granting the classes the permissions for that domain.

Noncompliant Code Example (Security Policy File)

This noncompliant example grants AllPermission to the klib library.

```
// Grant the klib library AllPermission
grant codebase "file:${klib.home}/j2se/home/klib.jar" {
  permission java.security.AllPermission;
};
```

The permission itself is specified in the security policy file used by the security manager. Program code can obtain a permission object by subclassing the java.security. Permission class or any of its subclasses (BasicPermission, for example). The code can use the resulting object to grant AllPermission to a ProtectionDomain.

Compliant Solution

This compliant solution shows a policy file that can be used to enforce fine-grained permissions.

```
grant codeBase
   "file:${klib.home}/j2se/home/klib.jar", signedBy "Admin" {
  permission java.io.FilePermission "/tmp/*", "read";
  permission java.io.SocketPermission "*", "connect";
};
```

To check whether the caller has the requisite permissions, standard Java APIs use code such as the following:

```
// Security manager check
FilePermission perm =
    new java.io.FilePermission("/tmp/JavaFile", "read");
AccessController.checkPermission(perm);
// ...
```

Always assign appropriate permissions to code. Define custom permissions when the granularity of the standard permissions is insufficient.

Noncompliant Code Example (`PermissionCollection`)

This noncompliant code example shows an overridden getPermissions() method, defined in a custom class loader. It grants java.lang.ReflectPermission with target suppressAccessChecks to any class that it loads.

```
protected PermissionCollection getPermissions(CodeSource cs) {
  PermissionCollection pc = super.getPermissions(cs);
  // permission to create a class loader
  pc.add(new ReflectPermission("suppressAccessChecks"));
  // other permissions
  return pc;
}
```

Compliant Solution

This compliant solution does not grant java.lang.ReflectPermission with target suppressAccessChecks to any class that it loads.

```
protected PermissionCollection getPermissions(CodeSource cs) {
  PermissionCollection pc = super.getPermissions(cs);
  // other permissions
  return pc;
}
```

Exceptions

ENV03-EX0: It may be necessary to grant `AllPermission` to trusted library code so that callbacks work as expected. For example, it is common practice, and acceptable, to grant `AllPermission` to the optional Java packages (extension libraries):

```
// Standard extensions extend the core platform
// and are granted all permissions by default
grant codeBase "file:${{java.ext.dirs}}/*" {
  permission java.security.AllPermission;
};
```

Risk Assessment

Granting `AllPermission` to untrusted code allows it to perform privileged operations.

Rule	Severity	Likelihood	Remediation Cost	Priority	Level
ENV03-J	high	likely	low	P27	L1

Automated Detection   Static detection of potential uses of dangerous permissions is a trivial search. Automated determination of the *correctness* of such uses is not feasible.

Related Vulnerabilities   CVE-2007-5342 describes a vulnerability in Apache Tomcat 5.5.9 through 5.5.25 and 6.0.0 through 6.0.15. The security policy used in the JULI logging component failed to restrict certain permissions for web applications. An attacker could modify the log level, directory, or prefix attributes in the `org.apache.juli.FileHandler` handler, permitting them to modify logging configuration options and overwrite arbitrary files.

Related Guidelines

MITRE CWE   CWE-732. Incorrect permission assignment for critical resource

Bibliography

[API 2006]   Class `AllPermission`, `ReflectPermission`, `RuntimePermission`

[Gong 2003]

[Long 2005]   Section 2.5, Reflection

[Permissions 2008]   Section `ReflectPermission`

[Reflect 2006]

[Security 2006]   Security Architecture, Section `RuntimePermission`

■ ENV04-J. Do not disable bytecode verification

When Java source code is compiled, it is converted into bytecode, saved in one or more class files, and executed by the JVM. Java class files may be compiled on one machine and executed on another machine. A properly generated class file is said to be *conforming*. When the JVM loads a class file, it has no way of knowing whether the class file is conforming. The class file could have been created by some other process, or an attacker may have tampered with a conforming class file.

The Java bytecode verifier is an internal component of the JVM that is responsible for detecting nonconforming Java bytecode. It ensures that the class file is in the proper Java class format, that illegal type casts are avoided, that operand stack underflows are impossible, and that each method eventually removes from the operand stack everything pushed by that method.

Users often assume that Java class files obtained from a trustworthy source will be conforming and, consequently, safe for execution. This belief can erroneously lead them to see bytecode verification as a superfluous activity for such classes. Consequently, they might disable bytecode verification, undermining Java's safety and security guarantees. The bytecode verifier must not be suppressed.

Noncompliant Code Example

The bytecode verification process runs by default. The `-Xverify:none` flag on the JVM command line suppresses the verification process. This noncompliant code example uses the flag to disable bytecode verification.

```
java -Xverify:none ApplicationName
```

Compliant Solution

Most JVM implementations perform bytecode verification by default; it is also performed during dynamic class loading.

Specifying the `-Xverify:all` flag on the command line requires the JVM to enable bytecode verification (even when it would otherwise have been suppressed), as shown in this compliant solution.

```
java -Xverify:all ApplicationName
```

Exceptions

ENV04-EX0: On Java 2 systems, the primordial class loader is permitted to omit bytecode verification of classes loaded from the boot class path. These system classes are protected through platform and file system protections rather than by the bytecode verification process.

Risk Assessment

Bytecode verification ensures that the bytecode contains many of the security checks mandated by the *Java Language Specification*. Omitting the verification step could permit execution of insecure Java code.

Rule	Severity	Likelihood	Remediation Cost	Priority	Level
ENV04-J	high	likely	low	P27	L1

Automated Detection   Static checking of this rule is not feasible in the general case.

Bibliography

[Oaks 2001]   The Bytecode Verifier
[Pistoia 2004]   Section 7.3, The Class File Verifier

■ ENV05-J. Do not deploy an application that can be remotely monitored

Java provides several APIs that allow external programs to monitor a running Java program. These APIs also permit the Java program to be monitored remotely by programs on distinct hosts. Such features are convenient for debugging the program or fine-tuning its performance. However, if a Java program is deployed in production with remote monitoring enabled, an attacker can connect to the JVM and inspect its behavior and data, including potentially sensitive information. An attacker can also exert control over the program's behavior. Consequently, remote monitoring must be disabled when running a Java program in production.

JVM Tool Interface (JVMTI)

Java 5 introduced the JVM Tool Interface (JVMTI) [Sun 2004d], replacing both the JVM Profiler Interface (JVMPI) and the JVM Debug Interface (JVMDI), which are now deprecated.

The JVMTI contains extensive facilities to learn about the internals of a running JVM, including facilities to monitor and modify a running Java program. These facilities are rather low level and require the use of the Java Native Interface (JNI) and C language programming. However, they provide the opportunity to access fields that would normally be inaccessible. Also, there are facilities that can change the behavior of a running Java program (for example, threads can be suspended or stopped). The JVMTI profiling tools can also measure the time that a thread takes to execute, leaving applications vulnerable to timing attacks.

The JVMTI works by using agents that communicate with the running JVM. These agents must be loaded at JVM startup and are usually specified via one of the command-line options –agentlib: or –agentpath:. However, agents can be specified in environment variables, although this feature can be disabled where security is a concern. The JVMTI is always enabled, and JVMTI agents may run under the default security manager without requiring any permissions to be granted.

Java Platform Debugger Architecture (JPDA)

The Java Platform Debugger Architecture (JPDA) builds on the JVMTI and provides high-level facilities for debugging Java systems while they are running [JPDA 2004].

The JPDA facilities are similar to the reflection API, which is described in rule SEC05-J. In particular, the JPDA provides methods to get and set field and array values. Access control is not enforced, so that even the values of private fields can be set by a remote process via the JPDA.

Various permissions must be granted for debugging to take place under the default security manager. The following policy file was used to run the JPDS Trace demonstration under the default security manager:

```
grant {
  permission java.io.FilePermission "traceoutput.txt", "read,write";
  permission java.io.FilePermission "C:/Program
Files/Java/jdk1.5.0_04/lib/tools.jar", "read";
  permission java.io.FilePermission "C:/Program", "read,execute";
  permission java.lang.RuntimePermission "modifyThread";
  permission java.lang.RuntimePermission "modifyThreadGroup";
  permission java.lang.RuntimePermission "accessClassInPackage.sun.misc";
  permission java.lang.RuntimePermission "loadLibrary.dt_shmem";
  permission java.util.PropertyPermission "java.home", "read";
  permission java.net.SocketPermission "<localhost>", "resolve";
  permission com.sun.jdi.JDIPermission "virtualMachineManager";
};
```

Because JPDA supports remote debugging, a remote host can access the debugger. An attacker can exploit this feature to study sensitive information or modify the behavior of a running Java application unless appropriate protection is enabled. A security manager can ensure that only known, trusted hosts are given permissions to use the debugger interface.

Java SE Monitoring and Management Features

Java contains extensive facilities for monitoring and managing a JVM [JMX 2006]. In particular, the Java Management Extension (JMX) API enables the monitoring and control of class loading, thread state and stack traces, deadlock detection, memory usage, garbage collection, operating system information, and other operations [Sun 2004a]. It also has facilities for logging monitoring and management.

The Java SE monitoring and management features fall into four broad categories:

- *The JMX technology:* This technology serves as the underlying interface for local and remote monitoring and management.
- *Instrumentation for the JVM:* These facilities enable out-of-the-box monitoring and management of the JVM and are based on the JMX specification.
- *Monitoring and management API:* These facilities use the `java.lang.management` package to provide the monitoring and management interface. Applications can use this package to monitor themselves or to let JMX technology–compliant tools monitor and manage them.
- *Monitoring and management tools:* Tools such as JConsole implement the JMX interface to provide monitoring and management facilities.

These facilities can be used either locally (on the machine that runs the JVM) or remotely. Local monitoring and management is enabled by default when a JVM is started; remote monitoring and management is not. For a JVM to be monitored and managed remotely, it must be started with various system properties set (either on the command line or in a configuration file).

When remote monitoring and management is enabled, access is password-controlled by default. However, password control can be disabled. Disabling password authentication is insecure because any user who can discover the port number that the JMX service is listening on can monitor and control the Java applications running on the JVM [JMXG 2006].

The JVM remote monitoring and management facility uses a secure communication channel (Secure Sockets Layer [SSL]) by default. However, if an attacker can start a bogus remote method invocation (RMI) registry server on the monitored machine before the legitimate RMI registry server is started, JMX passwords can be intercepted. Also, SSL can be disabled when using remote monitoring and management, which could, again, compromise security. See *The Java SE Monitoring and Management Guide* [JMXG 2006] for further details and for mitigation strategies.

There are also provisions to require proper authentication of the remote server. However, users may start a JVM with remote monitoring and management enabled, but with no security; this would leave the JVM open to attack by outsiders. Although accidently enabling remote monitoring and management is unlikely, users might not realize that starting a JVM so enabled, without any security, could leave their JVM exposed to attack.

If exploited, the monitoring and management facilities can seriously compromise the security of Java applications. For example, an attacker can obtain information about the number of classes loaded and threads running, thread state along with traces of live threads, system properties, VM arguments, and memory consumption.

Noncompliant Code Example (JVMTI)

In this noncompliant code example, the JVMTI works by using agents that communicate with the running JVM. These agents are usually loaded at JVM startup via one of the command-line options -agentlib or -agentpath. In the following command, libname is the name of the library to load while options are passed to the agent on startup.

```
${JDK_PATH}/bin/java -agentlib:libname=options ApplicationName
```

Some JVMs allow agents to be started when the JVM is already running. This is insecure in a production environment. Refer to the JVMTI documentation [JVMTI 2006] for platform-specific information on enabling/disabling this feature.

Platforms that support environment variables allow agents to be specified in such variables. "Platforms may disable this feature in cases where security is a concern; for example, the Reference Implementation disables this feature on UNIX systems when the effective user or group ID differs from the real ID" [JVMTI 2006].

Agents may run under the default security manager without requiring any permissions to be granted. While the JVMTI is useful for debuggers and profilers, such levels of access are inappropriate for deployed production code.

Noncompliant Code Example (JPDA)

This noncompliant code example uses command-line arguments to invoke the JVM so that it can be debugged from a running debugger application by listening for connections using shared memory at transport address mysharedmemory.

```
${JDK_PATH}/bin/java -agentlib:jdwp=transport=dt_shmem,
    address=mysharedmemory ApplicationName
```

Likewise, the command-line arguments -Xrunjdwp, which is equivalent to -agentlib, and -Xdebug, which is used by the jdb tool, also enable application debugging.

Noncompliant Code Example (JVM monitoring)

This noncompliant code example invokes the JVM with command-line arguments that permit remote monitoring via port 8000. This may result in a security vulnerability when the password is weak or the SSL protocol is misapplied.

```
${JDK_PATH}/bin/java
    -Dcom.sun.management.jmxremote.port=8000 ApplicationName
```

Compliant Solution

This compliant solution starts the JVM without any agents enabled. Avoid using the -agentlib, -Xrunjdwp, and -Xdebug command-line arguments on production machines. This compliant solution also installs the default security manager.

```
${JDK_PATH}/bin/java -Djava.security.manager ApplicationName
```

Clear the environment variable JAVA_TOOL_OPTIONS in the manner appropriate for your platform, for example, by setting it to an empty string value. This prevents JVMTI agents from receiving arguments via this mechanism. The command-line argument -Xnoagent can also be used to disable the debugging features supported by the old Java debugger (oldjdb).

This compliant solution disables monitoring by remote machines. By default, local monitoring is enabled in Java 6. In earlier versions, the system property com.sun.management.jmxremote must be set to enable local monitoring. Although the unsupported -XX:+DisableAttachMechanism command-line option may be used to disable local Java tools from monitoring the JVM, it is always possible to use native debuggers and other tools to perform monitoring. Fortunately, monitoring tools require at least as many privileges as the owner of the JVM process possesses, reducing the threat of local exploitation through privilege escalation.

Local monitoring uses temporary files and sets the file permissions to those of the owner of the JVM process. Ensure that adequate file protection is in place on the system running the JVM so that the temporary files are accessed appropriately. See rule FIO03-J for additional information.

The Java SE Monitoring and Management Guide [JMXG 2006] provides further advice:

> Local monitoring with jconsole is useful for development and prototyping. Using jconsole locally is not recommended for production environments because jconsole itself consumes significant system resources. Rather, use jconsole on a remote system to isolate it from the platform being monitored.

Moving jconsole to a remote system removes its system resource load from the production environment.

Noncompliant Code Example (Remote Debugging)

Remote debugging requires the use of sockets as the transport (`transport=dt_socket`). Remote debugging also requires specification of the type of application (`server=y`, where y denotes that the JVM is the server and is waiting for a debugger application to connect to it) and the port number to listen on (`address=9000`).

```
${JDK_PATH}/bin/java -agentlib:jdwp=transport=dt_socket,
    server=n,address=9000 ApplicationName
```

Remote debugging is dangerous because an attacker can spoof the client IP address and connect to the JPDA host. Depending on the attacker's position in the network, he or she could extract debugging information by sniffing the network traffic that the JPDA host sends to the forged IP address.

Compliant Solution (Remote Debugging)

Restrict remote debugging to trusted hosts by modifying the security policy file to grant appropriate permissions only to those trusted hosts. For example, specify the permission `java.net.SocketPermission` for only the JPDA host and remove the permission from other hosts.

The JPDA host can serve either as a server or as a client. When the attacker cannot sniff the network to determine the identity of machines that use the JPDA host (for example, through the use of a secure channel), specify the JPDA host as the client and the debugger application as the server by changing the value of the `server` argument to n.

This compliant solution allows the JPDA host to attach to a trusted debugger application.

```
${JDK_PATH}/bin/java -agentlib:jdwp=transport=dt_socket,
    server=y,address=9000 ApplicationName
```

When it is necessary to run a JVM with debugging enabled, avoid granting permissions that are not needed by the application. In particular, avoid granting socket permissions to arbitrary hosts, that is, omit the permission `java.net.SocketPermission    "*"`, `"connect,accept"`.

Exceptions

ENV05-EX0: A Java program may be remotely monitored using any of these technologies if it can be guaranteed that no program outside the local trust boundary can access the program. For example, if the program lives on a local network that is both completely trusted and disconnected from any untrusted networks, including the Internet, remote monitoring is permitted.

Risk Assessment

Deploying a Java application with the JVMTI, JPDA, or remote monitoring enabled can allow an attacker to monitor or modify its behavior.

Rule	Severity	Likelihood	Remediation Cost	Priority	Level
ENV05-J	high	probable	low	P18	L1

Automated Detection   The rule is not amenable to automated static analysis.

Related Vulnerabilities   CVE-2010-4495 describes a vulnerability in the TIBCO ActiveMatrix product line where a flaw in JMX connection processing allowed remote users to execute arbitrary code, cause denial of service or obtain potentially sensitive information.

Bibliography

[JMX 2006]

[JMXG 2006]

[JPDA 2004]

[JVMTI 2006]

[Long 2005]   Section 2.6, The JVM Tool Interface; Section 2.7, Debugging; Section 2.8, Monitoring and Management

[Reflect 2006]   Reflection, Sun Microsystems, Inc. (2006)

Chapter 18

Miscellaneous (MSC)

■ Rules

■ Risk Assessment Summary

Rule	Severity	Likelihood	Remediation Cost	Priority	Level
MSC00-J	medium	likely	high	P6	L2
MSC01-J	low	unlikely	medium	P2	L3
MSC02-J	high	probable	medium	P12	L1

(continued)

Rule	Severity	Likelihood	Remediation Cost	Priority	Level
MSC03-J	high	probable	medium	P12	L1
MSC04-J	low	unlikely	high	P1	L3
MSC05-J	low	probable	medium	P4	L3
MSC06-J	low	probable	medium	P4	L3
MSC07-J	low	unlikely	medium	P2	L3

■ MSC00-J. Use SSLSocket rather than Socket for secure data exchange

Programs must use the `javax.net.ssl.SSLSocket` class rather than the `java.net.Socket` class when transferring sensitive data over insecure communication channels. The class `SSLSocket` provides security protocols such as Secure Sockets Layer/Transport Layer Security (SSL/TLS) to ensure that the channel is not vulnerable to eavesdropping and malicious tampering.

The principal protections included in `SSLSocket` that are not provided by the `Socket` class are [Java API]:

- *Integrity protection:* SSL protects against modification of messages by an active wiretapper.

- *Authentication:* In most modes, SSL provides peer authentication. Servers are usually authenticated, and clients may be authenticated as requested by servers.

- *Confidentiality (privacy protection):* In most modes, SSL encrypts data being sent between client and server. This protects the confidentiality of data so that passive wiretappers cannot observe sensitive data such as financial or personal information.

It is also important to use SSL for secure remote method invocation (RMI) communications because RMI depends on object serialization, and serialized data must be safeguarded in transit. Gong, Ellison, and Dageforde [Gong 2003] describe how to secure RMI communications using `SSLSocket`.

Note that this rule lacks any assumptions about the integrity of the data being sent down a socket. For information about ensuring data integrity, see rule SER02-J.

Noncompliant Code Example

This noncompliant code example shows the use of regular sockets for a server application that fails to protect sensitive information in transit. The insecure code for the corresponding client application follows the server's code.

```
// Exception handling has been omitted for the sake of brevity
class EchoServer {
  public static void main(String[] args) throws IOException {
    ServerSocket serverSocket = null;
    try {
      serverSocket = new ServerSocket(9999);
      Socket socket = serverSocket.accept();
      PrintWriter out = new PrintWriter(socket.getOutputStream(), true);
      BufferedReader in = new BufferedReader(
          new InputStreamReader(socket.getInputStream()));
      String inputLine;
      while ((inputLine = in.readLine()) != null) {
        System.out.println(inputLine);
        out.println(inputLine);
      }
    } finally {
      if (serverSocket != null) {
        try {
          serverSocket.close();
        } catch (IOException x) {
          // handle error
        }
      }
    }
  }
}

class EchoClient {
  public static void main(String[] args)
                      throws UnknownHostException, IOException {
    Socket socket = null;
    try {
      socket = new Socket("localhost", 9999);
      PrintWriter out = new PrintWriter(socket.getOutputStream(), true);
      BufferedReader in = new BufferedReader(
          new InputStreamReader(socket.getInputStream()));
      BufferedReader stdIn = new BufferedReader(
          new InputStreamReader(System.in));
      String userInput;
      while ((userInput = stdIn.readLine()) != null) {
        out.println(userInput);
        System.out.println(in.readLine());
      }
    } finally {
      if (socket != null) {
```

```
      try {
        socket.close();
      } catch (IOException x) {
        // handle error
      }
    }
  }
 }
}
```

Note that the sockets are properly closed in accordance with rule ERR05-J.

Compliant Solution

This compliant solution uses SSLSocket to protect packets using the SSL/TLS security protocols.

```
// Exception handling has been omitted for the sake of brevity
class EchoServer {
  public static void main(String[] args) throws IOException {
    SSLServerSocket sslServerSocket = null;
    try {
      SSLServerSocketFactory sslServerSocketFactory =
          (SSLServerSocketFactory) SSLServerSocketFactory.getDefault();
      sslServerSocket = (SSLServerSocket) sslServerSocketFactory.
                        createServerSocket(9999);
      SSLSocket sslSocket = (SSLSocket) sslServerSocket.accept();
      PrintWriter out = new PrintWriter(sslSocket.getOutputStream(),true);
      BufferedReader in = new BufferedReader(
          new InputStreamReader(sslSocket.getInputStream()));
      String inputLine;
      while ((inputLine = in.readLine()) != null) {
        System.out.println(inputLine);
        out.println(inputLine);
      }
    } finally {
      if (sslServerSocket != null) {
        try {
```

```
            sslServerSocket.close();
        } catch (IOException x) {
            // handle error
        }
      }
    }
  }
}
}

class EchoClient {
  public static void main(String[] args) throws IOException {
    SSLSocket sslSocket = null;
    try {
      SSLSocketFactory sslSocketFactory =
          (SSLSocketFactory) SSLSocketFactory.getDefault();
      sslSocket =
          (SSLSocket) sslSocketFactory.createSocket("localhost", 9999);
      PrintWriter out = new PrintWriter(sslSocket.getOutputStream(),true);
      BufferedReader in = new BufferedReader(
          new InputStreamReader(sslSocket.getInputStream()));
      BufferedReader stdIn = new BufferedReader(
          new InputStreamReader(System.in));
      String userInput;
      while ((userInput = stdIn.readLine()) != null) {
        out.println(userInput);
        System.out.println(in.readLine());
      }
    } finally {
      if (sslSocket != null) {
        try {
          sslSocket.close();
        } catch (IOException x) {
          // handle error
        }
      }
    }
  }
}
```

Programs that use SSLSocket will block indefinitely if they attempt to connect to a port that is not using SSL. Similarly, a program that does not use SSLSocket will block when attempting to establish a connection through a port that does use SSL.

Exceptions

MSC00-EX0: Because of the mechanisms that SSLSocket provides to ensure the secure transfer of packets, significant performance overhead may result. Regular sockets are sufficient when

- the data being sent over the socket is not sensitive.
- the data is sensitive, but properly encrypted. See rule SER02-J for more information.
- the network path of the socket never crosses a trust boundary. This could happen when, for example, the two end points of the socket are within the same local network and the entire network is trusted.

Risk Assessment

Use of plain sockets fails to provide any guarantee of the confidentiality and integrity of data transmitted over those sockets.

Rule	Severity	Likelihood	Remediation Cost	Priority	Level
MSC00-J	medium	likely	high	P6	L2

Automated Detection   The general case of automated detection appears to be infeasible because determining which specific data may be passed through the socket is not statically computable. An approach that introduces a custom API for passing sensitive data via secure sockets may be feasible. User tagging of sensitive data is a necessary requirement for such an approach.

Related Guidelines

MITRE CWE   CWE-311. Failure to encrypt sensitive data

Bibliography

[API 2006]
[Gong 2003]   11.3.3, Securing RMI Communications
[Ware 2008]

■ MSC01-J. Do not use an empty infinite loop

An infinite loop with an empty body consumes CPU cycles but does nothing. Optimizing compilers and just-in-time systems (JITs) are permitted to (perhaps unexpectedly) remove such a loop. Consequently, programs must not include infinite loops with empty bodies.

Noncompliant Code Example

This noncompliant code example implements an idle task that continuously executes a loop without executing any instructions within the loop. An optimizing compiler or JIT could remove the while loop in this example.

```
public int nop() {
  while (true) {}
}
```

Compliant Solution (Thread.sleep())

This compliant solution avoids use of a meaningless infinite loop by invoking Thread. sleep() within the while loop. The loop body contains semantically meaningful operations and consequently cannot be optimized away.

```
public final int DURATION=10000; // in milliseconds

public void nop() throws InterruptedException {
  while (true) {
    // Useful operations
    Thread.sleep(DURATION);
  }
}
```

Compliant Solution (yield())

This compliant solution invokes Thread.yield(), which causes the thread running this method to consistently defer to other threads.

```
public void nop() {
  while (true) {
    Thread.yield();
  }
}
```

Risk Assessment

Rule	Severity	Likelihood	Remediation Cost	Priority	Level
MSC01-J	low	unlikely	medium	P2	L3

Related Guidelines

CERT C Secure Coding Standard   MSC40-C. Do not use an empty infinite loop

Bibliography

[API 2006]

■ MSC02-J. Generate strong random numbers

Pseudorandom number generators (PRNGs) use deterministic mathematical algorithms to produce a sequence of numbers with good statistical properties. However, the sequences of numbers produced fail to achieve true randomness. PRNGs usually start with an arithmetic seed value. The algorithm uses this seed to generate an output value and a new seed, which is used to generate the next value, and so on.

The Java API provides a PRNG, the `java.util.Random` class. This PRNG is portable and repeatable. Consequently, two instances of the `java.util.Random` class that are created using the same seed will generate identical sequences of numbers in all Java implementations. Seed values are often reused on application initialization or after every system reboot. In other cases, the seed is derived from the current time obtained from the system clock. An attacker can learn the value of the seed by performing some reconnaissance on the vulnerable target and can then build a lookup table for estimating future seed values.

Consequently, the `java.util.Random` class must not be used either for security-critical applications or for protecting sensitive data. Use a more secure random number generator, such as the `java.security.SecureRandom` class.

Noncompliant Code Example

This noncompliant code example uses the insecure `java.util.Random` class. This class produces an identical sequence of numbers for each given seed value; consequently, the sequence of numbers is predictable.

```java
import java.util.Random;
// ...

Random number = new Random(123L);
//...
for (int i = 0; i < 20; i++) {
  // Generate another random integer in the range [0, 20]
  int n = number.nextInt(21);
  System.out.println(n);
}
```

Compliant Solution

This compliant solution uses the `java.security.SecureRandom` class to produce high-quality random numbers.

```java
import java.security.SecureRandom;
import java.security.NoSuchAlgorithmException;
// ...

public static void main (String args[]) {
  try {
    SecureRandom number = SecureRandom.getInstance("SHA1PRNG");
    // Generate 20 integers 0..20
    for (int i = 0; i < 20; i++) {
      System.out.println(number.nextInt(21));
    }
  } catch (NoSuchAlgorithmException nsae) {
    // Forward to handler
  }
}
```

Exceptions

MSC02-EX0: Using the default constructor for `java.util.Random` applies a seed value that is "very likely to be distinct from any other invocation of this constructor" [API 2006] and may improve security marginally. As a result, it may be used only for noncritical applications operating on nonsensitive data. Java's default seed uses the system's time in milliseconds. When used, explicit documentation of this exception is required.

```java
import java.util.Random;
// ...

Random number = new Random(); // only used for demo purposes
int n;
//...
for (int i = 0; i < 20; i++) {
  // Re-seed generator
  number = new Random();
  // Generate another random integer in the range [0, 20]
  n = number.nextInt(21);
  System.out.println(n);
}
```

For noncritical cases, such as adding some randomness to a game or unit testing, the use of class Random is acceptable. However, it is worth reiterating that the resulting low-entropy random numbers are insufficiently random to be used for security-critical applications, such as cryptography.

MSC02-EX1: Predictable sequences of pseudorandom numbers are required in some cases, such as when running regression tests of program behavior. Use of the insecure java.util. Random class is permitted in such cases. However, security-related applications may invoke this exception *only* for testing purposes; this exception may not be applied in a production context.

Risk Assessment

Predictable random number sequences can weaken the security of critical applications such as cryptography.

Rule	Severity	Likelihood	Remediation Cost	Priority	Level
MSC02-J	high	probable	medium	P12	L1

Related Vulnerabilities

CVE-2006-6969

Related Guidelines

CERT C Secure Coding Standard	MSC30-C. Do not use the rand() function for generating pseudorandom numbers
CERT C++ Secure Coding Standard	MSC30-CPP. Do not use the rand() function for generating pseudorandom numbers
MITRE CWE	CWE-327, Use of a broken or risky cryptographic algorithm
	CWE-330, Use of insufficiently random values
	CWE-332, Insufficient entropy in PRNG
	CWE-336, Same seed in PRNG
	CWE-337, Predictable seed in PRNG

Bibliography

[API 2006]	Class Random
[API 2006]	Class SecureRandom
[Find Bugs 2008]	BC. Random objects created and used only once
[Monsch 2006]	

■ MSC03-J. Never hard code sensitive information

Hard coding sensitive information, such as passwords, server IP addresses, and encryption keys can expose the information to attackers. Anyone who has access to the class files can decompile them and discover the sensitive information. Consequently, programs must not hard code sensitive information.

Hard coding sensitive information also increases the need to manage and accommodate changes to the code. For example, changing a hard-coded password in a deployed program may require distribution of a patch [Chess 2007].

Noncompliant Code Example

This noncompliant code example includes a hard-coded server IP address in a constant `String`.

```
class IPaddress {
  String ipAddress = new String("172.16.254.1");
  public static void main(String[] args) {
    // ...
  }
}
```

A malicious user can use the `javap -c IPaddress` command to disassemble the class and discover the hard-coded server IP address. The output of the disassembler reveals the server IP address 172.16.254.1 in clear text:

```
Compiled from "IPaddress.java"
class IPaddress extends java.lang.Object{
java.lang.String ipAddress;

IPaddress();
  Code:
    0:  aload_0
    1:  invokespecial #1; //Method java/lang/Object."<init>":()V
    4:  aload_0
    5:  new #2; //class java/lang/String
    8:  dup
    9:  ldc #3; //String 172.16.254.1
    11: invokespecial #4; //Method java/lang/String."<init>":(Ljava/lang/String;)V
    14: putfield #5; //Field ipAddress:Ljava/lang/String;
    17: return
```

```
public static void main(java.lang.String[]);
  Code:
   0:    return

}
```

Compliant Solution

This compliant solution retrieves the server IP address from an external file located in a secure directory. Exposure is further limited by clearing the server IP address from memory immediately after use.

```java
class IPaddress {
  public static void main(String[] args) throws IOException {
    char[] ipAddress = new char[100];
    BufferedReader br = new BufferedReader(new InputStreamReader(
        new FileInputStream("serveripaddress.txt")));

    // Reads the server IP address into the char array,
    // returns the number of bytes read
    int n = br.read(ipAddress);
    // Validate server IP address
    // Manually clear out the server IP address
    // immediately after use
    for (int i = n - 1; i >= 0; i--) {
      ipAddress[i] = 0;
    }
    br.close();
  }
}
```

To further limit the exposure time of the sensitive server IP address, replace `BufferedReader` with a direct native input/output (NIO) buffer, which can be cleared immediately after use.

Noncompliant Code Example (Hard-Coded Database Password)

The user name and password fields in the SQL connection request are hard coded in this noncompliant code example.

```java
public final Connection getConnection() throws SQLException {
  return DriverManager.getConnection(
      "jdbc:mysql://localhost/dbName",
      "username", "password");
}
```

Note that the one- and two-argument `java.sql.DriverManager.getConnection()` methods can also be used incorrectly.

Compliant Solution

This compliant solution reads the user name and password from a configuration file located in a secure directory.

```java
public final Connection getConnection() throws SQLException {
  char[] username = new char[16];
  char[] password = new char[16];
  // Username and password are read at runtime from a secure config file
  return DriverManager.getConnection(
      "jdbc:mysql://localhost/dbName",
      username, password);
  for (int i = username.length - 1; i >= 0; i--) {
    username[i] = 0;
  }
  for (int i = password.length - 1; i >= 0; i--) {
    password[i] = 0;
  }

}
```

It is also permissible to prompt the user for the user name and password at runtime.

Risk Assessment

Hard coding sensitive information exposes that information to attackers.

Rule	Severity	Likelihood	Remediation Cost	Priority	Level
MSC03-J	high	probable	medium	P12	L1

Related Vulnerabilities GERONIMO-2925[1] describes a vulnerability in the WAS CE tool, which is based on Apache Geronimo. It uses the Advanced Encryption Standard (AES) to encrypt passwords but uses a hard-coded key that is identical for all the WAS CE server instances. Consequently, anyone who can download the software is provided with the key to every instance of the tool. This vulnerability was resolved by having each new installation of the tool generate its own unique key and use it from that time on.

---

1. http://issues.apache.org/jira/browse/GERONIMO-2925

Related Guidelines

CERT C Secure Coding Standard	MSC18-C. Be careful while handling sensitive data, such as passwords, in program code
ISO/IEC TR 24772:2010	Hard-Coded Password [XYP]
MITRE CWE	CWE-259. Use of hard-coded password
	CWE-798. Use of hard-coded credentials

Bibliography

[Chess 2007]   11.2, Outbound Passwords: Keep Passwords Out of Source Code
[Fortify 2008]   Unsafe Mobile Code: Database Access
[Gong 2003]   9.4, Private Object State and Object Immutability

■ MSC04-J. Do not leak memory

Programming errors can prevent garbage collection of objects that are no longer relevant to program operation. The garbage collector collects only unreachable objects; consequently, the presence of reachable objects that remain unused indicates memory mismanagement. Consumption of all available heap space can cause an OutOfMemoryError, which usually results in program termination.

Excessive memory leaks can lead to memory exhaustion and denial of service (DoS) and must be avoided. For more information, see rule MSC05-J.

Noncompliant Code Example (Off-by-One Programming Error)

The vector object in this noncompliant code example leaks memory. The condition for removing the vector element is mistakenly written as n > 0 instead of n >= 0. Consequently, the method fails to remove one element per invocation and quickly exhausts the available heap space.

```
public class Leak {
  static Vector vector = new Vector();

  public void useVector(int count) {
    for (int n = 0; n < count; n++) {
      vector.add(Integer.toString(n));
    }
```

```
  // ...
  for (int n = count - 1; n > 0; n--) { // Free the memory
    vector.removeElementAt(n);
  }
}

public static void main(String[] args) throws IOException {
  Leak le = new Leak();
  int i = 1;
  while (true) {
    System.out.println("Iteration: " + i);
    le.useVector(1);
    i++;
  }
}
}
```

Compliant Solution (>=)

This compliant solution corrects the mistake by changing the loop condition to n >= 0.

```
public void useVector(int count) {
  for (int n = 0; n < count; n++) {
    vector.add(Integer.toString(n));
  }
  // ...
  for (int n = count - 1; n >= 0; n--) {
    vector.removeElementAt(n);
  }
}
```

Compliant Solution (clear())

Prefer the use of standard language semantics where possible. This compliant solution uses the vector.clear() method, which removes all elements.

```
public void useVector(int count) {
  for (int n = 0; n < count; n++) {
    vector.add(Integer.toString(n));
  }
  //...
  vector.clear(); // Clear the vector
}
```

Noncompliant Code Example (Nonlocal Instance Field)

This noncompliant code example declares and allocates a HashMap instance field that is used only in the doSomething() method.

```
public class Storer {
  private HashMap<Integer,String> hm = new HashMap<Integer, String>();

  private void doSomething() {
    // hm is used only here and never referenced again
    hm.put(1, "java");
    // ...
  }
}
```

Programmers may be surprised that the HashMap persists for the entire lifetime of the Storer instance.

Compliant Solution (Reduce Scope of Instance Field)

This compliant solution declares the HashMap as a local variable within the doSomething() method. The hm local variable is eliminated after the method returns. When the local variable holds the only reference to the HashMap, the garbage collector can reclaim its associated storage.

```
public class Storer {
  private void doSomething() {
    HashMap<Integer,String> hm = new HashMap<Integer,String>();
    hm.put(1,"java");
    // ...
  }
}
```

Localizing or confining the instance field to a narrower scope simplifies garbage collection; today's generational garbage collectors perform well with short-lived objects.

Noncompliant Code Example (Lapsed Listener)

This noncompliant code example, known as the *Lapsed Listener* [Goetz 2005a], demonstrates unintentional object retention. The button continues to hold a reference of the reader object after completion of the readSomething() method, even though the reader object is never used again. Consequently, the garbage collector cannot collect the `reader` object. A similar problem occurs with inner classes because they hold an implicit reference to the enclosing class.

```java
public class LapseEvent extends JApplet {
  JButton button;
  public void init() {
    button = new JButton("Click Me");
    getContentPane().add(button, BorderLayout.CENTER);
    Reader reader = new Reader();
    button.addActionListener(reader);
    try {
      reader.readSomething();
    } catch (IOException e) {
      // Handle exception
    }
  }
}

class Reader implements ActionListener {
  public void actionPerformed(ActionEvent e)  {
    Toolkit.getDefaultToolkit().beep();
  }
  public void readSomething() throws IOException {
    // Read from file
  }
}
```

Noncompliant Code Example (Exception before Remove)

This noncompliant code example attempts to remove the reader through use of the `remove-ActionListener()` method.

```java
Reader reader = new Reader();
button.addActionListener(reader);
try {
  reader.readSomething();  // Can skip next line of code
  // Dereferenced, but control flow can change
  button.removeActionListener(reader);
} catch (IOException e) {
  // Forward to handler
}
```

If an exception is thrown by the readSomething() method, the removeActionListener() statement is never executed.

Compliant Solution (`finally` Block)

This compliant solution uses a `finally` block to ensure that the reader object's reference is removed.

```
Reader reader = new Reader();
button.addActionListener(reader);
try {
  reader.readSomething();
} catch (IOException e) {
  // Handle exception
} finally {
  button.removeActionListener(reader);  // Always executed
}
```

Noncompliant Code Example (Member Object Leaks)

This noncompliant code example implements a stack data structure [Bloch 2008] that continues to hold references to elements after they have been popped off the stack.

```
public class Stack {
  private Object[] elements;
  private int size = 0;
  public Stack(int initialCapacity) {
    this.elements = new Object[initialCapacity];
  }

  public void push(Object e) {
    ensureCapacity();
    elements[size++] = e;
  }

  public Object pop() { // This method causes memory leaks
    if (size == 0) {
      throw new EmptyStackException();
    }
    return elements[--size];
  }
}
```

```
/*
 * Ensure space for at least one more element, roughly
 * doubling the capacity each time the array needs to grow.
 */
private void ensureCapacity() {
  if (elements.length == size) {
    Object[] oldElements = elements;
    elements = new Object[2 * elements.length + 1];
    System.arraycopy(oldElements, 0, elements, 0, size);
  }
}
}
```

The object references are retained on the stack even after the element is popped. Such *obsolete references* cause objects to remain live; consequently, the objects cannot be garbage-collected.

Compliant Solution (null)

This compliant solution assigns null to all obsolete references.

```
public Object pop() {
  if (size == 0) {
    throw new EmptyStackException(); // Ensures object consistency
  }
  Object result = elements[--size];
  elements[size] = null; // Eliminate obsolete reference
  return result;
}
```

The garbage collector can then include individual objects formerly referenced from the stack in its list of objects to free.

Although these examples appear trivial and may not represent significant problems in production code, obsolete references remain a concern when dealing with data structures such as hash tables containing many large records. It is prudent to assign null to array-like custom data structures; doing so with individual object references or local variables is unnecessary because the garbage collector handles these cases automatically [Commes 2007].

Noncompliant Code Example (Strong References)

A common variation of the obsolete object fallacy is the unintentional retention of objects in collections such as maps. In this noncompliant code example, a server maintains temporary metadata about all committed secure connections.

```
class HashMetaData {
  private Map<SSLSocket, InetAddress> m = Collections.synchronizedMap(
      new HashMap<SSLSocket, InetAddress>());

  public void storeTempConnection(SSLSocket sock, InetAddress ip) {
    m.put(sock, ip);
  }

  public void removeTempConnection(SSLSocket sock) {
    m.remove(sock);
  }
}
```

It is possible to close a socket without removing it from this map. Consequently, this map may contain dead sockets until removeTempConnection() is invoked on them. In the absence of notification logic, it is impossible to determine when to call removeTempConnection(). Moreover, nullifying original objects or referents (Socket connections) is unwieldy.

Compliant Solution (Weak References)

This compliant solution uses *weak references* to allow timely garbage collection.

```
// ...
private Map<SSLSocket, InetAddress> m = Collections.synchronizedMap(
  new WeakHashMap<SSLSocket, InetAddress>()
);
```

Strong references prevent the garbage collector from reclaiming objects that are stored inside container objects, such as in a Map. According to the Java API [API 2006], weak reference objects "do not prevent their referents[2] from being made finalizable, finalized, and then reclaimed."

Keys held in WeakHashMap objects are referenced through weak references. Objects become eligible for garbage collection when they lack strong references. Consequently, use of weak references allows the code to refer to the referent without delaying garbage collection of the referent. This approach is suitable only when the lifetime of the object is required to be the same as the lifetime of the key.

Simply facilitating garbage collection of unneeded objects through use of weak references is insufficient. Programs must also prune the data structure so that additional live entries can be accommodated. One pruning technique is to call the get() method of WeakHashMap and remove any entry that corresponds to a null return value (polling). Use of reference queues is a more efficient method [Goetz 2005b].

---

2. A referent is the object that is being referred to.

Compliant Solution (Reference Queue)

Reference queues provide notifications when a referent is garbage-collected. When the referent is garbage-collected, the HashMap continues to strongly reference both the Weak-Reference object and the corresponding map value (for each entry in the HashMap).

When the garbage collector clears the reference to an object, it adds the corresponding WeakReference object to the reference queue. The WeakReference object remains in the reference queue until some operation is performed on the queue (such as a put() or remove()). After such an operation, the WeakReference object in the hash map is also garbage-collected. Alternatively, this two-step procedure can be carried out manually by using the following code:

```
class HashMetaData {
  private Map<WeakReference<SSLSocket>, InetAddress> m =
      Collections.synchronizedMap(
        new HashMap<WeakReference<SSLSocket>, InetAddress>());
  ReferenceQueue queue = new ReferenceQueue();

  public void storeTempConnection(SSLSocket sock, InetAddress ip) {
    WeakReference<SSLSocket> wr =
      new WeakReference<SSLSocket>(sock, queue);

    // poll for dead entries before adding more
    while ((wr = (WeakReference) queue.poll()) != null) {
      // Removes the WeakReference object and the value (not the referent)
      m.remove(wr);
    }
    m.put(wr, ip);
  }

  public void removeTempConnection(SSLSocket sock) {
    m.remove(sock);
  }
}
```

Note that the two-argument constructor of WeakReference takes a Queue argument and must be used to perform direct queue processing. Dead entries should be pruned prior to insertion.

Compliant Solution (Soft References)

Use of soft references is also permitted. Soft references guarantee that the referent will be reclaimed before an OutOfMemoryError occurs and also that the referent will remain live until memory begins to run out.

```
class HashMetaData {
  private Map<SoftReference<SSLSocket>, InetAddress> m =
      Collections.synchronizedMap(
        new HashMap<SoftReference<SSLSocket>, InetAddress>());
  ReferenceQueue queue = new ReferenceQueue();

  public void storeTempConnection(SSLSocket sock, InetAddress ip) {
    SoftReference<SSLSocket> sr =
        new SoftReference<SSLSocket>(sock, queue);
    while ((sr = (SoftReference) queue.poll()) != null) {
      // Removes the WeakReference object and the value (not the referent)
      m.remove(sr);
    }
    m.put(sr, ip);
  }

  public void removeTempConnection(SSLSocket sock) {
    m.remove(sock);
  }
}
```

Weak references are garbage-collected more aggressively than soft references. Consequently, weak references should be preferred in applications where efficient memory usage is critical, and soft references should be preferred in applications that rely heavily on caching.

Risk Assessment

Memory leaks in Java applications may be exploited in a DoS attack.

Rule	Severity	Likelihood	Remediation Cost	Priority	Level
MSC04-J	low	unlikely	high	P1	L3

Related Guidelines

ISO/IEC TR 24772:2010	Memory Leak [XYL]
MITRE CWE	CWE-401. Improper release of memory before removing last reference ("memory leak")

Bibliography

[API 2006]	Class Vector, Class WeakReference
[Bloch 2008]	Item 6. Eliminate obsolete object references
[Commes 2007]	Memory Leak Avoidance

[Goetz 2005a]   Lapsed Listeners
[Goetz 2005b]   Memory Leaks with Global Maps; Reference Queues
[Gupta 2005]

■ MSC05-J. Do not exhaust heap space

A Java `OutofMemoryError` occurs when the program attempts to use more heap space than is available. Among other causes, this error may result from

- a memory leak (see rule MSC04-J).
- an infinite loop
- limited amounts of default heap memory available.
- incorrect implementation of common data structures (hash tables, vectors, and so on).
- unbounded deserialization.
- writing a large number of objects to an `ObjectOutputStream` (see rule SER10-J).
- creating a large number of threads.
- uncompressing a file (see rule IDS04-J).

Some of these causes are platform-dependent and difficult to anticipate. Others are fairly easy to anticipate, such as reading data from a file. As a result, programs must not accept untrusted input in a manner that can cause the program to exhaust memory.

Noncompliant Code Example (`readLine()`)

This noncompliant code example reads lines of text from a file and adds each one to a vector until a line with the word "quit" is encountered.

```java
class ReadNames {
  private Vector<String> names = new Vector<String>();
  private final InputStreamReader input;
  private final BufferedReader reader;

  public ReadNames(String filename) throws IOException {
    this.input = new FileReader(filename);
    this.reader = new BufferedReader(input);
  }

  public void addNames() throws IOException {
    try {
```

```
      String newName;
      while (((newName = reader.readLine()) != null) &&
             !(newName.equalsIgnoreCase("quit"))) {
        names.addElement(newName);
        System.out.println("adding " + newName);
      }
    } finally {
      input.close();
    }
  }

  public static void main(String[] args) throws IOException {
    if (args.length != 1) {
      System.out.println("Arguments: [filename]");
      return;
    }
    ShowHeapError demo = new ShowHeapError(args[0]);
    demo.addNames();
  }
}
```

The code places no upper bounds on the memory space required to execute the program. Consequently, the program can easily exhaust the available heap space in two ways. First, an attacker can supply arbitrarily many lines in the file, causing the vector to grow until memory is exhausted. Second, an attacker can simply supply an arbitrarily long line, causing the readLine() method to exhaust memory. According to the Java API documentation [API 2006], the BufferedReader.readLine() method

> Reads a line of text. A line is considered to be terminated by any one of a line feed ('\n'), a carriage return ('\r'), or a carriage return followed immediately by a linefeed.

Any code that uses this method is susceptible to a resource exhaustion attack because the user can enter a string of any length.

Compliant Solution (Java SE 7: Limited File Size)

This compliant solution imposes a limit on the size of the file being read. This is accomplished with the Files.size() method, which is new to Java SE 7. If the file is within the limit, we can assume the standard readLine() method will not exhaust memory, nor will memory be exhausted by the while loop.

```
class ReadNames {
  public static final int fileSizeLimit = 1000000;

  public ReadNames(String filename) throws IOException {
    if (Files.size(Paths.get(filename)) > fileSizeLimit) {
      throw new IOException("File too large");
    }
    this.input = new FileReader(filename);
    this.reader = new BufferedReader(input);
  }

  // ... other methods
}
```

Compliant Solution (Limited Length Input)

This compliant solution imposes limits both on the length of each line and on the total number of items to add to the vector. (It does not depend on any Java SE 7 features.)

```
class ReadNames {
  // ... other methods

  public static String readLimitedLine(Reader reader, int limit)
                                        throws IOException {
    StringBuilder sb = new StringBuilder();
    for (int i = 0; i < limit; i++) {
      int c = reader.read();
      if (c == -1) {
        return null;
      }
      if (((char) c == '\n') || ((char) c == '\r')) {
        break;
      }
      sb.append((char) c);
    }
    return sb.toString();
  }

  public static final int lineLengthLimit = 1024;
  public static final int lineCountLimit = 1000000;
```

```
public void addNames() throws IOException {
  try {
    String newName;
    for (int i = 0; i < lineCountLimit; i++) {
      newName = readLimitedLine(reader, lineLengthLimit);
      if (newName == null || newName.equalsIgnoreCase("quit")) {
        break;
      }
      names.addElement(newName);
      System.out.println("adding " + newName);
    }
  } finally {
    input.close();
  }
}
```

The `readLimitedLine()` method takes a numeric limit, indicating the total number of characters that may exist on one line. If a line contains more characters, the line is truncated, and the characters are returned on the next invocation. This prevents an attacker from exhausting memory by supplying input with no line breaks.

Noncompliant Code Example

In a server-class machine using a parallel garbage collector, the default initial and maximum heap sizes are as follows for Java SE 6 [Sun 2006]:

- Initial heap size: Larger of 1/64 of the machine's physical memory or some reasonable minimum.
- Maximum heap size: Smaller of 1/4 of the physical memory or 1GB.

This noncompliant code example requires more memory on the heap than is available by default.

```
/** Assuming the heap size as 512 MB
 *    (calculated as 1/4th of 2 GB RAM = 512 MB)
 * Considering long values being entered (64 bits each,
 * the max number of elements would be 512 MB/64bits =
 * 67108864)
 */
```

```
public class ReadNames {
  // Accepts unknown number of records
  Vector<Long> names = new Vector<Long>();
  long newID = 0L;
  int count = 67108865;
  int i = 0;
  InputStreamReader input = new InputStreamReader(System.in);
  Scanner reader = new Scanner(input);

  public void addNames() {
    try {
      do {
        // Adding unknown number of records to a list
        // The user can enter more IDs than the heap can support and,
        // as a result, exhaust the heap. Assume that the record ID
        // is a 64 bit long value
        System.out.print("Enter recordID (To quit, enter -1): ");
        newID = reader.nextLong();

        names.addElement(newID);
        i++;
      } while (i < count || newID != -1);
    } finally {
      input.close();
    }
  }

  public static void main(String[] args) {
    ShowHeapError demo = new ShowHeapError();
    demo.addNames();
  }
}
```

Compliant Solution

A simple compliant solution is to reduce the number of names to read.

```
// ...
int count = 10000000;
// ...
```

Compliant Solution

The OutOfMemoryError can be avoided by ensuring the absence of infinite loops, memory leaks, and unnecessary object retention. When memory requirements are known ahead of time, the heap size can be tailored to fit the requirements using the following runtime parameters [Java 2006]:

```
java -Xms<initial heap size> -Xmx<maximum heap size>
```

For example,

```
java -Xms128m -Xmx512m ShowHeapError
```

Here the initial heap size is set to 128MB and the maximum heap size to 512MB.

These settings can be changed either using the Java Control Panel or from the command line. They cannot be adjusted through the application itself.

Risk Assessment

Assuming infinite heap space can result in DoS.

Rule	Severity	Likelihood	Remediation Cost	Priority	Level
MSC05-J	low	probable	medium	P4	L3

Related Vulnerabilities The Apache Geronimo bug described by GERONIMO-4224[3] results in an OutOfMemoryError exception thrown by the WebAccessLogViewer when the access log file size is too large.

Related Guidelines

CERT C Secure Coding Standard	MEM11-C. Do not assume infinite heap space
CERT C++ Secure Coding Standard	MEM12-CPP. Do not assume infinite heap space
ISO/IEC TR 24772:2010	Resource Exhaustion [XZP]
MITRE CWE	CWE-400. Uncontrolled resource consumption ("resource exhaustion")
	CWE-770. Allocation of resources without limits or throttling

---

3. http://issues.apache.org/jira/browse/GERONIMO-4224

Bibliography

[API 2006]	Class `ObjectInputStream` and `ObjectOutputStream`
[Java 2006]	Java—The Java application launcher, Syntax for increasing the heap size
[SDN 2011]	Serialization FAQ
[Sun 2003]	Chapter 5, Tuning the Java Runtime System, Tuning the Java Heap
[Sun 2006]	Garbage Collection Ergonomics, Default Values for the Initial and Maximum Heap Size

■ MSC06-J. Do not modify the underlying collection when an iteration is in progress

According to the Java API documentation [API 2006] for the `Iterator.remove()` method:

> The behavior of an iterator is unspecified if the underlying collection is modified while the iteration is in progress in any way other than by calling this method.

Concurrent modification in single-threaded programs is usually a result of inserting or removing an element during iteration. Multithreaded programs add the possibility that a collection may be modified by one thread while another thread iterates over the collection. Undefined behavior results in either case. Many implementations throw a `ConcurrentModificationException` when they detect concurrent modification.

According to the Java API documentation [API 2006] for `ConcurrentModificationException`:

> It is not generally permissible for one thread to modify a `Collection` while another thread is iterating over it. In general, the results of the iteration are undefined under these circumstances. Some `Iterator` implementations (including those of all the general purpose collection implementations provided by the JRE) may choose to throw this exception if this behavior is detected. `Iterators` that do this are known as fail-fast iterators, as they fail quickly and cleanly, rather that risking arbitrary, non-deterministic behavior at an undetermined time in the future.
>
> Note that fail-fast behavior cannot be guaranteed because it is, generally speaking, impossible to make any hard guarantees in the presence of unsynchronized concurrent modification. Fail-fast operations throw `ConcurrentModificationException` on a best-effort basis. Consequently, it would be wrong to write a program that depended on this exception for its correctness: `ConcurrentModificationException` should be used only to detect bugs.

Reliance on `ConcurrentModificationException` is inadequate to prevent undefined behavior resulting from modifying an underlying collection while simultaneously iterating over the collection. The fail-fast behavior may occur only after processing an arbitrary number of elements. In *Java Concurrency in Practice* [Goetz 2006a], Goetz and colleagues note:

> [Fail-fast iterators] are implemented by associating a modification count with the collection: if the modification count changes during iteration, `hasNext` or `next` throws `ConcurrentModificationException`. However, this check is done without synchronization, so there is a risk of seeing a stale value of the modification count and therefore . . . that the iterator does not realize a modification has been made. This was a deliberate design tradeoff to reduce the performance impact of the concurrent modification detection code.

Note that the enhanced `for` loop (for-each idiom) uses an `Iterator` internally. Consequently, enhanced `for` loops can also participate in concurrent modification issues, even though they lack an obvious iterator.

Noncompliant Code Example (Single-Threaded)

This noncompliant code example (based on Sun Developer Network [SDN 2011] bug report 6687277[4]) uses the `Collection`'s `remove()` method to remove an element from an `ArrayList` while iterating over the `ArrayList`. The resulting behavior is unspecified.

```
class BadIterate {
  public static void main(String[] args) {
    List<String> list = new ArrayList<String>();
    list.add("one");
    list.add("two");

    Iterator iter = list.iterator();
    while (iter.hasNext()) {
      String s = (String)iter.next();
      if (s.equals("one")) {
        list.remove(s);
      }
    }
  }
}
```

Compliant Solution (`iterator.remove()`)

The `Iterator.remove()` method removes the last element returned by the iterator from the underlying `Collection`. Its behavior is fully specified, so it may be safely invoked while iterating over a collection.

---

4. http://bugs.sun.com/bugdatabase/view_bug.do?bug_id=6687277

```
// ...
if (s.equals("one")) {
  iter.remove();
}
// ...
```

Noncompliant Code Example (Multithreaded)

Although acceptable in a single-threaded environment, this noncompliant code example is insecure in a multithreaded environment because it is possible for another thread to modify the widgetList while the current thread iterates over the widgetList. Additionally, the doSomething() method could modify the collection during iteration.

```
List<Widget> widgetList = new ArrayList<Widget>();

public void widgetOperation() {
  // May throw ConcurrentModificationException
  for (Widget w : widgetList) {
    doSomething(w);
  }
}
```

Compliant Solution (Thread-Safe Collection)

This compliant solution wraps the ArrayList in a synchronized collection so that all modifications are subject to the locking mechanism.

```
List<Widget> widgetList =
    Collections.synchronizedList(new ArrayList<Widget>());

public void widgetOperation() {
  for (Widget w : widgetList) {
    doSomething(w);
  }
}
```

This approach must be implemented correctly to avoid starvation, deadlock, and scalability issues [Goetz 2006a].

Compliant Solution (Deep Copying)

This compliant solution creates a deep copy of the mutable widgetList before iterating over it.

```
List<Widget> widgetList = new ArrayList<Widget>();

public void widgetOperation() {
  List<Widget> deepCopy = new ArrayList<Widget>();
  synchronized (widgetList) { // Client-side locking
    for (Object obj : widgetList) {
      deepCopy.add(obj.clone());
    }
  }

  for (Widget w : deepCopy) {
    doSomething(w);
  }
}
```

Creating deep copies of the list prevents underlying changes in the original list from affecting the iteration in progress. "Since the clone is thread-confined, no other thread can modify it during iteration, eliminating the possibility of ConcurrentModification-Exception. (The collection still must be locked during the clone operation itself)" [Goetz 2006a]. However, this approach is often more expensive than other techniques. There is also a risk of operating on stale data, which may affect the correctness of the code.

Compliant Solution (CopyOnWriteArrayList)

The CopyOnWriteArrayList data structure implements all mutating operations by making a fresh copy of the underlying array. It is fully thread-safe and is optimized for cases where traversal operations vastly outnumber mutations. Note that traversals of such lists always see the list in the state it had at the creation of the iterator (or enhanced for loop); subsequent modifications of the list are invisible to an ongoing traversal. Consequently, this solution is inappropriate when mutations of the list are frequent or when new values should be reflected in ongoing traversals.

```
List<Widget> widgetList = new CopyOnWriteArrayList<Widget>();

public void widgetOperation() {
  for (Widget w : widgetList) {
    doSomething(w);
  }
}
```

Risk Assessment

Modifying a collection while iterating over it results in undefined behavior.

Rule	Severity	Likelihood	Remediation Cost	Priority	Level
MSC06-J	low	probable	medium	P4	L3

Automated Detection   Some static analysis tools can detect cases where an iterator is being used after the source container of the iterator is modified.

Related Vulnerabilities   The Apache Harmony bug HARMONY-6236[5] documents an `ArrayList` breaking when given concurrent collections as input.

Bibliography

[API 2006]	Class `ConcurrentModificationException`
[SDN 2011]	Sun Bug database, Bug ID 6687277
[Goetz 2006a]	5.1.2. Iterators and `ConcurrentModificationException`

■ MSC07-J. Prevent multiple instantiations of singleton objects

The singleton design pattern's intent is succinctly described by the seminal work of Gamma et al. [Gamma 1995]:

> Ensure a class only has one instance, and provide a global point of access to it.

Because there is only one Singleton instance, "any instance fields of a Singleton will occur only once per class, just like static fields. Singletons often control access to resources such as database connections or sockets" [Fox 2001]. Other applications of singletons involve maintaining performance statistics, system monitoring and logging, implementing printer spoolers, or even ensuring that only one audio file plays at a time. Classes that contain only static methods are good candidates for the Singleton pattern.

The Singleton pattern typically uses a single instance of a class that encloses a private static class field. The instance can be created using *lazy initialization*, which means that the instance is not created when the class loads but when it is first used.

---

5. http://issues.apache.org/jira/browse/HARMONY-6236

A class that implements the singleton design pattern must prevent multiple instantiations. Relevant techniques include

- making its constructor private.
- employing lock mechanisms to prevent an initialization routine from running simultaneously by multiple threads.
- ensuring the class is not serializable.
- ensuring the class cannot be cloned.
- preventing the class from being garbage-collected if it was loaded by a custom class loader.

Noncompliant Code Example (Nonprivate Constructor)

This noncompliant code example uses a nonprivate constructor for instantiating a singleton.

```
class MySingleton {
  private static MySingleton Instance;

  protected MySingleton() {
    Instance = new MySingleton();
  }

  public static synchronized MySingleton getInstance() {
    return Instance;
  }
}
```

A malicious subclass may extend the accessibility of the constructor from protected to public, allowing untrusted code to create multiple instances of the singleton. Also, the class field Instance has not been declared final.

Compliant Solution (Private Constructor)

This compliant solution reduces the accessibility of the constructor to private and immediately initializes the field Instance, allowing it to be declared final. Singleton constructors must be private.

```
class MySingleton {
  private static final MySingleton Instance = new MySingleton();
```

```
  private MySingleton() {
    // private constructor prevents instantiation by untrusted callers
  }

  public static synchronized MySingleton getInstance() {
    return Instance;
  }
}
```

The MySingleton class need not be declared final because it has a private constructor.

Noncompliant Code Example (Visibility across Threads)

Multiple instances of the Singleton class can be created when the getter method is tasked with initializing the singleton when necessary, and the getter method is invoked by two or more threads simultaneously.

```
class MySingleton {
  private static MySingleton Instance;

  private MySingleton() {
    // private constructor prevents instantiation by untrusted callers
  }

  // Lazy initialization
  public static MySingleton getInstance() { // Not synchronized
    if (Instance == null) {
      Instance = new MySingleton();
    }
    return Instance;
  }
}
```

A singleton initializer method in a multithreaded program must employ some form of locking to prevent construction of multiple singleton objects.

Noncompliant Code Example (Inappropriate Synchronization)

Multiple instances can be created even when the singleton construction is encapsulated in a synchronized block.

```
public static MySingleton getInstance() {
  if (Instance == null) {
    synchronized (MySingleton.class) {
      Instance = new MySingleton();
    }
  }
  return Instance;
}
```

This is because two or more threads may simultaneously see the field Instance as null in the if condition and enter the synchronized block one at a time.

Compliant Solution (Synchronized Method)

To address the issue of multiple threads creating more than one instance of the singleton, make getInstance() a synchronized method.

```
class MySingleton {
  private static MySingleton Instance;

  private MySingleton() {
    // private constructor prevents instantiation by untrusted callers
  }

  // Lazy initialization
  public static synchronized MySingleton getInstance() {
    if (Instance == null) {
      Instance = new MySingleton();
    }
    return Instance;
  }
}
```

Compliant Solution (Double-Checked Locking)

Another compliant solution for implementing thread-safe singletons is the correct use of the double-checked locking idiom.

```
class MySingleton {
  private static volatile MySingleton Instance;
```

```
  private MySingleton() {
    // private constructor prevents instantiation by untrusted callers
  }

  // Double-checked locking
  public static MySingleton getInstance() {
    if (Instance == null) {
      synchronized (MySingleton.class) {
        if (Instance == null) {
          Instance = new MySingleton();
        }
      }
    }
    return Instance;
  }
}
```

This design pattern is often implemented incorrectly. Refer to rule LCK10-J for more details on the correct use of the double-checked locking idiom.

Compliant Solution (Initialize-on-Demand Holder Class Idiom)

This compliant solution uses a static inner class to create the singleton instance.

```
class MySingleton {
  static class SingletonHolder {
    static MySingleton Instance = new MySingleton();
  }

  public static MySingleton getInstance() {
    return SingletonHolder.Instance;
  }
}
```

This is known as the initialize-on-demand holder class idiom. Refer to rule LCK10-J for more information.

Noncompliant Code Example (Serializable)

This noncompliant code example implements the java.io.Serializable interface, which allows the class to be serialized. Deserialization of the class implies that multiple instances of the singleton can be created.

```
class MySingleton implements Serializable {
  private static final long serialVersionUID = 6825273283542226860L;
  private static MySingleton Instance;

  private MySingleton() {
    // private constructor prevents instantiation by untrusted callers
  }

  // Lazy initialization
  public static synchronized MySingleton getInstance() {
    if (Instance == null) {
      Instance = new MySingleton();
    }
    return Instance;
  }
}
```

A singleton's constructor cannot install checks to enforce the requirement that the class is only instantiated once because serialization can bypass the object's constructor.

Noncompliant Code Example (`readResolve()` Method)

Adding a `readResolve()` method that returns the original instance is insufficient to enforce the singleton property. This is insecure even when all the fields are declared transient or static.

```
class MySingleton implements Serializable {
  private static final long serialVersionUID = 6825273283542226860L;
  private static MySingleton Instance;

  private MySingleton() {
    // private constructor prevents instantiation by untrusted callers
  }

  // Lazy initialization
  public static synchronized MySingleton getInstance() {
    if (Instance == null) {
      Instance = new MySingleton();
    }
    return Instance;
  }

  private Object readResolve() {
    return Instance;
  }
}
```

At runtime, an attacker can add a class that reads in a crafted serialized stream:

```
public class Untrusted implements Serializable {
  public static MySingleton captured;
  public MySingleton capture;

  public Untrusted(MySingleton capture) {
    this.capture = capture;
  }

  private void readObject(java.io.ObjectInputStream in)
                           throws Exception {
    in.defaultReadObject();
    captured = capture;
  }
}
```

The crafted stream can be generated by serializing the following class:

```
public final class MySingleton
                    implements java.io.Serializable {
  private static final long serialVersionUID =
      6825273283542226860L;
  public Untrusted untrusted =
      new Untrusted(this); // Additional serial field

  public MySingleton() { }
}
```

Upon deserialization, the field `MySingleton.untrusted` is reconstructed before `MySingleton.readResolve()` is called. Consequently, `Untrusted.captured` is assigned the deserialized instance of the crafted stream instead of `MySingleton.Instance`. This issue is pernicious when an attacker can add classes to exploit the singleton guarantee of an existing serializable class.

Noncompliant Code Example (Nontransient Instance Fields)

This serializable noncompliant code example uses a nontransient instance field `str`.

```
class MySingleton implements Serializable {
  private static final long serialVersionUID = 2787342337386756967L;
  private static MySingleton Instance;

  // non-transient instance field
  private String[] str = {"one", "two", "three"};
```

```
    private MySingleton() {
      // private constructor prevents instantiation by untrusted callers
    }

    public void displayStr() {
      System.out.println(Arrays.toString(str));
    }

    private Object readResolve() {
      return Instance;
    }
}
```

"If a singleton contains a nontransient object reference field, the contents of this field will be deserialized before the singleton's readResolve method is run. This allows a carefully crafted stream to 'steal' a reference to the originally deserialized singleton at the time the contents of the object reference field are deserialized" [Bloch 2008].

Compliant Solution (Enumeration Types)

Stateful singleton classes must be nonserializable. As a precautionary measure, classes that are serializable must not save a reference to a singleton object in their nontransient or non-static instance variables. This prevents the singleton from being indirectly serialized.

Bloch [Bloch 2008] suggests the use of an enumeration type as a replacement for traditional implementations when serializable singletons are indispensable.

```
public enum MySingleton {
  private static MySingleton Instance;

  // non-transient field
  private String[] str = {"one", "two", "three"};

  public void displayStr() {
    System.out.println(Arrays.toString(str));
  }
}
```

This approach is functionally equivalent to, but much safer than, commonplace implementations. It both ensures that only one instance of the object exists at any instant and provides the serialization property (because java.lang.Enum<E> extends java.io.Serializable).

Noncompliant Code Example (Cloneable Singleton)

When the singleton class implements java.lang.Cloneable directly or through inheritance, it is possible to create a copy of the singleton by cloning it using the object's clone() method. This noncompliant code example shows a singleton that implements the java.lang.Cloneable interface.

```
class MySingleton implements Cloneable {
  private static MySingleton Instance;

  private MySingleton() {
    // private constructor prevents
    // instantiation by untrusted callers
  }

  // Lazy initialization
  public static synchronized MySingleton getInstance() {
    if (Instance == null) {
      Instance = new MySingleton();
    }
    return Instance;
  }
}
```

Compliant Solution (Override clone() Method)

Avoid making the singleton class cloneable by not implementing the Cloneable interface and not deriving from a class that already implements it.

When the singleton class must indirectly implement the Cloneable interface through inheritance, the object's clone() method must be overridden with one that throws a CloneNotSupportedException exception [Daconta 2003].

```
class MySingleton implements Cloneable {
  private static MySingleton Instance;

  private MySingleton() {
    // private constructor prevents instantiation by untrusted callers
  }

  // Lazy initialization
  public static synchronized MySingleton getInstance() {
    if (Instance == null) {
      Instance = new MySingleton();
    }
```

```
    return Instance;
  }

  public Object clone() throws CloneNotSupportedException {
    throw new CloneNotSupportedException();
  }
}
```

See rule OBJ07-J for more details about preventing misuse of the `clone()` method.

Noncompliant Code Example (Garbage Collection)

A class may be garbage-collected when it is no longer reachable. This behavior can be problematic when the program must maintain the singleton property throughout the entire lifetime of the program.

A static singleton becomes eligible for garbage collection when its class loader becomes eligible for garbage collection. This usually happens when a nonstandard (custom) class loader is used to load the singleton. This noncompliant code example prints different values of the hash code of the singleton object from different scopes.

```
{
  ClassLoader cl1 = new MyClassLoader();
  Class class1 = cl1.loadClass(MySingleton.class.getName());
  Method classMethod =
      class1.getDeclaredMethod("getInstance", new Class[] { });
  Object singleton = classMethod.invoke(null, new Object[] { });
  System.out.println(singleton.hashCode());
}

ClassLoader cl1 = new MyClassLoader();
Class class1 = cl1.loadClass(MySingleton.class.getName());
Method classMethod =
    class1.getDeclaredMethod("getInstance", new Class[] { });
Object singleton = classMethod.invoke(null, new Object[] { } );
System.out.println(singleton.hashCode());
```

Code that is outside the scope can create another instance of the singleton class even though the requirement was to use only the original instance.

Because a singleton instance is associated with the class loader that is used to load it, it is possible to have multiple instances of the same class in the JVM. This typically happens in

J2EE containers and applets. Technically, these instances are different classes that are independent of each other. Failure to protect against multiple instances of the singleton may or may not be insecure depending on the specific requirements of the program.

Compliant Solution (Prevent Garbage Collection)

This compliant solution takes into account the garbage-collection issue described previously. A class cannot be garbage-collected until the `ClassLoader` object used to load it becomes eligible for garbage collection. A simple scheme to prevent garbage collection is to ensure that there is a direct or indirect reference from a live thread to the singleton object that must be preserved.

This compliant solution demonstrates this technique. It prints a consistent hash code across all scopes. It uses the `ObjectPreserver` class [Grand 2002] described in rule TSM02-J.

```
{
  ClassLoader cl1 = new MyClassLoader();
  Class class1 = cl1.loadClass(MySingleton.class.getName());
  Method classMethod =
      class1.getDeclaredMethod("getInstance", new Class[] { });
  Object singleton = classMethod.invoke(null, new Object[] { });
  ObjectPreserver.preserveObject(singleton); // Preserve the object
  System.out.println(singleton.hashCode());
}

ClassLoader cl1 = new MyClassLoader();
Class class1 = cl1.loadClass(MySingleton.class.getName());
Method classMethod =
    class1.getDeclaredMethod("getInstance", new Class[] { });
// Retrieve the preserved object
Object singleton = ObjectPreserver.getObject();
System.out.println(singleton.hashCode());
```

Risk Assessment

Using improper forms of the singleton design pattern may lead to creation of multiple instances of the singleton and violate the expected contract of the class.

Rule	Severity	Likelihood	Remediation Cost	Priority	Level
MSC07-J	low	unlikely	medium	P2	L3

Related Guidelines

MITRE CWE   CWE-543. Use of Singleton pattern without synchronization in a multithreaded context

Bibliography

[Bloch 2008]   Item 3. Enforce the singleton property with a private constructor or an enum type; and Item 77. For instance control, prefer enum types to `readResolve`

[Daconta 2003]   Item 15. Avoiding singleton pitfalls

[Darwin 2004]   9.10 Enforcing the Singleton Pattern

[Fox 2001]   When Is a Singleton Not a Singleton?

[Gamma 1995]   Singleton

[Grand 2002]   Chapter 5, Creational Patterns, Singleton

[JLS 2005]   Chapter 17, Threads and Locks

Glossary

alien method From the perspective of a class C, an alien method is one whose behavior is not fully specified by C. This includes methods in other classes as well as overridable methods (neither private nor final) in C itself [Goetz 2006a].

anti-pattern An anti-pattern is a pattern that may be commonly used but is ineffective and/or counterproductive in practice [Laplante 2005].

availability The degree to which a system or component is operational and accessible when required for use. Often expressed as a probability [IEEE Std 610.12 1990].

big-endian "Multibyte data items are always stored in big-endian order, where the high bytes come first" [JVMSpec 1999] Chapter 4 "The `class` File Format." This term refers to the tension between Lilliput and Blefuscu (regarding whether to open soft-boiled eggs from the large or the small end) in Jonathan Swift's satirical novel *Gulliver's Travels*; it was first applied to the question of byte-ordering by Danny Cohen [Cohen 1981].

canonicalization Reducing the input to its equivalent simplest known form.

class variable A class variable is a field declared using the keyword `static` within a class declaration, or with or without the keyword `static` within an interface declaration. A class variable is created when its class or interface is prepared and is initialized to a default value. The class variable effectively ceases to exist when its class or interface is unloaded [JLS 2005].

condition predicate An expression constructed from the state variables of a class that must be true for a thread to continue execution. The thread pauses execution, via `Object.wait()`, `Thread.sleep()`, or some other mechanism, and is resumed later, presumably when the requirement is true and when it is notified [Goetz 2006a].

conflicting accesses Two accesses to (reads of or writes to) the same variable provided that at least one of the accesses is a write [JLS 2005].

data race Conflicting accesses of the same variable that are not ordered by a happens-before relationship [JLS 2005].

deadlock Two or more threads are said to have deadlocked when both block waiting for each other's locks. Neither thread can make any progress.

error tolerance The ability of a system or component to continue normal operation despite the presence of erroneous inputs [IEEE Std 610.12 1990].

exploit A piece of software or a technique that takes advantage of a security vulnerability to violate an explicit or implicit security policy [Seacord 2005a].

fail safe Pertaining to a system or component that automatically places itself in a safe operating mode in the event of a failure—for example, a traffic light that reverts to blinking red in all directions when normal operation fails [IEEE Std 610.12 1990].

fail soft Pertaining to a system or component that continues to provide partial operational capability in the event of certain failures—for example, a traffic light that continues to alternate between red and green if the yellow light fails [IEEE Std 610.12 1990].

fault tolerance The ability of a system or component to continue normal operation despite the presence of hardware or software faults [IEEE Std 610.12 1990].

happens-before order Two actions can be ordered by a happens-before relationship. If one action happens-before another, then the first is visible to and ordered before the second.... It should be noted that the presence of a happens-before relationship between two actions does not necessarily imply that they have to take place in that order in an implementation. If the reordering produces results consistent with a legal execution, it is not illegal.... More specifically, if two actions share a happens-before relationship, they do not necessarily have to appear to have happened in that order to any code with which they do not share a happens-before relationship. Writes in one thread that are in a data race with reads in another thread may, for example, appear to occur out of order to those reads [JLS 2005].

heap memory Memory that can be shared between threads is called shared memory or heap memory. All instance fields, static fields and array elements are stored in heap memory.... Local variables (§14.4), formal method parameters (§8.4.1) or exception handler parameters are never shared between threads and are unaffected by the memory model [JLS 2005].

hide One class field hides a field in a superclass if they have the same identifier. The hidden field is not accessible from the class. Likewise, a class method hides a method in a superclass if they have the same identifier but incompatible signatures. The hidden method is not accessible from the class. See [JLS 2005] §8.4.8.2 for the formal definition. Contrast with override.

immutable When applied to an object, this means that its state cannot be changed after being initialized. "An object is immutable if:

- its state cannot be modified after construction;
- all its fields are final; and
- it is properly constructed (the `this` reference does not escape during construction).

It is technically possible to have an immutable object without all fields being final. `String` is such a class but this relies on delicate reasoning about benign data races that requires a deep understanding of the Java Memory Model. (For the curious: `String` lazily computes the hash code the first time `hashCode` is called and caches it in a nonfinal field, but this works only because that field can take on only one nondefault value that is the same every time it is computed because it is derived deterministically from immutable state.)" [Goetz 2006a].

Immutable objects are inherently thread-safe; they may be shared among multiple threads or published without synchronization, though it is usually required to declare the fields containing their references volatile to ensure visibility. An immutable object may contain mutable subobjects, provided the state of the subobjects cannot be modified after construction of the immutable object has concluded.

initialization safety An object is considered to be completely initialized when its constructor finishes. A thread that can only see a reference to an object after that object has been completely initialized is guaranteed to see the correctly initialized values for that object's final fields [JLS 2005].

instance variable An instance variable is a field declared within a class declaration without using the keyword `static`. If a class T has a field a that is an instance variable, then a new instance variable a is created and initialized to a default value as part of each newly created object of class T or of any class that is a subclass of T. The instance variable effectively ceases to exist when the object of which it is a field is no longer referenced, after any necessary finalization of the object has been completed [JLS 2005].

interruption policy An interruption policy determines how a thread interprets an interruption request—what it does (if anything) when one is detected, what units of work are considered atomic with respect to interruption, and how quickly it reacts to interruption [Goetz 2006a].

invariant A property that is assumed to be true at certain points during program execution, but not formally specified. They may be used in `assert` statements, or informally specified in comments. Invariants are often used to reason about program correctness.

liveness A property that every operation or method invocation executes to completion without interruptions, even if it goes against safety.

memoization An optimization technique used primarily to speed up computer programs by having function calls avoid repeating the calculation of results for previously processed inputs [White 2003].

memory model "The rules that determine how memory accesses are ordered and when they are guaranteed to be visible are known as the memory model of the Java programming language" [JPL 2006]. "A memory model describes, given a program and an execution trace of that program, whether the execution trace is a legal execution of the program" [JLS 2005].

normalization Lossy conversion of the data to its simplest known (and anticipated) form. "When implementations keep strings in a normalized form, they can be assured that equivalent strings have a unique binary representation" [Davis 2008a].

normalization (URI) Normalization is the process of removing unnecessary "." and ".." segments from the path component of a hierarchical URI. Each "." segment is simply removed. A ".." segment is removed only if it is preceded by a non-".." segment. Normalization has no effect upon opaque URIs [API 2006].

obscure One scoped identifier obscures another identifier in a containing scope if the two identifiers are the same, but the obscuring identifier does not shadow the obscured identifier. This can happen when the obscuring identifier is a variable while the obscured identifier is a type, for example. See [JLS 2005] §6.3.2 for more information.

obsolete reference An obsolete reference is a reference that will never be dereferenced again [Bloch 2008].

open call An alien method invoked outside of a synchronized region is known as an open call [Bloch 2008], [Lea 2000a].

override One class method overrides a method in a superclass if they have compatible signatures. The overridden method is still accessible from the class via the `super` keyword. See [JLS 2005] §8.4.8.1 for the formal definition. Contrast with hide.

partial order An order defined for some, but not necessarily all, pairs of items. For instance, the sets {a, b} and {a, c, d} are subsets of {a, b, c, d}, but neither is a subset of the other. So "is a subset of" is a partial order on sets [Black 2004].

program order The order that interthread actions are performed by a thread according to the intrathread semantics of the thread. "Program order [can be described] as the order of bytecodes present in the .class file, as they would execute based on control flow values" (David Holmes, JMM Mailing List).[1]

---

1. https://mailman.cs.umd.edu/mailman/private/javamemorymodel-discussion/2007-September/000086.html

publishing objects Publishing an object means making it available to code outside of its current scope, such as by storing a reference to it where other code can find it, returning it from a nonprivate method, or passing it to a method in another class [Goetz 2006a].

race condition "General races cause nondeterministic execution and are failures in programs intended to be deterministic" [Netzer 1992]. "A race condition occurs when the correctness of a computation depends on the relative timing or interleaving of multiple threads by the runtime" [Goetz 2006a].

relativization (URI) [Relativization] is the inverse of resolution. For example, relativizing the URI `http://java.sun.com/j2se/1.3/docs/guide/index.html` against the base URI `http://java.sun.com/j2se/1.3` yields the relative URI `docs/guide/index.html` [API 2006].

safe publication To publish an object safely, both the reference to the object and the object's state must be made visible to other threads at the same time. A properly constructed object can be safely published by:

- Initializing an object reference from a *static* initializer.
- Storing a reference to it into a *volatile* field.
- Storing a reference to it into a *final* field.
- Storing a reference to it into a field that is properly guarded by a (*synchronized*) lock.

[Goetz 2006a, Section 3.5 "Safe Publication"]

safety Its main goal is to ensure that all objects maintain consistent states in a multithreaded environment [Lea 2000a].

sanitization Sanitization is a term used for validating input and transforming it to a representation that conforms to the input requirements of a complex subsystem. For example, a database may require all invalid characters to be escaped or eliminated prior to their storage. Input sanitization refers to the elimination of unwanted characters from the input by means of removal, replacement, encoding or escaping the characters.

security flaw A software defect that poses a potential security risk [Seacord 2005].

sensitive code Any code that performs operations forbidden to untrusted code. Also, any code that accesses sensitive data (*q.v.*). For example, code whose correct operation requires enhanced privileges is typically considered to be sensitive.

sensitive data Any data that must be kept secure. Consequences of this security requirement include:

- Untrusted code is forbidden to access sensitive data.
- Trusted code is forbidden to leak sensitive data to untrusted code.

Examples of sensitive data include passwords and personally identifiable information.

sequential consistency "Sequential consistency is a very strong guarantee that is made about visibility and ordering in an execution of a program. Within a sequentially consistent execution, there is a total order over all individual actions (such as reads and writes) which is consistent with the order of the program, and each individual action is atomic and is immediately visible to every thread.... If a program is correctly synchronized, all executions of the program will appear to be sequentially consistent (§17.4.3)" [JLS 2005]. Sequential consistency implies there will be no compiler optimizations in the statements of the action. Adopting sequential consistency as the memory model and disallowing other primitives can be overly restrictive because under this condition, the compiler is not allowed to make optimizations and reorder code [JLS 2005].

shadow One scoped identifier shadows another identifier in a containing scope if the two identifiers are the same and they both reference variables. They may also both reference methods or types. The shadowed identifier is not accessible in the scope of the shadowing identifier. See [JLS 2005] §6.3.1 for more information. Contrast with obscure.

synchronization The Java programming language provides multiple mechanisms for communicating between threads. The most basic of these methods is *synchronization*, which is implemented using monitors. Each object in Java is associated with a monitor, which a thread can lock or unlock. Only one thread at a time may hold a lock on a monitor. Any other threads attempting to lock that monitor are blocked until they can obtain a lock on that monitor [JLS 2005].

starvation A condition wherein one or more threads prevent other threads from accessing a shared resource over extended periods of time. For instance, a thread that invokes a synchronized method that performs some time-consuming operation starves other threads.

tainted data Data that either originate from an untrusted source or result from an operation whose inputs included tainted data. Tainted data can be sanitized (also *untainted*) through suitable data validation. Note that all outputs from untrusted code must be considered to be tainted [Jovanovich 2006].

thread-safe An object is thread-safe if it can be shared by multiple threads without the possibility of any data races. "A thread-safe object performs synchronization internally, so multiple threads can freely access it through its public interface without further synchronization" [Goetz 2006a]. Immutable classes are thread-safe by definition. Mutable classes may also be thread-safe if they are properly synchronized.

total order An order defined for all pairs of items of a set. For instance, <= (less than or equal to) is a total order on integers, that is, for any two integers, one of them is less than or equal to the other [Black 2006].

trusted code Code that is loaded by the primordial class loader, irrespective of whether or not it constitutes the Java API. In this text, this meaning is extended to include code that is obtained from a known entity and given permissions that untrusted code lacks. By this definition, untrusted and trusted code can coexist in the namespace of a single class loader (not necessarily the primordial class loader). In such cases, the security policy must make this distinction clear by assigning appropriate privileges to trusted code while denying those privileges to untrusted code.

untrusted code Code of unknown origin that can potentially cause some harm when executed. Untrusted code may not always be malicious, but this is usually hard to determine automatically. Consequently, untrusted code should be run in a sandboxed environment.

volatile "A write to a volatile field (§8.3.1.4) happens-before every subsequent read of that field" [JLS 2005]. "Operations on the master copies of volatile variables on behalf of a thread are performed by the main memory in exactly the order that the thread requested" [JVMSpec 1999]. Accesses to a volatile variable are sequentially consistent, which also means that the operations are exempt from compiler optimizations. Declaring a variable volatile ensures that all threads see the most up-to-date value of the variable if any thread modifies it. Volatile guarantees atomic reads and writes of primitive values; however, it does not guarantee the atomicity of composite operations such as variable incrementation (read-modify-write sequence).

vulnerability A set of conditions that allow an attacker to violate an explicit or implicit security policy [Seacord 2005].

References

[**Abadi 1996**] Martin Abadi and Roger Needham, Prudent Engineering Practice for Cryptographic Protocols, *IEEE Transactions on Software Engineering*, Volume 22, Issue 1, 1996, 6–15.

[**API 2006**] Java Platform, Standard Edition 6 API Specification, Sun Microsystems, 2006. Available at http://download.oracle.com/javase/6/docs/api/.

[**Austin 2000**] Calvin Austin and Monica Pawlan, *Advanced Programming for the Java 2 Platform*, Addison-Wesley Longman, Boston, 2000.

[**Black 2004**] Paul E. Black and Paul J. Tanenbaum, partial order, in *Dictionary of Algorithms and Data Structures* [online], Paul E. Black, ed., U.S. National Institute of Standards and Technology, December 17, 2004. Available at http://xlinux.nist.gov/dads/HTML/partialorder.html.

[**Black 2006**] Paul E. Black and Paul J. Tanenbaum, total order, in *Dictionary of Algorithms and Data Structures* [online], Paul E. Black, ed., U.S. National Institute of Standards and Technology, March 30, 2006. Available at http://xlinux.nist.gov/dads/HTML/totalorder.html.

[**Bloch 2001**] Joshua Bloch, *Effective Java: Programming Language Guide*, Addison-Wesley Professional, Boston, 2001.

[**Bloch 2005a**] Joshua Bloch and Neal Gafter, *Java™ Puzzlers: Traps, Pitfalls, and Corner Cases*, Addison-Wesley Professional, Boston, 2005.

[**Bloch 2005b**] Joshua Bloch and Neal Gafter, Yet More Programming Puzzlers, JavaOne Conference, 2005.

[**Bloch 2007**] Joshua Bloch, Effective Java™ Reloaded: This Time It's (Not) for Real, JavaOne Conference, 2007.

[**Bloch 2008**] Joshua Bloch, *Effective Java*, 2nd ed., Addison-Wesley Professional, Boston, 2008.

[**Bloch 2009**] Joshua Bloch and Neal Gafter, Return of the Puzzlers: Schlock and Awe, JavaOne Conference, 2009.

[**Boehm 2005**] Hans-J. Boehm, Finalization, Threads, and the Java™ Technology-Based Memory Model, JavaOne Conference, 2005.

[**Campione 1996**] Mary Campione and Kathy Walrath, *The Java Tutorial: Object-Oriented Programming for the Internet*, Addison-Wesley, Reading, MA, 1996.

[**CCITT 1988**] CCITT. *CCITT Blue Book*, Recommendation X.509 and ISO 9594-8: The Directory-Authentication Framework, International Telecommunication Union, Geneva, 1988.

[**Chan 1999**] Patrick Chan, Rosanna Lee, and Douglas Kramer, *The Java Class Libraries: Supplement for the Java 2 Platform*, v1.2, 2nd ed., Volume 1, Prentice Hall, Upper Saddle River, NJ, 1999.

[**Chess 2007**] Brian Chess and Jacob West, *Secure Programming with Static Analysis*, Addison-Wesley Professional, Boston MA, 2007.

[**Christudas 2005**] Internals of Java Class Loading, ONJava, 2005. Available at http://onjava.com/pub/a/onjava/2005/01/26/classloading.html.

[**Cohen 1981**] On Holy Wars and a Plea for Peace, *IEEE Computer*, Volume 14, Issue 10, 1981.

[**Conventions 2009**] Code Conventions for the Java Programming Language, Sun Microsystems, 2009. Available at http://www.oracle.com/technetwork/java/codeconv-138413.html.

[**CVE 2011**] Common Vulnerabilities and Exposures, MITRE Corporation, 2011. Available at http://cve.mitre.org.

[**Coomes 2007**] John Coomes, Peter Kessler, and Tony Printezis, Garbage Collection-Friendly Programming, Java SE Garbage Collection Group, Sun Microsystems, JavaOne Conference, 2007.

[**Core Java 2004**] Cay S. Horstmann and Gary Cornell, *Core Java™ 2 Volume I— Fundamentals*, 7th ed., Prentice Hall PTR, Boston, 2004.

[**Cunningham 1995**] Ward Cunningham, The CHECKS Pattern Language of Information Integrity, in *Pattern Languages of Program Design*, James O. Coplien and Douglas C. Schmidt (eds.), Addison-Wesley Professional, Reading, MA, 1995.

[**Daconta 2000**] Michael C. Daconta, When Runtime.exec() Won't, JavaWorld.com, 2000. Available at http://www.javaworld.com/javaworld/jw-12-2000/jw-1229-traps. html.

[**Daconta 2003**] Michael C. Daconta, Kevin T. Smith, Donald Avondolio, and W. Clay Richardson, *More Java Pitfalls*, Wiley Publishing, New York, 2003.

[**Darwin 2004**] Ian F. Darwin, *Java Cookbook*, O'Reilly, Sebastopol, CA, 2004.

[**Davis 2008a**] Mark Davis and Martin Dürst, Unicode Standard Annex #15, Unicode Normalization Forms, 2008. Available at http://unicode.org/reports/tr15/.

[**Davis 2008b**] Mark Davis and Michel Suignard, Unicode Technical Report #36, Unicode Security Considerations, 2008. Available at http://unicode.org/reports/tr36/.

[**Dennis 1966**] Jack B. Dennis and Earl C. Van Horn, Programming Semantics for Multiprogrammed Computations, *Communications of the ACM*, Volume 9, Issue 3, March 1966, pp. 143–155, DOI=10.1145/365230.365252. Available at http://doi.acm. org/10.1145/365230.365252.

[**DHS 2006**] Build Security In, U.S. Department of Homeland Security, 2006. Available at https://buildsecurityin.us-cert.gov/bsi/home.html.

[**Dormann 2008**] Will Dormann, Signed Java Applet Security: Worse than ActiveX?, CERT Vulnerability Analysis Blog, 2008. Available at http://www.cert.org/blogs/ certcc/2008/06/signed_java_security_worse_tha.html.

[**Doshi 2003**] Gunjan Doshi, Best Practices for Exception Handling, ONJava.com, 2003. Available at http://onjava.com/pub/a/onjava/2003/11/19/exceptions.html.

[**Dougherty 2009**] Chad Dougherty, Kirk Sayre, Robert C. Seacord, David Svoboda, and Kazuya Togashi, *Secure Design Patterns*, CMU/SEI-2009-TR-010, Defense Technical Information Center, Ft. Belvoir, VA, 2009.

[**Eclipse 2008**] The Eclipse Platform, 2008.

[**Encodings 2006**] Supported Encodings, Sun Microsystems, 2006. Available at http:// download.oracle.com/javase/6/docs/technotes/guides/intl/encoding.doc.html.

[EMA 2011] Java SE 6 Documentation, Extension Mechanism Architecture, Sun Microsystems, Inc. (2011). Available at http://download.oracle.com/javase/6/docs/technotes/guides/extensions/spec.html.

[Enterprise 2003] The O'Reilly Java Authors, *Java Enterprise Best Practices*, O'Reilly, Sebastopol, CA, 2003.

[ESA 2005] Java Coding Standards, prepared by European Space Agency (ESA) Board for Software Standardisation and Control (BSSC), 2005.

[Fairbanks 2007] *Design Fragments*, Defense Technical Information Center, Ft. Belvoir, VA, 2007. Available at http://reports-archive.adm.cs.cmu.edu/anon/isri2007/abstracts/07-108.html.

[FindBugs 2008] FindBugs Bug Descriptions, 2008. Available at http://findbugs.sourceforge.net.

[Fisher 2003] Maydene Fisher, Jon Ellis, and Jonathan Bruce, *JDBC API Tutorial and Reference*, 3rd ed., Addison-Wesley, Boston MA, 2003.

[Flanagan 2005] David Flanagan, *Java in a Nutshell*, 5th ed., O'Reilly, Sebastopol, CA, 2005.

[Forman 2005] Ira R. Forman and Nate Forman, *Java Reflection in Action*, Manning Publications, Greenwich, CT, 2005.

[Fortify 2008] A Taxonomy of Coding Errors That Affect Security, Java/JSP, Fortify Software, 2008. Available at https://www.fortify.com/vulncat/en/vulncat/index.html.

[Fox 2001] Joshua Fox, When Is a Singleton Not a Singleton? Sun Developer Network, 2001. Available at http://www.javaworld.com/javaworld/jw-01-2001/jw-0112-singleton.html.

[FT 2008] Function Table, Class FunctionTable, Field detail, public static FuncLoader m_functions, 2008. Available at http://www.stylusstudio.com/api/xalan-j_2_6_0/org/apache/xpath/compiler/FunctionTable.htm.

[Gafter 2006] Neal Gafter, Neal Gafter's blog, 2006. Available at http://gafter.blogspot.com.

[Gamma 1995] Erich Gamma, Richard Helm, Ralph Johnson, and John M. Vlissides, *Design Patterns: Elements of Reusable Object-Oriented Software*, Addison-Wesley Professional, Boston, 1995.

[Garfinkel 1996] Simson Garfinkel and Gene Spafford, *Practical UNIX & Internet Security*, 2nd ed., O'Reilly, Sebastopol, CA, 1996.

[**Garms 2001**] Jess Garms and Daniel Somerfield, *Professional Java Security*, Wrox Press, Chicago, 2001.

[**Goetz 2002**] Brian Goetz, Java Theory and Practice: Don't Let the this Reference Escape during Construction, IBM developerWorks (Java technology), 2002. Available at http://www.ibm.com/developerworks/java/library/j-jtp0618/index.html.

[**Goetz 2004a**] Brian Goetz, Java Theory and Practice: Garbage Collection and Performance, IBM developerWorks (Java technology), 2004. Available at http://www.ibm.com/developerworks/java/library/j-jtp01274/index.html.

[**Goetz 2004b**] Brian Goetz, Java Theory and Practice: The Exceptions Debate: To Check, or Not to Check?, IBM developerWorks (Java technology), 2004. Available at http://www.ibm.com/developerworks/java/library/j-jtp05254/index.html.

[**Goetz 2004c**] Brian Goetz, Java Theory and Practice: Going Atomic, IBM developerWorks (Java technology), 2004. Available at http://www.ibm.com/developerworks/java/library/j-jtp11234/.

[**Goetz 2005a**] Brian Goetz, Java Theory and Practice: Be a Good (Event) Listener, Guidelines for Writing and Supporting Event Listeners, IBM developerWorks (Java technology), 2005. Available at http://www.ibm.com/developerworks/java/library/j-jtp07265/index.html.

[**Goetz 2005b**] Brian Goetz, Java Theory and Practice: Plugging Memory Leaks with Weak References, IBM developerWorks (Java technology), 2005. Available at http://www.ibm.com/developerworks/java/library/j-jtp11225/.

[**Goetz 2006a**] Brian Goetz, Tim Peierls, Joshua Bloch, Joseph Bowbeer, David Holmes, and Doug Lea, *Java Concurrency in Practice*, Addison-Wesley Professional, Boston, 2006.

[**Goetz 2006b**] Brian Goetz, Java Theory and Practice: Good Housekeeping Practices, IBM developerWorks (Java technology), 2006. Available at http://www.ibm.com/developerworks/java/library/j-jtp03216/index.html.

[**Goetz 2007**] Brian Goetz, Java Theory and Practice: Managing Volatility, Guidelines for Using Volatile Variables, IBM developerWorks (Java technology), 2006. Available at http://www.ibm.com/developerworks/java/library/j-jtp06197/.

[**Goldberg 1991**] David Goldberg, What Every Computer Scientist Should Know about Floating-Point Arithmetic, Sun Microsystems, March 1991. Available at http://download.oracle.com/docs/cd/E19957-01/806-3568/ncg_goldberg.html.

[**Gong 2003**] Li Gong, Gary Ellison, and Mary Dageforde, *Inside Java 2 Platform Security: Architecture, API Design, and Implementation*, 2nd ed., Prentice Hall, Boston. MA, 2003.

[Grand 2002] Mark Grand, *Patterns in Java*, Volume 1, 2nd ed., Wiley, New York, 2002.

[Greanier 2000] Todd Greanier, Discover the Secrets of the Java Serialization API, Sun Developer Network (SDN), 2000. Available at http://java.sun.com/developer/technicalArticles/Programming/serialization/.

[Green 2008] Roedy Green, Canadian Mind Products Java & Internet Glossary, 2008. Available at http://mindprod.com/jgloss/jgloss.html.

[Grigg 2006] Jeffery Grigg, Reflection on Inner Classes, 2006. Available at http://www.c2.com/cgi/wiki?ReflectionOnInnerClasses.

[Grosso 2001] William Grosso, Java RMI, O'Reilly, Sebastopol, CA, 2001.

[Gupta 2005] Satish Chandra Gupta and Rajeev Palanki, Java Memory Leaks—Catch Me If You Can, 2005. Available at http://www.ibm.com/developerworks/rational/library/05/0816_GuptaPalanki/.

[Haack 2006] Christian Haack, Erik Poll, Jan Schafer, and Aleksy Schubert, Immutable Objects in Java, 2006. Available at https://pms.cs.ru.nl/iris-diglib/src/getContent.php?id=2006-Haack-ObjectsImmutable.

[Haggar 2000] Peter Haggar, *Practical Java™ Programming Language Guide*, Addison-Wesley Professional, Boston. MA, 2000.

[Halloway 2000] Stuart Halloway, Java Developer Connection Tech Tips, March 28, 2000.

[Halloway 2001] Stuart Halloway, Java Developer Connection Tech Tips, January 30, 2001.

[Harold 1997] Elliotte Rusty Harold, *Java Secrets*, Wiley, New York. 1997.

[Harold 1999] Elliotte Rusty Harold, *Java I/O*, O'Reilly, Sebastopol, CA, 1999.

[Harold 2006] Elliotte Rusty Harold, *Java I/O*, 2nd ed., O'Reilly, Sebastopol, CA, 2006.

[Hawtin 2008] Thomas Hawtin, Secure Coding Antipatterns: Preventing Attacks and Avoiding Vulnerabilities, Sun Microsystems, Make It Fly 2008, London, 2008.

[Heffley 2004] J. Heffley and P. Meunier, Can Source Code Auditing Software Identify Common Vulnerabilities and Be Used to Evaluate Software Security? *Proceedings of the 37th Annual Hawaii International Conference on System Sciences (HICSS'04)*, Track 9, Volume 9, IEEE Computer Society, January 2004.

[Henney 2003] Kevlin Henney, Null Object, Something for Nothing, 2003. Available at http://www.two-sdg.demon.co.uk/curbralan/papers/europlop/NullObject.pdf.

[Hitchens 2002] Ron Hitchens, *Java™ NIO*, O'Reilly, Sebastopol, CA, 2002.

[**Hornig 2007**] Charles Hornig, Advanced Java™ Globalization, JavaOne Conference, 2007.

[**Hovemeyer 2007**] David Hovemeyer and William Pugh, Finding More Null Pointer Bugs, But Not Too Many, *Proceedings of the 7th ACM SIGPLAN-SIGSOFT Workshop on Program Analysis for Software Tools and Engineering*, 2007.

[**Howard 2002**] Michael Howard and David C. LeBlanc, *Writing Secure Code*, 2nd ed., Microsoft Press, Redmond, WA, 2002.

[**Hunt 1998**] J. Hunt and F. Long, Java's Reliability: An Analysis of Software Defects in Java, *Software IEE Proceedings*, 1998.

[**IEC 60812 2006**] *Analysis Techniques for System Reliability: Procedure for Failure Mode and Effects Analysis (FMEA)*, 2nd ed. Internation Electrotechnical Commission, Geneva, 2006.

[**IEEE 754 2006**] IEEE, Standard for Binary Floating-Point Arithmetic (IEEE 754-1985), 2006. Available at http://grouper.ieee.org/groups/754/.

[**ISO/IEC TR 24772:2010**] ISO/IEC TR 24772. *Information Technology—Programming Languages—Guidance to Avoiding Vulnerabilities in Programming Languages through Language Selection and Use*, October 2010.

[**J2SE 2000**] Java™ 2 SDK, Standard Edition Documentation, Sun Microsystems, J2SE Documentation version 1.3, Sun Microsystems, 2000.

[**J2SE 2011**] Java™ SE 7 Documentation, J2SE Documentation version 1.7, Oracle Corp., 2011.

[**JarSpec 2008**] J2SE Documentation version 1.5, Jar File Specification, Sun Microsystems, 2000.

[**Java 2006**] Java—The Java Application Launcher, Sun Microsystems, 2006.

[**Java2NS 1999**] Marco Pistoia, Duane F. Reller, Deepak Gupta, Milind Nagnur, and Ashok K. Ramani, *Java 2 Network Security*, Prentice Hall, Upper Saddle River, NJ, 1999.

[**JavaGenerics 2004**] Oracle, Generics, Sun Microsystems, 2004. Available at http://download.oracle.com/javase/1.5.0/docs/guide/language/generics.html.

[**JavaThreads 1999**] Scott Oaks and Henry Wong, *Java Threads*, 2nd ed., O'Reilly, Sebastopol, CA, 1999.

[**JavaThreads 2004**] Scott Oaks and Henry Wong, *Java Threads*, 3rd ed., O'Reilly, Sebastopol, CA, 2004.

[JDK7 2008] Java™ Platform, Standard Edition 7 documentation, Sun Microsystems, December 2008.

[JLS 2005] James Gosling, Bill Joy, Guy Steele, and Gilad Bracha, *The Java Language Specification*, 3rd ed., The Java Series, Prentice Hall, Upper Saddle River, NJ, 2005. Available at http://java.sun.com/docs/books/jls/index.html.

[JMX 2006] Monitoring and Management for the Java Platform, Sun Microsystems, 2006. Available at http://download.oracle.com/javase/6/docs/technotes/guides/management/index.html.

[JMXG 2006] Java SE Monitoring and Management Guide, Sun Microsystems, 2006. Available at http://download.oracle.com/javase/6/docs/technotes/guides/management/toc.html.

[JNI 2006] Java Native Interface, Sun Microsystems, 2006. Available at http://download.oracle.com/javase/6/docs/technotes/guides/jni/index.html.

[Jovanovic 2006] Nenad Jovanovic, Christopher Kruegel, and Engin Kirda, Pixy: A Static Analysis Tool for Detecting Web Application Vulnerabilities (Short Paper), *Proceedings of the 2006 IEEE Symposium on Security and Privacy (S&P'06)*, pp. 258–263, May 21–24, 2006.

[JPDA 2004] Java Platform Debugger Architecture (JPDA), Sun Microsystems, 2004. Available at http://download.oracle.com/javase/6/docs/technotes/guides/jpda/index.html.

[JPL 2006] Ken Arnold, James Gosling, and David Holmes, *The Java™ Programming Language*, 4th Ed., Addison-Wesley Professional, Boston, 2006.

[JSR-133 2004] JSR-133: Java™ Memory Model and Thread Specification, 2004. Available at http://www.cs.umd.edu/~pugh/java/memoryModel/jsr133.pdf.

[JVMTI 2006] Java Virtual Machine Tool Interface (JVM TI), Sun Microsystems, 2006. Available at http://download.oracle.com/javase/6/docs/technotes/guides/jvmti/index.html.

[JVMSpec 1999] The Java Virtual Machine Specification, Sun Microsystems, 1999. Available at http://java.sun.com/docs/books/jvms/.

[Kabanov 2009] Jevgeni Kabanov, The Ultimate Java Puzzler, February 16, 2009. Available at http://dow.ngra.de/2009/02/16/the-ultimate-java-puzzler/.

[Kabutz 2001] Heinz M. Kabutz, *The Java Specialists' Newsletter*, 2001.

[Kalinovsky 2004] Alex Kalinovsky, *Covert Java: Techniques for Decompiling, Patching, and Reverse Engineering*, SAMS Publishing, Boston, 2004.

[Knoernschild 2001] Kirk Knoernschild, *Java™ Design: Objects, UML, and Process*, Addison-Wesley Professional, Boston, 2001.

[Lai 2008] Charlie Lai, Java Insecurity: Accounting for Subtleties That Can Compromise Code, 2008. Available at http://ieeexplore.ieee.org/xpl/freeabs_all.jsp?reload=true&arnum ber=4420062.

[Langer 2008] Angelica Langer, Practicalities—Programming with Java Generics, 2008. Available at http://www.angelikalanger.com/GenericsFAQ/FAQSections/ ProgrammingIdioms.html.

[Laplante 2005] Phillip A. Laplante, Colin J. Neill, *Antipatterns: Identification, Refactoring and Management*. Auerbach Publications. 2005.

[Lea 2000a] Doug Lea, *Concurrent Programming in Java*, 2nd ed., Addison-Wesley Professional, Boston, 2000.

[Lea 2000b] Doug Lea and William Pugh, Correct and Efficient Synchronization of Java™ Technology-based Threads, JavaOne Conference, 2000.

[Lea 2008] Doug Lea, The JSR-133 Cookbook for Compiler Writers, 2008. Available at http://g.oswego.edu/dl/jmm/cookbook.html.

[Lee 2009] Sangjin Lee, Mahesh Somani, and Debashis Saha, Robust and Scalable Concurrent Programming: Lessons from the Trenches, JavaOne Conference, 2009.

[Liang 1997] Sheng Liang, *The Java™ Native Interface, Programmer's Guide and Specification*, Addison-Wesley Professional, Reading, MA, 1997.

[Liang 1998] Sheng Liang and Gilad Bracha, Dynamic Class Loading in the Java™ Virtual Machine, *Proceedings of the 13th ACM SIGPLAN Conference on Object-Oriented Programming, Systems, Languages, and Applications*, 1998.

[Lieberman 1986] Henry Lieberman, Using Prototypical Objects to Implement Shared Behavior in Object-Oriented Systems, *Proceedings on Object-Oriented Programming Systems, Languages and Applications*, pp. 214–223 (ISSN 0362-1340), Massachusetts Institute of Technology, 1986.

[Lo 2005] Chia-Tien Dan Lo, Witawas Srisa-an, and J. Morris Chang, Security Issues in Garbage Collection, *STSC Crosstalk*, October 2005.

[Long 2005] Fred Long, Software Vulnerabilities in Java, CMU/SEI-2005-TN-044, Software Engineering Institute, Carnegie Mellon University, 2005.

[LSOD 2002] Last Stage of Delirium Research Group, *Java and Java Virtual Machine Security*. Poland: Last Stage of Delirium Research Group, 2002.

[Low 1997] Douglas Low, Protecting Java Code via Obfuscation, *Crossroads* Volume 4, Issue 3, 1997.

[Macgregor 1998] Robert MacGregor, Dave Durbin, John Owlett, and Andrew Yeomans, *Java Network Security*, Prentice Hall PTR, Upper Saddle River, NJ, 1998.

[Mahmoud 2002] Qusay H. Mahmoud, Compressing and Decompressing Data Using Java APIs, Oracle, 2002. Available at http://java.sun.com/developer/technicalArticles/Programming/compression/.

[Mak 2002] Ronald Mak, *Java Number Cruncher: The Java Programmer's Guide to Numerical Computing*, Prentice Hall, Upper Saddle River, NJ, 2002.

[Manson 2004] Jeremy Manson and Brian Goetz, JSR 133 (Java Memory Model) FAQ, 2004. Available at http://www.cs.umd.edu/~pugh/java/memoryModel/jsr-133-faq.html#finalRight.

[Manson 2006] Jeremy Manson and William Pugh, The Java™ Memory Model: the building block of concurrency, JavaOne Conference, 2006.

[Martin 1996] Robert C. Martin, Granularity, 1996. Available at http://www.objectmentor.com/resources/articles/granularity.pdf.

[McCluskey 2001] Glen McCluskey, Java Developer Connection Tech Tips, April 10, 2001.

[McGraw 1999] Gary McGraw and Edward W. Felten, *Securing Java, Getting Down to Business with Mobile Code*, Wiley, New York, 1999.

[McGraw 1998] Gary McGraw and Edward W. Felten, Twelve Rules for Developing More Secure Java Code, JavaWorld.com, 1998. Available at http://www.javaworld.com/javaworld/jw-12-1998/jw-12-securityrules.html.

[Mettler 2010a] Adrian Mettler, David Wagner, and T. Close, Joe-E: A Security-Oriented Subset of Java, 17th Network & Distributed System Security Symposium, 2010.

[Mettler 2010b] Adrian Mettler and David Wagner, Class Properties for Security Review in an Object-Capability Subset of Java, *Proceedings of the 5th ACM SIGPLAN Workshop on Programming Languages and Analysis for Security (PLAS '10)*, ACM, Article 7, DOI=10.1145/1814217.1814224, 2010.

[Miller 2009] Alex Miller, Java™ Platform Concurrency Gotchas, JavaOne Conference, 2009.

[MITRE 2011] MITRE Corporation, Common Weakness Enumeration, 2011. Available at http://cwe.mitre.org/.

[Mocha 2007] Mocha, the Java Decompiler, 2007. Available at http://www.brouhaha.com/~eric/software/mocha/.

[**Monsch 2006**] Jan P. Monsch, Ruining Security with java.util.Random, Version 1.0, 2006.

[**MSDN 2009**] Microsoft Corporation, Using SQL Escape Sequences, 2009. Available at http://msdn.microsoft.com/en-us/library/ms378045%28SQL.90%29.aspx.

[**Muchow 2001**] John W. Muchow, MIDlet Packaging with J2ME, ONJava.com, 2001. Available at http://onjava.com/pub/a/onjava/2001/04/26/midlet.html.

[**Müller 2002**] Dr. Andreas Müller and Geoffrey Simmons, Exception Handling: Common Problems and Best Practice with Java 1.4, Sun Microsystems GmbH, 2002.

[**Naftalin 2006a**] Maurice Naftalin and Philip Wadler, *Java Generics and Collections*, O'Reilly, Sebastopol, CA, 2006.

[**Naftalin 2006b**] Maurice Naftalin and Philip Wadler, Java™ Generics and Collections: Tools for Productivity, JavaOne Conference, 2007.

[**Netzer 1992**] Robert H. B. Netzer and Barton P. Miller, *What Are Race Conditions? Some Issues and Formalization*, University of Wisconsin, Madison, 1992.

[**Neward 2004**] Ted Neward, *Effective Enterprise Java*, Addison-Wesley Professional, Boston, 2004.

[**Nisewanger 2007**] Jeff Nisewanger, Avoiding Antipatterns, JavaOne Conference, 2007.

[**Nolan 2004**] Godfrey Nolan, *Decompiling Java*, Apress, Berkeley, CA, 2004.

[**Oaks 2001**] Scott Oaks, *Java Security*, O'Reilly, Sebastopol, CA, 2001.

[**Open Group 2004**] The IEEE and the Open Group, The Open Group Base Specifications Issue 6, 2004. Available at http://pubs.opengroup.org/onlinepubs/009695399/mindex.html.

[**Oracle 2010**] Oracle Corporation, Java SE 6 HotSpot Virtual Machine Garbage Collection Tuning, 2010.

[**OWASP 2005**] The Open Web Application Security Project, A Guide to Building Secure Web Applications and Web Services, 2005.

[**OWASP 2007**] The Open Web Application Security Project, OWASP Top 10 for Java EE, 2007. Available at https://www.owasp.org/images/8/89/OWASP_Top_10_2007_for_JEE.pdf.

[**OWASP 2011**] Open Web Application Security Project (OWASP), 2011. Available at https://www.owasp.org/index.php/Main_Page.

[**PCI 2010**] PCI Security Standards Council. Payment Card Industry (PCI) Data Security Standard v 2.0, October 2010. Available at: https://www.pcisecuritystandards.org/security_standards/index.php.

[**Permissions 2008**] Permissions in the Java™ SE 6 Development Kit (JDK), Sun Microsystems, 2008. Available at http://download.oracle.com/javase/6/docs/ technotes/guides/security/permissions.html.

[**Philion 2003**] Paul Philion, Beware the dangers of generic Exceptions, JavaWorld.com, 2003. Available at http://www.javaworld.com/javaworld/jw-10-2003/jw-1003-generics. html?page=2#sidebar1.

[**Phillips 2005**] Addison P. Phillips, Are We Counting Bytes Yet? 27th Internationalization and Unicode Conference, webMethods, 2005.

[**Pistoia 2004**] Marco Pistoia, Nataraj Nagaratnam, Larry Koved, and Anthony Nadalin, *Enterprise Java Security: Building Secure J2EE Applications*, Addison-Wesley Professional, Boston, MA 2004.

[**Policy 2002**] Sun Microsystems, Default Policy Implementation and Policy File Syntax, Document revision 1.6, 2002. Available at http://download.oracle.com/javase/6/docs/ technotes/guides/security/PolicyFiles.html.

[**Pugh 2004**] William Pugh, The Java Memory Model (discussions reference), 2004. Available at http://www.cs.umd.edu/~pugh/java/memoryModel/.

[**Pugh 2008**] William Pugh, Defective Java Code: Turning WTF Code into a Learning Experience, JavaOne Conference, 2008.

[**Pugh 2009**] William Pugh, Defective Java Code: Mistakes That Matter, JavaOne Conference, 2009.

[**Reasoning 2003**] Reasoning Inspection Service Defect Data Tomcat v 1.4.24, November 14, 2003. Available at http://www.reasoning.com/pdf/Tomcat_Defect_Report.pdf.

[**Reflect 2006**] Sun Microsystems, Reflection, 2006. Available at http://download.oracle. com/javase/6/docs/technotes/guides/reflection/index.html.

[**Rogue 2000**] Vermeulen, Ambler, Bumgardner, Metz, Misfeldt, Shur, and Thompson, *The Elements of Java Style*, Cambridge University Press, New York, 2000.

[**Rotem 2008**] Arnon Rotem-Gal-Oz, Fallacies of Distributed Computing Explained, 2008. Available at http://www.rgoarchitects.com/Files/fallacies.pdf.

[**Roubtsov 2003a**] Vladimir Roubtsov, Breaking Java Exception-Handling Rules Is Easy, JavaWorld.com, 2003. Available at http://www.javaworld.com/javaworld/javaqa/ 2003-02/02-qa-0228-evilthrow.html.

[**Roubtsov 2003b**] Vladimir Roubtsov, Into the Mist of Serialization Myths, JavaWorld com, 2003. Available at http://www.javaworld.com/javaworld/javaqa/ 2003-06/02-qa-0627-mythser.html?page=1.

[Saltzer 1974] J. H. Saltzer, Protection and the Control of Information Sharing in Multics, *Communications of the ACM 17*, 7 (July 1974): 388–402.

[Saltzer 1975] J. H. Saltzer and M. D. Schroeder, The Protection of Information in Computer Systems, *Proceedings of the IEEE* Volume 63, Issue 9, 1975, 1278–1308.

[SCG 2009] Sun Microsystems, Secure Coding Guidelines for the Java Programming Language, version 3.0, 2009. Available at http://www.oracle.com/technetwork/java/seccodeguide-139067.html.

[Schildt 2007] Herb Schildt, *Herb Schildt's Java Programming Cookbook*, McGraw-Hill, New York, 2007.

[Schneier 2000] Bruce Schneier, *Secrets and Lies—Digital Security in a Networked World*, Wiley, New York, 2000.

[Schönefeld 2002] Marc Schönefeld. Security Aspects in Java Bytecode Engineering. Blackhat Briefings 2002, Las Vegas, August 2002.

[Schönefeld 2004] Marc Schönefeld. Java Vulnerabilities in Opera 7.54, BUGTRAQ Mailing List (bugtraq@securityfocus.com), November 2004.

[Schwarz 2004] Don Schwarz, Avoiding Checked Exceptions, ONJava, 2004. Available at http://www.oreillynet.com/onjava/blog/2004/09/avoiding_checked_exceptions.html.

[Schweisguth 2003] Dave Schweisguth, Java Tip 134: When Catching Exceptions, Don't Cast Your Net Too Wide, Javaworld.com, 2003. Available at http://www.javaworld.com/javaworld/javatips/jw-javatip134.html?page=2.

[SDN 2011] Sun Microsystems, SUN Developer Network, 1994–2008.

[Seacord 2005] Robert C. Seacord, *Secure Coding in C and C++*, Addison-Wesley Professional, Boston, 2005.

[Seacord 2008] Robert C. Seacord, *The CERT C Secure Coding Standard*, Addison-Wesley Professional, Boston, 2008.

[Seacord 2010] Robert C. Seacord, William Dormann, James McCurley, Philip Miller, Robert Stoddard, David Svoboda, and Jefferson Welch, Source Code Analysis Laboratory (SCALe) for energy delivery systems, CMU/SEI-2010-TR-021, Software Engineering Institute, Carnegie Mellon University, Pittsburgh, PA, December 2010.

[SecArch 2006] Sun Microsystems, Java 2 Platform Security Architecture, 2006. Available at http://download.oracle.com/javase/6/docs/technotes/guides/security/spec/security-spec.doc.html.

[Secunia 2008] Secunia ApS, Secunia Advisories, 2008. Available at http://secunia.com/advisories/.

[**Security 2006**] Sun Microsystems, Java Security Guides, 2006. Available at http://download.oracle.com/javase/6/docs/technotes/guides/security/.

[**SecuritySpec 2008**] Sun Microsystems, Java Security Architecture, 2008. Available at http://download.oracle.com/javase/1.5.0/docs/guide/security/spec/security-specTOC.fm.html.

[**Sen 2007**] Robi Sen, Avoid the Dangers of XPath Injection, IBM developerWorks, 2007. Available at http://www.ibm.com/developerworks/xml/library/x-xpathinjection/index.html.

[**Steel 2005**] Christopher Steel, Ramesh Nagappan, and Ray Lai, *Core Security Patterns: Best Practices and Strategies for J2EE, Web Services, and Identity Management*, Prentice Hall PTR, Upper Saddle River, NJ, 2005.

[**Steele 1977**] G. L. Steele, Arithmetic Shifting Considered Harmful, *ACM SIGPLAN Notices* Volume 12, Issue 11 (1977), 61–69.

[**Steinberg 2005**] Daniel H. Steinberg, Java Developer Connection Tech Tips Using the Varargs Language Feature, January 4, 2005.

[**Sterbenz 2006**] Andreas Sterbenz and Charlie Lai, Secure Coding Antipatterns: Avoiding Vulnerabilities, Sun Microsystems, JavaOne Conference, 2006.

[**Steuck 2002**] Gregory Steuck, XXE (Xml eXternal Entity) Attack, 2002. Available at http://www.securityfocus.com/archive/1/297714.

[**Sun 1999**] Why Are Thread.stop, Thread.suspend, Thread.resume and Runtime.runFinalizersOnExit Deprecated? Sun Microsystems, 1999. Available at http://download.oracle.com/javase/1.4.2/docs/guide/misc/threadPrimitiveDeprecation.html.

[**Sun 2002**] Reflection, Sun Microsystems, 2002. Available at http://download.oracle.com/javase/1.5.0/docs/guide/reflection/index.html.

[**Sun 2003**] Sun Microsystems, Sun ONE Application Server 7 Performance Tuning Guide, 2003. Available at http://download.oracle.com/docs/cd/E19199-01/817-2180-10/.

[**Sun 2004a**] Java Management Extensions (JMX), Sun Microsystems, 2004. Available at http://download.oracle.com/javase/1.5.0/docs/guide/jmx/index.html.

[**Sun 2004b**] Java Object Serialization Specification, Version 1.5.0, Sun Microsystems, 2004. Available at http://download.oracle.com/javase/1.5.0/docs/guide/serialization/spec/serialTOC.html.

[**Sun 2004d**] JVM Tool Interface, Sun Microsystems, 2004. Available at http://download.oracle.com/javase/1.5.0/docs/guide/jvmti/jvmti.html.

[**Sun 2006**] Java™ Platform, Standard Edition 6 documentation, Sun Microsystems, 2006. Available at http://download.oracle.com/javase/6/docs/index.html.

[**Sun 2008**] Java™ Plug-in and Applet Architecture, Sun Microsystems, 2008. Available at http://download.oracle.com/javase/6/docs/technotes/guides/jweb/applet/applet_execution.html.

[**Sutherland 2010**] Dean F. Sutherland and William L. Scherlis, Composable Thread Coloring, *Proceedings of the 15th ACM SIGPLAN Symposium on Principles and Practice of Parallel Programming*, Association for Computing Machinery, New York, 2010.

[**Tanenbaum 2003**] Andrew S. Tanenbaum and Maarten Van Steen. *Distributed Systems: Principles and Paradigms*, 2nd ed., Prentice Hall, Upper Saddle River, NJ, 2003.

[**Techtalk 2007**] Josh Bloch and William Pugh, The PhantomReference Menace. Attack of the Clone. Revenge of the Shift, JavaOne Conference, 2007.

[**Tomcat 2009**] Apache Software Foundation, Changelog and Security fixes, Tomcat documentation, 2009. Available at http://tomcat.apache.org/tomcat-6.0-doc/index.html.

[**Tutorials 2008**] The Java Tutorials, Sun Microsystems, 2008.

[**Unicode 2003**] The Unicode Consortium, *The Unicode Standard*, Version 4.0.0, defined by The Unicode Standard, Version 4.0, Addison-Wesley, Reading, MA, 2003.

[**Unicode 2007**] The Unicode Consortium, *The Unicode Standard*, Version 5.1.0, defined by The Unicode Standard, Version 5.0, Addison-Wesley, Reading, MA, 2007, as amended by Unicode 5.1.0.

[**Unicode 2011**] The Unicode Consortium. *The Unicode Standard*, Version 6.0.0, The Unicode Consortium, Mountain View, CA, 2011.

[**Venners 1997**] Bill Venners, Security and the Class Loader Architecture, Java World. com, 1997. Available at http://www.javaworld.com/javaworld/jw-09-1997/jw-09-hood.html?page=1.

[**Venners 2003**] Bill Venners, Failure and Exceptions, A Conversation with James Gosling, Part II, Artima.com, 2003. Available at http://www.artima.com/intv/solid.html.

[**W3C 2008**] Tim Bray, Jean Paoli, C. M. Sperberg-McQueen, Eve Maler, and François Yergeau, *Extensible Markup Language (XML) 1.0, 5th ed.*, W3C Recommendation, 2008. Available at http://www.w3.org/TR/REC-xml/#include-if-valid.

[**Ware 2008**] Michael S. Ware, *Writing Secure Java Code: A Taxonomy of Heuristics and an Evaluation of Static Analysis Tools*, Master's thesis, James Madison University, Harrisonburg, VA, 2008. Available at http://mikeware.us/thesis/.

[Weber 2009] Chris Weber, Exploiting Unicode-enabled Software, CanSecWest, March 2009. Available at http://www.lookout.net/wp-content/uploads/2009/03/chris_weber_exploiting-unicode-enabled-software-v15.pdf.

[Wheeler 2003] David A. Wheeler, Secure Programming for Linux and Unix HOWTO, 2003. Available at http://www.dwheeler.com/secure-programs/Secure-Programs-HOWTO/index.html.

[White 2003] Tom White, Memoization in Java Using Dynamic Proxy Classes, August 2003. Available at http://onjava.com/pub/a/onjava/2003/08/20/memoization.html.

[Zukowski 2004] John Zukowski, Creating Custom Security Permissions, Java Developer Connection Tech Tips, May 18, 2004.

Index

Testing conformance to the CERT® secure coding standards

Secure coding can represent a significant investment, particularly when it is necessary to refactor or otherwise modernize existing software systems. Unfortunately, it is difficult to promote security and code quality as market differentiators because unsubstantiated claims are frequently discounted by software consumers.

CERT® staff can help by providing independent conformance testing of your software to *The CERT Oracle Secure Coding Standard for Java* or *The CERT C Secure Coding Standard*. Software that passes conformance testing is listed in a registry of conforming systems at https://www.securecoding.cert.org/registry. The developer is entitled to use the CERT Conformance Testing seal to promote the corresponding product or service.

Conformance testing to CERT secure coding standards provides a differentiator in a market that is increasingly concerned about the security of deployed software. For more information about conformance testing, visit the secure coding area of the CERT website:

www.cert.org/secure-coding

CERT is a registered mark owned by Carnegie Mellon University.

Software Engineering Institute
Carnegie Mellon®

The SEI Series in Software Engineering

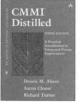

ISBN 0-321-46108-8

ISBN 0-321-22876-6

ISBN 0-321-11886-3

ISBN 0-201-73723-X

ISBN 0-321-50917-X

ISBN 0-321-15495-9

ISBN 0-321-17935-8

ISBN 0-321-27967-0

ISBN 0-201-70372-6

ISBN 0-201-70482-X

ISBN 0-201-70332-7

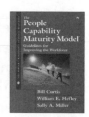

ISBN 0-201-60445-0

ISBN 0-201-60444-2

ISBN 0-321-42277-5

ISBN 0-201-52577-1

ISBN 0-201-25592-8

ISBN 0-321-47717-0

ISBN 0-201-54597-7

ISBN 0-201-54809-7

ISBN 0-321-30549-3

ISBN 0-201-18095-2

ISBN 0-201-54610-8

ISBN 0-201-47719-X

ISBN 0-321-34962-8

ISBN 0-201-77639-1

ISBN 0-201-73-1134

ISBN 0-201-61626-2

ISBN 0-201-70454-4

ISBN 0-201-73409-5

ISBN 0-201-85-4805

ISBN 0-321-11884-7

ISBN 0-321-33572-4

ISBN 0-321-51608-7

ISBN 0-201-70312-2

ISBN 0-201-70-0646

ISBN 0-201-17782-X

Please see our web site at informit.com/seiseries for more information on these titles.

FREE Online Edition

Your purchase of **The CERT® Oracle® Secure Coding Standard for Java™** includes access to a free online edition for 45 days through the Safari Books Online subscription service. Nearly every Addison-Wesley Professional book is available online through Safari Books Online, along with more than 5,000 other technical books and videos from publishers such as Cisco Press, Exam Cram, IBM Press, O'Reilly, Prentice Hall, Que, and Sams.

SAFARI BOOKS ONLINE allows you to search for a specific answer, cut and paste code, download chapters, and stay current with emerging technologies.

Activate your FREE Online Edition at
www.informit.com/safarifree

> **STEP 1:** Enter the coupon code: EKCMMXA.

> **STEP 2:** New Safari users, complete the brief registration form.
> Safari subscribers, just log in.

If you have difficulty registering on Safari or accessing the online edition, please e-mail customer-service@safaribooksonline.com

Addison
Wesley

ALPHA

Cisco Press

FT Press

IBM Press

lynda.com

Microsoft Press

O'REILLY

Peachpit Press

PRENTICE

QUE

SAMS

SAS Publishing

Sun microsystems

WILEY